CLASSICAL HOLLYWOOD COMEDY

AFI Film Readers
a series edited by
Edward Branigan and Charles Wolfe

Psychoanalysis and Cinema
E. Ann Kaplan, editor

Fabrications: Costume and the Female Body
Jane Gaines and Charlotte Herzog, editors

Sound Theory/Sound Practice
Rick Altman, editor

Film Theory Goes to the Movies
Jim Collins, Hilary Radner, and Ava Preacher Collins, editors

Theorizing Documentary
Michael Renov, editor

Black American Cinema
Manthia Diawara, editor

Disney Discourse
Eric Smoodin, editor

The American Film Institute
P.O. Box 27999
2021 North Western Avenue
Los Angeles, California 90027

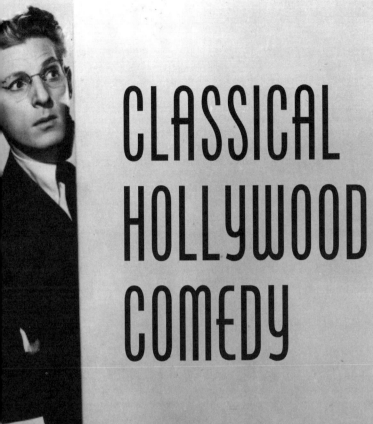

CLASSICAL HOLLYWOOD COMEDY

EDITED BY

KRISTINE BRUNOVSKA KARNICK
and HENRY JENKINS

ROUTLEDGE
New York • London

Published in 1995 by

Routledge
29 West 35th Street
New York, NY 10001

Published in Great Britain by

Routledge
11 New Fetter Lane
London EC4P 4EE

Photo Credits: Pages 35, 48, 145, 240, 241, and 345 courtesy of Photofest; both photographs on page 204 courtesy of the BFI Stills, Posters and Designs; page 212 courtesy of the Academy of Motion Picture Arts and Sciences; pages 296 and 297 courtesy of the Museum of Modern Art/Film Stills Archive; page 306 courtesy of the George Eastman House.

Library of Congress Cataloging-in-Publication Data

Classical Hollywood comedy / edited by Kristine Brunovska Karnick and
    Henry Jenkins.
        p.   cm.—(AFI film readers)
    Includes bibliographical references.
    ISBN 0-415-90639-3 (hb)—ISBN 0-415-90640-7 (pbk)
    1. Comedy films—United States—History and criticism.
I. Karnick, Kristine Brunovska,   . II. Jenkins, Henry,   .
III. Series.
PN1995.9.C55C56   1994
791.43′617—dc20   94-3859
                                                       CIP

British Library Cataloguing-in-Publication Data also available.

Contents

Acknowledgments

The two editors contributed equally to this book's development. The order of the listing of their names on the book's cover was determined arbitrarily by the flip of a coin. The sequencing of the names in the introductory essays privileges the primary author responsible for its contents but, in each case, ideas and often sections of the texts were contributed by the coeditor.

The editors wish to acknowledge the tremendous support they have received from the contributors, each of whom has struggled to meet deadlines and to be responsive in their revision of manuscripts, and each of whom has made here a substantial contribution to our understanding of film comedy. We also appreciate their cooperation with some last minute cuts for length. We would also like to express thanks for the support we have received from the American Film Institute and Routledge, especially the wise and tireless editing of Edward Branigan and Charles Wolfe. We appeciate the faith they showed in asking us to edit this volume, and hope that they will continue to be satisfied with the results.

In addition, Henry Jenkins wishes to thank Eve Diana, Peter Donaldson, John Hildebidle, Briony Keith, Wynn Kelly, Alvin Kibel, Marty Marks, Chris Pomiecko, Lynn Spigel, David Thorburn and Edward Baron Turk for their advice and assistance in preparing this manuscript and Jane Shattuc for her sharp editorial suggestions and close readings of many sections of this manuscript. I want to especially thank Cynthia Benson Jenkins for being there each and every time I needed her and for putting up with the fact that I often was not there when she needed me. This book grew from many discussions Kristine Karnick and I had in graduate school, so it is fitting that we have been able to bring it into print together as part of our ongoing conversation about comedy and life. I want to dedicate this book to Lucile Puckett Jenkins, whose passionate laughter was the musical backdrop for my childhood, who shared with me my discovery of the movies, and whose support has been a constant of my adult years.

Kristine Karnick would like to thank Virginia Wright Wexman, Russell Merritt, David Bordwell, Dorothy Webb, Dennis Bingham, K. C. D'Alessandro, Alan Reynolds and, of course, Sam Karnick (the best editor in the business) for their invaluable help during various stages in the preparation this manuscript, Katrina Coxe, whose thoughtfulness allowed me to get lots of work done in a very few days, Stuart Schleuse and Melody Johnson for their technical assistance, and Sam, Aleksandr, and Lukas Karnick for their unfaltering patience and understanding. I would especially like to thank Henry Jenkins for his wonderful insights, critical eye, and editorial judgement, which has made a world of difference in my work and in my life. I want to dedicate this book to my mother, Raita Brunovskis and my grandmother Vilhelmine Eglite whose love, guidance and fortitude are responsible for whatever good I do.

Introduction: Golden Eras and Blind Spots— Genre, History and Comedy

Henry Jenkins and Kristine Brunovska Karnick

> Genres were always—and continue to be—treated as if they spring full-blown from the head of Zeus. It is thus not surprising to find that even the most advanced of current genre theories, those that see generic texts as negotiating a relationship between a specific production system and a given audience, still hold to a notion of genre that is fundamentally ahistorical in nature.
>
> Rick Altman[1]

"Vagrant Smoke-Curls of Nostalgia": Agee, Kerr and Silent Comedy

James Agee's autobiographical novel, *A Death in the Family*, opens with a trip to the movies. In the summer of 1915, a Knoxville boy and his father go to the Majestic in search of a William S. Hart Western and, more importantly, of Charlie Chaplin, "that horrid little man" as the boy's mother calls him.[2] Agee writes of the ability of laughter to break down barriers, between the many classes of people attending the film, between the father and son.[3] Agee's description of the boy's delight in the Chaplin film captures a moment too precious to last. Soon Rufus's father will die, and Agee depends upon this powerful image of bonding through laughter to color our experience of what Rufus has lost. The plot of *A Death in the Family* mirrors Agee's critical account of the silent slapstick cinema as "comedy's greatest era," and of its traumatic decline. Just as Rufus's enjoyment of Chaplin's unnamed comedy ends with the father's death, the noise and chatter of the talkies destroys the critic's pleasures in an age of slapstick and pantomime, another moment too precious to last.

A remarkably similar memory frames Walter Kerr's *The Silent Clowns*, though Kerr is more self-conscious about the way nostalgia influences his account. Kerr contrasts the "dawnlike freshness" of the early films against his generation's "own aging, our own altered sense, our own vivid and restless acquaintance with sound." His account captures the "smell of tile and leather and nitrate and buttered popcorn" alongside the sounds of passionate laughter.[4] Like Agee, Kerr recalls a boyhood trip to the movies with his father. He remembers nothing of the William S. Hart feature, but cannot forget a glass slide featuring "the black silhouette of Charlie Chaplin against a red background." The vividness of his memories sets a standard no actual experience could satisfy: "When I first saw Keaton I didn't simply laugh at him, I fused with him, psyche locked to psyche; I recognized him as something known before birth."[5] Kerr's scholarship, like Agee's criticism, was motivated by a nostalgic return not only to old movies but to his lost childhood, his responses to the film colored by "vagrant smoke-curls of nostalgia . . . somewhere just beyond vision, just beyond smell, just beyond touching."[6]

These two autobiographical accounts remind us how much our conceptions of the history of film comedy have been seeped in personal memories and fantasies. The construction of the genre's history in terms of a series of golden ages and declines reflects the personal needs of the writers as much as an institutional need to understand our cultural past. Before archives and videotapes made these prints accessible for careful scrutiny, much of film history was written from memory, shaped by the writer's ability to recall films seen decades before, with a resulting distortion of descriptive detail and a simplification of the historical record.[7] What got discussed was what the writers could remember, often removed from its larger cultural context. Later writers adopted, almost without question, established canons of silent comedy, with the result that lesser-known figures became hazy memories and then disappeared altogether.

Nostalgia is a powerful emotional force, a central element of our experience of films, and one which has often gone unacknowledged as the language of scholarly distance denies itself the "immediate experience" of popular culture. Nostalgia motivates the construction and circulation of popular memory, making the public past meaningful for the personal present.[8] Yet nostalgia is *not* history, cannot replace the difficult task of reconstructing and interpreting the past. Nostalgia displaces collective history into either personal reminiscence (what these films meant to me when I was a child) or universalizing claims (the image of laughter transcending traditional barriers between class or gender). Nostalgia works by simplifying the past, removing all contradictions and nuances in favor of an oft-told narrative of innocence lost. The "infantile" quality of comedy, its presocial or antisocial impulses harkening back to the unregulated urges of childhood, makes it a ripe field for nostalgic recollection.

Synchronic and Diachronic Models

Apart from its roots in the exercise of nostalgia, the conceptualization of the history of screen comedy as a succession of golden ages and declines reflects tendencies toward synchronic rather than diachronic accounts of film genres. Many critics treat genre as a static or synchronic system, drawing on works across a broad range of historical periods in order to locate fixed formulas or consistent thematic oppositions. Synchronic models map the set of conventions in place at a particular historical juncture and are preoccupied with defining genre boundaries; diachronic approaches are interested in how genre formulas change over time and are aware of the range of different possibilities each genre contains. Few actual accounts of genres are fully synchronic or wholly diachronic, yet these terms allow us to identify general tendencies within critical discourses.

Synchronic approaches to genre often abdicate their role in developing historical explanations. Steve Seidman's work on the comedian comedy, for example, attempts to locate a "tradition" within the classical Hollywood cinema according to both formal and thematic attributes, a tradition illustrated by examples drawn from films by many different performers, ranging from the early shorts of John Bunny through the recent features of Woody Allen and Mel Brooks.[9] Seidman's important work allowed us to make meaningful connections across a range of films that had previously been treated in a more atomistic fashion. He facilitated a move from the study of individual comic performers to a consideration of comedian comedy as a genre. His synchronic approach, however, was limited by its ahistoricism. Seidman shows little interest in such diachronic issues as the popular roots of this comic tradition, its relationship more broadly to the history of the classical Hollywood cinema, and its transformations in response to a shifting cultural and social climate.[10]

If genres are defined in relatively static terms, then there is no way to account for changes within the structure or style of comic texts except in terms of declines or advances. The accounts of critics such as Donald McCaffrey and Gerald Mast presuppose the centrality of classical criteria of thematic significance, character consistency, narrative unity, causal logic and psychological realism at all stages of the genre's development.[11] These norms, which are never acknowledged as such, result in their embrace of the feature films of the silent clowns as the standard against which subsequent comedian comedies are to be evaluated. McCaffrey, for example, argues that what separates the great silent classics from less satisfying comedies is the fact that the "four great comedians" were "concerned, first of all, with the comedy character and the development of a well-motivated dramatic story that sprang from the roots of the leading comic character."[12] For McCaffrey, even Chaplin can be faulted for "his inability to tell an effective, unified dramatic story"; He often "patched together a brilliant series of scenes but was weak in his handling of his overall story development."[13] The silent classics emerged at a period when the classical norms were in place and comedians sought a fuller integration within the mainstream of Hollywood production. Earlier comic performers, such as Max Linder, or later stars, such as the Marx Brothers, enjoyed a different relationship to dominant screen practice, responding to alternative aesthetic traditions (the vaudeville aesthetic) and institutional contexts (early cinema, the transition to sound).

Employing this fixed standard, Mast, McCaffrey and others in their tradition devalue works within the "non-hermetic" tradition of comedian comedy, which are characterized by their fragmentation, their privileging of performance over characterization, their focus on spectacle over narrative, and their stylistic self-consciousness. Viewed in this fashion, the coming of sound and, the cinema's reconciliation with the vaudeville aesthetic can only be read as a fall from "Comedy's Greatest Era" rather than the emergence of a new and different style of screen comedy. Such rigidly held norms result in a profoundly conservative treatment of film genres; what corresponds to the critic's account of the genre attracts praise, while change, particular change that calls into question the universality of those norms, is suspect.

Comedy and the Masterpiece Tradition

Despite recent efforts to reconsider the place of comedy in film history, most existing accounts of the genre, most notably Gerald Mast's widely taught *The Comic Mind*, fit within what Robert Allen and Douglas Gomery have called the "masterpiece" approach to film history.[14] Its basic assumptions creep into standard film history textbooks and influence how we arrange syllabuses for teaching film comedy. Its framework structures television documentaries and critical responses to film retrospectives. For that reason, it is important to spend some time looking critically at the assumptions which underlie Mast's *The Comic Mind* and other traditional accounts of screen comedy.

Allen and Gomery have identified many of the blind spots characteristic of such accounts. First, the "masterpiece" tradition sees the study of cinema primarily in terms of the "evolution" of film art, with only passing attention given to "economic, technological, cultural" factors. Doug Riblet suggests, for example, that Mast's treatment of Mack Sennett and of the development of silent comedy is divorced from larger histories of Hollywood institutions and practices, including a consideration of the economic rationale and aesthetic consequences of the star system, the rise of the feature film, censorship and regulation struggles, the formation of the vertically integrated studio and shifting modes of production. Similarly, the works of the Marx Brothers have been isolated from the broader consideration of the star recruitment practices characteristic of the transition to sound. Mast's insularity reflects a general retreat from historical explanation and towards a vocabulary of "connoisseurship" and film appreciation.

Second, the "masterpiece" tradition focuses on the "individual work of cinematic art," with the film understood as reflecting "the personal vision of the artist." Gerald Mast, like many who preceded and followed him, organizes his history around a succession of "comic minds" and exceptional works:

> This is not a history of film comedy or comedians but a historical survey of the most significant minds that have worked with the comic-film form. The study will predictably neglect those comic performers who exerted little control over how the antics were shot, edited, and scored. Further, the book's focus is not only how or why these comic minds were funny, but what they had to "say" and how (or if) they were successful in "saying" it.[15]

In Mast's approach, all that matters is the individual work and the individual personality, with the autonomy of the artist a criteria of historical importance. Donald McCaffrey similarly dismisses "minor comedians" such as Charlie Chase or Ben Turpin because they lacked creative control over their own efforts and were at the mercy of their directors; Chaplin, Lloyd and Keaton, on the other hand, "needed only minimal guidance" and "took a strong hand in every phase of creation."[16] Even within the account of the career of a recognized "comic mind" like Buster Keaton, the focus is on those films over which Keaton is presumed to have creative control, while others, such as *The Saphead*, are read as marginal and uninteresting because they are "someone else's film."

Third, the masterpiece tradition holds that "the meaning of a film and its aesthetic significance transcend that film's historical context." These universalizing tendencies result, for example, in the assumption that, because Sennett's films do not produce laughs from contemporary audiences, they were also regarded as "unfunny" by their original and intended spectators. More recent work in genre history, on the other hand, has focused on the shifting criteria by which comic works were appreciated, the debates between proponents of "true comedy" and "new humor" in the pages of turn-of-the-century literary magazines or between advocates of Sidney Drew's classicism and Mack Sennett's slapstick in the pages of *Moving Picture World*.[17]

Fourth, the masterpiece tradition excludes the overwhelming bulk of films produced, since only a small number qualify as "great works of art." The four great comedians (Keaton, Langdon, Lloyd and Chaplin) stand apart from any contemporaries, with the result that these other films go unstudied, unrevived and, in many cases, have been lost altogether. The gender bias behind this canon formation has resulted in the all-but-total exclusion of women (such as Mabel Normand) from most accounts of the genre's history. One consequence of this value-laden approach to history has been the focus on Sennett as the "father of film comedy," while ignoring the large number of comic films produced before the establishment of Keystone in 1908. More recent work on early cinema, on the other hand, has led to a dramatic reassessment of those claims. The essays by Tom Gunning and Donald Crafton in this volume reflect the debates about gag and narrative which have emerged from this reconsideration of the role of comedy within the "cinema of attractions." This new approach presupposes that the history of the comic film requires attention to the works of countless minor artists, that genre conventions emerge across large numbers of films rather than in response to exceptional masterpieces.

Another consequence of the "masterpiece" approach has been a curious account of the impact of sound upon film comedy. Mast, for example, treats silent comedy in terms of comic performers, such as Chaplin and Keaton, associated with the comedian comedy, while he deals with sound comedy in terms of comic directors associated with romantic comedy, such as Frank Capra, George Cukor or Howard Hawks. Silent comedy, Mast argues, was a comedy of "personalities," while sound comedy is a "literary" comedy centering around character relationships. Such an account sees sound as representing a dramatic break with previous comic practice, while more recent work has tended to see comedian comedy and romantic comedy as two distinct traditions, existing side by side from the very outset of screen comedy. A recognition of the larger history of these two traditions—specifically of silent romantic comedy and sound comedian comedy—requires a considerable reassessment of Mast's basic claims about the differences between sound and silent comedy. Charles Musser, for example, has shown the degree to which the silent divorce comedies of Cecil B. DeMille fit within the same generic tradition as the "comedies of remarriage" Stanley Cavell associates with the 1930s and 1940s. A focus on outstanding films, therefore, results in a history of radical disjunctures, since it requires us to overlook the large number of ordinary films which fill in the gaps between periods of remarkable accomplishment.

Fifth, the primary purpose of the masterpiece tradition is the "critical evaluation of films," rather than the attempt to understand historical causality. One may, by this point, wonder what value can be attached to evaluations of films which are formed without regard to the specific aesthetic traditions that produced them. Just as the masterpiece tradition has worked to isolate films from history, rather than to construct the films as historical artifacts, it must necessarily ignore historical factors in making evaluations. Moreover, as Doug Riblet notes, this approach does not allow us to investigate the more interesting historical question—

what made people laugh in different time periods, and why. Often, the most important questions arise not from evaluating works which please us in the present, but rather in trying to more fully understand works we find puzzling or unpleasurable. As cultural historian Robert Darnton writes on earlier forms of popular humor:

> The perception of that distance may serve as the starting point of an investigation, for anthropologists have found that the best points of entry in an attempt to penetrate an alien culture can be those where it seems to be most opaque. When you realize that you are not getting something—a joke, a proverb, a ceremony—that is particularly meaningful to the natives, you can see where to grasp a foreign system of meaning in order to unravel it.[18]

Perhaps the slapstick of Mack Sennett seems closer to our modern sensibility than the cat massacre at the Rue Saint-Severin Darnton deciphers, yet Darnton's observation suggests the importance of not assuming a commonality in audience evaluation and response to jokes and comic representations. Donald McCaffrey, on the other hand, focuses his account of silent comedy only around those figures who enjoy significant recognition from present-day audiences with little interest in figures who had strong but transient appeal at the time of their initial release. The exclusion of such figures from historical accounts of silent comedy distorts our understanding of more canonical works, making it impossible to evaluate what is conventional and what is innovative in films which have been isolated from their larger generic context.

Finally, the "masterpiece" tradition explains change in terms of "an internal process of evolution" (the model of "golden ages" and declines found in Agee or Kerr) or "as a result of artistic genius" (Mast's "comic minds"). Similarly, the shifts of individual comic artists, such as Chaplin, from short films which were largely outside the classical norms of the Hollywood system towards more classically constructed feature films are read in terms of personal progress and maturity. Gerald Mast, for example, discusses Chaplin's career in terms of "lessons at Keystone," "Growth at Essanay," and "Mutual Maturity," while sound begins the process of his decline. The author-based model of the "masterpiece" tradition has often been a way of avoiding tricky questions of artistic control and of the relationship between the individual artists and the system of production. Most Hollywood directors had limited say in project selection, scripting, casting, editing or scoring, decisions which had a tremendous impact on the finished films.[19] Artistic values and thematic significance are ascribed to these "auteurs" in total disregard of these historical conditions; critical analysis substitutes for history writing. Moreover, the auteur theory has often stressed individual expression over the conventions and traditions which are shared between artists. Auteurists often praised filmmakers for resisting the demands of genre conventions, for maintaining a consistency of vision across multiple genres (as in Peter Wollen's discussion of Howard Hawk's oeuvre).[20] As Andrew Sarris writes, "The *Auteur* theory values the personality of a director precisely because of the barriers to its expression. It is as if a few brave spirits had managed to overcome the gravitational pull of the mass of movies."[21] Genres were read as a set of constraints on artistic production ("barriers to expression") rather than enabling conditions for the production and reception of popular texts.

An Alternative Approach

How might we write an alternative history of classical Hollywood comedy, one which avoids the blind spots associated with the masterpiece tradition? First, an alternative approach would situate comic films within a broader conception of film history, applying the same rigorous standards that govern other areas of history writing. It would display a healthy skepticism of secondary accounts (such as "Comedy's Greatest Era" or *The Comic Mind*) and would scour primary sources and trade press discourses in reconstructing the historical record. This revisionist impulse can be found in many of the essays found in this collection, including Doug Riblet's reconsideration of Mack Sennett's place in early film history and Peter Krämer's investigations of the factors shaping Buster Keaton's first feature film.

Second, an alternative approach would investigate film comedy's relationship to the larger history of popular humor, considering it in relation to the predominant forms of comic representation in nineteenth- and twentith-century America (vaudeville, theatrical farce, comic strips, humor magazines) and in relation to the larger Western tradition (Shakespearian New Comedy, Attic Old Comedy). Here, one might cite as examples Tom Gunning's exploration of the prank film in relation to comic strips or Kathleen Rowe's feminist reworking of New Comedy criticism.

Third, an alternative approach will dramatically broaden the narrowly constructed canon of the masterpiece tradition, seeking out the widest possible corpus of comic films and performers. It will investigate convention as well as invention, standardization as well as differentiation. It will map the basic norms and codes against which any given text, canonical or otherwise, gains its meaning. Even when writing about canonical figures like Preston Sturges, Mae West and Buster Keaton, the tendency here is to focus on lesser-known works which often are of interest because of their problematic relationship to the established canon. The writers' claims for these films center not on their perceived status as comic masterworks but rather on the ways that they may shed light on the contradictory impulses or institutional pressures which shaped comic film production at a specific historic moment.

Fourth, an alternative approach would situate comedy within its institutional context, within histories of the vertically integrated film industry, the star system, the emergence of classical norms, and self-regulation. It would understand the aesthetic choices made in individual films in relation to the classical Hollywood cinema as a legal, economic, technological and cultural institution. Ramona Curry's discussion of Mae West and the Production Code Administration, for example, fits comic films more fully within the history of self-regulation, while suggesting how Freud's work on jokes might shed light on the scandal that surrounded this controversial star.

Fifth, an alternative history would investigate the conditions of reception as well as the conditions of production. Rather than ranking comic texts, it would explore the criteria governing the historical construction and reconstruction of cultural hierarchies. It would focus on laughter as a social act, looking at what provokes and what restrains laughter and its relationship to class, racial, ethnic, sexual and gender difference. Alex Doty's treatment of *The Women*'s reception in the queer community provides a vivid model for how we might investigate comic texts from the perspective of their audiences rather than simply from the vantage point of the guiding "comic mind."

Sixth, an alternative approach will deal with film comedy as part of a larger system of genres, as one response among many to the process of social change. *Film noir*, gothic romance, family melodrama and comedian comedy may all express male anxieties about their loss of heroic status or female anxieties about their domestic containment following the war. Melodrama and romantic comedy, as Kathleen Rowe suggests, provide competing accounts of women's experience within the domestic sphere; heroic action stories and comedian comedies may, as Henry Jenkins argues, provide alternative ways for men to adjust to threats to their self-esteem. Looking at shifts within genres, as well as the interplay between competing genres, allows us to more fully trace the cultural repercussions of political, economic and social changes.

Genre and Classical Hollywood Cinema

Such an approach would integrate the study of film comedy more fully into our emerging understanding of the classical Hollywood cinema. David Bordwell, Janet Staiger and Kristin Thompson see the classical Hollywood cinema as a mode of film practice which survived almost unchanged from 1917 to 1960, and which made the American film industry the most powerful in the world, in terms both of its economic reach and its cultural/social influence.[22] Their book maps the formal conventions governing all film production within the classical era, norms which privilege continuity, causality, linearity and legibility as key criteria for creating and evaluating works. Their research stresses both the importance of standardization and the possibilities of innovation within the studio system. The vertical integration of the American film industry (the centralized control of production, distribution and exhibition by a limited number of studios) insured a steady market for its films. Yet, at the same time, this market required the regular production of films at a predictable cost and with a predictable audience. As Mary Beth Haralovich notes, dependence on genres allowed the studio executives to insure this steady flow of cultural goods to the market place.[23] Repetition of generic formulas minimized production costs, since special units, including stars, directors, screenwriters and production personnel, can be organized around the steady manufacture of comedies, horror films, musicals, melodramas or swashbucklers. The predictable concentration on specific genres allowed the studio to make intelligent purchases of literary and theatrical properties, to insure continuous employment of all contracted personnel and to reduce overhead. Comedy stars of the early sound era, such as Joe E. Brown or Wheeler and Woolsey, might appear in four or five vehicles a year, often with the same directors, writers, gagmen, songwriters and choreographers.

Genre films, as Haralovich notes, "sell themselves to audiences not on the basis of their meaning as particular films but because they meet audience expectations generated by their genre conventions."[24] *Variety* and other trade press publications constantly monitored the box office returns and exhibitor demands for specific genres. Differences in regional responses to alternative genre traditions was a subject of extensive discussion. Early sound comedies, for example, were designed so that they could be sold as musicals along the North Atlantic seaboard, where the appeal of Broadway entertainment was strong and as comedian comedies in the hinterland, where audiences had limited enthusiasm for the "sophistication" of stage-bound talkies. Broadway stars, such as Eddie Cantor, had to dramatically adjust their performance styles and personas to accommodate a more diverse national box office. Advertising foregrounded the generic features of films—their stars, their settings, their emotional address to the spectator—as major attractions.

Genre specialization became the central means by which the studios built their own distinctive identities. One could point to Mack Sennett's Keystone studios as an early example of a production company which sought to define its place in the marketplace through genre specialization, though many other early film companies similarly focused their efforts around comedy shorts.[25] While all of the majors of the mature studio system produced films within multiple genres, each singled out a few areas where their accomplishments dominated the field (such as Paramount's role as a comedy producer in the 1930s). The minors and poverty-row studios, as Paul Seales has suggested, were even more dependent upon genre specialization in order to appeal to independent exhibitors or to cut distribution and exhibition deals with the majors.[26]

Moreover, different genres allowed for the inflection of the dominant aesthetic norms which shaped all Hollywood production, defining the "bounds of difference" by which novelty could be introduced into an otherwise formula-based system.[27] Each genre, thus, constitutes an idiolect of the dominant system of aesthetic norms characterizing the classical Hollywood cinema; each genre also represents a site of contestation, as alien norms are pulled into the classical system alongside diverse cultural materials borrowed from elsewhere within popular culture. Bordwell documents, for example, the ways that *film noir* builds upon conventions of popular fiction and pulp journalism, Donald Crafton traces the emergence of film animation to graphic arts traditions in nineteenth-century Europe, and Henry Jenkins has shown how early sound comedy borrowed from vaudeville and Broadway revue.[28]

Such an approach links film comedy to a much larger history of popular amusements, investigating what it shares and how it breaks with classical norms. As John Cawelti notes, all cultural production depends upon a careful mixture of "conventions and inventions."[29] Narratives which are highly, though not totally, conventional are frequently the most popular, because they are accessible to a broader audience and require less effort on the part of the viewer to comprehend. They provoke an immediate and intense affective response, a criteria which was of particular interest to the producers of comedy. Comedy's dependence upon stereotypical characters and situations, for example, would be one example of the way that redundancy gets built into the system of genres. Yet, at the same time, the absence of novelty would make the repeated consumption of genre films a pointless and pleasureless activity. If genres provide the framework of shared and redundant assumptions which makes a popular film understandable, genre also defines the space for potential innovation and invention.[30]

Genre's ideological or mythic functions are similarly linked to the play of invention and convention, standardization and differentiation within the classical Hollywood cinema. The choices we make about what entertains us are not innocent or random decisions. We choose popular texts which speak to us in some basic fashion, which reflect our tastes and reaffirm our basic beliefs about the social order. Writers such as Cawelti, Thomas Schatz or Rick Altman argue that popular art has displaced religious ritual as the central means for "articulating and reaffirming primary cultural values."[31] Genre formulas, according to Cawelti, serve both conservative and progressive functions, allowing a culture to negotiate, through symbolic representation, both commonly shared values and the possibility of change in response to competing desires and needs. Such a system of conventions is marked by its repetitive and predictable qualities, with meaning achieved through the cumulative impact of many works rather than the unique statement of any given film. At the same time, this system of formulas cannot be static, since it must continually respond to the process of social change and cultural transformation. Genres thus allow us a common basis from which to measure this process of change. Shifting conceptions of romance or of masculinity and femininity can be traced through the shifts within the romantic comedy; historic changes in popular attitudes towards the social order, especially the demands for conformity, can be understood through looking at the permutations of the comedian comedy.

These accounts of the mythic functions of popular formulas do not offer a crude reflection theory, not even one which sees comedy as a "crazy mirror" through which to understand larger social ideologies.[32] Rather, as Tina Lent suggests in this volume, cultural change is communicated and examined through a multitude of representations within simultaneous circulation. No single representation reflects dominant social attitudes in a simple or straightforward fashion. All representations mediate social thinking through sets of generic and aesthetic conventions, and the history of those conventions must be central to our attempt to read the ideological construction of any given work. The same social change, the transformation in gender roles in postwar America for example, will be expressed in different ways across a range of different genres.

Many popular texts may, in fact, operate within multiple genre traditions; the reader's attempts to determine which genre model(s) to use in making sense of such a work become a vital part of the emotional experience of these films. One might cite, for example, John Cromwell's *Made For Each Other*, which features James Stewart and Carole Lombard, two actors commonly associated with romantic comedies, and opens with the comic problems encountered when a young couple meets their in-laws for the first time. As the film progresses, however, the euphoria of comic romance is displaced by a dramatic treatment of the difficulties the couple faces in maintaining their commitments to each other. The film's final scene has the couple reunited at the hospital bed of their dying son, a moment of pure melodrama. The film thus depends upon the emotional jolt which comes from transforming romantic comedy into melodrama, two genres which, as Rowe suggests, are closely related but which operate according to profoundly different expectations. Historical research might allow us to more fully trace the audience expectations which shaped the circulation and reception of genre texts, further refining our understanding of these films' social impact and cultural implications.

About This Book

Although no single essay or even a single volume can hope to address all of these different issues, the essays in *Classical Hollywood Comedy*, both individually and collectively, rewrite the history of American screen comedy and its relationship to classical Hollywood cinema. Each complicates many of the generalizations governing previous accounts, and examines the historiographical, critical and theoretical "tools" which will shape future investigations. If many of these essays still center around canonical figures, such as Buster Keaton and Preston Sturges, these essays read film "classics" in relation to broader movements within the film industry and the larger culture, introducing new frameworks to explain qualities in these films which perplexed and frustrated earlier writers. In other cases, such as work on pre-Mack Sennett screen comedy or the romantic comedy tradition during the silent era, these essays open up periods and topics which have received scant attention elsewhere.

This book is divided into four basic parts. The first part consists of two essays, one on comedian comedy, the other on romantic comedy, which provide broad overviews of the major traditions in classical Hollywood comedy. The essays in this part seek to identify the dominant ideological assumptions and narrative conventions structuring these two traditions, drawing on works from across the full range of the classical and postclassical cinema. The remaining three sections center on the central issues which govern contemporary research on screen comedy. In Part II, articles trace the narrative development of film comedy, focusing on the shifting relationship between comedy and classical narrative conventions and on the complex interplay between gags and plots. Part III addresses the role of performance traditions within comic films, considering the ways that comedy allows for the foregrounding of performance that exceeds the dominant acting conventions of the classical cinema and looking at the various strategies by which comic films sought to balance the demands of performance and characterization. Finally, Part IV examines issues of ideology, offering three case studies of the romantic comedy tradition and its sexual politics.

Two Traditions

1

A Spanner in the Works?
Genre, Narrative and the Hollywood Comedian

Frank Krutnik

As a genre, Hollywood comedian comedy differed from mainstream fiction films in one important respect:[1] comedian-centered films were not organized simply in accordance with the narrative-based aesthetic of classical cinema.[2] They exhibit, instead, a combination of fiction-making and performative entertainment spectacle. In these films, aspects of the classical representational paradigm coexist with a presentational mode of attraction that has its roots in such variety forms as vaudeville and burlesque.[3] My main concern here is with a distinct period in the history of the genre: the late 1930s to the early 1960s. In the comedian films of this period, the twin demands of representation and presentation are articulated and contained within a stable and predictable formal mode. This formal mode suited and was generated by the demand of the Hollywood film industry for product standardization, following the destabilizing effects of the introduction of sound. Compared to other genres, the standardization of the comedian comedy came comparatively late. (It is a curious fact that comedian comedy has always been slower than other genres to fall in line with industrial practices of standardization.)

In relation to earlier comedian comedies, the films produced from the late 1930s to the early 1960s reveal a greater degree of consistency in formal organization, regardless of the particular talents on display. Because these films gave a definite form and shape to the genre during this period, I will refer to them as formalized comedian comedies. The history of the genre is not simply a history of individual creative performers: the star comedians operated within specific formal contexts that were in themselves determined by the institutional and industrial context of Hollywood cinema.

Hollywood Comedian Comedy: Historical Forms

Gag-based slapstick comedy began to be channeled into comedian-centered comedy with the exploitation of the star performer in the 1910s. Besides foregrounding dynamic chase sequences and the spectacular choreography of thrown pies, Mack Sennett's influential Keystone studios recruited comic performers from vaudeville, circus, pantomime and British music hall. Peter Kramer has suggested, however, that the Keystone shorts of the 1912 to 1916 period—featuring star comedians like Mabel Normand and Roscoe "Fatty" Arbuckle—focused "on comic action rather than on the characterization of its protagonists."[4] It is only later, Kramer argues, that comic performers emerge as the organizing force within gag-based comedy:

> Slapstick "comedian comedies" of the late 'teens and early '20's [were] more exclusively concerned with the character and performance of the star comedian than early slapstick, differentiating his/her status and performance from that of all the other actors, thus turning the star into the film's main attraction.[5]

Centralizing the star performer in slapstick comedy was one move towards greater formal stability. A further significant factor was the innovation of the comedian-centered feature film. Early feature narratives, of the 1910 to 1915 period, tended to draw upon the structural models provided by literature and drama. The majority of film comedians, however, were experienced in performance contexts more readily suited to the short film format (the variety act was similar in length to the comedy short—from eight to twelve minutes). After the feature film was standardized as the dominant form of cinematic product, comedian-centered films remained ghettoized within the "confines" of the short. Consequently, they suffered from a relatively inferior status, playing as supporting attractions rather than the principal draw (Chaplin's shorts being the most famous exceptions).

The transition from the gag-based short to feature-length narratives was a major and difficult step for the established film comedians—although their films did increase gradually in length. As Steve Neale has suggested, the 1920s features of Charlie Chaplin, Buster Keaton and Harold Lloyd were transitory hybrids produced in response to changing conditions of industrial practice and economic profitability:

> features were privileged over shorts at the points both of production and exhibition, and features earned more money . . . these films are a specific and unstable combination of slapstick and narrative elements

rather than the final flowering of an authentic slapstick tradition, which is how they have generally tended to be seen."[6]

There were two significant formal paradigms in the feature-length comedian comedies of this time: (a) the Keystone films starring Ben Turpin; and (b) the feature films of Harold Lloyd, which combined slapstick comedy with a form of "genteel" comedy.[7] Extending a form already established in the Keystone shorts, Turpin vehicles such as *Down on the Farm* (1920), *A Small Town Idol* (1921) and *The Shriek of Araby* (1923) were slapstick parodies of contemporary (melo)dramatic or adventure films, and, as such, they were able to borrow and exploit an already formulated narrative framework. Harold Lloyd's major feature films of the 1920s, by contrast, are a much smoother, more integrated blend of gags and narrative. Lloyd's most successful screen persona (the "glasses" character) differs substantially from the physical grotesques and social outcasts who populate the Keystone comedies. Unlike Chaplin's Tramp figure, which was the model for Lloyd's earlier "Willie Work" and "Lonesome Luke" personas, the "glasses" character actively seeks social integration, and is not so readily barred from it. In films like *Safety Last* (1923), *Girl Shy* (1924), *The Freshman* (1925) and *The Kid Brother* (1927), the Lloyd figure overtly aspires to upward mobility, a wish that is given literal expression when he scales a skyscraper in *Safety Last*. Moreover, he possesses no insurmountable physical or psychological handicap that will ultimately frustrate the realization of his goals—attaining success, esteem and the love of a woman. Through determination, hard work and initiative Lloyd's hero proves himself and becomes accepted.

This drive towards integration is reflected by the structure of Lloyd's films: gags tend to *arise from* the narrative rather than competing with it. Both the status of Lloyd-as-comedian and the gags themselves are "naturalized" within a narrative process. Lloyd plays down his character's misfit connotations, and the films also downplay his special status as a comic performer, laying far more stress upon his role as a character. In their feature films of the 1920s, Chaplin, Keaton and Lloyd all accommodated themselves to the principles of "genteel" social comedy, while more traditional forms of slapstick comedy remained prevalent in the subsidiary realm of the short film.[8]

However, the innovation and standardization of the sound film resulted in a renewed and concerted exploitation of performative comedy by the Hollywood studios.[9] In their drive to capitalize upon the novelty attraction of sound in the late 1920s and early 1930s, Hollywood film companies recruited many of the top Broadway and vaudeville performers, including Burns and Allen, Olson and Johnson, Jack Benny, Eddie Cantor, Wheeler and Woolsey, W.C. Fields, Joe E. Brown and Ed Wynn. The short format served as the initial framework for many of these performers. Hollywood also exploited these stage comedians in other contexts: in feature-length comedian comedies centered upon such performers as the Marx Brothers and Wheeler and Woolsey; in revue films that brought together a range of musical and comedy performers (for example, *The Hollywood Revue of 1929*; *New Movietone Follies of 1930*); and in what Henry Jenkins has termed showcase films (Paramount's *Big Broadcast* series (1932–38) and *International House* (1933)), where comic and musical performance sequences are embedded within a slender narrative.[10]

Jenkins defines the most distinctive form of feature-length comedian centered film in this period as "anarchistic comedy."[11] The films of Wheeler and Woolsey and the Marx Brothers represented a shift away from the genteel slapstick mode dominant in the feature comedies. Where the films of Chaplin, Lloyd and Keaton seek to integrate comic performance and narrative, the anarchistic films present a "highly fragmented and disruptive style of comedy."[12] For example, the Marx Brothers' films from *The Cocoanuts* (1929) to *Duck Soup* (1933) show a determined resistance to principles of narrative integration. In each instance, plot continuity is dissipated rather than consolidated from scene to scene. The gangster/kidnap narrative of *Monkey Business* (1931) and the political conspiracies of *Duck Soup*, for example, develop in a haphazard, seemingly impromptu manner, with little regard for "classical" norms of motivation and causality. The comedians function as invaders of the diegetic world. Significantly, there is no attempt to establish stable, unified, character identities for them.

Anarchistic comedian comedy was inevitably short-lived, as these films were the products of a transitional period in which established norms were momentarily destabilized. The anarchistic films of the early 1930s were superseded later in the decade by a more standardized brand of comedian centered film.[13] This increased generic standardization was motivated by the declining box office revenues from the anarchistic films in the mid-1930s, "a decline which the trade press attributed to the overexposure of their comic stars and their failure to produce a consistently high quality product."[14] The Hollywood studios responded either by releasing these comic performers or by demanding "greater conformity with classical storytelling conventions."[15] The most famous example is what happened to the Marx Brothers: Paramount dropped them after the box office failure of *Duck Soup*, and MGM signed them for *A Night at the Opera* (1935), a film that situates the comic performance of the team within the structural conventions of a musical comedy plot and set the model for subsequent vehicles. In the Marx Brothers' MGM films, the move towards "formalization" resulted in a more emphatic ordering of their "disruptive" comic performance in relation to a clearly defined narrative process.

Groucho, Chico and Harpo Marx operate as figures who are peripheral to the narrative—they are not protagonists. In this sense, films like *A Night at the Opera* and *A Day at the Races* (1937) differ significantly from the formalized star vehicles of Bob Hope, Danny Kaye and the team of Dean Martin and Jerry Lewis. For example, in *A Night at the Opera*, the Marx Brothers cooperate with the romantic plot, in that they machinate to bring Rosa (Kitty Carlisle) and Ricardo (Allan Jones) together, but they are not fully bound by this plot, and have no deep personal stake in it. They are able to shift from disruptive to avuncular presences, circulating around the romance plot, but never overwhelming it. The comic subplot between Otis B. Driftwood (Groucho Marx) and Mrs Claypool (Margaret Dumont) introduces a parodic romance, but this in itself is not allowed to contaminate the Rosa-Ricardo love story.

As suggested earlier, the comedian comedies of the late 1930s to the early 1960s provided a standardized framework that suited the demands of the oligopolistic structure of the classical Hollywood film industry. The star vehicles of such comedians as Hope, Kaye, Red Skelton and Martin and Lewis provided a familiar and predictable combination of fiction-making and entertainment spectacle/comic performance.

From the late 1950s, the genre experienced substantial reorientations as Hollywood's established mode of production was subjected to widespread transformations. One of the results was the eccentric self-directed work of Jerry Lewis, which inflated the customary procedures of the formalized comedies beyond recognition.[16] Another development was the dispersal of "personality" found in epic slapstick spectacles like *It's a Mad Mad Mad Mad World* (1963), *The Great Race* (1965), *Those Magnificent Men in Their Flying Machines* (Britain, 1965) and *Monte Carlo or Bust / Those Daring Young Men in Their Jaunty Jalopies* (Britain-France-Italy, 1969). Unlike comedian comedies, these grandiose chase narratives are not unified by a central comic presence. Instead, they feature a range of performers who literally compete for the central focus. This range includes comedians like Peter Cook and Dudley Moore, Jerry Lewis, The Three Stooges, Milton Berle and Phil Silvers; situational comedy performers like Jack Lemmon, Tony Curtis, Terry-Thomas; and such dramatic actors as Spencer Tracy, George Macready and Stuart Whitman. The sustaining principle, then, is the competition between opposed modes of performance and spectacle. More recent trends offer a similar displacement of gag comedy away from the unifying presence of the comedian. For example, there are the team-based films of the National Lampoon and Police Academy series, and the scattershot generic burlesques of Zucker/Abraham/Zucker (the *Airplane* and *Naked Gun* films; *Top Secret!*, 1984; *Hot Shots*, 1991). The central presence of *Naked Gun: From the Files of Police Squad* (1988) and *Naked Gun 2: The Smell of Fear* (1991) is Leslie

Neilsen, who is not so much a comedian as a perpetually befuddled straight-man.

It seems that since the breakdown of classical Hollywood, the attractions previously presented by the genre of comedian comedy have been dispersed across a range of contrasting forms. There have been few prominent film comedians over the last 20 years.[17] Woody Allen specialized in gag comedy from the late 1960s to the mid-1970s (for example, *Take the Money and Run* (1968), *Bananas* (1971), *Sleeper* (1973)), but then shifted to "neurotic" romantic comedy (*Annie Hall* (1977), *Manhattan* (1979)), and subsequently to the more idiosyncratic auteurist films (*Zelig* (1983), *September* (1987), *Crimes and Misdemeanors* (1989)). Steve Martin's "crazy" comedy (*The Jerk* (1979), *Dead Men Don't Wear Plaid* (1982), *The Man With Two Brains* (1983)) has also been followed by more emphatically situational comedy (*Roxanne* (1987), *Dirty Rotten Scoundrels* (1988), *Parenthood* (1989), *L.A. Story* (1990), *Father of the Bride* (1992)). Where earlier comedians tended to work predominantly within their specialty genre, with occasional excursions into other forms, more recent comedians generally aim to establish a broader base of operations. A notable exception is Mel Brooks, who has systematically revived an old-style mixture of "low" comedy and generic parody (*Blazing Saddles* (1974), *Young Frankenstein* (1974), *Silent Movie* (1976), *High Anxiety* (1977), *Spaceballs* (1987)).

The Comedian and the Fiction

> The traditional film is presented as story [histoire], not as discourse [discours]. And yet it is discourse . . . but the basic characteristic of this kind of discourse, and the very principle of its effectiveness as discourse, is precisely that it obliterates all traces of the enunciation, and masquerades as story.
>
> Christian Metz[18]

The experience of the "historical" film is analogous to that provided by "fourth wall" realist theatre. Although it knows full well that the characters are impersonated by actors, and that the drama has been written, rehearsed and previously enacted, the theatre audience also knows that it has certain obligations, that it is "contracted" to observe the "rules of the game". Investing the stage-space with the illusion of reality, the audience asserts its own presence only when cued to do so, through bodily ruptures of applause, laughter, tears or shock. Other forms of theatrical entertainment, however, offer contrasting regimes of pleasure, meaning and engagement. Vital to the spectrum of attractions offered by the mainstream cinema are such entrenched traditions as the musical/dance film and the comedian comedy. These genres establish an interactional dynamic: the attractions of performance and entertainment spectacle (explicitly or implicitly dialogic) are set in competition with the "historical" priorities of fiction-making. For the Broadway musical, the proscenium arch demarcates a space for magical artifice; the show permits a temporary triumph over the restrictions of the "real" (and of realist drama). The Hollywood musical film is, likewise, freed from the orthodox demands of dramatic verisimilitude, from the conventions of the well-made play. Instead, the genre invests in flourishes of spectacle and in the choreography of voice, music and movement. In both stage and screen musicals, narrative tends to fulfill a crucial dual function: the story both motivates the scenes of performance and serves to register their difference.

The comedian-centered comedy has been most influenced by a third form of (theatrical) entertainment—variety. Prior to their film work, most Hollywood comedians gained experience, and even stardom, within one or several of the variety contexts provided by vaudeville, burlesque, British music hall, the theatrical revue, cabaret, radio and television. Variety forms differ from "historical" enactment and musical comedy in that the ordering framework is not provided by narrative. Instead, the audience is offered a package of acts that contrast with each other but which, in themselves, fit into familiar generic forms (the comic skit, the monologue, the dramatic sketch, the popular singer, the dance act, the conjuror, the juggler, the acrobatic team, the animal act and so on). Although variety entertainment eschews narrative continuity, it nevertheless operates within its own principles of coherence and structure. The variety program provides not only a structured contrast between familiar yet different acts, but it also builds toward a prime attraction, or "headliner." There are also structuring principles within individual acts themselves—such as the buildup towards a "wow climax."

The variety mode had a general influence on cinema, and not just in the period of early film when movies were shown as part of vaudeville bills. Prior to the 1950s, film exhibition often provided a similar program of diverse yet regulated attractions. The main act, the principal feature, served to cap a program that included cartoons, shorts, newsreels, a support feature or even live acts. Not only was the individual film located within a variety context but, as Leo A. Handel has suggested: "A picture is never a hundred per cent western, mystery, or comedy, but it usually includes many other basic story types. A western picture might, and often does, include elements such as mystery, romance and so on."[19] No matter what the signaled generic discourse, the particular film tends towards the polyglottic, speaking through a variety of affective "tongues." In order to maintain the spectator's engagement with a fictional narrative of ninety minutes or longer, the Hollywood film relies upon changes in scene and shifts in tone—in short, upon regulated diversity.

The Hollywood comedian comedy operates as a highly specialized form of star-centered film. All star vehicles involve some tension between the specific requirements of the fictional role and the signifying effects of the star image,[20] but the prime rationale of comedian comedy is to showcase the comic performance.[21] The fictional framework organizes and motivates scenes of performance. In most cases, the comedian's persona is initially developed and stabilized within a nonfictional performance context that relies upon interaction with an audience. Comedian-centered films seek to maintain the sense of witnessing or participating in the performer's act, but this inevitably requires some form of compromise between the interactive performance mode and the structuring process of narrative, resulting in the instability of the comedian's character identity. In the comedian comedy, the fictional character signifies a bounded form, a potential constraint for the star performer. But at the same time, the comedian has a privileged status in regard to character identity, a fact highlighted by the "straight" characters and actors who surround the comedian figure. Not only is he less integrated within the fictional regime—less bounded by conventions of motivation, for example—but he is also a presence who either knowingly or unknowingly disrupts the codes of behavior and action which sustain the fictional regime.

Steve Seidman takes this further, claiming that "in comedian comedy, both the comedian's awareness of the spectator's presence and the assertion of his own presence are factors which work toward described enunciation."[22] But Seidman seems closer to the point when, a few lines earlier, he suggests that, in regard to enunciative activity, the comedian is "a usurper (or at least a stand in)." No performer in a film can ever really function as an enunciator—but the comedian is allowed, at specific and regulated moments, to masquerade as enunciator. He is permitted fictional ruptures: through looks to the camera (Oliver Hardy), or by direct address (Groucho Marx, Bob Hope, Woody Allen).[23] While such gags overtly mock the principle of historical effacement, they simultaneously reaffirm the specialness both of the comedian (as performer, as licensed eccentric) and of the comedian comedy as generic carnivalesque (as a generic space in which the conventional rules of fiction and identity are turned upside down).

Whatever the role of narrative, all forms of comedian-centered film reveal a structuring conflict between eccentricity and conformity. This conflict is foregrounded through set-piece gag sequences in which the comedian disrupts a formalizing, rule-bound process concerned with work, sexual behavior, communication or even other forms of performance. For example, there is a sequence in *Modern Times* (1935) in which Chaplin's eccentric misfit conflicts with the mechanized regimentation of assembly-line factory work. Chaplin's worker finds that he cannot accommodate himself to the accelerated rhythm of the conveyor belt. He falls into the mouth of the machine, and is stranded on one of its giant cogs. Despite this, he continues to tighten nuts with the spanners seemingly welded to his hands. The Chaplin figure's breakdown precipitates a dizzying mime-ballet in which the worker confronts the outside world with the determination to tighten every nut he sees. The conveyer belt is shut down and Chaplin moves to his own idiosyncratic rhythm, applying his spanners to ears, noses, the buttons on women's clothing. Where the first part of the sequence incorporates Chaplin within the machine (so that he becomes a "spanner in the works"), the second is based upon the incorporation of the machine within Chaplin. But the comic effect does not derive simply from the mechanization of Chaplin's body, but from a more complex combination of mechanization and eccentricity. The machine inspires the mutation but does not determine its character. The dance with the spanners suggests the Chaplin figure's appropriation and deformation of mechanized procedures—so that they are effectively canceled out.

This sequence has been read as a critique of the dehumanizing effects of the capitalist labor process. But, more generally, it operates in accordance with the generically familiar conflict between excessive regimentation and the gifted misfit. Chaplin incorporates and nullifies the machine: the spanner-dance highlights his special individualism, his talent for rule dislocation, his innate superiority to the procedural decorum of work.[24] A sequence from *The Circus* (1927) makes this point in a different fashion. Mistaken for a pickpocket, Chaplin's Tramp is pursued by a patrolman; he seeks refuge in a circus tent, where he ends up disrupting both a conventional clown act and a conjuring performance. When the Chaplin figure hurls his disruptive presence into the two familiar circus acts, he transforms the expected process of the spectacle into an explicitly comic piece of performance. The circus clowns fail to move the diegetic audience to laughter, but the Tramp's intuitive, unforced actions do. Scenes of creative disruption like this abound in the genre: a procedure that excludes or demeans the misfit character is transformed into a showcase for the comedian's privileged individuality.

These moments encapsulate the overarching thematic of the comedian comedy—the conflict between the gifted outsider and demands for social conformity.[25] The comedian functions as a "spanner" thrown into the conventional workings of narrative, genre, communication, bodily decorum and mature manhood. In the formalized movies, the codifications of narrative logic provide the coordinates for a rule-bound fictional world.

A Spanner in the Works: Charlie Chaplin in *Modern Times* (1936).

The comedian is thrown into this world, in the guise of a fictionally specific identity, and proceeds to deform the rules and procedures that sustain it.

Not surprisingly, the most common structure for the comedian comedy involves setting the comedian figure in the midst of a familiar, highly coded genre. Examples abound in Bob Hope's solo films: the Western genre was co-opted for *The Paleface* (1948) and *Son of Paleface* (1952); the spy thriller for *My Favorite Blonde* (1942); the *noir* detective film for *My Favorite Brunette* (1947); the horror film for *The Cat and the Canary* (1939) and *The Ghost Breakers* (1940); the armed-services picture for *Caught in the Draft* (1941); the swashbuckler for *The Princess and the Pirate* (1944). In such films, the comedian figure's deviance is read against the familiar generic register. He signifies, at one extreme, a refusal or, at the other extreme, an inability to conform to the fictional role mapped out for him. Harpo Marx and Jerry Lewis embody these respective poles, with Bob Hope's comic persona often combining both tendencies. As noted earlier, in the pre-1935 Marx Brothers films, the comic performers remain to one side of the fiction, intruding into it from the periphery. But in the formalized comedian comedies, the narrative process is grounded in a fictionally inscribed identity thematic. The comedian is dropped into the center of a ready-made fictional world, and the fictional identity he assumes is torn between the demands of conforming (as a character) and the need to deviate (as performer).

The fictional process and the extrafictional process have a symbiotic relationship: each feeds energy to the other, and the friction between them generates many of the comic effects. The comedian interferes with the trajectory of the fiction, and the fiction constrains the comedian. A highly conventional problematic is provided by the frame-story; it establishes tasks to be accomplished, obstacles to be overcome, a clearly signaled order to be asserted or restored. The frame narrative contains few surprises: the plot intrigues and characters are readily familiar, and at times ostentatiously cliched. At the start of *The Paleface*, for example, the plot is handled seriously for quite some time. Jane Russell plays a bandit who is sprung from prison by the federal authorities to help track down a band of gun runners. But instead of meeting the federal agent who will set her on the trail of the villains, Russell is thrown into an allegiance with Bob Hope's "Painless" Peter Potter. With Hope's appearance, the narrative drive is arrested by the first of his comic routines—a vaudeville-style sketch which elaborates Potter's incompetence as a dentist. The frame narrative serves a valuable function in providing both a context and a register for the process of disruption set in motion by the comedian figure.[26] In *The Paleface*, the Hope figure patently inverts the typical qualifications of the Western hero. "Painless" Potter is a braggart, a coward and a useless gunslinger, and he is sexually inept—failing repeatedly to consummate the marriage that Russell tricks him into. Potter, however, is but a temporary vehicle for the mobilization of the familiar Hope persona. The deficiencies of Hope's character become signs of the comic performer's talent. The comedian *plays* the misfit, plays with generic expectations, plays—at the extreme—for the sake of play itself. Harpo Marx, for example, also displays this kind of extremity. There is no attempt to motivate much of his eccentric behavior, such as cutting off ties, bisecting cigars, burning hats, offering up an exposed leg and so on. He just *does* these things. The deficiencies of Hope's characters, however, tend to be more strongly motivated—they signify a limited range of character predicates which are more directly inversions of normal or ideal standards of behavior and identity.

Besides featuring performative comedy, formalized vehicles like *The Paleface* also generate comedy through familiar narrative procedures. Potter, for example, is frequently unaware that he is being manipulated by the Jane Russell character. Her contrivances are narratively motivated by the need to disguise her true identity as a federal agent, and they set in motion a structured play of discrepancies of knowledge, throughout

"Deforming Familiar Conventions of Film-Heroism:" Bob Hope and Bing Crosby in *Road to Rio* (1947).

which Potter is perpetually ignorant. On their wedding night, Russell sneaks out of the log cabin to sleep in the wagon outside. Returning with the pitcher of water she had requested, Potter does not realize Russell has made her exit. Furthermore, he is unaware that an Indian, who has just sampled the laughing gas in Potter's wagon, has stolen into the cabin and is hiding behind Russell's dressing-screen. Hearing the irrepressible giggling from the other side of the screen, Potter assumes they derive from Russell's sexual excitation. He reaches over the screen and fondles the Indian's bare arm. The misapprehension is extended as Potter fails to realize that the muscular arm does not belong to his wife. He closes his eyes and proceeds to kiss the Indian. The recipient of the kiss hits Potter on the head with his axe, knocking him unconscious. This corresponds with an earlier kiss, where Russell similarly immobilized him with a pistol. In each instance, Potter ascribes the effect to the woman's sexual power. At the end of the sequence he remains unaware that he has kissed the Indian. As this gag sequence suggests, the comedian's performance is often unified with a narratively articulated form of comedy that depends upon suspense or an unequal distribution of knowledge.

The comedian figure deforms familiar conventions of film heroism, unified identity and mature sexuality. Steve Seidman draws attention to instances of dressing up (for example, Woody Allen's impersonation of a robotic servant in *Sleeper*, 1973); to cross-dressing (for example, Bob Hope in drag in *The Princess and the Pirate*); to the feigning of madness (for example, Hope in *My Favorite Brunette*); to dual or multiple roles (for example, Danny Kaye in *Wonder Man*, 1945); to the preference for play and fantasy over reality (especially Kaye in *The Secret Life of Walter Mitty*, 1947).[27] At such moments, the comedian's performance intrudes into the fictional masquerade. But such intrusions can also have fictional consequences, where the *character* is afflicted with an unresolved or unevolved personality.[28] Through the intrusion, the comedian figure demonstrates that unified character identity is a fictional mask. But the fictional identity is not simply destroyed. Rather, it is momentarily overwhelmed, and held in suspension. When the comedian slides back into character, he carries with him repercussions from the performative rupture.

The fictional impetus is to subjugate deviance and disruption to the demands of stability and coherence. The performative impetus is to transform the narrative into a stage for a denarrativizing entertainment spectacle. The dialectic between the two can be articulated and resolved in various ways. For example, two distinct tendencies can be found within the comedies of Martin and Lewis. On the one hand, films like *That's My Boy* (1951) and *The Stooge* (1952) feature identity-thematic frame narratives that are articulated in a relatively serious manner. The narrative of *That's My Boy* bears similarities to such contemporary melodramas of masculine crisis as *Rebel Without a Cause* (1955), *Tea and Sympathy* (1956) and *Home from the Hill* (1960). Lewis's character Junior Jackson, is the hypochondriac son of the overbearing football star, Jarring Jack Jackson (Eddie Mayehoff). The father wants the son to follow in his footsteps, but Junior is a psychosomatic casualty of Jarring Jack's obsessive masculine success ethic and he cannot fulfill these expectations. The

Martin figure, Bill Baker, steps into this Oedipal impasse as a mediator. Baker is a reversed image of Junior: he is the superathletic son of a frail and impoverished father. Consequently, he is able to stand in as both idealized son for Jarring Jack and idealized father/buddy for Junior. His intervention enables father and son to achieve a mutual understanding: under Bill's guidance, Jackson Jr. is ultimately able to achieve legitimacy—recognition and acceptance, by the father, as a "man"—when he takes Bill's place in a crucial football game for the Jackson *alma mater*, Ridgeville University, where he leads the team to victory.

That's My Boy sticks closely to the structuring dynamic of the masculine melodrama. Its scenes of comic disruption are closely integrated within and motivated by the fiction. The frame narrative establishes the Martin-Lewis team in relation to a conformist regime of masculine success and identity. Two other Martin-Lewis films, *Sailor Beware* (1951) and *Jumping Jacks* (1952), represent a contrasting tendency. Their narratives are set within the context of the armed services—respectively, the navy and the paratroopers—where finding a place involves achieving an identity not in relation to the father but in relation to the institution: the individual has to fit in as part of a hierarchically structured community of men. Not only is the identity thematic differently conceptualized in these service comedies, but their narratives are also more loosely elaborated than in *That's My Boy*. The frame-story is developed in a far more episodic manner, serving to encompass a range of entertainment attractions: compressed plot sequences; solo comic spots by Lewis; Martin's songs; Martin-Lewis duo performances; and other musical/dance numbers. The principal function of the narrative in these two films, then, is to provide a legitimate linking structure for a variegated entertainment spectacle.

Conclusions and Irresolutions

The formalized comedian comedy, then, encompasses a range of possibilities for combining narrative and performative entertainment spectacle. Not all such films invest to the same degree in the fictional concept of character identity. At one extreme, the comedian figure's character can function as a mere painted backdrop (for instance, in *Sailor Beware*, *Jumping Jacks*, the Hope-Crosby *Road* movies, Abbott and Costello's films) or, at the other extreme, as a more lavishly equipped *mise-en-scène* (for instance, in *That's My Boy*, *The Stooge* and the films of Danny Kaye and Red Skelton). But, whatever the degree of fictional integration, the comedian figure is never fully bound within the constraints of character consistency—a fact that is often flamboyantly celebrated in the films' concluding scenes. Few of the formalized comedies end with the comic misfit earning his spurs as a *bona fide* hero. Like *That's My Boy*, *The*

Secret Life of Walter Mitty presents a conventional Oedipal narrative resolution. Danny Kaye's eponymous protagonist is a proofreader for a publisher of lurid pulp magazines. At the start of the film, the meek and mild Mitty is unable to stand up for himself, being totally dominated by his boss, his mother, his poodle-obsessed fiance, Gertrude, and his potential mother-in-law, Mrs. Griswald. The fantasy industry he works for furnishes a generic *mise-en-scène* for the daydreams through which Mitty seeks temporary escape from his real-life oppression. He fantasizes himself as captain of a sailing ship, a brilliant surgeon, an RAF flying ace-cum-entertainer, a cool and possessed gambler on a Mississippi riverboat, a singing milliner and a cowboy. The fantasy sequences which punctuate the film are compressed forms of the generic parody prevalent in the comedian film. They also set up opportunities for performative entertainment, such as the two comic novelty songs rendered by Kaye.

A divided character, Mitty is a hero in the world of his daydreams and a henpecked misfit in his day-to-day life. The narrative moves towards a unification of these internal and external realms by integrating fantasy and reality, as Mitty meets in "real life" the beautiful woman who has already featured in his daydreams. Towards the end of the film, Rosalind van Horn (Virginia Mayo) is kidnapped by a criminal gang of enemy agents. Mitty attempts to rescue the girl of his dreams in real life. To overcome the kidnappers, Mitty uses his extensive knowledge of pulp fiction. The unification of fantasy and reality is bolstered when the villains refer to Rosalind as a damsel in distress and a "sleeping beauty." Mitty is able to overcome his inadequacy when he saves Rosalind "for real". He then asserts himself over the "real-life" figures who had earlier forced him into submission, and he ends up with both Rosalind and a promotion.[29] In its final scenes, *The Secret Life of Walter Mitty* presents the assimilation of the comedian figure within the cultural and fictional order, stabilizing his identity (through the abolition of the multiple fantasy personas) and his sexuality (signaled by the reward of the bride).

It is debatable, though, whether such integrative resolutions are ever fully convincing. Coming at the end of the film, the integration of the comic misfit escapes the demands of narrative testing. It is often explicitly presented as a *figuration* of stability rather than a proper and irreversible stabilization. Even with a classically articulated Oedipal resolution like the ending of *That's My Boy*, it is difficult to accept Junior Jackson as a self-consistent character, rather than as Jerry Lewis. Bosley Crowther raises a similar question in his review of Lewis's first solo vehicle, *The Delicate Delinquent* (1957):

If there appears in this presentation a certain sobriety that was not a detectable feature in the old Dean Martin-Jerry Lewis films, it may respectfully be acknowledged as a purpose of the new Mr. Lewis. But it must also be discovered as the cause of an unevenness in this film. Mr. Lewis, as the star of his own picture, runs a gamut from Hamlet to clown . . . Mr. Lewis warding off a judo wrestler or trying to fit odd-shaped blocks into odd-shaped holes is a delirious comedian. Mr. Lewis trying to act hard like a man, with a policeman's hat planted on his noggin, is a mite incredible and absurd. The good intention of his message may be missed in this eccentricity.[30]

Like *That's My Boy*, *The Delicate Delinquent* ends with the Lewis figure finding his place through the intervention of an idealized masculine figure—in this instance, the police patrolman Mike Damon (Darren McGavin). But, as Crowther suggests, the more eccentric the comedian figure, the more difficult it becomes to accept his transition to maturity, although Lewis is, admittedly, a pretty extreme example.

The integrative ending is common in the comedies of Danny Kaye, the comedian of the 1940s and 1950s closest to Harold Lloyd. Other formalized comedies avoid such straightforward resolutions. A good example is *The Paleface*. "Painless" Potter misperceives himself to be a fearless Indian fighter, not realizing that his fame is due solely to Russell's sharpshooting prowess. This reversal of familiar Western film gender roles extends into *The Paleface*'s parodic treatment of the conventions of romantic love. Heroism and expectations of mature heterosexuality are firmly linked throughout, and Potter is deviant in both respects. *The Paleface*, like *The Secret Life of Walter Mitty*, asserts a clear separation between role-playing and reality, and then blends them together when, despite his ineptitude, Hope rescues Russell from the Indians and succeeds in vanquishing the gunrunners. Like Kaye's Walter Mitty, Potter defeats the villains and is awarded a beautiful woman as his bride. But instead of concluding with this, *The Paleface* ends with the Hope figure losing the woman, so reaffirming his unintegrated status.

The film's coda overturns the seemingly ordered resolution by subjecting the integrative tableau to a last-minute comic reversal. Hope and Russell are about to drive off in their wagon, a "happy honeymoon" placard on its side. As Hope prepares to urge the horses on, Russell interrupts him and takes over the reins herself. This refers to a running gag in the film—similar to the motorcycle sidecar routine in *Duck Soup*—where the wagon had remained stationary as Hope was pulled away by the horses. But now it is Jane Russell who is dragged off by the team of horses. Sitting on the wagon, Hope then turns to the camera, and cracks: "So what do you want, a happy ending?"

This final gag is the equivalent of a stage bow: Hope blatantly steps outside the fictional identity of "Painless" Potter, and into the role of performer. The fictional significance of the gag (Potter once more failing to consummate the marriage) is overwhelmed by its status as an extrafictional intrusion (the comedian commenting upon fictional conventions). The closing gag is a knowing wink to signal that the character identity "Painless" Potter, perpetually duped throughout the film by Russell's character, is a guise under the control of comedian Bob Hope. Similar endings which strip away an integrative resolution can be found in *Sailor Beware* and *Jumping Jacks*. The latter is especially interesting for the way that it sets up and deforms conventional procedures of narrative resolution by producing an overemphatic series of resolving scenarios that are overwhelmed by comic irresolutions.

As is common in the Martin-Lewis films, the narrative of *Jumping Jacks* is concerned with finding a place for the Lewis figure, Hap Smith. Hap is a talented comic entertainer who, at the start of the film, plays a supporting role in a variety act with Betsy Carver (Mona Freeman). The film opens with a number performed by the team, with Betsy mocking Hap's puny body. As she sings of her ideal military man, she tears the sleeves from Hap's army tunic, and embraces other, more likely soldiers behind his back. Betsy also forbids any backstage dalliances ("We do a swell act on stage. Let's just keep it that way, huh?"). Hap is rescued from this unsatisfying heterosexual act when his erstwhile partner, Chick Allen (Dean Martin), tricks him into a one-shot performance for the army show he has organized. After the success of this show Hap is forced by various circumstances, but largely by the manipulations of Chick, into masquerading as a paratrooper, assuming a false identity. When Hap manages to escape, Chick pursues him. He disrupts the audition that Betsy and Hap have arranged with a major Broadway agent, and in the process, Betsy falls in love with him. When Hap once more breaks away from the army camp, Chick follows him again—with the result that the Chick and Betsy romance is consolidated (as he serenades her on the dance floor of the Serviceman's Club).

At this point, where the potential alienation of Hap from both partners is strongly signaled as a dramatic problem, the film shifts to a relatively self-contained sequence where Hap is tested in the context of armed combat. As with the conclusions of Bob Hope's *Caught in the Draft* (1941) and Danny Kaye's *Up in Arms* (1944), the comedian is thrown into an arena of masculine activity which requires that he prove himself as a man. In a war-games exercise, the paratroopers are pitted against the army's tank division. Through sheer ineptitude, Hap manages both to rescue his pals and to capture the "enemy" general. He is then brought before General Timmons (Ray Teal) and is offered a choice: either to join up for real, or rejoin civilian life and face imprisonment. Hap thus allows himself to be legitimized as a corporal, under his real name. Hap's success in combat represents a deformation of the rules of acceptable masculine achievement decreed by the army, but the ending of the film presents a dislocation of the principles of narrative resolution. Indeed, the film teases with three of the permissible scenarios with which the narrative can conclude:

(a) the sequence at the Servicemen's Club raises the possibility of a resolution through heterosexual coupling. Chick is united with Betsy, and the film also summons up a potential girlfriend for Hap—an adoring young fan named Julie. No matter how casually it is motivated, heterosexual union tends formally to signify social integration through marriage, and hence the possible termination of the outsider or misfit status of the comedian figure;

(b) like the football game in *That's My Boy*, the mock-combat sequence is a trial by fire that permits Hap to gain recognition from the father figure, General Timmons, and thereby to consolidate his identity as a man;

(c) a coda presents Corporal Smith supervising the men under his command as they pass through the jump-door on a training exercise. But Hap falls out of the aircraft without a parachute. As he tumbles through the air, he manages to land on top of Chick's parachute, and he crawls down its side—to clasp hold of his buddy. Martin and Lewis are here unified as star team/male couple, at the expense of the two Oedipal scenarios of narrative integration.

The film then offers a closing gag that is directed at this third form of resolution—the unification of the familiar comedy partnership—but which simultaneously serves to reaffirm it. When the parachute touches down, Hap and Chick land upon a motorcycle and sidecar. Hap says "After what we've been through, nothing can separate us," and they then ride off together. But at a fork in the road, they are pulled apart, Hap and the motorcycle taking one path, Chick and the sidecar the other.

The final maneuvers of both *The Paleface* and *Jumping Jacks* suggest how formalized comedian comedies set in play the stabilizing process of most mainstream dramatic narrative: the dialectic between individuality and acculturation. But *Jumping Jacks* is also fed by a more pervasive tension—between the straight and the disordered, the serious and the comic, the adult and the child—that is embodied within the Martin-Lewis team itself. Andrew Sarris has suggested that, despite the apparent similarity to comedy duos like Laurel and Hardy, Abbott and Costello and fellow Paramount performers Bob Hope and Bing Crosby, Martin and Lewis represented a widely contrasting union of opposites:

Dean Martin and Jerry Lewis in *Jumping Jacks* (1952).

Most comedy teams . . . have a certain internal cohesion that unites them against the world outside. That is to say that members of a comedy team have more in common with each other than with anyone else. Martin and Lewis at their best . . . had a marvelous tension between them. The great thing about them was their incomparable incompatibility, the persistent sexual hostility. . . .[31]

Martin and Lewis embody polarized extremes of masculinity.[32] The team was by no means simply a 1950s version of Hope and Crosby: Bob and Bing each had separate and successful screen and extrafilmic careers prior to their teaming, but Martin and Lewis were firmly established as a male couple from the very start of their mainstream success.[33] In the public eye, each was incomplete without the other, and this made their split in 1956 all the more difficult for them. For Martin and Lewis to function successfully as a team across a range of films, this tension, and the homoerotic circuitry which underlies it, must be maintained, rather than resolved in any permanent fashion (as either total union or total separation). Hap Smith loses Chick Allen, his ideal ego, at the end of the film. But this restores the very instability and lack of balance that characterizes the Martin-Lewis team itself. Martin and Lewis are separated, so that they can be reunited once more (as a team) in their next film, where the process begins all over again.

The endings of films like *The Paleface* and *Jumping Jacks* are not in themselves determinate. They nevertheless emblematize both the degree to which the formalized comedian comedy must oscillate between fiction and comic performance, and the extent to which each process is conventionalized. The main point about comedy, whatever form it takes, is that it provides the site for an allowable disruption of fictional rules. Disruption is a crucial formal requirement—and expectation—of the comic text. Moreover, the comic effect itself involves not disruption alone but a dialectic between disruption and (re)ordering (and between the forms of pleasure associated with each process). It is crucial, then, to examine the role that deviation plays within the system. To take a basic example: Groucho Marx's lovemaking-as-insult (or insult-as-lovemaking) may breech the rules of romance familiar both from other texts and from everyday life, but it is a standardized and expected element within the Marx Brothers comedies. The representational machine of mainstream cinema comprises a complex series of interacting systems—including narrative, star systems, generic systems. The comedian may serve as a spanner in the works of the historical film, but this same spanner works simultaneously to tighten the nuts of the carnivalesque machinery of comedian comedy.

The Comedian and Gender: A Brief Note

The films considered in this essay highlight a certain important respect in which comic play within the comedian film is trammeled. They feature male comedians whose interventions into familiar fictional forms and genres inaugurate a play of disruption and containment that circulates around questions of gendered identity. An Oedipal model of male identity formation provides the principal structural paradigm for the frame narratives of the formalized comedian comedies. Even when this is flagrantly distorted, as in Lewis's *The Geisha Boy* (1958), *Rockabye Baby* (1958) and *The Ladies' Man* (1961), it remains the yardstick for the disruptions. Hollywood comedian comedy is a male-centered genre, in which female performers are traditionally marginalized. The genre repeatedly offers controlled assaults upon, or inversions of, the conformist options of male identity, sexuality and responsibility. Once more, the ending of *The Paleface* provides a pertinent illustration.

The Russell character's departure is the only joke in the film that is at the expense of the woman. Throughout the film, Russell is coded in terms of a sexual troubling, a confusion of conventional gender roles. From the start of the narrative, she usurps the traditional active role performed by the male hero. Dressed in the familiar buckskin of the cowboy, she is an overtly "masculine" woman, and by comparison Hope seems markedly deficient ("Mr and Mrs 'Painless' Potter," he announces as they join up with the wagon train. "I'm mister"). In relation to the Hope figure, Russell's character occupies a complex and shifting series of positions. Her expertise with the gun suggests a paternal masculine force, yet at times she is a more conventional maternal presence ("You poor kid," she says tenderly, after knocking Potter unconscious, "I'm sorry I had to do that"). And, over and above this, Jane Russell is familiar as an object of desire, an erotic icon for both Potter and the spectator. Instead of trying to reconcile these conflicting tendencies, the ending of the film ejects the woman. *The Paleface* links the refusal of the final integration to a refusal of women. Through doing so, the familiar Hope persona of controlled inversion can remain uncomplicated. Eliminating the woman sidesteps the problem of sexual placement. It is thus much easier for the comedian figure to remain a child.

This final gag feeds off a vein of sexual hostility that runs throughout the history of comedian comedy. Within the genre, women tend to signify the demands of integration and responsibility for the male. *The Paleface* offers a not uncommon final frisson that explicitly presents the woman as the target of the male comedian's revolt against order. A famous example is the final shot of *Duck Soup*, where the Marx Brothers' pelting of Margaret Dumont provides a parting testimonial to the comedians' characteristic "anarchy." The woman embodies everything that has to be assaulted to maintain their independence. *Sailor Beware* ends in a similar manner: immediately after Al Crowthers (Dean Martin) and Melvin Jones (Jerry Lewis) are united with female partners,[34] a final gag has them fleeing from the women, and back to the all-male haven of the waiting submarine. Once more, the ending provides a symptomatic indication of the sexual specificity of comedian comedy.

Molly Haskell's comments on the misogyny of knockabout comedy are relevant here. She suggests that the male comedy duo—Laurel and

Hardy, Abbott and Costello, Martin and Lewis—excludes heterosexuality to form a latently homosexual "union of opposites (tall/short, thin/fat, straight/comic) who, like husband and wife, combine to make a whole."[35] With this in mind, the bodily embrace of Martin and Lewis, as they descend through the air in *Jumping Jacks*, can be seen to substitute for the heterosexual embrace which concludes many classical Hollywood fiction films. In narrative terms, the film teases with the Lewis figure's possible unwillingness to perform as either hero or heterosexual male. The knowledge that Martin and Lewis belong together overwhelms all fictionally established heterosexual attachments—just as the final moments of *The Paleface* assert the independence of Bob Hope as solo comedian. In each instance, the comedian's prized eccentricity is defined in opposition to the responsibilities and limitations signified by the women. For the gendered machinery of Hollywood comedian comedy, the woman takes on the role of a potentially disruptive spanner who has to be kept away from the heart of the machine. A spanner that, in both *The Paleface* and *Sailor Beware*, causes the nuts to bolt.

2

Comedy, Melodrama and Gender:
Theorizing the Genres of Laughter

Kathleen Rowe

Poetics must begin with genre.
Medvedev/Bakhtin (*The Formal Method*, 175)

If on the high dramatic plane it is the son who kills and robs, it is
the wife who plays this role on the plane of comic Gallic tradition.
She will cuckold the husband, beat him, and chase him away.
Bakhtin (*Rabelais and His World*, 243)

Norman Jewison's 1987 film, *Moonstruck*, opens with an enormous
moon hanging over the skyline of Manhattan, followed by a montage of
shots of the "moonlit" city, from its bridges festooned with lights, to the
Metropolitan Opera House, to a poster advertising Giacomo Puccini's
opera, *La Bohème*. Within moments, the sky brightens and the streets
awaken with the activity of the day. A truck marked "Metropolitan Opera"
moves through the traffic, its path crossed by Loretta Castorini, a supersti-
tious Italian-American widow, walking to her job at a funeral parlor. The
film concludes in the Castorini kitchen, where the newly expanded family
is celebrating Loretta's engagement to Ronny and her mother Rose's
reconciliation with her husband Cosmo. Panning across the grandfather's
rowdy pack of dogs as it retreats into the parlor, the camera passes over
a series of family portraits, until it rests finally on those of an aged couple,
the matriarch and patriarch of the extended family gathered nearby.[1]

These two scenes bracket *Moonstruck*'s thematic and formal tensions.
Moving between darkness and daylight, images of death and those of
life, the film repeatedly shifts from the pathos of romantic melodrama,
most strongly represented by the story-within-the-story of the opera, to
the irony and humor of romantic comedy, two of the genres most typically
used to narrate fictions about women's lives.[2] The film's musical score
reinforces these tensions by playing the soaring melodies of Puccini against
"That's Amore," a corny but charming popular song sung by Dean Martin
("When the moon hits your eye like a big pizza pie, that's amore").[3]

Moonstruck's interplay of romantic comedy and melodrama does not
give equal weight to the two genres, however. After all, it is Dean Martin's
voice that closes the film, as well as opens it, and Puccini's arias that
are modulated into the schmaltzy pop style of "That's Amore." In the

Olympia Dukakis and Cher in *Moonstruck* (1987).

same way, the film uses romantic comedy to mirror, contain and ultimately transform the melodramatic themes and motifs of *La Bohème*. *Moonstruck* moves from the dying Mimi, the doomed bride-to-be in the opera, to the comic rebirth of the film's heroine Loretta; from Loretta's tears as opera spectator to the smiles and laughter of the film spectator; and from the opera's glorification of a romantic love based on woman's loneliness and pain to an alternative which, unlike most romantic comedy, refuses to make a woman's heterosexuality contingent on the symbolic death of her mother. Dramatizing the tensions between melodrama and romantic comedy, testing the values of one against the other, the film argues finally for comedy.

Romantic comedy might well rival melodrama as the narrative form most typically used to shape fictive accounts of women's lives. Yet feminist critics have been slow to direct much sustained attention to the genre. At the same time, feminist film theory since the late 1980s has found itself haunted by what Mary Ann Doane and Janet Bergstrom have described as a "kind of ennui," which they attribute to unresolved issues of female spectatorship (15).[4] I would like to suggest that this ennui has arisen in part from the powerful hold of melodrama on the female imagination. For many women, the social contradictions of gender have been played out most compellingly in narrative forms (the sentimental and Gothic novels, the woman's weepie film, the television soap opera) that are centered on female suffering and tears. Unlike comedy, which addresses a more active spectator, these forms position the spectator as powerless to avert the catastrophes they enact, and in fact produce their tears out of that powerlessness. Although the study of melodrama has yielded much ground-breaking feminist work, it has also reinforced feminist film theory's ambivalent but close relation to psychoanalysis, an interpretive paradigm that (despite its many variations) ties femininity to castration, pathology and an exclusion from the symbolic. As a result, texts that might suggest less deterministic views of female subjectivity have not received the scrutiny they deserve. I am referring in particular to those which position women as subjects of a laughter that expresses anger, resistance, solidarity and joy.[5]

Traditionally, the genres of laughter associated with the social practice of carnival and the narrative structures of comedy have proven elusive and difficult to theorize.[6] Humanist cultural criticism has neglected gender almost altogether in its studies of comedy and the carnivalesque. At the same time, feminists, with a few exceptions, have yet to fully investigate the potential of these forms to produce a theory that is not only explanatory but emancipatory.[7] Such an investigation would not disavow melodrama; genres, after all, do not exist as discrete formal categories but in relation to one another and to the social formations that produce them. Instead it would place melodrama within a wider range of cultural practices and genres as diverse as the television sitcom and the avant-garde, where women have made pointed use of the comic, the parodic and the grotesque.

This essay takes a step in that direction by approaching the study of romantic comedy in terms of gender. Seeking, as Robin Wood advises, not the "what" of a genre but the "why," I locate one of the why's of romantic comedy in the ideological tension surrounding the "excessive" woman who "desires too much." Whereas the transgressive male finds his home in the heroic genres of what Mikhail Bakhtin has called "the high dramatic plane," the transgressive woman finds hers in the "lower" forms of melodrama and romantic comedy. But whereas melodrama allows the transgressive woman to triumph only in her suffering, romantic comedy takes her story to a different end, providing a sympathetic place for female resistance to masculine authority and an alternative to the suffering femininity affirmed by melodrama. Making fun of and out of inflated and self-deluded notions of heroic masculinity, romantic comedy is often structured by gender inversion, a disruption of the social hierarchy of male over female through what might be called the *topos* of the unruly woman or the "woman on top." When romantic comedy most fully realizes the potential of this *topos*, it dramatizes a resistance to the law of Oedipus, a carnivalizing of sexual identities and gender hierarchies that posits a new and more inclusive basis for community than the social order it takes as its point of reference.[8]

Comedy and the Feminine

An understanding of the transgressive woman's placement in romantic comedy begins with her exclusion from the genres of the "high dramatic plane"—tragedy, the epic and genres associated with realism. It has become a critical commonplace that tragedy is a deeply "masculine" form, charting the progress of the male hero on a quest through alien landscapes, war, corporate battlefields for his Oedipal patrimony. While the term tragedy is most often used in connection with historical periods centuries removed from our own, Hollywood has produced its own versions of the excessive, larger-than-life tragic hero in such figures as Charles Foster Kane and Michael Corleone of the *Godfather* saga.[9]

The story of a woman with heroic aspirations, however, is rarely told in a tragic form. As Carolyn Heilbrun has argued, women's lives can be narrated only within the boundaries of heterosexual love, motherhood and loneliness. As a result, the female counterpart to the excessive male hero can rarely define herself except as a *romantic* heroine, who is placed in relation to a man and whose heroism is subordinated to that relationship. Her story must be "emplotted," to use historian Hayden White's term, in those genres oriented toward the private sphere and the family: melodrama, which emphasizes loneliness and/or motherhood (and is commonly considered debased or feminized tragedy) and romantic comedy, which emphasizes love.[10] *Moonstruck* casts all three of its major female characters— Loretta, Rose and Mimi—into stories that intermingle loneliness and love, with Rose appearing in the motherhood plot as well. It would seem that a man's presence, or conspicuous absence, keeps a woman's desires, accomplishments and failures in the proper perspective.

If tragedy is the most masculine of genres, the implications of gender for comedy are less clear. What is the correspondence between the son who "kills and robs in the high dramatic plane" and the wife who "plays this role" in the comic tradition? Why does changing the gender of the transgressive protagonist require a change in genre? And does the movement from tragic hubris to comic unruliness necessarily tame female transgressiveness?

Some feminist historians consider comedy a feminine form: "ancient, tribal, used to celebrate family bondings like marriage . . . always moving dramatically towards conclusions in which people are united and conflict dissipated" (Linda Jenkins, 11). Lisa Merrill asks: "If tragic form is associated with a specifically male psychological experience, might comedy be an affirmation of female experience?" (272). The title of Linda Bamber's study of Shakespeare, *Comic Women, Tragic Men*, suggests such a correspondence. Thomas Schatz identifies the film genres of order (the Western, gangster film, detective film) with male dominance and the individual hero, and the contrasting genres of integration (the musical, screwball comedy, family melodrama) with female dominance and the couple/collective hero (35). Such a characterization is surely apt. However, the very dearth of theory and criticism about comedy in general and the "unbearable lightness" (in Andrew Horton's words) of what does exist (1), in contrast to the voluminous work on tragedy, already suggest that no simple symmetry between the two forms exists. Despite (and probably because of) its enormous and enduring popularity, comedy has never enjoyed the critical prestige of tragedy and its descendants. Like melodrama, comedy is more often confined to the realm of amusement than art because of its popular accessibility and its connections with gossip, intrigue and the everyday, areas of culture tied to the feminine. The introduction to a classic anthology of American humor notes that "the world likes humor, but treats it patronizingly. It decorates its serious artists with laurels, and its wags with Brussels sprouts" (White, xvii).[11]

Like literary criticism, film criticism has gravitated toward genres more aligned with tragedy than comedy. Early genre criticism in the mid-1960s and early seventies focused on the Western, the gangster film, the war film, the detective film, the crime film and the horror film. More recently, film critics on the left have been wary of granting comedy a critical edge.[12] The lessons about comedy, politics and pleasure learned by the idealistic but naive director John L. Sullivan in Preston Sturges's *Sullivan's Travels* (1941) seem to have remained unlearned or at least inadequately studied. The consequences for film criticism of this lack of critical attention to comedy have been complex and, I believe, unfortunate. In "*The Nutty Professor*: A 'Problem' in Film Scholarship," Michael Selig ties the absence of rigorous genre analysis of comedy to a critical practice that does not acknowledge its rootedness in auteurism or its role in producing film canons based on the accomplishments of individual (male) directors and, in the case of comedy, male performers.

Narrative comedy is notoriously difficult to define, let alone explain, and those theories that do exist diverge widely. Emerging from them are two apparently contradictory but closely related characteristics. The first, which is often a prelude to the second, is comedy's *antiauthoritarianism*— its attack on the Law of the Father and drive to level, disrupt and destroy hierarchy, to comment on and contest the values tragedy affirms. Comedy breaks taboos and expresses those impulses which are always outside social norms.[13] Where comedy is, so are food, sex, excrement, blasphemy, usually presented obliquely enough to be socially acceptable. Comedy, in contrast to tragedy, inflects the Oedipal story that underlies most narratives by shifting the son's guilt to the father. Youth (the small, the petty and the powerless) triumphs over old age (authority, repression and the law), and the "happy ending" fulfills the son's transgressive desires. In one sense, comedy might be seen simply as staging a generational struggle between masculine forces to ensure the victory of the son. However, the weapons it deploys are also available to women and all oppressed people to express aggression and rage at the forces of the father.

Comedy, of course, can also be turned against those people in a movement of displaced abjection, when it shifts its destructive impulses from socially powerful groups that might be considered its proper target to even weaker ones. In this case, comedy may express the hostility to women Freud described in his analysis of the joke, or may express fears about what would happen if social justice were achieved and oppressed groups liberated. When comedy takes such a turn in narrative form, it emphasizes the first part of the Oedipal story—the rivalry between father and son, between forces of authority and repression and those of rebellion and release—but does not allow the son to wander far from existing structures of power. Much film comedy follows this tendency, and either excludes the feminine or subsumes it in its male figures.

Comedy's second tendency expresses an impulse toward *renewal* and *social transformation*. Emphasizing the second part of the Oedipal story, or the formation of the couple, this tendency finds its fullest expression in romantic comedy.[14] Male theorists, such as Northrop Frye, have often claimed too much virtue for this type of comedy, seeing its form as neutral rather than patriarchal. However, romantic comedy demands a place for women, in the narrative and in its vision of a social order that is not only renewed but also, ideally, transformed. Romantic comedies such as *Moonstruck* that mock male heroism through gender inversion and female unruliness retain a strong element of antiauthoritarianism, and so combine both comedic tendencies, holding sentiment and skepticism in a balance that characterizes, I believe, the most successful examples of the genre.

Sons and Fathers: Antiauthoritarianism in Comedian Comedy

Almost all comedic forms—from jokes to gags to slapstick routines to the most complex narrative structures—attempt a liberation from authority. Like carnival, comedy levels the lofty and erases distinctions, replacing the exalted hero of tragedy with one reduced to the level of Everyman, or lower. Consider, for example, the blockbuster 1990 film, *Home Alone* and its 1992 sequel, *Home Alone 2*. Like many comedies of the 1980s and early nineties (*Big, Pee Wee's Big Adventure, Bill and Ted's Excellent*

Adventure, *Ferris Bueller's Day Off*, *Wayne's World*), *Home Alone* exaggerates the comic male hero's infantilization. Its hero is a precocious little boy, who turns his accidental abandonment by his distracted, thoughtless parents into an opportunity for an anarchic vacation from their repressive and alienating rules.

In some ways, comedy's interest in the social, as opposed to tragedy's in the individual, aligns it with values that are conventionally associated with the feminine: community over separation, and the preservation of life rather than its sacrifice for principle, power or the quest for a Faustian knowledge. Comedy often mocks the masculinity that tragedy enobles. The very centrality of sex to comedy and the comedic agenda of renewing life open up space for the presence of women that does not exist in the more masculine world of tragedy. Because sex is to comedy what death is to tragedy, the heterosexual couple that is a mainstay of Hollywood narrative film is also one of comedy's most fundamental conventions. In comedy, sex is not a means toward knowledge or transcendence of the self, as in tragedy, but social. Sex is part of comedy's overall attack on repression and a celebration of bodily pleasure, a means of connection within the space of family and the time of generation.

Despite this apparent accord with the feminine, however, comedy in mainstream narrative film usually makes its case against the father with very little attention to the mother or daughter; it may show Oedipus to be a fool, but it still places him at the heart of the story. As Lucy Fischer has argued, comedy—in both theory and practice—is generally guilty of "matricide," of "throwing Momma from the train," to borrow a phrase from a recent, particularly misogynist film. The canon of (primarily U.S.) film comedy consists almost entirely of male directors and performers, from the Keystone Kops through Woody Allen, Eddie Murphy and many more.[15] Mae West is the only woman who is regularly included among them.

While some of these actors and directors have worked in romantic comedy, most of their films fall into a category Steve Seidman and others have described as "comedian" comedy and Stuart Kaminsky has called comedy "in the mode of the individual." Because "individual" usually means individual *male*, this kind of comedy might more aptly be described as "male-centered comedy," with male referring to an individual (Buster Keaton, Steve Martin), a couple (Laurel and Hardy, Dean Martin and Jerry Lewis, Cheech and Chong) or entire troupe or ensemble (the Marx Brothers, Monty Python). Women have performed in comedian comedy since its earliest days, but until recently, their absence from the canon of comedian comedy, as well as the cultural and institutional reasons for that absence, have remained largely unexamined.[16]

When comedian comedy mocks the heroic masculinity affirmed in serious drama, it often does so by creating a feminized, antiheroic male hero who appropriates the positive, anarchic, "feminine" principles comedy affirms. From Charlie Chaplin to Harpo Marx to Woody Allen to Danny DeVito, these figures are often small and feminine or androgynous in appearance, and positioned as feminine through their roles as underdogs. The films they appear in tend to emphasize their comic performance rather than a narrative trajectory to the altar; even if a bride exists in a romantic subplot, the son remains the primary agent of liberation and new (social) life.[17]

Comedian comedy often compounds its erasure of the bride by directing its corrective laughter onto the matriarch, displacing hostility from the father onto the repressive, phallic mother. In such comedy, consistent with Freud's analysis of the joke, women do not stand as essential subjects in a drama of new social life but as fearsome or silly symbols of repression and obstacles to social transformation. The matriarch represents a dreaded domesticity and propriety, a fearful symbol of a community that includes women, or even excludes men. Her ranks include spinsters, dowagers, prohibitionists, mothers-in-law, librarians, suffragettes, battle-axes, career woman, "women's libbers" and lesbians.[18] They serve as targets for the hatred of repression mobilized by comedy and especially by the infantile, regressive and misogynistic male hero of the comedian comedy.

Margaret Dumont played such a matriarch, although sympathetically, in the Marx Brothers films. In the futurist black comedy *Brazil* (1985), the "terrible mother" is only one of many female grotesques, who include an enormous secretary, an old woman who decomposes after the failure of her plastic surgery, an innocent-looking little girl who asks the hero if she can "see his willy." In *The Goonies* (1985) and *Throw Momma From the Train* (1987), Anne Ramsey plays an evil, comic mother. One of the most vicious treatments of such a matriarch appears in *It's a Mad Mad Mad Mad World* (1963), where Ethel Merman plays a terrible mother-in-law—matronly, loud, aggressive and abrasive. Her humiliations culminate in a final pratfall that makes her the target of unsympathetic laughter within the film and outside it. The film exemplifies the hostility of much male-centered comedy toward women. While critiquing much that is repressive about the father, such comedy often only reinforces his subjugation of women, and ensures that after his defeat he will be replaced by a new but hardly improved version of himself.

Sons and Brides: Renewal and Transformation in Romantic Comedy

Comedy celebrates excess not only for itself but because it paves the way for a community liberated from structures grown so rigid and unyielding that they threaten its very existence. Comedy that emphasizes this principle harnesses the genre's antiauthoritarian energy, and directs it toward creating a new vision of community based on the assumption that the renewal of both biological and social life depends on connection or relation to others. In this regard, comedy insists that community does not repress individual desire, but in fact represents its very fulfillment.

Romantic comedy treats the social difference that impedes community as a matter of sexual difference, and so it builds the feminine into both the construction and the resolution of narrative conflict. The formation of the heterosexual couple, of course, powerfully reasserts the supposedly universal law of kinship and the institution of what Adrienne Rich has called compulsory heterosexuality, buttressed historically by the ideology of romantic love. But the couple's union must also be seen, I believe, as a sign of the partial suspension of conflict—the tolerance for difference—on which community depends.[19] The utopian possibilities of a new social order lie in the couple's victory over the obstacles between them, and in the child or new life implicit in their union. This utopianism is traditionally represented in the public ceremony of the wedding or feast. As Laura Mulvey suggests, the triumph of the Law of the Father represented in narrative is not always absolute. During times of social transformation, and especially in the genres of laughter, narratives can reabsorb "the abnormal back into a sense of an order that is altered," although it is still recognizably subject to the law (170).[20]

Few critics have surpassed Northrop Frye's insights into comedy's utopian dimension, its mapping of an "order that is altered." Frye, in fact, can be credited with finding a profundity in romantic comedy, and in comedy itself, that had eluded earlier generations of critics.[21] For Frye, all narrative reworks a common story of community, struggle and renewal; of birth, death and rebirth. Comedy emphasizes the renewal element of the cycle. A world wilting under repressive law is liberated through a temporary movement into a dimension Bakhtin would call the carnivalesque, Victor Turner the liminal, and C. L. Barber the "green world" of festivity and natural regeneration.[22]

In romantic comedy, this movement follows the remarkably tenacious pattern of New Comedy: "What usually happens is that a young man wants a young woman, that his desire is resisted by some opposition, usually paternal, and that near the end of the play some twist in the plot enables the hero to have his will" (Frye, 163). The lovers are tested, and finally find themselves by retreating from the ordinary world, where their union seems impossible, to a "magical" place apart from everyday life, such as the moonlight island in *It Happened One Night* (1934), the Connecticut forest in *Bringing Up Baby* (1938), the cruise ship in *The Lady Eve* (1941), and the enchanting moments at the Metropolitan Opera and on the streets of New York City in *Moonstruck*. When the couple

Clark Gable and Claudette Colbert in *It Happened One Night* (1934).

returns, their union, in Frye's words, "causes a new society to crystallize" around them. The family gathered at the end of *Moonstruck* represents just such a crystallization.

Within the overarching narrative structure of birth, death and rebirth, every comedy contains a potential tragedy. But every tragedy can also be seen as an incomplete comedy. In the larger perspective of history, community or even biology, the life and death of the individual are no longer tragic. By shifting the guilt to the father and allowing the victory of the son, comedy gets the last word, just as on the Greek stage a satyr play always concluded a trilogy of tragedies. Chaplin's comment that tragedy should be filmed in close-up and comedy in long shot is suggestive here. Comedy not only requires a certain emotional detachment from the fate of the individual—ultimately death—but makes such detachment possible by showing that fate in a broader perspective, in long shot.

There is much to fault about Frye's work. His assertions about comedy as wish-fulfilling fail to ask *whose* wishes; his impulse, and it is the impulse of a liberal humanism, is to seek a common ground of shared desire, rather than to investigate the divisions which make such common ground difficult if not impossible to achieve. It is a mistake compounded by Stanley Cavell, in his work on romantic comedy and melodrama, which presents itself as apolitical but in fact is not.[23] Frye assumes too readily that desire in romantic comedy is the sole possession of the male hero: "What usually happens is that a young man wants a young woman," the woman can only be "bride to be redeemed." While this may be so in the Greek and Roman New Comedies, it is not true of Shakespearean comedy or such romantic film comedies as *Moonstruck*, with which it has much in common.

Female characters such as Loretta and Rose, or Susan Vance in *Bringing Up Baby*, Sugarpuss in *Ball of Fire* (1941) and Billie Dawn in *Born Yesterday* (1950)—like Rosalind in Shakespeare's *As You Like It* and Viola in *Twelfth Night*—function as far more than simply "brides to be redeemed." Instead, they are obstacles to desire, objects of desire, and subjects of desire often initiating and controlling the movement of the plot. As "women on top," they enjoy a dramatic weight comparable to that of the male hero in tragedy.

Despite such shortcomings, however, Frye has much to offer feminist approaches to comedy. Like Fredric Jameson, Frye sees narrative as an epistemological category, a structure which gives meaning to those other phenomena that also contribute to comedy—performance, gags, jokes, laughter. As in the case of auteurist studies of comedian comedy, when these factors are emphasized apart from narrative, gender has tended to disappear. By asserting the priority of narrative, Frye directs attention to the space, albeit limited, ensured for women in the comedic inflection of the Oedipal narrative; this space is most pronounced when the narrative privileges the son's quest for a bride over his battle with the father, and especially when it places the couple—or the woman—at its center. In addition, by asserting that comedy in effect contains tragedy, Frye implicitly reverses the hierarchy that has so long privileged tragedy: "The watcher of death and tragedy has nothing to do but sit and wait for the inevitable end; but something gets born at the end of comedy, and the watcher of birth is a member of a busy society" (170).

Melodrama and Romantic Comedy

Romantic comedy exists in the same kind of generic tension with melodrama that Frye finds between comedy and tragedy.[24] As *Moonstruck* suggests, romantic comedy usually contains a potential melodrama, and melodrama, like *La Bohème*, contains a potential romantic comedy. Melodrama depends on a belief in the possibility of romantic comedy's happy ending, a belief that heightens the pathos of its loss. Similarly, romantic comedy depends on the melodramatic threat that the lovers will not get together and that the heroine will suffer a fate like Mimi's—becoming a spinster, marrying the wrong man, suffering, even dying. In *Moonstruck*, we fear that Loretta will marry doltish Johnny rather than dashing Ronny. But while critics have exerted considerable effort to preserve the distinctions between drama on the high plane and its others (such as melodrama), no such stakes are involved in preserving the distinction between melodrama and romantic comedy. Both forms are set squarely in the province of women—the private, the domestic, the home or the heart. Both narrate the stories of "excessive" women who assert their own desire and whose stories are emplotted in narratives which depend on the ideology of heterosexual romance. Both use the deferral of sexual fulfillment not only to reinforce the fantasies of romance but as plot devices to prolong narrative suspense. Both depend to varying degrees on the structure of gender inversion.

Obvious and important differences, of course, distinguish the forms. For my purposes, the most critical one concerns the issue of motherhood. Noting that the maternal missing from romantic comedy surfaces in melodrama, Cavell asks: "What is it that makes the absence of the mother a comedy, and her presence a melodrama?" ("Psychoanalysis and Cinema" 20). Mothers and mother substitutes exist in some romantic comedies (*The Philadelphia Story*, *Bringing Up Baby*, *My Man Godfrey*). However, the heroine usually neither has nor is a mother, and the father fills the critical parental role. This situation arises in part from the traditional place of the woman as a token of exchange between men, mediating the transfer of power from one generation to the other. Mothers rarely hold any power to transfer; figures like the aunt in *Bringing Up Baby* are rare exceptions.

More suggestively, the mother's absence from romantic comedy occurs because of the genre's attention to the heroine's Oedipal passage to femininity, her acceptance of the terms of heterosexuality, the subjugation of female by male. To do so, she must reject the most important feminine identification of her life, her mother, in favor of an exclusive attachment to a man, a stand-in for her father. This rent between mother and daughter, ignored in our culture, is "the essential female tragedy," according to Adrienne Rich (237). This tragedy makes possible the story of masculine victory which patriarchy writes as comedy. Romantic comedy ironically allows its heroine to participate in its utopian, symbolic rebirth only by abdicating her literal connections with maternity, her bond to her mother and eventually to her own daughters. In *Philadelphia Story* (1940), it is Tracy's relationship with her estranged father, not her mother, that is crucial; until she reconciles with him, she cannot complete the maturation into femininity signaled by her acceptance of her proper mate. In *It Happened One Night*, the hostilities between Ellie and her father end when she accepts her father's choice, Peter, instead of her initial choice,

King Westley. Covering up the costs of a woman's heterosexuality with laughter and pleasure, romantic comedy tolerates, and even encourages, its heroine's short-lived rebellion because that rebellion ultimately serves the interest of the hero. It either disciplines the unruly bride, or prepares the hero for his Oedipal legacy by moderating or refining in some other way a masculinity shown as initially deficient.[25]

As *Moonstruck* suggests, the stronger the presence of women, the more a romantic comedy is likely to undercut or problematize the heterosexual couple. In *Bringing Up Baby*, for example, the aunt's position as bearer of social power reinforces the critique of conventional gender roles that runs through the film, culminating in its precarious resolution over a collapsing mountain of dinosaur bones. In the "working girl" comedies of the early thirties, female roommates highlight the cost to women of leaving a female-centered world of support and community to become part of a heterosexual couple. In rare cases, sisters and female friends provide a utopian element that transcends the closure represented by the couple. *The Women* (1939), for example, might be described as an *anti*romantic comedy, in which matrimony is undone and men remain a structural absence superfluous to the film's pleasures. Mary, the heroine, finally returns to her husband, but what is most memorable about the film is its comic and campy rendering of the texture of women's relationships.

In contrast to such comedies, melodrama not only teaches that a woman's lot under patriarchy is to suffer, but makes that suffering pleasurable. As Loretta says in *Moonstruck*, overwhelmed by Mimi's fate, "It's awful, beautiful, sad. She died." Melodrama, like romantic comedy, ties a woman's rebellion to her acceptance or refusal of the terms of heterosexuality. But unlike romantic comedy, it dooms her rebellion from the start. Exposing the male villainy repressed in romantic comedy—or shown as simple foolishness—melodrama takes up the story of the heroine for whom romantic comedy's happy ending never will be possible, or the story of what *follows* that happy ending. Melodrama, in fact, is the only cinematic genre (with the possible exception of the horror film) that has traditionally been available for that sequel. Because melodrama concerns the heroine who fails to resolve the Oedipal passage, it leaves the pre-Oedipal mother/daughter bond intact. It is no surprise, then, that under patriarchy the stories of such women are told in forms that guarantee their punishment. From *Mildred Pierce* (1945) to *Terms of Endearment* (1983), mothers and daughters caught up in each other's lives can only tear each other apart. Melodrama thus insists that women's deviance from the norms of our culture can lead only to isolation and tears, their pleasures can come only in pain, and the stories of their rebellion can be the occasions only of grief.

Stella Dallas (1937), a melodrama that has attracted much attention from feminist critics, illustrates the structural relation between melodrama and romantic comedy and the place of the mother in each. Stella's story eventually encompasses all three "women's" narratives—love, motherhood and, finally, loneliness. The film begins in the love plot, where Stella's desire to cross the boundaries of class and gender by actively pursuing the boss's son appears in the positive light of romantic comedy.[26] As the film follows her story past love into motherhood and loneliness, it moves into melodrama. Here, the assertion of her desire takes on a tragic cast, as it begins to signify her transgressive refusal to submerge her own identity into that of her husband, as well as the impossibility of preserving that identity and being a "good mother" at the same time.

Romantic comedy returns a second time in the film with the story of Stella's daughter Lollie. In this part of the film, Stella's unruliness becomes a source of pathos and horror when it nearly costs Lollie the "happily ever after" ending of romantic comedy; the most dangerous expression of female unruliness, after all, is the love between mother and daughter, which must be shattered to enable the daughter's narrative to end on a note of romantic comedy. Stella has no choice but to destroy the bond between them, which she does in a *tour-de-force* performance of the unruliness that has come to stand for a dangerous female independence from men. Lollie begins the painful transfer of her allegiance from her mother to her father and to the suitor who will be his successor. Lollie's story—with the important exception of her relation to her mother—remains confined to the structure of romantic comedy: a handsome and wealthy young man courts her, the obstacles to their union are overcome, and they marry.

As in most romantic comedies, Lollie's story stops short at the altar. But the film allows the viewer to experience romantic comedy from the point of view—quite literally—of the mother whose "death" is required to bring about its happy ending. In the film's most wrenching moment, the climax of Lollie's romantic comedy coincides with Stella's redemption in melodrama, after she has enacted the self-annihilation that ideology demands of mothers. Outside the house, excluded from Lollie's wedding, Stella watches Lollie, while Lollie watches only her new husband. With tears streaming down her face, radiant in her self-denial, Stella is banished from the occasion that in comedy stands above all for inclusiveness, renewal and festivity.

Moonstruck Again

Moonstruck offers a very different version of the relations between mothers and daughters and the dynamics of romantic love. Whereas *Stella Dallas* ends resolutely as a melodrama, *Moonstruck* concludes as a romantic comedy—but one that comes close to having it both ways in its intermingling of the two forms. The film retains those elements of melodrama that are most positive from a feminist point of view—the recognition of masculine guilt and acknowledgment of women's suffering, the presence of the mother and the connection among women. It rewrites romantic comedy's "happily ever after" love story to include a serious dose of pain, from Mimi's to Rose's, reminding us that romantic comedy never tells the whole of a woman's story. But the film rejects one of the most crucial elements of melodrama, the suffering, victimized femininity represented by Stella and by Mimi in *La Bohème*. While retaining the couple as an emblem of the fulfillment of all desire, the film ironizes romantic love, especially male melodramatics about romantic love.[27] In addition, it places the couple in the context of a community in which male authority is under gentle but continual assault.

Despite the immediate presence of melodrama in the film, *Moonstruck* is above all a comedy, and its generic tensions must be seen in that light. Like most comedy, its conflicts, choices and dilemmas are organized along the axis of life and death rather than the moral polarities of melodrama. Loretta speaks her first words of the film in a wry exchange with her boss about a corpse; Mamma Cammereri lies on her deathbed in Sicily; the grandfather socializes with his friends in a graveyard; Loretta and Ronny confess that they were "dead" before they met. Throughout, the film examines how to deal with life's pain, from aging to broken hearts and broken dreams to mortality, arguing finally that such pain can be avoided only by avoiding life itself.

In *Moonstruck*, it is the men, more than the women, who retreat from life, through fear, self-pity or self-absorption. In so doing, they demonstrate a lack of self-knowledge that not only hurts the women who love them, but makes them prime subjects for comic critique. Cosmo's fear of death causes him to withdraw from Rose and take a mistress. Perry, the middle-aged communications professor, has become "dead" in his work, and feels alive only when he sees himself through the eyes of young female students. Ronny hides in the inferno of his bakery. When he tells Loretta his life story, he rages like a villainous romantic hero of melodrama, while an adoring female employee weeps, saying "He's the most tormented man I know. I'm in love with him." It is important to note from the outset that the film's comic critique of masculinity is made possible in part by its use of ethnicity, for foolish men who are Italian-American can more readily be made the subject of comedy than those (like the professor) who are WASP.

While male pain is played for comedy, female pain is not; and *Moonstruck*'s women are shown as having a clearer sense of their identity than the men do. That clarity and strength authorize the film's use of gender inversion, which it introduces in an early scene, when Johnny and Loretta witness the professor being humiliated in a restaurant by his date, a young female student. Johnny giggles, then tells Loretta that a man who cannot control his woman is funny. The remark signals Johnny's lack of self-awareness, but more importantly, it establishes a model of love—based on male dominance—that the film will eventually replace with another far more appealing one. As a "woman on top," a characterization enhanced by the unruly star persona Cher brings to the part, Loretta challenges her father and the other men in her life. She dominates Johnny, and initiates the romance with Ronny, seeking him out, luring him from his cave, feeding him raw meat to restore his strength, and bringing him back to life. At the same time, by dramatizing the conflict between her desire for Ronny and her desire to remain independent, she exposes the contradictions lived by heterosexual women under patriarchy.

Cosmo's name means world, but the *social* cosmos or community the Castorini family represents is organized around Rose, whose deadpan wisdom and clear-eyed perceptiveness contrast with the melodramatic suffering of the film's male figures. When she turns down Perry's invitation to a tryst, she tells him that she knows who she is, implying that he lacks a comparable degree of self-awareness. When she counters Cosmo's self-pitying speech with: "Your life is *not* built on nothing. *Te amo*," she reminds him that the love that binds people together is not "nothing," but in fact all that there is. The prominence of Rose's story, and her intimacy with Loretta, displace romantic film comedy's conventional focus on the isolated heterosexual couple. Throughout the film the two women confide in each other, and their paths often cross. In this female-centered community, the crystallization of a new society does not occur until Cosmo capitulates to Rose, and Loretta does not have to give up her mother to get her man.

Not surprisingly, the moon is *Moonstruck*'s most important visual and thematic motif. Hanging over the film like the moon over the city is a sense of the mythic, the magic, the miraculous. The film is drenched in celestial imagery, from the moon itself to the stars and moons on the charm bracelet Cosmo gives Mona, the chandeliers at the Metropolitan Opera, the bags of "Sunburst Flour" piled next to Ronny in his dungeon bakery. Comparing himself to Orlando Furioso, a figure from Italian romance, Uncle Raymond sings, "Hey there, you with the stars in your eyes," and Ronny speaks of "storybook love" as having the unreal perfection of "stars and snowflakes." A familiar symbol of the feminine, the moon also suggests madness and the demonic, and it is accompanied by the masculine counterpart of the wolf, most comically rendered in the grandfather's pack of yapping dogs.

The grandfather has a privileged connection with the imagery of magic and romance. Observing the events that unfold with the same balance of engagement and detachment that the film asks of its viewers, he is the story's other Fool. Like Johnny, he is both puzzled and possessed of a naive wisdom. At one point he follows his dogs past a "No Trespassing" sign into a cemetery. This gentle act of transgression, of mixing death and life, is followed by another when the dogs dig up flowers and defecate on the new grave of his friend Alphonso. For the grandfather, this is no sacrilege. Alphonso is dead (or "asleep," he says), and the dogs are alive. Where Cosmo surrounds death with the aura of melodrama, the grandfather takes the attitude of the carnivalesque. He confronts death's inevitability as a fact of life, and worries only about threats to the living— for how Cosmo endangers the family by refusing to pay for Loretta's wedding. As Rose tells Cosmo, "No matter what you do, you're going to die, just like everyone else." She accepts this inevitability with a gaze as sober and direct as those of the old matriarch and patriarch of the family portraits.

As the grandfather knows, the moon and the wolf are real. To be moonstruck—to give oneself over to forces outside the rational—is to court danger, for as Uncle Raymond recalls, the moon can "crush the house." Yet those, like Loretta and Ronny, who attempt to deny its power and intensity cut themselves off from life. To be moonstruck is to acknowledge the wolf within, to give it its due, to grant that howling at the moon is the very foundation of social institutions.

Melodrama, with its heightened emotion, is the generic equivalent of being moonstruck, and the film argues that it, too, must be given its place in the more utopian narratives of comedy. That place is most clearly occupied in the film by the opera *La Bohème*. Mimi epitomizes the suffering, passivity and self-denial of the melodramatic heroine, consumed by romantic love. The opera's music literally orchestrates the pathos of her story and the emotions of the spectator.[28] Mirroring and inverting the film's play with genre, the opera contains a comic subplot based on the romances of Musetta, an unruly flirt. Musetta is spared Mimi's heartache and death, but she also does not experience the intensity of Mimi's passion, and takes second place dramatically and musically to her.

From its earliest moments, the film doubles the comic couple of Loretta and Ronny with the melodramatic couple of Mimi and Rudolpho. At the film's turning point, when Ronny and Loretta return home from the opera, they replay a scene they had just witnessed, only to a different end, coming together rather than separating as Mimi and Rudolpho do. Urging Loretta not to fight her desire for him, Ronny tells her, "We're here to ruin ourselves, and break our hearts, and love the wrong people." If Ronny appears still situated in the mode of melodrama, he is also arguing for the position of comedy, and the film resists the temptation to sentimentalize him or any of its male characters. By the end, Ronny has become a full-fledged romantic hero, but not until he has shown himself to be as much a fool as Cosmo and the professor. The very rhyming of his name with his clownish brother Johnny's shows that, at least initially, the two have more than a little in common. As a result, the film succeeds in exploiting comedy's double allegiance to anarchy and order, its centrifugal assault on authority and its centripetal drive toward community.

Moonstruck is not unique in playing comedy against melodrama, or in giving comedy the last word. Indeed, many more explicitly feminist texts invite us to look at melodrama through the lens of comedy. Jacques Rivette's *Celine and Julie Go Boating* (1974), Joan Braderman's *Joan Does Dynasty* (1986), and Allison Anders' *Gas Food Lodging* (1992), for example, use comedy to denaturalize not only melodrama but the "romance" in romantic comedy. *Moonstruck* remains faithful to the ideology of heterosexuality that defines both romantic comedy and melodrama. On the other hand, these explicitly feminist films, and others like them, posit other forms of family and community where passion, play and love can thrive, especially among women.

In the broadest sense, *Moonstruck*'s message about finding life in social connection and embracing its totality is entirely conventional. That very conventionality, however, suggests that romantic comedy persists as a narrative genre in part because it speaks to powerful needs to believe in the utopian possibilities condensed on the image of the couple; it addresses the wish for friendship between men and women, and for moments of joy in relationships constrained by unequal social power. Romantic comedy also offers an alternative to the passive and suffering heroines of melodrama. If Loretta finally submits to the same lunacy Mimi does when she agrees to "ruin herself" with Ronny, she differs from Mimi in one critical way: unlike Mimi, who lives and dies only to give Rudolpho a reason to sing, Loretta remains a woman on top. Where Mimi wastes away in isolation, Loretta will draw strength from the company of her mother and a community that extends beyond the individual couple. By giving centrality and weight to its women, *Moonstruck* not only demonstrates the flexibility of a popular and enduring narrative form, but takes a step toward more fully realizing its potential to foster new and more inclusive images of community.

Works Cited

Bakhtin, Mikhail. *Rabelais and His World*, trans. Helene Iswolsky. Bloomington: Indiana University Press, 1984.

Bamber, Linda. *Comic Women, Tragic Men: A Study of Gender and Genre in Shakespeare*. Stanford: Stanford University Press, 1982.

Barreca, Regina, ed. *Last Laughs: Perspectives on Women and Comedy*. New York: Gordon and Breach, 1988.

Bergstrom, Janet and Mary Ann Doane. "The Female Spectator: Contexts and Directions." *Camera Obscura* 20–21 (1989): 5–27.

Blaetz, Robin. "Explanation by Emplotment: Joan of Arc and the Romance." Society for Cinema Studies Conference. Washington, May 1990.

Bordwell, David, Janet Staiger and Kristin Thompson. The *Classical Hollywood Cinema*. New York: Columbia University Press, 1985.

Britton, Andrew. "Cary Grant: Comedy and Male Desire." *CineAction!* 3–4 (1986): 37–49.

Cavell, Stanley. "Psychoanalysis and Cinema: The Melodrama of the Unknown Woman." *Images In Our Souls*, Cavell, *Psychoanalysis and Cinema*, eds. Joseph H. Smith and William Kerrigan. Psychiatry and the Humanities 10. Baltimore: Johns Hopkins University Press, 1987). 11–43.

————. *Pursuits of Happiness: The Hollywood Comedy of Remarriage*. Cambridge, MA: Harvard University Press, 1981.

Cohan, Steven. "Cary Grant in the Fifties: Indiscretions of the Bachelor's Masquerade." *Screen* 33.4 (1992): 394–413.

Curry, Ramona. "Power and Allure: The Mediation of Sexual Difference in the Star Image of Mae West." Diss. Northwestern University, 1990.

Davis, Natalie Zemon. "Women on Top." *Society and Culture in Early Modern France*. Stanford: Stanford University Press, 1975.

Doane, Mary Ann. *The Desire to Desire: The Woman's Film of the 1940s*. Bloomington: Indiana University Press, 1987.

Fischer, Lucy. "Sometimes I Feel Like a Motherless Child: Comedy and Matricide." *Comedy/Cinema/Theory*, ed. Andrew Horton. Berkeley: University of California Press, 1991, pp. 60–78.

Frye, Northrop. *Anatomy of Criticism: Four Essays*. Princeton: Princeton University Press, 1957.

Heilbrun, Caroline G. *Writing a Woman's Life*. New York: Ballantine, 1988.

Henderson, Brian. "Romantic Comedy Today: Semi-Tough or Impossible?" *Film Quarterly* 31.4 (1978): 11–22.

Holland, Norman N. *Laughing: A Psychology of Humor*. Ithaca: Cornell University Press, 1982.

Horton, Andrew, ed. *Comedy/Cinema/Theory*. Berkeley: University of California Press, 1991.

Jenkins, Henry. "Don't Become Too Intimate With that Terrible Woman!" *Camera Obscura* 25–26 (1991): 202–233.

————. *What Made Pistachio Nuts? Early Sound Comedy and the Vaudeville Aesthetic*. New York: Columbia University Press, 1992.

Jenkins, Linda. "Locating the Language of Gender Experience." *Women and Performance: A Journal of Feminist Theory* 2 (1984): 5–20.

Kaminsky, Stuart. *American Film Genres*. 2nd ed. Chicago: Nelson Hall, 1985.

Kintz, Linda. *The Subject's Tragedy: Political Poetics, Feminist Theory and Drama*. Ann Arbor: University of Michigan Press, 1992.

Krutnik, Frank. " 'The Faint Aroma of Performing Seals': The 'Nervous' Romance and the Comedy of the Sexes." *The Velvet Light Trap* 26 (1990): 56–72.

———. "The Clown-Prints of Comedy." *Screen* 25.4–5 (1984): 50–59.

Lauter, Paul, ed. *Theories of Comedy*. New York: Doubleday, 1964.

Medvedev, P. N./Bakhtin, Mikhail. *The Formal Method in Literary Scholarship*, trans. A. J. Wehrle. Baltimore: Johns Hopkins University Press, 1978.

Mellencamp, Patricia. "Situation Comedy, Feminism and Freud." *Studies in Entertainment*, ed. Tania Modleski. Bloomington: Indiana University Press, 1986. 80–95.

———. *High Anxiety: Catastrophe, Scandal, Age and Comedy*. Bloomington: Indiana University Press, 1992.

Mirza, Candace. "The Collective Spirit of Revolt: An Historical Reading of *Holiday*." *Wide Angle* 12.3 (1990): 98–116.

Modleski, Tania. *Feminism Without Women: Culture and Criticism in a "Postfeminist" Age*. New York: Routledge, 1991.

Mulvey, Laura. "Changes: Thoughts on Myth, Narrative and Historical Experience." *Visual and Other Pleasures*. Bloomington: Indiana University Press, 1989, 159–76.

Neale, Steve. "The Big Romance or Something Wild?: Romantic Comedy Today." *Screen* 33.3 (1992): 284–299.

Neale, Steve, and Frank Krutnik. *Popular Film and Television Comedy*. New York: Routledge, 1990.

Polan, Dana. "The Light Side of Genius: Hitchcock's *Mr. and Mrs. Smith* in the Screwball Tradition." *Comedy/Cinema/Theory*, ed. Andrew Horton. Berkeley: University of California Press, 1991: 131–152.

Rich, Adrienne. *Of Woman Born: Motherhood as Experience and Institution*. New York: W. W. Norton and Co., 1986.

Roberts, Shari. " 'The Lady in the Tutti-Frutti Hat': Carmen Miranda and the Spectacle of Ethnicity." *Cinema Journal* 32. 3 (1993): 13–23.

Robertson, Pamela. " 'The Kinda Comedy That Imitates Me': Mae West's Identification With the Feminist Camp." *Cinema Journal* 32:2 (1993): 57–72.

Rowe, Kathleen. "Roseanne: Unruly Woman as Domestic Goddess." *Screen* 31.4 (1990): 408–419.

Russo, Mary. "Female Grotesques: Carnival and Theory." *Feminist Studies, Critical Studies*, ed. Teresa De Lauretis. Bloomington: Indiana University Press, 1986: 213–229.

Ryan, Michael, and Douglas Kellner. *Camera Politica: The Politics and Ideology of Contemporary Hollywood Film*. Bloomington: Indiana University Press, 1988.

Schatz, Thomas. *Hollywood Genres: Formulas, Filmmaking and the Studio System*. Philadelphia: Temple University Press, 1981.

Scheman, Naomi. "Missing Mothers/Desiring Daughters: Framing the Sight of Women." *Critical Inquiry* 15 (1988): 63–89.

Seidman, Steve. *Comedian Comedy: A Tradition in Hollywood Film*. Ann Arbor: UMI Research Press, 1981.

Selig, Michael. "*The Nutty Professor*: A 'Problem' in Film Scholarship." *The Velvet Light Trap* 26 (1990): 42–56.

Shumway, David R. "Screwball Comedies: Constructing Romance, Mystifying Marriage." *Cinema Journal* 30.4 (1992): 7–23.

Solomon, Stanley J. *Beyond Formula: American Film Genres.* New York: Harcourt, Brace, 1976.

Turner, Victor. "Frame, Flow and Reflection: Ritual and Drama as Public Liminality." *Performance in Postmodern Culture*, eds. Michel Benamou and Charles Caramello. Milwaukee: University of Wisconsin-Milwaukee Press, 1977: 33–55.

Walker, Nancy A. *A Very Serious Thing: Women's Humor and American Culture.* Minneapolis: University of Minnesota Press, 1988.

White, E. B., and Katharine S. *A Subtreasury of American Humor.* New York: Random House, 1948.

Wood, Robin. "Ideology, Genre, Auteur." *Film Comment* 13. 1 (1977): 46–51.

Woodward, Katherine S. "College Course File: American Film Comedy." *Journal of Film and Video* 42 (1990): 71–84.

Narrative

3

Introduction: Funny Stories

Kristine Brunovska Karnick and Henry Jenkins

Gags and Narrative

We are often accused of not having much of a story in our pictures, but I think you will find that when the mass of comedy business has been scraped away and the bare plot is left exposed, a genuine situation is sticking around in it somewhere. This, however, is usually so skillfully and humorously covered by Mack Sennett's directing, that a careless observer is inclined to overlook it.

Craig Hutchinson, Keystone Story Editor[1]

My feature comedies would succeed best when the audience took the plot seriously enough to root for me as I indomitably worked my way out of mounting perils.

Buster Keaton[2]

When the last reel has been run off, the audience does not remember merely a "gag" here and there that was especially funny, but while laughing at the humor, still retains a clear idea of and a strong sympathy for the character.

Harold Lloyd[3]

These three statements characterize a general shift in the conception of humor and its relationship to narrative in silent cinema. Hutchinson's conception of story as an element largely extraneous to the more visible and pleasurable gags of Sennett's comedies reflects the spectacle orientation of the preclassical cinema, which Tom Gunning has called a "cinema of attractions." Keaton's focus on a character-centered, goal-driven plot as a locus of audience identification and Lloyd's hope that the audience will

63

remember not the gags but the character suggest a greater assimilation into the mainstream of the classical Hollywood cinema. All three comments demonstrate the problematic relationship between gag and narrative which is central to any understanding of film comedy. This first section will outline the ways that the history of film comedy can be read in relation to the larger transition from "primitive" to classical Hollywood cinema.

The "Cinema of Attractions," which dominated early filmmaking until about 1906–1907, differs fundamentally from the later classical cinema in both its narrative structure and its address to the spectator. In this cinema, parts are often more important than wholes, with an emphasis on emotion-laden spectacles or "attractions," a term Gunning borrows from Sergei Eisenstein. As Gunning writes,

> The cinema of attractions directly solicits spectator attention, inciting visual curiosity, and supplying pleasure through an exciting spectacle.
> . . . Theatrical display dominates over narrative absorption, emphasizing the direct stimulation of shock or surprise at the expense of unfolding a story and creating a diegetic universe.[4]

In stark contrast to the effacement of classical cinema, direct address

> is here undertaken with brio. . . . From comedians smirking at the camera, to the constant bowing and gesturing of the conjurors in magic films, this is a cinema that displays its visibility, willing to rupture a self-enclosed fictional world for a chance to solicit the attention of the spectator.[5]

The roots of this aesthetic have been traced to vaudeville. Cinema's economic dependence on vaudeville as an institutional base for its early exhibition and distribution, as Kristin Thompson notes, helped to determine the genres and formal norms of its primitive period, the years between 1895 and 1909.[6] The cinema of attractions, Henry Jenkins argues, was at least partially "a response to the presentation of early films within existing forms of variety entertainment; the formal practices of early cinema reflected the need to appeal to audiences schooled in the vaudeville aesthetic."[7]

The fragmented, spectacle-oriented style of the "cinema of attractions" was ideally suited for the presentation of a gag-centered mode of comedy. In this volume, Gunning examines an early genre of film comedy, short gag or prank films, which, he argues, played a key role in shaping the tradition of silent film comedy. The problematic position of slapstick comedy within the classical cinema can be attributed in part to its development from an alternative model which takes shape in this early period.

Gags, as Gunning suggests, are at once elements of visual spectacle and rudimentary narratives.

When the cinema of attractions became displaced by a more narratively centered cinema, it did not disappear completely. Rather, it survived within certain genres, most notably the avant-garde, the musical, animation and comedy. The shift away from a cinema of attractions toward a more classical cinema represented a reformulation of the conception of the cinema in response to a shifting mode of production, a changing venue for exhibition and an alternative conception of its desired audience. Gag narratives were not simply a primitive story form on which later narrative films would be built; they comprised a unique structure which more fittingly addressed a particular moment in film history.

The years 1909 to 1917 comprised a transitional period during which the balance between narrative and spectacle was renegotiated. Filmmakers began to control the disruptive spatiotemporal effects of multiple shots and locations by making a unified narrative the top priority. As Thompson notes, "with such a unified structure as the grounding for the entire film, cutting, ellipses, repetitions of events, could all come to serve a clear function."[8] Short fiction, novels and legitimate drama emerged as the dominant models for film narrative, displacing the early influence of vaudeville, as filmmakers sought greater inroads into middle-class audiences. The demand for more product led manufacturers to increase the length of films, adding shots and incidents and providing for character traits that could motivate a more plot-centered work.[9] Comedy, however, continued to occupy a unique position within the film industry, as a genre in which the centrality of character-driven, goal-oriented narrative was less strongly felt. In 1911, *The Moving Picture World* declared that "in farce-comedy alone can characterization be *subordinated* to incident and action."[10] Critics such as Epes Winthrop Sargent continued to push for a greater conformity within comic films to the narrative conventions that increasingly dominated other sectors of the cinema, suggesting that more classically constructed comedies would attract greater emotional sympathy from a more refined class of filmgoers.

During this transitional period, comic films, like other productions, grew longer. At the same time, the number of comedies produced also increased. By 1912, the year Keystone initiated production, comedy vied with drama for a dominant position on the motion picture bill.[11] While the films became longer, however, they continued to be highly episodic, adopting what Jenkins has called an "accordian-like structure." The opening and conclusion follow a familiar structure of action and reaction or prank and punishment, but the core of the narrative remains open to easy expansion or condensation, depending on the needs of the particular production. Whole units could be added or subtracted with no noticeable effect on continuity.[12] In *See the Point?* (Lubin, March 1908), for example,

> a mischievous youngster puts a sharp nail at the end of a long stick and starts out for mischief. The colored butler is the first one to suffer. He falls into the water. The boy then goes on the street where his idle pranks create much disturbance. At last he is caught and given a good spanking." (*Moving Picture World*)

A longer and more complex variation on the earlier prank comedies, *See the Point?* still shares much with its single-shot predecessors. There is still a rascal, but now there is more than one victim and more than one prank. In the end, as in these earlier films, the effect of the rascal's actions is also shown, as he is eventually punished. In another variation on this structure, film comedies concentrated on the performance of some basic task, as when characters have to move an unwieldy and/or fragile object from place to place and are thwarted by a series of obstacles.[13] Much of the episodic action in such films was expandable or collapsible to fit a predetermined film length.

As film length grew to one thousand feet, comic film structure appears to have undergone a series of transformations. Characters became more individualized, with unique motivations and situations which would require more extensive exposition and would allow for more complex plot development. Prototypical romantic comedies began to appear during this period, focusing on the romantic entanglements of young couples and their attempts to overcome parental opposition to their marriage. *The High Cost of Living* (Edison, June 1912) centered on the efforts of Mr. Lord, president of the International Food Products exchange, to block a budding romance between his daughter, Mildred, and his private secretary, Tracy, on the grounds that Tracy's salary was too low to support a family. Mildred's determination to overcome her father's prohibition results in a series of misadventures, including her organizing a national boycott of her father's products. In the end, Mr. Lord grants Tracy a raise, thus facilitating their marriage. Such a complex plot clearly could not be made comprehensible within a three hundred-foot film, and it points to the narrative sophistication and middle-class aspirations of transitional-period comedies.

Extending film length also resulted in what Jenkins has called a "hybridization of comic formulas."[14] It becomes increasingly difficult to classify comic texts into subgenres as elements from various narrative patterns become intertwined to generate longer and more complex films. One such film, *A Narrow Escape* (Great Northern, March 1912), draws upon conventions from almost all of the narrative formulas in circulation at the time, including husbands sneaking out on their wives, misadventures due to intoxication, encounters with tramps, and a frantic chase. This breaking down of old distinctions between comic formulas, and the increased complexity of comic narratives, set the stage for the Keystone shorts.

Keystone, as Douglas Riblet notes, is often cited as the "birthplace" of American film slapstick, with its chief executive, Mack Sennett, figured as the "father" of this tradition.[15] Almost paradoxically, however, many such accounts also proclaim Keystone's reputation as overblown, denigrating the actual Keystone films as crude, primitive and unfunny, especially in comparison to the later "classic" features of Chaplin, Keaton, Lloyd and Langdon. Riblet's analysis of Keystone and early slapstick examines the elements that coalesced into a distinctive and influential style of comedy, albeit one still more centrally concerned with comic spectacle than narrative complexity. Keystone's emerging studio style featured knockabout physical humor, which emphasized kicking, punching, stumbling and falling. Keystone and early slapstick also relied on piecemeal bits of comic business rather than the extended gag sequences of later slapstick. Instances of comic violence in Keystone films are not random and disconnected. They usually feature extended chase or fight sequences which link a series of gags, stunts, and assorted comic business, as the gags escalate into bigger and bigger laughs. Often these films lack narrative and character motivation for the violent behavior they feature. Riblet argues that Keystone's comic protagonists from 1913 onward became even less individuated and complex. Similarly, Peter Kramer has argued that whereas Vitagraph studio films featured star comedians such as Mabel Normand and Fatty Arbuckle, the Keystone films from the period focused on "comic action rather than on the characterization of its protagonists."[16]

During the three years of Keystone's operation, the star system was becoming institutionalized within the American film industry, and with it came a more psychologically rounded and "realistic" conception of character. Studios increasingly marketed films around stars, and publicity about their comic personas and offscreen lives proliferated. In his essay in this collection, Kramer traces the process by which a vaudeville knockabout comedian, Buster Keaton, shifted from prank-centered shorts toward a fuller integration into conventions of narrative and character construction characteristic of the classical cinema. The result of this transition was the period James Agee and others have called "Comedy's Greatest Era," a period dominated by the feature-length comedies of Chaplin, Langdon, Lloyd and Keaton. Whereas Agee's original *Life* magazine essay constructed this pantheon of great comic stars around the dynamic quality of their screen performances, later writers such as Gerald Mast and Donald McCaffrey have praised these same canonical works for their narrative complexity, thematic ambition and psychological nuances. The accomplishment of these later works is seen as emerging from the stars' apprenticeship within the more rough-and-tumble world of comic shorts.

These films have more recently been recontextualized, as a new focus has been placed on the early cinema and the emergence of the classical paradigm. Revisionist accounts argue that the major 1920s features of Chaplin, Keaton and Lloyd exemplify a kind of transition—hybrids produced in response to changing conditions in the film industry. The films exhibit a specific and unstable combination of slapstick and narrative, rather than representing the final stage of an authentic slapstick tradition, which is how they have usually been described.

For many slapstick comedians, having to adjust to the demands of feature-length films resulted, at times, in a rather awkward juxtaposition of narrative and gags. Many of the earliest comic features were adaptations of existing stage farces reworked to suit the talents of emerging screen stars (*The Saphead*), melodramatic narratives with isolated comic moments (*Mickey*) or curious hodgepodges that cobbled together discrete set pieces that, in other situations, might have formed the basis for a series of two-reelers (*Three Ages*). Chaplin's films placed greater emphasis on plot, as they grew by gradual stages from two-reelers toward semifeature length (*Sunnyside*) into features (*The Kid*). Soon, however, there emerged plot formulas that allowed for a smoother linkage between gag and plot. Bordwell and Thompson's analysis of Buster Keaton's *Our Hospitality*, for example, suggests that virtually every bit of the film advances the narrative. Comic actions "support and advance the cause and effect chain," tightening the "narrative economy and insuring a high degree of conformity to classical conventions."[17] They describe the structure of gags within the narrative according to a formal principle of theme and variations. In an example they cite, a string of gags during a train trip is based on the idea of people encountering the train: "Several people turn out to watch it pass, a tramp rides the rods, and an old man chucks rocks at the engine."[18] Later, in the film's climax, the hero, Willie, dangles from a log over a waterfall like the fish on the end of his fishing pole. Bordwell and Thompson argue that in this case there is a complete containment of gags into the narrative: "The fish-on-the-line device advances the narrative, becomes a motif unifying the film, and takes its place in a pattern of parallel gags involving variations of Willie on the rope."[19]

Because of the uneasy relationship between gag and narrative, early film comedy took longer to adopt and fully assimilate the demands of classical Hollywood structure than did most other genres. Even with its greater accommodation to those norms, the comic film continued to push the boundaries of acceptable film practice. The performance-centered comedies of the early sound period, for example, have been alternately praised and dismissed for their relative disinterest in narrative continuity and character motivation. The fragmented, discontinuous quality of the films of Frank Tashlin and Jerry Lewis led many French critics to praise them for their "modernist" qualities, and *Cahiers du Cinema* cited Lewis's *The Bellboy* as a prime example of a work which contested dominant ideology through its formal structure. The imperfect fit between comedy and classicism has allowed Woody Allen's films to bridge the gap between the popular cinema and the art film, exploring the fragmented and self-conscious qualities that unite these two traditions.

The relationship between comedy and narrative remains a complex and vexing one, which will be explored in the next two sections. Issues central to this exploration include: Are there plot formulas characteristic of comic films and which therefore constitute a recognizable generic tradition? Do comedies tell particular types of stories? How does film comedy fit within the older narrative traditions of literary and theatrical comedy? Finally, how has the tension between gag and narrative been conceptualized by critics?

Narrative in Comedy

Is film comedy a genre? If we are tempted to argue that it is, what are its distinctive features? There are no elements of setting and iconography that distinguish comedy as a genre. There is no plot structure that encompasses all comedies. Nor is there shared subject matter. Bordwell and Thompson have argued that a genre "forms a set of 'rules' for narrative construction that both filmmakers and audience know," and that comedies seem "to be defined chiefly by a type of story situation."[20] However, by referring only to some well-known comedies the complexity of this issue becomes abundantly clear. What pattern of narrative development can we point to that could encompass films as diverse as *The Awful Truth*, *Dr. Strangelove*, *Tampopo*, *Monty Python's Meaning of Life*, and *Modern Times*?

Even if we narrow the discussion to one type of comedy, romantic comedy, critics offer divergent definitions of its boundaries and conventions. For example, recent years have seen the proliferation of books addressing romantic and screwball comedies. Some works distinguish between these generic terms; some use them interchangeably.[21] Although these accounts provide valuable insights into 1930s romantic and screwball comedies, and have expanded the corpus of romantic comedy texts, they lack concrete definitions of the terms and generic divisions involved. And although they provide a specific historical context, they are essentially atheoretical. Brian Henderson has addressed one of the dilemmas surrounding screwball: "We have chased the notion of screwball around the clock of filmic elements. We went in one door and came out another without encountering an iota of certainty or consistency, not even a vector between two points that pointed in a definite direction."[22] Henderson's own concentration on theoretical rather than historical explanations, however, may result in his reproducing some of the same blind spots he describes. Henderson cites the absence of a master theory of comedy as blocking other understandings of the genre:

> It is a scandal of culture that there has never been a widely accepted theory of comedy to organize the general sense of the subject and to orient particular studies within it. Since Aristotle's *Poetics* there has been a theory of tragedy, more or less the same one. . . . Lacking such a founding text and oddly unable to form a later tradition, theorists of comedy have operated in a vacuum, each writer setting out boldly to do the whole job.[23]

This image of an academy paralyzed by its lack of an Aristotelian account of comedy is, well, comic. There is, of course, no shortage of theoretical works on the subject of comedy, a question that has occupied many key thinkers throughout human history. In the absence of Aristotle, Freud, Bergson, Sartre, Darwin, Spencer and Meredith may have to do. Alan Williams' call for genre studies to "return to film history and try to produce individual genre studies with real historical integrity" may address an issue of more crucial concern to studies of comedy. One of the main goals of this volume is to provide studies of film comedy that possess such historical integrity.

Of particular value to such studies are examinations of genre grounded in historical specificity. Genre has been defined by Tzvetan Todorov as the historically attested codification of discursive properties. Historical reality and discursive reality represent two major components of this definition. In the absence of historical reality, "we would be dealing with the category of poetics that are called modes, registers, styles, or even forms, manners, and so on."[24] Similarly, in the absence of discursive reality, we would be dealing with notions that belong to literary history in the broad sense, such as trend, school or movement. A historical definition of genre (as opposed to a theoretical one) therefore holds genres to be classes of texts that have been historically perceived as such. This view is expressed by Todorov:

> Genres are entities that can be described from two different viewpoints, that of empirical observation and that of abstract analysis. In a given society, the recurrence of certain discursive properties is institutional-

ized, and individual texts are produced and perceived in relation to the norm constituted by that codification. A genre, whether literary or not, is nothing other than the codification of discursive properties.[25]

This codification can occur at a variety of levels, and any aspect of discourse can be made obligatory. Generic properties can stem from "the semantic aspect of the text, or from its syntactic aspect (the relation of the parts among themselves), or from the verbal aspect (everything connected with the material manifestations of the signs themselves)."[26]
 The historical specificity of genres makes them distinguishable from broader categories such as the comic, tragic and heroic. Such categories are more properly known as modes. By way of definition, Alistair Fowler has suggested the distinction between mode and kind (by "kind" Fowler refers to what is commonly known as historical genre):

> The terms for kinds, perhaps in keeping with their obvious external embodiment, can always be put in noun form ("epigram"; "epic"), whereas modal terms tend to be adjectival. But the adjectival use of generic terms is a little complicated. Consider the expressions "comedy," "comic play," "comic." "Comic play" is nearly equivalent to "comedy." But "comic" is applied to kinds other than comedy, as when *Emma* is by kind a novel, by mode comic. In the same way, Fielding invited his readers to treat *Tom Jones* as a comic epic not meaning that it is a comedy (it has few dramatic features), but that it is modally comic.[27]

In principle, argues Fowler, any genre might be extended as a mode, thus paralleling Todorov's argument that the absence of historical reality shifts discussion from a consideration of genre to one of "general poetics," and thus a consideration of mode.
 In describing features of genres, Fowler draws on Wittgenstein's concept of family resemblance. Representatives of a genre can be regarded as making up a family whose members relate in various ways without necessarily having any single feature shared in common by all. Family resemblance theory, according to Fowler, holds out the best hope to genre critics.
 Comedy is a category that transcends epochs and cultures, and it thus adds little to a consideration of historical genres. In film, the designation "comedy" provides the spectator and/or the creator of a text with little more that is concrete about the text than that it is funny, thus returning us to one of the initial questions posed in this section: What can be said to unify the diverse group of films commonly regarded as comedies? The term comedy can establish a mood and set a tone for a work, but one probably needs additional description before moving to the level of generic

expectation. Whereas Fowler's kinds may be characterized by any of the elements of the generic repertoire, modes involve a more elusive generic idea. Modes lack an overall external structure, so that when a modal term is linked with the name of a kind, it refers to a combined genre, in which the overall form is determined by the kind. American films comedies often transcend genre, making comedy a routine element in films of other genres, including Westerns (*Wild and Woolly* (1917)), mysteries (*The Cat and the Canary* (1927 and 1939)), and gangster films (*A Slight Case of Murder* (1938)). In such cases, comedy approaches the definition of mode rather than historical kind. Comedy also lacks the historically specific features that would define it as a historical kind, as well as any group (or family) of salient features which might constitute a genre of comedy. A historical account of genre is dependent upon such specificity, because genres function to provide a set of expectations for readers/spectators, as well as models of writing for authors.

Genres communicate indirectly within societies through their institutionalization. This factor has bearing on the historian, because each epoch has its own system of genres which stands in some relation to the dominant ideology. Genres highlight constitutive features of the society to which they belong, because a society chooses and codifies the acts that correspond most closely to its ideology.[28]

Critics have examined potential constitutive features of film comedy from a number of perspectives. A number of theories foreground plot structure in comedies as a generic feature. In *The Comic Mind*, Gerald Mast draws on a very narrowly defined canon of film comedy in arguing that the plots of film comedies can be classified into eight groups.[29] As Jerry Palmer has argued, however, Mast's categories are flawed on a number of levels. First, several of the categories, such as one in which "young lovers succeed in marrying despite various obstacles," are not specific to comedy. In addition, several of his categories do not refer to plot structure but rather are based on individual jokes or gags.[30]

The possibility of specifically comic plots has been more widely explored in literature, and it is possible to locate a number of significant points of intersection between film comedy and earlier forms of comic narrative. If, as Henderson notes, Aristotle did not provide us with an account of comedy, he did offer a very precise discussion of the role of plot within tragedy. In the *Poetics*, Aristotle saw plot, which he defined as the "structure of events," as "the goal of tragedy, and the goal is the greatest thing of all."[31] Of tragedy's six constituent elements (plot, characters, verbal expression, thought, visual adornment and song composition), plot is the most important. Many critics, notably Northrop Frye and Elder Olson, have adopted Aristotle's theory to construct a theory of comedy. Frye classifies all fiction into five categories: myth, romance, high mimetic, low mimetic and irony. These categories are determined by the plot of each work. In distinguishing between the categories, Frye interprets Aristotle's concept of plot as meaning "the hero's power of action, which may be greater than ours (myth, romance, high mimetic), less (irony), or roughly the same (low mimetic)."

Frye also distinguishes between two types of comedy, Old and New Comedy. An example of high mimetic comedy is the Old Comedy of Aristophanes. The New Comedy of Menander is more clearly low mimetic. There has always been a strongly low mimetic bias to social comedy. Old Comedy is a blend of the heroic and the ironic. The characters are older and more experienced, and the themes often revolve around a hero who constructs a society or is an integral part of a society, and who must fight off opposition in the form of characters who try to exploit him. The humor is satirical and comes from the actions the protagonist takes.

In New Comedy oppressive forces are in control of the society and humor arises out of the protagonist's attempt to gain control of and change the oppressive society. A typical feature of New Comedy is the struggle between the hero and a *senex* figure, an older, usually paternal figure. "At the beginning of the play the forces thwarting the hero are in control of the play's society, but after a discovery in which the hero becomes wealthy or the heroine respectable, a new society crystallizes on the stage round the hero and his bride."[32] The heroes in New Comedy are, in Frye's words, innocents, seldom interesting but typically socially attractive. The humor often centers around misunderstandings involving the protagonist. The hero is usually of the low mimetic mode. He is like one of us, and we respond to a sense of his common humanity. In low mimetic comedy, hence most New Comedy, the ending usually brings about a social promotion for the hero, thus creating the traditional success-story, boy-gets-girl, happy ending. A Shakespearean comedy, for example, may marry off eight or ten people of approximately equal dramatic interest.

Frye's work has been analyzed from a number of perspectives and is adopted in this volume by Kathleen Rowe to discuss generic structure in romantic comedy. She finds in Frye's description of romantic comedy a "profundity that had eluded earlier generations of critics." Rowe argues that for Frye, all narrative reworks a common story of community; struggle and renewal; and birth, death and rebirth. This leads to a liberation of a world "wilting under repressive law." In romantic comedy that movement follows the pattern of New Comedy. Rowe argues that Hollywood romantic comedies, *Moonstruck* in particular, possess this type of structure, but with some profound differences attributable to their historical context. Whereas Frye assumes that desire is the sole possession of the male hero, with the woman assuming the role of "bride to be redeemed," female characters often initiate and control the movement of the plot in Shakespearean comedy and in romantic film comedies such as *Moonstruck*. "As 'woman on top,' they enjoy a dramatic weight comparable to that of the male hero in tragedy," writes Rowe.[33]

There is a great deal that Frye's work can offer generic film studies. Many romantic comedies do follow what Rowe refers to as the "tenacious pattern of New Comedy." Others exhibit characteristics of Old Comedy. The plot paradigms outlined by Kristine Karnick are based on differences in plot structure and characterization within two types of romantic comedy. Here a reliance on Frye can help examine possible origins of such patterns.

In Hollywood's variation on the New Comedy tradition, what Karnick refers to as "commitment comedies" center on young protagonists who do not yet have a place in society. The society is oppressive in keeping the protagonist couple apart. This oppression is expressed in a number of ways. In *Bringing Up Baby*, David Huxley struggles with forces at the museum to find a role for fun in his life. When he expresses a moment of lightheartedness at the beginning of the film, his fiancée chides him: "Please, David, remember who and what you are!" Commitment comedies emphasize the struggle between the young couple and an older, usually paternal, *senex* figure, a blocking character who keeps the couple apart. Romantic comedies such as *Bringing Up Baby*, *Hands Across the Table*, and *It Happened One Night* proliferated in the mid-1930s, and the low mimetic mode of the hero found resonance in Depression-era America. The hero is like one of us: the hero works for a living and is not necessarily male. Some comedies—such as *Theodora Goes Wild*, *Hands Across the Table*, and *Nothing Sacred*—concentrate on working-class women who become involved with upper-class men. Rowe similarly argues for the woman as dramatic core in *Moonstruck* as well as in *Bringing Up Baby*, *Ball of Fire*, and *Born Yesterday*. In the resolutions of these films, lovers often retreat from everyday life to a "magical" place where their union is possible. When they return, a new society crystalizes around them and the new couple is integrated into a revised social order.

American romantic comedies often focus on young protagonists coming together despite social obstacles. Their integration into a reconstituted society points to patterns similar to those of New Comedy. A number of other American romantic comedies, however, exhibit characteristics of Old Comedy, particularly in their focus on older, established characters. Stanley Cavell's genre of remarriage comedy provides a locus for the kinds of characters that inhabit Old Comedies. Although some of the films in Cavell's taxonomy are undoubtedly not remarriage comedies (*Bringing Up Baby* and *It Happened One Night*) the emphasis in many Hollywood comedies on a previously married, socially established couple who struggle with the existing social order they had earlier bought into and had helped to maintain clearly expresses concerns of Old Comedy. Karnick's consideration of reaffirmation comedy puts particular emphasis on the relationship between the central couple as they find a way back to each other in the face of various social forces that try to keep them apart. Comedies such as *The Awful Truth*, *My Favorite Wife*, and *Adam's Rib* center on experienced, socially established characters who find themselves losing control of aspects of their personal and professional lives. These characters must fight to regain their place in society.

Frye's difficulty in dealing with gender also emerges in his discussion of Old Comedy, though, again, parallels are visible between the original Greek tradition and recent romantic comedies. He argues that Old Comedy "puts particular stress on the heroine, who may hold the key to the successful conclusion of the plot, who may be disguised as a boy, and who may undergo something like a death and restoration."[34] This formulation again reflects problems in the gender-specific thrust of Frye's argument. In reaffirmation comedies, disguise is often a key feature in plot resolution, though it is not necessarily tied to the role of the heroine.[35] It is often the heroine who uses disguise to help bring about the conclusion of the plot, as when Lucy Warriner disguises herself as husband Jerry's sister Lola in order to break up his relationship with his new fiancée, Barbara, in *The Awful Truth*. However, it is not the heroine who undergoes something like a death and restoration, but rather the central couple as a distinct identity. Disguise helps to bring about that restoration. At the end of these films the protagonists' role in society, both sexually (as a married couple) and professionally (a career placed into "proper" perspective), is again restored.

Although, as several writers have noted, the comedian comedy is also significantly influenced by both Old and New Comedy traditions, this genre is more closely linked to trickster myths and the picaresque romance. If the romantic comedy is marked by a strong focus on plot development, the comedian comedy is usually more episodic. If the romantic comedy moves towards a predictable resolution, the wedding feast or marriage of its protagonists, the comedian comedy often centers around the exclusion of its protagonist from any stable social relations. If the protagonists of romantic comedies are often central to the social order they reform and reaffirm, the comedian never enjoys such a close relationship, and is a perpetual wanderer or trickster.

Trickster stories are among humanity's earliest narratives, and can be found in almost all of the world's cultures. Anthropologist Madhev Apte has looked cross-culturally at this figure, identifying a number of common traits which run through most trickster stories. As he writes,

Tricksters are primarily preoccupied with satisfying their basal desires and with deriving pleasure. In pursuit of this goal, they steal, cheat, injure or even kill animals and humans, and they seduce women. They find enjoyment at the expense of others and take great delight in deceiving and depriving other people. In pursuit of such aims, tricksters totally disregard the established social norms. They break many taboos, and their behavior is antisocial. The tricksters often lack the ability to carry out their tasks successfully, however, and frequently act in a haphazard manner. As a result, they do not always achieve their objectives, their misdeeds are discovered, and they too suffer the injuries and pains that they try to inflect on others. They are punished for breaking taboos. Sometimes the very tricks that they try to carry out get them into trouble.[36]

In this description, one may recognize the basic narrative of the antisocial trickster hoist with his/her own petard as a prototype for the prank films which Tom Gunning describes. The misadventures of this desire-driven, often antisocial figure, and its abrupt shifts between craftiness and incompetence, give rise to periodic episodes of slapstick and masquerade, two of the defining characteristics of the comedian comedy tradition. Steve Seidman notes the "animalism" associated with film comedians, who are often equated visually or verbally with animals, children or other liminal figures on the margins of the social order.[37] In *Monkey Business*, for example, Groucho gets on all fours and meows like a cat, and in *Go West* he tells Lulubelle that "There's something about you that brings out the animal in me" and then proceeds to bark and jump up and down. This animalism points toward the comic character's "countercultural drives."[38]

Screen comedians, like their trickster predecessors in folklore, are often defined through their pursuit of pleasure: of alcohol, sex, money or food. This pleasure-driven mentality pits them against a succession of killjoys, dupes, and other representatives of the social order, who work to contain and constrain their impulsiveness. In Marx Brothers comedies, the brothers' spontaniety is continually contrasted with Margaret Dumont's formal and serious attitude and appearance.

The most literal embodiment of the trickster myth may come in cartoons, where figures like Bugs Bunny and Wile E. Coyote borrow both the names and personalities of their counterparts in native American folklore. Yet the various tramps, con-men and "wanderers" who have dominated the comedian comedy tradition display a similar degree of joblessness, uncleanliness and rootlessness, adhering to no fundamental beliefs and practices. These tramp figures, as Seidman notes, are often shown "undermining authority and having encounters with the law." Also like the trickster, the screen comedians are often shape-shifters, constantly engaging in a series of diegetic performances, impersonations and impressions which display their showmanship and indicate a fluidity of personality that cannot be contained within fixed cultural categories.

The trickster story is a highly episodic form that uses recurrent plot situations and the protagonist's personality to link together an otherwise unrelated string of incidents. Although Trickster stories often constitute a cycle built around a recurrent figure such as Wile E. Coyote or Br'er Rabbit, the events of one story may have limited impact on subsequent narratives. As Apte notes, even the trickster's death in one episode may not "preclude his having another adventure in the next tale."[39] This cyclical conception of narrative can be traced across a large number of films. For example, critics have often argued that Chaplin's films constitute one master narrative centering around the Tramp's eternal quest for his proper place within the social order, for food, shelter, a job and romance. Yet, like the trickster, the Tramp makes no reference to his previous film adventures, and nothing that happens here will have any consequence in the next narrative. Chaplin may wander away with the Gamine at the end of *Modern Times*, but she is nowhere to be seen when the Jewish barber makes his first appearance in *The Great Dictator*. Chaplin, Laurel and Hardy, the Three Stooges and their many counterparts go through a succession of jobs, but their adventures typically end as they began, with them expelled from the social order, out of work and looking for new employment.

This same episodic structure can be found in these performers' feature films, which are also highly fragmented and show limited causal unity, often breaking down into a series of set pieces. In that sense, a strong comparison may be made between the comedian comedy and the literary tradition of the picaresque. The picaresque, which literary critics identify as "one of the most important stages in the transition between earlier literary prose and the modern novel," can be traced back to sixteenth- and seventeenth-century Spanish writers, a tradition that reached its fruition in Cervantes, and influenced later works such as *Moll Flanders* and *Tom Jones*.[40] Like the comedian comedy, the picaresque centers on "nonaristo-cratic characters" searching for a place within a social order, which is itself undergoing dramatic social change. As Richard Bjornson writes:

> Essentially this story involves a rootless, unattached individual who must secure his own survival and psychological well-being in a society that openly espouses traditional ideals, while actually sanctioning the most dehumanizing modes of behavior. . . . This outsider (or "half-outsider") inherits no place which can be considered a home, no trade by means of which he can sustain himself, and no social position to provide him with well-defined relationships to other people. . . . Because he lacks the strength and absolute integrity to impose his

will upon a hostile world, he adapts himself to diverse situations by serving different masters, inventing clever ruses, or wearing a variety of masks during a peripatetic life of alternating good and evil fortune.[41]

The resulting story is highly episodic and brings together moments of comedy and pathos. Time and again its heroes confront "a choice between social conformity (which is necessary for survival) and adherence to what they have learned to consider true or virtuous."[42] Many picaresque narratives end unhappily or ambiguously, with the protagonist unable to put down roots, continuing down the open road or, in darker versions, toward the gallows, while some stories depict his successful integration into the world, once he has learned its lessons through his adventures.

Bjornson's description of the picaresque would hold true for the comedian comedy as well, with many of his claims overlapping the account of the genre that Seidman and Frank Krutnik have provided. Chaplin's *Modern Times*, to cite an obvious example, closely follows this basic plot outline, dealing with the Tramp's movements through a factory, a prison, a department store, a restaurant and, finally, the open road, as he searches for a way to reconcile social demands and personal integrity. Other comedian comedies, however, such as those associated with Keaton and Lloyd, conclude with the comedian's mastery of basic skills necessary to function in the established order, and his inclusion within a romantic couple, which marks his acceptance of dominant values and institutions.

The picaresque can also be embedded within another genre tradition, as when the trickster protagonist finds himself within the Western or the swashbuckler (as in Bob Hope's comedies) as if he had wandered out of his typical terrain and into another genre territory altogether. Often the anarchistic (or picaresque) plot of the trickster clown exists alongside the traditions of romantic comedy. Comic stars such as Harold Lloyd, Buster Keaton, Joe E. Brown and Eddie Cantor may form one part of a romantic couple. Peter Kramer has argued, for example, that Harold Lloyd's major feature films of the 1920s are a much smoother, more integrated blend of gags and narrative than those of Chaplin and Keaton. His most successful screen persona (the "glasses" character) is quite different from the much more physically grotesque characters of Ben Turpin and Fatty Arbuckle and social outcasts such as Chaplin and Keaton. Unlike Chaplin's tramp figure, the Lloyd character actively looks for social integration. Though he is not consciously or overtly barred from this social integration, it is difficult for him to attain. Lloyd also possesses no insurmountable physical or psychological handicap that will ultimately frustrate him and prevent him from attaining his goals. At the end of *Safety Last*, for example, he is able to attain success, esteem and the love of a woman. Through determination, hard work and initiative, he proves himself. Lloyd's drive toward social integration is reflected in the structure of his films. In *Safety Last*, Lloyd plays down the misfit aspects of his character, and he also downplays his own special status as a comic performer.

In other situations, the comedian may become one point of a romantic triangle, as in the *Road* comedies, where Bob Hope represents the traditional comic trickster, Bing Crosby the romantic young man, and Dorothy Lamour the woman they both desire. Here, as in many comedy teams, the interweaving of the picaresque and New Comedy is achieved through the splitting or doubling of the film's protagonist, so that one remains a rootless wanderer while the other finds a wife and a place within the social order. The comic character can also function as a comic servant who helps to facilitate the uniting of the couple, as in most of the Marx Brothers' comedies. The "hybridization" of the picaresque with New Comedy provides for the stronger causal unity and tighter narrative progression demanded by the classical Hollywood cinema, while still providing a space for slapstick pranks and other comic spectacles.

While one can draw strong parallels between romantic comedy and Shakespearean New Comedy or between comedian comedy and the picaresque, such an analysis leaves unaddressed a more basic question. Are these plots unique to comedy? Bordwell, for example, notes the centrality of romantic coupling to almost all classical Hollywood narratives. Melodrama and romantic comedy, as Kathleen Rowe notes, are closely related genres, and one can find something akin to New Comedy plots in melodramas such as *Since You Went Away*, where the war separates the young lovers at the beginning, and the husband's return reunites them at the end. Similarly, the picaresque can become the focus of dramatic narratives, as in *The Fugitive*, *North by Northwest*, and any number of *film noir* classics. The character of the outsider, the social outcast and the wanderer can be seen as a structuring element in Westerns such as *The Searchers*, *Shane* and *Unforgiven*. Whereas Hollywood comedies may exhibit these familiar plot characteristics, these characteristics appear in a broad range of other screen genres. These narrative formulas cannot, then, be seen as a definitive basis for the identification of comedy as a specific generic tradition.

Gags and Humor in Comedy

A focus on comic stories or plots presupposes the centrality of narrative to our experience of comedy. Most work on gags, however, suggests a fundamental tension within most comic texts between our interest in narrative and our interest in gags and humor. Various writers resolve this tension in different ways, making this question a center of debate within recent work on film comedy. This section outlines a range of positions advanced on this question.

One approach, advanced by Kristine Karnick, argues that humor in Hollywood romantic comedies constitutes a paradox: an expected disruption within a highly structured and formulaic narrative. Humor is based on the incompatibility and incongruity evident in two or more conflicting ideas, concepts or events. Consequently, if a narrative is understood as the process a spectator undergoes in constructing a continuum, or "a set of events occurring in defined settings and unified by principles of temporality and causation," comedy arises as a momentary break in some aspect of this continuum. Humor is not a sustained progression of funny events, ideas or concepts with an overarching logic that functions across an entire film. Rather, the incongruous nature of humor arises from unexpected shifts away from narrative logic and continuity. Therefore, we most likely watch *Young Frankenstein* utilizing schemata derived from horror films and other sources. Screwball comedies may be understood by utilizing cognitive structures derived from romance and/or melodrama. This possibility is suggested by Rowe's discussion of *Moonstruck*, a film which combines elements of romantic comedy and melodrama. This kind of combination, argues Karnick, is actually quite common. Spectator knowledge that such films are comedies does not provide a stable set of generic expectations about upcoming actions. The spectator may try to predict the outcome of a particular joke, gag or comic moment, but successful humor depends on the inability of the spectator to predict accurately the humorous result of the joke or gag. Individual jokes and gags also exhibit a logical structure until the punch line, at which time they rely on surprise to achieve their comic result.

Work on schema construction indicates that, as a spectator becomes familiar with a schema's components, and forms increasingly strong links among those components, it becomes more difficult to fit incongruous information into that structure. For example, spectators possess well-developed schemata that enable them to make sense of melodramatic structure, based on repeated exposure to such structures. A melodrama that diverges from the norm will give spectators considerable difficulty in accommodating it into existing structures. Therefore, the very highly structured and formulaic plots of commitment and reaffirmation comedies provide an extremely firm base from which to draw generic assumptions and hypotheses. The role which comedy plays in such a narrative is to provide divergences from these patterns.

In *Logic of the Absurd*, Jerry Palmer concentrates on the structures of gags themselves, arguing that gags function as micronarratives and possess what he calls the "logic of the absurd." He argues that any given sequence of gags is in fact a narrative in itself, albeit a miniature one. The individual gag is organized on the basis of two chronologically distinct stages— preparation and punch line. This in itself implies that the single gag is already a narrative. However, the narratives of individual gags encompass a single event. When gags combine into larger narratives, they are characterized by a plot that is essentially noncomic. He argues that there is no such thing as a specifically comic plot, and that, therefore, every comic narrative uses some genre plot schema or other and turns it into the comic mode through the inclusion of comic material.[44] The rules for interpreting the comedy in such a structure are based on the conventions of the genre on which the humor is mapped. This type of structure, characteristic of Hollywood comedies, and in this case the relationship between gag and narrative, can take one of two forms. Either the noncomic narrative is no more than a series of links between jokes, or the narrative serves some further aesthetic purpose beyond the creation of humor.[45]

Kevin Sweeney adopts a similar conception of gags in his work on Buster Keaton's comedies:

> Triparte disruptive gags open with the initial positing of a norm (sometimes stated as a rule or maxim) of human behavior. In the second stage, a variation of this norm is introduced which strains the norm but contains it; and, in the gag's final stage, the norm is exploded with comic results.[46]

In one of Sweeney's examples from *Sherlock Junior*, Buster Keaton finds a dollar while sweeping a theatre. A young woman inquires after the lost bill, and Keaton returns it (the norm). A little while later, a tearful older woman also approaches him, looking for a misplaced dollar, and he takes out a dollar from his own pocket and gives it to her (a variation or strain on that norm). Finally, Keaton spots a threatening-looking man shifting through the trash and, anticipating his request, Buster first starts to flee and then hands him over his last dollar with resignation (the explosion of the norm). Sweeney sees this structure working not only at the local level within individual comic situations, but more globally; a "gag logic" structures Keaton's entire film. As Sweeney explains, "Keaton seeks to make gag structure and plot line equally important. He is experimenting with a new conception of comedy, one in which comedic organization is neither subservient nor extraneous to narrative economy."[47] The triparte structure of *Sherlock Junior's* narrative, with its norms, variations and disruptions, mirrors the structure of Keaton's characteristic gags, achieving remarkable unity between them.

The essays in this volume by Don Crafton and Tom Gunning represent intriguing viewpoints on gag and narrative, and comprise a fascinating dialogue between two positions. Crafton sees the relationship between gag and narrative as a dynamic process, in which gags disrupt an original stasis while the narrative seeks to contain and limit disruption in order to regain the original equilibrium. He argues that the distinction between slapstick and narrative has been properly perceived, but incorrectly interpreted:

> I contend that it was never the aim of comic filmmakers to "integrate" the gag elements of their movies. I also doubt that viewers subordinated gags to narrative. In fact, the separation between the vertical domain of slapstick (the arena of spectacle I will represent by the metaphor of the thrown pie) and the horizontal domain of the story (the arena of the chase) was a calculated rupture, designed to keep the two elements antagonistically apart.[48]

Every narrative begins by establishing a schema, or set of spectator expectations, then systematically disrupts this initial stasis. "When the gag spectacle—the Pie—begins, the diegesis—the Chase—halts." Although Crafton distinguishes between slapstick (the generic term for nonnarrative intrusions) and gag (the specific forms of intrusions), he finds in gags a structure and logic that transcend cinema. He also argues that the narrative content of gags can be "nil" (as in the jarring close-ups of Ben Turpin's eyes). He refers to such cases as "attractions," elements of pure spectacle, using the term in a manner similar to its usage in Gunning's description of pre-1907 gag films.

A major distinction between the position held by Crafton and that of Gunning involves that moment when a gag and narrative collide. Crafton sees the two as opposing forces ("the centripetal force of the narrative meeting the centrifugal force of the gag"). Whereas other genres work to contain their excesses, in slapstick the opposition *is fundamental.* Furthermore, "it is carefully constructed to remain an unbridgeable gap."[49]

Gunning, on the other hand, questions the "unbridgeability" of the two forces, arguing that Crafton underestimates their interaction. Gunning sees narrative as a system of regulation that ultimately "absorbs nonnarrative elements into its pendulum sways." More specifically, Gunning argues, "gags become absorbed into the narrative economy of most films, marking perhaps an excess that is necessary to the film's process of containment."[50] Far from antagonistic, gags are what set the narrative into motion and what delay its potential resolution, all part of the process by which comic stories are constructed and told.

Much like Crafton, Sylvain Du Pasquier sees gags as subversive of narrative logic. Gags originate in realistic or "normal" discourse specifically in order to disturb it. "Thus the gag unmasks the character of the hidden ambiguity that exists in the harmless look of realistic film discourse." When a gag "explodes," two operations come into play. The normal operation belongs in any plot that is not a parody. The disturbing operation subverts the meaning of that normal operation by "revealing the fragility inherent in the norm."[51] He draws an intriguing distinction between the comic and the gag:

> Comic film discourse presents only a comic version of realism because of its fixed number of strings: rhetorical figures that make a discourse comic on the denotative plane, without "unmarking" other non-comic discourses. In fact, instead of reaching, as the gag does, the heart of the denotated message, the comic merely peels away connotations from the message. In this sense, we can say that the comic does not in any way disturb the operation of signification in the film message.[52]

The gag, then disturbs the film and "corrupts" the plot, and thereby exposes multiple meanings which are hidden in normal or realistic discourse. "The gag is a sharp and sudden utterance which does not fill out realistic discourse with meaning, but rather denies the realistic signifier the signification it presumed to possess."[53]

Noel Carroll has similarly focused on the sight gag as "a form of visual humor in which amusement is generated by the play of alternative interpretations projected by the image or image series."[54] Like Karnick and DuPasquier, Carroll grounds his account in an incongruity theory of humor, with the sight gag creating a confusing or unexpected situation which forces us to focus on everyday processes of perception and inference. Carroll ascribes to the sight gag our first recognition that cinema constituted an interpretive art rather than one doomed to the mechanical reproduction of empirical reality. Carroll is less interested in the narrative structure and function of gags than in the perceptual ambiguities and interpretive confusion they provoke.

Other writers see closer links between gag and narrative. Steve Neale and Frank Krutnik offer a helpful distinction between "comic events," which "can exist only within a narrative context—as a consequence of the existence of characters and a plot," and "gags," which "constitute digressions within a story or story-based action."[55] Neale and Krutnik's account can be seen as negotiating a middle ground between Crafton and Gunning, seeing gags and comic incidents not as systematically antagonistic to narrative but sometimes inside, sometimes outside its logic.

Peter Kramer has examined the relationship between gag and narrative in an analysis of Buster Keaton's *The Blacksmith*. There he draws on Frank Krutnik's characterization of spectator positioning as "a dialectic between disruption and (re)ordering," as "a play between engagement and distanciation."[56] Kramer argues that gags in comedian comedies are moments that transgress an otherwise firmly established filmic fiction—a fiction with which the spectators must be engaged, and to which they must return after the gag. Kramer discusses one of the more disruptive gags in *The Blacksmith*:

> The way Buster as the blacksmith's assistant treats the horse as a woman with the horse in turn acting as a human is funny in itself. It further destroys the very coherence of the fictional world in which the assistant's story is supposed to occur. Yet the full force and meaning of this incident can only be realized if it is placed in the context of the assistant's preceding desirous look at the horse's female owner, of the contrast between his present state as an employee and the lady's high class, and of his following mistreatment of the horse, which leads directly (albeit accidentally) to the formation of the couple. . . . In this manner, the ongoing narrative invests the gags with meaning, which in turn they contribute to its advancement.

For Kramer, gags pose and resolve specifically narrative issues, have plot consequences, and inform us about the characters and their worlds, even if their functions and pleasures cannot be reduced to the demands of story construction. As he explains, "Comic incidents are thus both funny and meaningful in terms of narrative issues, with a great deal of their humor deriving precisely from this meaning."

Bordwell and Thompson make an even stronger claim for the gags in Keaton's *Our Hospitality*, a film which they see as an exemplary example of the narrative economy and formal integration of the classical Hollywood cinema.[57] Their analysis concludes that virtually every element of the mise-en-scène advances the cause-and-effect chain of the film. They emphasize the importance of narrative economy, stating that most of the elements that create this narrative economy also function to yield comic effects. Thus, for example, settings are exploited for amusement. Gags revolve around costume. Comedy arises from the behavior of the figures. Comic motifs are patterned as strictly as the other motifs. The result is a complete integration of gags into narrative.

While acknowledging that gags may serve a variety of functions, both within and outside the narrative, Henry Jenkins argues that gags are primarily a source of affective immediacy within comic texts. Jenkins contrasts gags, which are highly memorable because of their unexpectedness and emotional charge, with narrative details, which simply convey necessary information without calling attention to themselves. As he explains, drawing an example from Roland Barthes:

> We may not remember that [James] Bond puffed on a cigarette before answering the phone; we have already translated that action into abstract data about his character and his attitudes toward story situations. We would remember, however, if Bond was struck by a pie before answering the phone and that unexpected image would linger in our mind longer than the phone call or even the entire event chain within which it participates.[58]

Gags, unlike other narrative details, are never invisible, never function quietly, but always demand our attention, even at the expense of other aspects of narrative comprehension. The most literal demonstration of this principle may be found in recent gag-centered comedies, such as *Airplane* and *Hot Shots*, where a comic detail buried in the background of a shot may distract our attention from foregrounded actions and dialogue. Gags, Jenkins argues, are "focal points of our cognitive and affective experience" of comic films.

These various views on the relationship between gags and narrative can be seen as points along a continuum. Karnick and Palmer represent views in which jokes or gags are experienced within non-comic narratives. Crafton argues for the ultimate irreconcilability of gags and narrative. Du Pasquier, by contrast, argues that gags subvert narrative logic, which implies a close relationship between the two. Kramer, Neale and Krutnik find a closer connection between gag and narrative. Kramer, for example, argues that comic gags may disrupt the narrative, but that the gag also reestablishes the fiction. Finally, Bordwell and Thompson link these two elements in the most fundamental ways.

There is one note of caution about this rather neat explication of a number of complex theories about the narrative/gag relationship. In these writings the authors are not all addressing the same issues and questions. Inherent in these works, for example, are distinctions between gag, joke, humorous incident, and so forth, which require closer consideration than this general overview allows. Second, inherent in any analysis of the gag/narrative relationship is the role of the spectator and his/her relationship to the text. This relationship can be constructed in a variety of ways: one may argue the role of gag within narrative from a purely psychological perspective, analyzing thought processes inherent in humor comprehension; the relationship can also be examined from an ideological position that foregrounds gag and narrative function on a broader scale, as epistemological considerations, as in Gunning's suspicion that narrative may carry a taint of conformity and containment within much contemporary theory. Other views emphasize aesthetic dimensions of this relationship; for example, how narratives and gags create pleasure, provoke affective responses, defamiliarize familiar patterns, introduce novelty, or destabilize our perceptions of the world around us.

The three essays in this section represent three approaches to the study of humor and narrative in Hollywood film. The methodologies vary, as do the authors' perceptions of the link between jokes and gags on the one hand and narrative progression and plot structure on the other. These essays deal with a number of comic genres and a variety of historical contexts. They stand together as an examination of the ways in which we make sense of, enjoy and, most importantly, laugh at Hollywood comedies.

4

Crazy Machines in the Garden of Forking Paths: Mischief Gags and The Origins of American Film Comedy

Tom Gunning

Even if Offissa Pupp should go crazy and start chasing Krazy, and even if Krazy should go crazy and start chasing Ignatz, and even if Krazy should swallow crazy Ignatz and crazy Offissa Pupp should swallow crazy Krazy and it was the millennium—there'd still be the brick. And (having nothing else to swallow) Offissa Pupp would then swallow the brick. Whereupon, as the brick hit Krazy, Krazy would be happy.

e.e.cummings on George Herriman's comic strip Krazy Kat

Bad Boys and the Art of the Device
Of course all boys are not full of tricks, but the best of them are. That is, those who are readiest to play innocent jokes, and who are continually looking for chances to make Rome howl, are the most apt to turn out to be first class business men.

George W. Peck, *Peck's Bad Boy and his Pa*, 1883

On the screen we see a French garden from the turn of the century (1895, to be exact) and a gardener watering the foliage with a hose. A boy about 14 years old enters and his shy look and stealthy body language immediately identify him as a rascal. As the gardener is occupied with his spraying, the rascal steps on the hose, cutting off the flow of water. Surprised by this interruption in the normal functioning of his apparatus, the gardener takes a closer look, bending over the large nozzle to examine it for blockage. This is the moment the rascal has been waiting for, and he raises his foot, liberating the building flood of water directly into the gardener's face. The gardener pursues the boy into the background, and catching him, administers an immediate punishment for his act of mischief, spanking him soundly on the behind.

This film carries a heavy freight. It is one of the first films projected before a public audience at the first exhibitions of Lumiere's Cinematographe. It is likewise one of the first films that students see in film history courses around the world, replaying every semester without variation this century old joke. Over and over the gardener gets soaked (the film's original French title is *L' Arroseur arrosé*—roughly, "the sprayer sprayed") and the boy punished. And equally, predictably, the film is used to demonstrate a series of "firsts." Undeniably it is one of the first projected films. But in addition, in contrast to most films shot by the Lumière brothers in 1895, which were primarily short films of real-life events, *L'Arrosseur arrosé* can also be described as the first fictional (that is, staged) narrative film and the first film comedy.

"Firsts" are the bane of film history. Not only are they usually dubious (given how many films have disappeared), they also obscure the issues history involves. If this Lumière film has a significance for the history and theory of film comedy, as I shall argue it does, that significance comes precisely from the films that came after it, from the way it set up a widely imitated prototype. Its interest lies not in its uniqueness but in its similarity to at least a decade's-worth of later films, its generic quality. But if *L'Arroseur arrosé* sheds light on the role and structure of comedy in cinema's first decade, we must avoid simply seeing it as a primitive ancestor of later comedy. The attraction that this and other early comic films had for early audiences must be reconstructed through a careful examination of filmic structures, and the attitudes that they imply towards their spectators. The early comedies I will describe in this essay reveal key aspects of the tradition of film comedy, but not necessarily in the simple, straight lineage one might expect. The history of early film comedy is a garden of forking paths.

It must be understood that when Parisians filed into the Salon Indien (where the Lumières held their first showing before a paying public), they did not come to see *films*, let alone any particular film (such as *L'Arroseur arrosé*) or a genre of films (such as comedies). They came to see a new machine, the Cinematograph, and the films were simply a demonstration of the machine's process and functioning. These early demonstrations of the filmic apparatus (which spread around the world before the end of the nineteenth century) came out of a tradition that has nearly been forgotten, the display of new technologies as entertainment. Cinema simply joined a long list of new inventions that had been presented to a paying public. During the latter part of the nineteenth century, audiences had gathered to listen to concerts given over the phonograph and the telephone, and to watch demonstrations of such new scientific marvels as X rays or incubators. Audiences were not attracted by the musical quality of telephonic concerts, but applauded the music for what it revealed about the new technology. Likewise, *L'Arroseur arrosé* may have provoked laughter from its first spectators, but it was the Cinematograph rather than the film which received praise. This show-biz strategy, called the "operational aesthetic" by Neil Harris, reflected a fascination with the way things worked, particularly innovative or unbelievable technologies.[1]

Early audiences for Lumière's watery slapstick were excited more by its lifelike portrayal of motion than the originality of its humor. An American film catalogue from 1897 hawked this film (or a near imitation), under the title *Gardener and Mischievous Boy*, to potential exhibitors by announcing that it contained "fine water effects" and "lots of action."[2] As Georges Sadoul pointed out, the basic scenario for *L'Arroseur arrosé* had circulated for nearly a decade as a comic strip drawn by Herman Vogel and published in 1887 by the Librairie Quantin in Paris.[3] Vogel's comic strip presented in a series of panels the action later represented in the film. It was not the originality of its humor that drew early audiences to *L'Arrosseur arrosé*, but is magical animation of a scenario of mischief previously represented through discrete and static images. The new technology of motion picture photography was capable of portraying even the complex motion of such ephemera as the spray of a garden hose.

But the history of cinema turns on the fact that it did not remain the history of cinematic apparatuses but became the history of films with titles, as inventors ceded pride of place to filmmakers. And *L'Arroseur arrosé* inspired a genre, rather than simply demonstrating the technology of reproduced motion. From 1896 to 1905 one of the major genres of motion pictures closely paralleled the structure of this Lumière film: short films, consisting of a single shot, chronicling a gag or bit of mischief, and frequently featuring a youthful rascal. During a period in which the largest number of films produced were short, nonfictional scenes, comedies and trick films were the most common type of fictional films produced.

Although I believe this early genre of short gag films plays a key role in shaping the tradition of silent film comedy, it also has its own identity which differs in some respects from what has been described as classical narrative film, the model that Hollywood films, from about the beginning of the twenties until at least the sixties, seemed to follow.[4] I would also maintain that this early film genre helped shape the later genre of film comedy, which frequently seems to teeter in a precarious position within the classical model. The rather deviant relation that film comedy sometimes displays to the classical norms of narrative structure and character development derives from an alternative model that begins to form in this early period—the gag.

Since a gag is basically a comic action, defining it can be as difficult (and self-defeating) as defining what makes us laugh. Therefore I will speculate on what makes a gag funny only at a later point in this essay. For the moment I will restrict myself to a descriptive and historical project: defining the structure of what I will call "mischief gags," which follow a pattern already evident in *L'Arroseur arrosé*. While this description does not fit all films which early film catalogues classed as comedies, it does cover many comic films which involve extended action. Further, while the sight gags of later comedians are often more complex, I believe a large number of them can be seen as elaborations of the schemata and approaches laid down by these early films.[5]

The first pattern found in these early gag films delineates an action, precisely laying it out in two clearly defined phases. First, a preparatory action is undertaken with a very precise aim in view. The audience usually anticipates what the result of this preparatory action will be (which is sometimes obvious, sometimes surprising). In *L'Arroseur arrosé* this preparatory phase consists of a boy stepping on the water hose (one could also add his stealthy approach) and then stepping off. The second phase of the action is the result and effect of this preparatory phase; in our example, the gardener getting sprayed in the face. The structure of mischief also assigns two basic roles in this action, which I will call "the rascal" and "the victim." The rascal undertakes the preparatory action, while the victim suffers its consequences.

Further modifications could be added to this basic schema. The two actions may have a number of stages; In our example, the preparation has two obvious ones—the stepping on the hose, which blocks the flow, and the stepping off, which frees it. Likewise, the result could be divided into two stages: the gardener's examination of the nozzle, and his consequent soaked face. However, these do not affect the basic structure of mischievous preparation and laughable consequence. Similarly there is an optional concluding action to the mischief gag, a sort of counteraction, meting out punishment to the rascal, either by the victim or some figure of authority (parents or police). *L'Arroseur arrosé* ends with this counteraction, but a number of other early mischief films omit it. The mischief can also backfire and the rascal can suffer the consequences of his action directly, hoist by his own petard. A delightful title of a Mutoscope film from 1902 exemplifies this sort of reversal: *The Boys Think They Have One on Foxy Grandpa, But He Fools Them.*

Linking the rascal and his victim is an apparatus that makes the mischief work. In our example, this is the garden hose. Although such devices may not be universal in early mischief gags, they seem to predominate. The device makes these early films somewhat more complex than the simplest forms of slapstick, such as the circus act Henri Bergson described, in which a pair of clowns repeatedly smack each other over the head,[6] or the violent routines of the Three Stooges. The device not only mediates between the rascal and the victim; it also allows the temporal development indicated by the separation between preparation and consequence. Further, in most cases it provides a visual correlative of the mischief. Although the human actants of rascal and victim are certainly essential to the gag, a detour is taken through an inanimate object, or an arrangement of objects. As a mediatory visual element which takes some time to operate, the device possesses its own fascination, one which brings us back in an unexpected way to the operational aesthetic. Although some mischief gag films are very simple, most of them make use of the possibilities such devices offered. The enjoyment of the gag lay at last partly in watching the device work.

Dozens of mischief gag films can be found in early American cinema. One finds them particularly frequently in films made by the American Mutoscope and Biograph Company, probably because they fit the short length and slightly off-color humor required by their Mutoscope peep show machines. One of the most frequent mischief gags was the flour in the lantern trick. Biograph's *The School Master's Surprise*, from around 1897, provides an early example (the gag later appeared in Edison's *Grandma and the Boys*, and would be reprised by Biograph in 1903 in *The Fate of a Gossip*).[7] Two boys enter their schoolmaster's bedroom, remove the lantern hanging above, fill its glass cylinder with flour, and replace it. They then hide under the beds in the room. When the schoolmaster enters, he lifts the glass cylinder to light the lamp and receives a cascade of flour in the face. He staggers back out of the door, brushing flour from his eyes, as the boys laugh.

Like many mischief films, this gag involves the victim getting besmirched. While this gag undoubtedly betrays a scatological origin, a sort of toilet-training reversal children inflict on adults, the device makes it somewhat more complex than the simpler, pie-in-the-face, infantile revolt against adult regimes of cleanliness and propriety. A similar sort of mischief in early American Mutoscope & Biograph films comes with a series of umbrella jokes. In such films as *A Boarding School Prank* (1903) and *A Black Storm* (1903), mischievous children fill umbrellas or parasols with flour or ashes. When the victims raise and open their umbrellas, a cloud of debris descends. Other variations include a hat filled with ashes (*Let Uncle Reuban Show You How*, 1904); a suddenly opened bag of flour suspended in a feed store (*A Blessing from Above*, 1904); a bucket of water set over a doorway (*A Boomerang*, 1903, *Why Foxy Grandpa Escaped a Dunking*, 1904); an atomizer filled with ink (*The Borrowing Girl*, 1904); and even a jerry-rigged camera which shoots soot into the sitter's face (*Willie's Camera*, 1903). All of these scenes of dirtied victims and delighted rascals involve the setting up of a device and a brief temporal, delay between the preparatory action and its risible results. Like any device, they can go awry, and occasionally catch the perpetrators in their coils.

The same structure also occurs in what we could call "connection devices," where the mischievous children create a comic device by linking objects and people together with a bit of string. An early example appears in *A Wringing Good Joke*, which served as the title for both Edison (1900) and Biograph (1898) films with identical gags. In a working-class kitchen, a mother does the laundry, as the father sits in a nearby chair, reading. A mischievous boy enters and attaches a string from the wringer of the washtub to the back of his father's chair. As the mother turns the crank to wring out her laundry, the father's chair is pulled over. Such strings wreak havoc on a number of domestic scenes: a boy servant ties the butler's coattails to a china cabinet (*How Buttons Got Even with the Butler*, 1903); a vengeful boy attaches a string to a woman's wig and lifts it onto the chandelier, just as a suitor was about to propose (*You Will Send Me to Bed, Eh?*, 1903); a boy in a rooming house attaches a woman's covers to a neighbor's doorknob (*Pulling Off the Bed Clothes*, 1903); a young boy strings a hanging fishbowl to the back of an old man's rocking chair (*Mischievous Willie's Rocking Chair Motor*, 1902); a little brother ties a visitor's coattails to the tablecloth (*Maude's Naughty Little Brother*, 1900).

Such mischief films display a number of formal characteristics. Since they generally consist of a single shot, they have to make good and economical use of the space of the frame. In most cases, separate areas are needed for tricksters and victims (the tricksters occasionally leave the frame before the device is triggered, but more often they stick around to enjoy the fruits of their labor). Further, the gag device usually takes up some space, and many of these early films are composed with the clarity of the turn-of-the-century comic strips that were their inspiration. The upper part of the frame, often ignored in classical film composition, frequently lodges gag devices. Further, to keep their victims in the dark about impending disasters, the films provide them with a series of absorbing tasks which direct their attention away from the mischief being prepared behind their backs or over their heads. Likely victims remain hard at work (like Lumière's gardener), asleep, or making love as their ridicule is devised.

Although watching a large number of mischief films end to end (an arrangement that would never be projected in an era which stressed variety in film programs) may make them seem tiresomely repetitive, early film-makers exercised a fair amount of ingenious variation within familiar formulas. Tricksters may themselves become butts of the joke, or have it turned against them. The basic premise of Biograph's *Foxy Grandpa* series (and of the comic strip by Charles E. Schultz and its musical theater adaptation by William S. Brady that inspired the films) was that Grandpa always saw the joke coming and turned the tables. In *Why Foxy Grandpa Escaped a Dunking*, he watches the boys set a water bucket over his doorway, and switches the pull string from the doorknob to the door bell. When the boys ring the bell to get Grandpa to open, *they* get drenched. An elaborate redirected joke appears in *A Trick on the Cop*, from 1904.

A brother and sister rig a bowl of flour on a shelf over a pantry door which will collapse when they pull a string. The trick is set up to humiliate their cook's cop boyfriend. However, the cook discovers the device and cuts the string. When the kids pull it, nothing happens. However, when the cop's superior officer comes searching for him, the kids and cook collaborate in rerigging the device. They pull it when the officer is about to discover the cop's pantry hiding place, temporarily blinding him with flour so the patrolman lover can make his escape.

Mischief Gags and the Attraction of Explosive Interruption

> And the more it breaks down, the more it schizophrenizes, the better
> it works, the American way.
> Deleuze and Guattari, *Anti-Oedipus*

Not all films which early film catalogues classified as "humorous" or "comic subjects" have gags, that is, a clearly structured comic action. Many are what I will call "comic views," which simply present a mirthful scene of some subject that was considered humorous by the culture of the filmmakers—such as scantily clad women, infringements of propriety, or children at play. An example of this basically nonnarrative form of humor would be the genre of facial expression films, which show in close framing an actor making a series of grotesque grimaces, as in Edison's *Facial Expressions*, from 1902. There is no narrative motivation given for this attractive woman's bizarre facial transformations, other than a laughable display of physiognomic agility. Such films do not display even the simple development of action found in the gag films. Rather they revolve around the presentation of a view whose content, usually some deviation from proper adult behavior, alone supplied the humor.

The most popular genre of comic views captured women in moments of erotic display. While such films obviously shade into pornography, they frequently supplement their voyeuristic pleasures with an accidental violation of social propriety in scenarios that come close to gags. For instance, in a Mutoscope reel from 1903, *Getting up in the World*, two women balance a ladder on a picket fence to create an improvised seesaw. While enjoying this childish amusement, the woman nearest the camera suddenly slips between the rungs, hiking her dress up around her waist and exposing her rear end and underwear to the camera. Staging this flash of erotic revelation as an accident certainly fulfills voyeuristic desires, but it also creates a comic scene, with the seesaw device both invoking childhood, and delivering an accidental victim of social humiliation.

Such early comic films exemplify what I have termed the cinema of attractions, a dominant tendency in early cinema which addresses spectators directly with a visual display, rather than a developed narrative action.[8] The simplest mischief films also serve as attractions, presenting a brief scene of fairly harmless aggression. However, the very structure of the mischief gag as I have defined it—with preparatory action and comic result, the necessary roles of rascal and victim, and the frequent mediating device—also shows a rudimentary narrative structure of cause and effect, characters and audience anticipation. The mischief films are of great importance to early film comedy precisely because they show an elementary form of narrative based on the gag which seems perched between a nonnarrative attraction and the later character-driven narrative forms. However, I would claim that these gag narratives are not simply a primitive story form on which later narrative films will build, but rather a unique structure, differing considerably from the narrative forms introduced by the dramatic films which became dominant around 1907 to 1908. This unique gag structure helps explain the difference between many film comedies and the narrative structures of later classical film.

Donald Crafton's important essay "Pie and Chase" defines a dichotomy in later comic films between what we might call the centrifugal energy of the comic gag and the centripetal energy of narrative.[9] Whereas classic narrative films establish a logic of action in order to create a linear and coherent story, gags, Crafton states, tend to interrupt and subvert the progressive order of narrative:

> the narrative is the propelling element, the fuel of the film that gives it its power to go from beginning to end. (To continue the automotive metaphor, one would say that the gags are the potholes, detours and flat tires encountered by the Tin Lizzie of the narrative on its way to the end of the film.)[10]

Crafton beautifully captures the lurching stop-and-start rhythm of silent comedies of the teens and twenties, as they veer between action that develops their often rather thin plot lines, and pure nonsense gags. However, if one approaches the gag from the other end of film history, it is clear that gags such as those found in early mischief films provide one of the earliest forms of narrative structure in early cinema. As I have shown, they present an unfolding action in such a way that the audience has a special knowledge in relation to other characters (the spectator can see the disaster coming which the victim does not foresee), and this audience anticipation can even be played with (as when the jokers themselves receive the force of the gag).

But Crafton's insight shows how closely early gag films still relate to the cinema of attractions, with its immediate pleasure in seeing a simple action displayed. The most obvious difference that separates these early gag films from even such early narrative films as *The Great Train Robbery* is length. Mischief gag films are short, abbreviated few of them lasting more than a minute. It takes some time for the gag to work itself out, but this time is of necessity limited—or the direct cause and effect relation between rascal and victim would become obscure, the gag gummy and blunted. Once again, this brevity is not the sign of the primitive state of this early period of film history. While in some cases it may be technologically determined (by the length of a Mutoscope reel, for instance), the gag form was selected for early films because it fit so perfectly into these constricted requirements. Early film dramas fit these procrustean requirements only by presenting highlights from longer works, while the gag structures and short film lengths make a perfect fit.

Brevity is the soul of the gag, while stretching out action provides an essential structure for narrative development. While most gags work on principles of surprise, narrative more frequently makes use of suspense, the elongation of action and consequent heightening of audience anticipation. Crafton relates narrative development to the "chase" with its linear progress over extensive space, and the gag to the pie in the face, with its temporality as custard slams into the kisser.[11] The gag film's single shot, therefore, reflects an essential economy of temporal form, rather than a primitive inability to edit.

But could the gag form not be seen as an elementary building block of narrative, one which could be expanded, and therefore a direct ancestor of later classical narrative film, as *L'Arroseur arrosé* is often claimed to be? I would maintain this would be a misleading way of looking at these films. Although they share with the classical film a form structured by purposeful action, it is not the sort of purpose around which a more lengthy, character-building drama can be built. Mischief films and other early gag films have roles, but one could hardly say they have psychological characters. The rascal and victim are entirely defined by the actions they perform; we know little about what they think or feel, and care less. Character and motivation formed the crux of the development of the dramatic film that began around 1908, and was characterized by films D. W. Griffith made for the Biograph Company—films sharply contrasting with the short gags the same company had cranked out earlier.[12]

As the standard length of films increased with the rise of the nickelodeon, multishot mischief films were made by most early film companies. But the process by which mischief stretched out into more extended narratives actually shows how recalcitrant the form is to development. Films such as Edison's *Buster Brown and his Dog Tige* (1904), Biograph's *Night of the Party* (1906) or *The Truants* (1907) or the delightful French versions, Pathé's *Les Farces de Toto Gate-Sauce* (1905) or *Ah, Le Sale Gosse* (1906) simply string together a number of one-shot scenes of mischief with a recurring character providing the film's unity, and punishment (occasionally) providing closure. This additive structure, a concatenation of single-shot gags, is a frequent form for comedy films until at least 1908, competing with the somewhat more popular (and certainly more linear and narrativized) form of the comedy chase. The chase allowed greater narrative development, because a single overarching action of chase and pursuit could be extended naturally. The mischief gag, on the other hand, was structured around a quick payoff, and so could not flow easily into a longer temporal progression. As Crafton points out, chases create continuity, while gags are essentially discontinuous. Each gag ends in such a way that the gag machine must be started all over again to produce an additional one. Rather than a flow, the longer gag films are structured as a series of explosions. After the explosion there is little to do, except possibly punish the culprit.

Mischief (and these mischief gags display this clearly) works through interruption rather than development. Sudden interruptions of order or actions characterize a large number of early film comedies, extending beyond the subgenre of mischief films. Two popular schemata in early film comedy become clearer when we look at them in this context: interrupted lovemaking and the explosion. These schemata sometimes appeared in mischief films, and sometimes became comic views on their own without fitting into a gag structure. But in either case their humor revolved around an unexpected disruption.

Early film catalogues are filled with titles such as *Love's Ardour Suddenly Cooled, Interrupted Lovers, An Interrupted Kiss,* and a youngster's mischief is frequently the cause of these erotic curtailments. By showing a gag pulled on a smooching couple (such as the shower bath given to the pair cuddling in front of a beachside bathhouse in *A Poor Place for Love Making,* 1905), these films release both erotic voyeurism and pent-up aggression. The transition from all-absorbing lovemaking to the shock of its sudden interruption reveals the comic effect that comes from a derailment of action rather than its continuation. The shock of a disastrous disruption becomes extremely literal in the explosion film, in which little happens other than something blowing up and inflicting injury on the characters (*The Finish of Bridget McKeene, They Found the Leak, Algy's Glorious Fourth of July, Brannigan Sets Off the Blast*).[13] The comedy in these films seems to come from the pure thrill of the explosion, its absolute disruption of the order of normality. If we think of the mischief gag structure as having two essential temporal moments, the preparation and then the explosive payoff, we can see why the gag did not provide a model for extensive narrative development. Mischief gags make things fall apart, whereas narrative structures put things back together.

For this early period of film exhibition, the comic role of interruption was not only an aspect of the film's structure but also frequently reflected its position in the film program. I noted earlier that film production in this period (and in most film programs before 1903) was dominated by actuality films. But even in film programs dedicated primarily to actuality films (such as the High Class Moving Pictures of traveling exhibitor Lyman Howe), comic films were by no means excluded. Instead, they were integrated into an evening's entertainment precisely to interrupt the flow of informative nonfiction. As Charles Musser phrases it, such short comic films provided a "respite" within a program dominated by other material.[14]

Similarly, in the later period of film comedy, when comedians were saddled with plots and characterization, gags appear in their films as attractions, momentary and hilarious distractions from the narrative aims of the plot. As Crafton indicates, many later comedies make a rough weave between gags and narrative events.[15] Although gags may become subordinated to simple plot lines, and can be intricately worked into comic personas (as in the films of Chaplin, Keaton, Lloyd and later Jerry Lewis), their role as interruption is still primary.[16] This show-stopping character of gags in longer works has long been recognized in the theatrical forms that films drew on. The Commedia dell'Arte *lazzi* (which provided schemata for many gags which survive into film comedy) were devised precisely as autonomous routines which could be inserted willy-nilly into almost any comic plot, at the whim of the company manager or even an individual performer. Plot development would be shunted aside momentarily, while the *lazzi* action took over the main track. Like early film gags, *lazzi* had their own development, but it was a self-enclosed one which contributed little or nothing to the unfolding plot action.[17] Like modern comic routines, they are "bits," self-contained fragments. Considered as a structure of explosive interruption, the early gag film shows its relation to the cinema of attractions, a display of an action whose temporal development is prompt, rather than setting up an extensive working out of plot and characterization. The pleasure gags gave audiences may relate more closely to the spectators amazed by the operation of Lumière's new invention than to a contemporary audience laughing over a Neil Simon comedy.

The Gag Machine and the Graceful Mechanics of the Unconscious

Descend, Unconscious, through our reflexes Reshuffle the cards, our lexicons, and sexes.
    Jules Laforgue "Complainte de Lord Pierrot"

Although the Lumière Company continued to privilege actuality films of travel or current events over their next four years as a production company, they did produce a number of other comic films. These include not only a number of mischief films, but a somewhat unique film which had both a long tradition preceding it and a long list of descendants in early film. This was the *Charcuterie Mecanique,* "Mechanical Butcher," a version of the famous sausage machine routine. In this film a group of men in an outdoor location operate a eccentric apparatus shaped like a large box with a wheel crank. The men herd a pig into one end of the box, turn the wheel, and from the other end come cuts of meat and links of sausage.

The sausage machine had been a joke apparatus for at least a century (one tradition claims its inventor was the famous early nineteenth-century, British clown, Joseph Grimaldi) and had appeared in circuses, vaudeville and minstrel shows for decades.[18] It became a standard attraction in early film catalogues, with films by Biograph (*The Sausage Machine,* 1897) and Edison (*Fun in a Butcher Shop* 1901) and other companies. The device was so well known that Edison even reversed the process in 1904 with *The Dog Factory,* in which sausages are fed into the device and puppies come out the other end. Although mischievous, these early sausage machine films do not precisely follow the pattern of the mischief films. However, the sausage machine itself shows again how adaptable such elaborate mechanical devices were to early film comedy. Such devices, in interaction with gags, provided the central heritage that early film comedy hands on to later silent comedy, from Lumière's garden hose and sausage machine to Chaplin's assembly lines and Keaton's locomotives.

The qualities we traced in early film gags—their explosive action, their interruption of the normal course of things—are embodied in the mischief devices I have described. These devices are machines whose purpose is to stop things from working, or make them work in an explosive counterproductive way. The Lumière company's garden hose again provides a perfect prototype. As the gag gets under way, the hose first simply doesn't work. Then, on closer examination, it works too well, but has been diverted from watering plants to dousing faces. Similarly the bad boys and girls in these early films convert lamps, cameras, umbrellas and doorways into dousing mechanisms and laundry wringers into paternal dethroners. Such devices can rarely be used more than once.[19] As they accomplish their tasks, they tend to destroy themselves. As a structure based on interruption, rather than a character developing action which can serve as a phase in a broader plot (in other words, which would be useful for a classical narrative structure), the gag presents an exquisite moment of the operating of a device, a device which produces an explosion of laughter.

Not only is the mischief device a machine that undermines productive rationality by connecting things which should not be connected, and not only is it a machine whose mode of operation is to destroy itself, it also provides vivid non-psychological action. As the device does its stuff, we become observers of how something works, rather than speculating on its motives. Here lies the core of truth in Bergson's identification of comedy with the mechanical[20]: the best gags unfold in such a way that everything, both devices and human actants, seem to perform like interlocking gears in a grand machine. A number of early gag films display this mechanical nature beautifully, such as *A Good Shot* (1903). In a tenement backyard a woman on one side of a fence does laundry, while a boy and girl with a rifle and target approach on the other. The girl holds the target against the fence, the bullet hits the woman in the rear, the woman jumps into her laundry tub, the kids realize they're in trouble and, as the woman rounds the fence, they jump into the tenement window behind them. The whole action is so beautifully laid out and synchronized it looks like an absurdist cuckoo clock.

This vision of the world as a crazy machine whose very regularity and precision manufactures mirthful disruption lies at the core of many masterpieces of American silent comedy. This goes beyond the actual comic use of machines, seeping into the very nature of extended gags. Keaton possessed the deepest understanding of these mechanics. On the literal level his films are filled with complex gadgets, from the devices of *The Electric House* (1922) through the motion picture camera of *The Cameraman* (1928).

But the very structure of a Keaton gag reflects a vision of absurdist mechanics. The pattern which Walter Kerr described as the "Keaton curve" envisions a universe structured like a karmic merry-go-round. As Kerr puts it, "set something in motion away from you and you can count on meeting it face to face."[21] Kerr's examples trace the circularity of some of Keaton's gags, such as his slide down a clothesline out of his girlfriend's window in *Neighbors,* which then accelerates and loops him up the bannister in the opposite building, back onto the clothesline and into the house he just left; or the steamboat paddle wheel which become a Keaton treadmill in *Day Dreams.*[22] The circularity of these gags depends on nonproductive devices which capture Keaton in their mechanical cycles, like an inert object. Keaton overcomes the mischief film's simple duality of rascal and victim as he merges with the central device, becoming a projectile in thrall to the laws of mechanics.

Keaton and other later comedians brilliantly elaborated on the basic structures of early mischief devices. Take, as one example, a moment in Keaton's *Our Hospitality.* Keaton's character, Willie McKay, stranded on a rocky ledge, has tied the end of a rope dropped to him around his waist. He soon discovers, however, that the other end of the rope is attached to his would-be murderer, a member of the rival Canfield clan, who has Willie in the sight of his rifle. As Willie tries to scramble out of the field of fire, he unwittingly tugs the rope and causes the rifleman to fall from his perch. Willie watches first the rope and then Canfield plummet past him, and then looks up at the camera as he realizes the connecting rope will soon drag him off the ledge too. And it does.

Keaton here brings the connection device to a sublime stage, merging roles of victim and rascal in a mutual subjection to the force of gravity and the structure of the device. A fascination with the way things work fuels the gag. In so many of his films, Keaton's character carries on a romance with the devices of a heroic but already fading age of machines and energy (the locomotive, the steamboat), a romance which reveals once again the American silent comedy's inheritance from the operational aesthetic. This fascination with the way things come together, visualizing cause and effect through the image of the machine, bridges the end of the nineteenth century and the beginning of the twentieth, shaping many aspects of popular culture.

The transformation that the comic strip undergoes in Europe and the U.S. during this period often depends on similar device gags. Moving away from satirical caricature heavily dependent on written captions, the modern comic strip began to unfold a successive action over a number of panels. As the model for Lumière's *L'Arroseur arrosé* indicates, devices frequently supplied the connecting link for the successive phases of comic action. What historian of the comic strip David Kunzle calls "the permutation of objects and people along certain vectors"[23] provided a direct visual means of conveying stages within a single gag action. Crafton has also described certain film gags as being structured through "comic strip" logic,[24] a clear delineation of the stages of an action and its results, such as those found in the early mischief gags. But I am less concerned with discovering the sources for early film gags than in pointing out that both forms of popular culture portrayed action by tracing the trajectories and chain reactions of people and objects via gag devices.

Cartoonist Rube Goldberg provides the ultimate expression of this form of humor. The famous Rube Goldberg inventions began as addendums to his comic strip in the teens, *Boob McNut*. Becoming a feature in their own right, they continued in American funny papers for decades. Although Goldberg's earliest inventions are simply elaborate machines designed to do simple tasks (such as the room full of gears that sharpen a pencil in a strip from 1919),[25] elaborate and improbable series of chain reactions defined his most famous devices. The diagrams that portrayed Goldberg's devices were accompanied by captions which explained how they functioned, referring to the different elements of the device through letter labels. One Goldberg invention, "a simple device for removing ice cubes from tray" bore this caption:

When you turn on faucet (A), string (B) uncorks bottle of ammonia (C)—fumes temporarily blind dwarf (D) who is looking for collar button—He falls off platform (E), causing foot (F) to pull lever (G) of slot machine (H), Hitting the Jackpot—When pile of nickels drops into holder (I), Hindu fakir (J) gets up from bed of nails to grab dough—Tray [of ice] (K) falls on hinge (L), landing on nails (M) which puncture tray and release ice cubes.[26]

Comic strip gags like this are only the most extreme development of the devices found in earlier twentieth-century comic strips, which are frequently put together by mischievous kids—whether the Kazenjammers, Hans and Fritz, Buster Brown, Little Jimmy or any one of a dozen nasty cartoon tykes—to wreak havoc on their adult oppressors.

But besides the appeal to anarchistic impulses, these devices, particularly when developed by imaginative craftsmen like Goldberg or Keaton, also make a direct appeal to the tinkerer and bricoleur, and the operational aesthetic. Like such magazines as *Popular Mechanics,* they come from a time when technology was still primarily a matter of the hand and the tool, and within the reach of most folks. As contemporary device gagster Philip Garner has said of Goldberg:

> Goldberg's inventions are "homemade" consisting of components available to the backyard tinkerer of his time. Pulleys and rope, springs, funnels, gears, levers and dripping sponges are common in Goldberg's repertory of devices, all of which demonstrate a functional clarity which makes the concept obvious. . . . It is satisfying to follow the chain of actions and reactions, matching the caption to the correct letter in the drawing. This sense of "How it works" has been all but eliminated in modern industrial products which are shrouded, silenced and styled to discourage any curiosity about their working parts.[27]

These homey components were also the stuff of devices in the mischief films and in the gags of later silent comedians. Within the bad boy lurks an engineer, calculating the amount of water pressure or the trajectory of a spray of ashes.

The calculation and precision of these rascal engineers also depended on the absorbed distraction or lack of attention of their victims.[28] Once again, the genius of Keaton lies in blending these two character roles. Keaton was a consummate engineer, master of mechanics, and in both films and private life constructed Rube Goldberg-type devices such as the nutcracker described by Rudi Blesh in his biography of Keaton: "A three-foot crane supplied one walnut at a time and a pile driver cracked it. But woven through before and after these two essential performances was a bewildering maze of utterly useless mechanical happenings."[29] A

Keaton film is also a maze of such devices, gags that often serve little narrative purpose, but which provide the essential fascination of the films.

But as Kerr's examples of the Keaton curve show, Keaton's characters are not only the master designers of such gadgets; they frequently become inert objects, a sort of freight hauled along by these devices. Most often Keaton is both, sometimes successively and sometimes—sublimely— simultaneously. If Keaton recurringly shows the masterful cleverness of a mischievous boy engineer, he also frequently displays the distracted unconsciousness of a victim. But Keaton raises this temporary absence of mind to a state of being, the near-Nirvana that Keaton's immobile mask has evoked for some commentators. It is Keaton's apparent mind-lessness and abstraction, his renunciation of will, that allows him at points to blend with the curve and be swept along by the device and its chain reactions, rather than be humiliated or destroyed by them.

Again, *Our Hospitality* provides a perfect instance. Towards the end of the film, Willie is swept down a raging stream and nearly over a waterfall, his umbilical-cordlike rope now tied to an inert log. His girl, while attempting to save him, has also been swept up in the current and is bobbing along not far behind him. Suddenly, at the edge of the falls, through the sort of magical alignment of elements that occasionally appear in Keaton's universe, the log wedges into a rock and Willie, suspended from his rope, becomes—a device. Saved from his fall, but caught dan-gling from his rope, Willie recognizes in a flash the mechanical possibility of his position. Setting himself swinging, he reaches out like a trapeze artist and rescues his beloved as she plunges over the falls. Through the perfect arc he describes as he catches her, Keaton merges with his device, swinging, as Daniel Moews describes it, "like a weight on a pendulum,"[30] inert, mechanical, attuned to the laws of gravity, and impossibly graceful.

If one wants to avoid the metaphysical connotations which seem to attach themselves to such acts of Keaton, one can stress the very physical nature of this grace, the mechanics of this perfection. Keaton here literally functions like the marionette which Heinrich von Kleist described in his famous essay, in which a dancer claims that marionettes possess greater grace than human beings, because a marionette's "limbs are what they should be: dead, mere pendulums, governed only by the laws of gravity." Human grace, on the other hand, has been destroyed by the onset of consciousness. "Grace appears purest in that human form which has either no consciousness or an infinite one, that is, in a puppet or in a god."[31]

Is this great romantic ironist too far a stretch from the lowly devices of the mischief film or even the acrobatic perfection of Keaton? And can such considerations really be related to a modern fascination with mechanical devices and the chain reactions of cause and effect? While Kleist may be beyond the reach of the Biograph bad boys of the turn of the century, I believe that there is a continuous tradition of American silent comedy stretching from these devices and the operational aesthetic that inspired them through to the works of Keaton and other silent comedians. And the central issues of this tradition involve an interaction between devices, consciousness (and unconsciousness) and grace. If a romantic, Continental writer like Kleist seems too distant a reference point, we can turn directly to a central figure in the tradition of American humor, Mark Twain.

Twain's training as a Mississippi steamboat pilot places him in direct lineage with Keaton's locomotive engineer Johnny Gray, both the heroes of young boys for their control of huge and powerful machines. In Twain's account of his years as a riverboat pilot, "Life on the Mississippi," he describes an extraordinary feat of piloting. A pilot named Ealer was navigating a particularly tangled and complex section of river in a dead-dark night. All lights in the pilot house were extinguished, so that no glare might distract his gaze as he attempted to peer into the darkness and pilot his craft.

Suddenly an obscure shape appeared in the pilot house, whose voice Ealer recognized as his fellow pilot, who had been sleeping in his cabin below. The man offered to take over the wheel, since he had been over this stretch of river more recently. Ealer gladly surrendered control and looked on in amazement as his partner guided the ship smoothly through the difficult channel in the gloom of night. Secure after watching "the sweetest piece of piloting that was ever done on the Mississippi River,"[32] Ealer went below to get a cup of coffee. While there he encountered the nightwatchman, who asked who was at the wheel. Learning it was the other pilot, the watchman ran to the pilot house in alarm. The replacement pilot, it turned out, was a well-known somnambulist, and had been steering the ship in his sleep. Ending the yarn, Ealer expressed his hope the pilot would continue to have fits of sleepwalking, exclaiming, "And if he can do such gold-leaf, kid-glove, diamond-breastpin piloting when he is sound asleep, what *couldn't* he do if he was dead?"[33]

Silent American comedy developed a form which drew its inspiration from gags rather than plotting. These gags have their origins in acts of anarchy, infantile revolts against authority and propriety. But their explosive counterlogic also found embodiment in devices of balance and trajectory, antimachines which harness the laws of physics to overturn the rules of behavior. Simultaneously revolt and engineering, these devices mine the fascination that spectators of the industrial age had with the way things work, the operational aesthetic. The most extraordinary development of this gag humor does not necessarily involve submitting it to narrative development and complex characterization. Rather the comedy of gags which begins with the tricks of naughty boys extends to images of an unbelievable grace, as the human blends with the unconscious functioning of the machineries of physical laws.

Filmography

Ah, Le Sale Gosse, Pathe, 1906
Algy's Glorious Fourth of July, American Mutoscope and Biograph Co (AM&B), 1902
L'Arroseur arrosé, Lumière Company, 1895
A Black Storm, AM&B, copyright 1903
A Blessing from Above, AM&B, 1904
A Boarding School Prank, AM&B, 1903
A Boomerang, AM&B, copyright 1903
The Borrowing Girl, AM&B, copyright 1904
The Boys Think Have One on Foxy Grandpa, But He Fools Them, AM&B, 1902
Brannigan Sets Off the Blast, AM&B, 1906
Buster Brown and his Dog Tige, Edison, 1904
The Cameraman, Metro-Goldwyn–Mayer, 1928
Charcuterie Mecanique, Lumière Company, 1896
Day Dreams, Metro, 1922
Dog Factory, Edison, 1904
The Electric House, Metro, 1922
Facial Expressions, Edison, copyright 1902
Les Farces de Toto Gate-Sauce, Pathé, 1905
The Fate of a Gossip, AM&B, 1903
The Finish of Bridget McKeene, Edison, 1901
Fun in a Butcher Shop, Edison, 1901
Getting up in the World, AM&B, 1903
A Good Shot, AM&B, 1902
Grandma and the Boys, Edison, copyright 1900
The Great Train Robbery, Edison, 1903
How Buttons Got Even with the Butler, AM&B, 1903
An Interrupted Kiss, Biograph catalogue, 1902
Interrupted Lovers, Edison catalogue, 1901
Let Uncle Reuben Show You How, AM&B, 1904
Love's Ardour Suddenly Cooled, Edison catalogue, 1901
Maude's Naughty Little Brother, Edison, 1900
Mischievous Willie's Rocking Chair Motor, AM&B, copyright 1902
Neighbors, AM&B, 1912
Night of the Party, AM&B, 1906
Our Hospitality, Metro, 1923
A Poor Place for Love Making, AM&B, 1905
Pulling Off the Bed Clothes, AM&B, copyright 1903

The Sausage Machine, AM&B, 1897
The School Master's Surprise, AM&B, 1897
They Found the Leak, AM&B, copyright 1902
A Trick on the Cop, AM&B, 1904
The Truants, AM&B, 1907
Why Foxy Grandpa Escaped a Duncking, AM&B, 1903
Willie's Camera, AM&B, 1903
A Wringing Good Joke, AM&B, 1898
A Wringing Good Joke, Edison, 1900
You Will Send Me to Bed, Eh?, AM&B, 1903

Most of the Edison and Biograph films listed above are in the Library of Congress Paper Print Collection and can be purchased on film or video through the Library.

5

Pie and Chase: Gag, Spectacle and Narrative in Slapstick Comedy[1]

Donald Crafton

Whether judged by production statistics, contemporary critical acclaim, audience popularity or retrospective opinions, it is abundantly clear that the American silent film comedy was flourishing in the mid-twenties, rivaling drama as the dominant form of cinematic expression. My aim in this essay is to rethink the function of the gag in relation to the comic film as a classical system. I seek not to examine or catalog all the possible variations of the gag (as joke, as articulation of cinema space or as thematic permutations) but rather to examine its operation in the slapstick genre.[2]

Let us introduce the subject by way of an amusing account of a screening of Charlie Chaplin films in Accra (Ghana, Africa), reported in the *New York Times* in 1925:

> It was a film from the remote antiquity of filmdom; a film from the utter dark ages of the cinematograph, so patched and pieced and repieced that all continuity was gone; a piebald hash chosen from the remains of various comedies and stuck together with no plot. Just slapstick. But Charlie had survived even that, and how they did love it![3]

The anecdote provides several insights into both the reception of films in a non-western culture and the status of film comedy in its "golden age." Most important for us, it expresses the opinion that this assemblage of Chaplin shorts is primitive, in the view of the reporter, because it lacks continuity. The writer intuitively distinguishes between linear aspects of film (plot, narrative, diegesis) and nonlinear components (spectacle and gag). Take away the story and what do you have left? "Just slapstick."

Much criticism of silent film comedy still hinges on the dichotomy between narrative and gag. Gerald Mast remarks in *The Comic Mind* that Max Linder's film *Seven Years' Bad Luck* "is interested in a gag, not a story to contain the gags or a character to perform them," or that the plots of Sennett's Keystone films "are merely apparent structures, collections of literary formulas and clichés to hang the gags on."[4] In such statements, there is an implicit valorization of narrative over gags. These films are flawed because the elements of slapstick are not "integrated" with other elements (character, structure, vision, cinematic style—Mast's criteria).

In this reading of film comedy, slapstick is the bad element, an excessive tendency that narrative must contain. Accordingly the history of the genre is usually teleological, written as though the eventual replacement of the gag by narrativized comedy was natural, ameliorative or even predestined.

While viewing dozens of short comedies from the teens and twenties in preparation for the Slapstick Symposium, it became clear that there was no such selective process operating. On the contrary, slapstick cinema seems to be ruled by the principle of accretion: gags, situations, costumes, characters and camera techniques are rehearsed and recycled in film after film, as though the modernist emphasis on originality and the unique text was unheard of. Unlike "mainstream" dramatic cinema, which progressed rapidly through styles, techniques and stories, nothing was discarded in slapstick. Camera tricks perfected by Méliès and Zecca are still in evidence a quarter-century later; music hall turns that were hoary when Chaplin, Linder and Keaton introduced them to cinema in the teens were still eliciting laughs by those clowns and others at the end of the silent period. We are forced to ask, if gags were so scorned, then why did the gag film linger on for so long, an important mode of cinematic discourse for at least forty years? And is there not something perverse about arguing that what is "wrong" with a film form is that which defines it to begin with?

The distinction between slapstick and narrative has been properly perceived, but incorrectly interpreted. I contend that it was never the aim of comic filmmakers to "integrate" the gag elements of their movies. I also doubt that viewers subordinated gags to narrative. In fact, the separation between the vertical domain of slapstick (the arena of spectacle I will represent by the metaphor of the thrown pie) and the horizontal domain of the story (the arena of the chase) was a calculated rupture, designed to keep the two elements antagonistically apart. In *Narration in the Fiction Film*, David Bordwell asks, "Is there anything in narrative film that is not narrational?"[5] My answer is yes: the gag.

If we examine typical Hal Roach two-reel comedies from 1925 and 1926, we find a laboratory for what some film analysts have described as the series of symmetries and blockages that define the systematicity of classical American cinema. At the same time, it is important to differentiate these films from the contemporaneous feature. While at first the narrative structures of the shorts may resemble condensations or abridgments (features with the boring bits taken out), the high concentration of gag and spectacle defines the genre as unique. Among other features, the frequent intrusions of spectacle produce a kind of narrative lurching that often makes the plots of slapstick comedies distinctively incoherent (and delightfully so).

The Pie

Let us first look more closely at those nonnarrative gag elements that the term slapstick usually encompasses. This usage is appropriate when we consider the origin of that word, referring to a circus prop consisting of two thin slats joined together, so that a loud clack is made when one clown hits another on the behind. The violent aural effect, the "slap," may be thought of as having the same kind of disruptive impact on the audience as its visual equivalent in the silent cinema, the pie in the face. In fact, very few comedies of the twenties really used pies, but nevertheless their humor in a general sense frequently depended on the same kind of emphatic, violent, embarrassing gesture.

The lack of linear integration that offends some slapstick commentators can trace its roots to popular spectacle. For example, in his 1915 home correspondence manual, Brett Page advised would-be vaudeville writers that their scripts must account for the actors' *business*. He meant the visual, nonverbal performance component, "done to drive the spoken words home, or to 'get over' a meaning without words."[6] His pupils learned that:

> So large a part does the element of business play in the success of the two-act that the early examples of this vaudeville form were nearly all built out of bits of business. And the business was usually of the "slap-stick" kind. (p. 98)

Page defined slapstick as physical gags, and consistently emphasized its nonverbal nature:

> Every successful two-act, every entertainment-form of which acting is an element—the playlet and the full-evening play as well—prove beyond the shadow of a doubt that what audiences laugh at—what you and I laugh at—is not words, but actions and situations. (p. 108)

Page easily generalized and shifted his focus from the nonverbal to the nonnarrative. About the vaudeville sketch he wrote,

The purpose of the sketch is not to leave a single impression of a single story. It points no moral, draws no conclusion, and sometimes it might end quite as effectively anywhere before the place in the action at which it does terminate. It is built for entertainment purposes only and furthermore, for entertainment purposes that end the moment the sketch ends. (p. 147)

Recalling the African projection of the fragmented Chaplin films, the movie might have been incomprehensible as a narrative, but it worked fine as a filmic sketch, an assembly of nonverbal gags. Such an aesthetic of spectacle for its own sake is clearly inimical to the classical narrative feature, but not at all hostile to slapstick cinema of the teens and twenties.

Again, we can use this concept to discriminate between the comic shorts and the comic feature. The latter purposefully (and more or less successfully) sought to produce an "integrated" spectacle. Certainly *The General* and *The Gold Rush* are exemplary in their attempt to set the hero's struggles within a determinant Griffithesque historical fiction. But when one examines the two-reelers, even late in the twenties and well into the sound era one finds a preponderance of anarchistic non- and quasinarratives that pass for movie stories.

Generally, there is a simple plot which frames the gags, with an opening premise and a closing scene which provides a resolution. The gags may or may not be thematically related. Whether this is a narrative depends on how insistently one defines it. I argue that despite a weakly structured set of causes and effects, many of these films remain, at best, quasinarratives. Although the shorts emulate feature film narrative structures, the audience is scarcely aware of it, navigating the film from laugh to laugh as though enjoying a sketch. This is gag-driven cinema.

There can be no concrete definition of a gag because it is marked by affective response, not set forms or clear logic. Further, gag and slapstick are not synonymous. Slapstick is the generic term for these nonnarrative intrusions, while gags are specific forms of intrusions. Like verbal jokes, to which they are closely related, gags have their own loose structures, systems and "fuzzy" logic that exist independently of cinema. The gag may also contain its own microscopic narrative system that may be irrelevant to the larger narrative, may mirror it, or may even work against it as parody. "Sight gags," those that depend primarily on visual exposition, still have characteristic logical structures, the same that one finds in multipanel comic strips.[7] Think, for example, of the gag in *Jus' Passin' Through*, a Will Rogers film from 1923, produced by Hal Roach and directed by Charles Parrott (a.k.a. Charley Chase). We see a hobo checking the gates of houses for the special chalk tramp-sign that indicates whether there is a mean dog inside. One can easily see how the sequence could be presented effectively as a wordless comic strip. In the first two frames we would see images of the tramp eschewing those yards with the mark on the gate (the exposition of the nonhumorous part of the joke that vaudevillians would have called the "buildup"); in the penultimate panel we would see him fleeing a yard through an unmarked gate with a dog in hot pursuit; the final panel would show him adding his own beware-the-dog sign to the gate. Whether this corresponds to a "punch line" depends on how much visual/narrative information is perceived, and how the viewer's expectations are subverted.[8]

Other examples of "comic strip logic" might be mistaken identity gags (accomplished by fluid montage and parodic sight line constructions) such as the one that begins the Charley Chase film *Looking for Sally* (1925): from a ship's deck, the arriving hero waves to a girl on the dock whom he incorrectly assumes to be his fiancée; she waves back, not to Charley (as he thinks) but (as we see) to *her* friend on another deck. (See also Chaplin's *A Dog's Life* for the same gag.)

Also commonplace are camera tricks, for instance, double exposures and animation, that exploit the film medium's capability of disrupting the normal vision that the narrative depends on for its consistency and legibility. Manipulation of cause and effect—for example, when a little action produces a disproportionate reaction—is another form of cinematic excess characteristic of the sight gag. It is important to remember that the narrative content of the gag may be *nil*—for example the jarring close-ups of Ben Turpin's eyes. Such cases are illustrations of what Eisenstein called "attractions," elements of pure spectacle.

Writing in 1923, Eisenstein defined the "attraction" as: "every aggressive moment in [the theater], i.e. every element of it that brings to light in the spectator those senses or that psychology that influence his experience."[9] Eisenstein also referred to those moments as "emotional shocks," and insisted that they are always psychologically disruptive (for example, the gouging out of an eye). He contrasted the attraction to the lyrical, that being the part of the presentation readily assimilated by the spectator. Probably referring to *The Kid* (1921) he notes that the lyrical may coexist with the disruptive attraction, for example, the "specific mechanics of [Chaplin's] movement." In slapstick comedy, I am claiming, there is a variant of this concept: the "lyrical" is the narrative, functioning as the regulating component; the "attraction" is the gag or, again in Eisenstein's words, the "brake" that has to be applied to sharpened dramatic moments."[10] In another context, Tom Gunning has described early cinema (pre-1906) as a "cinema of attraction:"

> Whatever differences one might find between Lumière and Méliès, they should not represent the opposition between narrative and nonnar-

rative filmmaking, at least as it is understood today. Rather, one can unite them in a conception that sees cinema less as a way of telling stories than as a way of presenting a series of views to an audience. . . . In other words, I believe that the relation to the spectator set up by the films of both Lumière and Méliès (and many other filmmakers before 1906) had a common basis, and one that differs from the primary spectator relations set up by narrative film after 1906. . . . Although different from the fascination in storytelling exploited by the cinema from the time of Griffith, it is not necessarily opposed to it. In fact the cinema of attraction does not disappear with the dominance of narrative, but rather goes underground, both into certain avant-garde practices and as a component of narrative films, more evident in some genres (e.g. the musical) than in others.[11]

Gunning's observation is astute; the disruptive gags of slapstick can be regarded as an anachronistic manifestation of the cinema of attraction. I disagree, though, with his unwillingness to polarize the two components. While other genres work to contain their excesses, this opposition is fundamental to slapstick. Furthermore it is carefully constructed to remain an unbridgeable gap. In this sense it is *not* underground, but instead overt, flagrant and flamboyant.

The Chase

Let us look briefly at the other component, the Chase, or the narrative dimension of film comedy. Again, rather than examining specific narrative structures, it is enough for our purposes to say that the narrative is the propelling element, the fuel of the film that gives it its power to go from beginning to end. (To continue the automotive metaphor, one would say that the gags are the potholes, detours and flat tires encountered by the Tin Lizzie of the narrative on its way to the end of the film.) Film narrative has been the subject of considerable recent scholarly exposition, and rightly so. But its other, that is, those elements that block narrativity— the Pie—has been dismissed as textual excess, if it has been considered at all. Although, in the twenties, actual chases were more frequent than pie-throwings, I am also using the term Chase metaphorically, suggesting the linear trajectory of the narrative in general, not a specific instance. The term includes many characteristic twenties plots, such as pursuing a criminal, retrieving a lost object, restoring a family, and—most importantly—reuniting a separated couple in a presumed marriage. Of course the same themes predominate in dramatic films as well, and we should bear in mind that, as Gunning, Eileen Bowser, Andrew Horton and others have noted, the line between comedy and melodrama can be very fine.[12] One thinks, for example, of Anita Loos's claim that she tried to turn the screenplay of Griffith's *The Struggle* (based on *Ten Nights in a Barroom*) into a comic farce, while the film that Griffith made from the screenplay turned out to be a "serious" temperance melodrama. The disruptive elements, the parodic "attractions" concocted by Loos, were recuperated by Griffith's narrative priorities.

So Much for Theory . . .

When Steve Neale writes of "the emergence of terms like Fate, Chance and Destiny," or "a character's mistaken perception, or lack of knowledge,"[13] instead of melodrama, he could just as well be discussing *His Wooden Wedding*, a short produced in 1925 by Hal Roach, directed by Leo McCarey, and starring Charley Chase.[14]

Rich playboy Charley is marrying Katherine (Katherine Grant) on Friday the 13th. The date is a portent of the loss of stasis that is about to occur, and an explanation, couched in the uncanny, of several aspects of bad luck that will inevitably mar the wedding: the best man (unknown to Charley) is Katherine's rejected suitor, who is spiteful and, besides, would like to steal the diamond engagement ring. He plants false knowledge, in the form of a note to Charley informing him that his fiancée is not what she seems: "Beware! The girl you are about to marry has a wooden leg." By coincidence (extraordinary in life, but typical in fiction), Katherine sprains her ankle just before the wedding, causing her to limp down the aisle, apparently substantiating the outrageous rumor. Charley shouts "Stop! I've been engaged to a girl with a wooden leg—I must break it off." When he confronts Katherine in her room after the aborted wedding ceremony, he is unaware that he is actually speaking to a manikin. In the course of his explanation, her leg falls off and he walks out.

Drowning his sorrows in a bottle of wine, Charley then boards a cruise ship to forget Katherine's presumed treachery. On board he discovers the plot, recovers the diamond, and turns the boat around to meet Katherine, who has learned independently of the hoax and is following the ship on her father's yacht. When she arrives, Charley and the rival are struggling in the water. She strips down to her bathing suit to save Charley and, when the villain is hauled aboard, she displays her very real bare leg and uses it to kick him back into the water, thus cancelling the effects of his libelous false knowledge with this empirical demonstration of her corporeal integrity.

What is especially interesting, and also very typical of many shorts of the period, is the manner in which the apparent narrative closure, eliminating the villain, is not really final. There is a coda reunion scene as the lovers pose in an embrace. The formal tableau ending suggests that the symmetry of the narrative is insufficient by itself to properly close the film.

It is as though the narrative's validity must be confirmed by subsuming it into spectacle showing that the initial promise of order—the protagonists' marriage—will be fulfilled. To put it another way, the man and woman must be rejoined and visually wed before they can be wed in the later fiction, the one after the film ends, the one the spectator (not the filmmaker) creates.[15]

Also typical of comedy as well as melodrama is the insistence on a woman's body as the site for restoring natural order through heterosexual coupling. In this reading, the imagery in Chase's film is essentially a castration nightmare: the revelation to the groom on his wedding day that his bride has a horrifying lack (a symbolic missing leg) and an intolerable replacement (the metonymic wooden member). Charley contemplates his future children and the family dog all sporting peg legs, as if the wound were a genetic flaw passed on by the wife. The woman is being projected as the scene of the man's fears and anxieties concerning familial responsibility and sexual performance. Only when the threat of the woman's repugnant phallic intrusion into their relationship, the despised wooden leg, is removed ("broken off") can the wedding—of flesh and not of wood—take place.

This film is an excellent example of how gag and narrative interact and regulate each other by means of a lively dialectic. One cannot help but compare the complex system of alternation of spectacle and diegesis to the same systems observable in Eisenstein's films of the period. While space does not allow a thorough analysis, we can point out some of the ways in which gags disturb the narrative.

The film's opening scenes of wedding preparations provide the armature for an "instant" narrative form, since viewers understand the protocol of such ceremonies. But expectations for a normal unfolding of events are soon derailed. Instead of providing background information on the story or characters,the intertitles make gratuitous jokes that interfere with our comprehension: "The happy bridegroom—So excited he telephoned the minister to bring along a shotgun and a good bird dog." The verbal content diverts the narrative rather than advancing it. The rival's note about the wooden leg similarly challenges the viewer to rationalize a motive for its effect. Why would the rival choose this particular lie (instead of the "usual" marital impediments: bigamy, secret lovers, dreaded diseases, racial taint, illegitimate children)? Would not even the most priggish of grooms already be aware of this physical trait of his fiancée? Would having a prosthesis really be sufficient grounds for halting a marriage? To "explain" Charley's motives, the viewer sees a subjective vision of Charley's family in the future; but what Charley imagines is biologically impossible. However improbable, it nevertheless convinces *him* to interrupt the wedding. The spectacle of the wooden-legged family also halts the deployment of the ready-made narrative of the wedding ceremony. In a trope that will be replayed several times in the film, a small action (the bogus note) prompts a massive and irrational overreaction (the cancellation).

But the disjunctive titles are inserted into a very ordinary *mise-en-scène* quite typical of any 1920s feature (complete with characteristic matchcuts, eyeline matches, and so on). The exception is when Charley looks at the camera and performs his signature "slow burn," for instance when the manikin (whom he has mistaken for Katherine) loses her leg.

The advancement of the wedding ceremony is frequently halted by Charley's inappropriate actions: he attempts to shake the hand of an old friend, he is distracted by the crying mother-in-law-to-be. And fate intervenes when Katherine sprains her ankle. When Charley exits the wedding, the restoration of the narrative commences by way of a triple pursuit structure. Katherine, learning of the hoax, follows Charley; the rival pursues Charley to get the diamond; and Charley seeks the diamond (and thence Katherine). These three motives are articulated in parallel montage sequences.

Each pursuit has its own trajectory, which is protracted by fate's intervention: The rival retrieves the diamond, but loses it to Charley in a hat mix-up; Katherine and her father pursue Charley but keep just missing him; Charley finds the diamond but loses it in a woman passenger's clothing.[16] Neale's description of melodrama structure is once again applicable here:

> The constantly changing and apparently arbitrary course of events articulates and intensifies these vicissitudes, and, in turn, is motivated by them. Blockages, barriers and bars to the fulfillment of desire are constantly introduced as events change course.[17]

There are running gags involving hats (thrown overboard, blown by wind, knocked off). There are sight gags (the manikin) and spatial gags (the double door keyhole in the woman's stateroom). An example of another kind of block is Charley's subjective insert, in which he fantasizes the "future," set in faraway 1934. While the viewer understands the diegetic time to be in the character's future, the diegetic tense is nevertheless the present. For, though it takes a few seconds to unfold on the screen, for Charley, the vision is an instantaneous flash of clairvoyance. The confusion of tense is something like the effect of the temporal lapses in musicals.

Special effects also break into the diegetic world. When the boat swerves there is a cut to a small model ship, hilarious in its obviousness. Similarly, the effect of the ship's turning is done simply by having the actors lean in one direction and fall over. A splice creates the effect of Charley picking up a full decanter of wine and setting down an empty one.

Many of the gags are based on inversions of normal logic. As mentioned, small actions that spark big reactions are a *leitmotif*. When Charley's servant tosses his suitcase out the window it destroys a parked car; the policeman tells Charley he cannot park his car on the quay, so he pushes it into the ocean. There is also the truncated syllogism. The joke is set up as a set of logical relations, but the expected conclusion does not follow. Charley throws his hat (with the diamond in it) over the ship's rail, and it returns three times. But when he throws the captain's hat it sails away. These subversions of logic undermine the viewer's ability to match effects with causes.

The most elaborate set piece occurs when Charley entices the woman passenger to dance the Charleston with him in the hopes of shaking loose the diamond. This important scene is semidiegetic; that is, it furthers the narrative in a crucial way—it produces the object of the chase, the diamond—but it is also predominantly a spectacle, and the sequence which provokes the most belly laughs in viewers. Again there is a humorous failure of logic. The dancers' contortions become more frenetic and gymnastic, causing the woman to shed first her watch, her powder puff, then her brassiere. This progression *ad absurdum* is anticlimactically cut short when the envelope containing the diamond falls out, and Charley strolls out without a word, as though the episode never took place.

The three pursuits wind down, but are again prolonged by inserting a spectacle—Katherine's exposed leg—and by the "business" of kicking the rival back into the water. By the time the final closure is achieved, sealed with a kiss between the betrothed, the audience experiences relief, but also a temporal waste, a *temps perdu* because the "story" has been set back to a time before the film began (the plans for a new wedding have to be made). All that transpired was "excess"—slapstick.[18]

The opposition of Pie and Chase may be outlined in a chart:

"Pie"	"Chase"
Gag Titles	*Glance-object editing style*
Inappropriate actions (Charley recognizes old friend as he walks down the aisle)	*Expected chain of events* (structure of wedding ceremony)
	Triple pursuit:
Fate (sprained ankle)	• Katherine → Charley
Mistaken perception (cane for leg)	• Rival → diamond
Subjective insert (temporal confusion)	• Charley → diamond

Attenuated reaction/direct address (long glance at camera when manikin's leg falls)

Drunken gags

Running gags (e.g. hats)

Small action → large reaction

Repeated action (car destructions)

Inappropriate action

Truncated syllogism (hat over rail)

Sight gags

Spatial gags

Semidiegetic insert (dance scene)

Progression ad absurdum (dance scene)

Exaggerated reaction (boat turning → dancers falling)

Special effects (obvious model boat)

Revelation (display of "real" leg)

Final tableau (apotheosis)

Motivating action (duplicitous note)
Parallel action in different spaces
Actions to restore order:

• Rival retrieves diamond
• Diamond in Charley's hat

• Katherine's father discovers note; she and he pursue Charley

• Charley pursues his hat, finds diamond, hides it on old maid

• Charley wins old maid's admiration and tricks rival (keyhole)

• Charley tries to recover ring

Closures

• Charley retrieves diamond

• Katherine intercepts ship; Charley turns boat around; jumps into ocean (with rival)

• Katherine kicks rival with "real" leg

In his response to this paper in its original version, reprinted following this essay, Tom Gunning made some valuable criticism that I should address briefly. First, he drew attention to the two-dimensionality of my picture of the "forces that disrupt and the forces that contain," and insisted on the complexity of the relationship. I agree. But I disagree that the narrative is always a complex "process of integration in which smaller units are absorbed into a larger overarching pattern and process of containment," or that gags are "an excess that is necessary to the film's process of containment." This may be an accurate description of other genres, but slapstick seems to actively construct this "failure" of containment and to resist bourgeois legibility and rationality.

Gunning cites the dance sequence as an example of the recovery of gags by narrativization. True, the purpose served by the scene is to retrieve the engagement ring from the "virgin wilderness of the old maid's underclothes," but at what lack of economy! The same function would have been satisfied by Charley's finding the ring on the deck. Instead the woman is presented in such a way as to reward the audience's desire to see an old maid making a shimmying spectacle of herself. The abruptness of Charley's desertion after he gets the ring is funny in part because his offhand gesture points up the irrelevance of the ring to the narrative; it's a MacGuffin. It is the diegetic content of the scene (ring as object of the chase) that becomes the excessive part of the elaborate joke.

Gunning also rightly notes that my chart contains several elements (such as truncated syllogisms) that, as inversions, are possible only through the gag's deceptive assimilation of narrative form. He points out that parodies of narratives are still narratives "in which narrative logic is not so much ignored as laid bare."

No one will argue that *His Wooden Wedding* is lacking in parody. Charley's "courting" of the old maid, for example, is a parody of his court ship with Katherine and its vicissitudes (the woman's agility contrasting with Katherine's lameness). But again, I maintain that in these instances, the tail *really is* wagging the dog! To say that the gags' assimilation of narrative structure is laying bare the illusionist invisibility of the fictional mechanism is simply another way of saying that spectacle is here "containing" narrative, and not the other way around. The "message" of this and other slapstick films is that the seeming hegemony of narrative in the classical cinema is being assaulted by the militant forces of spectacle. The film's multiple narrative closures are overly redundant, even by classical standards. The obstacles mounted by fate are overcome, but not at the cost of annihilating the impact of the gags. It is the *non sequitur* components of the humor that we recall best—as in one of Brett Page's ideal sketches. Like the wedding of the title, the absorption of all the disruptive elements by the narrative never takes place.

If there is a controversy here, it may be resolved simply by asserting that while films generally are not all-or-nothing, spectacle-versus-narrative propositions, there are certain cases that encourage the viewer to see them in just this binary fashion. *Don Key, Son of Burro* (Roach, 1926) is a good illustration of the slapstick genre's awareness of its own ambivalent attitude toward narrative containment.

The "story" of the film is minimal: a movie writer enters a producer's office to pitch his screenplay. As he speaks, the actions of his screenplay appear as a series of vignettes, separated from the main narrative by conventional dissolves. These usually denote another narrative level (dream, fantasy, and so on), but in this case, the vignettes show us the writer's fiction.

The joke is that the writer's "story" is only a succession of sight gags and business that ultimately fail the test of a narrative: there is no cause and effect, no consistent pattern or development of the represented events. The "episodes" vary from the surrealistically strange to the hilariously funny. In one sequence the leading lady's boyfriend is getting a shave. Every time the barber applies the razor, a dog runs up to the chair as though begging for a bone. The barber explains, "He's such an optimist. Once he got an ear."[19]

As best as can be reconstructed, the writer's "story" begins with a boy who has a chimp as a baby-sitter. They live next to a den of lions. An old, ugly playboy (Jimmy Finlayson) is spying on the girl and her boyfriend. There is a bank robbery, and a sheriff who chases the bandits over railroad tracks and fields. The chimp runs away with the boy, and the playboy falls into the lion's den. All this is punctuated with numerous "pie" elements: Finlayson's constant mannerism of looking at the camera; the chimp's victimization by a pesky duck; Finlayson's kissing the chimp instead of the girl; and extensive animated effects: Finlayson's beating heart, the robbers' car careening around a curve on a cliff; a strange car that bucks off the passengers.

As the writer tells his incomprehensible tale, we cut back to the reactions of the producer and his flunkies. His assistants appear with a sledgehammer, a bomb, and a bow and arrow and ask their boss, "Now?" The producer replies, "Not yet," and finally dismisses the writer. (He shoots the next writer who walks in without even listening to his screenplay.)

The film recounts vividly the antagonism between slapstick business and the institutional drive to subdue it to the demands of Hollywood. By showing plural interpretations of the "screenplay," the film exploits the viewer's conflicting associations. On the one hand, the writer's gags are truly funny, his sight gags successfully crafted; on the other, his film will never be produced (existing only as an unrealized fiction). For the writer it works, for the producer it fails, but we can see it both ways: successful as a comic spectacle; a flop as a movie melodrama.

We can see it binocularly because we know the parameters of film narrative. Our *de facto* orientation is that of the producer. But unlike him and his yes-men, we do not reject the writer's proposal because of its nonconformity; we relish it precisely because it flaunts conventions of Hollywood storytelling. Certainly this is parody. And the film finally "recuperates" Hollywood by throwing out the writer. But like inadmissible evidence at a trial, the point of the film was understood, and lingers subversively in the minds of the viewers. Slapstick gags are more effective than melodramatic tears.

Conclusion

It may be that the tendency to suppress the antinarrative elements of film history results from a hasty overclassicism of actual Hollywood output in the 1920s. Richard Koszarski has reminded us that cinema in the twenties was *an evening's* entertainment.[20] The slapstick short took its place among the travelogues, cartoons, 3-D novelties, sing-alongs, live prologues and musical performances. Like these expressive forms, spectacle "attraction" was the primary characteristic; narrative was greatly diminished, if present at all. Some features—*The General* is a good example—even contained color sequences that were narratively expendable, but contributed visual novelty.

One way to look at narrative is to see it as a system for providing the spectator with sufficient knowledge to make causal links between represented events.[21] According to this view, the gag's status as an irreconcilable difference becomes clear. Rather than providing knowledge, slapstick misdirects the viewer's attention, and obfuscates the linearity of cause-effect relations. Gags provide the opposite of epistemological comprehension by the spectator. They are atemporal bursts of violence and/or hedonism that are as ephemeral and as gratifying as the sight of someone's pie-smitten face.

6

Response to "Pie and Chase"

Tom Gunning

The term "narrative" has been something of a dirty word in film studies for the last few decades. It was assumed that telling stories was the most simple and boring thing a film could do. Narrative was associated with "content" or "thematics," and understood as clearly a less sexy thing for a film theorist to be involved with than form or style. When Truffaut said that he loved the moments in film when the narrative stops, he seemed to announce a whole generation's preoccupation with the contingent and nonnarrative elements of film practice.

The recent refocusing on narrative has somewhat redressed the balance, calling attention to what we might term the structural aspects of narrative, seeing story not as content but as a structuring force. However, narrative seems to still carry an ambivalent reaction, a taint of ideological conformity and containment. The Bellour-Heathian view of narrative which Don Crafton cites may announce narrative as a respectable topic for investigation, but still approaches it with a lingering suspicion. Narrative, in this view, is a dynamic process which charts, as Crafton puts it, a disruption of an original stasis and a consequent process of containment that seeks to limit the violence of disruption and regain the original equilibrium.

The usefulness of the description is obvious, and although there may be doubts about its universality, its range of application is certainly broad in commercial narrative films. However, what needs to be emphasized is that this view sees two elements to narrative: the forces that disrupt and the forces that contain. While most narratives operate so that containment dominates disruption, thus providing closure, it should be emphasized that the forces of disruption *are essential* to even the most conventional narrative.

I think that Crafton's paper is fairly clear on this point, but the relation between the disruptive elements of narrative and the "pie" elements of pure nonnarrative spectacle is complex. Like the disruptive elements, gags are, as he puts it, the potholes, detours and flat tires of narrative, that which Barthes and the Russian Formalists would call the "delays" of narrative.

This is not at all to deny that slapstick comedies (along with a number of other popular genres, most obviously the musical) involve an interrelation of narrative and nonnarrative elements. I like very much the relation Crafton draws between gags and Eisenstein's concept of theatrical attractions, a relation which I have also made dealing with elements in pre-1907 films. However I believe that Crafton opens here a subject for further analysis. The interrelation of these nonnarrative and narrative features is quite complex, precisely because narrative acts as a system of regulation which ultimately absorbs nonnarrative elements into its pendulum sways.

Ben Brewster recently pointed out to me the limitations to our conception of narrative as linear. Useful as this two-dimensional metaphor may be in describing the goal-directed aspect of many narratives and narrative's own rush to containment, it also makes narrative appear more simple than I think it is in practice. Rather, we could think of narrative as a process of integration in which smaller units are absorbed into a larger overarching pattern and process of containment.

Crafton underestimates the interplay between the pie and the chase. First, gags become absorbed into the narrative economy of most films, marking perhaps an excess, but an excess that is necessary to the film's process of containment. The dancing sequence in *His Wooden Wedding* is a good example. This is, as Crafton notes, a progression *ad absurdum*. However, along with the delightful absurdity, we also get an important progression in the narrative: Chase's regaining of the diamond lost in the virgin wilderness of the old maid's underclothes.

But only the most boring of semioticians could feel that the regaining of the diamond was the *point* of this sequence. It is, rather, its excuse. But it is important to maintain this double vision: the excess of the gags and their recovery by narrativization.

The most important aspect which this double view allows is the realization that, in their contact with narrative, gags do not simply lose their independence, but precisely subvert the narrative itself. This is done not through their nonnarrative excess, their detouring of narrative concerns into pure attraction, but precisely through their integration with narrative, their adoption of narrative's form of logical anticipation, and then their subversion of it.

For instance, in Crafton's excellent list of gags from *His Wooden Wedding*, a number are quite correctly described as inversion in narrative logic ("inappropriate action," "truncated syllogism," "small action-large reaction"). The point here is that such inversions are possible only through the gag's deceptive assimilation of narrative form. It is by seeming to resemble certain narrative situations that narrative anticipation is subverted. This is not simply an issue of two separate forms, but of a dialectical interrelation. It is in fact the process of parody, in which narrative logic is not so much ignored, as laid bare.

When, as in *Don Key, Son of Burro*, the pie in the face (or its equivalent) is repeatedly delayed, it takes on one of the basic aspects of narrative. And when narrative situations are repeatedly rendered absurd by laying bare their devices, this subversion brings them close to gags. Eisenstein called, of course, for a *montage* of attraction, and noted that, in this structure, elements of narrative could be introduced in such a way as to lose their usual claim to coherence and diegetic realism. Slapstick comedy takes us not simply into the realm of the pie, but into the land of carnival, where narrative reveals the absurdity of its principle of integration, as legs transform from flesh to wood and back again, and pies end up in the face rather than the mouth.

7

Commitment and Reaffirmation in Hollywood Romantic Comedy

Kristine Brunovska Karnick

The story begins on a note of distrust. A husband is on his way home early one morning, having spent two weeks in Florida. But he has not really been in Florida. Before the husband arrives home, a friend wonders how this behavior will affect the husband's marriage, while asking where the husband has really been. The husband answers, "What wives don't know won't hurt them, and it won't hurt you either." However, when the husband arrives home, his wife is not there. She comes home a few minutes later, wearing an evening gown from the night before, accompanied by another man, a young Continental type. As the husband expresses his shock at the situation, the wife realizes that he has been dishonest with her. On a note of mutual distrust, the couple decide to divorce.

The situation described above could well have provided the premise for a Hollywood melodrama. There is certainly nothing in the plot structure that would necessarily designate this as a comedy. However, if we fill in details of this scene, a different sense of the situation emerges.

The husband, Jerry Warriner (Cary Grant), is first seen at the Gotham Athletic Club getting an artificial tan, in order to pull off the fiction of his having been in Florida. He comes home carrying a big fruit basket for his wife, Lucy (Irene Dunne), and is accompanied by a few friends whom he has invited over for breakfast. When they arrive at Jerry's house, Lucy is not home. Jerry hypothesizes that she is with her maiden aunt, Patsy. Then Patsy arrives, alone. Soon after, Lucy arrives home with another man, Armand Duvalle. Adapting two classic clichés to explain the situation, Lucy tells the group that Armand has been giving her voice lessons, and that they went to a recital the night before, their car broke down, and they were forced to spend the night in a small inn. The friends decide that it is time to leave. As Armand is leaving, Lucy

Jerry Warriner greets his wife and . . .

responds to Jerry's characterization of Armand as a "great lover," with the statement that "no one can accuse you [Armand] of being a great lover." Jerry and Lucy argue about trust. Lucy marvels at Jerry's fine tan, considering the rain in Florida the past two weeks. Then she picks up an orange from her basket and tosses the piece of fruit to Jerry. He glances at the stamp of the word "California" on the orange and winces. They call their lawyer to set plans in motion for a divorce. On the phone, the lawyer alternates between dissuading the couple from divorcing, with clichés such as "marriage is a beautiful thing," and responding to his wife's requests to come to breakfast: "Shut up! I'll come when I'm good and ready, and if you don't like it, you know what you can do."

The scene takes place in Leo McCarey's *The Awful Truth*, a screwball comedy, and it illustrates one of the difficulties involved in analyzing this genre. Specifically, what makes this a comedy? While this plot is not necessarily comic, its treatment of the story is. Humor is a means of expressing a plot which is not generically comic. This essay examines the relationship between narrative structure and humorous treatment in screwball comedies, looking for the ways in which humor inflects and transforms nongeneric storylines into comedies.

. . . Armand Duvalle: Cary Grant, Irene Dunne, and Alexander D'Arcy in *The Awful Truth* (1937).

Rick Altman has argued that a major stage of any genre study involves identifying and describing certain traits and systems present and operative within a large number of texts considered to be examples of the genre.[1] Then, adopting a particular methodology, one can constitute a revised corpus. For this analysis, the preliminary corpus is that group of films popularly known as screwball comedies. The term "screwball" itself became codified in the mid-1930s, as representing films with certain common features. James Harvey argues that "screwball" was originally a publicist's term that came into wide usage in around 1936, when *My Man Godfrey*, "with Carole Lombard's dizzy rampaging heroine, seemed to compel the description."[2] Screwball, however, came to represent a wider category of films than simply those that emphasized "scattiness or derangement." Screwball named a style associated with "a paradoxical kind of liberation, with romantic exaltation of a very down-to-earth kind. This paradox was the peculiar, energizing complication that made the style so congenial to Hollywood—so expressive of both the place and the fantasy."[3] Ted Sennett's examination of screwball traces the genre to an evolving optimism emerging by the mid-thirties, while still stressing the bleak character of the time. Screwball comedies brought "nervous explosions of slapstick and occasional touches of asperity [to] alleviate the frustrations and bitter disappointments of the time."[4]

It is difficult to define screwball comedy according to such easily identifiable elements as setting and iconography. Unlike the West of the Western, the urban milieu of the gangster film or the monsters of the horror film, the screwball comedy has no identifiable setting or easily definable character types. Thomas Schatz, for example, has argued that screwball comedies are "fast-paced, witty comedies of manners exploiting the foibles of America's leisure class."[5] However, such commonly accepted examples of the genre as *His Girl Friday* and *Ball of Fire* resist even this broad definition.

Finally, classifying films as comedies because they contain jokes, comic moments and humorous situations is problematic, because obvious non-comedies contain a great many such situations. The George Stevens film, *Penny Serenade*, for example, stars Cary Grant and Irene Dunne, as does *The Awful Truth*. Much of this film also contains comic moments and humorous situations. However, as the film progresses, the tone becomes increasingly darker and more melodramatic, the plot culminating with the death of a child.

Many critics would agree with Harvey that "there was almost nothing in the screwball mode that wasn't familiar from long usage in theater, vaudeville, popular fiction, or earlier films."[6] It is relevant to an analysis of the screwball comedy, then, to examine which elements came together, and in what form. The first part of this essay examines the interplay between narrative structure and humor in a large number of Hollywood comedies typically referred to as screwball. The nature of this relationship determines the methodology, which is then employed to look at these films' particular structures in order to establish the borders of a revised corpus.

Theorizing Narrative and Humor

Many of these films share a common narrative structure. Some of the most popular and most often cited examples of the genre not only tell the same story but do so within the parameters of a remarkably similar plot. Many more screwball comedies pick up and emphasize key elements of what I will refer to as this basic plot paradigm. Given this structure, humor in screwball comedies serves to complicate a structure which might otherwise be quite predictable. Therefore, the humor offers additional challenges to the spectator's hypothesis-making ability.

This model presupposes a cognitive approach to meaning production. When watching a film, spectators actively produce meaning. Narratives are constructed either to reward, modify or frustrate this search for coherence.

Spectators come to a text prepared to focus their energies toward story construction. Advertising, for example, and exposure to similar texts, such as films from the same genre, help structure the expectations the viewer brings to the individual viewing experience. As Peter Rabinowitz has argued, genres are strategies that readers use to process texts.[7] Readers develop or acquire reading competence through repeated exposure to representative texts.

In this hypothesis-forming process, the spectator is aided by the existence of schemata. While this term has been variously defined, many definitions agree that a schema is "a cognitive structure that contains units of information and the links among these units."[8] In other words, schemata are organized clusters of knowledge.[9]

Gordon Bower has argued that we understand simple narrative stories as the working out of a protagonist's plan to achieve some goal. The action sequence is instrumental in overcoming some obstacle blocking that goal. However, "actions and events that are not on this main, goal-directed sequence of the story will be soon forgotten. Texts which list a series of events not connected by an overall plan or goal of some agent, are poorly understood and easily forgotten."[10] The motive or plan of a character provides a strong framework for interpreting and organizing the events in which that character participates.[11]

Story comprehension research suggests that, in our culture, perceivers tend to presuppose a particular master schema, an abstraction of narrative structure which embodies typical expectations about how to classify events and relate various parts to an overall narrative. Perceivers use this schema as a framework for understanding, recalling and summarizing a particular narrative. In the most common template schema (or filing system schema), which Bordwell refers to as the canonical story format, the setting and characters are introduced, a state of affairs is established, an action disrupts this state of affairs, ensuing events result, and there is a final outcome.[12] A narrative that violates this ideal scenario or creates ambiguities distorts and complicates the viewer's comprehension and recall.

Jean Mandler has found that story schemata consist of sets of expectations about stories, about the units of which they are composed, the way in which those units are sequenced, and the types of connections between units that are likely to occur. Experimenting with this concept, Mandler found that subjects hearing stories presented in an unusual interleaved fashion showed a strong tendency to recall stories in their canonical form rather than in the correct input order.[13] In other words, the underlying ideal structure of the story schema played an important role in retrieval.

Humor is one element which continually distorts this canonical form.

Humor depends on unpredictability, which often takes the form of incongruity. Humor complicates and frustrates the spectator's inferences about the narrative. Humorous moments within comedies are approached by the spectator in a manner akin to his/her comprehension of other formal aspects of the text. Such an approach is supported by an incongruity-resolution model of humor comprehension and appreciation. An incongruity involves some difference between what one expects and what one gets, a lack of consistency and harmony.[14] Incongruity can be found at the root of the views of Bergson, Schopenhauer and Kant.[15] Incongruity theories, in one or another of their manifestations, are the most generally accepted theories of humor. One such widely accepted account sees incongruity as fitting together with resolution, so that at some, often not immediately recognizable, level the incongruous elements cohere.

An incongruity-resolution model holds that humor results when the perceiver meets with an incongruity (usually in the form of a punch line or a cartoon) and is then motivated to resolve the incongruity either by retrieval of information in the joke, or from his/her own storehouse of information. According to this account, humor results "when the incongruity is resolved; that is, the punch line is seen to make sense at some level with the earlier information in the joke. If there is no resolution, the respondent does not 'get' the joke, is puzzled, and sometimes even frustrated."[16] The presence of incongruity and resolution can be found in the vast majority of cases of humor, even in non-Western, nontechnological societies.[17]

Numerous empirical studies on humor comprehension suggest that humor is based on mental operations, and that thought-based theories are most appropriate in understanding the nature of humor. Daniel Berlyne, for example, found that a degree of cognitive congruence exists between the cognitive demand features of humor stimulus and the cognitive resources of the individual.[18] Other researchers have examined the problem-solving efforts involved in humor, and the links between the cognitive processes and affective experience at work in humor comprehension.[19]

This model's emphasis on incongruity, or incongruity-resolution, leads to an interesting situation when examining humor *within* narrative structure. If a narrative can be understood as a continuum—"a set of events occurring in defined settings and unified by principles of temporality and causation"[20]—humor arises during a momentary break in this continuum. Humor is not a sustained progression of funny events, ideas, concepts or thoughts which exhibit logical conceptions of temporality and causation. Rather, humor arises out of unexpected breaks in narrative logic and continuity. Our generic expectations may allow us to predict that a romantic comedy like *The Awful Truth* will contain humor. This knowledge, however, does not provide us with a set of assumptions about upcoming humorous events or actions. Successful humor involves our expectations being thwarted. On the other hand, the highly codified narrative structure of Hollywood romantic comedies provides the spectator a fairly firm set of assumptions about upcoming events and actions.

In screwball comedies, humor serves to complicate a structure which might otherwise be quite predictable. It therefore adds interesting challenges to the spectator's attempts to form hypotheses about an otherwise familiar narrative structure. Although we may expect humor in an abstract sense when we encounter a comedy, we surely don't anticipate its concrete instances, that is, the punch lines to jokes and individual comic moments. Even if we predict a particular line of dialogue in a joke, humor in film contains a visual component as well. Often it may be a joke's visual dimension which cannot be predicted. Though the dialogue or the broad lines of an event may be predictable, variations in other elements of the scene may make the moment seem fresh and funny. Take, for example, Jerry Warriner's actions in *The Awful Truth*. Convinced that Lucy is having an affair, Jerry forces his way past Armand's butler, determined to catch the lovers in The Act. Instead, he bursts in on Lucy's vocal recital. He takes a seat at the back of the room, and tries to get comfortable by leaning his chair back against the wall, until finally he and it crash to the floor.

This scene operates at a number of levels. First, it conveys story information crucial to the plot, which has revolved around questions of Lucy's fidelity. Jerry's and perhaps our suspicions are at least temporarily assuaged in this scene, as we find out that Lucy has indeed been taking voice lessons. Second, the relationship between narrative and gag in this scene raises interesting questions about generic expectations within comedy. Having seen this sequence numerous times, I am fascinated by the fact that I still find it hilarious.

Because humor depends on unpredictability, it is easy to explain the humor's impact upon a first viewing. There is certainly incongruity present in the juxtaposition of the very formal restrained performance at the front of the room, as Lucy sings, and the performance at the back of the room, as Jerry crashes to the floor. Incongruity is also present in Jerry's (and perhaps our) expectations about what he will find as he bursts into the recital hall, as contrasted with what he actually finds. Upon repeated viewings, however, this incongruity becomes folded into our expectations about what will happen, and at that point the scene, at the narrative level at least, ceases to be unpredictable. So why is it still funny?

Jerry's fall may retain much of its humor in subsequent viewing of the film precisely because of its rich visual component. Even though we may predict that Jerry will fall as he leans backwards in his chair, we may not predict (or remember) the peculiar look on his face, his disheveled hair, his foot getting stuck in the drawer of the table he has just knocked over, or Lucy's quiet chuckle upon seeing the fall. The humor in this very rich comic moment is an amalgam of all of these distinct elements.

A Morphology of the Screwball Comedy

This scene from *The Awful Truth* represents a comic moment in a larger narrative which is highly codified, and at many levels, quite predictable. Establishing a morphology of the screwball comedy allows us to examine not only recurring elements within a number of comedies, but also the role of humor within this highly codified structure. The comedy itself (the jokes, comic situations, humorous banter) provides the novelty necessary for a text to be able to tell a story which is virtually identical to that in other screwball comedies.

This analysis traces narrative structure across a number of screwball comedies by adopting the methodology created by Vladimir Propp in *Morphology of the Folktale*.[21] Propp compared the themes of 150 Russian magic tales by separating the component parts of these tales into what he termed "functions," "spheres of action" and "moves." What resulted was a description of the tales according to component parts and their interrelationships.[22] Propp found that while the characters' names and their personal attributes changed between these tales, neither their actions nor their functions within the narrative changed. Functions are the actions of characters defined from the point of view of their significance for the course of the action. Propp saw functions as "stable, constant elements in a tale, independent of how and by whom they are fulfilled. They constitute the fundamental components of a tale."[23]

While the core of Propp's analysis centers on functions, he also examined how functions are distributed among characters. Many functions logically join together into certain "spheres"; these spheres "in toto correspond to their respective performers. They are spheres of action."[24] Propp argued that there are three possible ways in which spheres of action can be distributed among the characters. A sphere of action can either exactly correspond to a character, one character can be involved in several spheres of action, or a single sphere of action can be distributed among several characters.

A tendency in film studies has been to apply Propp's categories directly to Hollywood films. David Bordwell has correctly questioned this enterprise: "Why should a method derived for the analysis of oral narratives of a pre-feudal era hold good for a modern medium developed in a capitalist economy and a mass society?"[25] Bordwell contends that the arguments used to construct such an analysis are "fatally flawed, both empirically and conceptually,"[26] and concludes that film studies should abandon its concentration on Propp, and, instead, focus on the "far more subtle and flexible narratological concepts" of his contemporaries.[27]

However, although the application of Proppian categories directly to Hollywood films is at best questionable, use of a Proppian methodology can provide rich insights into the study of genre. In the case of screwball comedy, for example, the establishment of functions based on Propp's criteria allows us to concentrate on a corpus of films that can perhaps be classified as a genre. A Proppian analysis can quantify those aspects of a filmic text that recur in a number of films and that spectators might come to recognize as generic elements. Once that structure is established, the role of humor becomes clear as an element that continually pushes against the boundaries of that structure without altering it fundamentally.

In adapting this framework for the present study, a distinction first needs to be made between the story—the event chain which constitutes the narrative—and the plot—the form with which it is presented in a given work.[28] The screwball comedies in this study tell essentially the same story. The plots of the films, however, often arrange story events out of chronological order, or begin their narratives at an advanced point and then recount relevant previous events. Therefore, it is important to note that the establishment of functions occurs on the basis of story rather than plot.

A Proppian framework allows us to discern two groups of films which tell two distinct but related stories, Comedies of Commitment and Comedies of Reaffirmation. The commitment comedies include *Bringing Up Baby, It Happened One Night* and *Holiday*. Reaffirmation comedies are represented by *The Awful Truth, The Philadelphia Story, My Favorite Wife* and *His Girl Friday*.

These films illustrate a paradigm structure of the screwball comedy, with a virtually identical distribution of functions and consistent spheres of action. In both types the focus is on sexual confrontation and courtship. However, whereas commitment comedies focus on the establishment of the central couple, reaffirmation comedies concentrate on the reestablishment of the couple after circumstances at the beginning of the film have succeeded in separating them.

These two types of screwball comedy stem from the same cultural myth of the American Dream. The viability of the American work ethic and conservative notions of marriage and the family are present in both forms. They are, in a sense, elements of the same story: hard work and socially acceptable notions of heterosexual love and marriage lead to the establishment of the comic/romantic couple at the end of commitment comedies. Reaffirmation comedies simply continue this basic theme, beginning some time after the establishment of the comic/romantic couple. The characters in reaffirmation comedies have fallen short of these ideals.

The emphasis of the narrative is on steering the couple back toward the goals and commitments they have abandoned. Such films often begin with the separation of the couple, and the film then traces their reconciliation.

The Commitment Comedy

Like most Hollywood films, commitment comedies develop along two plot lines. One of these concerns a character's commitment to career and social advancement. In *It Happened One Night*, reporter Peter Warne needs a juicy story in order to get his job back after being fired. David Huxley, in *Bringing Up Baby*, is trying to obtain a financial contribution for his museum, and later wants his intercostal clavicle back so that he can complete his brontosaurus. Reporter Bill Chandler, in *Libeled Lady*, is sent by his newspaper to blackmail Connie Allenbury out of suing his newspaper. In *Holiday*, Johnny Case needs to succeed in business so that he can go on a long vacation to "find himself."

These films juxtapose the working protagonist with a love interest for whom attaining wealth is unimportant. The working characters in commitment comedies do not give up their professions and accept the easy lives of their counterparts. On the contrary, the upper-class hero/heroine leaves a life of inherited wealth so that the couple can be united. In *It Happened One Night*, the only thing Peter Warne wants from Ellie Andrews' father is a reimbursement of the money he spent in getting Ellie home, not the reward money that he is offered. At the end of the film, Peter and Ellie spend their first married night together in a cheap motel in rural Michigan, the implication being that they will live the kind of life in which Peter will earn his own living and support his family. At the end of *Holiday*, Johnny has earned his long-held goal, taking a long trip to find himself. He and Linda Seton embrace on the floor of a boat headed for Europe. In *Bringing Up Baby*, Susan and David are united on a scaffold in his museum, where she manages to destroy his dinosaur. The final image implies that David will have a great deal of work to do to rebuild what has just crumbled. In *Theodora Goes Wild*, wealthy Michael Grant goes to work as a handyman for Theodora's aunts.

These characters' professional obligations are balanced with personal, or romantic, commitments. These comedies all end in marriage or the promise of marriage. These films' narratives center around the ideal couple coming to realize that their fun and play together indicate their compatibility and thus form a sound basis for a successful marriage. Financial and personal commitments are linked in the resolutions of commitment comedies. Commitment comedies link professional and romantic commitments, often at the expense of other, previously held goals. Both partners must make some sacrifice to reach the correct balance between professional and personal concerns. In all cases, the working character's willingness to give up single life is presented as a desirable goal. The working partner is often presented as too heavily focused on career commitments, and he/she is forced to relinquish some career-oriented goal. Peter Warne must choose between Ellie and his career. He refuses to capitalize on the 'scoop' that he's been working toward and forgoes his $10,000 reward; David Huxley loses his clothes, his glasses, his intercostal clavicle, his dignity, and a million dollars in *Bringing Up Baby*; and John L. Sullivan gives up his job and his comfortable life and ends up on a chain gang in *Sullivan's Travels*.

The upper-class partners in these films must also give up something. Because they have focused their energies on the relationship, they must be willing to give up their life of wealth to secure the relationship, a tension vividly expressed by the contrast between Ellie's lavish wedding and the run-down motel in Michigan in *It Happened One Night*. In *My Man Godfrey*, Irene Bullock fully intends to live on the city dump with Godfrey. She is surprised when she arrives at the dump and sees that it has been turned into a nightclub. The road to happiness is not a smooth one. The couple will need to work to maintain a happy equilibrium among the various aspects of their life together. In the films' resolutions, the distinctions between professional and personal commitments are bridged, with each partner giving up something to create the final balance between social/financial and personal commitments in one's life.

Commitment comedies share more than merely these general themes. They share a great many plot elements. By examining character roles or spheres of action we can begin to see how character types perform identical actions across a number of films.

Spheres of Action

	Holiday	It Happened One Night	Bringing Up Baby
First Partner	Johnny Case	Ellie Andrews	David Huxley
Initial Partner	Julia Seton	King Wessley	Miss Swallow
Second Partner	Linda Seton	Peter Warne	Susan Vance
Conscience Figure	Mr. Andrews	—	Sarah, Nick and Ned
Blocking Figure	Mr. Gordon	Aunt Elizabeth	Mr. Seton

The first partner in commitment comedies is initially involved in an unsuitable relationship. Ellie Andrews is married at the beginning of *It Happened One Night*. Both David Huxley and Johnny Case are engaged to be married. This character represents one half of the ideal couple, and much of the action will involve these characters' gradual realization that his or her prospective spouse, the initial partner, is not a good mate. The second partner is the second half of the ideal couple. Conscience figures are those people who advise one or both of the ideal partners on their relationship. In *Holiday*, Linda's brother Ned and Johnny's friends Nick and Sarah all criticize Johnny's relationship with Julia and recognize that Linda and Johnny are far more compatible. The blocking figures are characters who complicate the relationship between the ideal couple. In *It Happened One Night*, Peter Warne's editor, Mr. Gordon, wants a juicy story regardless of what Peter wants. In *Bringing Up Baby*, Aunt Elizabeth continually warns Susan to stay away from David. Julia's father, Mr. Seton, is concerned only with Johnny's career in *Holiday*. In any number of ways, these characters either purposely or inadvertently strive to keep the ideal couple apart.

FUNCTIONS

Initial Situation   The initial couple (first partner and initial partner) is indicated. In *Bringing Up Baby* (*Baby*) and *Holiday*, the initial couple plans to marry. In *It Happened One Night* (*One Night*), Ellie Andrews and King Wessley have just gotten married, but have not yet slept together. This is also the initial situation in *Theodora Goes Wild*.

I *A Flaw Is Shown in the Initial Relationship*   In *Baby*, Miss Swallow is portrayed as a cold, emotionless woman. She states: "Our marriage must entail no domestic entanglements. I see our marriage purely as a dedication to your work." In *Holiday*, Julia Seton is likewise frigid and reserved. Even when she and Johnny are alone, she says, "Johnny, mind your manners." Ellie's father in *One Night* calls King Wessley a pompous fake and a self-absorbed fortune hunter. All these couples represent potentially loveless and sexless marriages.

II *Introduction of the Ideal Partner*   In *One Night* Ellie meets Peter on a bus to New York. Susan Vance meets David Huxley on a golf course in *Baby*. Linda Seton is introduced to Johnny by sister Julia in *Holiday*. In *My Man Godfrey* (*Godfrey*), Irene Bullock meets Godfrey only after he has encountered her cold, emotionless sister Cornelia.

III *The Conscience Figure Is Introduced*   In *Holiday*, Linda's brother Ned Seton meets Johnny. Later, Linda and Julia are introduced to Johnny's friends Nick and Sarah Potter. In *One Night*, Ellie's father organizes a search for Ellie.

IV *The Initial Couple Finalizes Marriage Plans* Usually the couple plans to marry in a very short time (within twenty-four hours in *Bringing Up Baby* or within two weeks in *Holiday*) and thereby establishes a deadline for the narrative action.

V *The Ideal Couple Expresses Hostility Toward Each Other* The main character's sparky encounters with the second partner in films like *One Night*, *Baby* and *Twentieth Century* express the sense of spirit and excitement which distinguishes them from the initial partners. As Susan so aptly tells David in *Baby*, "The love impulse in man shows itself first in conflict."

VI *Second Partner Expresses His/Her Decision to Pursue the First Partner* Susan Vance tells Aunt Elizabeth that she plans to marry David. Irene Bullock expresses her interest in Godfrey to the maid (and a number of other characters). Linda Seton acknowledges her desire for Johnny Case early on.

VII *One Partner Manipulates the Other into an Inextricable Situation [a Dilemma]* Peter Warne blackmails Ellie. Susan Vance steals David Huxley's clothes. Linda Seton encourages Johnny to retain his dreams, and reminds him that he does not feel comfortable in such swanky surroundings.

VIII *Ideal Couple Is Trapped in a Situation Which Is not of Their own Making* The relationship between this function and the previous one involves the conditions under which the ideal couple will become romantically involved. Whereas all of these films feature one partner manipulating the other into a relationship, this is not presented as an ideal foundation on which to build such a relationship. Therefore, this function operates to draw the couple together without the previous manipulation. It is only on this basis that the next function (IX) is presented as genuinely romantic. In *Baby*, George steals David's intercostal clavicle and sends Susan and David off on a hunt for George and the bone. In *One Night*, Ellie Andrews is robbed on her way to New York, and she must learn to trust and rely on Peter.

IX *The Ideal Couple Comes Close to Sharing an Intimate Moment but Stops Short* This signals the beginning of their romantic relationship. Ellie Andrews and Peter Warne almost kiss in the hayloft. Susan and David almost kiss by the campfire in the woods. Linda and Johnny almost kiss in the playroom at midnight on New Year's Eve.

X *The Conscience Figure Gives Advice* Linda Seton discusses her love for Johnny with brother Ned and friends Sarah and Nick. Irene and the maid have a conversation about Godfrey. Lily and O'Malley discuss her relationship with Oscar Jaffe in *Twentieth Century*.

XI *The Ideal Couple Separates* In order for the ideal couple to passionately come together at the conclusion of the film, there must first be a separation, with the implicit threat that they may not be united at the end. Peter Warne leaves Ellie at the hotel. She misunderstands and decides not to marry him. David Huxley returns to the museum alone. Godfrey quits work at the Bullocks's and goes to the city dump. Linda avoids Johnny while he is still engaged to Julia.

XII *Initial Couple Formally End the Relationship*   The initial couple, not having been married, separates permanently. Miss Swallow leaves David, calling him "just a butterfly." Ellie runs away from her wedding. Julia is happy when Johnny breaks off their engagement.

XIII *One of the Partners Tracks Down the Other and Forces Him/Her to Make a Quick Decision About the New Relationship*   Linda must evaluate her future with Johnny before his boat sails. She decides to meet Johnny at the boat. Ellie decides her future while walking down the aisle at her wedding. Irene brings a minister with her when she decides to move in with Godfrey. As the minister begins the ceremony, Godfrey must decide whether to marry Irene.

XIV *The Ideal Couple Is United*   Susan and David kiss on the scaffold. The trumpet sounds as the "walls of Jericho" fall. Linda and Johnny kiss on the floor of the boat. Godfrey and Irene are married at the nightclub.

Commitment comedies begin with a couple about to be married. Their relationship is flawed due to those characters' unwillingness or inability to balance the various commitments that marriage and career entail. The ideal partner is then introduced, and shown to possess the qualities that keep the initial partner from becoming a well-rounded person. The ideal partner provides the missing piece which has kept the initial partner from attaining true happiness. At the end, the ideal couple achieves the right balance between their personal and professional lives. The struggle to maintain that balance then becomes the subject of reaffirmation comedies.

The Reaffirmation Comedy

In many ways, reaffirmation comedies are continuations of the stories established in commitment comedies. The tensions between personal and professional concerns which were resolved (or at least forgotten) in commitment comedies resurface in reaffirmation comedies as lost or perverted goals. This issue is one that distinguishes reaffirmation comedies from what Stanley Cavell calls comedies of remarriage. For Cavell, the issue of remarriage is peripheral: almost half of his examples are not about remarriage at all. He justifies the inclusion of *Bringing Up Baby*, for example, by arguing that the principle pair shares "capacities for recognition of one another such that what they are is revealed by imagining them as candidates for the trials of remarriage."[29] Cavell dismisses fundamental differences between *It Happened One Night* and *Bringing Up Baby*, on the one hand, and *The Philadel-*

phia Story and *His Girl Friday* on the other. It is central to the later films that the couple has been married previously.

At the beginning of these films the comic/romantic couple is married or has been married previously. Their marriage, however, is shaky and in most cases leads quickly to divorce if it has not already done so when the plot begins.

One spouse leaves the other in all reaffirmation comedies. However, often the spouse who is left has abandoned the relationship emotionally long before the physical separation. In *His Girl Friday*, for example, Walter Burns's preoccupation with his career has diverted his attention from his relationship with his wife, Hildy Johnson. Consequently, she leaves him. In the opening shot of *The Philadelphia Story*, Tracy leaves (or rather throws out) C. K. Dexter-Haven because of his drinking. Yet the film attributes his drinking, in part, to Tracy's emotional/sexual coldness.

The characters in reaffirmation comedies have already attained financial security. Their problems are related to lost goals and values, and to the imbalance between the various commitments they have made. The rich cannot remedy their problems and conflicts by using their financial resources. The story in *His Girl Friday*, for example, begins with Walter Burns shifting all of his attention to his career, at the expense of his commitment to Hildy. At this point in their relationship, Walter is not a struggling reporter trying to get ahead. He is the editor, and he is motivated by blind ambition rather than the needed balance between ambition and concern for family. Similarly, in *The Palm Beach Story* Tom is willing to give up his marriage because of career insecurities. In *The Women*, Mary Haines's husband Steven rejects the values inherent in marriage when he enters into an affair with Crystal Allen. His power and success make him an easy target for what the film clearly presents as Crystal's manipulation. Consequently, he and Mary break their marital commitment.

All of these films focus on the romantic couple's road toward recapturing some important yet temporarily missing aspect of their relationship. These films reaffirm the value of the characters' original goals and ideals, ending in the reunion of the couple and a restored balance between various commitments. *The Philadelphia Story* makes the implicit assumption that the second marriage of Tracy and Dexter-Haven will permit a tolerance of each other's imperfections and idiosyncrasies. In *His Girl Friday*, remarriage implies that a balance will be struck between Walter's concerns with his career and his commitment to Hildy. Again, however, in these films the endings are rather tenuous. Walter and Hildy's problems are not *solved* at the end. These films do not effect the actual working out of the conflicts but simply indicate that the characters have acquired the tools with which to solve future problems without divorcing. They have learned to improvise together and work together. One of the most important and telling moments in *Adam's Rib*, for example, occurs when Adam Bonner shouts, "Competitor! Competitor!" at his wife Amanda. By the end of the film, however, as in all reaffirmation comedies, Adam and Amanda have learned to cooperate, not compete, even if it is clear that putting their new knowledge into practice will be difficult.

In this regard, it is interesting to note the time at which the majority of reaffirmation comedies appeared. Both types appeared throughout the 1930s and into the 1940s. Elements of reaffirmation comedy appear as early as 1934 in *Twentieth Century*. However, most reaffirmation comedies were made in the years following the height of commitment comedies. Commitment comedies—such as *It Happened One Night* (1934), *The Gilded Lily* (1935), *My Man Godfrey* (1936), *Nothing Sacred* and *Easy Living* (both 1937), *Holiday* and *Bringing Up Baby* (both 1938)—appear to peak by the mid- to late 1930s. Reaffirmation comedies, in general, appear to peak somewhat later, with films such as *The Awful Truth* (1937), *His Girl Friday*, *My Favorite Wife* and *The Philadelphia Story* (all 1940) and *Mr. and Mrs. Smith* (1941).

In commitment comedies, narratives focus on ways to establish a society based on the conservative values inherent in the work ethic and heterosexual love and marriage. Many of the reaffirmation comedies emerged in later years to reinforce these values, and restate their viability and their importance during times which, although still bleak, were not as desperate as were the early to mid-1930s.

Spheres of Action

	The Awful Truth	The Philadelphia Story	My Favorite Wife	His Girl Friday
First Partner	Lucy Warriner	Tracy Lord	Nick Arden	Hildy Johnson
Second Partner	Jerry Warriner	C. K. Dexter-Haven	Ellen Wagstaff-Arden	Walter Burns
First Blocking Figure	Dan Leason	George Kittridge	Bianca Arden	Bruce Baldwin
Second Blocking Figure	Barbara Vance	MacCauley Connor	Steven Burkett	—
Conscience figure	Aunt Patsy	Diana Lord	Mrs. Arden (Nick's mother)	the "chorus" of newspaper reporters
Common denominator	Mr. Smith	Tracy's family, the *Spy* magazine story	Children	The newspaper

In reaffirmation comedies, the first and second partners constitute the ideal couple. The first partner initiates a new relationship first. The first blocking figure is the new love interest of the first partner. In most of these films there are at least two possible "new" relationships. The second new relationship is usually much shorter and/or more tenuous than that involving the first partner and the first blocking figure. The new character involved in this second relationship is the second blocking figure. In *The Awful Truth*, for example, Jerry Warriner becomes engaged to Barbara Vance long after Lucy has become involved with Dan Leason. Tracy Lord is not only engaged to George Kittridge in *The Philadelphia Story*; she also becomes briefly "involved" with MacCauley Connor. Similarly, in *My Favorite Wife*, Ellen's relationship with Steven Burkett is not substantive, and occurs only after Nick seems unwilling to leave Bianca. The conscience figure functions in much the same way as in commitment comedies, advising the central couple on various aspects of their reconciliation. The common denominator is the element that keeps the ideal couple in contact with each other. In *My Favorite Wife* Nick and Ellen have children, and through them the couple is able to keep in contact. At the beginning of *The Awful Truth*, Lucy and Jerry's divorce stipulates that Lucy gets custody of Mr. Smith, the couple's fox terrier, but that Jerry can have visitation privileges.

FUNCTIONS

Initial Situation   Reaffirmation comedies begin by establishing the ideal couple. In *The Awful Truth* (*Truth*), Jerry tells his friend at the gym that he is married. In *The Philadelphia Story* (*Story*), Tracy and Dex fight at the door of their house when Tracy throws Dex out. In *My Favorite Wife* (*Wife*), Nick is in court with Bianca to have his wife Ellen pronounced legally dead. In *His Girl Friday* (*Friday*), Hildy and Bruce are first shown outside of Walter's office. Even if one of the partners is first shown with his or her new fiancée (as in *Friday* and *Wife*), the occasion is marked by the new couple having to deal with that partner's previous marriage. Though Hildy and Bruce, for example, are together, their first discussion is about Walter. Nick and Bianca are together but are first seen in court discussing Ellen. In this way the second half of the ideal couple is indicated at the beginning of the film as a central force, as a potential disruption to the new relationship.

I   *One Partner Leaves Home for an Extended Period of Time*   In *Truth*, Jerry Warriner returns home after having spent two weeks "in Florida." Ellen Wagstaff-Arden went on a business trip and has been lost at sea for seven years in *Wife*. Hildy has left Walter, obtained a divorce, and become engaged to Bruce when she returns to the newspaper office to talk to Walter in *Friday*.

II *A Fault or Flaw Is Established in the Second Partner*   Walter Burns's preoccupation with his career, Jerry Warriner's possible infidelity, and C. K. Dexter-Haven's drinking are revealed as causes for their separations. Ellen's preoccupation with her career results in her disappearance.

III *Introduction of Conscience Figure*   In *Truth*, Aunt Patsy advises Lucy on her marriage to Jerry. Diana Lord comments to Tracy about her aversion to George Kittridge in *Story*. Ellen discusses her marriage to Nick, and his new relationship with Bianca, with Nick's mother in *Wife*. Hildy's "buddylike" relationship to the rest of the reporters in *Friday* results in their assessment that her new marriage will fail and that she will eventually return to the paper.

IV *Fault in the First Partner Is Established*   Lucy's distrust of Jerry and her possible infidelity (*Truth*), Tracy Lord's pride and emotional coldness (*Story*), Hildy's inability to come to terms with her true desires (*Friday*), and Nick's bad judgment in marrying Bianca (*Wife*) constitute character flaws.

V *The Ideal Couple Dissolves Their Relationship*   *Story* and *Friday* open with the issue of divorce. Ellen (*Wife*) is pronounced legally dead, and Jerry and Lucy (*Truth*) divorce fairly early in the story. In all of these films, the story components occur in the same order. For example, the faults of both partners are established as reasons for their divorce, even if, in terms of plot development, the divorce occurs first.

VI *Common Denominator Is Introduced as the Link Between Both Partners*   This element keeps the ideal couple in contact with each other. Jerry Warriner is given visitation rights to see their dog, Mr. Smith. Dex visits the Lord home to keep them from being blackmailed by *Spy* Magazine. Ellen Wagstaff-Arden keeps in contact with Nick through their children, and Hildy visits Walter and the other newspaper reporters at the newspaper office and the press room.

VII *First Blocking Figure Is Introduced*   Hildy plans to marry Bruce Baldwin. Tracy Lord plans to marry George Kittridge. Lucy Warriner meets Dan Leason, and Nick Arden marries Bianca.

VIII *Blocking Figure Exhibits an Underlying Flaw*   Neither Dan Leason nor Bruce Baldwin is particularly dynamic, though both are kindhearted. George Kittridge is socially clumsy, inconsiderate and indiscreet. Bianca's attention to herself and her appearance in the courtroom make her appear self-centered.

IX *Conscience Figure Expresses Objections to the New Relationship*   Aunt Patsy warns Lucy not to marry on the rebound. Diana Lord makes numerous disparaging remarks about George, and asks how she can get smallpox in order to stop Tracy's wedding. Nick's mother tells

Ellen that she does not like Bianca. The reporters in *Friday* take bets on how long Hildy's new marriage will last.

X *Second Partner Attempts to Disrupt the New Relationship* Jerry Warriner tries to embarrass Lucy and Dan at the nightclub. Dex gives Tracy and George a model of his and Tracy's boat, the "True Love," as a wedding gift. Ellen goes to Yosemite to break up Nick and Bianca's honeymoon. Walter Burns convinces Hildy to do "just one more story."

XI *The Compatibility of the Ideal Couple Is Made Explicit* Lucy and Jerry Warriner discuss past happiness in front of Dan at his apartment. Walter and Hildy do the same at the restaurant with Bruce. Nick and Ellen gaze longingly at each other when they first meet at the hotel at Yosemite.

XII *An Extended Conversation between the Ideal Couple Establishes Their Inability to Solve Their Problems* Jerry Warriner asks Lucy what she sees in Dan. Dex and Tracy argue about each other's faults at the pool. Hildy and Walter argue repeatedly about what led to their divorce. Ellen and Nick argue in her hotel room about Nick's reluctance to tell Bianca the truth.

XIII *First Partner Expresses Doubts about the New Relationship* Lucy confesses to Aunt Patsy that she does not want to marry Dan, and asks for her help. Tracy worries when George "threatens" to idolize her. Nick agrees to annul his marriage to Bianca.

XIV *First Partner's New Relationship Suffers a Serious Setback* Lucy's "two men in a bedroom farce" causes a fight between Jerry and Armand, and shocks Dan. Tracy angers George by swimming with Connor after the party.

XV *A New Relationship, with a Second Blocking Figure, Becomes an Expressed Possibility* Jerry Warriner becomes involved with Barbara Vance. Connor tries to establish a relationship with Tracy. Steven Burkett proposes marriage to Ellen.

XVI *First Partner's Relationship Ends* Dan Leason leaves Lucy. George Kittridge discovers Tracy with Connor and leaves her. Bruce Baldwin leaves town with his mother.

XVII *Ideal Couple Hold a More Civil Conversation, Raising Hopes for Reconciliation* Lucy visits Jerry on the eve of his wedding to Barbara. Tracy and Dex talk in her garden on the morning of her wedding. Ellen and Nick talk at the cabin. Walter and Hildy discuss their situation in the press room.

XVIII *Ideal Couple Become Trapped in Confined Situation* Jerry and Lucy are driven to Aunt Patsy's cabin. The "Wedding March" begins, and Tracy and Dex must quickly decide whether to marry. Nick and Ellen are driven to their cabin, and left there without a car. Walter and Hildy are left alone in the press room of the county court building.

XIX *Under Pressure, Conflicts Are Resolved or, at Least, Temporarily Forgotten*   Jerry and Lucy resolve their questions of trust. Dex and Tracy go through the wedding ceremony. Ellen and Nick resolve their difficulties just before their divorce is to become final at midnight.

XX *Ideal Couple Is Reconstituted*   Lucy and Jerry, like Nick and Ellen, are joined in bed at the end of the films. Dex and Tracy are last seen at the altar. Walter and Hildy leave the press room to get remarried and cover a story/have a honeymoon in Albany.

By arranging the narratives of these films into functions, it is possible to examine and establish the importance of single actions to the overall structure. An argumentative conversation between two characters, for example, may seem unique until we see that it occurs in a large number of films. These comedies are much more homogeneous in terms of narrative structure than is usually recognized; narrative actions bear striking similarities from film to film.

"In Some Humpty Dumpty Way, That Was True Love": The Case of *Twentieth Century*

The fact that these two types of films express two parts of the same overall myth is particularly clear when examining films that explore both parts of the myth. One such film, *Twentieth Century* (1934), combines commitment and reaffirmation narratives in one film. The first third of *Twentieth Century* functions as an abbreviated commitment comedy. Lily Garland, the working protagonist, gives up her freedom to be with Oscar Jaffe. Oscar is a theatrical producer who "discovers" lingerie model Mildred Plotka, and transforms her into Broadway star Lily Garland. The two characters are first seen together on the theatrical stage during a rehearsal. At this time a conscience figure, Owen O'Malley, is also introduced. These actions represent functions II and III in the commitment comedy formula. During this first rehearsal, Lily and Oscar argue over Oscar's directions, and Lily threatens to quit (function V). Lily's success in the theatre in the following scene culminates with Oscar visiting Lily in her dressing room to compliment her performance. The scene ends as Lily thanks Oscar, and asks if there is any way she can repay all that he has done for her. She and Oscar embrace as he looks offcamera slyly while pushing the dressing room door closed with his foot (functions VI and XIV). This is the point at which most commitment comedies end. *Twentieth Century*, however, continues—as a reaffirmation comedy.

Three years after her initial success, Lily is still in her relationship with Oscar, but she complains to Owen that Oscar's jealousy is stifling her. She tells Owen one evening that she is going out to a nightclub without Oscar. This scene reestablishes the ideal couple and indicates their unhappiness together. Lily's conversation with Owen emphasizes her transformation into a rather self-absorbed, egotistical star, not unlike Oscar Jaffe's character (function II). In this scene she and Owen discuss her relationship with Oscar (function III). Toward the end of this conversation, Oscar arrives. He and Lily argue about her plans for the evening, and as she prepares to leave he opens a window, and implies that he will jump. In this way the film reestablishes Oscar's faults, the most obvious being his jealousy (function IV). Lily, however, does not believe Oscar's threats, calling him a cheap ham and a fake. She stays home nevertheless. The next morning Oscar admits his jealousy, but assures Lily that he has changed, and that he now trusts her. As soon as she leaves the house, however, he hires a private investigator to follow her. When she finds out, she leaves Oscar (function V).

When Lily and Oscar meet again, it is on the "Twentieth Century," a train between Los Angeles and New York. Lily is accompanied by another man, George (function VII). When Owen and Oliver try to convince Oscar to reconcile with Lily, he responds, "I wouldn't take that woman back if she and I were the last people in the world and the future of the human race depended on it . . . besides, she's two thousand miles away." When George tells Lily that he is accompanying her to New York, she impatiently tries to convince him not to. Like the blocking figures in both *The Awful Truth* and *His Girl Friday*, George exhibits a decided lack of dynamism (function VIII). When Owen O'Malley meets Lily and George, he tries to convince Lily to see Oscar (function IX). When Oscar first sees Lily on the train, she is embracing George. Oscar is outraged. He visits Lily and succeeds in starting an argument between Lily and George (function X). As George leaves the room, Oscar and Lily are left arguing, but in doing so they exhibit the passion that was pointedly missing from her other relationship. After Oscar leaves, Lily takes out and looks at a locket that is a keepsake from their previous involvement (function XI). The argument between Oscar and Lily also establishes their inability to solve their problems. They are virtually identical in how they communicate with each other. Each acts childishly, as they yell at each other without ever pausing to listen to what the other has to say (function XII). A later conversation between Lily and George begins with Lily proclaiming her love for George, telling him that she wants to elope. George, however, is distrustful of her intentions, and the conversation ends angrily with Lily telling George that Oscar was the only man in her life (function XIV). George tells Lily that he is leaving her (function XVI). When Oscar goes to see Lily again, she asks, "What do you want, Scorpion?" This conversation is more civil, however, and raises hopes for reconciliation. Each admits to being selfish. Oscar apologizes, and Lily cries. They come close to embracing (function XVII), but Lily becomes skeptical of

Oscar's motives and the scene ends with Lily and Oscar arguing again. Because both characters are trapped on a train (function XVIII), neither can escape the situation which keeps them in contact with each other. When Oscar is superficially wounded, he convinces Lily that he is dying. He pressures her into signing a contract, telling her that it is his last request and that he only wishes to be buried with it (XIX). After signing the contract, Lily finds out the truth. The last scene begins as did the first, with Oscar and Lily together again on the stage, arguing (function XX).

In this reading of *Twentieth Century*, not all functions of both commitment and reaffirmation comedy occur. Only the first third of the film functions as a commitment comedy. However, the film does correspond to the broad narrative outline exhibited in commitment comedies. Quite a few of its functions occur in this film, and in approximately the same order as in other commitment comedies. Most of the film concentrates on the second half of this myth of commitment, and it concerns Lily and Oscar finding their way back to each other. In the end, their commitment to their relationship is seen as part of their commitment to the theatre, much as Hildy and Walter's commitment to each other at the end of *His Girl Friday* is seen primarily in terms of their commitment to the newspaper.

The plot of *Twentieth Century* is more complex than those of most commitment and reaffirmation comedies, in part because it contains a number of functions from each category. This attests to the high degree of standardization present in this plot formula. Rather than integrating elements from other formulas, other plot structures, and so on, this film extends the commitment and reaffirmation formulas diachronically. The movement of the plot, however, like the formula itself, is not dependent on humor as a structuring element. There are no recurrant gags in screwball comedies. There are no pies in the face, no comic chases, and few set-piece gags that have an extended and logical progression.

It is far more common for romantic comedies to emphasize comic lines of dialogue and short, often abrupt, sight gags that do not build and develop like those in many comedian comedies. It is difficult to describe the relationship between humor and narrative in these films, because it involves seizing on those individual lines of dialogue, which do not have a great deal of meaning apart from the function of characterization.

The humor in commitment and reaffirmation comedies defines characters rather than advances the plot. Much of the humor surrounding Owen, for example, centers on his drinking and the funny things he says when he is drinking. His drinking, however, never becomes a component of the chain of events. Lily tries to forget Oscar by proposing to George. She describes her vision of married life as including a home "with a little

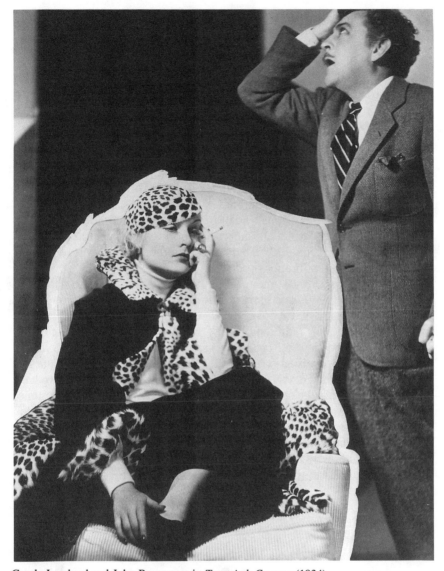

Carole Lombard and John Barrymore in *Twentieth Century* (1934).

attic and a cookie jar." This comment, like many such lines of dialogue, adds little to narrative progession. It has a more central function synchronically, adding to Lily's characteristics an outrageously simplistic outlook on marriage. Similarly, much of the humor characterizing Oscar emphasizes his all-encompassing theatricality. He fires employees by stating, "I close the iron door on you." When Lily leaves him, Oscar responds by splashing black paint on huge posters of Lily while calling her "child of Satan." When he first sees Lily in George's arms, Oscar responds, "This is the final irony, mousing around with boys . . . after Oscar Jaffe." Here again, these humorous moments define characters rather than advance the plot.

This structure constitutes a screwball comedy world which is in some important ways different from that of comedian comedies. The comedian's world is one of order, which the comedian disrupts, often in very pronounced and important ways. The screwball comedy universe does not structure the humor around a comedian; in screwball comedies most characters participate in humor production. Not only are Lily and Oscar involved in making jokes; Owen, Oliver, Lily's maid and numerous other characters participate in the humor. Although almost none of the jokes or gags are as well-developed as those in comedian comedies, they are more evenly spread around. Rather than portraying a central humorous character, these films portray a generally humorous world whose inhabitants all have roles in humor production.

Within a remarkably homogeneous narrative structure, the screwball comedies of the 1930s and early 1940s dealt with issues of commitment to and reaffirmation of a set of culturally determined, though nevertheless powerful, goals and ambitions. These goals were reinscribed and reaffirmed with each new telling of the same story. The Hollywood film industry clearly benefited through such repetition. Generic formula has always been perceived as a less risky endeavor than nongeneric product. However, although the stories in screwball comedies remained the same, humor in these films provided a crucial component that differentiated them from one another and from films of other genres. The incongruity of screwball humor allowed the genre to balance audiences' desire for a familiar formula with the desire for variation and originality. Without the humor, the stories in these films would have simply been . . . the same.

Performance

8

INTRODUCTION: Acting Funny

Henry Jenkins and Kristine Brunovska Karnick

James Agee's influential essay, "Comedy's Greatest Era," organizes the history of the genre around the distinctive contributions of the major silent clowns and their virtuoso performances. Agee is interested in the play between, on the one hand, a shared vocabulary of stock gestures and performance tricks which constituted the legacy of variety entertainment upon silent slapstick, and on the other, the unique personalities and expressive potential of individual comic stars:

> The man who could handle them [these clichés] properly combined several of the more difficult accomplishments of the *acrobat*, the *dancer*, the *clown* and the *mime*. Some very gifted comedians, unforgettably Ben Turpin, had an immense vocabulary of these clichés and were in part so lovable because they were deeply conservative classicists and never tried to break away from them. The still more gifted men, of course, simplified and invented, finding out new and much deeper uses for the idiom. They learned to show emotion through it, and comic psychology, more eloquently than most language has ever managed to, and they discovered beauties of comic motion which are hopelessly beyond the reach of words.[1]

Agee valued the immediacy of comic expression, the physicality of this gestural language and its ability to express a range of human emotions, tapping into the "cult of personality" surrounding performers with the vaudeville tradition.[2] Unlike the classicism associated with later writers, such as Gerald Mast, Agee focuses on moments of performance virtuosity and spectacle which demand our attention regardless of their narrative framework, on comic actions and reactions rather than on comic plots and characters.

Perhaps more words have been spent trying to analyze and interpret the performances of Charles Chaplin, Buster Keaton and their contemporaries than have been devoted to any other aspect of screen performance. Yet there is often a kind of insularity to this writing. A cult of personality still shapes how we talk about comic performance, with our focus often in celebrating the distinctiveness of individual performers at the expense of any attempt to map the lexicon of "clichés" Agee suggests constituted the basic building blocks of even the greatest comic performances.

This situation is not, of course, unique to screen comedy, though the self-consciousness of comic performance poses the issue in a particularly vivid fashion. While performance has been central to our understanding of many different genres, acting style has long taken a back seat to other aspects of mise-en-scene (such as lighting, setting and costume), narrative construction and camerawork.[3] The words, performance and acting, are often used interchangibly yet it is important to distinguish between them. Acting will be used here to refer to the task of constructing characterization. The more expansive term, performance, includes not only skills of acting but other aspects of showmanship, such as acrobatics, dance, musical performance, magic, and slapstick, which reflect the non-narrative traditions of variety entertainment. Issues of performance, thus, include but exceed the demands of characterization. Key questions center around the relationship between performance sequences and plot development (narrative integration) and between the performer and the character (character integration), the consistency of the performance signs (expressive coherence), the relative conformity of all of the performers in a film to a single acting style (ensemble consistency) and the actor's address to the camera (audience consciousness). Writing about screen acting, then, pulls us towards a closer consideration of narrative construction and character development; writing about screen performance, on the other hand, often focuses on the ways that performance excess or spectacle disrupts or escapes the demands for narrative causality or character psychology.

Any understanding of performance within classical Hollywood comedy needs to be situated in relation to the conventions of the classical film more generally. Comic performance can not be simply read as a rejection of the traditions of screen acting. Rather, comic stars took full advantage of the spaces provided by the classical system for excessive or spectacular performance. A novelistic (or "realist") conception of the rounded, psychologically motivated, goal-driven protagonist shaped the narrative conventions of the classical Hollywood cinema. Characters' goals, desires, ambitions and conflicts motivated the forward movement of the films' plots, with causal links forged primarily around the actions of individual protagonists. Hollywood actors strove towards what James Naremore calls "expressive coherence," so that all of the features of a performance worked together to create a plausible character.[4] Even classical realism, however, provides some space for performers to display their skills as performers above and beyond the task of conveying the emotional and social lives of psychologically rounded characters. Naremore is interested in moments within classical films where characters must themselves become performers, adopt alternative identities, lie, exaggerate, impersonate or masquerade. Such moments test an actor's skill, while remaining heavily motivated in terms of character consistency and plot development. Such moments of layered performance are central to a large number of comic films within both the comedian comedy and the romantic comedy tradition, where these diagetic performances invite our awareness of the construction and maintenance of social and personal identities.

Naremore's discussion suggests a central tension within the classical Hollywood cinema between the need to develop and showcase the talents of movie stars (who play a central economic and aesthetic role within the overall system of production) and the creation and maintenance of individualized characters. As Richard Dyer has noted, the star always brings to a given role much more semiotic significance than can be successfully contained within the individual film narrative. Dyer identifies a range of possible relationships between stars and fictional characters, including situations where the performer perfectly embodies the character traits (Clark Gable in *Gone With the Wind*, Humphrey Bogart in *Casablanca*) as well as situations where there is a more "problematic fit" (Bette Davis in *Now Voyager*).[5] Film comedy might allow for an even broader range of relations between performers and roles, with the comedian comedy tradition, particularly, relying upon extreme mismatches between performers and roles, as in Groucho Marx's performance in *Duck Soup*. The flatness of many comic characters contributes to the dominance of performer-centered criticism rather than character-centered criticism within most accounts of film genres. Performers show little interest in realizing the particularity of these characters; rather, the characters function as a vehicle for comedians to display their repertoire of performance skills.

Audience fascination with film stars cannot be reduced to the actors' abilities to convey character psychologies. The star system also exploits what Roland Barthes has described as "the grain of the voice," those aspects of performance which are expressive, sensual, connotative, affective and pleasurable without being reducible to "signifiance." For Barthes, who was writing about musical performance, the "grain of the voice" has to do with the qualities of the body, "the cavities, the muscles, the membranes, the cartilages." These expressive materials are not fully under the performer's control, but define the distinctive sound and "feel" of a particular performance.[6] Comic film stars, such as W. C. Fields or Groucho Marx, developed idiosyncratic ways of speaking and moving, eccentric facial and bodily gestures, which fully exploited these nonrepresentational aspects of performance.

Hollywood entertainment depends upon this pleasure in pure performance, yet too much indulgence in our fascination with performance threatens narrative coherence and continuity. Certain genres, most notably the musical, the comedian comedy and pornography, allow for a freer expression of performance as performance than would be typical of the classical Hollywood cinema. Different genres, as David Bordwell argues, create their own "idiolects" within the classical Hollywood norms, defining the "bounds of difference" by which they may deviate from dominant screen practice. As Bordwell explains, many accounts of the classical or realist film "see the stylization of certain films as outrageous and jolting." Stylization, however, was a conventional aspect of many generic traditions, particularly those which "descend from episodic and composite forms in the American popular theater (e.g., vaudeville, melodrama)." These genres allowed for a constant play between storytelling and showmanship, characterization and performance.[7] Naremore contrasts the "expressive coherence" associated with most classical films to the "expressive anarchy" associated with the comedian comedy. In his examples (Charlie Chaplin in *The Gold Rush*, Steve Martin in *All of Me*, Peter Sellers in *Dr. Strangelove*), the performer's skills are displayed through the fragmentation of the character's unstable subjectivity or a loss of bodily control.[8] Integration between these performance numbers and the narrative trajectory is always a matter of degree. In considering the comedian-centered comedies of the early sound period, for example, Henry Jenkins distinguishes between revue films (*Paramount on Parade*), which consist of discrete performance sequences; showcase films (*International House*), where various performance sequences are embedded within a narrative frame; comic romances, where comic performers adopt secondary roles within a more classically constructed narrative (*Rio Rita*); anarchistic comedies, where the focus of the fragmented narrative is on a single clown or comic team (*Duck Soup*) and affirmative comedies, where plot development constrains comic performance (*Local Boy Makes Good*).[9]

While the codes marking the transition from narrative to number in a musical are fairly conventional and well documented, a more ambiguous shift demarks the space between performance spectacle and narrative development within film comedy. Certain set pieces, such as Groucho's comic monologues, W. C. Field's pool or golf tricks, Charlie Chaplin's dancelike pantomimes or Jerry Lewis's extended slapstick sequences, are recognized and anticipated from film to film, becoming a source for audience fascination apart from their narrative functions. Such acts are often performed before diagetic audiences (who may or may not be aware of their entertainment value) and in spaces which echo the structures of the vaudeville stage. Such performances are marked by frontality and direct address to the camera. These sequences are often filmed in long take and from a more distant camera position to preserve the comic performance's integrity. These performances involve highly stylized movements which call attention to *how* an act is performed more than *what* is being done. Finally, such sequences involve shifts in costume which reflect the performer's play with identity, as in Eddie Cantor's blackface, Bert Wheeler's drag, or Danny Kaye's impersonations. Such performance sequences enjoy a semiautonomous status within the film narrative, functioning as "set pieces" pleasurable in their own right, apart from any specific plot functions they might serve.

Many writers have seen such genres as falling outside the norms of the classical Hollywood cinema, or as posing a serious threat to its aesthetic and ideological coherence. Writers within what Barbara Klinger calls the "progressive genre" tradition, for example, attribute "deconstructive capabilities and a subversive effectivity" to all differences from their otherwise monolithic conception of the classical text. In his important study of the comedian comedy, Steve Seidman makes a similarly sharp distinction between hermetic and nonhermetic genres. Hermetic genres, such as the Western, the melodrama, the private eye film the gangster film, and the situation comedy, follow the dominant tendencies of the classical Hollywood narrative: "[hermetic films] present an impression of reality by way of a closed narrative structure and uninterrupted narrative exposition."[10] Hermetic genres invite spectator identification with characters rather than audience awareness of performance, and maintain narrative continuity and character consistency rather than fragmenting into a series of discrete performance sequences. Nonhermetic genres, such as the comedian comedy, the animated cartoon and the musical, are marked by "a more open and expansive narrative structure which acknowledges the spectator, narrative exposition that is 'spoiled' by actors who 'step out' of character, a foregrounding of its marks of production, essential artificiality, and a deconstruction of its signifying practices."[11] However, the classical Hollywood cinema was never as inflexible nor as perfectly "illusionistic" as these critics suggest, allowing a fair degree of latitude for performance spectacle within a system nevertheless centrally concerned with telling coherent stories and developing plausible characters. Rather than focusing on hermetic and nonhermetic genres as radically distinctive modes of screen practice, it might be more constructive to consider the ways that these different genres evoke and contain the potential disruptiveness of the vaudeville aesthetic while operating, more or less, fully within the classical Hollywood cinema.

If, as Bordwell suggests, the classical norms (rooted in theatrical realism) were primarily interested in narrative causality and character motivation, the aesthetics of vaudeville placed particular emphasis upon performance virtuosity and audience response.[12] Performers, who held sole responsibility for the selection, rehearsal and presentation of the comic material, built the act to foreground their own performance skills. Vaudevillians often developed a broad range of talents, including singing, dancing, joke-telling, magic, juggling and acrobatics. Characters played a limited role, often reduced to familiar stereotypes. Sometimes, vaudevillians invited audience awareness of the gap between their own personalities and the stock characters they assumed, layering identities to showcase their performance skills. Scenery was paired down to insure ease of transportation and to direct maximum attention onto the performer. Vaudevillians directly addressed their audiences, sometimes pulling them directly into the act, often adjusting both the performance's style and content to spectator response. The vaudeville manager made detailed records of the spectator reactions to various acts, measuring the performer's merits according to the ability to provoke outward displays of emotion. The act was, as a consequence, built to intensify affective experience and heighten awareness of the performer's skills and expertise; the simple plot became a "string" upon which loosely associated bits of comic and musical material might be attached. Most acts built towards a "wow climax," closing upon a spectacular moment to maximize the audience's final response.

The fragmentation and intensity of vaudeville shocked many middle-class critics and reformers, who preferred the emotional restraint and realism associated with theatrical farce or "true comedy." "True comedy," the tradition preferred by bourgeois critics, preserves the imaginary fourth wall separating audience from performers. "True comedy" depended upon exaggerated characters, often possessing a "comic flaw" (such as egotism, absentmindedness, jealousy, greed, false piety) which, when taken to extremes provided the motor for the farcical action. Actors in "true comedy," much as in other forms of theatrical realism, sought to blend into the characters, adopting their personal performance styles to the demands of the script and the director. Influential *Moving Picture World* critic Epes Winthrop Sargent was a strong advocate of this "true comedy" tradition, which he found more compatible with middle-class decorum and more consistent with the emerging classical norms.[13] "True comedy," as embodied by performers such as Sidney Drew, placed tremendous emphasis upon audience identification with plausible characters engaging in realistic situations and upon the subordination of gags and performance to the development of a coherent plot. If comedian comedy, as Seidman suggests, drew heavily upon the vaudeville tradition, the roots of romantic comedy can be found in "true comedy."

It is no accident that the stars most closely associated with romantic comedy (Cary Grant, Katharine Hepburn, Gary Cooper, Clark Gable, Carole Lombard) moved back and forth in the course of their career between comic and dramatic films, or that certain films, such as *Made For Each Other*, *Stage Door*, *Dinner at Eight* or *Penny Serenade* merge comic and dramatic elements within a single narrative. Their acting style maintains the realism and character integration expected elsewhere within the classical cinema. The same mobility was not enjoyed by film comedians, such as the Marx Brothers or Laurel and Hardy, who adopted more radical performance techniques. As a rule, the more the film invites our awareness of comic performance as performance, the less likely that character can attract sympathetic identification. Charlie Chaplin, for example, often spent some time developing the realistic base of his narratives before opening the possibility for more stylized performances, allowing him to shift between comedy and pathos.

Chaplin, as a star, thus, helped to negotiate the competing demands of the vaudeville aesthetic (embodied in such moments as the dance of the dinner rolls in *The Gold Rush*, the roller-skating sequence in *Modern Times* or his play with the globe balloon in *The Great Dictator*) and the "true comedy" tradition (suggested by the oft-discussed final confrontation with the flower girl in *City Lights*). Chaplin's conformity to many aspects of the classical Hollywood cinema has insured his critical respectability, yet Chaplin, like many other screen clowns, sought and exploited the spaces for performance spectacle available within the classical paradigm.

Performance in Comedian Comedy

Seidman's account of comedian comedy identifies both formal conventions (stressing particularly the self-conscious acknowledgment of the performer as performer through direct address, masquerade and impersonation) and thematic concerns ("the dialectic between eccentric behavior and social conformity," the imperfect integration of the comedian into the adult social order).[14] Seidman sees the relationship between these formal and thematic features as essentially stable, even static, throughout the full history of the genre's development. As subsequent writers, such as Peter Kramer and Frank Krutnik, have worked within Seidman's model, they have come to recognize the problems caused by its ahistoricism.[15] Comedian comedy has not been a static genre, but has undergone a series of dramatic shifts as the Hollywood system has negotiated the competing demands of the classical norms and the vaudeville aesthetic.

To begin with, it may be useful to distinguish between clowns and comedians, words which have often been used interchangeably but which suggest somewhat different social roles and thematic structures. The term "clown" derives from two Old German terms, *Klonne*, meaning "clumsy lout, lumpish fellow" and *Klunj*, meaning "a clod, a clot or lump." The clown constitutes a liminal figure, existing on the edges of civilization and contesting its dictates; the clown resists the civilizing process, celebrating social transgression, fluid identity and bodily pleasure. The clown historically had a ritual role, as in the ritual clowns who allowed worshippers to explore the cosmic interplay of order and disorder, and later, a civic role, as in the court jester who both amused and questioned the king. As Parker Tyler notes, the rise of Western democracy diminished the clown's official or sacred status, and made the figure more accessible to popular audiences.[16] The clown became an entertainer, a comedian and, as such, sought increasingly to please rather than critique the larger social community.

Building on this opposition, one might distinguish between clown comedies (such as those of the Marx Brothers), which stress a resistance or contesting of dominant social categories, and comedian comedies (such as those of Bob Hope or Harold Lloyd), which stress social integration and affiliation. The comedian's comedy stems from mistakes and mishaps arising from efforts to conform to social roles, the clown's comedy from disruptions and transgressions arising from a desire to break free from constraint. This distinction implies more than simply the thematic values we ascribe to performance in these films; there is a linkage between the film's celebration of personal rebellion and a looser conformity to classical norms, a more fragmented narrative structure and less coherently constructed character. As Seidman suggests, the performer in the comedian comedy pulls the character into the mainstream, muting the signs of "expressive anarchy" as the plot develops. The performer in a clown comedy, on the other hand, maintains a highly stylized acting style which marks the clown's separation from the larger social order. The clown wanders away from the crowd at the end, while the community embraces the comedian into its celebration. Historically, there has been a movement from clown comedy towards comedian comedy, as the demands of classical storytelling conventions made themselves more strongly felt.

Tom Gunning's account of "cinema of attractions" stresses the nonhermetic qualities of early cinema, including its tendency towards stereotypical rather than individualized characters, various forms of direct address and "mugging" to the camera, and an emphasis on spectacle over narrative.[17] In the early prank films Gunning analyzes, comic actions were performed by stock comic characters, most often by wayward youths or foxy grandpas, rather than by comic stars. The audience lacked the awareness of the performer as an extratextual and intertextual personality which would become the defining characteristic of the later comedian comedies. French and Italian filmmakers were among the first to put a name to the faces of comic performers, though here the tendency was for character names to continue from film to film, rather than to construct the performers as stars.[18] For the most part, these French and Italian clowns came from circuses and variety entertainment. Traces of those show business traditions can be found in their film's consistent use of various acrobats, jugglers, "freaks" (giants, midgets, bearded ladies), trained animals, and tightrope walkers. Stars such as Polydor and Cretinetti developed many of the stock performance tricks Seidman would link to the comedian comedy tradition, including the impersonation of children, animals and women, and often appeared in plots centering around their attempts to perform basic jobs and to find a place for themselves within the social order. The French and Italian clown comedies based their appeal primarily on the creation and marketing of comic personas, while the comedian comedy tradition, as described by Seidman, presumes the existence of the star system and the creation of star images. Mack Sennett operated during a transitional period within the construction and marketing of film stars. Sennett's films depended more upon an ensemble of clowns, many of whom possessed recognizable comic personas, rather than the marketing of star images.

As the star system took shape in the silent era, and as feature-film narratives became the industry norm, however, comic films tended to lag behind dramatic films, retaining aspects of the earlier "cinema of attractions" even as the classical Hollywood norms came to dominate film production. In slapstick films, Peter Kramer notes, "star performers and popularity seem to have been less balanced by . . . the story and its 'proper' presentation." Tensions within and between aesthetic traditions arose as these comic stars were fitted within feature films: "the quality standards connected with feature film production clashed with the specific qualities of the slapstick comedians, the former being mainly concerned with narrative, the later with a form of screen presence, of performance, which is often directly opposed to narrative integration and coherence."[19] Kramer's essay, thus, traces a movement from slapstick comedies, primarily concerned with showcasing the star comedian, towards classically constructed comedian comedies of the 1920s, where a much stronger effort was made to integrate the performer into a coherent story and a rounded character. These comedian comedies often borrowed their narrative situations and character types from the generic traditions of the dramatic cinema, while allowing space for comic turns and set pieces which harkened back to the earlier slapstick tradition. Kramer's essay in this volume describes how Buster Keaton's first feature, *The Saphead*, participated in this process. This important and generally overlooked film required Keaton to mesh his individualistic performance style with a theatrical farce originally written to showcase his costar, William H.

Crane. *The Saphead* balances slapstick and "true comedy," the vaudeville aesthetic and the classical norms.

The transition to sound led Hollywood to a new reconciliation with the vaudeville aesthetic.[20] The studios grappled with difficult questions surrounding the place of sound film within their overall production output and the aesthetics which should govern the sound track. Hollywood raided Broadway, with the recruitment of stage stars intended less to displace film stars with limited vocal ability than to provide styles of entertainment familiar to urban northeastern audiences who would become the key market for the first wave of talking pictures. Many of the comic stars of this period, such as Eddie Cantor, Will Rogers and W. C. Fields, had enjoyed some limited success in the silent cinema, but were still primarily associated with the New York stage revues. Others, such as the Marx Brothers, Wheeler and Woolsey, Olsen and Johnson and Jimmy Durante, came to Hollywood as part of the Broadway talent raids. The Hollywood studios sought formulas which would allow them to fully exploit these stars' diverse performance skills while maintaining some fidelity to classical norms. The sophisticated blend of music and comedy associated with the *Ziegfeld Follies* proved less marketable to regional audiences, who demanded a return to screen comedy's slapstick roots. What was sought, in the words of one *Variety* observer, was "a happy melding of sophistication and hoke."[21] Early sound comedies, such as *Diplomaniacs, Whoopee, Million Dollar Legs* and *Animal Crackers,* display a fascination with performance virtuosity at the expense of plot and characterization. The performers make only minimal effort to blend into their characters, often stereotypes possessing few individualizing traits. The films reflect the need to diversify entertainment through scattered set pieces. This highly fragmented subgenre has been called "anarchistic comedy."

These film's formal disruptiveness is also linked to a thematic iconoclasm. If the classic silent films represented the comedian's attempts to find an appropriate place in society, the clowns in these films often actively resist social integration. These clowns take pleasure in their ability to play with their identities and to thwart dupes, killjoys and counterfeits. The films often embrace the "expressive individualism" of the clowns as preferable to the repression, hypocrisy and narrow-mindedness of the dominant order, with exuberant performance linked to this liberation from social constraint. As a result, these comic performers often found themselves pushing against the moral standards enforced by the Production Code Administration. The PCA was initially prepared to accept a fairly loose interpretation of the Code's provisions when it came to comic films, feeling that moral transgression posed less of a threat if it was presented in a fashion that nobody could take seriously. Yet comic performers, such as Mae West and Wheeler and Woolsey, were often cited as among the worst offenders in the public fight to insure stricter enforcement of the code. Wheeler and Woolsey's *So This is Africa* (1934) not only pushed against the outer limits of the code provisions but broke them into a million pieces, including gags centering around prostitution, homosexuality, aggressive female sexuality, masturbation, transvestism, lesbianism, nudity and bestiality. In the film's final sequence, for example, Wheeler and Woolsey have been forced to disguise themselves as Amazon women, hoping to escape from a tribe of sex-crazed females, only to find themselves captives of a warring tribe of equally lascivious men. Two rather manly warriors grab them in their arms, carrying them away to their huts. A title suggests that a year has passed and then we see Wheeler and Woolsey, still dressed in drag, washing the men's clothes outside the same hut and tending to their babies, while the men go away on a hunting party. The juxtaposition clearly suggests that Wheeler and Woolsey have fully adopted to their new gender and sexual identities; only belatedly does the film coyly reveal that the two male comedians have, in fact, found wives and are engaged in an appropriate heterosexual relationship.

Mae West, as Ramona Curry suggests, represented an equally problematic figure. If initially West adopted her flamboyant comic style as a means of circumventing the potential censorship of her sexy stories, the PCA increasingly came to focus on West's style as itself licentious and potentially censorable. Curry identifies a number of problems associated with West's style, including her ties to the "dirty blues" musical tradition, her control over the gaze, her suggestive movements and her acknowledgment of feminine erotic pleasure. Curry's close examination of Mae West's *Goin' to Town* also reflects an emerging academic interest in female comic performers, such as West, Winnie Lightner, Charlotte Greenwood, Lupe Velez, Carmen Miranda, Gracie Allen, and more recent female clowns, such as Roseanne Barr and Lucille Ball.[22] Female clowns developed a style of comic performance at once similar to and markedly different from that associated with the male comedian comedy tradition. The focus of their comedy is often upon ridiculing the traditional construction of femininity (especially aspects of beauty, domesticity and passivity) and playing with stock female roles (the wife, the show girl, the prostitute). Such work illuminates long-standing feminist interests in the gaze (as in Mae West's appropriation of the gaze in her erotic looks at men), masquerade (as in the layering and play with identity in Winnie Lightner's films) and spectacle (the comic and dreadful spectacle of the "woman on top" as opposed to the erotic spectacle of female sexual display).

The late 1930s and early 1940s were marked by growing conservatism in both the formal and thematic construction of comedian comedies. The studio system was increasingly insistent that comic forms conform to the narrative conventions and the Code standards governing all Hollywood output. Many careers ended, others shifted to poverty row studios which were more tolerant of their transgressiveness, and still others were forced into the role of "eccentric uncle" in traditional romantic comedies. Many factors may have contributed to this shift, including increased public pressure to restrain moral content, declining box office returns for comedians who had been overworked and overexposed, exhibitor insistence that "stronger stories" might offset the uneven quality of the clown's comic set pieces, and critical hostility to the film's lowbrow humor.

The overwhelming majority of Seidman's examples of the comedian comedy come from postwar films, particularly those of Bob Hope and Bing Crosby, Dean Martin and Jerry Lewis, and Danny Kaye. Seidman's reclamation of these films as a subgenre coincided with the increased scholarly interest among French and British critics in Frank Tashlin and Jerry Lewis.[23] *Cahiers du cinema*, for example, offered an account of Jerry Lewis as a modernist artist who criticizes and exposes central American "mythologies" through the qualities of his performance (his elasticity, his inarticulateness, his stiffness, his "virtuosity") and his film's construction (their cartoonish stylization, their fragmentation, their unusual sound-image relations, their parodic quotation).[24] As Michael Selig notes, the focus on authorship rather than genre tended to isolate Lewis from his larger historical context.[25] Seidman's model moves beyond these celebrations of individual creativity towards a recognition of the broader generic traditions within which Hope, Tashlin and Lewis operated. All of these writers identified the comedian-centered comedies of this period as remarkably self-conscious, pushing the nonhermetic aspects of the genre to its logical extremes. Earlier critics, such as Parker Tyler, had noted a significant shift in tone and style among postwar comedies. Tyler contrasts Kaye's "madness"— the instability of his characters, the frenetic quality of his performances, his childishness and feminization, his tendency towards impersonation and masquerade—to the "concerted goofiness" of the Marx Brothers, suggesting that he combines their assorted lunacies within a single figure. Tyler notes the way that Kaye's "obvious fixation on the camera" emerged from his solo nightclub performances, and became a dominant trait of his screen appearances.[26] Tyler's discussion of Kaye, thus, identifies many of the features the Seidman-Krutnik model associates with the "formalized" comedian comedy. Tyler's early fascination with psychoanalytic approaches to the popular cinema is echoed by later accounts of the comedian comedy, including Krutnik's interest in the comedian's "unresolved personality" and Seidman's concern with comic performance signs as paralleling neurotic symptoms. These psychoanalytic terms suggest the new conception of character which emerged in the postwar cinema, a period when many different genres responded to the American popularization of Freudianism. If silent comedies, such as those of

Chaplin, dealt with the outsider's search for a place within an exclusive society, or anarchistic comedies dealt with the expressive clown's rebellion against social conformity, these post-war films explore the problematic status of social identity, turning the comedy inward rather than directing it outward towards society. Performance traits which were once read as defiant to social conformity are now read as symptoms of neurosis which the film will work to resolve.

These "formalized" comedian comedies, as Frank Krutnik notes, also depended on generic parody. Parody can be found in the slapstick shorts of Mack Sennett, the later films of the Marx Brothers, and the wartime films of Abbott and Costello, but parodic quotation of other films and genres dominates the oeuvres of Hope, Lewis and Kaye. These shifts within the comedian comedy tradition reflect broader tendencies within Hollywood, as many different genres entered a "baroque" period.[27] How might the "formalized" comedian comedy be aligned, for example, with the move towards the adult Western (*Man From Laramie*), the self-reflexive musical (*The Band Wagon* and *The Pirate*), the excessive melodramas (*All that Heaven Allows*) and *film noir* (*Kiss Me Deadly, Touch of Evil*)? All of these subgenres are marked by a blurring of previous genre distinctions, increasingly flamboyant visual and performance styles, self-conscious acknowledgment of their own construction and destabilized identities.

This new phase of innovation and experimentation was the last gasp of the classical era. The comedian comedy as a genre has lost its distinctiveness since the early 1960s, reflecting the tendency towards hybridization within the postclassical Hollywood cinema. Perhaps the most interesting shift within the post-1960s comedian comedy has been the merger of the comedian comedy with horror, fantasy and science fiction. Where the "formalized" comedian comedies once dealt with eccentric individuals seeking a stable identity and a fixed place in the social order, these supernatural or fantastic comedian comedies (such as *All of Me, Innerspace, Big, Switch, Memoirs of an Invisible Man, The Incredible Shrinking Woman, Teen Wolf, Sleeper*) start with individuals who are comfortably positioned in the social order, who are upwardly mobile or who enjoy a stable (if dull and unsatisfying) identity. Instability, and hence the opportunity for comic performance, originates from outside the individual, often through the intrusion of some supernatural force or of some odd wish-fulfillment fantasy (such as those involving changing one's gender, race or age). The comedy centers around their efforts to restabilized their identity and potentially to resolve personality defects (misogyny, racism, self-doubt, noncommitment, infantilism, work obsession) in the process. Conversely, comedy may constitute an "other world" which the characters must enter and return from (as in films like *Stay*

Tuned) or may be figured as the source of supernatural disruption (as in *Oh, God* or *Beetlejuice*). These works provide opportunities for broad comic performances by veterans of variety-style television series (especially *Saturday Night Live* or *SCTV*) but also from dramatic actors not normally noted for their comic roles. Since these films merge comic conventions with other generic traditions, they are often marked by a shifting emotional tone, so that films like *Edward Scissorhands* or *Toys* include melodramatic as well as comic sequences. Here, again, the comedian comedy runs parallel to larger industry trends towards the mixing and matching of previously distinctive generic traditions, a increasingly fragmented and decentered narrative structure and a progressively more self-conscious visual style.

Rather than seeing the comedian comedy as a static tradition, remaining more or less constant from the silent films of Charlie Chaplin through the contemporary features of Eddie Murphy and Pee-Wee Herman, it is possible to see comedian comedy as a highly dynamic genre, constantly renegotiating the relative balance between narrative and spectacle, characterization and performance. Rather than seeing comedian comedy as a "nonhermetic" genre radically at odds with the dominant currents of the classical Hollywood cinema, one can productively trace the genre's history in terms of shifts within the classical cinema, including the emergence of the star system, the introduction of self-regulation standards, the transition to sound, the increased self-consciousness towards genre in the postwar cinema or the fragmentation and hybridization of genres within the postclassical period. In the next section, we will look more closely at the ways that romantic comedy, similarly, seeks a balance between the demands for plausible characters within this more realist tradition and the potential for performer expression and virtuosity.

Performance in Romantic Comedy

The overwhelming majority of work on comic performance has centered on comedian comedy, allowing us to move beyond generalizations to a fairly concrete consideration of its historical transformation. Most critical work on romantic comedy has focused on narrative and ideological questions and on a fairly finite set of texts (mostly the screwball comedies of the 1930s). The role of performance within romantic comedy remains a fertile area for exploration. We need to look more closely at the different styles of interactions between male and female stars within the divorce comedies of Cecil B. DeMille of the 1910s, the flapper comedies of Clara Bow in the 1920s, the sophisticated farces of Ernst Lubitsch, the screwball comedies of the 1930s, the postwar comedies of Preston Sturges, Billy Wilder or Frank Tashlin, and the more recent "nervous" romances of

Woody Allen and Neil Simon, to cite only a few of the genre's many permutations.

Much like the state of scholarship on comedian comedy prior to Steve Seidman's innovative work, the most sustained discussion on performance in romantic comedy consists of studies of individual stars, such as Katharine Hepburn, Marilyn Monroe or Cary Grant.[28] Such stars are read not as posing questions particular to romantic comedy, but rather as representative of the star system as a whole. Andrew Britton's monograph about Katharine Hepburn, for example, moves back and forth between comic and dramatic works, making comparisons most often to other dramatic stars, such as Dietrich or Garbo, rather than to her comic contemporaries. Britton is interested in the qualities of Hepburn's performances which resist ideological and narrative containment. As he writes, "Hepburn's presence is always more radical than her films. . . . Her presence forces her films to go in directions they cannot possibly go, adopt strategies they cannot fully sustain, raise issues they cannot adequately resolve."[29] Britton, however, does not associate Hepburn's disruptive presence with the romantic comedy tradition as a whole, even though the categories he adopts (such as tomboyishness, eccentricity, class, bisexuality, masquerade, camp, the female community, the independent woman) point towards traits with a larger history in romantic comedy, and his most common examples come from *Stage Door* and *Sylvia Scarlet*.

The tendency, across a range of critical traditions, has been to treat romantic comedy as more fully contained within the classical cinema than the comedian comedy tradition. Such critics, thus, see little need to distinguish the types of performances found there from the styles of dramatic acting found elsewhere in Hollywood movies. In romantic comedies, as in other classical films, the pleasures of performance are tied to the demands of character and narrative development. Performance signs are given a high degree of narrative motivation. Romantic comedy can be seen as an outgrowth of the notions of comic realism associated with the "true comedy" tradition, a tradition which, from the outset, was seen as more fully compatible with classical norms than the vaudeville aesthetic that governed the comedian comedy. Much as in the "true comedy" tradition, the narratives of romantic comedies are marked by the comic exaggeration of realist traits (such as Hepburn's pride in *Philadelphia Story* or Gary Cooper's small-town naivety in *Mr. Deeds Goes to Town*) yet retain rounded and plausible characters. Comic characters within romantic comedy, much as in "true comedy," are often defined through their comic flaws (such as Cary Grant's academic distance from life in *Bringing up Baby* or the competitiveness that charges the marriage of Katharine Hepburn and Spencer Tracy in *Adam's Rib*). Although these characters were often constructed with an eye towards particular actors, the history of romantic comedy points to many examples where scripts were written for one star and performed by another, either through accidents of production or the recasting of roles in screen adaptations of theatrical plays. If comedian comedy has depended upon the creation of flat, stereotypical characters who facilitate the performer's display of his or her personality and skills, the romantic comedy has created rounded characters who have an integrity and complexity that holds our attention, apart from the particularity of their realization within a given film. Casting Gary Cooper in *The Lady Eve*, James Stewart in *Ball of Fire* and Henry Fonda in *Philadelphia Story* would make a difference, but not as great as casting Groucho Marx in *Modern Times*, Charles Chaplin in *The Road to Utopia* or Bob Hope in *Duck Soup*.

Despite their closer conformity to classical norms, romantic comedy still provides some space for excess, virtuosity and spectacle. As James Naremore has suggested, classical films often provided plot rationales for the layering of identities, for impersonation or masquerade, which allow their stars a chance to display their performance skills. The bantering dialogue and rapid delivery which characterizes screwball comedy, for example, has been linked to the film's overall conception of male-female relationships. These aspects of performance style, as Tina Lent notes in her essay in this volume, fit comfortably within an ideology which sees men and women as potential playmates as well as lovers. The smooth interaction between two performers, as in the interplay between Cary Grant and Rosalind Russell in *His Girl Friday* or Myrna Loy and William Powell in *The Thin Man*, can suggest how much these characters belong together, and may contrast sharply with the slow, ponderous responses of mismatched couples (such as the exchanges between Irene Dunne and Ralph Bellamy in *The Awful Truth*). These playful interactions allow the most extreme forms of performance, such as Cary Grant's backflips in *Holiday*, safe within plot structures which link these stunts to larger character issues.

The contrasting styles of two performers, such as the sizzling "hot" sexuality of Barbara Stanwyck in *Ball of Fire* or *The Lady Eve* and the more pedestrian qualities of her costars (Gary Cooper, Henry Fonda) indicates issues which must be resolved before the couple can be brought together. The sounds of the actor's voices (Cooper's tongue-tiedness, Fonda's stammering, the clicking of Stanwyck's tongue and the suggestiveness of her slangy talk), their physical presence (the glistening of her hair, the shimmer of her legs, the sparkle of her costumes) and the movements of their bodies (her hip-swinging walk, his nervous stumble) all help to define the interplay between these two characters.

Many romantic comedies feature supporting characters who are marked by a broader comic style than their leading couples. Supporting actors, such as Edward Everett Horton or Franklin Pangborn, played roles within romantic comedies which parallel the traditional function of the comic servant in Shakespearean New Comedy. They may provide a staid, boring and befuddled contrast to the romantic lead's giddiness in love, a comic foil for their exuberance. Such performers are sometimes situated within older couples, who personify the staleness of old love as a counter to the freshness of new romance, or conversely may embody the flippancy of oft-divorced characters as a contrast to the need of the central couple to renew their marital commitments. If such characters provide straight-men for screen clowns, they often play a more buffoonish role in relation to romantic comedy leads, enjoying a broader range of performance techniques, in order to suggest their "otherness" and their exclusion from the game of love. An extreme example would be Toto, the character of unspecified European origins played by Sig Arno, in *The Palm Beach Story*. While Toto dogishly pursues the Princess (Mary Astor), he is constantly abandoned or ridiculed by her as she pursues Tom Jeffers (Joel McCrea). His foreign eccentricities makes him a laughable choice as a lover, while the character allows Arno a chance to ham it up, and to steal most of the scenes where he is featured. Mischa Auer plays a similar role within Frank Capra's *You Can't Take It With You*—an eccentric foreigner who offers ironic and deflating commentary on the central romance, putting the demands of his stomach above the dictates of love.

Romantic comedy narrativizes performance. Narratively motivated performance (impersonation, masquerade) is common within the comedian comedy tradition. In comedian comedy, however, our knowledge of the comedian as an extratextual performer often allows our fascination with the mechanics of the performance to distract attention from character development; little explanation is given to justify the ability of the character to perform in such a virtuoso fashion. In romantic comedy such performances are often closely linked to narrative goals (as in the cross-dressing plot which provides the core of *Some Like It Hot*) or to the resolution of character issues (as in Irene Dunne's impersonation of Cary Grant's lower–class sister in *The Awful Truth*). One might, for example, point towards the motel sequence in *It Happened One Night*, where Ellie and Peter must pretend to be a squabbling married couple in order to elude her father's detectives; their ability to improvise together, to take on a role in fiction, anticipates their transformation into a married couple by the film's conclusion.[30]

A more complex example arises in Billy Wilder's *One, Two, Three*, where the capitalist businessman (James Cagney) must remake the Marxist newlywed (Horst Buchholz) into an aristocrat in order to please Scarlet's father and Cagney's boss. Here, the bulk of the film is given over to preparations (scripting, casting, costuming and rehearsing) for a performance, inviting us to take pleasure in performance as a process rather than as a finished product. The film, moreover, involves a constant play with Cagney's preexisting screen image, with references to his most familiar roles (*Public Enemy*, *Yankee Doodle Dandy*) and his most characteristic mannerisms. The film's dependence upon a system of typage, of extremely stereotypical characters, does not allow us to see the characters as psychologically rounded individuals, but rather invites an exploration of the false perceptions that block understanding within its Cold-War context. *One, Two, Three* becomes an extreme example of the potentials for excessive or disruptive performance within the romantic comedy tradition.

Comedian comedy opens with "expressive anarchy" or identity confusion, marking the comedian's imperfect integration into the social order. Comedian comedy works towards the resolution of that "anarchy" either by the comedian's self-mastery and conformity to mature adult expectations (Danny Kaye, Bob Hope) or the comedian's disruption of and escape from the social order (Chaplin, the Marx Brothers). Romantic comedies, on the other hand, open with characters who possess coherent, if incomplete, identities, and work to destabilize those identities. Susan's (Katharine Hepburn)'s systematic assault on David (Cary Grant) in *Bringing Up Baby* throws his identity into crisis. She removes him from his normal context, strips him of his familiar clothes, forces him to enact unfamiliar roles and to hide his own name and occupation. In short, she destroys what little coherence he possessed at the film's opening. In the process, David frees himself from his obsession with work and his stifling romance with Miss Swallow, discovering the pleasures of play, and forging a romance with Susan. This process of transforming David's identity gives Grant a chance to perform broad slapstick and to mimic other characters (the gangster, the big game hunter). Fluid identities are necessary in order to reconcile the differences separating the male and female protagonists and to integrate them into a couple. If such fluidity poses a problem for social integration within the comedian comedy, it provides the solution to romantic isolation within romantic comedy.

The difference between romantic and comedian comedy may not rest on the distinction between restrained and excessive performance so much as on the alternate strategies by which virtuoso performance is expressed and contained. Many of the traits identified with comedian comedy, especially masquerade or the problem of unstable identities, function as well within romantic comedies, and may be defining characteristics of the comic tradition as a whole. Some romantic comedies, such as *The Seven Year Itch*, *Some Like It Hot*, *One, Two, Three* or *Unfaithfully Yours*, become every bit as self-conscious about the process of staging a performance as any of the "formalized" comedian comedies of Hope,

Kaye or Lewis. Much like comedian comedies, these films invite our familiarity with the extratextual images of stars, with the problem of constructing and maintaining a coherent image, with the mechanics of masquerade and impersonation; such films provide a fairly large stage upon which their stars can display their performance skills.

9

The Keystone Film Company and the Historiography of Early Slapstick

Douglas Riblet

Charles Bauman and Adam Kessel of the New York Motion Picture Company (NYMPCo.) and Mack Sennett, formerly director of Biograph's comedy unit, formed the Keystone Film Company in the summer of 1912, issuing its first releases on September 23 of that year. The new company's mandate was to produce weekly comedy releases under Sennett's direction for the Mutual program, the newest of the distribution alliances which provided American exhibitors with a daily supply of new films in one thousand-foot reel formats. Keystone continued releasing its product through Mutual until mid-1915, when it left to become part of the new Triangle Film Company.[1] Slapstick comedy was hardly new to cinema; the trade press had long used the term "slapstick," originally derived from vaudeville, to refer to the action-oriented, sometimes violent comedies produced in great numbers before 1908. Nonetheless, Keystone quickly developed a highly distinctive, popular and influential style of film comedy. Jay Leyda has coined the term "California slapstick" to refer to the new form of the genre created in the early 1910s at Keystone and other American comedy studios, a form which drew on a variety of influences—vaudeville, burlesque, the circus, early chase films, the French and Italian comedies which were widely imported into the U.S. market before 1914, even Griffith's melodramas.[2] Looking in the other direction, Keystone helped initiate a slapstick craze which continued more or less unabated to the end of the silent era, despite periodic predictions by hostile trade press critics of the genre's impending decline.[3]

The names of Mack Sennett and the Keystone Film Company are well known. Film historians universally acknowledge Sennett's importance in the history of American film comedy, and the "Keystone Cops" remain ingrained in the cultural vocabulary as a metaphor for chaotic or destructive incompetence. Yet despite a ground swell of revisionist research into preclassical cinema, Sennett and Keystone—and pre-1917 slapstick comedy more generally—have received surprisingly slight historical attention in recent years.[4] Traditional slapstick criticism, often driven by an enthusiastic connoisseurship toward the genre, has generally taken a highly negative view of Keystone and its style of film comedy. Walter Kerr's chapter on Sennett in *The Silent Clowns* represents the most eloquent expression of this position.[5] While acknowledging the studio's historical importance, Kerr and others have proclaimed Keystone's reputation to be overblown and its films crude, primitive, formulaic and—the worst thing one can say about comedies—not very funny. While James Agee celebrated the anarchic energy of the Keystones in his famous 1949 essay, "Comedy's Greatest Era," the later consensus among slapstick connoisseurs has seen Keystone comedy as lacking the comic subtlety and sophistication of the "classic" slapstick of Chaplin, Keaton, Lloyd *et al.*[6] Kerr summed up this view in a memorable phrase: "Sennett seems to me not so much the King as the Carpenter of Comedy. He built the house. It is hard now to believe that he ever entertained friends in it."[7]

Several historiographical assumptions underlie this treatment of Sennett and Keystone, some of which deserve to be problematized. First, these historians and critics tend to adopt a highly teleological model of film slapstick history, taking the classic 1920s slapstick of Keaton, Chaplin *et al.* as the genre's standard, and judging earlier forms against this standard. Presenting slapstick history as a process of maturation or progress from primitive prototypes toward *The General* and *The Freshman* inevitably distorts earlier forms of the genre which employed different conventions, aimed for different effects and developed within specific historical conditions. The slapstick produced by Keystone and its contemporaries should be examined as a distinctive, historically specific style of film comedy, not simply as a crude predecessor of later styles.

This teleological perspective derives, in part, from the great emphasis on evaluation of films and comedians in much slapstick criticism and history. As noted above, the general consensus among traditional slapstick critics finds the Keystone films to be singularly unfunny, Walter Kerr noting almost pityingly that "I have, in the past months, sat through dozens of Keystones and later Sennetts . . . without once being trapped into laughter."[8] My own observation of modern audiences (whose presence at the screenings discounts any generalized antipathy toward silent films) supports Kerr's negative evaluation of the Keystones' lasting appeal. Much analysis of Keystone's brand of slapstick concentrates on its failings in relation to the later classics or Sennett's failure to understand the principles of slapstick. Questions of evaluation are not uninteresting or irrelevant to film history, but problems arise when modern evaluations become the basis for historical arguments. Overemphasis on evaluation can lead to a reductive historical approach which simply assumes a linear progress from the "bad" films to the "good" films, without striving to understand the historical context or conventions in which those unfamiliar or unappealing films were produced.

Finally, traditional historians of slapstick have tended to examine slapstick in isolation from the film industry as a whole. However, the rapidly changing institutional structure and social status of the American industry affected the development of slapstick comedy in countless ways. A more nuanced understanding of Keystone (and early film slapstick more generally) must situate it within broader industrial trends, such as: changing systems of exhibition and distribution, the rise of the feature film, the development of the star system, censorship and regulation struggles, the industry's ongoing struggle for cultural respectability, and so forth.

Sennett and Keystone are ripe for historical reevaluation. This essay will trace the gradual development of Keystone's style of film comedy from 1912 to 1915. Slapstick of this period employed different conventions and aimed for different effects from the canonical 1920s slapstick more familiar today. A less teleological approach which situates the genre's development within the relevant historical contexts will shed light on those conventions and effects. Indeed, as Peter Kramer, Steve Neale and Frank Krutnik have recently argued, a less teleological approach to the genre's history may provide insight into the classical 1920s slapstick features as well.[9]

The Evolution of a Studio Style

The Keystone Film Company began production at a low point in American film comedy. As Eileen Bowser has documented, the percentage of output devoted to comedy by American studios gradually declined between 1908 and 1911. Among the comedy which was being produced, the action-oriented chase and "linked vignettes" films, which predominated before 1908, declined (though they did not disappear, especially at the smaller studios), while more narrative-oriented, less fantastic situation comedies, centered around middle-class characters, increased. Bowser attributes this shift mainly to the impact of reform movements, whose criticisms of the film industry posed the threat of heightened censorship and regulation, as well as the industry's own drive to attain a higher degree of cultural respectability, and thus to appeal to a middle-class audience with presumably less raucous tastes than their working class counterparts.[10] The licensed and independent distribution alliances continued to release French (and occasionally Italian) comedies which maintained a more farcical, physical style of comedy, but the amount of

European comedy released in the United States declined in the early 1910s. This decline was most likely due to both declining audience popularity and American companies' attempts to squeeze foreign competitors out of the market.[11] Meanwhile, exhibitor complaints about the lack of quality and quantity in film comedy, while not a new occurrence, became louder in the early 1910s.[12]

Keystone (and the new California slapstick more generally) quickly attained a somewhat contradictory position in the industry. On the one hand, Keystone's films became extremely popular with audiences and financially lucrative for NYMPCo. and exhibitors. Keystone and Sennett even achieved a level of prestige by 1913–14, with a reputation as the industry's best comedy producers amidst a flood of lesser-quality slapstick. A November 1913 *Variety* article entitled "Unfunny 'Funny' Films Hurt" quoted one exhibitor who claimed that "he voiced the opinion of more than 500 exhibitor associates" as saying that "to-day none of the companies save the Keystone was living up to the old laugh standards."[13] On the other hand, many industry personnel and trade press critics considered the slapstick genre something of an embarrassment, too vulgar and immoral to appeal to the "more refined audiences" which many in the industry wanted to cultivate. *The Moving Picture World*, whose staff contained many advocates of raising the film industry's cultural respectability, often praised or criticized a new release on the basis of the "class of picture goers" to whom it would or would not appeal.[14] Its comments on Keystone's *That Ragtime Band* (1913), for example, stated, "The vaudeville acts contain coarse touches, which are unfortunate, and the 'rough-house' ending will not appeal to refined audiences."[15] In many instances, *World* reviewers even suggested that exhibitors in "the better houses" cut certain offensive sequences out of a film before projecting it.[16] Conversely, the *World*'s more positive reviews of Keystone films often contained statements such as "Good burlesque, without objectionable features."[17] We should be wary, however, of accepting uncritically the assumption of slapstick's exclusive appeal to lower-class, "less refined" audiences; on the contrary, much evidence points to Keystone's vast popularity with audiences in those "better houses." The Strand, one of the most luxurious movie palaces in New York, used Keystones consistently after its opening in April 1914, on programs which customarily included a high-class dramatic feature, newsreels, travelogues and several orchestral interludes.[18] Nor was the Strand alone; *Motography* reported, in the fall of 1914, that five out of six Broadway theaters converted to cinemas were showing Keystone shorts along with their features.[19]

Keystone's trademark style of film comedy developed gradually during this three-year period. (Most obviously, the average length of its films increased from almost all split-reels in 1912 to two-reelers exclusively

in the summer of 1915.) The dearth of extant prints makes any generaliza-
tion about the films of the studio's first six months problematic. However,
those films which do survive bear great resemblance, unsurprisingly, to
the films of Sennett's Biograph unit and lack (or, at least, employ to a lesser
degree) many basic elements of Keystone's later style—for example,
grotesque makeup, rapid editing and violent physical comedy. These films
employed succinct narratives, with the rapid exposition and closure typical
of split-reel and one-reel cinema, often constructed around misunderstandings or pranks played by one character against another. The most
common plot in Sennett's Biograph and early Keystone comedies involved
a young couple plotting to fool his or her father into consenting to their
union. The comedy in these films relied mainly on hierarchies of knowledge between viewer and characters in the unfolding of the prank. In one
of the studio's first split-reel releases, *The Water Nymph* (September
1912), for example, Sennett convinces his fiancée, Mabel Normand, to
flirt with his philandering father, Ford Sterling, before he introduces her
to his parents. The film's narration clues the audience in on the prank,
so that we can revel in the spectacle of the father's humiliation along
with the pranksters. *The Cure That Failed* (January 1913) expands on
this pattern with the victim of a prank responding with a counterprank.
When Ford Sterling's wife kicks him out of the house for getting drunk,
his friends plot to cure him. Fred Mace dresses up as woman and, when
Sterling wakes up from a binge, tells him that they were married while
he was drunk. A glimpse of Mace's shoes, however, eventually reveals
the ruse to Sterling, who then pretends to have committed suicide to get
back at Mace and the others. Again, the comedy relies on a narrational
structure which aligns the viewer's knowledge with that of the prankster
in the planning and execution of the prank. The drunk characterization
gives free rein to Sterling's hammy mugging and pratfalls, but the level
of physical humor does not nearly approach the violent knockabout seen
in Keystones of less than a year later. Such prank narratives did not
disappear as Keystone developed, but narrational comedy became increasingly subordinate to comic action and performance in 1913 and beyond.

The physical comedy in early slapstick, termed "knockabout" in contemporary parlance, was far more violent than that in the classic 1920s
slapstick. Common bits of comic business in Keystone films included a
variety of cruel assaults on the human body: kicking unaware victims'
asses; poking pins into asses; firing guns into asses; burning someone's
flesh with a lit cigarette or a pan pulled off a hot stove; biting another
character's nose; spitting a mouthful of water into another character's
face; roundhouse punches to the face; and horseshoes, bottles, bricks and
other objects hurled at characters' heads. (The ass and the head were the
favored targets of knockabout abuse.) Keystone's knockabout comedy

also included much accidental, self-inflicted, physical abuse—stumbling, falling, tripping, bumping one's head, twirling and falling after a missed punch, and general clumsiness. Many Keystones also included elaborate stunts involving explosives and car crashes. (Notices about Keystone performers being injured on the set were common in the trade press, though some may have been exaggerated for publicity purposes.) While nostalgic treatment of slapstick has fetishized the throwing of custard pies as representative of slapstick assaults on the body, the more common projectile of choice in early slapstick was the brick. In some instances, characters even pounded bricks directly into each others' faces (for instance, Keystone's *Between Showers* and L-Ko's *Love and Surgery*, both 1914).[20]

Contrary to common statements that "no one ever got hurt" in slapstick films, facial registrations of pain, however exaggerated and brief, were a fundamental part of the comedy. *A Hash House Fraud* (1915), for example, employs close-ups of waiter Hugh Fay's convulsing face as cook Nick Cogley pulls a pan off the stove and presses it against his ass. In a somewhat more extreme example, the boxing match which comprises the second half of *Hogan's Romance Upset* (1915) ends with a close-up of Charlie Murray, having been kicked in the face, spitting a mouthful of broken teeth at the camera. Though a certain element of fantasy and unreality was essential to achieve a comic distance, a certain level of clearly expressed pain was also essential to the dark comic edge of these films. We might more accurately say that characters almost never died or suffered permanent, serious injury in these films, though even this proscription could be tested in places. At the end of *Barney Oldfield's Race for a Life* (1913), Ford Sterling, the cartoonish villain in the film's mock melodrama, shoots five policeman, then turns to the camera and shoots himself, falling to the ground in exaggerated death throes.

This style of physical comedy often seems too sadistic, unsubtle and narratively unmotivated to be genuinely funny to modern audiences. As noted above, many critics who delight in the later slapstick find the Keystone films crude or even distasteful. Walter Kerr criticizes Keystone's brand of comic violence and compares it unfavorably to Chaplin's later films on the basis of the former's lack of narrative and character motivation for violent behavior. Kerr writes:

> When, in an early Keystone comedy, Chaplin kicks Mack Swain in the stomach, it isn't particularly funny. When, in a later feature-length film called *The Pilgrim* (1923), he kicks a small boy in the stomach, it is marvelously funny. . . . Both acts are outrageous, in the original Sennett manner. . . . But the second is funny for a reason that goes deeper than the bizarre physicality of the act. Chaplin has taken great

pains earlier in the film to make us thoroughly detest the little monster, to make certain that we shall be immensely gratified when he gets exactly what is coming to him. . . . At Keystone, no kick ever needed to be justified. The invitation of an available backside was motivation enough.[21]

Kerr overstates the lack of narrative motivation for slapstick violence in Keystones, but this comparison nonetheless points to another crucial difference between Keystone and later forms of slapstick—a different conception of the comic character. While the figure of the prankster in the Sennett Biographs and early Keystones was usually pursuing some goal (for instance, winning a father's consent to marriage) or teaching a lesson to some flawed character (the philandering father in *The Water Nymph*, the drunken friend in *The Cure That Failed*), the typical later Keystone comic protagonist was fundamentally an unredeeming scoundrel, behaving in the most outrageous and barbarous fashion as a matter of course. Gilbert Seldes—who wrote admiringly of slapstick, and Keystone particularly, in the 1920s—referred to Keystone's stock characters as "scamps, scoundrels, shysters, fakers, tramps."[22] This character type differed not only from those in the earlier Sennett films but also from those which predominated in the classic 1920s slapstick, promoting a very different form of audience address. The 1920s slapstick most often portrayed the comic protagonist as a victimized misfit, and carefully established narrative motivation for any violent action, thus eliciting the audience's sympathies for the character. In contrast, the Keystone films generally revelled in the protagonist's outlandishly amoral, cruel behavior.

Theorists of comedy have debated the appeal of the figure of the comic rogue or scoundrel. In "The frames of comic 'freedom'," Umberto Eco begins his exploration of the relation between comedy and carnival by attempting to deduce the definition of comedy proposed in the lost or never-written second book of Aristotle's *Poetics*.[23] Working from fragments of Aristotle's other writings, as well as post-Aristotelian treatises on comedy (Eco calls this project "an exercise in the Peircean art of 'fair guesses' or abductions"[24]), he arrives at a definition based on social or moral transgression performed by a comic scoundrel.

[The] comic effect is realized when: (i) there is the violation of a rule (preferably, but not necessarily, a minor one, like an etiquette rule); (ii) the violation is committed by someone with whom we do not sympathize because he is an ignoble, inferior, and repulsive (animal-like) character; (iii) therefore we feel superior to his misbehavior and to his sorrow for having broken the rule; (iv) however in recognizing that the rule has been broken, we do not feel concerned; on the contrary we in some way welcome the violation; we are, so to speak, revenged by the comic character who has challenged the repressive power of the rule (which involves no risk to us, since we commit the violation only vicariously); (v) our pleasure is a mixed one because we enjoy not only the breaking of the rule but also the disgrace of an animal-like individual; (vi) at the same time we are neither concerned with the defense of the rule nor compelled toward compassion for such an inferior being. Comedy is always racist; only the others, the Barbarians, are supposed to pay.[25]

T. G. A. Nelson disputes Eco's model of the audience's response to this type of comic figure, arguing instead that such comedy more often elicits an audience's admiration for the protagonist's audaciously transgressive behavior.[26] Nelson refers to this appeal as "the magnetism of sensitive or enterprising villains," comparable to the public tolerance for and fascination with particularly artful and charismatic criminals.[27] Nelson's observation that the comic rogue's transgressions often go unpunished applies to a great many Keystones.[28]

Neither Eco's nor Nelson's model seems wholly able to account for all of Keystone's films of this period. Some follow Eco's model, encouraging the audience to delight in both the contemptible protagonists' low behavior and his eventual, brutal punishment (*Toplitsky and Company* (1913), *His Favorite Pastime* (1914), *Gussle Rivals Jonah* (1915)). Others lean more toward Nelson's model in their depiction of the comic protagonist as an endearingly nervy scoundrel who victimizes the pretentious, the arrogant and the overly serious (*Making a Living* (1914), *The Masquerader* (1914), *Fatty's Reckless Fling* (1915)). We might think of Nelson's and Eco's models less as alternatives and more as poles on a continuum of possible forms of comic representation and audience address. In either case, Keystone's protagonists were rarely genuinely likeable or sympathetically downtrodden in the fashion of Keaton, Chaplin, Lloyd and Langdon in most of their 1920s features, nor were they intended to be. Of course, as Nelson points out, the comic appeal of moral and social transgression has certain limits: "Few of us, perhaps, can resist the lure of the demonic in comedy, but we recognize that it can reach a point where it transforms itself into something that is not comical at all."[29] The wide range of responses to Keystone's films over the years indicates that the line between admirable comic roguery and reprehensible barbarity depends not only on the films themselves but on the differing sensibilities of audiences divided by class, taste, historical context and other factors.

Costume, makeup and performance style played key roles in the representation of this type of comic scoundrel. Keystone films constructed the comedian's body as stylized and grotesque through the use of dishevelled, ill-fitting costumes and bizarre facial hair, often building on the comedian's extreme body type and/or distinctive facial features. Comedians' performance styles continued to feature exaggerated mugging and broad gesturing, techniques which were declining in American dramatic films of the period (and which some critics still excoriate as "unsubtle"). Just as Keystone films derived comedy from aggressive assaults against the human body, so they constructed the comedian's body as stylized, incongruous, grotesque—in Eco's words, "animal-like." This construction of the comically grotesque body has roots in turn-of-the-century vaudeville's pervasive "rube," "tramp" and assorted racial and ethnic characterizations. Indeed, Keystone films often explicitly employed such racial, ethnic and religious stereotypes—Ford Sterling's Dutch or German persona (*A Strong Revenge*, 1913), countless Jewish and Irish characterizations (*Cohen Saves the Flag* and *The Riot*, both 1913), and the many blackface comedies which Keystone produced (*Rastus and the Gamecock*, 1913; *A Dark Lover's Play*, 1914; *Colored Villainy*, 1915).

Many later critics have criticized these racist characterizations as unfortunate lapses in good taste, or dismissed them as lighthearted jabs which offended no one, in either case just unconscious reflections of the times.[30] However, the use of ethnic, racial and religious caricatures in film comedy was widely considered to be in bad taste at the time, and became a subject for debate in the industry and in society. While the struggles over racist representations in *Birth of a Nation* have garnered much historical attention, many ethnic, racial and religious organizations also protested what they saw as demeaning characterizations in both comedies and dramas during the early 1910s.[31] *Moving Picture World* even editorialized against stereotypical depictions of nationalities in film comedy in 1913.[32] After 1913, for whatever reason, the use of racial and ethnic stereotypes as comic protagonists declined in Keystone films. The more permanent comic personae adopted by Chaplin, Swain, Conklin, Murray and others in 1914–1915 employed many of the elements of costuming, makeup and performance style associated with vaudeville rube, tramp and ethnic characterizations, but adapted and recombined them in such a way that these personas no longer bore such explicit signs of specific ethnicity. Character names such as "Hogan," "Ambrose," "Gussle" and "Mr. Droppington" replaced the ubiquitous "Cohen" and "Schnitz."

The comic types described by Kerr and the preceding passage refer mainly to male comedians and characters. However, Keystone's stock company contained several prominent female comic performers, who often participated fully in the knockabout—another aspect which differentiated the studio's style of comedy from the classic 1920s slapstick. Some female performers played vulgar scoundrels and took on grotesque appearances similar to Keystone's male comedians—for instance, Polly

Moran in *Their Social Splash, Caught in the Act* and other 1915 films which paired her with Charlie Murray as a comedy team. On the other hand, Mabel Normand—consistently the studio's most popular star apart from the 1914 Chaplin craze—developed a screen persona quite different from those of the studio's male comedians, one which generally played up her beauty against the backdrop of Keystone eccentricity. Many of Normand's films also displayed her athletic prowess, not only in the physical knockabout comedy but also in elaborate stunts similar to those seen in the contemporary "serial-queen melodramas."[33] In *Mabel's New Hero* (1913), for example, she climbs several hundred yards down a tethering rope from a hot-air balloon in which she had been imprisoned by a Desperate Desmond-type villain. Indeed, Normand's star image bore certain similarities to those of serial queens such as Pearl White—an attractive young woman in an action-oriented genre, straddling cultural conventions of gendered behavior. In the late 1910s, female participation in knockabout became increasingly less common, in part due to conflicts between the violent aggression associated with slapstick comedians and dominant cultural definitions of appropriate feminine behavior. Female roles in 1920s slapstick tend to be passive love interests who play no part in the physical comedy.

Keystone's style of comedy also often employed aggressively bad taste—sexually suggestive situations, evocations of disgusting smells and tastes, and amoral treatments of "serious" social and moral issues. In the typical prank narrative of *A Strong Revenge* (March 1913), for example, two romantic rivals (Ford Sterling and Mack Sennett as German shopkeepers) each try to undermine the other's chances of wooing Mabel Normand by secretly planting rancid-smelling cheese on the other's body before a party. Much of the film's comedy lies in the other characters' expressions of disgust at the foul smell.[34] *That Ragtime Band* (1913) features jokes about prostitution—during a vaudeville show, two successive female dance duos hold up signs announcing their acts, then turn over the signs to show the audience their addresses written on the back of the sign. In both instances, Ford Sterling, a bandleader waiting to go on next, feigns outrage to the stage manager, then quickly writes the addresses on his sleeve when the manager turns away. While the concurrent cycle of "white slave" films adopted tones of moral outrage and/or sociological detachment in exploiting such racy subject matter, the Keystone film mocked such appropriate responses and revelled in the vulgarity of the subject matter. Other Keystone films routinely dealt with drunkenness, suicide and adultery in a similarly amoral, burlesque fashion. Official censorship and regulation guides declared that comedy was granted no special license to treat such themes in a less than moralistic light. *The American Motion*

Picture Directory of 1914 to 1915, for example, stated in a section entitled "The Problem of Censoring Farces, Burlesques and Satire Which Deal with Questions of Morality":

> There are certain types of subjects which become at once objectionable if treated in any but a serious manner. Many themes are made immoral when their true importance in the relations of society is ridiculed and shown in a farcical and burlesquing light. Marital infidelity, degeneracy and sexual irregularities are notable examples. In the drama of life these themes are generally ones of tragedy, the causes or results of social forces that mankind has always struggled against, and to make of them low comedy is not only to progress in the direction of bad taste, but also to vulgarize the presentation of life itself. The [National Board of Censorship] will, therefore, act accordingly when such treatment is given these themes.[35]

Exhibitors and trade press critics complained often about vulgarity and suggestiveness in slapstick comedies during this period, but such complaints did not seem to have much effect on film content.[36] Moreover, Keystone and other slapstick companies did not receive undue attention from reformers and censorship boards, who generally targeted dramatic films more assiduously.[37] Comedy clearly did have a degree of license to exploit vulgarity and bad taste for humorous effect, and Keystone took advantage of this license.

The final essential element of Keystone's distinctive style of comedy lay in the manipulation of tempo and speed, primarily through editing. Many film historians have noted that Sennett learned his craft working under D. W. Griffith at Biograph, and that Keystone editing displays Griffith's influence. In a perceptive 1915 article entitled "Tempo—The Value of It," critic Wid Gunning grouped Griffith and Sennett together as "the two greatest living 'tempo builders' in the business today," and he identified this aspect of Keystone's films as the key to their superiority over the output of other comedy producers.

> Many people have wondered at the success of all Keystone comedies. They have failed to understand why men who have directed for the Keystone company have been unable, after leaving the Keystone forces, to put over the same successes. The answer is that the master hand of Mack Sennett was not there to officiate in the cutting room.[38]

Gunning also noted that Keystones adjusted the tempo across the course of the film for effect, building to the most rapid cutting and action toward the end of the film.

Possibly you have noticed that in almost every Keystone comedy, the action goes along smoothly with a few good laughs for about half the length of the film and then suddenly it begins to swing faster and faster, until it is moving at the rate of about a mile a minute with laugh following laugh, just the proper time being allowed each to carry from one to the other. That's "tempo."[39]

These second-half action sequences often involved crosscutting between up to four or five lines of action. Along with the fast-paced editing, the construction of these rapid-fire climactic sequences also generally featured rapid and/or violent movement in each shot, a withholding of intertitles which might interrupt the rhythm, and occasional slight undercranking. Even in sequences not involving crosscutting, Keystone films often employed quick cutting between adjacent spaces to follow knockabout action or interplay between characters.

As with the other elements of Keystone's style, the manipulation of tempo evolved gradually over this three-year period. The films of Sennett's Biograph unit and the earliest Keystones employed relatively restrained pacing (though quick by overall American industry standards), only occasionally exploiting the rhythmic possibilities of editing described by Wid Gunning. The Sennett Biographs (most of which survive in reliable versions) generally have Average Shot Lengths (ASL) of between ten and twenty seconds, with the 1912 films cut faster overall than the 1911 films.[40] The few surviving Keystones from September 1912 to February 1913 fall into this range. Most Keystones from later in 1913, however, have ASLs of between five and eight seconds, due in particular to the wild, second-half, action sequences. The ASL statistic, of course, cannot fully document shifts in editing style or their role in larger stylistic changes—partly because it cannot distinguish the different functions editing may serve, and partly because many films from this period survive only in reedited rerelease prints.[41] Nonetheless, these figures do reflect a new conception of editing in Keystone's later studio style. Whereas the Sennett Biographs and early Keystones generally employed crosscutting to give the viewer an omniscient perspective on comic narratives, the rapid editing in the later Keystones exceeded any narrative function, and created a more frantic, visceral effect. *Double Crossed* (January 1914) represents the fastest surviving Keystone to that point, with an ASL of 4.2 seconds, highlighted by a wild second-half chase which clocks in at less than three seconds per shot; several 1914 to 1915 Keystones surpassed even this speed of cutting and action.

Wid Gunning's insightful likening of Sennett to Griffith points to significant connections between their respective uses of rhythm in editing, and not simply because Sennett learned his craft as director at Biograph under Griffith's tutelage. Keystone's films included a great many chases and races to the rescue similar to those seen in many Griffith melodramas and serial melodramas in the early to mid-1910s, and, like Griffith, Keystone exploited the possibilities of rapid editing most vigorously in such sequences. Indeed, many Keystone films were takeoffs on stock melodrama plots, in some instances veritable remakes of specific Griffith Biograph films. (For example, Keystone's 1913 *At Twelve O'Clock* exactly reprises Griffith's 1908 *The Fatal Hour*, in which an ethnic villain attempts to kill a young woman by tying her up and setting a gun to shoot her when a clock strikes the hour). In his list of Sennett's failings as a maker of comedy, Walter Kerr cites the shallowness of his parodies of other genres. Keystone's use of melodrama, however, has motivations other than simply parodying those conventions. Certainly Keystone's films often employed exaggerated versions of cliched or anachronistic, melodramatic, acting styles for laughs, and the injection of knockabout into stock melodrama plots and situations served to deflate their usual emotional resonances. However, Keystone's 1913 publicity often referred to these films as "thrilling burlesque melodrama," a mixing of genre conventions designed to combine the exhilarating effects of comedy and action melodrama, both of which rely greatly on rapid physical action.[42] *Moving Picture World*, apparently paraphrasing a Keystone publicity release, described these "burlesque melodramas" thus: "The stories have a well-defined plot filled with thrilling incidents and intense moments, while a light vein of comedy running all the way through the picture provides excellent relief and much laughter."[43] Films such as *At Twelve O'Clock* and *Barney Oldfield's Race for a Life* (1913) did not so much parody melodrama and its emotional charge, as exploit its thrilling, suspenseful qualities, and use its stock situations as vehicles for knockabout comic action. Speed, action and exhilaration are fundamental qualities which Keystone slapstick shared with serials and Griffith's famed "race to the rescue" sequences. By stripping the familiar narrative situations of their usual emotional or moral weight, Keystone exploited these qualities more directly for purely visceral pleasures.

Slapstick, the Star System and Comedian Comedy

Keystone developed this style of comedy during a time of large-scale institutional changes in the American film industry, most notably the rise of the star system and the feature film. Far from stubbornly ignoring these new trends (a criticism often made of Sennett), Keystone experimented with different ways of adapting to them. In 1914, for example, Keystone produced a six-reel feature, *Tillie's Punctured Romance*, and moved to follow up its success in 1915 with both a second feature project and a new, parallel production company entitled "Sennett Features." However, this second feature project was never released (though apparently completed), and the incorporation of Keystone into Triangle as exclusive provider of comedy shorts ended any plans for a regular line of Sennett features.[44] The star system had a particularly strong impact on slapstick. Traditional histories of slapstick generally divide the subject into units on each major comedian's career. This model assumes, however, that slapstick was a highly comedian-centered genre across the course of its history, with slapstick films constructed mainly as vehicles for particular star comedians (or occasionally comedian teams, such as Laurel and Hardy). While this characterization applies readily to most 1920s slapstick, both shorts and features, Keystone (and many other early slapstick producers) initially employed a more ensemble form of comic performance. Indeed, the period from 1912 to 1915 was marked by struggles and shifts within the American film industry over the centrality of star comedians to the slapstick genre, with Keystone often diverging from or resisting majority practice.

In examining the development of the star system, Richard deCordova has distinguished between an initial period (roughly 1909 to 1914) of "picture personalities"—during which studios began to circulate actors' names, and many actors developed fan followings—and the fully developed star system characterized additionally by the circulation of extratextual discourses about the star's private life and the establishment of an integral relation between the extrafilmic star image and the fictional role.[45] During the earlier period, studios tended to promote their stock company of actors *en masse* as part of what distinguished the studio's output; the distribution alliance system, with its regular weekly release schedule, made it less necessary for the studios to promote individual films on the basis on a particular star's appearance. With the rise of features and the decline of exhibitors' exclusive dependence on one distribution alliance, however, studios increasingly designed and marketed films as vehicles for particular stars.

The changing role of star performers was particularly important in the historical development of silent film comedy. Peter Kramer has proposed a rough historical outline of American silent film comedy based upon "the changing relations between performer/star, fictional character and narrative."[46] Kramer rightly points out that Keystone's brand of slapstick "focuses on comic action rather than on the characterization of its protagonists," whereas most slapstick of the late 1910s and 1920s corresponded more to Steven Seidman's category of "comedian comedy," which was "more exclusively concerned with the character and performance of the star comedian than early slapstick, differentiating his/her status and performance from that of all the other actors, thus turning the star into the film's main attraction."[47] To better understand these shifts, we might draw a distinction between *star*—the star's name and "real life personality" as constructed and promoted by extratextual media—and *comic persona*— a recognizable screen presence based on continuities of performance style, comic business, character traits and external appearance created by costuming and makeup.[48] Comedian comedy requires not only a recognizable star but also a consistent comic persona from film to film, with the comedy designed specifically around and for this persona. Pre–1907 film comedy typically had neither stars nor comic personas.[49] French and Italian studios, from approximately 1907 onward, built series around comedians with consistent comic personas, with the titles of films usually featuring the name of the comic persona (*Rosalie et ses meubles fidèles, Onesime debute au théatre.*[50] Most American comedy production before 1912 was not organized around particular stars or comic personas. In the early 1910s, however, several American studios were moving toward a more comedian-centered format. For example, Essanay's *Alkali Ike* films followed the French format of building a series around a comic persona whose name was more well known than that of the star, while Vitagraph's Sidney Drew and John Bunny situation comedies featured recognizable stars with somewhat consistent comic personas. Thus Keystone and the new "California slapstick" appeared at a time when the role of individual comedians in film comedy—in terms of both formal construction and marketing—was in flux.

During 1912–1913, Keystone adopted the older stock company format which had characterized Sennett's Biograph unit. Rather than build comedy series around individual comedians, Keystone preferred to market its studio name as a trademark signaling a certain style and quality of comedy, touting its stock company of comedians as part of that quality. The studio did not lack stars, nor did it resist releasing their names or promoting them, as Biograph did until 1913. For example, Keystone provided exhibitors with eleven-by-fourteen-inch portraits of its top comedians (initially Sennett, Mabel Normand, Ford Sterling and Fred Mace, later Arbuckle and Chaplin) to display in their lobbies, and the titles of many films included the star's name (for instance, *Fatty Again, Mabel's Adventures*).[51] However, the films themselves generally relied on ensemble or "all-star casts," rather than focusing on a specific comedian's performance. Even films centered around a single comic protagonist always surrounded him or her with supporting players who carried much of the comedy. Moreover, even after branching out into multiple units, the studio had its star comedians appear together in as many films as possible. Though the top comedians developed their own idiosyncrasies of performance and comic business, each also played a variety of roles (sometimes starring, sometimes minor), and none immediately developed the consistent comic

An Ensemble of Stars: a 1915 *Motion Picture News* advertisement for the Keystone Film Company.

persona, including recognizable costume and makeup, typical of later slapstick.

The invention of the "Keystone Cops" may be seen as a response to the rising centrality of stars, one which allowed the studio to both exploit and resist this industry trend. The police troupe, usually numbering between four and eight, began to appear in Keystone films in early 1913, almost always during the rapid action/crosscutting sequences toward the ends of films. In one sense, the Keystone Cops served a similar function to actual, individual stars—their recurring appearances provided a unifying, exclusive, marketable quality to the studio's output. On the other hand, their acrobatic, group performance fit perfectly in the ensemble, action-centered format of Keystone's comedy, and did not focus attention on a single comedian's performance. Indeed, this device contributed to the studio's ability to promote its stock company and studio trademark over individual stars. And of course, since the actors playing the Cops were anonymous and interchangeable, they did not need to be paid as stars, and could not take their star capital to another studio.

The issue of individual star comedians versus stock companies soon came to the fore. In 1913, Universal, the main rival to Mutual as a non-MPPC distribution alliance, hired Augustus Carney (the actor who had played "Alkali Ike") away from Essanay, and established a new company for him entitled Universal Ike. In early 1914, Universal similarly raided Keystone, hiring Ford Sterling (along with Henry Lehrman, Fred Balshofer, Robert Thornsby and child star "Little Billy" Jacobs) and forming the Sterling Company to make films centered exclusively around the newly acquired star.[52] In many (though not all) of his 1913 screen roles, Sterling had developed a more consistent comic persona than the other Keystone stars, wearing an identical dark suit, top hat and circular chin beard to complement his recognizable facial expressions, gestures and character traits. This comic persona became much more rigidly defined in the Sterling Company films, even gaining a constant persona/character name, "Snookie," which would appear in many of the films' titles. Universal trumpeted its coup in a two-page trade press ad announcing the hiring of "Mr. Ford Sterling" in huge type, along with testimonials from managers of Universal-affiliated exchanges on Sterling's drawing power.[53] Universal further publicized its acquisition by running a contest for moviegoers to come up with a brand name for the new line of comedies, which resulted in the winning choice of "Sterling" being chosen. The trade press ads for the Sterling brand's initial releases showed eight photographs of Sterling's face—all in the makeup of his comic persona, and featuring familiar facial expressions from his repertoire—further emphasizing Sterling's performance as the center of the films' comedy and their main selling point.[54]

Meanwhile, Keystone responded with a series of trade press ads of its own, reaffirming the superiority of its noncomedian-centered format while hyping other Keystone stars. In the same issue of *Moving Picture World* in which Universal first trumpeted its Sterling hiring, Keystone ran an ad which did not mention Sterling but stated: "Comedies May Come and Comedies May Go, BUT Keystone Comedies Are With Us Forever." The ad went on to stress the role of Sennett, "the man who built up the wonderful organization that has made *Keystone Comedies* the most popular photoplays the world over," and also announced that Sennett "has decided to play leads in all comedies that he directs in the future, opposite to '*Keystone Mabel*' *Normand*."[55] Two weeks later, a full-page *Moving Picture World* ad for the four brands produced by the NYMPCo. (Keystone, Kay-Bee, Domino and Broncho) referred to this issue directly, though again without mentioning Sterling by name:

> A HIGHLY ADVERTISED STAR working under a poor director, with a weak scenario, dragging along a mediocre company, are methods that have never been employed by the NEW YORK MOTION PICTURE CORP. to hoodwink the exhibitor. Our strength lies in the fact that we have made it a point to get PRODUCERS whom we knew to have great executive abilities in addition to being the World's GREATEST DIRECTORS: THOS. H. INCE and MACK SENNETT, who organized and built up stock companies which did not require any of these so-called STARS to make KAY-BEE, BRONCO, KEYSTONE, DOMINO the most popular brands of film on the market today.[56]

Thus Keystone announced its intention to continue its established format and marketing strategies, relying on its distinctive style of comedy, its stock company of well-known comedians and its reputation for a certain quality, over the promotion of individual stars. Keystone ads during the spring of 1914 continued to tout Sennett's role as producer and director, as well as the "all-star casts" which appeared in the studio's films.

Nonetheless, Keystone's films and marketing practices displayed contradictory responses to this issue in 1914 and 1915. The films of 1914 generally maintained the ensemble or "all-star cast" format of the earlier period, drawing from the studio's constantly expanding stock company, and including the studio's top star comedians (Normand, Arbuckle, Sennett, Chaplin, Charley Murray, Chester Conklin, Mack Swain) in assorted combinations in as many films as possible. The studio trend toward performers directing their own films in 1914 did not immediately reverse this tendency, as even those who got the chance to direct also appeared regularly in other units' films. At the same time, several comedians began to develop more consistent and distinct comic personas, most noticeably in continuities of costume and makeup from film to film. For example, Chester Conklin began wearing his trademark baggy suit and "walrus" mustache with regularity, and Mack Swain developed his familiar "Ambrose" look. Many Chaplin scholars have traced the development of the "Little Tramp" persona and outfit to Chaplin's Keystone's films.[57] More importantly for my argument, Chaplin's case parallels that of other top studio comedians, and reflects an apparent studio-wide strategy for making these stars more individuated and recognizable from film to film.

The rapid, phenomenal popularity of Charlie Chaplin in 1914 provided a major impetus to the slapstick genre's shift toward a more comedian-centered format. By the summer of 1914, his appearance in a film drew audiences into theaters to a degree unparalleled by any previous film comedian. Exhibitors began to promote Chaplin wildly, outweighing their promotion of the name Keystone. In contrast to earlier Keystone lobby portraits which showed the star comedians out of character or in a variety of roles, the promotion of Chaplin depended precisely on the existence of a recognizable, consistent comic persona. For example, exhibitors used posters and banners depicting Chaplin in his standard costume and makeup on days when they had a Chaplin film, while others hired Chaplin imitators to walk along the street outside their theaters with flyers or sandwich boards. The Chaplin craze continued up to and beyond the star's departure from Keystone in late 1914. Keystone exploited the Chaplin mania by rereleasing his films during the summer of 1915 to compete with the newly released Essanay Chaplins.[58]

Throughout late 1914 and 1915, Keystone's films moved overall toward a more comedian-centered format. By January 1915, the studio's production system had been divided more rigidly into units built for the most part around a particular comedian or comedian team, though some films still featured ensembles of lesser-known performers without established comic personas. The establishment of consistent comic personas for the top star comedians, including standard names and appearances, became more entrenched. Indeed, Keystone announced in January 1915 that this practice had become official studio policy. *Motion Picture News* reported that:

> Keystone players are the first to be assigned definite names for all productions. Roscoe Arbuckle is to be known as Fatty, Miss Normand as Mabel, Mack Swain as Ambrose, Chester Conklin (fish face) as Mr. Droppington, and Sid (*sic*) Chaplin as Mr. Gussell (*sic*). Appropriate names are now being selected for all other players.[59]

The names of stars—"Fatty," "Mabel," and occasionally "Mack"— had appeared in Keystone titles for years. From December 1914 onward, films increasingly incorporated these persona/character names into the titles, following the practice of the French and Italian comedy series— for instance, *Ambrose's First Falsehood*, *Hogan's Annual Spree* and *Gussle the Golfer* (all from December 1914). This increasing emphasis on star comedians with consistent comic personas diminished but did not completely displace the studio's strategy of using ensemble or "all-star casts." Two, three or more top comedians still occasionally combined to appear in films together, and even the films centered on a single comedian usually featured large supporting casts of both eccentric and straight characters. Moreover, the studio continued to promote the Keystone brand name and Mack Sennett's role as producer in equal measure to its stars; a trade journal advertisement from March, 1915, demonstrates the studio hyping all three elements at once, while not allowing any one star to overshadow the studio as a whole (fig. 11).[60] Despite an increasing emphasis on star comedians and their distinctive performance styles, Keystone's 1915 films remained overall less comedian-centered, in both formal and marketing terms, than its main slapstick rivals, such as Essanay's Chaplin films or Kalem's Ham and Bud films.

New formal possibilities introduced into Keystone's films in 1914 and 1915 contributed to a more comedian-centered format, most notably the use of long takes to encompass extended, uninterrupted comedian performances within a single space. Unlike much Keystone comic action, these comedian performances in long takes tended to unfold at a slower pace and to call more attention to the idiosyncratic touches which the individual comedian(s) brought to the comic business. This use of long takes— ranging from 30 seconds to several minutes—represented a radical departure from the rapid editing and rapid action which was an integral part of Keystone's distinctive studio style.[61] However, those films which used this technique did not by and large forsake the earlier, established style of editing; rather, they generally used one or more such long takes while otherwise following the usual Keystone style. The most common strategy involved using a long take at the beginning of a film, often the first shot, to highlight a single comedian's performance, then shifting to the recognizable style of Keystone editing, which started out quick and built to a feverish pace during the climactic sequence—for instance, in *Making a Living*, *His Favorite Pastime*, *The Masquerader*, *Hogan Out West*, *A Lover's Lost Control*.[62] Elsewhere, occasional long takes were interspersed into the middle of an otherwise rapidly paced film. *His Talented Wife* (November 1914), for example, contains a ninety-second shot in which Sennett (otherwise a minor figure in the film) clowns around in the theater lobby and tries to cadge a ticket; in contrast, the chase which closes the film comprises forty-two shots over approximately 150 seconds.[63] Long takes are not, of course, essential to comedian comedy, nor do long takes necessarily function in this way. However, by concentrating the audience's attention on an extended routine featuring a single performer (occasionally a pair of performers), Keystone's use of long takes during this period helped to establish both the distinctive personality and the structural centrality of the star's comic persona necessary to more comedian-centered forms.[64]

By 1915, Keystone's studio style allowed a wide range of possibilities regarding the long take/comedian performance style and the rapid action/rapid editing style, with different units adapting particular stylistic choices to the performance styles of particular comedians or comedian pairs. Many films employed a small number of extended comedian performances within long takes, usually toward the beginning of the film, before building to a lengthy sequence of rapid action to close the film. Other films employed one or the other approach more consistently. David Robinson has rightly identified *His Musical Career* (November 1914), directed by and starring Charles Chaplin, as a bold experiment in using the long take/comedian performance style across the course of a whole film. This film consists almost entirely of long takes in which the comic action—much centered around extended Chaplin routines—gradually unfolds within the space of the frame, until a brief, final spasm of rapid action and editing as Chaplin and Swain chase a piano down a hill and off a pier.[65] Some units, especially those producing the Charley Murray "Hogan" films and the Syd Chaplin "Gussle" films, employed long takes more extensively in 1915. *Hogan's Aristocratic Dream* (February 1915) represents, along with *His Musical Career*, the studio's most radical exploration of this long take/comedian performance style, with only ninety-nine shots spread over two reels, for an ASL of almost nineteen seconds.[66] Moreover, much of the cutting in the film simply shifts back and forth between adjacent spaces in which Charley Murray and Bobby Dunn run through simultaneous, extended, solo comedian performances. On the other extreme, Ford Sterling's films as performer and director after his 1915 return to Keystone exploit the rapid editing/rapid action style most vehemently. His *Dirty Work in a Laundry* (July 1915) is a whirlwind of violent action and nonstop crosscutting, with 504 shots spread over two reels, for an ASL of 3.6 seconds.

In his chapter on Sennett in *The Silent Clowns*, Walter Kerr cites Sennett's apparent willingness to let his premier comedians leave the studio after they had achieved a degree of stardom as one of the major failings of his comic vision, the decision to allow Chaplin to leave Keystone at the end of his one-year contract being the primary example. Kerr and others attribute this tendency to Sennett's stubbornness, foolish penny-pinching, and a lack of appreciation for the fundamental role that a central, charismatic comedian played in good slapstick.[67] This concentration on one man's personality and limited vision slights the historical context in which these decisions were made. During the early to mid-1910s, the centrality of star comedians to the genre was a point of contention in the American film industry, with different companies adopting different strategies of exploiting stars. Sennett and Keystone's often contradictory strategies for dealing with stars must be seen as attempts to perceive and adapt to industry trends, while maintaining their dominant position in slapstick production. Having achieved enormous popularity and prestige within the industry, Keystone resisted the full-scale turn to comedian comedy which characterized the films of some rival studios, while assimilating some aspects into its studio style. Out of this transitional period, highly comedian-centered slapstick emerged as the genre's norm in the late 1910s and 1920s.

Within the history of silent film comedy, Keystone slapstick should be considered not as a primitive forerunner to the Chaplin, Keaton, Lloyd and Langdon classics, but as a distinct formal system with its own comedy and filmmaking conventions. Comparisons between Keystone slapstick and later forms of the genre can be fruitful, but only if historians resist the temptation to interpret the differences as signs of the genre's "maturation" or "progress." Many, perhaps most, modern viewers exposed to the 1912–1915 Keystone films will find themselves identifying with Walter Kerr's disappointment in finding them not particular funny. With a few exceptions, Chaplin's 1916–1917 Mutual films are the earliest film slapstick comedies which consistently appeal to modern audiences. The willingness to laugh and the curiosity to understand why one has laughed are probably necessary qualities for anyone researching film comedy. However, puzzlement and displeasure at unfamiliar, unappealing films may also provide an impetus to the film historian, forcing him or her to investigate the historical conditions under which these films were originally made and seen. (This principle has served early cinema researchers well over the last fifteen years.) The nostalgic aura surrounding silent film slapstick comedy has obscured the study of early California slapstick, and has contributed to the dismissal of these films as "primitive." A nonteleological, less masterpiece-centered, more industrially contextualized approach to slapstick will allow a fresher understanding of these films—and, I would argue, of the classic 1920s slapstick as well.

10

The Making of a Comic Star: Buster Keaton and *The Saphead*

Peter Kramer

In 1920, after three years of supporting roles in Roscoe Arbuckle's short films, Buster Keaton appeared in *The Saphead*.[1] The film is distinguished by the comedian's first feature film appearance and by his last ever smile on screen. When Bertie, the saphead of the title, is confronted by his sister Rose with a newspaper article about his presence at a gambling club raided by the police the night before, a proud smile appears on his face. Bertie is happy about the bad reputation he is acquiring, because an advice book tells him that a colorful lifestyle is the best way to impress the "Modern Girl." Anyone familiar with Keaton's work in the 1920s will appreciate the outstanding quality of Bertie's smile. Throughout the decade, and indeed during his later career, Keaton, on screen and off, was known as "The Great Stone Face."[2] What is the significance, then, of Keaton's smile in *The Saphead*? What does it reveal about Keaton's changing performance strategies, or about the historical moment at which Keaton made the transition from slapstick shorts to feature-length comic dramas and from supporting roles to starring roles? And what, finally, does the neglect of this smile and this film within the voluminous Keaton literature tell us about the workings of film criticism?[3]

From "Somebody Else's Film" to "A Star in His Own Right": Keaton Criticism and *The Saphead*

Most critics would probably agree with Gilberto Perez, who excludes *The Saphead* from consideration in his study of Keaton's comedy because it is "somebody else's film in which Keaton was merely an actor."[4] Whereas Keaton (co)directed his short films at the Comique studio from 1920 onwards, as well as his classic features, *The Saphead* was directed by Herbert Blache for Metro. As in most auteurist studies, directorial control, not the continuity of Keaton's performances, is the basic selection criterion for constituting the corpus under investigation.[5]

If *The Saphead* is discussed at all, it is subject to a negative critical evaluation. Since it is not a "proper" Keaton film, it is defined by what it lacks rather than what it possesses. *The Saphead*, Donald McCaffrey argues, "showed very little of the skill that was to make him an object of critical acclaim."[6] Walter Kerr notes that Keaton's role "was not at all tailored to his talents." Instead of structuring the film around his thematic concerns and performance skills, Keaton was merely "doing what the narrative required of him, modestly appropriating any opportunity to inflect a situation *his* way."[7] These inflections involve the insertion of "comic tumbling" and "eloquent knockabout" into the narrative.[8] In Kevin Brownlow's opinion, "many of the gags were his and the final riot in the stock exchange was a typical Keaton sequence."[9] The typicality of a sequence for Keaton's work can only be established retrospectively, after the critic has seen the films Keaton directed himself in the 1920s. The typical features of this corpus are then projected onto "minor" works, those before or after his classical period or those made in a particularly restrictive production context, so as to establish how much of the director's thematic vision and stylistic signature is already, or still, realized in them. The presence of typical features may be ascribed to the creative influence of the director, their absence to outside interference.[10]

In Keaton's case, the core corpus comprises the independently produced nineteen short films and ten features Keaton directed (with the assistance of various codirectors) and starred in between 1920 and 1928. Closely associated are his first two films as a contract actor for MGM (*The Cameraman*, 1928, and *Spite Marriage*, 1929—also his last two silent films). In their standard reference work on Keaton, George Wead and George Lellis foreground the problematic status of these films, yet include them in the annotated filmography, because, as an established star and experienced director, Keaton was able to shape the film's production; they "are still considered his films, though they were officially directed by Edward M. Sedgwick."[11] The filmography begins with *One Week* (1920) and excludes *The Saphead*, assuming that Keaton's impact as a relative newcomer was minimal. In fact, the most sustained analyses of Keaton's work also marginalize or ignore the short films he directed after his initial training in vaudeville and Arbuckle's films, because they are basically perceived as the second stage of his apprenticeship, or, rather, his journeyman years.[12]

The Saphead is given more space in biographical studies. In reconstructing Keaton's life and work as a whole, these studies complement critical evaluations with an account of important career moves and their determinants and consequences.[13] David Robinson argues that *The Saphead* was "probably crucial to his career," establishing him as "a star in his own right," and forcing him to realistically impersonate a highly individualized character rather than using caricatured stock figures as a launching pad for dazzling comic displays. This demand "encouraged" a shift from comic performance to dramatic characterization.[14] The part of Bertie, a "languid, spoiled, and wealthy character" was the "prototype" for Keaton's subsequent impersonations of spoiled rich young men in *The Navigator* and *Battling Butler*. Bertie's ability to overcome his limitations and "undergo a total transformation of character" became characteristic of all of Keaton's feature film protagonists.[15] Most biographical writers also note that the restraint of Keaton's acting in *The Saphead* focused attention on a key aspect of his earlier stage and screen performances, the "frozen face" which would ultimately become his trademark.[16]

Despite its obvious importance, Keaton's appearance in *The Saphead* is often reduced to a minor episode in a biographical narrative dominated by the production of Keaton's masterpieces. These accounts are remarkable for their reliance on anecdotal incidents occuring at crucial turning points in Keaton's career, and thus for their dependence on chance or fate. In 1917, an encounter on the streets of New York with an old vaudeville acquaintance introduced Keaton to film production, and despite his lucrative and prestigious contract for a Broadway revue, Keaton spontaneously decided on a career in the movies. In 1920, when casting for *The Saphead* ran into problems because the original costar of the 1913 stage production, Douglas Fairbanks, was not available, Fairbanks suggested Keaton, offering him the big break he needed after his cinematic apprenticeship in Arbuckle's films. Keaton's biographers are satisfied with such anecdotes, and reluctant to explore the historical determinants shaping Keaton's career. For them, the overall direction of his career is not in question; it is a foregone conclusion that Keaton will become a star comedian and great film director in the 1920s, because his success during this decade is, after all, the main justification for writing about him in the first place. Keaton's fundamental artistic vision is seen to be rooted in his unique personality, which is fixed at an early age. Change takes place only in terms of how he realizes this vision, with Keaton gradually gaining access to, and taking control of, various artistic means of expression.

Against these traditional auteurist approaches, I will investigate the historical determinants for Keaton's work. The choices made by him and his producer Joseph Schenck will be considered in relation to the cultural and economic framework in which they worked. Here, Keaton figures first and foremost as a performer, not a film director. *The Saphead* may be seen as the intersection of the careers of two stars, that of Buster Keaton, vaudeville veteran and rising screen clown, and that of William H. Crane, a theatrical legend returning from retirement to costar in the film version of his greatest stage hit. The film's fusion of two performance traditions (slapstick and legitimate acting) was the cornerstone of a complex marketing strategy employed by Joseph M. Schenck, an independent producer who, in cooperation with most of the major studios, specialized in the promotion of stars. The production and release of *The Saphead* served to highlight Keaton's transfer from the ranks of supporting players in Roscoe Arbuckle's short films to the position of a star, complete with directorial control (over a series of independently produced two-reel comedies), extensive publicity about his professional and private life, and a trademark (the famous stone-face). This prestige production temporarily moved him to the top of movie theater bills (whereas short films usually served as support acts), and thus established him as a comedian of substance and quality, who aspired to, and was able to deliver, more than routine slapstick entertainment. Keaton contributed an innovative characterization of a familiar stage part, making near-perfect facial restraint the key feature of his performance. His stone-face served both as the most visible marker of quality performance (restraint signifying refinement), and as a highly distinctive comic mask. Keaton's final smile in *The Saphead* indicates the gradual nature of the changes in his performance style, as well as the problematic status of the extreme deadpan style he used from this film onwards. Keaton's smile in *The Saphead* is the last occasion on which Keaton sacrificed the purity of his evolving comic mask to the demands of psychological realism; in the following decade, his refusal to comply with one of the basic tenets of classical Hollywood cinema had a negative influence on the contemporary reception of his star persona on and off screen.

Promoting Keaton: Joseph M. Schenck, *The Saphead* and Notions of Creative Control

Keaton's performances arose within precise institutional contexts, providing him with the necessary means of production as well as with channels of distribution and exhibition for his work; these institutions also shaped his work through their norms and rules and the specific demands made on him by producers, scriptwriters and directors. Keaton's appearance in *The Saphead* exemplifies the limited control he had over his work. Yet, despite the fact that he worked with a given script under someone else's direction at a major studio, Keaton was given space and considerable freedom to develop and highlight his performance skills, because the film was designed specifically as a showcase for his talents. At Comique, on the other hand, where Keaton started work on a series of two-reelers in 1920, he took over the position that Roscoe Arbuckle, a major star and also a co-owner of Comique, had vacated. With this position came considerable control over the production process, and Keaton was able to shape scriptwriting and directing. However, contractually power still rested with Keaton's producer, Joseph Schenck. As a promoter of stars, Schenck signed personal contracts with major stage and film talent, launched publicity campaigns raising their public profiles, and sought various ways of exploiting their appeal through production activities and leasing arrangements. Analyzing Schenck's role puts the chance encounters and big breaks apparently so crucial for Keaton's career into a more systemic framework, which sees performers as valuable properties carefully handled by an interconnected group of entrepreneurs operating in a variety of media.

Keaton entered the film industry in 1917, after a long and distinguished career in vaudeville as a member of the famous family act, The Three Keatons. The act had highlighted acrobatically executed violent exchanges between father and son. Due to his father's alcoholism and irascibility, which hampered both his ability to perform the physically demanding stage routine and to secure lucrative bookings, Keaton decided to go solo early in 1917. Through his agent, Max Hart, who specialized in the transfer of vaudeville performers to Broadway productions, he got a lucrative contract for that year's edition of the Shubert brothers' annual revue.[17] However, *The Passing Show of 1917* opened on April 26, 1917, without Keaton, who by then had joined the Comique studio in New York, a joint operation of vaudeville and film entrepreneur Joseph M. Schenck and former Keystone star Roscoe Arbuckle.[18] With a significantly reduced salary (down from 250 dollars to forty dollars per week), Keaton started work at the studio during the production of Comique's first film, *The Butcher Boy* (which was released on April 23, 1917).[19]

Keaton decided to take a salary cut and join Comique because physical comedy had become marginal in musical revue, while the half-a-million to a million-dollar contracts Arbuckle and Chaplin had signed in 1916 suggested enormous career opportunities for slapstick comedians in the cinema.[20] Comique was the ideal springboard for his film career. In various newspaper interviews published in September 1916, Arbuckle announced that he had formed his own company initially to produce a series of two-reel comedies which he would direct and star in. Yet the company would also "produce serious plays," and promising comedians who joined the outfit would in time be given separate production units to make their own starring vehicles. Eventually Arbuckle would withdraw from acting in comedy shorts altogether, and continue his performance career in five-reel dramas.[21] Arbuckle's plans exemplify the major stars' strivings to gain creative and economic control over their output and to raise their artistic profile with the public and with critics. Slapstick comedians (such as Mabel Normand and Arbuckle) hoped to improve the low regard accorded comedy by refining their comedy shorts, and eventually by leaving them behind altogether for the more prestigious and more lucrative field of feature production.[22]

On March 10, 1920, Famous-Players formally agreed to produce and release a series of feature films starring Arbuckle (for a period of up to seven years), paying Comique 194,000 dollars during the first year of the contract for the company's consent to this production deal, and 219,000 dollars for each of the following two years. Arbuckle continued to be under contract with Comique, and in effect was leased to Famous-Players, which paid both the studio and Arbuckle for the right to star him in features.[23] With Arbuckle making features at the biggest of the major studios, his costar Keaton was able to take over the Comique production unit and star in his own series of two-reelers.

Keaton's promotion to stardom in 1920 was part of a long-term strategy which reached back to the very beginnings of his film career. Rather than joining Comique after a chance encounter on the streets of New York, Keaton was probably carefully selected for his place at the studio and the possibility of future film stardom. Comique was only one branch of Schenck's varied enterprises, which included, amongst many others, the production of features starring his wife, Norma Talmadge, and her sister, Constance, and amusement parks in the New York City area.[24] His main activity in 1916 was with Loew's Theatrical Enterprises, a huge circuit of small-time vaudeville theaters, presenting a mixed bill of films and live acts. Schenck acted as Loew's's general manager in charge of booking. (He gradually withdrew from this post in the late 1910s, when his film deals became more central to his business.) Nicholas Schenck was one of the chief executives of Loew's, and the two brothers seem to have owned shares in Marcus Loew's business empire, while the Loew family, in turn, held stock in Joseph Schenck's many companies, including Comique.[25]

In his capacity as booking manager, Joseph Schenck maintained an ongoing correspondence with the Shubert brothers, concerning the exchange of performers that he and the Shuberts, the leading theatrical producers of their time, had under contract.[26] Schenck would frequently place his contract players in musical revues, and the Shuberts would in turn place their stars in vaudeville. For these transactions, they usually gained a share in the performers' salaries. Many of the Shuberts' contract players were, like Keaton, clients of Max Hart, who had also temporarily been Arbuckle's agent in 1916, before Arbuckle had set up a business with Schenck.[27] By early 1917, therefore, Schenck had a well-established business relationship with Keaton's employers and, more indirectly, with his agent. Furthermore, he must have had dealings with Keaton himself, because, in 1916, The Three Keatons had toured the Loew's circuit, for which Schenck did the bookings.[28] Under these circumstances, Keaton's transfer from the Shuberts to Comique was probably the result of a direct enquiry by Schenck to the Shuberts, asking for one of their contract players with whom he was already familiar and saw as a potential co-star in his new production outfit for Arbuckle. The career decisions of performers like Keaton were monitored by, and dependent on, entertainment entrepreneurs and managers. Dealing with the exchange of performers and the marketing of performances, they had established a communication network that transcended the boundaries between different entertainment institutions (vaudeville, legitimate theater, cinema). Keaton's move, first from vaudeville to Broadway, and then to a New York-based film production company, traversed the current career opportunities for performers opened up by the increasing integration of entertainment industries.[29]

After joining Comique in March of 1917, Keaton appeared in fifteen of the twenty-one Arbuckle two-reelers.[30] Due to his military service, which brought him to France during the last months of World War I, Keaton missed several productions between the autumn of 1918 and April 1919. Afterwards, only three more Arbuckle/Keaton films were produced. The last, *The Garage*, was released in January 1920. On December 23rd, 1919, the day after production had started on Arbuckle's first feature at the Famous-Players studio, Keaton signed a new agreement with Comique.[31] Since this contract is not available, we have to rely on a 1924 contract between Keaton and Comique, which by now had been reorganized as Buster Keaton Productions, Inc., to indicate the terms under which Keaton was employed during this period.[32] He offered his "exclusive services" to the studio, and agreed to "promptly and faithfully comply with the reasonable directions, requests, rules and regulations made by the producer." His involvement in other aspects of production appeared as an obligation rather than as a right: Keaton agreed to "render such other services in connection with directing, cutting, titling and editing of said pictures as may be requested by the producer." The contract allowed for a certain level of creative control by Keaton, if the producer chose to grant it, yet it clearly assigned ultimate control to the studio. The 1924 contract stipulated that the studio also had "the sole and exclusive right to make use of his name for advertising, commercial and publicity purposes." The studio was entitled to design (or let a distribution company design) advertising and publicity campaigns without consulting Keaton, and, in general, to control the dissemination of any information about or pictures of Keaton. Thus, even as the head of his own production unit, Keaton remained completely dependent on Joseph Schenck's goodwill and sustained effort to raise Keaton's profile through advertising, publicity and contracts with major distributors.

Keaton owed his promotion to his succesful contributions to the Arbuckle films, but also, possibly, to the fact that he was dating Schenck's sister-in-law, Natalie Talmadge (which would be in line with Schenck's general tendency to mix personal and business matters). However, at this point, Keaton was mostly seen in the trade press, fan magazines and newspaper reviews as an adjunct to Roscoe Arbuckle, rather than a performer and personality in his own right.[33] Keaton's performance showed more restraint than that of his fellow comedians, and in particular contrasted sharply with that of his main rival at Comique, Arbuckle's brother-in-law, Al St. John, who was known for his facial agility. Keaton, however, did engage in a fair amount of mugging (exaggerated smiling, laughing and crying directed at the camera). Both in terms of his public recognition and his acting style, Keaton in 1919 was far removed from the status and the distinctive identity he aquired in 1920.

Schenck bought Chaplin's former Lone Star studio in Los Angeles for the Keaton team, which included several people taken over from the Arbuckle group. The studio ran into problems soon after its opening in January 1920. During the first four months, only one two-reeler, *The High Sign*, was made at Comique (whereas Arbuckle had taken about six weeks for each of his shorts). When finally completed, the film was shelved because it did not satisfy Keaton's expectations for his first star vehicle, on which much of the success of the Keaton two-reelers depended.[34]

The opportunity to appear in a full-length comedy arose in this context. Metro intended to make a film version of the stage hit, *The New Henrietta* (a successful 1913 revival of Bronson Howard's classic, *The Henrietta*), bringing in playwright and stage director Winchell Smith, and producer John Golden, the men responsible for the revival. The film was to bring together the two stars of the 1913 production, William H. Crane and Douglas Fairbanks. Fairbanks's first film, *The Lamb* (1915), had been loosely based around the character of Bertie Van Alstyne, and was followed by a string of successes which, by 1920, had made Fairbanks one of the top film stars.[35] With Fairbanks tied up at United Artists, the studio he helped to found, a substitute was needed.

Rather than Keaton being cast in *The Saphead* exclusively on the basis of Fairbanks's suggestion, as other accounts have suggested, Keaton was chosen because of close links between Schenck and Metro. In January,

1920, Metro had been taken over by Loews.[36] While the film went into production in the spring of 1920, Metro was negotiating with Comique about the distribution of Keaton's two-reelers. The film, being based on a stage hit, and costarring a Broadway legend, was going to be a prestige production with considerable popular appeal. Casting Keaton gave Schenck the perfect vehicle to launch his latest star and Metro the opportunity to advertise their new comedy series. The Comique studio, where Keaton's shorts were produced, was aligned with the Loews-Metro combine through familial and long-standing business relationships. Joseph Schenck, however, ran the company as a largely independent unit, free from interference by outside interests. *The Saphead*, on the other hand, was produced by one of the major vertically integrated corporations (combining a theatre chain with a distribution network and a studio) which came to dominate the film industry around 1920. The film's production thus brought together two different sectors of the industry (majors and independents) as well as two different comic traditions (slapstick and legitimate Broadway comedy). Clearly, in this case at least, independents and majors, rather than being locked into a confrontational relationship, coordinated their actions for their mutual benefit. Indeed, Keaton's solo film career derived precisely from such collaborative efforts. Schenck promoted him to starring roles (and directorial control) when a vacancy arose at Comique, due to Arbuckle's lease to the major company and feature specialist Famous-Players/Paramount. The success of the Keaton vehicles depended largely on their being picked up for distribution by Metro, and on the added publicity and prestige that Keaton derived from costarring in a Metro feature production.

Metro had assigned its chief scenarist, June Mathis, the task of adapting the play for the screen.[37] The first two scripts, still using the stage title *The Henrietta*, had been written before Keaton joined the production team in April.[38] Keaton's presence led to fundamental changes in the script. These changes resulted in a shift in emphasis away from the stage original and Crane, and towards Keaton and his distinctive interpretation of the role of Bertie Van Alstyne, signaled by the film's new title, *The Saphead*.

On the same day (June 1, 1920) that Comique contracted with Metro for the distribution of eight Keaton two-reelers, the distributor issued a press release to film magazines and daily newspapers across the country, focusing attention on their new star attraction and his simultaneous launch in full-length comic drama and slapstick two-reelers.[39] As the first sustained publicity effort for Keaton as an independent comic star, the Metro publicity sheet explicitly placed Keaton at the intersection of two performance traditions. His "chief claim to fame hitherto has been his ability to hurl custard pies and perform pat (*sic*) falls" in Roscoe Arbuckle's comedies and, before that, on the vaudeville stage. His twenty years of experience in physical comedy would now be complemented by the "high comedy characterization" of Bertie "the lamb" in *The Saphead*, "being co-starred with William H. Crane at the head of a noteworthy cast." His appearance in the film version of a Broadway comedy was not a final departure from low comedy, but a temporary separation, after which he would return to the kind of comedy he was known for, with "a series of laughing two-reelers" for Metro. After his promotion from the ranks of supporting players, Keaton would combine the comic spectacle of stage and screen slapstick with the rounded characterization of legitimate comedy. Metro's Keaton would be a respectable slapstick comedian associated with the comedy tradition of Broadway, an actor as well as a clown. Keaton's own brand of two-reel slapstick comedy would draw, it was implied, on this tradition of quality, by injecting seriousness and depth into his acrobatics, and, most importantly, by leaving room for "moments of stabilizing gravity."

The Meaning of Restraint: Slapstick, Legitimate Acting and the Production of *The Saphead*

The stars dominating what James Agee has called "comedy's greatest era" did not operate in a cultural vacuum.[40] Although their unique art is seen to possess timeless and universal appeal, they were deeply rooted, and actively participated, in a rich and well-established performance tradition: slapstick. However, today this term tends to be reserved for early manifestations of screen comedy, most importantly Mack Sennett's Keystone comedies of the 1910s. The work, especially in the 1920s, of the great comedians such as Chaplin, Keaton and Harold Lloyd is characterized by qualities which set it apart from "plain slapstick": subtlety, poetry, beauty, grace, sentiment, restraint, a carefully worked-out gag and plot structure as well as a rounded characterization. Some of these qualities are indeed extraneous to the tradition of physical comedy which dominated the American variety stage until the end of the nineteenth century, and informed the majority of comic short films. Instead, narrativization, rounded characterization and refinement are associated with a second, "legitimate" performance tradition which dominated stage drama as well as feature films. The two traditions were not strictly separate, but often intersected, when, for example, comic performers moved from vaudeville to the cinema, or from short films to features. *The Saphead* marks one such intersection, exemplifying the negotiation of conflicting traditions and contradictory sets of demands in the work of the great comedians of the silent period.

Originally referring to two flat pieces of wood joined together at one end, used to produce a loud slapping noise creating the impression of someone having been dealt a hard blow on stage, the term "slapstick" came to cover various forms of violent comedy. To transform acts of willful maliciousness and intense pain into comedy, performers had to signal clearly that their actions were mere make-believe, and constituted highly accomplished athletic routines. The actions' excess, their fantastic exaggeration, as well as performers' self-conscious address of the audience, were the most obvious indicators of their professional and ritualistic nature.[41]

Keaton had gained recognition for his ability to take spectacular falls and engage in acrobatic fights, first with his father on the vaudeville stage, then with Arbuckle and Al St. John in their Comique shorts.[42] However, Keaton's performance skills were much more wide-ranging. On the variety stage, he had performed monologues, parodies, impersonations and songs; the melodramas he appeared in as a child, and also Arbuckle's two-reelers, had demanded a fair amount of straight acting. Unlike slapstick, such acting was not supposed to draw attention to its physicality and athletic accomplishment. Instead, it sought to transparently project a fictional character, evoking an interior, psychological realm of desires and ambitions, as well as external character conflicts. Without acknowledging the audience, the reality of the performer's body was subsumed into a fictional character. To achieve this aim, the overall trend both in the legitimate theater and, since about 1909, in dramatic films had been to deemphasize the performer's actual physical presence and activity; the actors restrained their movements so as to focus attention on subtle gestures and facial expressions that derived significance from their complex narrative context. Classical devices such as intertitles, close-ups and eyeline matches, for example, were used to convey mental processes and establish social relations. Thus they replaced, to some extent, the performer's actual physical activity. In particular, immobile faces shown in close shots served as blank screens onto which thoughts and emotions could be projected.[43] In addition to concern about looks at the camera which destroyed the illusion of a self-contained fictional world, a key issue in discourses about screen acting throughout the teens and early twenties was the need for actors, especially those coming from the stage, to restrain their performance.[44]

Typically working in short film production where the rules and norms of dramatic features did not apply, slapstick comedians systematically transgressed both of the above stipulations. They frequently and self-consciously directed their performance to the camera, and they constantly drew attention to their bodies through acrobatic stunts, contorted faces and overanimated gestures. This performance style aimed for an immediate impact on the audience, either laughter or breathless amazement. Yet their films usually also included quieter sections, where the dramatic situation was established or audience sympathy was evoked. Thus slap-stick comedies shifted back and forth between delayed gratification and immediate emotional release, restrained and excessive physical activity, one seen as the norm, the other as its amusing and/or astonishing trans-gression.

When Keaton made *The Saphead*, the balance between these two perfor-mance modalities shifted in favour of legitimate acting. The film's stage origin, its complex narrative, the presence of William H. Crane and, most importantly, the promotional campaign's objectives encouraged him to make restraint the centerpiece of his impersonation of Bertie Van Alstyne. Interestingly, against the explicit prescription of the script, Kea-ton decided to take the notion of restraint beyond the level of illusionistic acting, until his avoidance of facial expressions drew attention to itself as the clearest and most striking mark of his physical presence as a performer. Keaton's performance stood out both in those scenes where he engaged in traditional slapstick tumbling, that is an excess of activity, and in those where he acted straight, that is with an excess of restraint. In both cases, William H. Crane, who represented the traditions and highest achievements of legitimate acting in stage comedies, served Kea-ton as a perfect foil.

After twenty-four years of stage experience as a comedian on the legitimate stage, forty-two-year-old William H. Crane had found the role that he would be associated with for the rest of his life: Nicholas Van Alstyne, "the lion of Wall Street," in Bronson Howard's *The Henrietta*. Opening at the Union Square Theater in New York in 1887, the play had been such a success that even twenty-five years later it was considered a property valuable enough for a major revival. Winchell Smith and Victor Mapes's updated version, *The New Henrietta,* costarred Crane with Douglas Fairbanks, at the time one of the leading young comedians on Broadway. During the 1913 to 1914 season, the play enjoyed a long run at the Knickerbocker Theater in New York, and in the following year it went on the road.[45] In December 1915, Crane announced his retirement from the stage after the end of the *New Henrietta* tour, which was still going strong. In the future, he would "act only on special occasions."[46] A few months later, the *New York Sun* reported that Crane, "stage dean," had been honored at a special dinner, attended by "stars of all professions," and recognized by a note from president Woodrow Wilson.[47] Critics emphasized his exalted position in the theatrical profession, while noting the refinement of his comedy: He was "one comedian who did his training in the library in place of in the gymnasium." Both as an actor and a producer, he was said to have been involved only in plays that were "sane, and, to his eternal credit, sanitary."[48]

Crane represented a tradition of quality that was explicitly set against the verbally and physically aggressive comedy of musical comedy and vaudeville. However, when Crane came out of retirement in the 1917 to 1918 season, he appeared in a vaudeville playlet which brought him closer to lowbrow comic traditions.[49] Apart from his limited role, the sheer presence of the legendary star was expected to appeal to audiences. This thought must have also occured to Winchell Smith and John Golden, who, in 1920, wanted the seventy-five-year old Crane for their film adaptation of *The New Henrietta*. Crane had already appeared in a film version of his stage hit, *David Harum*, in 1915, but he was not prepared for the radical turn this particular adaptation would take.[50] "And they made Berty, the Lamb, a slapstick character," he complained in a newspaper interview in 1925: "Mr. Keaton was never suited for the role and the result was terrible."[51]

We can trace the gradual transformation of the stage play into a show-case for Keaton's performance by comparing the finished film with the material contained in the University of Southern California script file for *The Saphead*. The original play highlighted Nicholas Van Alstyne's romance with one Mrs. Opdyke. This romance, which spans most of the play, is a counterpart to Bertie's relationship with Nick's ward, Agnes. The play places Nick at the centre of his own love story and carefully intertwines the romances of father and son, as well as the themes of love and business. The first film script, dated March 1920, retains the play's dual focus.[52] Nick's romance foregrounds his subjectivity, his desire for love and companionship. Given the pressures of his work on Wall Street, Nick is unable to properly guide his children. His daughter, Rose, has married a crook, whom Nick mistakenly grants his power of attorney; his interference with the romance of his son and his ward delays their happiness. Yet Mrs. Opdyke, whose insight into people's characters and emotions enables her to tell right from wrong, helps him recognize and rectify his mistakes. His business is saved and the family unit reconstituted. In the classic theatrical tradition of New Comedy, the play ends with the reconciliation of father and son, and with two weddings.[53]

The narrative was reorganized once Keaton became involved, to foreground his part. Contrary to what one might expect, this was not done by adding slapstick material. The spectacular scenes of Bertie being violently initiated into the stock exchange fraternity by having his hat knocked off and being pushed around, and his subsequent acrobatically executed purchase of shares, which may seem "typically Keaton," are extensively described in the script. They were possibly derived from Douglas Fairbanks's acrobatic performance in the 1913 revival.[54] Other-wise, Keaton's physical stunts are limited to two brief and isolated in-stances of comic tumbling, in which Bertie's confrontation with his angry father causes him to slide down the stairs on his backside, and to jump off a windowsill. The transformation of the script into a Keaton vehicle was mainly achieved through drastic cuts in Crane's part, which subordinated Nick's previously dominant story line to that of his son. With the removal of Mrs. Opdyke from the film, Nick's activities lost their driving force and overarching goal, his story line now lacking cohesion, and disintegrating into a series of largely disconnected scenes. Nick became a mere blocking figure. In the light of Crane's old age and his perceived status as a bulwark against vulgar comedy, one could see the generational conflict between the two main characters as enacting a cultural conflict between the two performers playing them. The film's shift of narrative focus from father to son thus mirrored and facilitated the transfer of comic stardom from a master of the old school to the representative of a new generation. On both levels, the improved status of the younger man was finally validated by the handshake of his elder.

The centrality of Bertie's (and thus Keaton's) shortcomings, ambitions, misfortunes and final triumph is already signaled by the film's title. The original title introduced and foregrounded the narrative complexities associated with the name Henrietta and its multiple referents in the story.[55] *The Saphead*, however, makes Bertie the focus of attention, and in introducing his comic stupidity, it poses a problem for the narrative to resolve. Calling Bertie a saphead builds expectations that he will overcome his shortcomings. Plot complications constitute an obstacle course which will allow, and indeed force, the ignorant, passive fool to encounter the world at large and act in it. In the process, Bertie gains, if not knowledge and insight, then at least tangible success and an improved social standing. In the end, Bertie's new status is confirmed by his grateful father, and symbolized most effectively by the marriage to Agnes and the fathering of twins.

Bertie is first introduced by an intertitle as "his father's hope and pride," which, right from the start, signals the social pressures eventually forcing him to transcend his comfortably passive existence. Agnes is first mentioned as "the girl Bertie loved. He had confided this to his sister and his valet—but had never mentioned it to her." Bertie's failure to communicate his love reflects his painful awareness that he lacks those qualities that define contemporary manhood. An advice book on courtship, *How To Win The Modern Girl*, tells him, "The Modern Girl has no use for the old-fashioned man. She prefers sports to saints. Few girls now-a-days can resist a dashing, gambling, drinking devil." While the opposition is couched in moral terms (saint versus devil), what separates Bertie from the ideal of masculinity is decisive action. Accepting this ideal, Bertie starts playing the role of the good sport, forever in pursuit of a bad reputation, which leads him into the world of nightclubs and gambling dens obviously completely alien to him. He wins at roulette, yet never

Bertie Van Alstyne's Restraint . . .

and Physicality: Buster Keaton in *The Saphead* (1920).

even understands that he is playing for money. Initially, his role-playing backfires. Agnes cries when she first learns of his nightclubbing, clearly preferring the idiotic saint to the dashing devil. Only after Bertie has unknowingly revealed his love does Agnes fully understand his behavior. Yet he fails to explain himself to his father, who so strongly objects to his supposedly hedonistic life-style that he will not allow him to marry Agnes before he has proven his manhood in the world of business. Work, rather than leisure, is now defined as the sphere for manly activity. This second call for action is again met with mechanical obedience. Without any real interest or knowledge, Bertie goes into business. Watson Flint, his father's broker, buys him a seat at the stock exchange. For Bertie, a seat at the stock exchange is merely a physical object, and he therefore finds the price of one hundred thousand dollars rather high. Yet, he is willing to do whatever is necessary to satisfy his father, and thus be allowed to marry Agnes. When she indicates her willingness to marry him, even against his father's will, he is eager to quickly bring about the ceremony. The wedding gets under way in his father's house only after Rose and Agnes have taken preparations in their own hands. Bertie's subsequent failure to defend himself against Mark's accusation that he is the father of an illegitimate child constitutes the most dramatic instance of his complete inability to take appropriate action in crucial situations, and alienates him from his wife-to-be and his father. His isolation can only be reversed when he finally realizes his potential for aggressive self-assertion during the climactic scene at the stock exchange. Although Bertie remains completely ignorant about what is really going on around him, Watson Flint uses his anger about people shouting "Henrietta" to manipulate him into action. By vigorously defending his honor against those who seem to taunt him with the name of the woman who brought about his disgrace, he saves his father, and proves himself a man, a worthy son and suitor (and, at the same time, Keaton proves that his violent acrobatics are a socially useful skill after all). In the end, then, anger, athletic physicality and, of course, fatherhood, rather than hedonism, notoriety and business sense, are the cornerstones of Bertie's masculine identity.[56]

Keaton's deadpan performance departed radically from the characterization explicitly outlined in the script. Here, Bertie is highly expressive, "smiles," "grins," "becomes quite happy," "is delighted," and "stands smiling happily" on many occasions. Of these, only two smiles survive in the film, remnants of a construction of Bertie's character which Keaton otherwise rejects. Keaton's conscious choice of a deadpan performance derived from an innovative view of Bertie as a person who does not properly connect with his surroundings, his failure to understand being paralleled by his failure to respond emotionally. Keaton's deadpan performance not only serves to characterize Bertie as an intellectually and emotionally retarded young man, but also highlights Keaton's own distance from the fiction, his irreducible and transgressive presence as a comedian in the universe of serious drama. With relatively few opportunities to dominate the screen with violent acrobatics, Keaton turned his straight characterization into an excessively restrained piece of acting and thus into an extended comic turn.

The opening credits end with an oval insert showing silhouettes of the two featured actors. This dissolves into a shot, which still belongs to the credit sequence, of the two shaking hands, with Crane also putting his hand on the comedian's shoulder as if to welcome him as an actor in the world of legitimate drama. The drama then begins with a set piece for Crane. In his Wall Street office, Nick meets an old friend from his prospecting days, bringing good news about their gold mine. Crane portrays the character's excitement with expansive gestures and plenty of movements across the room. Keaton's first appearance presents a sharp contrast. While heartily tucking into his breakfast, Keaton does not make any unnecessary movement, holding his body still and keeping his face completely inexpressive, thus indicating his complete detachment from his surroundings.

When, in the film's climatic sequence, Bertie does learn to act vigorously in the world on his own behalf, Keaton's performance is again contrasted directly with Crane's. From his yachting trip, Nick returns to his office at a time when it is too late for him to do anything but wait for the final outcome of the trading at the stock exchange, the latest results of which are relayed to him by a ticker tape machine. Completely incapacitated, his emotions become the centre of attention. His anger and despair dominate the scene in the same way that his joy provided a key to the film's opening. In dramatic terms, however, Bertie's actions at the stock exchange are decisive, and the narrative focus soon shifts to them. Occasional cuts to Nick's office showing his reactions serve to set Keaton's athletic performance against Crane's acting. At the beginning of the film, Keaton's deadpan poses a narrative problem (Bertie's unmanly passivity) which needs to be solved. Towards the end, his slapstick speciality brings about the resolution. Bertie's dramatic transformation from passive idiot to angry fighter, which establishes him as a worthy protagonist for the narrative and a worthy suitor and son in the social world of its fiction, is pure slapstick. Running, jumping, sliding across the stock exchange, his dress disintegrating and his body bruised, Bertie's buying spree is a long-awaited return of Keaton's violent acrobatics.

The film's conclusion does not discard Keaton's restraint, which served to define the initial narrative problem. The final two scenes of the film bring father and son, Crane and Keaton, in direct contact. In the penultimate scene, Nick goes to his son's new house to make amends. With the father rushing to Bertie and enthusiastically thanking him for the rescue of his business, Bertie's success is confirmed and his new social identity is established. At the same time, the scene mirrors the end of the credit sequence, and the handshake signaling Bertie's arrival in the world of adults as an equal to his father echoes the extrafictional welcome Crane extends to the slapstick comedian Buster Keaton. While throughout most of the film, the narrative and the extrafictional discourse are interwoven seamlessly by matching Keaton's performance to Bertie's character, the two levels are separated and brought into conflict towards the end. The film's last scene, which moves ahead one year to show Bertie as an expectant father receiving the news about the birth of twins, would suggest that Bertie has changed fundamentally, that he has matured and at least partly overcome his intellectual and emotional retardation. Yet Keaton's refusal to show any response undermines the narrative resolution and the normality of Bertie's status as father. Keaton's deadpan contrasts sharply with the way Crane uses a little dance to express Nick's joy, and foregrounds Keaton's exceptional status as a comic performer.

Reviewing *The Saphead*: Performance Styles, Trademarks and the Success of Keaton's Promotion

Contemporary critical responses indicate that the simplistic and potentially dehumanized identity of stone-face Keaton contradicted basic assumptions of psychological realism in feature films and of psychological "normality" in everyday life. This issue was explicitly and complexly addressed in the film's reception in New York, the largest and most influential movie market in the United States. Reviewers were also debating the merits of *The Saphead*'s merging of performance styles and comic traditions, the cornerstone of the campaign to launch Keaton as a featured attraction. In particular, reviewers were concerned about the marginalization of William H. Crane, who was, after all, the better-known and more highly regarded of the two costars. Some, but by no means all, New York reviewers highlighted Crane's presence, seeing and judging the film primarily in relation to its origins as a stage classic, to Crane's long stage career, and to the traditions of legitimate comedy. Severely criticizing Keaton, who was seen merely as an additional player, the *New York American*, for example, stated that Crane had done "the real acting" and had "stood out" even though his role had been "cut down and subordinated."[57] Critics still celebrated the sheer weight of Crane's reputation, his "realism" and "understanding," the nobility the old man could bestow upon the screen.[58] However, virtually all acknowledged in one way or another the datedness of play and actor, and the necessity to introduce new elements. *Variety*'s positive comments on the film's stage origins, for example, were slightly defensive, claiming that, despite the "modern interpretation," "the plot remains the same." Crane was referenced "as a comedian of the old school," while the critic quickly added that this "does not mean that his methods are old, because they are as up-to-the-minute as those of his younger colleague." Clearly, the writer was at pains to avoid the impression of Crane as a mere relic of the past. Yet, in the context of critical remarks on the film's reliance on theatrical tableaux ("the sparsity of close-ups and the overplus of long shots"), Crane appeared highly anachronistic.[59] The *New York Times* welcomed the fact that he "yields place . . . to the younger Keaton." What made Keaton's performance so appropriate for screen comedy was precisely his restraint: unlike Crane, with his dependence upon the spoken word and grand gestures, Keaton was "a pantomimist, as all true screen actors are, . . . definitely and subtly expressive."[60]

Keaton's centrality to the film was noted in most reviews, yet opinions about his performance differed radically. The most damning judgment came from the *New York Morning Post*, which found Keaton "downright stupid and inane." Bertie comes across as a "simpleton" who is both "a menace" and "a bore." In this critic's view, Keaton's restraint merely proved he was not doing his job properly, causing the film to fall flat.[61] Equally, for the *New York American*, Keaton's "constant mournfulness," while initially amusing, became "tremendously monotonous."[62] Yet another critic, who basically liked his performance, nevertheless doubted that "Mr. Keaton is an artist who can depict human emotions."[63]

However, most reviews accepted and even celebrated Keaton's performance because it suited the character of Bertie, who, according to *Photoplay*, "has always presented a problem" for actors: "He either has to be made such a fool that the authorities would never have permitted him to roam the streets at large, and get his laughs by being a fool, or he has to be played as a reasonably normal, but quite irresponsible youth, and run the risk of being dismissed as neither funny nor interesting."[64] Keaton solved this problem, as the *New York Globe and Commercial Advertiser* noted, by emphasizing Bertie's essential stupidity to such a degree that his performance became an ironic comment on it: "Buster Keaton is not the only feeble-minded hero we have seen in the movies, but he is the first who has admitted it and taken no end of pleasure and merriment from his task."[65] Here, Keaton's restraint is perceived as an indication of his professional skill, and not of his personal moroseness.

Keaton's second major contribution to the film was seen to be his physical comedy. Even the very critical reviewers of the *New York Post* and the *New York American* admitted that the climactic scene at the stock exchange was "largely responsible for the entire picture's sense of enjoyment."⁶⁶ The *New York Herald* fit Keaton in the tradition of Fairbanks's spectacular stage and film performances, noting that he "becomes a human rocket at the finish almost as well as Doug could have."⁶⁷ The film's entertaining violence was foregrounded by the *New York World*, which praised "the ability of Keaton to survive the kicks and falls he receives throughout the play."⁶⁸ On the whole, critics accepted the violence and "nonsense" of slapstick sequences as effective comic entertainment, even if they cited the film's failure to achieve the realism and expressiveness of the legitimate stage. Obviously, the film was judged according to two different standards, one applying to the sequences of physical comedy, the other to the drama.⁶⁹ The *New York Times* saw *The Saphead* as a precariously balanced union of fundamentally different concerns, "a two-reel comedy stretched and padded to fill some 5,000 feet of film, but its scenes that count are so full of fun that the spectator does not mind the story stuff."⁷⁰ Story material was added to comic spectacle, potentially getting in the way of continuous enjoyment. Other critics, focusing on Crane and the legitimate tradition, approached the film differently, implying that comedy sequences were inserted into an otherwise perfectly respectable, if somewhat old-fashioned, narrative. All agreed that the film was a hybrid, resulting from the presence of Keaton and Crane, who, in their respective careers up to this point, had come to embody different comic traditions.

Whereas Crane and his followers saw his association with and intermittent displacement by a slapstick clown as potentially degrading, Keaton's admirers saw his teaming with the famous Broadway comedian as a new and very promising career departure from slapstick to the "more human field of straight comedy."⁷¹ Genuine stardom could only be achieved in the field of feature-length comedy, and depended on a restrained performance style. The hierarchical organisation of comic forms and the sense of Keaton's upward mobility was highlighted by the *New York Journal*: Keaton "rises to fine comedy heights here, and points distinctly to the fact that he is a player of promise as a legitimate comedian."⁷² This critical response indicates the success of Metro's promotional strategy. Yet the many criticisms of the film, especially of Keaton himself and his excessive restraint, indicated how difficult a fusion, how fragile a balancing act Keaton's rise to stardom was.

Following the release of *The Saphead* in February, 1921, the first extensive articles dealing with Keaton's screen work and offscreen life were published. Keaton's identity as a star on-screen and off was heavily influenced by his most characteristic performance trait. Elizabeth Peltret's biographical sketch, "Poor Child," for example, highlighted the possibility that Keaton's deadpan performance expressed his personal sadness. "He has a settled look of sadness, as though from a secret sorrow," she wrote, speculating that this sadness might be atttributed to the fact that "being laughed at is a serious proposition."[73] By May, 1921, when a flurry of publicity surrounded Keaton's marriage to Natalie Talmadge, Keaton's sadness had already been so firmly established as a fundamental personality trait in the press that it now clashed with the normalized image of the comedian's private existence as a lover and husband (in the same way that Keaton's deadpan clashed with the normalization of Bertie's status as a husband and father at the end of *The Saphead*). A headline described Keaton as "The Saddest Bridegroom in the World," and the fact that, on- or off-screen, he never smiled was seen as a unique feature of Keaton's personality, separating him from the rest of humanity, and creating a distance between him and his wife.[74] Contemporary reviews of Keaton's later features showed that the critical remarks about his gloomy and withdrawn personality in some reviews of *The Saphead* and in the articles about his wedding also applied to his sustained dramatic roles. When Keaton returned from slapstick two-reelers to feature film production in 1923, his deadpan performance became the object of increasing criticism. It was seen as a highly inappropriate response to the task of creating characters which were rounded and believable and could sustain audience interest for the duration of a feature. Consequently, Keaton's masterpieces were not very successful commercially, and his independent status was short-lived, with Keaton in 1928 becoming a mere contract actor at Loews/ MGM, without the creative control granted to him at Joseph Schenck's studio.[75]

11

Goin' to Town and Beyond: Mae West, Film Censorship and the Comedy of *Un*marriage

Ramona Curry

Genre studies of film comedy and historical analysis of U.S. movie censorship, traditionally distinct fields of film scholarship, intersect frequently at one point: in discussion of American film star and cultural icon Mae West. This essay explores connections between Mae West's status as a bawdy film comedienne and the extensive government and movie industry censorship of her work in the 1930s. A case study of one Mae West vehicle, *Goin' to Town* (1935), drawing on records of the Production Code Administration (PCA) and other materials documenting the production and reception of West's film performances, yields a basis for a historically grounded analysis of the structures and implications of West's comedy.[1]

The essay's aim is to suggest an approach to film comedy that integrates semiotics, feminist-inflected psychoanalytic theories and star studies with careful research in film and social history. Only a historically informed theoretical model can adequately address a crucial issue in contemporary media analysis: how the cinematic and comedic structures in a given film relate to the possible readings it engenders. Only by taking into account the circumstances of production and the historical reception of a given film can we engage the critical dilemma that recurs implicitly, and sometimes explicitly, in much discussion of film comedy: is the humor radical or recuperative? Does a given film comedy (or film comedian) generally "subvert" or predominantly reassert hegemonic ideologies? A historically anchored analysis shifts emphasis from a film's cinematic and narrative structuring to its discursive formation, rephrasing the question: what *documented ideological effects* has a film comedy occasioned? What relations obtain between structural elements of a comedy (for instance, a given joke or gag), and audience responses to that film at any given time?

Mae West wearing Delilah costume in *Goin' to Town* (1935).

These questions direct attention to the cultural workings of a film and its performers—in the present case, of Mae West.

A discursive, historically informed theory of film comedy offers a means of resolving disagreements about the ideological effects of West's films and persona that have arisen in the last two decades among feminist analysts. A recurrent point of contention in feminist analyses of West (as, more emphatically, of Madonna) runs something as follows: does this star represent nothing more than a superficial gender role reversal, just a woman telling men's jokes? Is Mae West merely another spectacle upholding the fetishistic workings of classical Hollywood cinema? Or is there justification for finding West and her films a feminist challenge to repressive dictates of female sexual morality? In sum: does the phenomenon "Mae West" illustrate the capacity of twentieth-century popular culture to promote hegemonic ideologies while appearing to oppose those, or do this star's films and persona represent a genuinely radical moment in U.S. media history?

I have argued elsewhere that West's star image was widely understood in the 1930s to transgress normative delineations of gender, class and race. Yet it was precisely *as an emblem of transgression* that the U.S. film industry sought and developed West as an exceptional and initially highly valued asset. West's well-established reputation as a bawdy comedienne attracted the major movie studios' interest as early as 1929. As an iconographic representation of willful, unrestrained female sexuality, Mae West benefited the major film corporations doubly: first, at a time of economic crisis, as a highly marketable commodity, beginning in 1932 when Paramount signed West and began planning an adaptation of West's highly successful Broadway play, *Diamond Lil* (filmed in 1933 as *She Done Him Wrong*); secondly, as a controversial cultural emblem which indirectly justified the major studios' oligopolistic trade practices, enabling them by the mid-1930s effectively to eliminate competition from independent producers and distributors.[2]

A historically informed analysis of West's films recognizes that these partook extensively of and contributed to Hollywood's dominance institutionally and as a set of filmic and narrative practices: Mae West's image and her film comedy performances were shaped within, not in opposition to, the U.S. media industry and the conventions of classical Hollywood cinema.[3] But Mae West was also frequently the target of criticism by leaders of 1930s U.S. cultural institutions working to maintain the middle-class values expressed in the Motion Picture Production Code of 1930 (including respect for law, "natural or human," the "correct standards of life," and "the sanctity of the institution of marriage and the home")[4] Certainly, censorship—which is an index of a work's being considered subversive—was a recurrent issue in the production and reception of West's films.

By the mid-1930s, it was the comedic elements in West's performance that were most extensively censored, both by the Production Code Administration in its *a priori* censorship of films during production, and by state boards that reviewed films before their release into a given area. Yet while, as we shall see, industry and state censors focused on West's comedic utterances and gestures in *Goin' to Town*, this does not necessarily indicate that it was West's comedic style itself that elicited censorship. Indeed, West herself claimed in interviews and in her 1959 autobiography, *Goodness Had Nothing to Do with It,* that she adopted her style of sexually suggestive humor early in her career precisely in order to circumvent censorship of dramatically presented sexual material in her vaudeville acts and plays.[5] A *Los Angeles Times* columnist, writing in 1943, reported West's account of her development as a comedienne:

> The wisecracks that are now her trademarks came about as a kind of last resort in *She Done Him Wrong.* On the stage Mae played *Diamond Lil* straight, as down-to-earth melodrama; she killed a dame, for instance, and then cursed her dead body, just like a gangster; but the Hays office wouldn't let her do anything like that in the picture, so she substituted "wisecracks for kids of school age." "And it stuck," she says.[6]

A 1932 letter from Dr. James Wingate, head of the MPPDA Studio Relations committee (precursor to the Production Code Administration, which the MPPDA organized in July 1934), indicates that, early in her film career, West's comedic performance was construed as a socially acceptable means of expressing what might be taboo if presented seriously. Wingate prefaced his written response to Paramount's initial script for West's first starring vehicle, *She Done Him Wrong,* with a cautionary remark:

> I am assuming that in making a picture of such a period and with such a background, you will develop the comedy elements, so that the treatment will invest the picture with such exaggerated qualities as automatically to take care of possible offensiveness. . . .[7]

PCA head Joseph Breen either did not share his predecessor's view that comedy automatically diffused social offense, or else had become convinced, after observing responses to West's films, that the star's style of comedic performance was not as ameliorative as anticipated. Within four years, it was precisely West's comedic style that the PCA sought to restrain. In an internal PCA memo following the release of the controversial *Klondike Annie* (1936), Breen wrote:

> Difficulty is inherent with a Mae West picture. Lines and pieces of business, which in the script seem to be thoroughly innocuous, turn out when shown on the screen to be questionable at best, when they are not definitely offensive.[8]

The divergent evaluations of West's comedic performance arise not solely from a shift in MPPDA personnel or policies over a four-year period. Rather, the later judgment incorporates a grasp of the cultural impact of West's film comedy, of its ideological workings. Analysis of these entails careful historical research, as well as close textual analysis and contextual evaluation of West's star image and performative style. A historical study of the production and reception of *Goin' to Town* anchors a subsequent textual analysis of West's comedy that draws critically on Sigmund Freud's work on jokes and on feminist psychoanalytic film theory. My evaluation of the ideological effects of West's comedy concludes in consideration of "censorability" as an element of West's comedic persona.

Goin' to Town in Production and Reception

Goin' to Town, released in the spring of 1935, was the fourth of five Mae West films that Paramount produced between 1933 and 1936.[9] West's first two star vehicles, *She Done Him Wrong* and *I'm No Angel*, had broken box office records and garnered wide publicity upon their releases in January and October 1933, respectively. Production and release of West's next film, *Belle of the Nineties* (September 1934), occurred amidst a public debate about the effects of movies on the criminal and sexual behaviors of audiences. This discourse, fostered by U.S. news and entertainment media, had gained national scope by the early 1930s, *prior* to West's first movie appearance in 1932. However, by 1934, Mae West had assumed an iconographic function in that public discourse, for she was held to embody the movie immorality that reform-minded interest groups strove to curb. The ongoing debate about morality in the movies significantly inflected the initial impact of West's films. A counterfactor impelling the films' production was the severe effects of the world economic crisis on the U.S. film industry in the early 1930s. These two well-documented and not-unrelated historical circumstances codetermined the parameters of the national public discourse within which *Goin' to Town* was produced and released.[10]

Goin' to Town opens in what appears to be the Wild West, but a scene about ten minutes into the film, in which Cleo Borden (Mae West) arrives in an automobile, brings her into the twentieth century and integrates in one film West's two primary personas: an irrepressible, Gay 1890s, dance hall queen and a wealthy, modern woman calling the shots. After she has wrangled the inheritance of an oil-rich cattle ranch, Cleo sets her sights on a reticent aristocratic English engineer, Edward Carrington (Paul Cavanagh), whom she literally lassos in the intensity of her desire. Her pursuit of him leads to the Buenos Aires racetrack; into a marriage of convenience with another man, which she contracts to acquire higher class status; and onto a stage in her South Hampton mansion to sing the female lead in the Saint-Saëns opera *Samson and Delilah*. It is in her performance as Delilah that Cleo ultimately beguiles the Englishman, who has in the interval inherited the title of Lord; the same evening she fortuitously becomes a widow and soon thereafter gains the title "Lady."

The narrative of *Goin' to Town* is typical of Mae West vehicles, hardly surprisingly, given that West wrote the screenplay for this film as well as most of her other film and stage material. West's role is that of her standard character: a talented, enterprising, musical entertainer (at the outset of the story implicitly a prostitute) who trades on her beauty and performative skills to amass male admirers and wealth. In keeping with her other sobriquets that bear associations with jewels or other valuable commodities (Diamond Lil, Ruby Carter), West's character name in *Goin' to Town*, Cleo(patra), implies that she is as unique and sexually irresistible a personage as the legendary Queen of the Nile.

The plot of *Goin' to Town* is not only typical of West's films, but also encapsulates the "rags to riches" fantasy common in many American films and an especially recurrent theme in 1930s Hollywood productions. The Westian twist to the tale, and a primary source of its humor, is that the protagonist Cleó boldly acquires and revels in the luxuries associated with a high-class existence, but repudiates the pretentious social conventions and other restrictions that usually accompany such a life. The colloquial expression that became the film's release title hints at the pleasures of consumerism and urbane romance that the lead character attains. Yet the film's working titles during production, first *Now I'm a Lady*, then *How Am I Doin'?*, suggest more directly the deliberate planning and effort that the character undertakes to achieve her marked rise in class standing.[11]

Critical response to *Goin' to Town*, which appeared just six months following the critical and popular success of *Belle of the Nineties*, was quite mixed. *The Motion Picture Herald*, a trade paper aimed at movie exhibitors, waxed eloquent in describing it as a "wild, woolly western," a comedy romance, a "swanky drama" and a "mystery melodrama," all in one (May 11, 1935, p. 54). However, another trade publication, *The Hollywood Reporter*, had declared on April 23, following an early press screening of the film, that *Goin' to Town* was the "weakest and most slipshod production that Madame West has taken credit for writing . . . that fine, exuberant spontaneity has been dragged out to where the pulling for the leering snicker is exhausting, and a 14-year-old is two jumps ahead of the answers." A *New York Times* review written by Andre Sennwald was even more critical, labelling the film "a vulgar, demoralizing exhibition" (May 11, 1935, p. 21).

Such diversity in critical response is evident even within the pages of a single trade journal. The *Daily Variety* reviewer asserted, on April 25, 1935, that the new film was "much more amusing than her last two pictures" and went on to summarize, "Miss West's performance is her standard effort which includes the hip wiggling, eyes, teeth and all. It's what the West fans love and there's plenty of everything they want." That reviewer's counterpart in the weekly edition of *Variety*, "Abel," concurred that the film contained the "crisp and unsubtle" dialogue expected of West, but called the film "West's poorest" and warned that "exhibs and exploiteers will have to go to town to sell *Goin' to Town*" as "no amount of [West's] epigrammatic hypoing can offset the silly story." (May 15, 1935, p. 19) The capsule summary in this weekly edition predicted poor box office for the film, but in its next issue, following the film's official opening, noted that *Goin' to Town* was a leading box office attraction.[12]

Citizen and church groups lobbying for movie reform did not share the general public's enthusiasm for West's new film, however, nor one reviewer's confident prediction that the film was "essentially of high moral tone and not at all likely to encounter any of the difficulties which either hindered or aided her previous pictures."[13] A spokesperson for a large Protestant church, which along with the Catholic Legion of Decency had denounced the films West made in 1933 and 1934, wrote indignantly to the Production Code Administration: "I cannot understand how this particular actor who stands for a particular phase of morals should have been permitted to put another one over on the American youth!"[14] This outraged response came despite numerous cuts and changes that the PCA had demanded in the original script. An overview of these changes elucidates the challenge that Mae West's comedic films may have represented in 1934 and 1935 to the social values which the PCA worked to maintain in the American film industry's productions.[15]

Joseph Breen had the following to say of an early script of the film, which Paramount submitted in December 1934 for Code approval: "As we read it, it is the boasting of a woman of loose morals who has had any number of men in her time, and has climbed over them to the top of the ladder where she has finally married respectability."[16] In detailing changes to be made, Breen insisted that there be no scenes of branding cattle (Cleo's first betrothed is a cattle rustler), no indication of toilets, and most particularly no indication of prostitution. It was to be clear that the unscrupulous character of Ivan, who courts Cleo with an eye on her wealth, comes from Russia, not from Argentina, for the South American market was sensitive to the portrayal of Argentinian men as gigolos.

Nor was any hint of homosexuality (referred to in the Production Code as "sexual perversion") to be allowed: the character of an interior decorator, subsequently deleted from the script, was not to be a "nance."

Breen also wrote with circumspection, "We suggest changing the line 'I made the bed and now you're laying in it,' substituting the proper grammatical word, 'lying'." That West's character, whose line that was to be, should speak in grammatically correct English was indeed *not* the point at issue, for no other instances of West's character's colloquial speech patterns, which supply material in the completed film for numerous jokes about class difference, were marked for change. The PCA's aim was clearly to delete the sexual innuendo embedded in the word "laying."

Potential sexual double entendres were also the focal point of Breen's copious red-penciled markings of lyrics to the closing song, "Now I'm A Lady," from which the film's initial working title was taken. These lyrics, written not by West herself, but by songwriter Irving Kahal in a style in keeping with West's dialogue and persona, were submitted and rejected several times before a shortened, rewritten version was finally accepted. In the earliest version of the song that was submitted for approval on January 14, 1935, Breen marked as offensive the italicized opening lines of the first verse:

> *I used to have a lot of sweet sugar daddies*
> *As much as 7 or 9*
> *But now I'm a lady*
> *I see 'em one at a time*
> I used to baby all those sweet sugar daddies
> to keep my cloud silver-lined
> But now I'm a lady
> I get my sugar refined.

Subsequent developments suggest that Breen offered these initial markings as guidelines to the studio about the style of lyrics to be avoided, not as the full extent of deletions necessary.[17] A version of the number the studio submitted ten days later is even more heavily marked in Breen's handwriting, with offending lines underscored and exclamatory comments scrawled in red pencil in the margins (for instance, "NO!" writ large at the top of the page of mimeographed lyrics). Two phrases in this version are emphatically marked for elimination, as follows:

> I'd flirt with handsome men and ask them no questions
> I met the best and the worst
> But now I'm a lady
> I see their pedigrees first.
> I used to play without any conscience,
> I just broke hearts left and right
> But now I'm a lady,
> *I only break one each night*

Let me see—there's many a boy friend that knew me
when
But today, they're the guys in the army of my forgotten
men
I used to put my heart and soul in my dancing
My hips would do a *jelly roll*
But now I'm a lady
I've got them under control.

Clearly, the aim of PCA censorship was to eliminate any suggestion of Cleo Borden's—or Mae West's—sexual promiscuity. The underlined phrase in the first stanza, which implies that even after attaining social status and economic security the singer chooses a new sexual partner every night, became in the film performance a mild report of her improved etiquette: "I've learned to be more polite." The vivid description of undulating hips in sexual performance ("jelly roll") was replaced by a line explaining the singer's prior enthusiasm for dancing in terms of the Protestant work ethic: "to keep the wolf from the door." (See the complete final lyrics below.)

This closing number serves structurally to summarize the plot and arguably to reiterate the film's overall ideology. It is thus perhaps not unexpected that its lyrics should have become the primary site of contention between Paramount and the PCA in the production of *Goin' to Town*. At issue was West's long-standing self-characterization as an openly sexually active woman, indeed, as a happily successful prostitute. The lyrics initially submitted strongly connote such characterization; later versions, which assert the singer's persistent promiscuity, may suggest the singer's economic and social advancement to higher-class "call girl": "I only break one each night."

The musical style of this number as well as the initial lyrics bear associations not only of gender and class (that is, lower-class female), but also of race, for this number evokes the tradition of the "dirty blues" made popular by African-American performers such as Ma Rainey and Bessie Smith. West had adopted a dirty blues musical style in her years in vaudeville and popular theater, and maintained its performance, albeit in ever more modified form, in her film roles. West performs distinctly blues-based numbers in her first four starring vehicles. In *She Done Him Wrong*, for example, she sings not only the popular tune "Frankie and Johnny," with which (in a "low-down" version) she had become closely identified during the run of *Diamond Lil*, but also two numbers clearly derived from the "dirty blues" tradition: "A Guy What Takes His Time" and "Easy Rider," a Bessie Smith song. West performs versions of "St. Louis Woman," "Memphis Blues," and "My Old Flame" in *Belle of the*

Nineties, accompanied by Duke Ellington and his Orchestra in an on-screen performance, as well as a hymnlike number entitled "Troubled Waters," which West sings against the backdrop of an African-American Christian revival meeting. "St. Louis Woman" is a song reminiscent of Ma Rainey's style that includes lyrics such as "I lived six flights up but he sure did like to climb" and "Oh, bring on those fancy loving papas!" West's opening song in *Goin' to Town*, "He's a Bad Man (But He Loves Me Good)," is also a blues-style number.

It is a mark of the dirty blues that the female singer (the first person narrator, the "I" in the lyrics) is eager for sex, promiscuous and intent on garnering financial gain for her sexual performance. The "dirty blues" tradition is an instance of stylized, humorous, sexual display which bears specific class and racial connotations. West's performance of dirty-blues-style songs underscored the star's characterization as an actively sexual, persistently "low-class" woman, notwithstanding all her wealth and fame (both as film character and as star), by associating her with the unbound sexual behavior that the dominant U.S. society frequently attributes to lower-class African-Americans.

West's star image was infused in the early 1930s with multiple associations to African-Americans along with to those evoked by her musical performance. Some such associations arose around the publication in 1930 of West's novel *Babe Gordon*, reprinted in 1931 and presented under the title *The Constant Sinner* as West's last theater production before her move in 1932 to Hollywood. Its protagonist is a character embodying the West persona who takes as one of her lovers "Money Jackson," "the Negro king of the Harlem numbers racket," in West's words.[18] Paramount studio publicity from 1934 to 1936 about West's private life included photographs of West's personal African-American maids and also her chauffeur in 1935 and 1936, boxer Chalky Wright. African-American women have roles as maids in *She Done Him Wrong* (Louise Beavers as Pearl), *I'm No Angel* (Gertrude Howard as Beulah, also Libby Taylor and Hattie McDaniel) and *Belle of the Nineties* (Libby Taylor as Jasmine). African-American men have roles as employees of the New Orleans "Sensation House" in *Belle of the Nineties*, in addition to appearing as entertainers (Duke Ellington and his Orchestra, as well as numerous unnamed singers who enact a revival meeting).

Only one scene in *Goin' to Town* directly reinforces these previous associations in West's star image with African-Americans performers. Her character Cleo's appearance on stage in the operatic role of Delilah is heralded by a small group of black male attendants. The train of the singer's long gown falls across the head of a bowed attendant, who brushes it away. West/ Cleo glances down and stops singing long enough to say, "Sorry, Joe." This gag disrupts the earnestness of Cleo's operatic entrance, and recalls thereby

Tira and her four African-American maids: Mae West, Libby Taylor, Hattie McDaniel, Gertrude Howard, and an unidentified actress in *I'm No Angel* (1933).

West's status as comedienne. It simultaneously underscores the star's good humor and apparent liberality in race and class relations.

While the presence of African-Americans in West's films diminished following *Belle of the Nineties*, other performers of color appeared in increasing numbers. There are two Native American characters in *Goin' to Town*. In *Klondike Annie* (1936), a number of Asian-American men appear in the film's initial San Francisco Chinatown setting, and West's character has a Chinese maid (Soo Young as Fah Wong), with whom she converses in Chinese. (In subsequent films, West's maids are all "French," that is, slightly foreign but white.) In *My Little Chickadee* (1940), set in "the West," a stereotyped Native American is the object of many of W. C. Fields' jokes, while Indians attacking a train are the butts of several of West's jokes, in conjunction with her marksmanship, as she shoots them.

West's recurrent juxtaposition on screen with actors of color emphasizes the star's own racial identity (white—enhanced through her blondeness) and gives her image an undercurrent of exoticism and sexual taboo. Particularly in the films from 1933 to 1936, these actors simultaneously represent the star character's accession to comparatively high social position, for they are stereotypically cast as servants. Such servants are standard characters in all of West's films, their number correlated with her character's rising status and wealth.[19]

It is a strong possibility that the reduction specifically of the African-American presence in West's films after *Belle of the Nineties* is associated with tightened censorship. PCA correspondence reports that censors eliminated the revival meeting scene in *Belle of the Nineties* in prints distributed in England.[20] It *is* quite clear that PCA efforts to efface West's depiction of an active female sexual performance motivated both by economic necessity and lust focused precisely on the strongest allusion in *Goin' to Town* to African-American cultural forms: the dirty-blues-style closing song. The version of "Now I'm a Lady" that West was permitted to sing in the film is a distinctly sanitized blues-style number:

> I used to put my heart and soul in my dancing
> To keep the wolf from the door.
> But now I'm a lady,
> Don't have to dance anymore.
>
> I'd flirt with handsome men and ask them no questions
> I've met the best and the worst
> But now I'm a lady
> I see their pedigrees first
>
> Let me say there is many a boyfriend that knew me when
> But today they're the guys in the army of my forgotten men.
>
> Oh, I used to play around without any conscience
> I just broke hearts left and right
> But now I'm a lady
> I've learned to be more polite.

The final verse of the number nonetheless retains some allusion to African-American musical performance. After West begins the song in the elaborately decorated boudoir her character has acquired, Cavanagh enters, and the two exchange a few lines of dialogue, before West sings a concluding verse:

> Hi de ho, baby, I'm goin' places
> I've made my plans
> Hi de ho, love is queen of the aces[21]
> I've got my man.
> [West links arms with Cavanagh and they exit]
> Now step by step I hit the top of the ladder
> It was a dangerous climb
> [West sings as she and Cavanagh descend stairs. Cavanagh exits.]

But now I'm a lady
Come up and see me sometime.
[camera dollies in to CU on West's face, fade to black and
end credits]

The phrase "hi de ho" was popularized as a musical phrase by jazz
band leader Cab Calloway in the early 1930s; West's use of it here relates
her to that dynamic African-American performer and to the exuberance
and urbanity associated with jazz performance generally. The final line
of the song, a much-quoted quip derived from West's first star vehicle
She Done Him Wrong, also invokes West's previously more evident
borrowing from African-American musical styles through its reference
to the star's earlier performances and established image.

Another element in *Goin' to Town* which draws on the extensive interracial associations in West's image appears to have been effaced at some
stage of the production. An article that appeared in the *Los Angeles Times*
soon after the release of *Belle of the Nineties*, in September 1934, notes
West's plans for her next starring vehicle:

> In my next film I'm going to have an Indian in one of the principal
> roles, and I want a real Indian. . . . He's got to be just right, and
> one that the ladies will love. Of course, you understand, I sort of like
> him myself, and when I meet him I look him over carefully. . . .[22]

The general topic of the article is West's response to the public "drive
against pictures" that had come to a head that summer. West is quoted
as finding film censorship an occasion to build a comic scene: "If you
can't go straight, then you've got to go around." She goes on to describe
a proposed scene with the "real Indian" under the new conditions of
comedy production:

> We're leaving the rancho; I'm going into racing. I say: "Let's take
> him along; he'll be useful."
>
> "What will he be good for," another character says, and I reply, "Oh,
> I dunno. I think he might be good in lots of ways," looking him over
> again (Mae demonstrated the eye work) and finally end up by saying,
> "Oh let him come along and take care of the horses." And there isn't
> a thing that anybody would quarrel about in any of those lines.
>
> A year ago I wouldn't have made half as much of that scene; I would
> have just stepped up to the Indian and slapped him on the shoulder
> and said: "How you doing, big boy!" The scene would have been
> done in a much broader way, and that's all there would have been to
> it."

In the completed film, *Goin' to Town*, two men are cast as Native Americans: Taho (Tito Coral, a Latino singer), who plays a stable hand, and the jockey Laughing Eagle (Joe Frye), who appears only briefly and has no dialogue. While Taho is a slightly developed character who exchanges a few lines with Cleo, the role and its casting by no means approximate that announced by West. The comic scene West purportedly had already scripted in September 1934 does not occur in the finished film, nor does *Goin' to Town* otherwise bear any suggestion in dialogue, gesture or editing that West's character finds Taho of sexual interest. This dialogue, if it was ever written, may have been made excised from the screenplay prior to the studio's submitting it to the PCA, for there is no mention of it in the PCA files. Breen's emphatic objections during the production of *Klondike Annie*, a few months later, about the sexual relationship between West's character and a Chinese gambler suggest that the PCA would well have called for the elimination of any sexual involvement between Cleo and Taho, had a script hinting at such liaison been submitted. From the perspective of the Code, and for many film reviewers, implications of interracial relations compounded the offense of representing extramarital sexual activity.[23]

West's on-screen interactions with minor Indian and African-American characters certainly are no indication of progressive racial politics. The "mammy" characters in West's first three star vehicles (*She Done Him Wrong*, *I'm No Angel* and *Belle of the Nineties*) contribute to the star's aura of power and sexual allure, not only through their roles as maids and vividly contrasting visual presence, but also in serving in West's comedic performance as "straight-man." In keeping with racial stereotypes in other 1930s Hollywood films, several of West's lines in the banter between mistress and maid take the African-American characters as the butt of the joke, implying that they are lazy, ignorant or untrustworthy. The sustained scenes in which these jokes occur nonetheless infused West's 1930s image with cross-racial associations which, combined with the star's signification of sexual transgression, rendered her on-screen exchanges with male characters such as Taho and even Joe, in the role of Delilah's herald, potentially taboo.

Notwithstanding the PCA's attempts to shepherd the production *Goin' to Town* through to a release that would give no occasion for state intervention, the film was subject to minor censorship in several U.S. states after gaining the Code's seal of approval. In all cases, excisions were of West's comedic retorts in dialogue with male characters. State censors in Ohio made four cuts in the film, the most extensive of all U.S. state censor boards that reviewed it.[24] All deletions were of quips by West which occurred during seduction scenes and that suggest, through the technique of double entendre, that character has an active, sometimes predatory sexual desire that is not constrained by matrimony or monogamy. For example, the Ohio board (as well as several others) deleted the word "twice" in the following exchange:

> WINSLOW: (Gilbert Emery, playing the distinguished older ac
> countant to Buck Gonzales, a rancher killed while
> rustling cattle) "You did consent [to marry Gonzales],
> didn't you?
>
> CLEO BORDEN: "I certainly did—twice!"

In eliminating the punch line of West's joke (for without the word "twice" there is no joke), the censors excised the suggestion that Cleo had consented to premarital sex. Other lines censored by Ohio's and other states' boards imply that West is sexually active outside matrimony—or intently wishes to be so. Consider, for example, the following lines exchanged between Cleo and Carrington in a discussion of the oil-bearing potential of her land:

> CARRINGTON: (pointing to a map, against which Cleo is leaning rather
> ostentatiously with her hips) This is the undeveloped
> territory.
>
> CLEO: Um, we'll have to do something about that.

Several censor boards eliminated this and other instances of sexual double entendre in the scene by cutting the entire exchange (designated in the reports as the "map scene").

The effect of postproduction state censorship was to eradicate residual hints of extramarital sexual activity or even desire. In several instances state censorship also addressed dialogue suggesting that Cleo might easily divorce her dissipated, upper-class husband, with whom, the film makes obvious, Cleo has never deigned to have sexual relations.[25] Both the PCA and the state censor boards clearly read the ironic reversal in Cleo's preferred site of sexual activity—only *outside* marriage—as a violation of the sanctity of matrimony, which the Motion Picture Production Code of 1930 expressly sought to uphold.

The case study of *Goin' to Town* demonstrates that many cultural arbiters in 1935 read West's comedy as violating conventional, middle-class values, particularly the constraint of female sexuality within marriage. The study also reveals the extent of institutional negotiation in the shaping of West's film performances, and their subsequent public reception. But, while censorship records and newspaper reviews indicate individual readings of a film, these documents do not cogently articulate or theorize relations between a film's specific components and its effects on viewers. Semiotic analysis can provide insight into how a film text may have elicited specific audience responses, as long as the approach avoids postulating an idealized reader, but instead relates the audience's possible reading strategies to genre conventions and other factors that historically circumscribe the film. I turn now to examine how cinematic devices, including *mise-en-scène,* costume, editing, camera framing, narrative address and dialogue delivery, inscribed West's comedic performance.

Goin' to Town with Freud

It is in keeping with her role as star as well as perceived author of her screenplays that Mae West tells virtually all of the jokes in her films. The *Goin' to Town* review in *Hollywood Reporter* (April 23, 1935) criticizes this pattern (implicitly as narcissistic and selfish): "Madame West gives herself the cream of the crap [*sic*] in lines, and what remains is left for the others to make the best of." West also perpetrates a range of physical and other visual jokes in her films, and functions, in effect, as a narrator of those performative jokes. An example of such physical humor in *Goin' to Town* is West's roping the character Carrington (Cavanagh). West's exaggerated stride and her gesture of rolling her eyes upward, often while patting her hair with one hand, are well-known and much-cited elements in West's physical comedic style.

Visual jokes created through cinematography and editing also center around West as narrator. For example, in a transitional montage between narrative sequences in *I'm No Angel* (1933), a medium shot opens on West's bejeweled hands patting the picture of her character's most recent male conquest; the camera pans as she places it next to a figurine of a deer, then tilts down to reveal further shelves laden with figurines and correlated portraits. A framed picture of one male character who has been shown to be unpleasant is adjacent to a glass skunk; that of another, a pickpocket and jealous former lover, next to a snake. Carnivalesque music, featuring a tuba, accompanies the sequence. The comic suggestion is that West has collected the men in the pictures on her way to her current status, just as she has collected the glass menagerie that typifies each.

West, in effect, delivers almost all of the visual as well as the verbal jokes in her films. West biographers George Eells and Stanley Musgrove describe how West successfully prevented Henry Hathaway, director of her 1937 film *Go West Young Man,* from making her character the butt of visual jokes in that film. Hathaway had planned a shot sequence that intercut shots of West's swaying walk with shots of jiggling tassels on a lamp shade, and another that called for West to walk away from the camera leading a bulldog, to be followed with a cutaway to the dog's behind. In interviews, Hathaway reported West's response: "Nobody gets laughs in my pictures but me, see?" The shots were not taken.[26]

The most frequent comedy pattern in West's films is a comic dialogue exchange in which Mae West delivers the punch line, while a supporting actor acts as straight-man. The straight-man helps set up West's jokes, and may sometimes be the apparent butt of them, as in the following dialogue exchange in *Goin' to Town*:

> IVAN: (an opportunistic and unscrupulous Russian gigolo character) Let me tell you I am an aristocrat and the backbone of my family!
>
> CLEO: Your family should see a chiropractor!

Frequently, however, the straight-man facilitates the narration of the joke in lines of dialogue in the absence on-screen of the named or implicit object of aggression. The actors who most often serve as West's straight-man play West's character's maids or other supporting figures with whom West's character has no prospective sexual relationship. The character Winslow (Gilbert Emery), who plays Cleo's accountant, and later, unclelike companion and butler, serves such a role in *Goin' to Town*.

Freud's treatise, *Jokes and Their Relation to the Unconscious*, offers an analysis of verbal humor that brings insights into the structures and effects of Mae West's comedic performances.[27] My considering West's comedic lines as jokes does not deny their original delivery as dialogue in a narrative and cinematic context, itself delimited by genre conventions of film comedy.[28] However, the extent to which West's comedic film quips have gained cultural currency as colloquial jokes (the lines retold in conversation following viewings of the films, and subsequently widely cited in other media such as radio, TV, and books of West's witticisms) invites analysis of West's comic lines as jokes. An example of how dialogue in *Goin' to Town* circulated as a joke occurs in a short program in interview format which Mae West gave in 1971 for broadcast to the American Armed Services. Along with numerous quips from her other films, West delivers these lines from the opening scene of *Goin' to Town*:

> MAE WEST: For a long time I was ashamed of how I lived.
>
> INTERVIEWER: (suitor/client in the film) You mean to say you reformed?
>
> WEST: No, I got over being ashamed![29]

Freud's analysis of the purposes of jokes and the nature of the pleasure derived from them focuses on what he calls *"tendentious"* jokes, those which have a specific object (90). This category comprises primarily *hostile* jokes, which "serve the purpose of aggressiveness, satire or defense," and *obscene* jokes, which serve the purpose of exposure (97). Most instances of West's comedic dialogue qualify as tendentious jokes: the comedic exchanges between Cleo and Ivan work as hostile jokes, while the plays on the words "twice" (consented) and "undeveloped territory" are obscene jokes, in Freud's terms. So, too, are the lyrics of "Now I'm a Lady" that were eliminated during production (for instance, "I used to break men's hearts left and right, but now I'm a lady, I break only one a night.")

Freud suggests that a person telling a joke which takes as its butt an individual or human type (for instance, member of an ethnic or other group, including gender) is expressing aggression towards that individual or group in a socially acceptable form: "Brutal hostility, forbidden by law, has been replaced by verbal invective" (102). The narrator of a hostile joke solicits simultaneously the listener's compliance and pleasure in the act of aggression. In Freud's argument, social aggression arises from a "powerful inherited disposition to hostility," which in adults has usually become constrained by social conventions; the hostile joke allows the teller to express aggression in a form that *"will evade restrictions and open sources of pleasure that have become inaccessible"* (102–3) [original italics]. The listener is put in the position of spectator to an act of aggression, and can thus gain voyeuristic pleasure from the joke (97).

An example of a hostile joke in *Goin' to Town* occurs when West's character Cleo encounters the smarmy gigolo Ivan at the Buenos Aires racetrack; Ivan has begun to shift his attentions from his current paramour, Mrs. Crane Brittany, to the even wealthier Cleo:

> IVAN: "For one kiss of your lips I would give half of my life!"
>
> CLEO: "See me tomorrow, I'll kiss you twice."

Cleo's retort employs the technique of joke formation Freud calls "displacement," to redirect attention from a seductive offer to its fatal consequence, if taken literally: two of Cleo's kisses would finish the would-be seducer! Another example of a hostile joke in *Goin' to Town* is the exchange between Cleo and the persistently opportunistic Ivan about his family needing to see a chiropractor. Cleo's retort plays on the metaphoric and literal meanings of the word of "backbone" and displaces the suitor's social boasting with an ostensible medical diagnosis—a crooked backbone—that aggressively impugns his character.

But Mae West's comedic style is primarily characterized for its frequent use of what Freud calls obscene or "smutty" jokes. An example of a smutty joke in *Goin' to Town* is West's state-censored utterance "twice," in response to the query about her having agreed to marry the rancher. As we have seen, the joke turns on the diversion of thought from the legal to the sexual implications of the word "consent." The smutty joke differs from simple smut in two ways: its reference to sex takes the form of an allusion, rather than being an undisguised indecency; and a person who is a desired object of seduction is usually absent at the telling of smutty jokes, whereas this person is often present at the utterance of simple smut. Freud attributes the elaboration of smutty jokes out of simple smut, which only "the common people" tolerate, to the power of repressions arising from "civilisation and higher education" (99–101). He thus correlates the occurrence of smutty jokes, as distinguished from simple smut, with social class standing.

Freud discusses the psychodynamics of both smut and smutty jokes in terms of a triadic model of narrator, object and listener. He presumes thereby a strict delineation of gender behaviors: a sexually aggressive male and sexually submissive but repressed female, who is the original object of the smut. Yet the enunciation of smutty jokes in Mae West's films clearly transgresses Freud's model of male narrator, male listener and female object of the joke. Besides West's transgressive performance as a female narrator of smutty and hostile jokes, it is the identity of the object or "butt" of the jokes that is most distinctive in West's film comedy. The butts of Mae West's hostile jokes are most frequently male characters in positions of ostensible authority, and with whom the West character does not contemplate sexual relations.[30]

Further, in a pattern that emphatically undercuts Freud's gender presumptions, men are also the butts of West's frequent smutty jokes. West's sexually suggestive comments are usually directed at male characters whom her character is trying to seduce, who are almost invariably the leading men. Following Freud's distinction, one might argue that the numerous lewd remarks (including throaty hums and suggestive facial expressions) that West's character makes to the male objects of her desire represent simple smut. Certainly, West's sexually suggestive lines and gestures were publicly condemned upon the films' initial release (and increasingly censored during subsequent productions) as smut. Like Freud, many censors and critics, such as the church representative and the critic from the *New York Times*, emphasized the lower-class associations of such material.

These observations suggest an explanation for some of the reactions to West's comedy, including its censorship. Following his initial discussion of hostile and smutty jokes as tendentious, Freud introduces *cynical* jokes as a further type of joke that serves a purpose. Cynical jokes take institutions, ideologies and persons who represent these as objects of aggression (107–110). Marriage, Freud notes, is the institution that cynical jokes most often attack. Asserting that a single example suffices to make his point, Freud relates the following joke: "A wife is like an umbrella—sooner or later one takes a cab" (110). Yet, while Freud's analysis yields insights into the construction and possible effects of West's comedy, that comedy distinctly negates the premise of gender distinctions that underpins Freud's tripartite model of joke exchanges. A single example also suffices to make this point. In *She Done Him Wrong*, the character played by Cary Grant (a detective posing as a settlement house worker) asks Lady Lou, the Mae West character, "Haven't you ever met a man that could make you happy?" West responds, "Sure, lots of times!" This exchange involves a play on the word "happy" (to imply specifically sexual rather than emotional satisfaction) and the technique of displacement, with the suggestion of a promiscuous search for sexual gratification displacing the apparent discussion of a search for a husband. This exchange works as a smutty joke, but also as a cynical joke, with its object the institution of monogamous marriage.

We have seen that censorship of *Goin' to Town* focused on lines that implied that West's character was happily promiscuous and regarded marriage primarily as a means of social and economic advancement rather than a locus of sexual intimacy or a repository of "family values." Extending Freud's analysis of cynical jokes, one might consider *Goin' to Town* in its entirety as a sustained cynical joke about marriage. Breen's initial evaluation of the project, and the church leader's letter, as well as the actions of some state censors, indicate that the film was widely regarded as such at the time of its production.

My use of psychoanalytic theories to explicate the workings of West's performance diverges from that of feminist media critics who have argued that West's films and image fit entirely within the bourgeois patriarchal institution of classical Hollywood cinema. These authors have concluded that the effect of West's representation of excessive, wanton sexuality is not to counter, but rather to reinforce sexist myths, especially through her presentation as fetishized spectacle.[31] Such analysis of West's performance, without regard to its historical and discursive effects, is inadequate to account for the workings of film comedy.

Cinematic Address and Comedy

The sets, choreographed musical numbers and costumes in West's star vehicles remain, especially in good prints of the films, an impressive cinematic spectacle, even sixty years after the films' release. A striking example in *Goin' to Town* is West's costume in the role of Delilah: West/Cleo appears on stage, preceded by a troop of slaves, in a long blond wig and a formfitting, dark, chiffon gown that is accented with gold lamé breastplates and a large, shield-shaped adornment directly over the pubic area. Ropes of gold lamé drape closely around the star's hips.

However exaggerated or "campy" contemporary audiences may find such costuming, publicity releases and media discussions of West's films on their release suggest that the star's initial appeal arose in part from an earnestly perceived attractiveness. West's early appeal encompassed both the conventional sexual allure of "glamour girls" and the visual pleasure of rich textures, luxurious settings, upbeat song and dance, of *spectacle* altogether.[32] In this, West's appearance fulfills the Hollywood convention established in the 1920s in Cecil DeMille's domestic dramas, following which only glamorized women are portrayed as sexually attractive.

British film scholar Claire Johnston argued, in an influential 1973 essay, that West's highly fetishized image supports "the collective fantasy of phallocentrism," through the "traces of phallic replacement in her persona":

> [West's] voice itself is strongly masculine, suggesting the absence of the male, and establishes a male/non-male dichotomy. The characteristic phallic dress possesses elements of the fetish. The female element which is introduced, the mother image, expresses male Oedipal fantasy. In other words, at the unconscious level, the persona of Mae West is entirely consistent with sexist ideology; it in no way subverts existing myths, but reinforces them.[33]

While Johnston's approach, an early attempt to adapt Lacanian psychoanalytic theories to feminist analysis of media, purports to analyze the workings of cinematic spectacle, it does so only by addressing a cinematic star entirely ahistorically. Johnston abstracts West's persona not only from the historically documented cultural functions it served (which formed contexts for its reception), but also from any of West's specific film performances.

Other semiotic and psychoanalytic approaches to the textual structuring of West's films suggest that the star's image need not entail such a deterministic, monolithic reading as Johnston offers. Even as those films employ conventional cinematic devices to present West as spectacle and fetishized object of male desire, other techniques and elements in West's performance offer spectators the potential of alternative patterns of identification and sources of pleasure. Key among these techniques are her manner of playing ironically to the film audience, and the inversion of traditional gender difference in the narratives (whereby her character motivates the action, including sexual and nominally criminal acts, but usually escapes the narrative punishment or containment female figures are usually subject to in classical Hollywood films). West's powerful star image (including her public persona as a narcissistic, independent, successful businesswoman) also codetermines viewer responses to her films.

While filmic devices establish in the leading man or men in West's films a male-identified position which partially fixes "the male gaze," a close analysis of West's films reveals a complex system of *gazes* that yields structures of narrative desire contrary to the Oedipal model that, according to Laura Mulvey, Stephen Heath and others, dominates Hollywood cinema. As star and performer, West is the object of the camera gaze, and in many scenes, especially when she is performing on stage, she is also the object of the gaze of a number of male characters as well as of supporting women characters. But in West's films, significantly, no one male character functions as a male identificatory position, fixing the gaze of desire.

Instead, West's characters themselves frequently initiate the gaze at male characters. For example, she addresses audience attention to her primary romantic interest in *Goin' to Town*, an English lord, Edward Carrington (Paul Cavanagh), by commenting, before his figure has been introduced on screen, "Ah, English, eh? I thought that body looked imported!" In their first joint scene, West wears trousers astride a horse as she arrives at her oil rigs, at which he works. Her first view of Carrington is in a medium shot from behind, as he leans over a forge. She calls, "Hey, handsome!" to attract his attention, and, getting no response, shoots off his hat and later lassos him to pull him over to her. Only in the scene, late in the film, in which West/Cleo performs Delilah, does Carrington fix his gaze on her. West, in all cases, returns the gazes of primary male characters, whether they prove narratively to be her romantic interests or not. She often accompanies her looking at men with a humorous comment, underscoring thereby her position of speaking subject, often to denigrate or dismiss the men to she addresses her comments.

Mae West is fundamentally a star rather than an actress, for she always plays herself, that is, her star image. A technique through which her performance signals star presence is her direct address to the film audience. The direct address, derived from the vaudeville and stage traditions in which West first performed, firmly positions West as the primary narrative voice within her films. Not only does each narrative take whatever character West plays as its subject, it is always the star, "Mae West," who relates the tale through her self-referential dialogue, gesture and performance.[34] The consistent promotion in the films' opening credits and general publicity of West as author of her own screenplays underscores her status as narrator of her stories extracinematically as well as diegetically.

As a star performing theatrically and ironically, West returns the camera's gaze in playing through it directly to her anticipated audience in the movie theater. From her position as narrator (author/star) of most of the humorous dialogue in the film, West also, in effect, returns the gaze of that cinematic audience: West's targeting of men in her jokes directs aggression (sexual and/or hostile) towards those portions of the audience who identify with the conventional, male-identified, spectator position in classical Hollywood cinema. Indeed, West's performance can be understood to invert the usual gender associations in the structuring of the look, with its sadistic or masochistic implications.[35]

West's film performances position the female as psychosexual aggressor, the male-identified spectator as passive exhibitionist or masochist. At the same time, her film performances invite identification with the position of the star herself. This identification can be variously understood as that of the exceptional female in male position (a perception which leads, in conjunction with her performance, to the view of West as a female impersonator or as "phallic woman"), or else as a female in an exceptional female position (a perception which can account particularly for the feminist interest in West as a "strong woman").[36] The cinematic presentation of Mae West exceeds that of a conventional female sexual icon as object, and instead encourages subject-identification with West.

Indeed, critics addressing West's popularity as a gay cult figure have argued that her performance style and persona encourage active transsexual identification. West's excessively ornate costume and exaggeratedly feminine walk and gestures occasioned her to be interpreted as early as 1934 as a female impersonator and a parody of conventional gender distinctions.[37] Comprehension of West as parody—as conscious "camp"—involves recognition of comedic elements in her performance. Lacanian psychoanalytic approaches to West, such as Johnston's, fail to take into account the impact West's performance *as comedienne* has on the workings of her image. A perspective combining a critical grasp of Freud's work on jokes with film semiotic analysis reveals instead how West's comedic performance undermines the usual structuring of the look in Hollywood cinema as well as the punitive narrative positioning to which female characters are usually subjected.

West's violation of these visual and narrative cinematic conventions is closely intertwined with her violation of PCA-enforced guidelines for film dialogue and gesture. The case study of *Goin' to Town* indicated how film industry and government-appointed censors targeted quips and gestures that implied West's character refused to be constrained by demure feminine roles or a morality dictating sex only within marriage. None of these censors could have approached the film *Goin' to Town* innocently, with red pencil or scissors in hand to excise offensive bits of a film for which they had no expectations or prior context, any more than a potential movie patron at that time could have done. Viewings of this film in 1935 occurred within a vigorous public discourse around West as a controversial emblem in debates about sexual morality and gender roles. A significant revelation about West, coinciding with the release of *Goin' to Town* in the spring of 1935, augmented that public discourse: that Mae West herself had cynically discarded and refused to recognize a long-secret husband. Publicity about West's own repudiation of marriage insured audience and institutional response to *Goin' to Town* as a comedically expressed attack on dominant sexual mores.

Censorship of the Comedienne

"[A]n insignificant hoofer chased Hitler, the N.R.A., and the quintuplets off the front page of every newspaper in America for the period of two weeks," noted a *Los Angeles Times* columnist on May 4, 1935, referring to Frank Wallace, the song-and-dance man who asserted, in a newspaper story that broke in New York on April 23, 1935, that he had married Mae West in 1911. In fact, it was not the "insignificant hoofer," but instead the Hollywood star who grabbed the headlines. In 1935 West was firmly ensconced as a leading American icon, with her image as a freewheeling, sexually active woman who resisted the constraints of matrimony both in her films and her life. And here was evidence that she herself had married but rapidly rejected her husband! For some, the story's primary newsworthiness rested in a bit of correlative information: the revelation of West's current age as forty-two, more than a decade older than other Hollywood glamour queens at that time. West immediately and repeatedly denied ever having married, and dismissed associated claims about her age.[38]

That news of West's twenty-four-year-old secret marriage broke within a month of the release of her new film did not go unnoticed. Hollywood gossip columnist Louella Parsons mused in the *Los Angeles Examiner* on April 27, 1935:

> Of all things, now comes the accusation that the Paramount publicity department cooked up the Mae West husband story simultaneously with the promised release of her Paramount picture, "Goin' to Town." I don't know about that, but yesterday the New York newspaper Women's Club wired Miss West that she was the woman who had attained the most front page prominence within the past year. This is the second time Mae has won that distinction. Of course, I wouldn't put it past some of those lads in the Paramount publicity department to think up this husband idea!

In fact, as West conceded more than two years later, she had, as a teenager, married Wallace and lived with him for a short time.[39] The veracity of Wallace's claim does not, of course, disprove Parson's suspicions: the Paramount publicity department may well have been involved in the timing of the revelation. Whatever its source or motivation, the widespread publicity about West's personal life certainly heightened interest in her new picture. And whether or not moviegoers in 1935 believed that West had quickly and callously abandoned a husband in her pursuit of fame, wealth and sexual freedom, the much-discussed possibility that she had done so dramatically augmented her previous image as a sexually promiscuous and financially successful woman who rejected matrimony. Most of the film's viewers in the year of its release would have gone into the movie theater with a fresh sense of the star's personal attitude toward marriage: avoid it or deny it.

This extracinematic information would have underscored for 1935 audiences the impact of West/Cleo's quips in *Goin' to Town* about marriage, such as her skeptical remark to the rancher, Buck Gonzales, upon his proposal, "Marriage—that'll be a new kind of racket for me!" Knowledge of the publicity would also have inflected audience response to West/Cleo's comment to the Russian gigolo, Ivan, in the scene in which she insults his character: "You're all right to play around with, but as a husband, you'd get in my hair!" Although Cleo does marry at the end of the film (as West's character had done, in a quite obviously tacked-on ending to her previous production, *Belle of the Nineties*), *Goin' to Town* concludes not with a shot of the happy couple but with the star recounting in song how she climbed to the "top of the ladder" through a sequence of lovers. Viewers may also recall that Cleo managed to catch and marry Lord Carrington only by first exploiting marriage to another man to gain social class advantage.

Goin' to Town's depiction of marriage predominantly as an economic institution was a rare exception among the myriad Hollywood productions that, by 1935, almost always promoted a romantic, idealistic view of matrimony.[40] But it was not only the narrative of *Goin' to Town* nor even the array of West's humorous quips in this and other films which censors and paying audiences understood to take marriage and men generally as "butts." Counter to initial industry expectations, the comedic mode did not adequately cushion the offensive blow of West's depicted violations of middle-class sexual mores, largely because reports about the star's personal life and values lent her performance a verisimilitude that exceeded the degree of social transgression conventionally allowed film comedy. It was as much West's evident personal rejection of tenets of sexual morality as her film performances that were being censored. A comment Breen made in the internal PCA memo he wrote following the controversial release of *Klondike Annie*, nine months after *Goin' to Town*, suggests the industry's recognition of West's excessive transgression of even the relatively wide parameters of film comedy: "Just so long as we have Mae West on our hands with the particular kind of story which she goes in for, we are going to have trouble."[41]

That West's comedic style should have eventually proven so problematic to the film industry is a paradox, for West's marketability as a movie star was rooted precisely in public perception that she violated conventions of female behavior. West's media-fostered notoriety for repeated confrontations with censors had helped build her fame and popularity beginning in the 1920s; her "censorability" was an integral aspect of the image that attracted movie executives' interest in West.[42] But, by the mid-1930s, aspects of West's performances and image were taken to *exceed* the transgression of social decorum and gender roles expected, even required, of Hollywood comedy as a genre.

The censorship and controversy that marked the production and reception of West's films, with *Goin' to Town* as an example, do indicate that her comedic performances violated dominant social mores in the 1930s in the U.S., particularly the ideal of romantic monogamous matrimony. However, claims that Mae West's comedy is intrinsically subversive are at once reductionistic and overgeneralized. The reception, in the mid-1930s, of West's comedy as transgressive arose not alone from particular jokes and gags in the film texts, but rather had the impact they did due to West's status as star and as a bawdy comedien*ne*, that is, as a highly successful *female* performer who blithely transgressed sexual mores and gender conventions in her life as well as films. The same jokes narrated by the same, albeit older, star do not necessarily function in opposition to the social values of audiences some twenty or thirty years later. For example, West's comedic lines from *Goin' to Town* about not being ashamed of how she lived (implicitly, as a prostitute) seemed anything but subversive when delivered in 1971 to a radio audience of U.S. soldiers in Vietnam. The workings of comedy are always historically inscribed in its reception.[43]

Knowledge of the historical reception of West's comedy and persona may inform but does not determine a contemporary audience's readings of West's films and jokes. Yet those who valorize Mae West as a censored iconoclast or a gay cult figure may well grasp and use the star's comedic persona as a mark of opposition to the current status quo. This obtains for the present, especially in view of hotly contested discourses about sexual practices with reference to the AIDS pandemic, civil rights for gays and lesbians, and reproductive rights for women. For example, a greeting card available in 1987 in novelty shops features a man made up, costumed and posed to impersonate Mae West. A phrase across the top of the picture reads, "I hear you practice safe sex." The punch line is printed inside: "Call me when you're through practicing."[44] In face of the currently well-warranted fear of unsafe sex, and the politically powerful conservative moral drives of the 1980s and early 1990s that condemn all sexual activity outside monogamous heterosexual matrimony, such gay celebration of Mae West as an emblem of sexual and gender transgression seems a subversive comedic moment indeed.

12

"The Laughingstock of the City": Performance Anxiety, Male Dread and *Unfaithfully Yours*

Henry Jenkins

"You've Made Rather a Mess of Your Castle": Male Failure and Female Laughter

> No man who employs detectives should ever be disappointed. I hope every time you've engaged these vermin you've discovered that you've got antlers out to here, that you were the laughingstock of the city, that you came crawling out of the agency, your face aflame and your briefcase stuffed with undeniable evidence of your multiple betrayal, dishonor dripping from your ears like garlands of sea weed.
>
> Sir Alfred, *Unfaithfully Yours*

Of all of Preston Sturges's comedies, *Unfaithfully Yours* (1948) centers most explicitly upon male psychology, specifically upon the gap between an aggrandized male self-perception and the comic reality of male incompetence and failure. *Unfaithfully Yours* is a comedy about an orchestra conductor, Sir Alfred (Rex Harrison), who is terrified of the possibility that he may be "unmade" by an unfaithful spouse, that he may be turned into "the laughingstock of the city." Sturges's innovative structure frames the film around a series of fantasy solutions to the perceived threat of female infidelity, each linked to a specific piece of classical music. Sir Alfred's attempts to act upon these fantasies are consistently foiled and frustrated, often within elaborate slapstick sequences. Eclecticism, fragmentation, juxtaposition of generic materials, properties characteristic of Sturges's oeuvre, are read here through the character's crisis of faith in his marriage and his inability to decide upon an appropriate course of action. The film's ideological structure can be mapped by considering a series of sequences involving the principal characters laughing at each other's expense.

A woman laughs. In the first of the three fantasies, Daphne (Linda Darnell), the wife suspected of adultery, is talking on the telephone with Tony (Kurt Kreuger), her husband's loyal assistant and her supposed lover. Her husband, Sir Alfred, has urged her to take Tony dancing. Her laughter is melodic yet duplicitous as she shares with Tony her amusement at being pushed into her paramour's arms: "No, I tell you it was his own idea!"[1] In this sequence, Daphne shares many of the traits of the "spiderwoman," a stock female role found in 1940s *film noir*.[2] Daphne is dressed in black, a long flowing gown spreading around her, revealing her shapely legs. As she sits perched on her dressing table in front of a large mirror, she clutches a slow-burning cigarette in one hand and a black telephone in the other. Seductive, beautiful, untrustworthy, Daphne is, at the moment, the dark woman of the male imagination, a figure of dread and of desire, and nothing is more dreadful about her than that ringing laughter.

A man laughs. Tony, his brow dripping with sweat, struggles against two policemen and cries out his innocence at the end of the first fantasy. His desperate pleas are met by triumphant yet maniacal laughter. The camera slowly pans from the terrified Tony to Sir Alfred, sitting in the courtroom, as he throws back his head and laughs at his former assistant's fate. Sir Alfred has murdered his wife and framed her lover for the crime. He has turned the tables on all of those who just a few scenes before were laughing at his expense, and he is free, at last, to laugh back.

As the camera draws in to his eyes and then pulls back again, Sir Alfred is still laughing in triumph, conducting the crescendo of a Rossini overture. Audience members, including Daphne and her sister, Barbara, watch his passionate performance with rapt attention. Here, Sir Alfred's laughter also connotes mastery, although of a more benign sort: he is the "great man" who, as his manager suggests, can "bring such music from that bunch of cat scratchers." Sir Alfred's laughter is loud, "brazen," and, most of all, "vulgar." Sir Alfred advises a cymbal player, whose mother has taught him to always avoid the vulgar, to cast aside maternally imposed inhibitions in favor of robust and rebellious music: "Be vulgar, by all means, but let me hear that brazen laugh."

The other man laughs. Sir Alfred has left the concert without saying a word to anyone and returned to his apartment with plans to kill his wife. Sir Alfred's attempts to enact his fantasies become the stuff of slapstick. Concerned by Alfred's abrupt disappearance, Tony and Daphne come home to find the apartment in a shambles, and the embarrassed husband sprawled on the floor, unable to stop sneezing. There is no music here, only the warped bass of a phonograph record of his own voice

Male Mastery . . .

playing at the wrong speed. Struggling to his feet, the irate conductor
boldly proclaims his male privilege: "I'm well within my rights. I'm
doing what I like in my own home. They say in England that an Englishman's home is his castle." Daphne looks at him with bemusement
and affection: "You've made rather a mess of your castle." Unable to
ignore the ridiculousness of his boss's situation, Tony laughs. Sir Alfred
growls, "What are you laughing about?" Tony's laughter confirms what

. . . and Male Incompetence: Rex Harrison in *Unfaithfully Yours* (1948).

Alfred already knows, that he has become a laughingstock, and all attempts to extract himself from that situation simply make him more comical.

And what of our laughter? *Unfaithfully Yours* is, after all, a comedy. How is our laughter implicated within the scenario of male dread which is at the center of Preston Sturges's film? How does our laughter fit within the complex power relations Sturges charts through these successive images of characters laughing?

Sigmund Freud's *Jokes and Their Relations to the Unconscious* proposed a tripartite structure to account for the pleasures of the "smut" joke. Such jokes, according to Freud, become exercises of male power, as the male joker seeks to embarrass (as well as seduce), the female listener and seeks confirmation of his triumph from a male third party. Freud asserts this shared male laughter comes at the expense of a woman and, by logical extension, all women. He distinguishes between the joke (which is staged with the knowledge and unwitting cooperation of all three parties) and the comic (which represents "an unintended discovery from human social relations," and therefore involves two parties, "the one who is comic and the one who laughs").[3] Viewing comic films, Steve Neale suggests, involves both a pleasure in observing the comic and a pleasure in responding to the joke. In so far as we laugh at the joke, we endorse the exercise of male power over women. In so far as we respond to the comic, we most often laugh at the expense of a male character (often, in the process, expressing our superiority in the face of his bungling incompetence). Our relationship to the scenes from *Unfaithfully Yours* described above is more complex still, since Sturges invites us to consider the male dread which the perceived threat of feminine laughter provokes. Daphne's laughter is neither a joke nor comic; it occurs during the film's most prolonged dramatic sequence. Since the comedy has unrelentingly invited us to identify with Sir Alfred's plight, Daphne's laughter does not spark our laughter, and may pain us. Yet it also colors our response to the film as a whole, since we are later invited to share Daphne's laughter at Alfred's expense when we take glee in his slapstick bungling.

Perhaps this accounts for why so many male critics have described this sequence as painfully unfunny, as a failure either of Preston Sturges the director to discipline his comedy, or of Rex Harrison the performer to master slapstick comedy. As Richard Corliss writes:

> In *Unfaithfully Yours*, Sturges submits us to a fifteen-minute sequence in which Rex Harrison falls through a chair several times, trips over a phone cord several times, hurls a roulette wheel out of his apartment window, dismantles—and is dismantled by—an insane voice-recording machine . . . the catalogue is unnerving, and endless, and the sequence is so grating that it demolishes the cumulative appeal of the film. Its only value is in the opportunity it affords us to analyze Sturges' most notorious weakness. . . . Rex Harrison is no Keaton, so his disgrace at the hands of some demonical objects evokes only fear. . . . The failure of the film is ominous because it seemed for once as if Sturges himself didn't know what these things were.[4]

Sir Alfred's humiliation extends outward to sully all who touch it, the actor, who pales by comparison to Keaton; the director, who displays his loss of control over the film's narrative (and thus looks forward to his own declining control over the mode of production for his films), and the critic, who finds it all "unnerving," "ominous," fearful and "grating."

Unfaithfully Yours has generally been ranked as the last and probably the most flawed of Sturges's string of comic masterpieces. Sturges himself regarded the film a failure, because of its protagonist's inability to act decisively upon the world: "The audiences laughed from the beginning to the end of the picture. And they went home with *nothing*. Because *nothing* had happened. He hadn't killed *her*; he hadn't killed *himself*."[5] Sturges's biographers mark the film as the last over which the director had substantial control, and trace his declining power within Hollywood, in part, to Darryl Zanuck's discomfort with the finished production. Other critics suggest strong links between the character of Sir Alfred and Sturges himself, noting his original plans to cast his own paramour, Francie Ramsden, as Daphne.[6] This correspondence between character and director allows us to read Sir Alfred's failure as a reflection of Sturges's own, dwindling self-confidence and his diminished control over both his personal and professional relations. Moreover, *Unfaithfully Yours* was released under the shadow of a scandal. Rex Harrison had been publicly implicated in the suicide of his lover, Carole Landis, and while he was never actually accused of murdering her (at least not publicly), there remained some gossip about his role in the affair, and many held him indirectly responsible for the events surrounding her death, particularly since the motivations behind her suicide were never publicly established.[7] Harrison's performance in the film thus raised issues which were already a matter of public gossip, linking the death of Carole Landis with the threatened death of Daphne. So Sir Alfred's loss of control can be read in relation to both the declining authority of the film's director and a crisis in the career of its lead actor, so that a cloud of "failure" engulfs the entire production.

On another level, however, *Unfaithfully Yours* represented a highpoint in Harrison's career, a film structured to display his full range as a performer, and to connect his performance skills with the potency and virtuosity of the film's protagonist. Sturges directed the other actors in the film to underplay their roles, allowing Sir Alfred to dominate the narrative and pull the other characters into his orbit. Sir Alfred's virtuosity is linked to his status as a musician and as a foreigner (traits which often motivate excessive performance in romantic comedy). These traits, among others, make his behavior and psychology suspect to his prim, Bostonian brother-in-law, August Finchler (Rudy Vallee) but they are not sufficient to explain the emotional extremes of Harrison's performance. As Daphne exclaims, "Even if you are a musician and an Englishman, don't you think you are carrying things just a little too far." To understand what motivates Sir Alfred's comically excessive response, one must consider the psychology of male dread and its expression in the film.

Champagne and Prune Juice: The Duality of Masculine Identity

Some men just naturally make you think of brut champagne. With others, you think of prune juice.

Barbara, *Unfaithfully Yours*

Writing in 1932, Karen Horney offered a complex account of male "dread of woman" and its impact upon male identity. The more familiar Freudian account of male subject formation focuses on the boy's Oedipal struggle with the father for possession of the mother. Horney, on the other hand, focuses on the mother as an object of the boy's dread in two ways: first, because she first voices social prohibitions against instinctual activities, and second, because she becomes a reminder of the boy's own impotence and inadequacies. Horney posits a series of initial erotic speculations and fantasies which both boys and girls project onto the parent of the opposite gender. For the girl, these fantasies become a source of fear, since she recognizes that she is too small to contain her father: "if her wishes were fulfilled, she herself or her genital would be destroyed."[8] For the boy, the matter of size works in the opposite direction, since he envisions himself as far too small to satisfy his mother, becoming, as a result, "rejected and derided." As Horney writes, "his original dread of women is not castration-anxiety at all, but a reaction to the [perceived] menace to his self-respect."[9] Castration anxiety, which is central to the Freudian account, represents, for Horney, only "a secondary process (by way of frustration-anger)," an elaboration and rethinking of that initial experience of insecurity and dread.

What Horney evokes, then, is the boy's fear of the mother's derisive laughter at his expense. The boy fears that his claims towards masculinity may be a bad joke, and reacts often in rage and self-aggrandizement—hypermasculinity. Hypermasculine masquerade exaggerates the myths of male potency, strength, hardness, rigidity, and masks the male's fundamental sense of his own ridiculousness.[10] The phallus, as a symbolic and mythic structure, compensates for the inadequacies and vulnerabilities of the penis.[11]

Male projects, goals, creative acts, Horney suggests, stem from a male need to prove to himself and others that the mother's laughter is misdirected and undeserved. Male creative activity, she suggests, constitutes a vehicle for exploring and exorcising male dread of women: "the violent force with which the man feels himself drawn to the woman, and, side by side with his longing, the dread lest through her he might . . . be undone."[12] These urges motivate a highly polarized account of feminine sexuality (the Madonna and the whore, the *femme fatale* and the nurturing woman). The demonic image of the woman as vampire, as destroyer of men, constitutes a direct manifestation of male dread, while the romanticized conception of a pure woman needing male protection allows a space for an ennobling male control over women and their threatening sexuality. What Horney does not consider is the way that this same tension produces an equally dualistic conception of male subjectivity, represented by the contrast between the larger-than-life screen hero who becomes the focus for male identification (an ego-ideal) and the comedian who becomes the focus for male self-doubt (a comic Other). Here, the difference between an account based in male dread and more traditional accounts of castration anxiety becomes apparent. The theory of castration anxiety positions the formation of male identity within a heroic account of the son's struggle against his father, and ultimately offers reassurance to the male; the issue comes to rest on masculine possession and the feminine lack of the phallus. Undergoing "Oedipalization" is the process by which the boy "secures" his masculinity. The concept of male dread, on the other hand, sees the formation of male identity in more comic terms; the male becomes the cloddish suitor, a laughingstock. Masculinity becomes a way of coping with what the male lacks—self-confidence, a sense of his own potency—and what the male must therefore compensate for.

Horney's account does not shift the blame for the more negative aspects of male subjectivity from the father to the mother, nor does it implicate a matriarchy within the psychic structures that define the patriarch. The slights the male child experiences are a product of his own speculations, a projection of his own insecurities, not of the mother's actual responses and actions. These fears are as much a product of patriarchal culture as the swagger that tries to mask them. An approach anchored in Horney's theory tries to locate the contradictions and instabilities within male identity; masculinity is seen not as monolithic and unassailable but rather as always on the verge of toppling under the weight of its own self-doubts. Masculinity is as much a process as a structure. Masculinity constructs a set of rigid rules and social norms restricting men's affective and psychic lives, but it also must produce a succession of cultural spaces which allow the momentary suspension of those rules, or at least an acknowledgment of their arbitrary nature. The rigidity of masculinity is bound to its self-perceived instability. The more wobbly the base, the more men strike out blindly against any threat to their equilibrium, and the more severely the traditional codes of male conduct are enforced. The specific sexual character of this threat (the matter of size) seems less important than the fact that this fear has such dramatic repercussions on how men think about themselves, and how they act within the social world (a matter of gender identity).

Although, in this myth of the origins of male identity, male dread originates in response to maternal laughter, it can also be contained through laughter, particularly laughter at the expense of women (as in Freud's smut joke scenario) or laughter at the expense of another male (as might be suggested by the familiar formulation of laughter as a response to "sudden superiority.") As both of these theories suggest, laughter is an exercise of social power, while to be laughed at, to be the passive *butt* of a joke, is a degrading position of submission and subordination. The comedian's performance of incompetence or social maladjustment, thus, functions alongside the hero's embodiment of exaggerated male competence and mastery as cinematic figures which help to manage masculine self-doubt and dread.

Although he does not acknowledge the gender-specific qualities of this duality, Parker Tyler cites the complementary mythic functions played by the hero and the fool within wartime and postwar American cinema. Tyler notes that comedians such as Bob Hope were often called upon to entertain the troops in the field during World War II, inviting the soldiers to draw a sharp contrast between the warrior and the clown.[13] As Tyler notes:

> One of the great characteristics of the fool, a part of his natural unfitness, was that, unlike his masters, the king and the knight, his blood was presumably mixed with water. He had the opposite of a warrior's courage; he was a coward. . . . The role of the clown, mythologically speaking, is still to provide a contrast to the knight, to illustrate by a kind of magic that the knight may project on the fool—who accepts it—every base qualm or cowardly quaver and thus purify his knighthood.[14]

The fool's presence allows the man to overcome his sense of his own ridiculousness and to construct a self-image of courage, mastery and potency.[15]

Since the knight and the fool are two sides of the same male insecurity, it is perhaps not surprising that the same actors may play both roles at various points in their careers. Paul Smith, for example, compares the roles Clint Eastwood plays in his action films (*Dirty Harry*, *Unforgiven*) and his comedies (*Pink Cadillac*, *Every Which Way But Loose*). The "burlesque body" of the clown offers a "bundle of symptoms" which contrasts with "the pained and beaten masochistic body" of the action hero.[16] While the comic body is only acted upon, the heroic body's actions have a dramatic impact within Eastwood's "melodramas of beset masculinity," which center around the suffering and pain he experiences in the pursuit of his goals.[17] Andrew Britton has argued for a similar duality in the film career of Cary Grant.[18] Across a wide range of films, Grant appeared as both a romantic hero (*North by Northwest*, *Notorious*, *Only Angels Have*

Wings) and a clown (*Bringing Up Baby, The Awful Truth, I Was a Male War Bride*). In contrast to his more heroic roles, which allow Grant to prove his manliness in the face of competition or opposition, Grant's comedies are "often bound up with the undermining of masculinity, or at the least, of male prestige and dignity." Britton characterizes these films as "comedies of male chastisement," suggesting that the values of traditional masculinity (such as professionalism, reason, logic, rational inquiry) take a terrible drubbing and that, as a consequence, the comedies establish a heterosexual couple "whose sexuality is no longer organized by the phallus."

One reason why Sir Alfred becomes such a problematic figure for critics writing about *Unfaithfully Yours* is that he shifts so abruptly between these polarized male identities.[19] Here the Knight (Sir Alfred) becomes the Fool, and if an inscrutable woman can so easily make a fool of a "great man" like Sir Alfred, any man is at risk. Sir Alfred is a *collieshangie*[20] of contradictory traits, both masterful and incompetent, powerful and passive, heroic and comic. The film's shifts between drama and slapstick are extensions of these competing notions of male identity. Such shifts place tremendous demands upon Rex Harrison. What Eastwood or Grant do across an entire career must here be done within the context of a single film, and in such a way that these brawling conceptions of male identity may be reconciled to create a rounded and psychologically coherent character.

Sir Alfred displays his hypermasculinity, first and foremost, through his professional activities. The film's opening image shows Sir Alfred conducting, casting a giant shadow on the wall, a heroic image of the male maestro remarkably similar to the larger-than-life treatment of Leopold Stokowski in Walt Disney's *Fantasia*. Hugo, his manager, describes him as a "hypnotist," who can magically produce magnificent music through total control over his orchestra. Sir Alfred proclaims, "All I do is wave a wand and out comes the music." This discussion of his "little magic wand . . . dipped in stardust," as Daphne describes it, suggests the phallic power associated with conducting, while a latter scene contrasts Stokowski's effeminate hands ("so beautiful, so large, so white, so free and easy on the draw") with Sir Alfred's more traditionally masculine hands which "look more like nutcrackers." If classical music has often been seen as a suspect sphere of male activity, Sturges presents the orchestra as a site of male mastery, with Sir Alfred remarking at one point that classical music should be enjoyed surrounded by beautiful women and with a bottle of beer.

Secondly, Sir Alfred displays signs of omniscience and omnipotence in his three compensatory fantasies. As Sturges suggested, Sir Alfred exerts a power over the production of these fantasies, and maintains a powerful role as a character within them: "Imagining his own role vividly, the marionettelike behavior of the other characters during the prospects is the natural result of Sir Alfred's ability to have them say and do *exactly* what he wants them to say and do."[21] The three fantasies involve different figures of male mastery: the cunning fox, the noble patron of women and the brave soldier. In the first fantasy, Sir Alfred masterminds his wife's murder, while successfully framing her lover for the crime. Here, Sir Alfred displays calculation, planning, cunning, precision, in short, intellectual mastery. In his second fantasy, he magnanimously gives Daphne her freedom, while writing her a check insuring she will never worry about life's necessities. He treats her as an innocent child ("a baby with bows in her hair") who knows nothing of the world and its hardships; he becomes her paternalistic protector, a role he intends to maintain even as he grants her the freedom to love another. He boasts, as well, of his superior insight into women's emotional life: "I couldn't understand music as well as I do if I didn't know the human heart a little." Here, his power arises from his emotional control and insight, his wise and forgiving heart, and his vast economic resources. The shift between his self-presentation as a monstrous murderer and as a nurturing benefactor is linked to an equally abrupt shift in Daphne's presentation, from "spiderwoman" to the child-woman: "That little head was never made to worry or these little hands to work, only to love, to love so dearly." In his third fantasy, his masculinity is preserved through the display of raw courage and brute force. Here, Sir Alfred confronts Tony, proposing a mutual test of their manhood. Daphne's responses are of little interest to either man, since what is at stake is the power relations between men as defined through the exchange of women. Pulling out a revolver from his desk drawer and inserting a single bullet, Sir Alfred proposes a game of Russian roulette, "a magnificent opportunity for you to show Daphne how brave you are." Tony cowers, pleads and cries, demonstrating that he is made of inferior stock: "Could it be I detect a thread of saffron in this otherwise perfect fabric?" Sir Alfred, on the other hand, displays complete control over his emotions as he put the gun to his temple, and pulls the trigger which delivers a bullet to his head.

In all three fantasies, Sir Alfred relishes his verbal mastery, the way that the others hang on his every hyperbolic phrase and flamboyant gesture. Sir Alfred's pleasure comes through giving a showstopping performance, becoming a spectacle for public admiration as compensation for his fears of being a comic spectacle for public ridicule. Behind it all, the affective force of the film's orchestral selections intensify the dramatic impact of his actions: Rossini's Overture to *Semiramide* (the murder fantasy), Wagner's reconciliation theme from *Tannhauser* (the forgiveness fantasy) and Tchaikovsky's *Francesca da Rimini* (the Russian roulette fantasy).[22]

Rex Harrison, in turn, adopts dramatically different performance styles across the three fantasy sequences, mirroring Sir Alfred's search for a masculine identity appropriate to his current situation. His actions in the first fantasy are swift, smooth, decisive; his voice has a guttural edge, and there is a slight rise at the end of each sentence as he archly manipulates the other characters. Harrison commands our attention simply by the ceremonious way that he removes his scarf, or by the way he arches his back as he circles around her. In the second sequence, he moves more slowly, a slight slump in his shoulder, and resignedly drops his scarf to the floor. His voice is soft, slightly raspy, at times caressing, as he looks lovingly and dejectedly at his beautiful wife. Each movement commands thought, as if he must force himself to go ahead with his all-too-noble sacrifice. In the third sequence, Harrison adopts an erect, stiff-backed posture appropriate to the scene's martial imagery. He moves towards them and they back away from him as if his very presence posed a threat. As he delivers Sturges's long, convoluted lines, Harrison shows no apparent need to take a breath, the actor's physical control connoting the character's emotional restraint and discipline. All of this control contrasts sharply with his all-but-inarticulate rage in the earlier, real-world scenes, where he confronts first August and then the Detective. Here, he struggles over the words, spitting out his *B*s and popping his *P*s with revulsion, each line delivered in staccato. In each case, Harrison projects some variant of hypermasculinity, demonstrating Sir Alfred's authority and mastery, the heroic ideal which becomes a bulwark against mounting male dread.

Harrison's performance during the slapstick sequences, however, exaggerates Sir Alfred's failure, the loss of his masculinity, as he is "undone" by his mounting suspicions and self-doubts. Here the comic side of male identity comes to the forefront. As Sir Alfred tries to enact each fantasy, the same three pieces of music are reprised, and the same props and situations are repeated, this time with comic rather than dramatic effect. The tones and rhythms of the classical compositions are "mickey-moused," so that what once rang forth with power becomes instead an ironic commentary on his repeated failure to fulfill his anticipated roles. If, in his fantasies, everything seemed perfectly planned and everything worked according to his plans, nothing works here, and Sir Alfred finds himself confused, baffled, lost in his own apartment. If he demonstrates extraordinary intellectual rigor in his fantasies, he is completely dumbfounded by the instructions for the recording machine. If his movements are precise in his fantasies, he stumbles, slips and slides here, knocking over the furniture. If he suggests emotional control in his fantasies, he is unable to stop sneezing here, his body turning against him and completely undercutting his grand speeches. If his imagined verbal agility wowed his associates in his fantasies, Daphne displays bafflement over what he is talking about here. In short, Sir Alfred demonstrates the "paralysis in motion" Scott Bukatman associates with Jerry Lewis, a constant movement and expenditure of energy producing no tangible results.[23] Sir Alfred can accomplish nothing except humiliating himself, and making a mess of his "castle."

Sturges exaggerates the contrast between Sir Alfred's empowering fantasies and his emasculating performance by the film's systematic opposition between music and noise. Classical music dominates the fantasy sequences, amplifying Sir Alfred's grandiloquent self-perceptions, and demonstrating his professional control. Sound effects are minimized, with the music broken primarily by the spoken word, another source of Sir Alfred's authority. In the slapstick sequence, however, sound effects exaggerate each clumsy gesture and ill-considered step with rips, crashes and squeaks; the music itself disintegrates into fragmented sounds and notes, while Sir Alfred's eloquent speech is disrupted by his sneezes. As Jacques Attali suggests, the opposition between music and noise is a basic one within any culture. Music is regimented noise, sound which has been controlled, directed, mastered by composer, conductor, musician. Noise is undisciplined and uncontrolled; noise defies authority and mastery.[24] Insofar as male myths of the knight involve an exercise of control over oneself and one's environment, music becomes the sonic equivalent of that myth, while noise assumes many of the traits of the comic myths of the ineffectual clown who, through his incompetence, his loss of control, brings about disorder. A throwaway gag early in the film points towards just such an opposition. In Sir Alfred's apartment, there is a clock which chimes the hour by playing "Jingle Bells." Each time the song plays, a loud, grinding sound silences the music and, as Hugo suggests, "leaves you hanging up on a meathook." The clock establishes the basic opposition between pleasing and predictable music and grating and unpredictable noise. Significantly, the only time in the film when the clock completes its musical selection is within Sir Alfred's fantasies.

Fantasy in *Noir* and Purple

> The only trouble with you is I never feel like getting up. I never feel like getting dressed. I never feel like going out into the world to wrestle it and bring it to its knees. I think the successful energetic men must all have been married to women who look like ———.
>
> Sir Alfred, *Unfaithfully Yours*

The knight becomes the fool. The man who rules his professional sphere is incompetent within the domestic space. These myths seem basic to the American comic tradition, and are, in fact, repeated many times in *Unfaithfully Yours*, as other male characters face a similar breakdown of their control and a loss of their dignity. In the film's opening sequence, an airport announcer is besieged with questions from Hugo, Tony, Daphne and August about the whereabouts of Sir Alfred's much-delayed airplane. (An earlier shot shows the plane flying through a dense fog.) Each time, he responds with absolute confidence, as if he were in complete control of the situation: "I tell you, you've got nothing to worry about. The plane is perfectly safe." Each time, his information keeps changing. Sir Alfred's plane, he explains with the patronizing tone of a man used to exercising unquestioned authority, has set down in Aroostook, Antigonish, or Apple-hockey, somewhere in "the general neighborhood of Nova Scotia." "Some neighborhood," Hugo grumbles. Then, with an air of triumph, the announcer points towards the large picture window behind them, announcing the arrival of the plane, regaining control of events which seconds before seemed totally beyond his control. August's assurance to his distressed sister-in-law proves no more effective: "There is one reassuring thing about airplanes; they always come down." His wife tells him, "shut up, stupid," and drags him along to meet the returning hero. (Here, as else-where in the film, Barbara's jokes at August's expense embody the male fear of becoming the object of feminine ridicule, yet even where the specifically sexual dimensions of this humiliation are not present, as in the treatment of the airport announcer, few men are allowed to enjoy unchallenged authority or mastery in this film. Women, on the other hand, are reduced to passive complainers and worriers, unable to change their situation through their actions, but often harsh in their judgments of men.) This sequence thus encapsulates the problem of male attempts to exert authority and exercise control within a world which is resolute in its refusal to bend to male will, the constant struggle to remain one step ahead of being made to look "stupid."

The opening scene's focus on the arriving plane, Sir Alfred's return from Europe, and his uncertainty about his wife's actions in his absence suggests a way of understanding the place of *Unfaithfully Yours'* within postwar American culture. Like Sir Alfred, many male members of the film's 1948 audience would have recently returned from "abroad." These men were also trying to reconstruct their relationships with the women they left behind, and were uncertain what to make of the changes which had occurred in their absence. These men also might have returned with nagging questions about the fidelity of their wives and girlfriends during the long months of their absence. The postwar Hollywood cinema re-sponded to dramatic shifts in the social construction of gender. Women, who had become active contributors to American economic life during World War II, shed their "Rosie the Riveter" work clothes and donned their aprons again. Many women made this shift unwillingly, resulting in a good deal of frustration, domestic unhappiness and an acute sense of personal isolation (by comparison to the fulfillment, pleasures and female companionship the war years had offered).[25] Men also experienced a painful transition, as they left behind the heroic, male-centered sphere of their wartime activities to accept their new roles as heads of suburban households and anonymous corporate functionaries, or to return to roles of subordination in factories, and the possibility that their lives would not be substantially improved by their actions. The gap between appropriate forms of masculine action and the realm of lived experience widened for most men within the culture. Most men wanted to be heroic, kings and knights of their new suburban castles, while many felt pathetically unheroic, the fools in their own comedy, laughingstocks at home and cogs at the office.

Many of the genres which came to prominence in the years immediately following the war (*film noir*, the family melodrama, the social problem film, the romantic comedy, the anti-Western) responded to these changes, offering various metaphors for the destabilization of gender identification within postwar America. The range of classical Hollywood genres, as Andrew Britton suggests, functions as an ideologically interlocking system, one which poses different strategies for confronting and resolving the same social tensions. Our tendency to discuss genres as discrete and synchronic categories does not allow us to explore the complex relationship between genres or the ways that many films, including *Unfaithfully Yours*, draw simultaneously upon multiple generic traditions. Melodramas like *Bigger than Life* and science fiction/horror films like *I Married a Monster From Outer Space* and *Invaders From Mars* function in remarkably similar ways, using drug addiction, alcoholism or alien thought control to provide a narrative justification for transforming hypermasculine behavior into a kind of monstrosity. These films exaggerate and intensify the gaps both between the masculine and feminine spheres and between masterful and emasculated conceptions of male identity. Other films, such as *The Incredible Shrinking Man*, dealt with men's fears of their dwindling role as economic provider or moral authority within the family. The postwar revival of the comedian comedy paradigm led to exaggerated representations of male inadequacy and incompetency, with Dean Martin and Jerry Lewis vividly expressing the polarized conceptions of male identity which characterized the period, while the films of Bob Hope or Danny Kaye dropped fools into generic situations (Westerns, swashbucklers, war movies) which demand knights.

Such concerns have been central to critics examining the emergence of *film noir*, perhaps the most complex of the postwar genres. *Film noir*, as critics such as Richard Dyer and Frank Krutnik suggest, represented a struggle over the shifting definitions of "masculinity and normality." Although they were not directly expressed, Dyer suggests that *film noir* became a means of exploring these shifting gender relations, often through a profound polarization of both feminine and masculine identity.[26] Much as *film noir* presents polarized views of women as figures of male dread or objects of male desire, a similar polarization and instability of male identities casts the male lead as simultaneously a heroic individual struggling against adversity and a pathetic victim of feminine deception. The gothic romances of the period (*Suspicion, Gaslight*) similarly express and resolve female anxieties about the ambiguities of masculinity, with the wife (and by extension, the audience) unable to judge throughout most of the film whether the husband is a murderous monster or simply misunderstood and benign.[27] The parallels between the polarized female identities in *film noir* and the polarized male identities in the gothic suggests important links between the two genres. The separation between the masculine and feminine sphere seemed enormous; men felt a perpetual threat to the stability of their masculine authority, while women were beginning to question the normality of traditional feminine roles.

If, as Mark Williams suggests, the wartime Sturges comedies anticipate *film noir*, his postwar comedies participate fully in the genre. That few critics have focused on the construction of gender within Sturges's works is somewhat surprising. Few American comedy directors seemed as obsessed with the "crisis of masculinity" as Sturges was. The unstable status of male identity and the potential downsides of the culture's obsession with success are the recurrent materials of his comedy. His protagonists are most often failures who enjoy male privileges by deception or confusion, and who stand to lose them the moment they attempt to exercise them, as McGinty (*The Great McGinty*) does, when he tries to move from being a pawn of the political machine and become an honest politician, as Sullivan (*Sullivan's Travels*) does, when he tries to turn his back on the comedies that made him a popular success in favor of a more realistic portrait of American life. Jimmy MacDonald, in *Christmas in July*, becomes a success through a practical joke: his friends convince him that he has won a slogan competition, and he tries to claim his prize money. Here, as in *Unfaithfully Yours*, Sturges explores the gaps between the character's self-perceptions and his actual situation. Woodrow Truesmith, in *Hail the Conquering Hero*, is crushed by his inability to live up to the heroic ideals of his ancestors, reclaiming his manhood by posing as the war hero he never was. Norval Jones, in *Miracle of Morgan's Creek*, becomes a national father figure when he claims the parentage of children who are not his. Sturges's films return over and over again to the gap between heroic male fantasies (which no real man can fulfill) and the comic reality of male inadequacies and failures. The same plots played from drama rather than comedy become the basis of tragedies such as *The Power and the Glory* or *The Great Moment*.

His obsession with deconstructing and reconstructing the myths of American masculinity reaches its peak in *Mad Wednesday*, where he literally rewrites the ending of *The Freshman* so that its upwardly mobile young protagonist becomes a middle-aged failure stuck in relentless repetition, falling in love with and losing an endless succession of sisters. *Unfaithfully Yours* digs deeper and more openly into masculine psychology, constructing a film which occurs almost entirely within its hero's tormented imagination and, in the process, pulling to the surface the male dread which is barely masked by some of these earlier representations. Much like Harold Diddlebock's love life in *Mad Wednesday*, the film becomes cyclical, ending as it began, resolving nothing, because its protagonist is completely unable to act.

Sir Alfred's fantasies are drawn directly from the thematic and visual vocabulary of the *film noir*. The conductor casts himself as the tormented protagonist who confronts a feminine sexuality and psychology which cannot be comprehended or contained within marriage. If, as Horney suggests, attempts to contain male dread exaggerate feminine power, making women into destroyers of men, or exaggerate masculine power, making women totally dependent upon men, Daphne's representation shifts between Sir Alfred's fantasies, sometimes the "spiderwoman," sometimes the innocent and idolized woman. In a speech cut from the final print of the film, Daphne explains to her husband, "None of us [women] are quite as good as men imagine—or as bad either."[28] Sir Alfred, caught in the throes of male dread, can find no such middle ground. Neither, it would seem, can critics, who have variously described Linda Darnell's performance as flat and uninspired or insipid and overplayed. Neither captures the nuances she brings to the thankless role of the "marionette" onto whom Sir Alfred projects both his fantasies and his fears.

Sturges wants to keep us guessing about Daphne, unsure whether she is too good to be true or simply untrue. Her constant flattering and fluttering, her cooing voice, and her doelike eyes invite us to see her lovemaking as a performance rather than an authentic expression. This suggestion is posed in the film's opening scene, when she embraces and pampers her returning husband. Their reunion is watched with varying degrees of interest and credulity by Tony, August, Barbara and Hugo. Barbara's first response, upon listening to her describe her sleepless nights awaiting her lover's return, is one of profound skepticism. "Is she kidding? If she wasn't my own sister, I'd have a name for her." Barbara never tells us what the name for Daphne might be, yet this is the film's central enigma. The women at the fashion salon also have a name for her. "What a lollipop," the saleswomen exclaims, with, perhaps, the hidden implication that her husband may be another kind of sucker.[29] Sir Alfred's doubts about Daphne first surface around the spectacular display of flowers she receives on the day of Sir Alfred's homecoming. He feigns indifference to this gift, uninterested in who might be sending his wife flowers, making jokes that they might have come from one of her former lovers. However, he seems remarkably relieved to learn that they were, in fact, the flowers he had ordered for Daphne. These anxieties intensify when he learns that August has had Daphne tailed, having misunderstood his instructions to "keep an eye on my wife while I am gone." Sir Alfred is outraged at this violation of his privacy and threat to his family honor. While he treats questions of her fidelity as absurdly misdirected, he nevertheless seeks her reassurance as soon as August has left. "You really do love me, don't you?" Sir Alfred asks, but her response is totally enigmatic. Daphne makes no definite statements, turning back questions with more questions, "I don't know what I would be doing here if I didn't. . . . How could I fall in love with anyone else when you took my heart with you?" Sir Alfred takes her words at face value, finding there what he wants to hear, "No man ever had a better answer than that." But she never answers his questions at all. Just as Barbara's barbed comments in the first scene of their lovemaking raised questions about the authenticity of her feelings, her evasiveness in this scene leaves us uncertain how far to trust this potentially duplicitous woman.[30]

Sir Alfred's love is totally narcissistic; he seeks through his wife the enhancement of his own self-esteem. The adoration of women has always been a means of resolving male self-doubts or, at least, of masking them from public view, "giving lie to male dread" (Horney). When he meets her at the airport, he wants only to examine her feelings for him: "Did you think of me every night? Did you take my picture to bed with you? Did you dream of me after you went to sleep?" He demonstrates his love by lavish displays of flowers, by ever more spectacular evening gowns. His contempt for his brother-in-law's cheapness is also expressed in terms of the display of women, "Every fur coat he gives his wife he inherited from his grandmother, every pearl from his aunt." (Note here, as well, that inherited money comes from women, while earned money comes from men.) For all of his playful disdain for social conformity, he is tremendously concerned by what others may think of him. In the midst of his fight with August, in which he threatens to murder his hapless brother-in-law, he takes the time to insure that they will still speak to each other on public occasions, since to do otherwise might raise specula-tion. The fantasy sequences seem particularly obsessed with which dress his wife will wear, "the purple one with the plumes on the hips," and no sooner does he achieve a reconciliation with her, than he wants to parade her around as a public demonstration of his marital bliss:

> Will you put on your lowest cut, most vulgarly ostentatious dress with the largest and vulgarest jewels that you possess and accompany me to the vulgarest, most ostentatious, loudest and hardest-to-get-into establishment the city affords. . . . I want to celebrate. I want to be seen in your exquisite company. I want the whole world to know that I am the most fortunate of men in the possession of the most magnificent of wives. I want to swim in champagne and paint the whole town not only red but red, white and blue. I want everybody to see how much I adore you—always have adored you, revered you, and trusted you.

His language is lush and passionate, but his passion stems from the prospect of becoming a romantic, erotic spectacle, the public image of a successful man and his beautiful wife. His love is only real when he displays it.

To some degree, Sir Alfred's obsession with public perception is presented as an issue of class, with the British conductor and his wealthy American brother-in-law sharing an upper-class preoccupation with "appearances." Yet this obsession can be read in relation to male dread as well, since Daphne's possible infidelity is seen as a public threat to Sir Alfred's self-esteem, a challenge to his pretenses of hypermasculinity (with much made of the difference in their ages). Because the scenario of male dread focuses on self-doubts which are projected onto women, it makes sense that Sir Alfred's primary concern may be whether his antlers are showing, rather than with the possible damage her adultery may cause to their storybook happy marriage.

Read in these terms, the detective report is doubly damaging: first, because it exists in tangible form and circulates between men, leading towards more and more exposure of Sir Alfred's humiliating predicament, and second, because it represents empirical evidence, depending on outward signs of affection rather than internal emotions. He tries to get rid of the report without reading it, yet it keeps coming back, and the indestructible report becomes the material manifestation of his own rising doubts and insecurities about a relationship with a woman substantially younger than himself. When he finally reads the report, sees the accusations with his own eyes, he can not help but believe them. The report suggesting Daphne's infidelity thus reconfirms his own doubts about whether such a beautiful young woman can really love a "seasoned traveler" like him.

Seeking assurance from the men around him, trying to find a counterexample, Sir Alfred finds only fellow cuckolds and potential cuckolds, as if the entire male sphere were constantly at risk of being "unmade" by feminine sexuality. His brother-in-law's marriage is loveless and sexless. August, like Sir Alfred, has married a younger woman, and his wife takes every opportunity to remind her husband of his own failed masculinity. When August complains about the spectacle of Sir Alfred's public lovemaking, she grumbles, "Better to do it in public than not to do it at all," and suggests that he reminds her of "prune juice" rather than "brut champagne." Barbara's nicknames for her husband, "Casanova" and "Sitting Bull," all represent ironic evocations of heroic male myths of conquest (sexual and otherwise). Here, the linkage between male dread and female ridicule comes closest to the surface.

Sweeney, the detective, is himself a cuckold, his marriage destroyed by an earlier detective's report: "We fall for these little dames and try to believe they are in love with us. But every morning our shaving mirror tells us they can't be. Then one day we find out that youth belongs to youth as you just did." Here female infidelity is again linked to a failure of masculinity, to Sweeney's sense of his own inadequacy and undesirability, while his professional life is spent investigating and unveiling the infidelity of other women. Only the valet speaks with assurance that his wife would never cheat on him; "I think it's most unlikely. First of all, where would she find anybody. In the second place, if she'd wanted anybody more attractive than me, she could have had him easily enough. I was awfully ugly when I was young, sir." In short, the valet has already confronted and resolved the gap between his own appearance and his culture's romantic ideals, finding security in the fact that his wife accepts him for who he is.

As his suspicions and insecurities mount, Sir Alfred becomes more controlling, dictatorial, patriarchal. These shifts vividly embody the links Horney identifies between male dread of women and the threat to male self-esteem. Feeling increased doubts about his own masculinity, Sir Alfred exaggerates his own power and authority. Sir Alfred threatens to flatten August, to beat his skull into a "nutburger." With Daphne, he exercises the male privileges he fears he is about to lose, complaining about his meal, refusing to answer her questions, attacking her unjustly for her fixation on clothes. He bellows, "I forbid you to talk to your husband with that tone!" and he threatens to strike her. If Sir Alfred, his manhood called into question, adopts what he sees as the trappings of a heroic male authority, he becomes, from Daphne's point of view, a monster, a lunatic and a "brute." Barbara asks, "Is there insanity in his family?" Such lines suggest that the male pathos of *film noir* is simply the inverse of the female fears evoked by the gothic. From the women's point of view, Sir Alfred's heroic struggle to reclaim his masculinity becomes either the stuff of horror (the insane "brute") or the stuff of comedy (the fool).

His fantasies erupt with the hyperbolic imagery of *film noir*, the canted angles, the extreme camera positions, the fragmented editing, the expressive *mise-en-scène*, the masking shadows, all of which contrast dramatically with the high-key lighting and long takes found elsewhere in the film. In these sequences (especially in the first fantasy), the camera seems to hold Daphne in suspicion, rarely taking its eyes off her, scrutinizing her every gesture and expression; such camerawork invites us to pay attention to what she says and does when Sir Alfred is looking elsewhere. Sir Alfred retreats into the compensatory fantasies of a patriarchal culture in crisis. And from there, he stumbles away, dazed, finding himself trapped inside a comedian comedy where he is the primary clown, bungling his way through the most prolonged slapstick sequence to be found in any Sturges film.

Sturges's play with narration and genre becomes a way of mapping different strategies for resecuring male identity in the face of the threat of public ridicule. The narrative conventions of the *film noir*, the gothic, and the melodrama offer no refuge from Sir Alfred's problems, since the film's comic tone renders their conventions ironic and hyperbolic. We know that, one way or another, Sir Alfred is going to be made the fool. On the other hand, we have trouble accepting Sir Alfred as the protagonist of a comedian comedy, since the shift from heroic ideal to comic reality becomes too abrupt to satisfy audience expectation, while Sturges's attempt to move from spectator identification with Sir Alfred in his fantasies to comic distance in his slapstick scenes is never fully achieved. We have too much invested in Sir Alfred's situation to find much pleasure in his total humiliation. Instead, Sturges seeks the film's resolution through a return to romantic comedy, reframing the events as something close to Kristine Brunovska Karnick's "comedies of reaffirmation."[31] Romantic comedy represents a compromise between the polarized extremes of male mythology, offering a space where male inadequacies can be acknowledged and contained within a relationship that chooses to ignore them.

Just as his world lies in shambles at his feet, his "castle" completely destroyed, Daphne tells a story and Sir Alfred takes it at face value. Daphne confesses that she has been to Tony's room, not to make love with him, but rather in search of her sister, Barbara, who, she believes, may be having an affair. Sir Alfred leaps on this explanation, screaming with joy as his feared humiliation dissolves into a situation that renders both Sweeney the detective and August the prying brother-in-law ridiculous. Such an ending evokes the tradition which Andrew Britton describes as "comedy of male chastisement," pitting the truth of feminine emotion against the evidence of male rationalism, the truth of the heart against the truth of the detective's report, and Sir Alfred bows before the feminine. In doing so, Alfred finds a way of separating himself (a man who reminds women of brut champagne) from his hapless brother-in-law (a man who makes women think only of prune juice), and of separating the dutiful Daphne from her acerbic sister. And he escapes the male fellowship of cuckolds, accepting himself, much as the valet has, by seeing himself through his wife's forgiving eyes.

The Final Sequence

I know what it is like to be a great man. That is, I don't really.
Daphne, *Unfaithfully Yours*

Taken at face value, *Unfaithfully Yours* becomes something close to the film Sir Alfred has described earlier, a "picture which questioned the necessity of marriage for eight reels and then concluded it was essential in the ninth." The restoration of Sir Alfred's trust in Daphne is both a convention of the romantic comedy and a resolution to the male dread which the film taps. Most critics have trusted Daphne's words, allowing the conventions of the romantic comedy to override the ambiguities of her previous speech and conduct. No other "comedy of reaffirmation" resolves itself this abruptly and this arbitrarily. Most critics feel compelled to assert, unambiguously, that *Unfaithfully Yours* is a film about a man who believes his wife is having an affair, only to find out that he is wrong. As eager as Sir Alfred to find a way out of this whole mess and preserve their faith in happy endings, they accept Daphne's claim that "I have no secrets from you, darling." (Sir Alfred fails to notice that Daphne is unsurprised by his knowledge of the events or of the detective's presence, suggesting that she may have learned through Barbara and/or August of the report and its contents. If she possesses no "secrets," she clearly knows more than she is saying.)

Yet the film's concluding scenes are far more ambiguous than these accounts would suggest; much of this ambiguity arises from the nuances of Linda Darnell's underrated performance. Much like the film's opening lovemaking, the couple's reconciliation is staged before an appreciative audience. Hugo, Tony, Barbara and August quietly enter the apartment and watch the couple's embrace and romantic reaffirmation: "A thousand poets dreamed a thousand years and you were born, my love." Yet, as Daphne professes her love, she rolls her eyes and looks just over his shoulder, a look which Sir Alfred clearly does not and was not intended to see. Sturges constructs the scene's space in a highly ambiguous fashion, never showing us a shot which positions the couple in relation to their observers, and so he makes it impossible to determine where Daphne is looking or who might share her look. In the group shot that precedes and follows that close-up, Barbara stands, her arms crossed, a smirk across her lips, looking like the proverbial cat who ate the canary. She rolls her eyes in the first shot and nods in the second, suggesting an exchange of meaningful glances with her sister. The view we get of Daphne is clearly not an eyeline match with Barbara, yet, as Edward Branigan has noted, point-of-view shots are often more suggestions or approximations than actual reproductions of a character's physical vantage point.[32] Even if we do not read this as a point-of-view shot, loosely defined, Daphne's rolling eyes would be visible from points other than the one from which the shot was framed, would be visible to someone standing behind her husband's back. What are we to make of this purposeful ambiguity? Are we witnessing the signs of a conspiracy between the two women to make dupes of their husbands? Who is covering for whom here and why? Does this glance call into question once again the validity of Daphne's proclamations of love, so that there are no statements in the film about her affections for Sir Alfred which go uncontested? Or does Barbara simply enjoy a good performance (with the concept of performance calling into question, here as in the opening, the authenticity of what is being performed)? These gestures are too small, too understated, to become proof positive of Daphne's deception, yet they keep alive ambiguities surrounding her trustworthiness.

What difference would it make whether Daphne is lying or telling the truth? Clearly, critics and conservative ideology have had a great deal invested in assuming the later. Such a reading helps to foreclose the indeterminacy that has structured the film, and to provide a means of containing the male dread Sturges evokes and explores. Yet Sir Alfred becomes a laughingstock in either case. If she is telling the truth, he becomes a object of ridicule because of his willingness to get so carried away by his own overactive imagination, because there is something comic in the entire psychology of male dread. If she is lying, he becomes an object of ridicule because of his willingness to allow himself to be duped by a deceptive woman, and, of course, because he is, as he feared, a cuckold. In either case, he becomes the object of laughter, and as such, never escapes the male dread of women which has structured the entire film.

Where do we stand in all of this? If such comedies were constructed to exorcise male dread by directing it against the figure of the fool, they do so by a kind of double positioning. We are asked to share the imagined feminine laughter at male foibles, to laugh at Rex Harrison's pratfalls and splattering ink, and we are asked to identify with him, to share his frustration, embarrassment, discomfort and, most of all, his suspicions about Daphne and his distrust of her words. The film positions us as both inside and outside the psychology of male dread. There can be no simple laughter at such a comedy. On the one hand, the film helps to reinforce traditional masculinity, to allow male spectators to displace male dread onto the body of the clown, and therefore to laugh at what might otherwise frighten them. On the other, the film exposes the basic mechanisms of male psychology to public ridicule, making explicit the process by which male self-doubts give rise to misogyny and sexual violence. The film's shifts between drama and comedy become painful reminders of the close relationship between the knight and the clown, reminders which will be experienced differently by those who function within and outside of masculine culture. A woman laughs, a man laughs, but not at the same time, not in the same way or for the same reason.

Ideology: The Case of Romantic Comedy

13

INTRODUCTION: Comedy and the Social World

Kristine Brunovska Karnick and Henry Jenkins

Comedy and Culture

In the case of comedy, the tendency is great to imagine the comic as outside of history, an essential force. On the one hand, the notion of comedy as transcendent celebration . . . imagines history is but a contingent pressure or resistance that the comic impulse can always overcome. On the other hand, the secular tradition . . . imagines that history always undoes pretension, that the pragmatic always triumphs over the idealistic. In both cases, comic tradition is imagined as self-contained, never losing its essential identity to the contingencies of a merely arbitrary history.

Dana Polan[1]

Comedy's tendency toward the scatological has often been read as a search for a universal humanity that transcends traditional boundaries of class, race and nationality. Comedy pulls everything down to its most basic level, and as such it transcends petty concerns of the moment and enters a space where the sacred and the profane merge. Critics have therefore searched comedies for messages of social transgression or social reaffirmation which emerge from a timeless and unchanging realm of playboys and killjoys, senexes and young lovers, tricksters and their foils. The auteurist orientation of most film comedy criticism invites us to focus on great "comic minds" such as Chaplin and Capra, whose "original visions" escape the mundane constraints of filmic convention and ordinary thought. The exclusive focus on films that retain their comic appeal to modern-day audiences tends to exaggerate their "universality" at the expense of an understanding of their particular address and meaning for their original audiences.

More recent work on Chaplin, however, has stressed his historical roots and context, his ties to a broader range of other tramp figures within early screen comedy and British music hall, his borrowings from less memorable comic works, his relations to contemporary aesthetic evaluations of what constituted an appropriate balance between comedy and pathos, and his evaluation by contemporary critics and audiences.[2] Charles Musser's account of the Marx Brothers comedies similarly stresses not their vaguely defined "anarchism" but their specific relation to Jewish culture, fitting them within a broader history of debates and representations surrounding cultural assimilation.[3] Within such accounts, the notion of a comic "mind" of the romantic artist is replaced by a broader history of comic "mentalities," of the relationship between comedy and sociocultural processes. Newer cultural historians are interested in a more broadly defined conception of culture, of how everyday people structured their lives and made sense of their social experience.

If we look up "culture" in Webster's Dictionary, we find two definitions: Culture is defined as "Enlightenment and excellence of taste acquired by intellectual and aesthetic training; acquaintance with taste in fine arts, humanities and broad aspects of science as distinguished from vocational and technical skills." Derived from a tradition of high-art criticism that can be traced back to Matthew Arnold and his search for "the best that man creates," this definition focuses on what culture excludes (that is, culture consists of "fine arts and humanities" as opposed to technical and vocational knowledge, exceptional works rather than conventional works, and so on). Most of human experience is thus defined as nonculture. Culture requires and mandates specialized learning and the transmission of knowledge from an educated elite (Arnold's "great men of culture") to an uneducated mass (which is presumed to lack a culture of its own). As this "High C" conception of culture is applied to the terrain of popular works, it rescues from nonculture selected works deemed worthy of serious consideration. This conception of culture demands a canon, and auteurists such as Gerald Mast or nostalgia buffs like Walter Kerr have been all too happy to provide it with one. Comedy, a genre known for its low cultural status, is reduced to the works of a small number of exceptional "comic minds," rather than being dealt with as a rich popular tradition consisting of a large number of films, some accomplished, some ordinary, but all defining the conventions and thematics of the genre.

Webster provides another definition of culture, one that offers more hope for the serious consideration of comedy as a genre rather than as a corpus of masterpieces: "The integrated pattern of human knowledge, belief and behavior that depends upon man's capacity for learning and transmitting knowledge to succeeding generations; the customary beliefs, social forms and material traits of a racial, religious or social group." If the first definition was marked by its exclusions, this definition, derived from the social sciences, is marked by its inclusions. We all participate in this broader, less hierarchical conception of culture. Such a notion of culture postpones the task of evaluation until after we have a fuller sense of what constitutes cultural experience and what it means to its partici-pants. This "Low C" culture would see comic films as completely inter-twined with a broad range of social, economic and cultural practices, as a site for examining the contradictory impulses that constitute modern experience. This more inclusive, Low C conception of culture has been the governing principle behind much cultural studies research, including the newer work in social and cultural history we would propose as a model for constructing a history of film comedy. The history of the "mentalities" movement (as represented by Henri Chartier, Norbert Elias, Robert Darnton and Natalie Zemon Davis) has worked toward a fuller understanding of the ways that cultural and social factors have shaped people's sense of themselves and their experiences, on the ways that books were read, on the "structure of feelings" characteristic of a particular time and place, and on shifting conceptions of the body, emotion and sexuality. Popular festivals and celebrations, and comic texts and jokes have been among the materials these new cultural historians examine, adopting sociological and anthropological models to understand why French peasants found it so amusing to burn cats alive, or how carnival provoked and contained popular transgressions of normal gender roles.[4] Though not specifically addressed to the problems of filmic genres, these studies offer models for a more culturally and socially complex account of comedy.

Carroll Smith-Rosenberg, for example, reads nineteenth-century Davy Crockett stories in relation to genre traditions (such as the figure of the trickster) and in relation to the social context that produced and distributed them (the class and generational politics of Jacksonian America).[5] More-over, she is attentive both to the larger social ideologies they expressed (particularly the dynamics of capitalist expansion) and to the particularity of comedy as a means for expressing those ideologies. What difference does it make that the Crockett stories initially functioned as jokes or that they have been read with ever more seriousness by each successive generation of Americans? What could be expressed within comedy that could not be expressed through more serious forms of representation? And what did it mean for young Jacksonians to be able to laugh at such themes as cannibalization, masturbation, homosexuality and racial genocide? Much as this new, "bottom-up" cultural history represents a break with top-heavy intellectual and event-centered political history, a new style of genre history might focus on the conventions and contexts that shaped a broad range of comic films, rather than centering around identifying and evaluating exceptional works.

Does Laughter Have a History?

Consider, for example, what a theoretically informed history of "mentalities" might tell us about "comedy's greatest era" and more particularly about the intense laughter Agee describes. In a provocatively titled essay, "Do Dogs Laugh?" anthropologist Mary Douglas asks us to reconsider what it means to laugh. Douglas's first move is to demystify laughter, which, she reminds us, is simply a bodily eruption, like farting, burping or sneezing. On the other hand, she argues, whereas burping or sneezing may be read as uncontrolled and unintentional acts, laughter is always taken to be a communication. Different cultural codes shape the display of laughter.[6] The cultural basis of these distinctions gets lost in traditional accounts of screen comedy, where, as we have suggested, nostalgia moves too quickly between personal and universal categories. Consider, for example, the description of laughter that opens Agee's essay:

> In the language of screen comedians four of the main grades of laugh are the titter, the yowl, the belly laugh, and the boffo. The titter is just a titter. The yowl is a runaway titter. Anyone who has ever had the pleasure knows all about a belly laugh. The boffo is a laugh that kills. An ideally good gag, perfectly constructed and played, would bring the victim up the ladder of laughs by cruelly controlled degrees to the top rung, and would then proceed to wobble, shake, wave and brandish the ladder until he groaned for mercy.[7]

On the one hand, Agee's description of different kinds of laughter resemble the legendary Eskimo distinctions between different kinds of snow—a specialized vocabulary that originates within a culture that demands the ability to provoke and measure affective response.[8] Emotional immediacy had become a defining characteristic of American popular humor and thereby a reasonable standard for measuring the success or failure of different comic films. Laughter was assumed to be a collective rather than a subjective response, one which his *Life* magazine readers would share with Agee. Silent comedy, he argues, provoked a pleasure in performance spectacle, in how actors moved, rather than in narrative complexity, thematic significance or character psychology. He praises a vocabulary of stock gestures and movements, a "poetry" of bodily responses which provoked laughter regardless of context. What Agee takes for granted, then, is the vaudeville aesthetic, a particular set of norms and conventions that rooted the silent slapstick comedies within the history of variety forms of entertainment. For later writers such as Mast, Raymond Durgnat and Donald McCaffrey, issues of character psychology and thematic importance supersede Agee's focus on comic performance, linking the evaluation of comic films to the broader aesthetic traditions of the classical cinema. Even Agee's nostalgia can be read in relation to broader, postwar, social and cultural movements that sought to reinscribe American national traditions at a time when America was emerging as a global leader. His appeal to a golden era set in the past would have had special relevance amid the social transformation American society was undergoing in the late 1940s, when Agee's essay first appeared.

On the other hand, Agee's nostalgia for these sounds of forgotten laughter effaces the social conflicts that surrounded this privileging of emotional response. Many bourgeois critics in turn-of-the-century America would have questioned and rejected Agee's basic assumptions that the goal of comedy was to provoke audience laughter, or that laughter should be a source of bodily pleasure. The conception of humor that ruled the Victorian era favored a mental rather than physical laughter. The emotional responses that Agee describes were linked to lower-class tastes and life-styles. For many late nineteenth-century observers, qualities of laughter could and did serve as a measure of class distinction: "the coarse guffaw is the mark of ill-breeding."[9] Moreover, there were gender-specific codes surrounding laughter. Rufus's mother in Agee's *A Death in the Family* rejects Chaplin not only because of the suggestive content of his performance, but because he provokes styles of laughter unbecoming in women. Women were presumed to be too sympathetic to take pleasure in slapstick. Thus, like all cultural practices, laughter has a history, a history that reflects tensions of class, race, gender and sexuality, a history that needs to be central to our attempts to understand film comedy.

In her writing on jokes, Mary Douglas explores more fully the cultural and social dimensions of the comic. The questions she poses are central to any understanding of comedy as a filmic tradition: "What is the difference between an insult and a joke? When does a joke get beyond a joke? Is the perception of a joke culturally determined so that the anthropologist must take it on trust when a joke has been made? Is there no general culturally free analysis of joking?"[10] Each of these questions, Douglas concludes, points toward the relationship between jokes and "social cognition." The structure of a joke brings together two alternative patterns of thought, often placing the image of control against the image of what is normally controlled, allowing license to win out over restraint. The joke responds to social instabilities, and provides a way of defusing the tensions within such a situation. The joke, however, can only be taken as comic when it expresses something that is already understood and accepted by the cultural community. Otherwise, what might be a joke in one context will be read as an insult in another. Jokes thus assert social values, not simply those commonly accepted but also values in the process of transformation and redefinition. Because jokes must often deal with questions of the body and sexuality, jokes get bound up with the social construction of gender and sexuality. Moreover, cultural codes restrict the number of occasions in which joking can occur; thus bawdy jokes may be appropriate at funerals or worship services in some cultures and not in others. In the case of film, genre distinctions—or what Mast called "comic climate"—determine whether a represented action should be met with laughter, tears or some other response. Finally, cultural codes determine who gets to joke and who gets to laugh. The issue of joking relations is a complex one which has long interested anthropologists. In our own culture, the relative absence of female clowns from the official canon can be seen as expressing a patriarchal culture's uneasiness at the image of a laughing and joking woman.

Is Humor Liberating?

Douglas's analysis of jokes and social cognition seeks to resolve one of the central paradoxes confounding our understanding of comic representation. On the one hand, we experience comedy as an exhilarating release from social control, as a source of transgressive pleasure. As Douglas writes, "the joke merely affords the opportunity for realizing that an accepted pattern has no necessity . . . it is frivolous in that it produces no real alternative, only an exhilarating sense of freedom from form in general." This abstracted sense of freedom is what is captured when critics characterize clowns such as the Marx Brothers as anarchists, and celebrate their disruption of filmic and social convention. On the other hand, comedy can confirm a cultural community's most fundamental beliefs and values, directing its scorn against outsiders and nonconformists who threaten this basic order. In Douglas's account, jokes can allow a public airing of transgressive views only at a price (that they can no longer be taken seriously), and only where these alternatives are already gaining some modicum of social acceptance. Jokes may just as often be conservative, ridiculing the possibility of social change, as they are radical.

This tension between comedy as a source of social transgression and comedy as a source of cultural cohesion or social control runs throughout discussions of the carnivalesque. Russian scholar and linguist Mikhail Bakhtin introduced the carnivalesque as a core concept in his rich and provocative reading of the comic works of Rabelais. His book is, first and foremost, a historical description of popular humor and folk culture in the Middle Ages and the Renaissance.[11] Bahktin describes the medieval cultural consciousness, arguing that in early modern Europe serious and comic aspects of the world and of the deity were equally sacred, equally "official." A wide range of humorous forms coexisted in one culture of folk carnival humor. Bahktin identified three distinct forms of this folk culture: ritual spectacle, such as carnival pageants and comic shows of the marketplace; comic verbal compositions and oral and written parodies; and various genres of billingsgate, curses, oaths and marketplace speech. These forms of folk humor reflected a single humorous aspect of the world. Carnival festivities and comic spectacles, and the rituals connected with them, played a central role in the lives of medieval men and women. In carnival, there was no distinction between actors and spectators. Everyone participated in the festivities, because "its very idea embraces all the people."[12] Bahktin was drawn to and here described the positive and regenerative power of carnival:

> While carnival lasts, there is no other life outside it. During carnival time life is subject only to its laws, that is, the laws of its own freedom. It has a universal spirit; it is a special condition of the entire world, of the world's revival and renewal, in which all take part.[13]

The carnivalesque style and spirit engendered a laughter that represented joyful and triumphant hilarity. It possessed a positive, regenerative power. The liberation offered by the carnivalesque contrasts sharply with the hierarchical social structure of the Middle Ages. Through carnival, fixed social roles were abandoned in favor of a more fluid conception of identity, the hierarchy was shattered, as fools were crowned kings and wives publicly beat their husbands. Although intended as a ritual for containing social tensions, such moments of carnivalesque sometimes sparked actual peasant uprisings and urban riots as people sought to extend the carnival into the realm of their everyday lives, making its resistance a permanent rather than temporary state.

Whereas Bahktin recognized in this type of folk culture a "regenerative spirit," that same spirit is viewed by Umberto Eco as regressive rather than liberating. Eco asks, for example, "why the most repressive dictatorships have always censured parodies and satires but not clowneries; why humor is suspect but circus is innocent; why today's mass media, undoubtedly instruments of social control (even when not depending upon an explicit plot), are based mainly upon the funny, the ludicrous, that is, upon a continuous carnivalization of life."[14] Eco uses this evidence to argue that the theory of "cosmic carnivalization as global liberation" will not bring about the desired results. Bahktin is right, argues Eco, in seeing the medieval carnival as a manifestation of a profound drive toward liberation and subversion. The hyper-Bakhtinian ideology of carnival as *actual* liberation, however, is wrong, in Eco's view.

Eco's argument stems from a comparison of tragic and comic; he sees the tragic as dealing with "eternal" problems (life and death, love and hate), while comedy seems more closely linked to specific social habits. Each tragedy features not only the story of a violation of a rule, but in so doing restates that rule. He cites, as an example, *Madame Bovary*, which he argues is a "long and passionate argument against adultery or, at least, about the impossibility of adultery in nineteenth-century bourgeois society."[15] By contrast, in comedy the broken frame must be "presupposed but never spelled out." A slapstick comedy situation provides an example:

> During a formal dinner somebody throws a cream pie in the face of somebody else. In order to recognize the situation as a comic one, one ought to know that (1) such behavior is usually forbidden by good manners and (2) food must usually be eaten and not wasted in unreasonable potlatches.[16]

Thus in tragedy the rule is explicitly stated, and in comedy it remains implicit. Eco goes on to argue that this is why the carnivalesque "liberation" seems suspect. In order for rules and rituals to be parodied, they must already be recognized and respected. "One must know to what degree certain behaviors are forbidden, and must feel the majesty of the forbidding norm, to appreciate their transgression."[17] Without a valid law to break, carnival is impossible. It is only the fact that the laws are obeyed during the rest of the year that makes their transgression joyous and pleasurable during carnival. Therefore, carnival can exist only as "an authorized transgression." The effect is thus not one of real transgression but simply a paramount example of law reinforcement. Here Eco seems to approach Mary Douglas's argument, that comic inversion is possible only within the limits of "social cognition."

This is not to say that transgression is impossible. On the contrary, Eco draws on Luigi Pirandello to argue that one can distinguish between the comic, as the perception of the opposite, and humor, as the "sentiment" of the opposite. Humor locates the spectator "halfway between tragedy and comedy." This is because humor attempts to reestablish and reassert "the broken frame." The performance of humor can act as a form of social criticism. Therefore, humor "does not promise us liberation: on the contrary, it warns us about the impossibility of global liberation, reminding us of the presence of a law that we no longer have reason to obey. In so doing it undermines the law. It makes us feel the uneasiness of living under a law—any law."[18]

The arguments of Bahktin and Eco can be viewed as opposing ends of a spectrum which includes a wide variety of views on the role which humor plays in society. A more modest claim for the possibility of transgression in comedy is advanced by Mary Russo, who argues that "the masks and voices of carnival resist, exaggerate, and destabilize the distinctions and boundaries that mark and maintain high culture and organized society."[19] Russo draws inspiration from Natalie Zemon Davis's examination of the trope of the "woman on top" in early modern France. Davis argues that social conceptions of woman as "the unruly sex," governed by the "lower" rather than the "higher" impulses, created a space for gender transgression and political revolt within comic representations, carnival festivities and political culture. The concept of the woman on top allowed both men and women to rethink social arrangements that held them in powerless positions. Looking at more-contemporary representations of disruptive and unruly women, Russo sees a possibility of transgressing and destabilizing the existing order through these carnivalesque images. The image of the woman on top "undermined as well as reinforced" the renewal of existing social structure:

> Play with an unruly woman is partly a chance for temporary release from the traditional and stable hierarchy; but it is also a part of the conflict over efforts to change the basic distribution of power within society.[20]

Thus the image of the unruly woman becomes a site for social transgression, with the potential to incite and embody popular uprisings. Kathleen Rowe expands on Russo's discussion of the feminine grotesque to examine a range of media representations of unruly women. She concludes that "comedic forms contain the potential for representing radical inversions of women's relation to power by not only unmasking the myths and heroes of patriarchal culture, but by opening up spaces for transgression, parody and exposure of the 'masks' of 'femininity'." The process of "making a spectacle of yourself" as a willful act, rather than as a consequence of a powerful male gaze, allows female clowns such as Winnie Lightner and Roseanne Barr to break down cultural assumptions about the female sex and traditional conceptions of femininity. Rowe argues that comedy may be ultimately as important for feminist debates as melodrama was for another generation of critics. Ramona Curry's discussion of Mae West's struggle against censorship shows how social institutions recognize and respond to the transgressive potential of comedy.

Arguments for and against the potential of comic resistance both assume that jokes and laughter hold considerable social and cultural power. Sigmund Freud's analysis of the smut joke, evoked here by both Ramona Curry and Henry Jenkins, suggests that joking can be an exercise of male control and sexual aggression against women. Jenkins pushes this argument further to suggest how the comic, another of Freud's categories, may simultaneously expose masculine vulnerability and contain it by displacing it onto a clownish other. Thus comedy's ability to expose uncomfortable truths about masculinity and femininity is both conservative and progressive. Film critics such as Andrew S. Horton, William Paul and Peter Brunette have used Bakhtin's notion of the carnivalesque to consider contemporary comedies of the Marx Brothers, Charlie Chaplin and the Three Stooges.[21] Such writers, however, rarely acknowledge the dramatic differences between the cultural ritual of the carnival and the mass entertainment of screen comedy. Anthropologist Victor Turner draws an important distinction between the liminal forms, such as carnival, which emerge in "tribal and early agrarian societies," and the liminoid forms, such as screen comedy, which function within contemporary mass societies. Liminal forms "tend to be collective, concerned with calendrical, biological, social-structure rhythms or with crisis in social processes." Liminoid forms allow for a great deal more individual expression, emerging in a context of leisure, recreation or entertainment. Liminal forms are "centrally integrated into the total social processes," as Bakhtin characterizes the complex place of carnival within the larger medieval culture. Liminoid forms exist on the periphery, are "plural, fragmentary and experimental," are often experienced as a break from social routines or as escapism. Liminal forms are "collective representations" within which all segments of society participate and find their identities, speaking to what unites a community. Liminoid forms tend to be "more idiosyncratic, quirky," linked to notions of personal expression and identities or at most to particular "schools, circles and coteries." As Turner concludes, "For most people, the liminoid is still felt to be freer than the liminal, a matter of choice, not obligation. The liminoid is more like a commodity— indeed, often *is* a commodity. . . . One *works* at the liminal, one *plays* with the liminoid."[22]

This shift in the function of the comic from carnival to commodity is reflected as well within the forms of transgressiveness each represents. Bakhtin saw the carnival as a historically specific practice, originating in response to social structures and thought processes characteristic of the medieval mentality. The leveling of social classes the carnivalesque enacted was a reaction against an otherwise rigid social structure where one's role was determined by birth and by an unchanging conception of the moral universe governed by the unquestionable authority of the church. The comic grotesque pulled everyone down to the most basic biological level, pointing towards those processes (eating, defecation, birth, death) that constituted a common humanity. Bakhtin traces the emergence of newer conceptions of the grotesque fundamentally at odds with the medieval carnival. David Kunzle has similarly examined the topos of the "world turned upside down" in medieval chapbooks, suggesting that the same images functioned at various times and places as expressions of the desirability *and* the absurdity of social change.[23] While the films of the Marx Brothers, for example, may superficially resemble the carnival culture Bakhtin describes, with their focus on biological pleasures and social disruption, with their opposition between grotesque and classical bodies, these films also affirm an expressive individualism fundamentally at odds with the communalism of medieval comedy. The Marx Brothers express a demand for personal freedom and self-expression; we recall what makes them different from the other characters, not what makes humans human.

Hollywood and Romantic Comedy

The complexity of comedy as an ideological force requires more particularized accounts of the interplay of social thought and comic representation. Generalizations about the medieval realm are hardly applicable to contemporary mass media, though analogies may help us more clearly see the continuities and differences within comedy. The essays in this section seek to explain the role of comedy and laughter in the social order of early twentieth-century America. These essays bring into focus issues of social relations by offering a case study of the romantic comedy, which here provides the site for a number of discourses surrounding gender and power relations, sexuality and class distinctions.

Too often film romantic comedy is seen as first emerging in 1930s sound comedies. A significant number of critics and historians have interpreted screwball comedy as, in some way, a reaction to the Depression. Lewis Jacobs, for example, writes that the "Screwball quality" of the films was a "cover for depression-bred alienation, felt by a depression generation that felt cheated of its birthright"—this being the earlier viability of the work ethic.[24] Arthur Knight noted, from a grimmer perspective, that these comedies had as their point of departure the terrible realities of the period—these being unemployment, hunger and fear.[25] Andrew Bergman argued that the comic technique of these films became a means of unifying a society that had been splintered and divided. "If earlier thirties comedy was explosive, screwball comedy was implosive: it worked to pull things together."[26]

All these accounts see these films as somehow fundamentally different from those produced only a few years earlier. Yet as James Harvey has noted, "there was almost nothing in the screwball mode that wasn't familiar from long usage in theater, vaudeville, popular fiction, or earlier films."[27] To understand screwball comedy, we must explore why certain

genres become popular at particular times and try to understand the historical ebb and flow of genres, without falling into the trap of seeing them
as determined by a single source.

Romantic comedy of the 1930s has been examined extensively during
the past decade. However, most analyses of the genre treat it as a discrete,
self-contained entity and chart its development from the arrival of recorded
sound motion pictures to World War II. In his essay "Divorce, DeMille
and the Comedy of Remarriage," Charles Musser argues that this approach
has increasingly marred our understanding of Hollywood romantic comedy, "a rich and evolving genre that dates back to the 1910s." Sources
for its initial appearance include a dramatic increase in the divorce rate
and shifting attitudes towards divorce:

> [in the 1910s] a minority was gradually laying the groundwork for
> the New Morality that ascended in the postwar era. Openly acknowl-
> edging the role of sexual gratification, proponents of companionate
> marriage sought to redefine the nature of this relationship if they did
> not overtly challenge it.[28]

As a result of this change, Musser argues, "it may be that the maintenance
of the legal bond will come to be held improper if the natural bond
ceases."

Responding to growing public awareness of the issue, Cecil B. DeMille
produced a number of films during the 1910s and 1920s depicting divorce
not as an evil associated with social degeneration "but as a way for couples
to escape dead marriages and find partners more suited to their current
needs and circumstance."[29] Musser's insightful analysis focuses on three
films from this period—*Old Wives for New* (1918), *Don't Change Your
Husband* (1919), and *Why Change Your Wife?* (1920), which he sees as
constituting the beginnings of the remarriage comedy. Musser's essay
examines social factors involved in the formation of this genre, institutional determinants, and DeMille's own attitudes about marriage and
divorce.

Tina Lent extends this discussion to the 1930s, focusing on romantic
comedies that expressed newer attitudes about friendship, love and marriage. In her essay in this volume, Lent defines screwball comedy in
relation to historical discourses about romance and gender of the late
1920s and early 1930s. Her work focuses on shifting conceptions of
courtship and the representation of "playful" relationships in these comedies. The widespread discourse on love and marriage appearing in popular
fiction and nonfiction signified a contemporary concern with the institution
of marriage, which was "perceived as being in crisis." Lent chronicles a
number of widespread social changes which make their way into romantic

comedies. Perhaps most importantly, films such as *Bringing Up Baby,* *It Happened One Night* and *His Girl Friday* built upon the contemporary ideology that love required a male/female friendship based on fun and play:

> A contemporary marriage required a union that took more than a license or certificate to forge. Many screwball comedies dismissed older ideas of marriage, including the importance of similarity to a matrimonial union and the importance of traditional aspirations, to advocate the newer ideas of a love-companionship between two complementary opposites.[30]

Lent argues that by repeatedly showing the redefined relations between the genders, screwball comedies created a heightened awareness of the new expectations for love and marriage.

Romantic comedies such as *It Happened One Night* and *My Man Godfrey* made the romance between the protagonist couple the major focus of the narrative. These films emphasized the importance of love and companionship in marriage but also dealt with other social issues. For example, films such as *It Happened One Night, My Man Godfrey, Bringing Up Baby, Sullivan's Travels* and *Holiday* explicitly posit work and the work ethic as preferable to a class-based system of inherited wealth, power and status. In numerous 1930s romantic comedies, rich protagonists leave a world of inherited wealth to struggle along with the working-class hero (but they almost never have to do any actual struggling). Irene Bullock fully intends to marry Godfrey and live with him at the city dump, when she goes to meet him at the end of *My Man Godfrey*. At the same time, working-class characters who single-mindedly pursue career goals are pushed into the realization that such single-mindedness leads to loneliness, that there is more to life than career, and that true happiness is found in the love and friendship inherent in companionate marriage. These films manage to uphold fidelity to the work ethic while downplaying its importance to happiness.

Such comedian comedy images as Charlie Chaplin caught in the gears of a machine in *Modern Times*, or Harold Lloyd dangling from a clock in *Safety Last*, are reformulated in romantic comedies. The twist, however, involves screwball characters who have no trouble coping with their work environment but are lost in other types of situations. Godfrey is a quite capable butler who has such trouble coping with Irene Bullock that he resigns his position in *My Man Godfrey*. David Huxley is lost in Connecticut, unable to cope with life outside the museum in *Bringing Up Baby*. His fiancee, Miss Swallow, is similarly preoccupied with his career, a trait which the film shows as undesirable. To celebrate his having received a valuable addition to the museum, David attempts to hug his fiancée, to which she responds, "Please, David, remember who and what you are!" Similarly, in *Holiday*, Johnny is so preoccupied with his career that he fails to recognize that his fiancée is also interested in only his career.

These traits move screwball romantic comedies away from an earlier characterization of the comic hero as an individual who no longer feels in tune with an increasingly industrialized environment, a character Wes Gehring calls the comic antihero.[31] Though this type of humor had become popular in literature of the 1920s and had been present in certain films of that decade, Gehring argues that in the 1930s the concerns of the antihero were cemented together in an identifiable genre; the screwball comedy.

The comic hero in screwball comedies has become too absorbed in his/her working environment at the expense of the rest of life. The romantic relationships that exist at the beginning of screwball comedies are almost always overcome. Miss Swallow breaks off her engagement to David Huxley, calling him "just a butterfly." The film replaces that unhealthy relationship with one in which the protagonists laugh and have fun. Lent emphasizes the importance of complementary traits:

> Each gender required the cooperation of the other to be complete and whole, and when their interests did not fuse, the complementary nature of the genders provoked the clashes described as sexual antagonism.[32]

In 1930s romantic comedies this emphasis on complementary traits extends to social characteristics, with the protagonist couple's "oneness" expressing the ideals of a classless society.

Economic and social factors that influenced screwball comedies have also been posited as the source of a conservative counterrevolution in the mid-1930s, a "Popular New Deal." This phenomenon coincided with and provided a reaction to the New Deal, and concerned not economic issues but rather how people felt about themselves and their institutions. According to Ralph Brauer, the Popular New Deal marked a "counterrevolution in consciousness,"[33] and "the victory of conservative values over some of the revolutionary values of the preceding years."[34] Comedies in the mid-1930s hence became more orderly, with sentiment leaning toward a conservative dream of comfortable surroundings and submission to the *status quo*. In this context, the adoption of the Production Code in 1934 is seen as part of this counterrevolution rather than its cause:

> The relative ease . . . with which the Code was instituted and the lack of wide protest by the general audience after its inception suggest that the public was closely in tune with the Code.[35]

The lack of social or political commentary is often cited as a defining characteristic of screwball comedy, in contrast to films of the early thirties, which are generally thought to contain biting social criticism. With the advent of screwball comedy, the anarchic spirit and sexual liberation that emerged in the early 1930s disappeared from America's movie screens. Films such as *Duck Soup*, *She Done Him Wrong* and *Blonde Venus* gave way to "innocuous" fare such as *It Happened One Night*, *My Man Godfrey* and *The Awful Truth*. Screwball comedies, according to Kristine Karnick, exhibit a remarkably homogeneous narrative structure. In the 1930s and early 1940s, these comedies dealt with issues of commitment to and reaffirmation of a set of culturally determined though nevertheless powerful goals and ambitions. These goals were reinscribed and reaffirmed with each new telling of the same story.

The romantic comedies of the postwar era represent yet another shift in the ideological construction of the romantic comedy, one responsive to what Henry Jenkins identifies as a reconceptualization of gender politics. Women who had worked during the war were being displaced back into the home, while men, returning from their heroic experiences overseas, felt dissatisfied with the more mundane life on the home front. Vague suspicions lingered in the air, suspicions about how faithful the women had remained. Jenkins links the anxious masculinity found in Preston Sturges's wartime and postwar comedies, most especially *Unfaithfully Yours*, to larger concerns about masculinity within the popular cinema and within American life.

The essays in this volume have focused on performance traditions, narrative structure, social ideologies and production conditions to better assess the role of film comedy in American culture. An alternative approach might focus on the reception of comic texts and their relationship to both their original and present-day audiences. As should be clear by this point, we do not all laugh at the same things or for the same reasons. Groups seen as marginal to the dominant attitudes and values of American society often must reclaim their laughter from the margins of texts produced for mass audiences. The final essay in this volume addresses issues of reception through its analysis of the ways that queer audiences find pleasure within the Hollywood romantic comedies of George Cukor, especially *The Women*. This film is doubly appropriate for an analysis of queer comedy and laughter since it is both directed by a gay auteur and has become a cult classic with queer audiences; Alexander Doty suggests some of the possible links between the two which help to facilitate an ironic camp reading of the film.

Camp, Doty argues, both originates within the text and its creator and within the reception context, within the extratextual information which circulates through gossip, within the subcultural knowledge and desires of the audience. As he writes, "the politics of the camp connected to the text or the reader can become contested ground, often negotiated scene by scene and character by character, as readers move between different camp positions, sometimes cued by textual codes, sometimes by their cultural background."[36] As many recent theorists have argued, homosexuality manifests itself in classical Hollywood cinema more through connotation than denotation, through suggestions and hidden references which invite savvy queer viewers to engage in a process of active interpretation and reclamation. As D. A. Miller writes, "For once received in all its uncertainty, the connotation instigates a project of confirmation . . . Pushing its way through the Text, it will exploit the remotest contacts, enter into the most shameless liaisons, betray all canons of integrity."[37] Romantic comedy becomes a particularly potent site for these queer reception practices, since it deals so directly with the issue of sexual desire and its influence upon our personal interactions. Camp readings offer ironic perspectives on what is said in these films, and often reintroduce what it was impossible for them to say in denotative language.

If, as Doty hints, George Cukor is having his own kinds of queer pleasures in his construction and staging of *The Women*, he would not be the first gay artist to toy with the conventions of romantic comedy in this fashion. Christopher Craft and other recent literary scholars have traced a similar fascination with impersonation, punning and connotative play within the works of Oscar Wilde. Craft traces the way that Wilde introduces into *The Importance of Being Earnest* a "parodic account of his own double life (the public thumbing of a private nose) as well as a trenchant critique of the heterosexist presumption requiring, here statutorily, that such a life be both double and duplicitous."[38] Wilde's romantic comedy becomes, in this reading, a narrative of closeted sexual pleasures (the fascination with the "Bunburrying" metaphor), building upon the play with identity inherent in the farce tradition, as well as about the absurd and arbitrary basis of heterosexual desires (both women's desires to marry a man named Earnest). Wilde, much like Cukor, makes romantic heterosexual love a matter of performance rather than substance. Much as *The Women* opens up a rich field for queer connotative interpretation, *The Importance of Being Earnest* enters into "the gay interspace of the pun" which remains totally invisible and inaccessible to straight audiences. Wilde, much like Cukor, "achieves these critical effects without the slightest breach in heterosexual decorum," though both Cukor and Wilde were known from their excessive verbal play and flamboyant *mise-en-scène*.

Yet even if we do not see Cukor as self-consciously introducing these queer subtexts into the film, Doty suggests, queer audiences have found *The Women* a rich space for mapping their own fantasies and desires, for focusing their own laughter at themselves and at heterosexual desire. Doty's focus on subcultural responses to romantic comedy, thus, becomes a vital example of the history of laughter we proposed at the outset of this essay, an investigation not only of *what* makes particular audiences laugh (a comic text) but *why* (a comic interpretation). Much like James Agee, Doty is interested in the laughter shared between filmmakers and audiences. For Agee, that laughter was universal and timeless. For Doty, that laughter is contingent and particularized. Agee is interested in the laughter that unites us across class boundaries; Doty is interested in how those who have been excluded from the cultural center nevertheless find laughter a powerful means of expressing their collective identities. This is merely one way in which classical Hollywood comedies stay lively and meaningful to audiences sixty years after their production.

14

Divorce, DeMille and the Comedy of Remarriage

Charles Musser

Over the past decade, film critics and historians have provided diverse perspectives on Hollywood's romantic comedy. Highlights include William Paul's fine book on Ernst Lubitsch's sound films, James Harvey's loving look at movies from Lubitsch to Preston Sturges, Gerald Weales's intertextual examination of comic masterpieces, Ed Sikov's glossy yet serious look at screwball comedy, and Elizabeth Kendall's investigation of female stars and their directors in 1930s comedy.[1] Yet all these studies share one characteristic: they treat film comedy from the arrival of recorded sound motion pictures to World War II as an essentially discrete, self-contained entity. They accept and extend a longstanding approach to American classical film comedy by isolating two distinct, almost unrelated phases of high achievement—the slapstick work of "silent clowns" such as Charles Chaplin, Buster Keaton and Harold Lloyd; and the screwball comedies of such directors as Howard Hawks, Frank Capra and Sturges.[2]

Without denying the benefits that have been derived from these studies, I would suggest that their disjunctive periodization has increasingly impinged upon our overall understanding of romantic comedy, a rich and evolving genre that dates back to the 1910s.[3] The classical Hollywood cinema was well-established by the 1920s, and genre practices from this decade continued to be crucial for those making and seeing films in the 1930s, despite the technological changes and social dislocations that separate the two periods. Although today's video stores and television offer comparatively few silent films, we should not allow the immediate absence of historical antecedents to skew our appreciation of either individual cinematic achievements or the genre's social relevance. Our understanding of depression era romantic comedy is both altered and enhanced by a deeper exploration of prior films in that genre.

The first and arguably most provocative study in this cycle of books on 1930s film comedy, Stanley Cavell's *Pursuits of Happiness: The Hollywood Comedy of Remarriage*, shares their periodization. As its subtitle suggests, Cavell's book examines a subgenre of romantic comedy that he calls "the Hollywood comedy of remarriage." It's basic narrative type involves a couple who divorce but then remarry each other by the story's conclusion. For Cavell, however, this comic trope of remarriage is not sufficient to define the genre, since:

> then the genre would begin in 1931, with Noel Coward's *Private Lives*, a work patently depicting the divorce and remarrying of a rich and sophisticated pair who speak intelligently and who infuriate and appreciate one another more than anyone else. But their witty, sentimental, violent exchanges go nowhere; their makings up never add up to forgiving one another (no place they arrive at is home to them); and they have come from nowhere (their constant reminiscences never add up to a past they can admit together). They are forever stuck in an orbit around the foci of desire and contempt. This is a fairly familiar perception of what marriage is. The conversation of what I call the genre of remarriage is, judging from the films I take to define it, of a sort that leads to acknowledgment; to the reconciliation of a genuine forgiveness; a reconciliation so profound as to require the metamorphosis of death and revival, the achievement of a new perspective on existence, a perspective that presents itself as a place, one removed from the city of confusion and divorce.[4]

Cavell goes on to focus on seven films, six from the 1934 to 1941 period, asserting that "this group of films is the principal group of Hollywood comedies after the advent of sound and therewith one definitive achievement in the history of the art of film." (p. 1) They include such admitted classics as *It Happened One Night* (1934), *The Awful Truth* (1937), *Bringing Up Baby* (1938), *The Philadelphia Story* (1940), *His Girl Friday* (1940), and *The Lady Eve* (1941).

Cavell studied this popular but little-recognized genre in a provocative and often fascinating manner, even though his insights were little acknowledged by Harvey, Kendall and others in the following decade. Perhaps because Cavell consciously constructs this genre so subjectively, by selecting films that he considers "masterpieces" and "Shakespearean" (are not the two for him almost the same?), its heuristic value for broader examinations of romantic comedy was questioned. Is the comedy of remarriage really a genre, or Cavell's quite private cannon of beloved films? In fact, I am convinced that Cavell has identified a crucial strand of American comedy which cannot easily be ignored. One of the most appealing features of *Pursuits of Happiness* is Cavell's interest in conversation, in dialogue occurring between the spectator and the film, and between himself and the reader. This essay is offered as part of conversation with Cavell, a historian's response to a philosopher's engagement with a group of films. Although Cavell argues that he is not "writing a history of the genre in question but proposing its logic," (p. 24), I am not convinced that these two operations can be as easily separated as he suggests.

Perhaps we are operating somewhat at cross-purposes, but Cavell's work raises, often explicitly, a whole series of questions about genre in general and the Hollywood comedy of remarriage in particular that I think still need to be answered (pp. 27–32). These seem to fall into two distinct if related sets. The first set involves issues of the genre's formation. How did this genre get started and what is its relationship to screwball comedy and/or romantic comedy? Cavell certainly raises these questions, but only to dismiss them casually with tentative and unsatisfactory answers. The second set of questions is more synchronic and more self-consciously polemical on Cavell's part. What constitutes a genre and how do we determine its domain? The comedy of remarriage, I would argue, does include *Private Lives*, as well as many additional films made both before and during the 1934 to 1941 period.[5] Cavell identifies a genre, but then seeks to limit its scope in a way that coincides with his philosophical project.[6] Turning Cavell's terminology against itself, I find his efforts to limit the genre's domain to be arbitrary, even unnatural. I will return to this polemic but want to look first at the issue of genre formation.

Locating and Historicizing Genre Formation

Cavell acknowledges that the comedy of remarriage might extend back to the silent era, but he does not find this crucial to his concerns, even to his speculations about the genre's first appearance (p. 27). He locates the genre's flowering in the eight years prior to U.S. involvement in World War II and associates the genre with a certain generation of actresses—Katharine Hepburn, Claudette Colbert, Irene Dunne, Rosalind Russell and Barbara Stanwyck—and a subtle if significant change in the place of women in American society. As daughters of a generation of women who fought for suffrage, these actresses embodied a new kind of equality that made comedies of remarriage possible (pp. 16–19). Certainly, these speculations about the social basis of the genre are weakened by the possibility of its origins in the silent period, as it would then be inaugurated by an earlier generation of actresses and actors. Moreover, while these performers may account for a certain reshaping of the genre, I am not persuaded they provide a sufficient explanation for its formation. A more thorough historical investigation can offer more fruitful reasons for the genre's appearance, locating causes that speak more deeply to its social and cultural relevance.

My own research indicates that the genre known as "comedy of remarriage" was created in the immediate post-World War I era, with three films by Cecil B. DeMille playing crucial roles: *Old Wives for New* (May 1918), *Don't Change Your Husband* (January 1919), and *Why Change Your Wife?* (March 1920). This assertion might itself seem hopelessly old-fashioned. Am I not guilty of sleuthing for first times—a practice still in disrepute among film scholars after being attacked some twenty-five years ago by Jean-Louis Comolli?[7] Am I not simply replacing one possible beginning with another, equally suspect? Certainly Stanley Cavell deemphasizes the importance of such formative moments by at least acknowledging the possibility of other starting points. In contrast, I wish to argue that the accurate identification of these moments is crucial for any serious historical enterprise. Whether the comedy of remarriage emerged as a genre in 1880, 1920, or 1934 is vital, since the timing of its initial appearance will inevitably signify different things in light of changing social and cultural trends. In each case, the shape and history of the genre will be radically altered. For example, in contrast to Cavell, I suggest that the genre of comedic remarriage originated in the Hollywood cinema and subsequently moved into theater, with Broadway later feeding the Hollywood genre via screen adaptations of its hits.[8] To make the most basic kinds of observations about genres, about relationships among different cultural forms or national cinemas, or about "influence," the historian must routinely sequence events in ways that acknowledge the value as well as the problem of firsts.

One can make a fetish of firsts. But in the 1970s, an era when theory dominated film studies, film scholars eagerly attacked "the myth of the first time" and often used it as a hammer to bludgeon historians into silence. Such attitudes tended to marginalize if not reject outright the time-consuming efforts of empirical historical work. Perhaps at a time when relatively little was known of preclassical (pre-1917) film practices, and claims to priority often generated unproductive national rivalries, an amnesty on firsts was beneficial. Now as film scholars increasingly use history and theory synergistically, we must value efforts to establish and understand initiatory moments.[9]

For purposes of comparison, we might turn to the historiography of the western, perhaps cinema's foremost genre, which exemplifies the neglected issue of genre formation. Scholars in film studies and American studies continue to view Edwin Porter's *The Great Train Robbery* (1903) as cinema's first Western. Yet, despite its Western locale and its oblique debt to Wild West shows, spectators did not initially interpret this film within that genre—which in any case did not yet exist in the cinema. In

1903, industry personnel and spectators would have seen *The Great Train Robbery* as part of a cycle of crime films, with immediate antecedents such as *Daring Daylight Burglary* and *Desperate Poaching Affray*, both imported from England earlier in the year. Moreover, the films that it directly inspired, Lubin's *The Bold Bank Robbery* (1904), Porter's own *Capture of "Yegg" Bank Burglars* (Edison, 1904) and his *The Train Wreckers* (Edison, 1905), were likewise crime films that lacked even a Western locale. Porter asserted that he made "the first Western" but identified it as *Life of a Cowboy* (Edison, May 1906), not *The Great Train Robbery*.[10] In fact, the film Westerns emerged in 1906 and 1907, helping to feed the new nickelodeons' voracious appetite for pictures.

Investigating the formation of genres across different cultural forms is one area that needs further attention. Unlike the comedy of remarriage, which seems to have first appeared in Hollywood movies, the Western was well-established both in literature and on the stage before appearing on the screen. Although *The Great Train Robbery* bears some similarities with Sam Peckinpah's *The Wild Bunch* (1969), *Life of a Cowboy* is much more connected to the immediate antecedents of the Western in literature and theater, notably Owen Wister's novel *The Virginian* (1902, adapted for the stage in 1904), Edwin Milton Royale's play *The Squaw Man* (1905) and David Belasco's *The Girl of the Golden West* (1905). In *Life of a Cowboy* the lone cowboy hero (dressed in white), the Eastern schoolmarm who claims the cowboy's affection at the end, the Mexican (or "greaser" as he was then called), the drunken Indian, the Indian maiden, the saloon, the chase, the hold up of the stage, the play of six-guns, the displays of frontier dexterity (lasso and other cowboy tricks) are all present and woven together in a narrative form that served as a powerful antecedent to the films of G. M. "Broncho Billy" Anderson and William S. Hart.[11] *Life of a Cowboy* helps us understand the ways in which the Western moved from more established cultural forms into the cinema, while an inappropriate privileging of *The Great Train Robbery* (which enjoyed such commercial longevity that it eventually changed its generic identity from crime film to Western) obscures such connections.[12]

Formative periods in a genre's history are typically complex and revealing. The reasons why a genre emerged at a particular historical juncture seem crucial, most often because it addressed compelling, usually unresolved or conflictual experiences within society. In the early 1900s, the screen Western evoked both a nostalgic escape from the regimentation of the new industrial workplace *and* an acceptance of new strictures and responsibilities. By returning to those initial moments of a genre's formation, the historian can investigate those elements that continued unaltered, or were subsequently excluded, replaced and reworked. After all, the films of a genre's formative period provided the framework within which pictures of a subsequent, perhaps more classical period were made, exploited and understood. The purpose of the following sections is to understand both DeMille's role in the formation of the comedy of remarriage and the genre's social and cultural underpinnings, particularly the marked shift in how Americans experienced the institution of marriage and the place of divorce.[13]

A Watershed in the History of Divorce

Our knowledge of American cinema of the late 1910s and 1920s—still largely limited to a few actors (Mary Pickford, Charles Chaplin, Rudolph Valentino), directors (D. W. Griffith, John Ford), and genres (slapstick, the Western)—has perhaps obscured the extent to which divorce preoccupied the motion picture world of the post-World War I era. Although the highly publicized divorces and marriages of stars such as Douglas Fairbanks and Mary Pickford focused this concern, these events resonated with broad-based changes in the social fabric. Divorce had become much more pervasive after the war, both in the United States and in Europe. As Roderick Phillips remarked, in his systematic look at divorce in Western society, the war "had important short- and longer-term implications that made it something of a watershed in the history of divorce."[14] In most of Europe and North America, both the number of divorces and the divorce rates rose dramatically. In the United States, the divorce rate, which had risen steadily since the 1860s, took another jump:

Year	Number of divorces	Number per 1,000
1860	7,380	1.2
1870	10,962	1.5
1880	19,663	2.2
1890	33,461	3.0
1900	55,751	4.0
1910	83,045	4.5
1920	167,105	7.7[15]

Between 1910 and 1920, the number of divorces per annum dramatically doubled. Moreover, divorces in the U.S. averaged 111,340 in the period 1914 to 1918, but 155,070 between 1919 and 1921. A forty percent increase thus came at the end of the decade.[16]

These increases, which suggest a quantitative crisis in the late 1910s, were matched by a sea change in how Americans thought of divorce. During the late nineteenth and early twentieth centuries, the role of, and grounds for, divorce were much debated, but a "conservative reaction" was generally ascendent. At the turn of the century, the Episcopal Church came very close to denying sacraments to anyone who was divorced, whether or not they were "at fault."[17] In 1916, its House of Bishops passed a canon that would have prohibited any remarriage of divorced persons during the lifetime of their former mates—only to have the proposal narrowly defeated in the House of Deputies.[18] Meanwhile a minority was gradually laying the groundwork for the new morality that ascended in the postwar era. Openly acknowledging the role of sexual gratification, proponents of companionate marriage sought to redefine the nature of this relationship, if they did not overtly challenge it. Herbert Spencer provided a touchstone for this movement when he declared,

> It may be that the maintenance of the legal bond will come to be held improper if the natural bond ceases. Already increased facilities for divorce point to the probability [that] there will come a time when the union by affection will be held of primary moment: whence reprobation of marital relations in which the union by affection has dissolved.[19]

Ultimately, William L. O'Neill argues, the new morality and the affirmation of companionate marriage did not produce the radical cultural transformation that was imagined, hoped for or feared, so much as establish divorce as a valid and perhaps necessary part of the family system.[20] Though not revolutionary, this still significant change in social mores created new hopes and freedoms, but also uncertainties and anxieties. The older, outmoded values were part of the genteel culture that collapsed in the wake of World War I.[21]

Given these quantitative and qualitative changes, it should hardly be surprising that many films participated in the discourse around divorce, either directly and indirectly, after the war. In this regard, the AFI catalog is perhaps deceiving. Under the subject heading of "divorce," it lists thirty-eight feature films in 1917, thirty-two in 1918, nineteen in 1919 and twenty-six in 1920.[22] Such numbers severely underrepresent the extent to which divorce had become a key structuring element for many films, even though they might not include an actual divorce. To cite two such films from 1920 that are not on the AFI list: *The Road to Divorce* and *Dollars and the Woman* have stories in which couples are clearly heading toward marital separation before dramatic events intervene. DeMille's *Forbidden Fruit* (1920–21) also fits this pattern, creating a situation in which divorce has become inevitable, but the ne'er-do-well husband dies before the act of marital dissolution actually begins.[23] The narrative logic was laid out, but the consequences were achieved by other means.

Particularly in the immediate postwar period, many pictures were working through the new social attitudes toward divorce, giving them a narrative form to which spectators could respond, perhaps as a way to incorporate this new belief system into their own psyche. Soaring divorce rates, the potential instabilities of companionate marriage and the increasing importance of consumerism in the dynamics of marriage all fostered anxiety for many who would never become part of the statistics. Even those couples for whom divorce was objectively remote must have had moments when marital dissolution seemed all too possible. With repetition one way to master uncertainty and anxiety, demand existed for a large number of films dealing with the subject. Yet repetition in the mode of melodrama could intensify feelings of guilt and anxiety, even induce social hysteria, rather than avoid it. Here comedy's ability to play with potentially explosive social topics such as divorce—to address the deep structures of social crisis—can make it vital to social well-being.

As Sumiko Higashi has remarked, divorce and the travails of married life were recognized as Cecil B. DeMille's specialty by the 1920s, due in large part to a series of very successful comedies and dramas.[24] As early as 1914, the "director general" at the Jesse Lasky Feature Play Company explored these problems in the dramatic film, *What's His Name* (October 1914), based on the novel by the well-known author George Barr McCutcheon. After rising from chorus girl to Broadway star, Nellie sends her husband Harvey to the country while she carries on an affair with a millionaire. Actors and stagehands soon refer to Harvey as "what's his name" during his increasingly infrequent visits to the city. Nellie abandons her husband and child and goes to Reno to get a divorce, only to discover that her millionaire lover is a true scoundrel. She returns to her husband and their sick child, reuniting the family. Although the film text is open to a range of readings, divorce is shown in strongly negative terms, as are various aspect of feminism, consumerism and the new morality. (It is revealing of changing attitudes, however, that Nellie does not have to pay some ultimate price—insanity, death or permanent rejection—for her transgression.) DeMille's *The Heart of Nora Flynn* (1916), which also touches on the possibility of divorce, remains consistent with these attitudes.

In both films, the breakdown of traditional gender identities has adverse consequences. The women (in both instances the guilty party) display remarkable immaturity as they forsake their morally superior role, while the men are weak and ineffective. In *What's His Name*, the husband is unable to provide an adequate income, impelling Nellie out into the public world. She is then seduced by the millionaire, who woos her with extravagances. In *The Heart of Nora Flynn*, the man is too busy earning the money. He is able to provide a luxurious home, but neglects his wife whose consumerist acquisitions include dapper younger men. The same dynamic operates in *The Cheat* (1915). Extramarital relationships are linked to the breakdown of public and private spheres. In *What's His Name*, the man is confined to a domestic space, while the wife asserts her independence by working on the stage. To some extent, women behave like men and vice versa. Divorce is understood as one manifestation of social degeneration, the inevitable result of a breakdown in social roles.[25]

DeMille and the New Morality

With *Old Wives for New* (1918), DeMille sharply shifted his public stance in the discourse on divorce, articulating views that were only then gaining wide acceptance. Divorce is no longer depicted as an evil associated with social degeneration, but as a way for couples to escape dead marriages and find partners more suited to their current needs and circumstance. Charles Murdock (Elliott Dexter) has become a successful oil king, whose physical charm and business powers are at their height. In contrast, Sophy (Sylvia Ashton), his once attractive wife, has become depressed and obese during twenty years of married life. In virtually every respect they have gone in opposite directions. Charles suggests the desirability of divorce to his wife, and then departs for a vacation, re-treating to the woods with his son. Amidst the beauties of nature, he meets and falls in love with Juliet Raeburn (Florence Vidor), who runs a fashionable dress shop in the city. Upon his return, Sophy rejects Charles's request for a divorce, and the nascent affair with Raeburn ends. Later, trying to cover up the murder of his business partner (Theodore Roberts) by a jealous mistress, Murdock is caught in a scandal that forces his wife to seek a divorce. His romance with Juliet revives, while his wife finds unexpected happiness in the arms of Murdock's male secretary Blagden (Gustav Seyffertitz). Divorce may be a difficult, painful business, but in the end everyone is happier. Even the children are remarkably understanding.

The film aroused some controversy, for the protagonist rejected his first wife to take a new one who was much younger, more attractive and self-sufficient. Charles was in no way punished, and presumably lived happily ever after, a fact that violated what would become the customary Hollywood ending. One female patron at the New York opening found *Old Wives for New* to be "a beautiful picture, but I am afraid it's a bit immoral."[26] The *Variety* reviewer who overheard this remark disagreed, employing double speak: "Laying aside the general theme, what may be considered immoral is counter-balanced by the pointing out of a moral and thus the picture should encounter no serious censorship."[27] This moral is summarized in the first dialogue title from the film, a title that functions emblematically in that it is extracted from the narrative in a way that introduced this theme:

> It's my belief Sophy, that we Wives are apt to take our Husbands too much for granted.
> We've an inclination to settle down to neglectful dowdiness—just because we've landed our Fish!
> It is not enough for Wives to be merely virtuous anymore, scorning all frills: We must remember to trim our "Votes for Women" with a little lace and ribbon—if we would keep our Man a "Lover," as well as a "Husband."

In fact, the speaker and context for this dialogue never become clear. And the term "we Wives" might easily embrace those women in the audience. The film thus offers itself as a moral tale, admonishing women to retain their physical attractiveness and girlish personality. In this brave new world of the postwar era, where women will soon have the vote, and only the fittest will survive the marriage contest, wives must keep their allure to hold their man.

Although DeMille supposedly agreed to produce this modern drama to satisfy Jesse Lasky, there is no doubt that he quickly identified himself with the film's position. In an interview appearing in *Motion Picture Classic* shortly after the film's release, DeMille maintained that "the normal man is satisfied to stay by his own fireside if the illusion and attraction are not entirely dispelled by marriage."[28] The new, companionate marriage and the new consumerism are intertwined. As Lary May has pointed out, this new type of marriage fostered a consumer life-style in which adults were "enhancing married life by purchasing victrolas, clothes and cars geared toward leisure fun."[29] Juliet Raeburn, whose first name embodies the essence of romantic love, is an attractive and elegantly dressed manager of a clothing shop for wealthy women, and so epitomizes the lure and eroticism of luxury items. She embodies a youth culture of which Charles Murdock is also a part. At different points in the film, both Murdock's son and daughter claim that he could be mistaken for their older brother. The picture thus affirms the social legitimacy of divorce based on personal incompatibility, but then suggests that women can overcome this ever-present threat through consumerism. The film resonates with a study that compares the causes of divorce in 1920 and 1880: the failure of the husband to provide the new consumer "necessities" was increasingly likely to serve as grounds for divorce.[30] Here, however, the situation is inverted: the wife could embrace these new consumer-oriented attitudes and perhaps hold on to her husband, but she refuses. On a more unconscious level, therefore, the increased anxieties now surrounding married life could be overcome through consumer purchases.

However much DeMille might have claimed that *Old Wives for New* was a moral tale for women, it was first and foremost a *drame à thèse* that advocated a new view on divorce. Divorce is now presented as a positive force that can bring social hypocrisy and counterproductive relationships to an end. And yet DeMille did not embrace the divorce thesis for himself. Rather he situated himself in relationship to the *Old Wives for New* moral in a quite explicit way. The picture contrasts the honorable Murdock, who seeks the new way to marital happiness (the path of divorce), to Murdock's business partner Berkeley, who pursues the old way by having a string of mistresses. Berkeley leaves his wife at home as he pursues his various affairs, and so did DeMille. As Charles Higham points out, DeMille was at that very moment romantically involved with both the film's scenario writer, Jeanie Macpherson, and the actress Julia Faye, who played the role of Berkeley's mistress.[31] Like Berkeley, DeMille spent his Saturday nights either on the town or at Paradise ranch, his rural retreat, with an entourage that might include both women. Despite the film's advocacy for a new conception of divorce, DeMille quietly, that is privately, signaled that his personal solution was somewhat different. The film can thus also be read either as an inside "joke" and/or a film *à clef*. In Macpherson's scenario, Berkeley throws off his mistress for a new one, and the jilted mistress kills him. In real life, Macpherson tolerated DeMille's new affair with Faye, even if she killed a DeMille stand-in on the screen. DeMille, perhaps amused by this narrative retort, had the last word: he cast Faye in the more substantial Macpherson role on screen, if not in his private life. Art may imitate life, but only to a point. In its politics of production, at least, the film appears resolutely amoral.

Despite its moralizing tone and outward advocacy for a modern attitude toward divorce, *Old Wives for New* "abounds in light comedy."[32] Among these comic elements is Sophy, the kind of matronly battle-axe who could have come out of a Max Sennett farce. There is also the double marriage, as both Sophy and Charles find new mates. Such doubling is, as Henri Bergson points out, a comic strategy. In fact, the romantic marriage of Charles and Juliet is balanced by the somewhat farcical marriage of Sophy and Blagden (a name perhaps evoking the French word for joke, blague).

Comedies of Remarriage

Old Wives for New is a film about remarriage which has comic elements, but it is not a "comedy of remarriage" in the way that Stanley Cavell uses the term in *Pursuits of Happiness*. That is, Charles and Sophy Murdock remarry, but to new and different mates, while Cavell properly focuses on those films in which married couples divorce but ultimately remarry each other. Cavell at one point argues that the comedy of remarriage might also be called the comedy of equality. It is therefore appropriate that the first film in the genre, *Don't Change Your Husband* (1919), was released the same year that the Woman's Suffrage Amendment was passed by Congress, while its creative remake, *Why Change Your Wife?* appeared the year it was ratified. Moreover, as the subtitle to his book makes clear, Cavell very much sees the comedy of remarriage as a Hollywood genre: DeMille's films are Hollywood products in a complex cultural sense much more than those made by D. W. Griffith, Maurice Tourneur or even Thomas Ince. Howard Hawks, who went on to make several comedies of remarriage, served his apprenticeship at Famous Players-Lasky under DeMille in the early 1920s.[33]

By examining DeMille's early comedies of remarriage, we can consider how this genre began. Initially *Don't Change Your Husband* could not function within the genre, because the genre did not yet exist. Rather, it appeared as part of a cycle of films dealing with divorce. That is, it was billed as a "New Angle on the Ever Present Divorce Problem" and a "companion story but not a sequel" to *Old Wives for New*.[34] Promotional materials reiterated the relation between the two films with a variety of lines such as "Remember the shabby wife in 'Old Wives for New'? Here's the untidy, neglectful husband."[35] There is at least the appearance of reciprocity between the two pictures: the slothful husband loses his wife just as the lazy wife did in the earlier film. While husband James Porter (Elliott Dexter) learns to shape up much as Sophy did in *Old Wives for New*, the film has a second thesis, a warning to women that they should not fall for the "male vampires." These "lounge lizards" seduce women burdened with neglectful modern husbands too preoccupied with business deals. While the husband made the proper decision in seeking divorce and a second marriage in *Old Wives for New*, the wife, Leila Porter (Gloria Swanson), clearly made a mistake in seeking a divorce in *Don't Change Your Husband*. That is, a warning to women against divorcing their husbands replaced the affirmation of divorce in *Old Wives for New*. This shift may be partially explained by the fact that the right to divorce was increasingly taken for granted. Its value no longer needed to be asserted so vehemently. If anything, the mushrooming rate of divorce seemed to require a note of caution—especially for women. However, it is no coincidence that these different "messages" are associated with different sexes.

The changes in structure enable the narrational stance of *Don't Change Your Husband* to remain patriarchal and consistent with DeMille's authorial voice. As before, the film was constructed to address women as its primary audience. The film's title makes this clear; it is a command made by DeMille, the self-acknowledged authority on marriage, seconded by his scenario writer, and directed at individual women sitting in the darkened theater, those who are or will be married. While the narrator does not seem to address a gendered audience as the story unfolds, the final intertitle reasserts the primacy of the female audience: "And now you know what every Woman comes to know—that Husbands at best, are pesky brutes; and at worst—are unfit for publication!" This would confirm the analyses of Miriam Hansen, Gaylyn Studlar and Sumiko Higashi, who point out that women were important audiences for Hollywood films, and that the industry recognized this both in the films and in the discourse around them.[36] In these DeMille films, however, male members of the audience are not marginalized but, rather, have a privileged place. A significant part of their enjoyment comes from the fact that the films are lecturing women (their wife, their girl friend, their date). Reversing the notion of the eternal female, these films tell women that men will be men and so they must adapt. Men are not above criticism, but beyond it. The moralizing seeks to ward off the woman as a Medusa that lodges in DeMille's psyche. At the same time, this film at least purports to speak to women as free agents, as their husbands' equals; it is not women as sisters or lovers but women as mothers whom DeMille fears.[38]

If, in moving from *Old Wives for New* to *Don't Change Your Husband*, DeMille reorganized narrative elements and introduced a filmic narrator in ways that foreclose a feminist perspective, these new factors also contribute to the comedy. Remarriage to an original partner inevitably involves circularity, a narrative structure conducive to comedy. Much effort brings this couple quite literally back to the same place (the living room of their home), when less traumatic solutions could have, in principle at least, achieved similar ends. With the husband winning back his wife, the story is now structured as a comic reversal. In this reversal, James Porter has reformed, becoming quite debonair. Leila's second husband, Van Sutphen, has become neglectful as he pursues an affair with Toodles Thomas (Julia Faye). That is, Van Sutphen's real business, seducing women, has pushed Leila to the periphery where she had been once before, with husband number one. Porter thus wins her back in a manner not unlike the way Van Sutphen won her away. The organizing comic trope or principle for *Don't Change Your Husband*, and for many if not all comedies of remarriage, is twinning and comic reversal.

To the extent that *Don't Change Your Husband* retrospectively represents the formation of a new film (sub)genre, the comedy of remarriage, the constant emphasis on reading it through its companion film, *Old Wives for New*, must be acknowledged and investigated. The earlier film is its twin, and so sets up opportunities for comic reversals on an intertextual level. Theodore Roberts, who played the old-fashioned, philandering husband in *Old Wives for New*, now plays "the Bishop," a comic, though not necessarily simple reversal of roles (while presumably playing a character that has a more respectable sense of personal morality, the Bishop, like Berkeley, probably opposes divorce). Other inversions also function in quite complex ways. Elliot Dexter, who had played romantic leads in several of DeMille's efforts, including *Old Wives for New*, is cast as the untidy husband whose favorite food is onions. Given Dexter's established persona, this identity is a comic mask. His persona is play-acting: the audience is already waiting for his transformation. Again, this can be contrasted to the construction of Sophy, the slothful wife played by character actor Sylvia Ashton in *Old Wives for New*: the actresses's established persona tells us she could not magically become a romantic lead. Moreover, Ashton reappears in *Don't Change Your Husband* as the somewhat elderly and asexual aunt, affirming the very different constructions of these parallel roles. That the rejected spouse, James Porter, wins back the divorcing partner is thus an intertextual inversion as well as a narrative reversal. It is the interplay between comic parallels, inversions and reversals that spark laughter in this film. It fulfills Henri Bergson's definition of comedy as a game that imitates life.[38]

Don't Change Your Husband is a comedy of manners in a tradition perceptively analyzed by Henri Bergson. As Wylie Sypher has said of Bergson, we might say of DeMille: they "were alike wearied by the 'heavy moralizings' of the nineteenth century, with its 'terrific tonnage,' and thus sought relief in comedy of manners."[39] Bergson's essay on laughter provides a useful key for understanding DeMille's comedy, in terms not only of form but of purpose and narrational stance. "A humourist," Bergson remarked, "is a moralist disguised as a scientist, something like an anatomist who practises dissection with the sole object of filling us with disgust; so that humour, in the restricted sense in which we are here regarding the word, is really a transposition from the moral to the scientific."[40] This tone is introduced in the very first intertitle, when the narrator suggests that Mr. and Mrs. Porter "should not have looked for their marital problems with a telescope—but a microscope." Although this observation ribs the many sociological studies advocating divorce, as well as the sexology tracts of Floyd Dell (*Love in the Machine Age*) and others, it also defines the narrator's stance throughout much of the film.

In *Don't Change Your Husband*, the narrational point of view is highly selective. There are seemingly arbitrary omissions: we are not shown the marriage ceremonies nor Leila's trip to Reno for her divorces. The narrator seeks parallels and contrasts as a way to measure or compare. The narration thus retains a somewhat distant and objective stance that we might label scientific. The husband's pungent onion breath is juxtaposed with the sweet words and incense of Van Sutphen. Ending the film as the couple sits in the living room by the fire not only brings the film back to its

Leila Porter finds the onion breath of her husband James unappealing . . .

beginning, it allows for a summarizing evaluation. The narrator considers what has changed and what has remained the same. James Porter's dress and appearance are much improved. He also remembers their wedding anniversary. But even after only a month of remarriage, Leila is once again playing solitaire as he falls asleep by the fire.

The final scene tells us that both husband and wife have learned much. They have grown, and grown together, even if they have not, because they *cannot*, completely transformed themselves. Some of what once annoyed Leila about her husband's character has been modified. She has learned to find endearing the flaws that remain. But she is moved most of all by his efforts to change. As Bergson might put it, they have shed their former rigidity, their inattention to self and consequently to others. At the end, they have ceased to be comic characters because each has renewed his or her attentiveness to self and to the world. They are wiser, an ideal example of companionate marriage. As Cavell might say, they have learned to carry on a conversation about what it means to be married, specifically married to each other. This conversation is also about what it meant to be married in postwar America, where divorce had become relatively common and no longer socially devastating, and where women have a new, more equal status symbolized by the vote.

. . . and so is vulnerable to the sweet words of Schuyler Van Stuphen: Gloria Swanson, Elliot Dexter, and Lewis J. Cody in *Don't Change Your Husband* (1919).

The couple's growth is also measured against the unchanging nature of Schuyler Van Sutphen: the final scene of the reunited Porters is interrupted by a brief scene of Van Sutphen wooing a new woman with the line, "Do you know that if I were King—I'd bring you three priceless gifts: 'Pleasure'—'Wealth' and 'Love' and the first should be *Pleasure*." This is an exact repetition of the line he earlier used on Leila. Van Sutphen has not changed, but rather continues using the same seductive words with the same apparent success, in an almost mechanical fashion. He remains a stock character, a "male vampire [who] is essentially a bachelor."[41]

The scientific stance of the film's comedy is reinforced by several texts that address the film's potential spectators. These purport to explore human nature, assuming the tone of serious discussions while in truth they act as publicity pieces. In interviews for *Motion Picture Classic* and *Photoplay Magazine*, DeMille offers himself as an expert on marriage and divorce, with a firm knowledge of sex psychology. Nine out of ten divorces, he assures his interviewer, are based on one thing: "Husbands leave home because their wives are no longer physically attractive."[42] In a slightly latter article, DeMille revises his analysis somewhat, based more on his

own experience: husbands leave home because their wives (the Medusa)
berate them when they stray.

> Why, take a horse. Because it is his nature, he will shy at things.
> If when he shies, you steady the rein, speak gently and ease him
> along, he settles down again and no harm is done. After a while he
> gets more sense and doesn't shy at all.
> But if when he shies, you take a rawhide whip and lash him with
> it, he will probably run away, upset the buggy, and kill you.
> I honestly believe that if I could show women the exact similarity
> I would have done the world a great, an inestimable good.[43]

Although Cecil B. DeMille did not spend a Saturday night with his wife
in eighteen years, she never complained (at least publicly) about this
arrangement, and they lived "happily" together the other six nights of
the week. What this suggests about Constance DeMille's ability to train
her husband using Pavlovian techniques may be questioned, but these
interviews extend the pseudoscientific tone of narration in DeMille's sex
comedies to their intertextual framework of publicity.

Two other articles take somewhat related attitudes toward their subject,
focusing on those actors who play vamplike characters in *Don't Change
Your Husband*. These characters help to establish the various triangles
that propel the narrative. The first profile features Lewis J. Cody, who
played Van Sutphen, the "male vampire" who woos Leila away from
James Porter and marries her. Again based on extensive experience, Cody
concludes that "The real male vampire is essentially a bachelor. His
freedom is his most cherished possession. His heaven is anticipation. His
hell is a woman he is tired of."[44] When Van Sutphen becomes bored, he
gets involved with Toodles Thomas, the so-called "vampette" created and
played by Julia Faye. According to the second article, a vampette or
"baby vamp" "is a youngish little rascal, with big innocent blue . . . eyes
. . . who knows naught of your city ways, but always managed to dress
well without any visible means of support."[45] It is Toodles whose affair
with the married Van Sutphen leads to the breakup of his marriage with
Leila. Again a comparison between the two is authorized by a moral-
scientific stance that allows for comic parallels, inversions and reversals
within the narrative. It is worth noting that these two articles appeared
in the same issue of *Photoplay Magazine*, facilitating this basis for comparison.

There are ways in which *Don't Change Your Husband* only makes
sense or is only fully appreciated intertextually. The Julia Faye character
is introduced at the beginning of the film, interrupting the first living
room scene between the Porters. She is as much a flashback to *Old Wives*

for New as a flash forward to the point, halfway through the film, when she will assume a narrative role in the story. (Again, this is the highly intrusive insertion of a dispassionate, omniscient narrator.) The remarriage of Leila to her first husband diverges from the parallels with *Old Wives for New*, and so breaks with the seeming mechanical or repetitious nature of a previously established story.

Why Change Your Wife?

Why Change Your Wife? was written by Cecil's brother, William C. DeMille, who rigorously constructed a plot that parallels *Don't Change Your Husband*, except that the genders have been reversed. In the earlier film, Van Sutphen tries to hold on to his wife by shooting her first husband—but misses. In *Why Change Your Wife?*, Sally (Clark) Gordon attempts to keep her husband by throwing "acid" on the first Mrs. Gordon's face and so ruin her beauty, only to discover the liquid is eye drops. Advertisements and reviews encouraged audiences to explore these parallels and the accompanying inversions. In this respect, it anticipates Howard Hawks' *His Girl Friday* (1940), which reworked Ben Hecht and Charles MacArthur's play *The Front Page* (the film adaptation of which was directed by Lewis Milestone in 1931) by making Hilde Johnson a woman. At the same time, DeMille manufactures other, more subtle comic upheavals. Bebe Daniels, who had played young ingenues for Harold Lloyd, is suddenly playing Sally Clark, the other woman or vampette. Julia Faye, who had previously played the role taken by Bebe Daniels, is not entirely absent: Toodles, the name of her character in *Don't Change Your Husband*, is now the name of Sally's black cat. The sexually charged Gloria Swanson displays comedic grace as she plays Beth Gordon, a priggish wife with schoolmarm glasses. And what Bergson calls "reciprocal interference of series" produces comic awkwardness as Robert Gordon (Thomas Meighan) introduces Mrs. (Beth) Gordon (Gloria Swanson) to Mrs. (Sally) Gordon (Bebe Daniels). DeMille's inversion is limited only in that, as a *Variety* reviewer noted, the woman does the complaining in both films.[46]

Publicity also placed *Why Change Your Wife?* in the larger context of DeMille's previous divorce films. This was an effort to sell *Why Change Your Wife?* based on a string of earlier successes, but also a strategy for audience reception, one that, once again, facilitated the film's comic value. As in *Old Wives for New*, the story begins with marital discord in the bathroom. And Sally Clark works as a model in a dress store almost identical to the one in that previous film. A flask of Forbidden Fruit liqueur anticipates a DeMille film of that title then in the planning stages. These are some of the many examples of "coincidence" which are "more laughable in proportion as the scene repeated is more complex and more naturally introduced."[47] An Aunt Kate character, played by Sylvia Ashton, appears in both *Don't Change Your Husband* and *Why Change Your Wife?*. Being asexual, there is no reason to invert her role. But Beth Gordon (Gloria Swanson) is accused of dressing like her aunt, that is like the wife Sophy (played by Ashton) in *Old Wives for New*. Thus the larger world of DeMille divorce films is constantly evoked.

The DeMilles also extended the ironic moralizing. The opening intertitle of *Why Change Your Wife?* reads: "Angels are often dead husbands, but husbands are seldom live angels. Wives know this but they can't seem to get used to it." The film's title and this opening intertitle speak to a male spectator, pretending his female companion is absent while in fact assuming she will "overhear." This pretense is then dropped in the closing intertitle:

> And now you know what every husband knows: that a man would rather have his wife for his sweetheart than any other woman: but ladies if you would be your husband's sweetheart, you simply *must* learn when to forget that you're his wife.

This reversal of address confirms what we have known all along: the film's narration appears to be addressing only the male spectator while it has actually been addressing women. The female spectator thus has the pleasure of gaining access to this conversation between the male narrator and the hypothetical male spectator, who is more concretely her date, her lover, her husband. If the woman is unaccompanied or with girlfriends, so much the better. The resulting voyeurism only furthers the titillation.[48]

Cecil B. DeMille's play with address is part of a more general continuity of style and directorial tropes. One of the most obvious instances is his fondness for sexualized close-ups (typically point-of-view shots) of attractively shod feet *à la The Gay Shoe Clerk* (Porter/Edison, 1903). In *Old Wives for New*, we see Juliet's ankle through the eyes of Charles Murdock's daughter, signaling her appreciation and approval of Juliet as a potential stepmother. In *Don't Change Your Husband*, Leila looks at Van Sutphen's dapper shoes, and then compares them to a mental image of her husband's unkempt footwear. Only in *Why Change Your Wife* does DeMille begin to give us close-ups of the woman's ankle from an overtly male point of view. And these shots proliferate. Correspondingly, the selection and playing of records has significance in all three films. In each film DeMille cuts to a close-up of a record which reveals the title of the song. In *Why Change Your Wife?* this is used repeatedly and in a stylized fashion. Robert Gordon, the sexually frustrated husband, wants to play the "Hindustan Fox-Trot," and dance with his wife Beth. Beth Gordon quickly replaces that record with one labeled "The Dying Poet." When Sally Clark lures Robert Gordon to her home, she puts on "Hindustan Fox-Trot" and they dance. At the film's close, both Robert and Beth have learned flexibility, mutual acknowledgment and forgiveness. He plays "The Dying Poet" for her. But she takes the record off the victrola and breaks it, putting on "Hindustan Fox-Trot" in its stead. As a *New York Times* reviewer noted, the film is filled with artificialities. Or, as Bergson might explain it, DeMille is "getting life to submit to be treated as a machine."[49] Yet the effects are "naturally" introduced, if we accept that "Hindustan Fox-Trot" is a popular hit, or that certain characters in DeMille's universe share his shoe fetish. As *Photoplay* critic Burns Mantle explains, "Having achieved a reputation as the great modern concoctor of sex stew by adding a piquant dash here and there to 'Don't Change Your Husband,' and a little something more to 'Male and Female,' he spills the spice box into 'Why Change Your Wife' and the result is a rare concoction—the most gorgeously sensual film of the month."[50]

Orientalism, Sexuality, and Cosumerism

Much of DeMille's spice box entails a rampant orientalism that has been discussed by Edward Said.[51] The Orient has served as a contrasting image, idea and experience for the West. As with Flaubert, DeMille associates it with "sexual promise (and threat), untiring sensuality, unlimited desire, deep generative energies" and fantasy.[52] DeMille's orientalism allows for an escape from Victorian moralism. The sexually repressed wife cannot stand listening to the Hindustan fox-trot or wearing a translucent negligee. If a negligee acts as a veil, concealing to accentuate, inviting rather than walling off, Beth ultimately conceals herself with a quilt. (When Bob enters the dress shop to buy this gift for his wife, he is greeted by an Asian, orientalized woman.) The Orient is thus a site around which DeMille associates alcohol (just prohibited by a Constitutional amendment), musical theater, cigarettes, sensuality, luxury and consumerism.[53] As Beth cries out to her husband in disgust, "Do you expect me to share your Oriental ideas? Do you want your wife to lure you like a— a—Oh why didn't you marry a Turk?" For her, divorce becomes a way to escape sensuality. The contrast of orientalism with conservative rigidity and prudishness is the film's core comic contradiction. If Beth is disgusted by Bob's cigarettes and takes one away from him, Sally seductively offers Bob a cigarette from her own dispenser, dominated by an orientalized Ibis. This inversion suggests how both rigid moralizing and oriental sensuality are associated with the feminine. On one hand, there is Medusa, on the other, Pandora. The possibilities of each make both terribly frightening. DeMille depicts the male of the species, in this case Bob Gordon, as the hardy victim of both. However imperfectly he may conduct his own life, in fact because he is so imperfect, the masculine figure escapes these extremes and achieves some kind of balance. The remarriage of Bob and Beth Gordon becomes an affirmation of life and of the possibilities of sexuality within marriage. It suggests a reconciliation of the two extremes, an integration of the exotic within the existing social framework.[54]

As Bergson might put it, the mystical force of the Orient allows for an escape from the mechanical to life itself.[55] This sensual world can be suggested, through record titles or through the partially revealed female body, rather than shown. Sensuality is made explicit not only by the contents of the film but by DeMille's filmic style. *Why Change Your Wife?* is labeled a "super-production" and yet the spectacle, like sex itself, is kept offscreen (except when orientalist fantasies are themselves being depicted). To a remarkable extent, DeMille avoids establishing shots. Scenes are built up out of an accumulation of medium shots. The spectator imagines the total space. The scientific stance of the narration, moreover, helps to justify what is not shown. The contents of a scene are there to be juxtaposed with something in some other scene. Establishing shots are thus not called for. Likewise, when Bob Gordon takes Sally Clark to the *Follies,* their trip to the theater is left out; it is not deemed pertinent to this "moral" comedy. Not coincidentally, this practice enabled DeMille to keep a cap on his production costs. Certainly, DeMille's simultaneous embrace of orientalism and scientism is one of the film's comic achievements.

Why Change Your Wife? claims to be a moral tale, warning wives (current or prospective) that their husbands "married a *woman* not a governess" and "want a *sweetheart*, not a judge!"[56] The film thus condemns excessive virtue. As a moral tale, it warns us not to be preoccupied with morality but with sensuality. *Variety* called it "a good everyday sermon in story form" with "good sex stuff camouflaged carefully for the benefit of the censor."[57] But as the *Times* reviewer concluded:

> Mr. DeMille's sermons may have the entertainment value of a popular novel for some, but their obvious artificialities and inconsistencies give one the impression that he isn't seriously preaching at all, but is simply seeking to please those who like preaching if it doesn't hurt and doesn't mean anything.[58]

Critics such as Burns Mantle found the comedy immoral. More accurately, the film might be seen as amoral, embracing either a pragmatic or an ironic perspective. As Bergson concluded his essay, laughter "indicates a slight revolt on the surface of social life. It instantly adopts the changing forms of the disturbance. It, also, is a froth with a saline base. Like froth, it sparkles. It is gaiety itself. But the philosopher who gathers a handful to taste may find that the substance is scanty, and the aftertaste bitter."[59]

Yet these two comedies of remarriage are not just some combination of surface glitter and dross. They touched on complex anxieties and fantasies in the new postwar era. On one level, they allayed anxieties by suggesting differences could be overcome. On another they indulged fantasies by allowing spectators to participate vicariously in the loosening of sexual bonds, an activity endemic to the remarriage narrative, with its intermediate sexual partners. In this respect, the very process of viewing a film replicates the narratives of these remarriage comedies. As the spectators sit in a darkened theater, the normal constraints of everyday life are temporarily lifted. Viewers become voyeurs, and can watch what is normally forbidden. They can partake in a unique, sensual freedom. But the film finally provides closure, if only in preparation for, and as signal for, the lights to come up and those obligations to be resumed. And so these films also reassured people that romantic or marital differences can be resolved or overcome. They kept the tone light, and celebrated the adaptability of their protagonists.

An Initial Expansion of the Genre

How the comedy of remarriage became a persistent and recognizable genre is something that requires still further research, but some tentative observations can be offered. In Hollywood, at least initially, DeMille was strongly identified with the comedic film of remarriage, one of several narrative tropes that the producer-director used to focus on the problems of marriage and divorce. A film such as *Male and Female* (1919), which comes between *Don't Change Your Husband* and *Why Change Your Wife?*, seems destined to be such a comedy, only to have such expectations frustrated.[60] In this film, the aristocratic Lasenby family is thrown up on a desert island, where their butler Crichton (Thomas Meighan) takes charge. He soon leads the group, and is at the altar and all but married to the eldest daughter (Gloria Swanson), when the castaways are rescued by a passing ship. The lovers are separated (divorced) by the return of class distinctions, even though she adores him and he also seems to love her. Finally he runs off with the maid (Tweeny) to America, where such class distinctions presumably do not exist. Here the comedy of remarriage fails, and such failure serves as an indictment of old-world values. Though based on J. M. Barrie's 1902 play, *The Admirable Crichton*, the narrative gains a new context and a new meaning by being situated within the emerging genre of comedic remarriage.

Certainly the theater, particularly Broadway, played an important role in establishing the comedy of remarriage as a significant genre, but it seems to have followed rather than anticipated Hollywood's lead. During the 1918 to 1919 season, theatrical farces that focused on marriage tended to treat "the time worn problem of the honest woman who, although living in an easy going society, as far as matrimonial obligations are concerned, succeeds to preserve her sense of morality and even to outwit her environment."[61] Divorce rarely figured prominently in these plays: one of the very few was the melodrama *The Woman in Room 13,* which was notable for its absence of comic relief.[62] During the next two theatrical seasons (1919 to 1920 and 1920 to 1921), divorce emerged as a significant theme: examples from 1919 to 1920 include *An Exchange of Wives* (a comedy by Cosmo Hamilton, which debuted on September 26, 1919), *The Dancer* (a drama by Edward Locke, which debuted on September 29, 1919), *Too Many Husbands* (a comedy by Somerset Maugham, which debuted on October 8, 1919) and *My Golden Girl* (a comedy by Frederic Kummer, which debuted on February 2, 1920). The 1920 to 1921 theatrical season again had a number of plays dealing with divorce and its possible confusions and ramifications, including *Scrambled Wives,* in which a divorcée is invited away for a weekend with her new fiancé, but her first husband and his second wife are also present. *Wedding Bells,* the sole comedy that enacted the remarriage narrative in this two-year period, opened on November 12, 1919, and ran for five months. Chosen by Burns Mantle as one of the best plays of that season, it is a comedy of errors, in which Reginald Carter is about to marry Marcia Hunter, when his first wife Rosalie appears on the scene. Their initial attraction is rekindled, and it is eventually revealed that a series of relatively innocent misunderstandings escalated into divorce. Reginald's marriage to Marcia is postponed (because an Episcopal bishop refuses to perform the ceremony for a divorcé) and then canceled as Marcia weds Douglas Ordway, the poet she really loved all along.[63]

Wedding Bells lagged behind DeMille's *Don't Change Your Husband* by nine months, enough time for the playwright to have found his inspiration from Hollywood. The synopsis and excerpted dialogue appearing in *Best Plays of 1919–1920,* however, suggest that *Wedding Bells* is comparatively superficial: DeMille was exploring more profound levels of discontent and reconciliation. A survey of Broadway shows, moreover, reveals one of DeMille's (and cinema's) real advantages. DeMille's comedies of remarriage resonated with issues raised in his other films of this period. DeMille could turn out a "super-production" every few months, and the rearrangement of themes and actors created a controlled, intertextual web of references that this essay has only begun to explore. Plays by a successful playwright generally appeared much less frequently (though a handful of authors had two or three works produced in a given season), and each play was likely to tie up a group of performers for the duration of its New York run. Thereafter the production was largely confined to the playgoers' fading memory, while films were easily and frequently rereleased. The intertextual web involving star personas, narrative reworkings and referencings of earlier works could be denser and more readily exploited for artistic purposes by a producer such as DeMille. It could also be more easily sustained and, most importantly, national in scope.

During Broadway's 1921 to 1922 and 1922 to 1923 seasons, divorce emerged as a dominant subject for treatment. This included such plays as *A Bill of Divorcement* (October 10, 1921), adapted for the 1932 film of the same name starring John Barrymore and Katharine Hepburn.[64] Comedies of remarriage assumed a striking prominence. In *Skylark* (July 27, 1921) the couple arrange a "temporary divorce," during which they remain married "in name only." Ultimately they call off their separation. In the musical comedy *Tangerine* (August 9, 1921), three men are in jail for refusing to pay alimony to their ex-wives. Though given the chance to escape to the exotic South Seas, they ultimately choose to remarry their former spouses. In *Why Not* (December 25, 1922), which Burns Mantle chose as one of the best plays of 1922 to 1923, two couples divorce, switch spouses, and ultimately begin to repeat/reverse the process. *The Goldfish* (April 17, 1922), *A Pinch Hitter* (June 1, 1922), *Banco* (September 20, 1922), *The Bunch and Judy* (November 28, 1922), *The Laughing Lady* (February 12, 1923), *The Sporting Thing to Do* (February 19, 1923), and *Pride* (May 2, 1923) also fit this mould of comedic remarriage.

Broadway, culturally significant in its own framework, also provided a testing ground for a significant number of films. Two comedies of remarriage from this period are *Bluebeard's Eighth Wife* (September 19, 1921), adapted by Charles Andrews from the French of Alfred Savoir, and *The Awful Truth* (September 18, 1922) by Arthur Richman. Both were quickly turned into screen comedies during the silent period, and then remade as screwball comedies in the late 1930s. In *Bluebeard's Eighth Wife*, which ran for 155 performances, the very rich American John Brandon essentially purchases his eighth wife (the other marriages having generally ended in divorce). Monna de Briac quickly divorces him as well, then "with her freedom and her self-respect restored Monna voluntarily remarries Brandon."[65] When the film version, starring Gloria Swanson in the Monna de Briac role, opened in August of 1923, it was considered "not only an amusing picture but one which is ably directed and beautifully staged" by Sam Wood.[66] Swanson and the production studio of Famous Players-Lasky provided an obvious continuity with the earlier DeMille comedies. *The Awful Truth* is "concerned with the efforts of a wayward and vexatious but frequently adorable woman to recapture

Gweynne Evans with her first husband Oliver, and her future husband Bob Hamilton: Leatrice Joy, Victor Varconi, and Raymond Griffith in *Changing Husbands* (1924).

the husband she had petulantly divorced some years before";[67] it ran for 144 performances and was translated onto the screen twice in the 1920s. Unlike the 1937 film remake, starring Cary Grant and Irene Dunne, the play presents a couple (Norman Satterly and Lucy Warriner) who have been thoroughly and completely divorced for two years before the action begins.[68] *The New York Times* found the 1925 film version consistently amusing, and praised the acting of Warner Baxter and Agnes Ayres.[69] Unfortunately, it does not appear to have survived. Nor does a sound version released by Pathé Exchange in 1929.

The comic trope of remarriage enjoyed a certain obvious popularity, and became a specialized genre within which producers, directors and writers could explore an array of possibilities. Although DeMille shifted much of his interest in sex and moralism from movies on marriage and divorce to biblical epics such as *The Ten Commandments* (1923) and *King of Kings* (1927), he did not abandon the genre completely. He supervised the production of *Changing Husbands* (1924), codirected by Frank Urson and Paul Iribe, two first-time directors who had worked on many earlier DeMille films.[70] A sophisticated comedy about life in the elite, upper-class world of New York, *Changing Husbands* contained an array of slapstick elements that make it a predecessor of 1930s screwball comedy. In this Lubitsch-like quadrangle, Leatrice Joy played the two principal female characters, who switch lives, and soon discover that their career choices and men are mismatched. Ultimately, one couple breaks off the engagement, and the other seeks a divorce, so all four can rearrange their attachments to better suit their temperaments. Divorce occurs without guilt or social condemnation. Marriage is viewed not as a holy sacrament but as a legal contract that can and should be manipulated to suit personal growth and even to respond to sexual attraction.

Changing Husbands is a clever, if minor effort in the Hollywood comedy of remarriage genre. If we agree with Stanley Cavell and others that the motion picture camera typically gives the actor primacy over the character he or she plays, then Leatrice Joy may play two different roles in *Changing Husband* but in a real sense she is playing two sides of herself.[71] This enables the male characters to (re)marry a woman who is different yet also the same. Given these two sides to Leatrice Joy's personality, her unstated task is to proffer that side which best fits her chosen spouse. As DeMille has moralized in his earlier films, it is the women who must accommodate to the fixed character of the male. In effect, it is a remarriage in which divorce is unnecessary or impossible, for these different characters are only projections of the actress's complex self, someone who—like most actresses, according to fan magazines—enjoys both acting and resting quietly at home, who wants to be free and yet secure. Like other films in the genre of remarriage, *Changing Husbands* plays with the collision of sexual desire and social convention, and with the fantasies and anxieties that result from that collision.

By 1924, critics found *Changing Husbands* a rather ordinary picture. A *New York Times* reviewer remarked, "There is so much packed into this picture that one leaves with the feeling of having witnessed a comedy and a circus on the same afternoon. Some parts of the film are fairly well produced, but the profusion of slapstick scenes cause one to groan as they are anything but funny."[72] *Variety* also complained about the "hoak comedy."[73] Both publications, however, frequently complained about slapstick elements in films of this period, whether Chaplin's *The Idle Class* or screwball comedies such as *Bringing up Baby*.[74] While these kinds of criticism may reveal a subterranean unease with the comic stance of much American film comedy, the depiction of lighthearted divorce in *Changing Husbands* aroused little or no explicit controversy.

Returning to Stanley Cavell: Genre and Comedies of Remarriage

Here again I find myself in conversation with Cavell, taking up the second set of questions regarding the genre's logic and domain. In some respects I agree with him that the genre of comedic remarriage emerged fully developed, though the first films that fulfilled these genre requirements and helped to establish the genre (*Don't Change Your Husband* and *Why Change Your Wife?*) functioned initially within a quite different intertextual system. At the same time they are much more explicitly about the process of divorce and remarriage than the films of the genre made fifteen to twenty years later. The very vibrancy and longevity of this comic form gave Capra and his writer Robert Riskin (*It Happened One Night*), as well as Howard Hawks and his writers Ben Hecht and Charles MacArthur (*Twentieth Century*), a firmly established framework in which they could maximize their comedic talents. In *Twentieth Century*, a business contract replaces a marriage contract. *It Happened One Night* (1934) flirts with bigamy as well as remarriage, for Ellie Andrews (Claudette Colbert) is legally married to one man but enjoys a companionate marriage with the another (Peter Warne, played by Clark Gable). Certainly she will remarry one of them, though without necessarily first getting a divorce. Both *The Philadelphia Story* (1940) and *His Girl Friday* (1940) focus on only one portion of the full remarriage narrative.

The comedic genre of remarriage thus provided knowledgeable and sophisticated viewers with a specific framework in which they could appreciate substitutions and displacements from previously established patterns. Because the thoroughgoing application of the Production Code from 1934 onward often forced filmmakers to conceal or modify certain tropes and scenes that had characterized the genre (for instance, adultery), the form's prior establishment allowed it to continue under these trying limitations. As the genre became established, layered and reworked, its narrative basis (the remarriage plot) could recede, and other features associated with the genre could be foregrounded (such as the excessive and eccentric behavior of the wealthy, the upper-class urban and/or country-estate milieu). In a way, one of Cavell's impressive achievements was to identify and reconstruct the genre from its more attenuated examples.

Nevertheless, I obviously wish to include many more films in the genre than Cavell, synchronically as well as diachronically—not only films from the 1920s but Lubitsch's *Design for Living* (1933). This kinky comedy of remarriage involves a triangle formed and, after being shattered, eventually reformed not by wedding vows but by a handshake, in which the agreement "no sex" takes on a completely different meaning for the characters and for us (a declaration that seems to invert the traditional marriage vow that asserts most basically "yes sex"). Cavell excludes *Twentieth Century* for the reasons he excludes *Private Lives*: because Oscar Jaffe (John Barrymore) and Lily (Carole Lombard) do not "grow," nor do they come to any new insight about their relationship (pp. 18–19).[75] He sees these films, like many others, in the tradition of French bedroom farces and comedies of manners, which he finds superficial. But I cannot accept these distinctions, and ultimately this denial of what might be considered the genre's natural diversity. Genres are not constructed based on a film's attitude towards its subject. Westerns, such as John Ford's *Stagecoach* (1939), typically celebrate the frontier as a place where good American values are forged and renewed. If a Western such as Sam Peckinpah's *Pat Garrett and Billy the Kid* (1973) sees it otherwise, it is nonetheless a part of the genre.

Nor are genres formed by the individual preferences of a critic, however illustrious. Stephen Neale has described genres as "systems of orientations, expectations, and conventions that circulate between industry, text, and subject," emphasizing the large-scale nature of spectatorship and other genre operations within dominant cinematic practices.[76] Genres functioned intersubjectively. Within the industry and larger film practice, there were numerous sophisticated comedies in which the narrative trope of remarriage had a significant presence. Although critics, moviegoers and industry personnel never had a specific name for this genre (as a general rule, these films being situated within the more broadly and vaguely defined nomenclature of sophisticated, romantic or screwball comedy), the plethora of films and plays that participate within this easily recognized framework suggests that Cavell has indeed retrospectively identified and labelled such a phenomenon. It is, for the most part, however, an implied genre now being contructed by retrospective writings, mirroring in a modest way the critical discourse that created *film noir*. But even if a genre is asserted as an intertextual category in retrospect, its contours cannot be arbitrary.

For better or worse, not all conversations are as caring and productive as Cavell might wish. Oozing red greasepaint from their endless exchange of barbs, Oscar Jaffe and Lily Garland in *Twentieth Century* are made for each other, and on some level they know it. Jaffe finally wins back Garland with a carefully faked death scene, straight out of *Dinner at Eight*, in which the Barrymore character carefully sets the stage for his own suicide. Garland, who plays out her own life story as if it were the life of one of her melodramatic stage characters, instantly assumes the role of grieving lover.[77] Whatever makes couples stay together, it is as much a mutual play into each others' weaknesses as a complement of their strengths. It is as much sadomasochism as the moments of bliss that come from reconciliation. For this reason, *Twentieth Century* has an edge, a cynical accuracy which sometimes seems truer. It is not that we (the "modern couple") do not enjoy wasting time together, or treasure those moments of epiphany that culminate some of Cavell's favorite films. The opportunities for wasting time in play just seem all too rare, while the periods of reconciliation and renewal are all too briefly sustained.

And so Hecht, MacArthur and Hawks remind us that marriage is in many ways a business contract, and involves playing some kind of role where, like it or not, power is often at stake. But, by acknowledging this unseemly side, we sometimes find it possible to move beyond it. There is, therefore, a potentially more complicated relationship between spectators and a film's narrative and its characters than Cavell is quite ready to acknowledge. Creative literature and film encourage kinds of responses from readers and viewers different from those of philosophy or literary theory. Rather than excluding these "non-Shakespearean" films from the genre, I want to make them one side of a dialectic—a dynamic which kept the genre alive. They are part of a larger conversation about marriage, love and romance.

If, following Cavell, we can contrast the cynical banter of *Twentieth Century* with the fun of *It Happened One Night*, such black-and-white distinctions are not so easy with DeMille. The equality of its women characters are at once acknowledged and undermined. Couples forgive and grow together even as the filmic narrator engages in moralizing double-talk that is at once patriarchal, cynical *and* anarchic. Nor is this ambiguity unique to DeMille. At the end of *His Girl Friday*, one of Cavell's select films, Walter Burns (Cary Grant) successfully wins back Hildy Johnson (Rosalind Russell) and then goes out of the door, leaving her to chase after him, dragging her heavy suitcase. One is left to wonder how much he has changed, and how much the dynamic of his relationship with his lover and star reporter has grown. Both *Twentieth Century* and *His Girl Friday* were based on plays by Ben Hecht and Charles MacArthur, and directed by Howard Hawks. Why should one film be "Shakespearean" and the other a simple bedroom farce? Gerald Mast, to cite one critic, found these films to be twins grappling with quite similar themes.[78]

Where does the comedy of remarriage fit in to the larger realm of comedy? We should first acknowledge that many films (and plays) mirror the structure of this comic narrative, even though they do not go to the extremes of divorce. After breaking up, the unhappy couple restores the marriage or relationship: new, more mutual understanding and deeper love are often the happy by-products. Lubitsch's *The Marriage Circle* (1924) and *So This is Paris* (1926) are two films in which divorce hovers over the entanglements. Even though divorce does not occur, Lubitsch's tone, as well as his reliance on coincidence, parallelism and reversal, place these films firmly within this comic genre. *Lady Windermere's Fan* (1925) can also be seen as part of this genre: Mrs. Erlynne is seeking to restore her place in proper society, a return dependent upon her marriage to Lord Augustus Lorton. In the 1920s, this might be seen as her own particular kind of remarriage, her remarriage to society. Her efforts end ambiguously, since she gets Lorton to propose, but then he demands that they escape to the Continent. Lubitsch's comic duel with Oscar Wilde, in which he challenges the original play's verbal wit with his visual wit (the so-called Lubitsch touch), involves the repetitions and inversions that are also part of the genre's formal domain.

These comedies are what has often been called sophisticated comedy, which grew out of the long-standing comedy of errors and of manners that played with infidelity among married couples. Here the ideological purpose has been to keep the couple/nuclear family together, despite its inherent frustrations and the specific stresses of contemporary life. Early examples might include such films as *Madame La Presidente* (1916) with Anna Held and *Meyer aus Berlin* (1919), directed and starring Ernst Lubitsch. There were some quite early Keystone comedies that operated along these lines as well, such as *Mabel and Fatty's Wash Day* (1915) and *For Better—But Worse* (1915), but because their characters were lower-middle-class, and the acting style was more slapstick, the films were typically identified as marital farces. Genre categories in this period were fluid and dynamic, with sophisticated comedy and farce not always as easily distinguished as one might think. Both were, of course, subgenres within the larger, more embracing category of comedy.

As already pointed out, *Don't Change Your Husband* and *Why Change Your Wife?* did not, because they could not, function within the intertextual framework of remarriage comedies that did not yet exist. One reviewer suggested that "satirical comedy would seem to be the best classification of *Don't Change Your Husband*,"[79] but most other critics and publicists were uncertain how to label it, and avoided even the most basic genre categories. When offering ways for prospective exhibitors to hype the film, one trade journal remarked, "You have something distinctly 'different' here. There never was another screen story like this one."[80] As a result, DeMille and the stars became even more important to push in advertisements. Genre categories were avoided again with *Why Change Your Wife?*, its close affinity to DeMille's previous remarriage comedy now being repeatedly emphasized. By the mid-1920s, films of remarriage, such as *Bluebeard's Eighth Wife* and *The Awful Truth*, were very clearly understood to be comedies with significant romantic aspects.[81] Terms such as satire were no longer mentioned. Comedies of remarriage had not only become a new subgenre of sophisticated comedy, but arguably restructured the entire genre, enabling it to continue serving the same function, but under fundamentally new social circumstances.

Looking Toward Cultural History

The Hollywood comedy of remarriage was a vital and key genre between the first and second world wars. It is against this background that Hollywood created Cavell's favorite examples of the genre. Although the genre hardly ended with Pearl Harbor, the comedies made in the twenty-two-year period between *Don't Change Your Husband* and *His Girl Friday* spoke to a generation of Americans seeking to accommodate to a new sexuality and a different conception of marriage and divorce. As Stephen Neale and Frank Krutnik have pointed out, this does not mean that sophisticated comedy did not change from the jazz age of the 1920s to Depression years of the 1930s.[82] These films succeeded because they engaged broader trends within the culture as well. We must, therefore, also understand DeMille's comedies of remarriage in relation to the changes in American social and cultural life that have been examined by Warren Susman, T. Jackson Lears, John Higham and others. To use a distinction made by Susman, in both *Don't Change Your Husband* and *Why Change Your Wife?*, the problematic spouse starts off with too much "character" but not enough "personality."[83] Each is a dutiful and responsible husband and wife. Only after they have lost their mates do they realize that this is not enough, and so they seek to redress the balance, ultimately abandoning old ways and values and embracing new ones. Through this process, the characters become new objects of desire for their former mates. This involves a new physicality and attention to appearance: James Porter works out and gets his body back in shape—and learns to dress chicly.[84] Beth learns how to display and commodify her body. Both embody the very process of self-realization: when Beth throws convention aside and wears dresses with plunging necklines, she becomes the Swanson character audiences recognized and adored.

These characters' self-realization is other-directed. In regaining their spouses, both James Porter and Beth Gordon become more conscious and concerned about the ways they are perceived by, and relate to, others. They judge their effect on other people and adapt. They achieve social poise, learning to be both popular and charming. The therapeutic ethos, which T. Jackson Lears defines as "an ethos characterized by an almost obsessive concern with psychic and physical health defined in sweeping terms," had fully emerged by around 1920 and permeates these films.[85] DeMille's depiction of James Porter's onion breath and its alienation of Porter's wife and social set came about a year before a new advertising campaign depicted Listerine, until then used as an antiseptic for wounds, as a cure for halitosis.[86] Porter learns to avoid onion breath, to be sensitive to its effect on others, foregrounding and even spoofing some of the social anxieties that would give rise to the market for mouthwash. Dress, particularly the stylishly shod foot, becomes a measure of social well-being. The depiction of these characters' marital relations is also a depiction of their larger place in and relations with society.

DeMille's comedies present a world in which anxiety about the self has been mobilized, in which social fears of ostracism are endemic. Yet if these films of the post-World War I era seem to embrace the culture of consumption as a way to allay this anxiety and so partake of this new ethos, they also can make light of these methods as a release from their potential oppression—as a means for filmmaker and spectators alike to retain a degree of social sanity. The costumes and consumer items are excessive, the coincidences and parallels turn oppressive moralizing into fun. DeMille's comedies of remarriage play with larger social anxieties in ways that offered release and refuge from some of the uncertainties and even dread of this new order, in which fulfillment always seemed just out of reach.[87] Like Bruce Barton and other renowned advertising men of this period, DeMille himself had a somewhat conflictual relationship to this new ethos.[88] These comedies hardy offered the corrosive wit of Chaplin or the early Marx Brothers. Perhaps, more accurately, they lightly spoofed what they also embraced: just as they made fun of divorce even as they made divorce fun, they made fun of consumption even as they made it fun. Many of these concerns were refigured in the screwball comedies of the 1930s, with a trajectory running through Elliot Dexter and Thomas Meighan fulfilled by Cary Grant with his vital, athletic personality, while Gloria Swanson perhaps anticipated much that we find in, for instance, Claudette Colbert. Comedies of the 1930s, an era of sound films and economic depression, engaged a different constellation of issues, and while some of these were new, and other were being worked through at a new stage, the break between decades is not as radical as Cavell and others would have us believe.

15

Romantic Love and Friendship: The Redefinition of Gender Relations in Screwball Comedy

Tina Olsin Lent

In the early 1930s, several popular Hollywood films depicted the relationship between men and women in a fresh, new way that focused on their enjoyment of each others' company, their shared sense of fun and companionship and the complementary nature of their partnership. Preeminent among such films was Frank Capra's *It Happened One Night* (1934), the archetype of the screwball comedy genre.[1] The screwball comedy adapted the new ideal love relationship, referred to by a contemporary writer as "love-companionship," to the realm of middle-class experience and to a variety of middle-class characters.[2] By repeatedly showing the redefined relations between the genders, the screwball comedy made this style of love its central focus, and thereby represented the theme's most in-depth exposition on the Hollywood screen.

Film was only one of several popular media that participated in the thoroughgoing exploration and reconceptualization of the ideal love relationship between men and women. During the 1930s, similar discussions appeared in commercial fiction, popular nonfiction (specifically college texts, marriage manuals and advice literature) and mass market periodicals.[3] Most of the popular media considered women to be their primary audience; female taste not only dictated the content of most periodicals, but also shaped the film and best-seller market.[4] The widespread discourse on love that permeated the popular media signified a contemporary concern (especially among women) about the institution of marriage, which experts and the public alike perceived as being in crisis.[5] This view rested, in part, on contemporary statistical evidence: during the 1920s the divorce rate had increased to approximately one in seven. Between 1929 and 1932, the marriage rate in the United States declined abruptly, reaching a record low in 1932.[6] Liberal reformers in the late 1920s and early 1930s sought to reappraise and redefine the institution of marriage. Their writings verified to the reading public that the older Victorian model of marriage had lost social credibility.[7] Margaret Sanger, Ernest Groves, Ben Lindsey and others predicated the new marriage on a revised model of male/female relationships, based on love and companionship. These changes came on the heels of a cultural revision of the ideology of femininity that repudiated the nineteenth-century cult of domesticity, and superseded it with the "New Woman" of the 1920s.[8] The widespread discourse on love and marriage in film and popular literature helped to disseminate, naturalize and sanction the newer male/female relationships during a time when Depression conditions caused Americans to focus greater attention on marriage. Marriage became more desirable during the 1930s due to its postponement. By the end of the decade, the marriage rate exceeded any previous year on record. The family became the locus of social interaction, emotional support and entertainment, due to declining financial resources.[9]

In the 1930s, screwball comedy specifically addressed love and marriage. The films' plots characteristically involved a sexual confrontation between an initially antagonistic couple whose ideological differences heightened their animosity. Their courtship entailed the verbal and physical sparring referred to as the battle of the sexes, and their recognition of mutual love and decision to marry (or remarry) ultimately reconciled the sexual and ideological tensions.[10] Class conflict frequently motivated the ideological clashes in the early examples of the genre; one of the romantic pair was often identified as being middle or working class. By interjecting their class perspective into the life and circumstances of the other, upper-class half of the pair, they exacerbated the sexual tension, but eventually humanized the wealthy partner.[11] Conflicts in class ideology gave way in many later (post-1937) screwball comedies to other ideological disputes (city/country, home/work, reason/intuition). However, the genre always retained its focus on the comedic situations arising from the dual tensions of sexual and ideological conflict between its romantic leads. By multiplying the couple's fundamental disagreements, screwball comedy intensified the normal concern of romantic comedy (whether a couple will marry) by decreasing the probability that they would overcome their significant and numerous differences.[12]

The *style* of male/female interaction was a central concern of screwball comedy. Many critics and historians have offered interpretations of which audience interests, needs and desires screwball comedies addressed. Some writers have asserted that the characters' eccentric behavior and "lunacy" provided models for sanity and survival in a crazy and overly conventional world.[13] Other writers have maintained that screwball comedy constructed a model for reconciling the socioeconomic disparities that threatened national unity.[14]

To read the screwball comedy as an exegesis on a new style of love is not to contradict these other readings. Rather, such an interpretation will situate these films within the historical context of the Depression years, and link screwball comedy with ideas prevalent in other forms of popular media. The lack of contextualization of specific films in their historical milieu has resulted in many film historians and critics making oversimplifications.[15] In 1975, Robert Sklar wrote that critics and historians could arrive at a "considerably more accurate idea" of the messages a work of art communicated if they were placed within the "broader framework of imaginative communication" in the culture to see how they relate to the "recurring themes, images, characters, situations and resolutions that make up the conventions of artists and entertainment workers in many media."[16] This idea has received greater theoretical grounding and articulation in the work of the new social historians and feminist historians, who have shifted their attention away from the public sphere of politics and policy to study the private sphere of daily life. Working from such materials as the mass market writings of sociologists and psychologists, advice literature, popular periodicals, general-interest and women's magazines, commercial fiction and advertisements, a historian can reconstruct a period's recurrent themes, images and rhetoric. Reading films in relation to other mass media firmly grounds them in their contemporary culture, suggesting the meanings they carried for their audiences.[17]

Screwball comedies focused on the primary intimate relationship most Americans would engage in during their lives, love and marriage, and provided an ideal model for successfully achieving this union based upon contemporary social thought. Departing from the traditional filmic depiction of love and marriage, screwball comedy built upon three major sources: a redefined image of woman, a redefined view of marriage and a redefined idea of cinematic comedy.[18]

The "New Woman," or the flapper, evolved from cinematic and literary sources of the 1920s, presenting a redefined image of the modern woman. This cultural revision of femininity, conducted primarily through the mass media, incorporated some of the features of radical female dissent, but altered them to conform to the needs of the hegemonic culture. The "sexual revolution" of the 1920s commercialized the more politically radical sexual revolution among the working class and the Greenwich Village bohemians in the previous decade. The political and economic critique of the *status quo* implicit in the prewar movements were lost, as the dominant culture used the popular media to sell the sexual revolution and its complementary cult of consumption to the middle class in the 1920s.[19] The flapper challenged earlier codes of feminine behavior through her consumption of such commodities as short and revealing clothing, silk stockings for everyday wear, cosmetics, cigarettes, perfume, jewelry, sweets, hairstyling and popular public entertainment (such as movies, dancing and amusement parks),[20] but broke with the feminist ideas of political and economic equality.[21]

The flapper's consumer-based "revolution" masked her continued and more profound conformity to the dominant ideology of women's subordination, economic dependency and powerlessness, and her acceptance of her primary role as wife and mother. The movies depicted the flapper's new manners and morals as integrally tied into a larger quest for self-fulfillment, a desire satisfied through the new " 'fun' morality and a consumer life-style."[22] The eminent psychologist G. Stanley Hall suggested, in the *Atlantic Monthly* in 1922, that the high school flapper imitated her favorite movie actress, and that films had fashioned her tastes and style, if not her very code of honor.[23] Robert S. Lynd and Helen Merrell Lynd's influential 1925 study of Muncie, Indiana, indicated the effect of movies on behavior (for example, on the use of clothing for social recognition) as well as on social mores.[24] Both contemporary sources indicated that the flapper was, above all, a consumer. The focus on consumption and behavioral freedom in the popular culture of the 1920s sidetracked the larger issue of women's real freedom through economic equality, hopes dashed with the failure of the Equal Rights Amendment in 1926.[25] Although the rubric of "the flapper" subsumed many different aspects of modern female behavior, and although the flapper image declined under Depression conditions, the female protagonists of screwball comedy were the repositories for some of her characteristics.[26]

In three significant areas, the screwball women protagonists perpetuated the attributes of the flapper: her personality and behavior, her participation in the paid labor force, and her more egalitarian relationship with men. Although they lacked the flapper's overt sexuality, the screwball heroines shared her vitality, physical freedom, spontaneity and vivaciousness.[27] Margaret Thorp commented in 1939 that the more natural, down-to-earth looks of the "screwball heroines" made them easier to identify with; discussing the change in the concept of "glamour" in Hollywood, she wrote:

> The glamorous star today is as natural as possible. She does not pluck her eyebrows and paint in new ones; she develops the natural line. She does not tint her hair to exotic hues. She does not try to be a fairy-tale princess, but an average American girl raised to the nth power. "Vivid" is the adjective she works for hardest.[28]

In the women's magazines of the 1930s, both advertisements for beauty products and feature articles on makeup and hairstyle frequently used

Hollywood stars as the epitome of the new, more natural style. Advertising copy featured words like "natural seductiveness," "nature's colorings," "vitality and buoyant grace," "radiance," "animation and vitality," to sell such diverse produces as face rouge, Max Factor make-up, health shoes and canned pineapple.[29] Max Factor ads featured Claudette Colbert and Joan Crawford, and Lux soap ads depicted Barbara Stanwyck and Mae West (the text accompanying Stanwyck tells the reader that nine out of ten Hollywood stars use Lux).[30] Even a General Mills brochure on bread commented that "motion picture stars take no chances with their diet; to insure the energy essential to glowing beauty and vitality, they include bread in every meal."[31]

In terms of her outward behavior, the movie and literary flapper enjoyed new personal freedom in manners and morals; she could work, smoke, drink, dance, dispense with constricting undergarments, and engage in "petting."[32] As a working woman, however, the only employment opportunities available to the flapper were pink-collar jobs whose low wages and limited promotions provided neither a living wage nor the possibility of economic independence; the dominant ideology had already predetermined that she defined her ultimate goal as a homemaker, wife and mother—not a wage earner.[33] The flapper did not challenge the social conventions of premarital chastity, matrimony and economic dependence.[34] Despite their freedom and assertiveness, the female protagonists of screwball comedy also conformed to contemporary expectations that a woman's ultimate goal was marriage, and that a married woman's place was in the home.[35]

A second characteristic of the flapper that the screwball heroine adopted was her participation in the paid labor force. The working-class movie flapper helped to legitimize the single woman's role in the work force (which had been increasing since the beginning of the twentieth century), and leading women in screwball comedies were frequently assertive "working girls."[36] Their premarital careers and jobs included newspaper reporters (*Mr. Deeds Goes to Town, His Girl Friday, Meet John Doe, Woman of the Year*); writers (*Easy Living, Theodora Goes Wild*); secretaries (*You Can't Take It With You, Mr. Smith Goes to Washington*); department store clerks (*Bachelor Mother*); and a factory worker (*Nothing Sacred*). Although married women were increasingly working, the ideology of the period, expressed in the films and popular literature of the 1920s, never fully supported their presence in the work force.[37] Despite these economic realities, public rhetoric strongly supported women's traditional role as homemaker.[38] The government and unions strongly opposed working wives out of fear of their displacing or competing with the supposedly more needy male breadwinners. Ironically, the gender-segregated work force, which prevented women from competing with men in the higher-paying, more depressed manufacturing sector of the economy, provided them with increased employment opportunities in the lower-paying, growth sectors of clerical and service work, where men did not want jobs.

The screwball comedy, as well as the popular literature of the 1930s, supported the ideology of domesticity that maintained that women could work while single, but should not pursue a career that superseded marriage and motherhood as their life goal. The majority of the screwball comedies with working heroines (with the possible exceptions of *His Girl Friday* and *Woman of the Year*) implied that they would "return" to the home after marriage.[39] Similar images of women and marriage emerged from *The Saturday Evening Post*, the largest-circulation magazine in the world in the 1930s, and the representative of American middle-class culture. The ideal *Post* story heroine of the early Depression years was "witty, athletic, self-possessed, urbane" and appeared as a "competent secretary, aggressive business woman, ambitious college graduate, adventurous aviator" as well as a successful author, show business star and athlete.[40] The majority of female characters fell into one of three traditional categories: the silly, irrational childish woman; the beautiful, vain parasitic woman; and the wholesome, supportive girl-next-door.[41] The stories' overriding message was that women were to subordinate their career ambitions to those of their husbands, and that the successful career women were single, preferably widowed. Severe censure was meted out to working married women, who ignored their maternal responsibilities and damaged their husband's egos.[42] As in screwball comedies, these widely popular magazine stories underwrote women's more liberalized manners and morals, while subscribing to the dominant ideology of female domesticity.

Thirdly, the screwball heroine adopted the flapper's more egalitarian relationship with men. Popular magazines depicted the high school and college coed flapper as one who treated men as "partners" and "pals," roles that carried an aura of adventure, innovation and equality with men.[43] Describing the flapper in 1922, G. Stanley Hall wrote, "In school, she treats her male classmates almost as if sex differences did not exist. Toward him she may sometimes even seem almost aggressive. She goes to shows and walks with him evenings, and in school corridors may pat him familiarly on the back, hold him by the lapel and elbow him in a familiar and even *'de-haut-en-bas'* way."[44] This type of relationship characterized many screwball comedies, where the leading romantic pair became partners in an enterprise (eluding detectives in *It Happened One Night*, tricking the newspaper and the public in *Nothing Sacred*, finding the intercostal clavicle in *Bringing Up Baby*, saving Earl Williams in *His Girl Friday*) and had fun as they shared the adventure. The image of the pal also appeared in contemporary advertisements. An ad for Woodbury's creams showed a woman and man on a bobsled (she driving, he steering), enjoying a "glorious sport" but one that roughened hands.[45] An ad for Frostilla lotion made the message even clearer:" 'Men want so much!' They expect their girls to be good pals—and good lookers! They want us to romp with them by day—and romance at night. They don't consider that wind and weather roughen our hands—but they do expect us to give them smooth hands to hold."[46]

Although the flapper viewed herself as a man's pal, her relationship with men was generally more sexualized, and thus more prone to overt tension and animosity than that of the screwball female protagonist. When the flapper was the protagonist in a film (as in *It*), she was usually more three-dimensional than the male characters with whom she interacted. She viewed men with a mixture of cynicism, distrust and disgust, seeing them as weak and easily manipulated; men were her ticket to economic security.[47] Responding to Production Code restrictions, screwball comedy downplayed the female lead's physical sexuality to the point of ignoring (or sublimating) it.[48] At the same time, the films strongly delineated the male lead and a playful companionship became their major focus. Here, the male represented an entertaining friend. Whereas the films featuring the flapper depicted gender inequality (she had strength of character, while he had social and economic power), the screwball comedy depicted greater gender equality.[49]

The redefinition of marriage in the 1920s was a second source for the altered image of gender relations in screwball comedy. Sociologists, psychologists, psychiatrists, jurists and physicians, writing in marriage manuals, college texts and in the popular literature of advice columns and mass-circulation magazines, attempted to shift the primary focus of marital happiness from the family to the romantic-sexual union between the husband and wife.[50] Marriage became less a social and economic institution based upon spiritual love and more a sexual and emotional union based upon sexual attraction.[51] The aims of the ideal contemporary marriage were romantic satisfaction achieved through sexual gratification and friendship—a "love-companionship."[52] Liberal reformers Ernest Groves and Margaret Sanger, among other writers, saw mutual sexual attraction and desire as the "virtual foundation and essence of love" and the primary basis for marriage.[53] The quality of friendship, companionship or fellowship also featured prominently in writings on marriage. Marriage was an "adventure in fellowship." Its "vitality and permanency" required a "common basis of interest, a cooperative give and take, a continuing delight in association."[54] Courtship "must be adventurous, daring, exciting, romantic. The great danger . . . is not that it be too recklessly romantic, but that it be too tamely accepted, too anemic, too lifeless."[55]

Cary Grant and Katharine Hepburn play in *Bringing Up Baby* (1938).

The screwball comedies were, above all, stories of courtship, where friendship developed along with love. The rapid pace and comedic nature of the physical movements and verbal exchanges served as courting rituals. These films depicted the energy and vitality generated by strong sexual attraction and a desire for personal happiness through fun. In Capra's *It Happened One Night* (1934), the alliance between Ellie Andrews (Claudette Colbert) and Peter Warne (Clark Gable) originally rested on mutual convenience and sexual attraction, feelings cemented into love (and marriage) by the fun and companionship which developed as they shared the adventure of traveling from Miami to New York. In Hawks's *Bringing Up Baby* (1938), Susan Vance's (Katharine Hepburn) attraction for David Huxley (Cary Grant) led to mutual love (and we assume marriage) as a result of their sharing adventures and fun. In Cukor's *Holiday* (1938), the relationship between Johnny Case (Cary Grant) and Linda Seton (Katharine Hepburn) originated as friendship and developed into love, as their anarchic personalities found their complement in the other's rebellion against the conventional and stultified atmosphere of the Seton mansion. In Hawks's *His Girl Friday* (1940), Walter Burns (Cary Grant) and Hildy Johnson (Rosalind Russell) had previously been married. She was about

In the playhouse: Cary Grant, Edward Everett Horton, and Binnie Barnes in *Holiday* (1938).

to remarry, to become a "real woman" with a home and children. Waltei combined his sexual charms and energy with a journalistic crusade, creating a shared adventure that rekindled their love and led to their remarriage.

The screwball comedy also illustrated the value of play as a means of establishing the companionship so essential to contemporary love. A fundamental aspect of the youth culture of the 1920s was its pursuit of fun through activities like dating, dancing, sports and other forms of mass entertainment. The "fun morality" advocated fun as a new obligation, and defined too little fun as something to be feared; one could not have enough fun, and it even became part of work.[56] *Bringing Up Baby* developed the idea of play as a metaphor for Susan's vitality, spontaneity and sexuality, qualities noticeably absent in David. From the beginning, David misunderstood the nature of play, seeing the golf game with Mr. Peabody as an extension of work, while Susan understood that it was "only a game." Later on, as she and David pursued George to find the missing bone, Susan commented, "Isn't this fun, just like a game." Immediately prior to the final embrace and declaration of mutual love, David admits that the day they spent together was the best he ever had, signifying his conversion to her worldview. *Holiday* went even further in advocating the benefits of play. Here play itself became the language by which the authentic lovers discovered their affinity. Suggested by its title, the concept of play permeated the film, surfacing in Johnny's exuberant entrance into Nick and Susan's apartment where he wrestled with them, then exited, doing a cartwheel, in the juxtaposition of the formal rooms in the Seton mansion (comfortably occupied by Mr. Seton and Julia) with the playroom (inhabited by Linda), in Johnny and Linda's pursuit of amusement through toys and acrobatics, and in Johnny's understanding that amassing money was not the ultimate goal of life, but the means to an end that he wanted to discover. In McCarey's *The Awful Truth* (1937), both Jerry Warriner (Cary Grant) and Lucy Warriner (Irene Dunne) actively and enthusiastically played with the dog, Mr. Smith, when their marital strife disrupted their ability to play together. The protagonists C. K. Dexter Haven (Cary Grant) and Tracy Lord Haven (Katharine Hepburn) in Cukor's *The Philadelphia Story* (1940) had shared fun and play aboard the sailboat *True Love* (and other activities like swimming and hunting) which provided the common language and experiential base uniting them despite their divorce. In Wellman's *Nothing Sacred* (1937), Wally Cook (Fredric March) and Hazel Flagg (Carole Lombard) played together on a sailboat, while in Capra's *You Can't Take It With You* (1938), the transforming power of play beneficially affected not only the lovers, but everyone else.

The screwball comedy also used role-playing to show how the companionable relationship emerged from separate, often hostile, identities. By playing fictional characters, the screwball characters freed themselves of their original personalities, expectations and value systems. Experimenting with other identities allows them to grow together. In *It Happened One Night*, Peter and Ellie played a married, working-class couple, while Hildy in *His Girl Friday* played Bruce's fianceé, the traditional, middle-class version of nurturing and respectable femininity. In *Nothing Sacred*, Hazel Flagg impersonated a strong and heroic dying woman, while David in *Bringing Up Baby* (whose identity had already been stripped of its professional signifiers when he donned a negligee, then hunting clothes and sandals) impersonated a big-game hunter, Mr. Bone, and a gangster, Jerry the Nipper ("a regular Don Swan").[57] In *The Philadelphia Story*, the entire Lord family put on an affected and obnoxious upper-class act for the benefit of the *Spy* reporters Mike and Liz. In *The Awful Truth*, both Lucy and Jerry Warriner put on elaborate acts to embarrass the other: Jerry feigned sincerity when waxing eloquently to Dan about his desires to live in Oklahoma, and to Dan's mother about how pure and above suspicion Lucy was. Lucy enacted the role of Lola Warriner, Jerry's "sister," to embarrass him in front of his wealthy new girlfriend and her family.

Several women's magazines from 1934 (the date of *It Happened One*

Night) carried stories dealing with the positive values of companionable love between active, enterprising women and men. In "The American Thing" (*Women's Home Companion*), a thirty-five-year-old single woman saved her family business and her town's economy. She found a lover-companion-husband in the lawyer who was going to foreclose on her house. His mind was changed by the fun of the endeavor to salvage the old way of life.[58] In "Marriage is Like That" (*McCalls*), the young wife feared she was losing her husband's affections to a widow at the office. After trying a new wave and facial, a new dress and his favorite dinner, to no avail, she regained his love by their companionable interest in their pet dog, who the widow found totally objectionable.[59] In "I'll Give You a Ring Some Day" (*McCalls*), a female dance teacher (again in her thirties) married a man who at first awakened a feeling of comradeship in her, due to their mutual interests and experiences. He was a temporary teacher whose music class was next door to her dance class.[60] Gaiety and vibrancy were codes for the desirable quality of fun in romance: a cover description of a serialized novel, *Modern Merry-Go-Round,* read, "A New Novel of Young Moderns in a Modern World . . . He brought gayety [*sic*] to love and, in some inexplicable way, drama."[61]

Not only were romantic love and friendship the basis for a love relationship; contemporary sources also defined the sexes as complements of one another. Due to the complementary nature of their physical and psychological characteristics, men and women were incomplete without each other. When their interests did not fuse, the complementary nature of the genders provoked the clashes described as sexual antagonism.[62] The battle of the sexes became a convention of the screwball comedy. In *It Happened One Night*, the mutual antagonism between Ellie and Peter stemmed from both sexual attraction and ideological conflict. Their clearly delineated socioeconomic differences compounded the tension arising from their erotic desire. By the end of the film, their shared experiences and interests allowed them to discover their complementary natures.

In *Bringing Up Baby*, perhaps more than any other screwball comedy, the romantic couple represented polar opposites, and their final pairing signified the perfect complementariness of the male/female relationship.[63] The conflict in this film, as in *It Happened One Night*, was also sexual and ideological, although here the ideological clash was between the intellect and emotion, reason and feeling, work and fun, confinement and freedom, rigidity and spontaneity. Hawks's *His Girl Friday* was a remake of Milestone's *The Front Page* (1931), which had focused on the companionable relationship of two male journalists and the conflict between them due to one's desire to leave the newspaper business to marry and settle down. The narrative's central opposition was between the spheres of work and domesticity, between the world of men and the world of women. Hawks's transformation of the male Hilde Johnson into a female compounded the ideological conflict between Johnson and Walter Burns, adding sexual conflict through the device of their recent divorce. The divorced couples in *The Philadelphia Story* and *The Awful Truth* also possess sexual knowledge from their earlier marriage. In the former film, the differences between Tracy and Dexter rested on his knowledge of her sexual coolness, her emotional remoteness and her disdain for human frailty (particularly emotional weakness). Tracy experiences a sexual awakening and an emotional "thaw," leading to their remarriage. In *The Awful Truth*, the couple was already perfectly matched but needed to experience their incompatibility with others (Dan Leeson and Barbara Vance) to realize their complementariness.

Dorothy Parker's short stories from the 1930s also depicted various male/female relationships during courtship and marriage, and revealed the complementary qualities that signified a well-matched pair. For Parker, the linguistic form of the argument became the mode of engagement for the battle of the sexes.[64] In "The Sexes," she depicted a courtship entirely through a bickering conversation dealing overtly with lack of communication and jealousy. Like the feuding couples of screwball comedy, the argument entailed their intense interaction with and concentration on each other and ended with harmony.[65] In "Here We Are," a couple departing on their honeymoon progressed from stilted conversation to full-scale bickering (complete with the man's continual, accidental and embarrassed references to sex), as they adjusted to being alone together.[66]

Building upon the contemporary ideology that love required a male/female friendship based on fun, and that play melded the complementary aspects of their natures into a harmonious whole, a contemporary marriage required a union that took more than a license or certificate to forge. Many screwball comedies dismissed older ideas of marriage, to advocate the newer ideas of a love-companionship between two complementary opposites. *It Happened One Night* explored the contrast between a legal marriage and a real one, in the triangular relationship of Ellie, her husband King Wesley, and Peter. Although they both come from wealthy, leisured backgrounds, Ellie and Wesley's marriage was nominal; they had experienced neither a sexual nor companionable union, and their marriage represented the older legalistic definition of the institution. Ellie's legal marriage was as bogus as the series of pretend marriages she and Peter enacted during their journey (for the benefit of a traveling salesman on the bus, various auto court owners and her father's detectives). Her legal marriage was actually more fraudulent, because as Ellie and Peter played married lovers, they built the necessary foundations (familiarity, friendship and nurturance) for an authentic marriage. By the journey's end,

Ellie declared her love for Peter, and at the film's end, they entered into an authentic marriage.

Marriage was also the central motif in *Bringing Up Baby*, and the film had recurrent references to it.[67] When David and his fiancée, Miss Swallow, discussed their upcoming marriage, she primly informed him they would have no honeymoon and no children, because his work came first. David's forthcoming marriage spurred Susan's virtual abduction of him to Connecticut, and it formed a continual refrain of his lament while there. In contrast to Miss Swallow's image of the brontosaurus-skeleton-as-child, Susan provided David with a live Baby (the leopard).[68] The audience learned of Susan's intentions to marry David early in the film, and by the end he finally recognized that the fun they had had together revealed the falseness (and sterility) of his previous relationship. The film clearly contrasted the formal, lifeless, work-oriented relationship between David and Miss Swallow with the unconventional, fun-filled adventures of David and Susan. Although David and Miss Swallow have more in common intellectually, the film championed David and Susan's relationship, based on shared experiences of fun and play.

Marriage was also the central motif in the films that featured divorced couples. *His Girl Friday* opened with Hildy's announced intentions to marry her fiancé Bruce (Ralph Bellamy), and ended with her planned remarriage to Walter. In between, contrasts were made between two different types of men (Bruce had good manners, was honest and sincere— qualities notably absent in Walter) and different types of marriage. Bruce offers a home, children and a mother-in-law, contrasted with a first honeymoon with Walter in a collapsed coal mine and a second one following up a story in Albany, which was, after all, on the way to Niagara Falls. As in the earlier examples, the film advocated the nontraditional marriage choices that incorporated fun, adventure and excitement. Just as *It Happened One Night* contrasted Ellie's legal marriage to King Wesley with her authentic relationship with Peter, *His Girl Friday* maintained that, although legally divorced, Hildy and Walter were still a couple. Similarly, the concept of what constituted a "real" marriage was the central concern of *The Awful Truth* and *The Philadelphia Story*, both of which began with couples separating, and ended with their reconciliation. Divorce as a legal institution did not sever the complex affectional ties between Lucy and Jerry Warriner nor between Dexter and Tracy Haven. Their separations appeared fraudulent when juxtaposed with the superficiality of their new relationships, the hopeless mismatches of Lucy and Dan (Ralph Bellamy) and Tracy and George Kittredge (John Howard). Their reconciliations seemed a natural outgrowth of their obvious complementary characteristics.

Dorothy Parker also dealt with the contrast between the traditional view of marital harmony and the contemporary perception of a "real" partnership in her story "Too Bad." Framed by the conversation of two women discussing the divorce of a mutual friend, Mrs. Weldon, whose marriage had seemed the one happy and congenial one, the story's central section depicted the actual relationship between Mr. and Mrs. Weldon. Although they laughed and talked easily in the company of others, they could not carry on even polite conversation when alone. Mrs. Weldon wondered, "What did married people talk about, anyway, when they were alone together? She had seen married couples . . . at the theater or in trains, talking together as animatedly as if they were just acquaintances. She always watched them, marvelingly, wondering what on earth they found to say."[69] Although the women discussing the Weldons concluded that they got along so beautifully that they must have been crazy to get a divorce, the disparity between what seemed an ideal marriage and what the marriage actually entailed was apparent.

Screwball comedy redefined film comedy in the 1930s and the conventions of this new genre were the third major source for the modification of the portrayal of gender relations on the Hollywood screen. Not only was there an equal teaming of a male and female star in screwball comedy, but for the first time the romantic leads were also the comic leads.[70] Screwball comedy combined the sophisticated, fast-paced dialogue of the romantic comedy with the zany action, comic violence and kinetic energy of slapstick comedy. The underlying premise of slapstick comedy was the "miraculous survival of the human in a world in which man is treated as a machine" and which depended upon collision as its dominant force.[71] In contrast to slapstick comedy, which relied upon a central actor (usually male) whose identity developed from film to film, who was misogynistic in vision and was innocent of sex, the screwball comedy divided the central figure into a male and female, was more egalitarian in its vision, and featured sexual antagonism as the motivating force.[72] The romantic leads often had eccentric qualities, and their unconventional behavior was both a form of social criticism and anarchic individualism. Although screwball comedy and the sophisticated romantic comedy of the early 1930s both demonstrated the limits of conventional morality, they differed in the physicality of the assault on society perpetrated by the romantic leads.[73] A contemporary film historian, Lewis Jacobs, who referred to the screwball comedies as "daffy" comedies and the activities of the heroine as "screwball," commented that in these films the "genteel tradition is 'knocked for a loop': the heroes and heroines are neither ladylike nor gentlemanly. They hit each other, throw each other down, mock each other, play with each other"[74] Another contemporary, Margaret Thorp, wrote that, "Today a star scarcely qualifies for the higher spheres unless she has been slugged by her leading man, rolled on the floor, kicked downstairs, cracked over the head with a frying pan, dumped into a pond, or butted by a goat."[75] The screwball antics also functioned as a substitute for expressions of overt sexuality. As such, they showed the influence of the prohibitions and restrictions imposed by the Production Code, as well as the ideology of the companionate marriage.[76] Allusions to sexuality replaced the overt, explicit physical sexuality depicted in earlier films, and double entendre, allusion, humor, symbol and metaphor abounded in screwball comedy. Many screwball comedies, in fact, ended without the lovers even kissing on screen.[77] The most famous sexual image in *It Happened One Night* was the blanket (referred to as the "Walls of Jericho" during the course of the film) hung between Ellie and Peter's beds in the auto courts, and which fell, to the sound of a toy trumpet, after Ellie and Peter married. During their first night together, Peter undressed in front of Ellie (performing a virtual striptease as he removed everything except his trousers), while giving her a lecture on how men remove their clothes. Ellie, undressing on her side of the blanket, inadvertently made the blanket move suggestively and then hung her undergarments on it. A traveling salesman named Shapely ("Shapely's the name and that's how I like them"), a lifted skirt as a hitchhiking ploy, and a hungry Ellie daintily munching on a carrot were other sexual referents.[78] Sexual innuendo ran rampant throughout *Bringing Up Baby*, from David's reference to the intercostal clavicle as his bone ("My bone. It's rare, it's precious!") to his explanation for dressing in Susan's negligee ("I've gone gay all of a sudden!"). Hildy and Walter, in *His Girl Friday*, already had a rich sexual-companionable relationship. Walter's attraction to Hildy was clear through his many antics to regain her affection both during and after their divorce. During the actual proceedings he had hired an airplane to skywrite, "Hildy, don't be hasty, remember my dimple . . . Walter." She told him that stunt delayed their divorce for twenty minutes while the judge went out to watch, and he responded, "Well I still have the dimple, and in the same place," implying it was not the one in his chin.

Aside from obvious sexual innuendo, screwball antics drew attention to both the sexual and companionable aspects of the developing romantic relationship, as the films seemed to have imposed a taboo on the clichés of romance.[79] The extreme physicality allowed the characters to touch intimately, but humorously, offering alternative outlets for repressed sexual energy.[80] Furthermore, the screwball antics paired the would-be lovers to show their physical harmony and compatibility, as in the parallel movements of David and Susan (tearing each others' evening clothes, falling down a hillside, submerging in a stream, and swaying on either side of the brontosaurus skeleton).[81] The harmony of Hildy and Walter's movements showed that these two characters were perfectly complemen-

"I never saw this woman before in my life:" Cary Grant, Gene Lockhart, Alma Kruger, and Rosalind Russell in *His Girl Friday* (1940).

tary. They carried on a rapid, bickering dialogue as they circled his desk in one scene, and traversed the pressroom in a later one. They were so familiar with each others' actions that Walter insulted her while simultaneously ducking to avoid the purse he knew she would throw at him and chiding her for loosing her aim. These antics intensified the fun and excitement the characters experienced together, and these feelings further heightened sexual awareness. The screwball antics reinforced the characters' growing friendship because, like the rapid dialogue that accompanied these actions, they focused the couple's attention on each other, and created familiarity. In *Nothing Sacred*, Wally and Hazel kissed behind some crates on the pier after he saved her from "suicide," but their most intimate physical moment came when they engaged in a fistfight to help her simulate the symptoms of pneumonia, after which they sat in parallel positions, each with a swollen jaw. In *Holiday*, the screwball antics, particularly the acrobatic tricks, performed by Johnny and Linda became the signifiers of their feelings for each other. Although such physical comedy characterized all the films in this genre, none has the sheer energy of *Bringing Up Baby*. The romantic couple's pranks and pratfalls dominated this film from the moment David and Susan met. The characters continually fell down, ran around, tore clothes, dug holes in the ground, smashed and stole cars, threw stones, chased animals all over the country-side, and sang "I Can't Give You Anything But Love, Baby."

The rapid-paced, constant dialogue of the screwball comedy also functioned as both sexual and companionable interaction, and provided an aural counterpoint to the physical action. The mode of verbal exchange was bickering; the argument, verbal wrangling, was the characteristic sound of screwball comedy, as if this high-spirited, intellectual repartee was a new symbolic language of love.[82] Talking together was being together, and their use of language forged the bond between them.[83] What was important to the lovers was not merely what they said or did, but the fact of saying or doing it together.[84] The screwball banter clearly differed from the nagging argument of a "traditional" marriage by its speed and its context of fun and adventure rather than domesticity. In *It Happened One Night*, Ellie and Peter staged a marital argument to elude discovery by her father's detectives. The tone, content and context of their quarrel convinces the detectives that they were a working-class married couple. From the moment of their first encounter in *Bringing Up Baby*, David and Susan engaged in fast, bickering conversation which not only contrasted with David's usual mode of communication with Miss Swallow, but became a gauge of his basic incompatibility with her when she could no longer understand the meaning of his discourse. The dialogue between Johnny and Linda in *Holiday* was faster and more playful than between Johnny and his fiancée, Julia. Julia's inability to engage in playful discourse with Johnny (or with his friends Nick and Susan) signified the deep ideological gap between them that could not be bridged. Hildy and Walter also engaged in rapid, bantering dialogue from the beginning of *His Girl Friday*, another sign that they, rather than Hildy and Bruce, belonged together. The image of the ideal male/female relationship that emerged from these and other screwball comedies is one that emphasized multiple levels of interaction and satisfaction: the couple was sexually attracted to each other, had fun together, shared adventures, and developed a singular mode of discourse—all of which resulted in the completion of each person by the complementary characteristics of the other.

Contemporary analysts of real-life gender relationships in the 1930s depicted a picture closer to Dorothy Parker's Weldons than to Walter Burns and Hildy Johnson or Dexter and Tracy Haven. In *Middletown in Transition*, the Lynds described the world of the two genders in 1935 as complementary and reciprocal, but as something akin to separate subcultures.[85] Although there was more change and choice open to women to enlarge their social roles, married women clearly saw themselves in a secondary role; high school girls, on the other hand, seemed to be showing more independence by their desire to work after leaving school, rather than immediately marrying and having families.[86] Adolescent behavior had changed the most since the earlier study in 1925, and the Lynds attributed some of the changes to the movies, the newer and more potent agent of cultural dissemination.[87]

The lessons taught by the movies were vivid reinforcements of those learned from other channels of the popular culture and meant different things to different viewers. While the younger, less tradition-bound audience had the values of their developing youth culture validated and substantiated, the older audience saw their values and beliefs, particularly those supporting the Victorian ideology of love and marriage, challenged. While movies, especially screwball comedies, provided an escape and a fantasy for contemporary viewers, it was an escape to a world that did not seem so remote and unattainable. Although that world may have been inhabited by heiresses with wealth and leisure (*It Happened One Night, My Man Godfrey, Holiday, The Philadelphia Story, Bringing Up Baby*) or working women suddenly transported into a realm of excitement, prominence and wealth (*Easy Living, Nothing Sacred*), the women in the movies had the same objective as the middle- and working-class female inhabitants of Muncie, Indiana: to find an emotionally satisfying, sexually exciting, physically compatible, fun-filled love-companionship was the goal of the female characters featured in the screwball comedy, as well as of the women who went to movies, read *The Saturday Evening Post* and women's magazines, consumed popular literature, and followed the advice of Dorothy Dix and other writers of advice literature. Through its discourse on the ideal relationship, the screwball comedy created a heightened awareness of the new expectations for love and marriage. While not a blueprint for actual gender relationships, the screwball comedy was part of the new liberal ideology that redefined gender relations and focused on the sexual and companionable components of intimacy.[88] Along with the other popular media, these films helped to sanction and naturalize these beliefs so that they attained social dominance during the 1930s.

16

Queerness, Comedy and *The Women*

Alexander Doty

How do queers—lesbians, gays, bisexuals, and other nonstraight people—make sense of, and take pleasure in, a mass culture that we have been told time and again is made by and for straight people (especially men)?[1] While our queer pleasures in film, television, music, videos and other forms are many and varied, they are almost always rooted in the tensions between understanding ourselves as members of a *sub*culture, which subversively or secretly reinterprets products not made with us in mind, and seeing our readings and pleasures as standing alongside (rather than as being alternatives to) those of straight people. This complicated positioning—simultaneously feeling within, outside and alongside mass, straight culture—is evident in the relationship of queers to comedy production and interpretation.

When queers and comedy come together, most people think of camp and "bitchy" wit (gays) and sociopolitical humor (lesbians). Simultaneously comic forms and reading strategies, camp and the sociopolitical continue to be mainstays of queer humor, particulary as gay and lesbian producers and audiences have been sharing and combining these two forms/strategies more and more since the mid-1970s. So what is a queer sociopolitical angle on comedy? In lesbian cultures, it has historically been linked to feminist concerns about critiquing the patriarchy's limited and oppressive notions regarding gender. Lesbian humor has expanded these gender concerns to include comic examinations of straight culture's misconceptions about homosexuality. Lesbian sociopolitical comedy production and reading practices also comment upon dyke cultural experiences (butchfemme roles; coming out to parents; fashion, dietary, and dating trends, and so on). Influenced by feminist and lesbian comedy over the past thirty years, many gays and bisexual men have adopted a more overt sociopolitical edge in their humor. This is perhaps most evident in recent uses of camp within progressive and radical queer politics (ACT-UP, Queer Nation). Camp had previously been considered either as apolitical or as a form of *implicitly* political gay humor.

Besides camp and the sociopolitical (or combined with them), comic texts and performers have been queerly understood through many other academic and nonacademic reading strategies: star cults, *auteurism*, gossip and other form of extratextuality, and various types of emotional-erotic connections between characters, or between actors and audiences. Major queer star cults have formed around comedy (and musical comedy) performers like Doris Day, Judy Garland, Lily Tomlin, Bette Midler, Sandra Bernhard, Cary Grant, Lucille Ball, Carmen Miranda, Pee-Wee Herman (Paul Reubens), Roseanne Barr, Reno, Lypsinka, Charles Busch, Divine and Mary Tyler Moore. Often, queer comedy readings will bring in material related to performers not generally considered comic actors: Greta Garbo (*Ninotchka, Two-Faced Woman*) and Katharine Hepburn (*The Philadelphia Story, Pat and Mike, Adam's Rib* and so on), for example. Of course, whether considering comic or dramatic actors, many queer star cults include erotic fantasies about performers.

In relation to film comedy, directors can challenge stars as important figures through which to read comic texts, particularly among queer scholars. While classic "cult of the director" *auteurism* has been reviled or revised within the academy, seeing film texts as the expression of a director's "worldview" is still a popular way to interpret films. This is particularly the case when the director is known, or rumored to be, queer (or "homosexual," "gay," "lesbian, "bisexual") as is the case with George Cukor, Dorothy Arzner, James Whale, Gus Van Sant, Ulrike Ottinger, Edmund Goulding and others. With knowledge of a director's queerness, some readers will construct readings that interpret certain visual and aural codes in their films with reference to specifically queer cultural contexts.

Queer readers do not really need to know about a director's sexual status to read their films from within queer cultural contexts. However, information about this status might come up as part of the general round of gossip and other extratextual information that circulates within queer communities about texts and personalities. Queer communities have always had their versions of *Entertainment Tonight* and the *National Enquirer* within an oral tradition that conveys, by word of mouth, news, opinions and rumors of interest to gays, lesbians and bisexuals. Until the 1950s, gossip, letters and personal diaries were how most queer mass culture history and opinion was recorded and transmitted; this material was considered too trivial, shocking or dangerous to commit to the public print and electronic media. Since the 1950s, a handful of gay, lesbian, bisexual, and queer journals, magazines, 'zines, radio programs, and cable access and public television shows have begun the process of publicly recording queer information and opinion about mass culture. Now even some "mainstream" magazines have gotten into the act, with articles on lesbian fashion and queer cinema. In any case, between gossip and gleaning information in print and on the air, queer cultures circulate a wide range of "background material" people can use as part of how they queerly understand mass culture texts and performers.

Of course, certain comic texts and performers present themselves as being *about* queerness (*Victor/Victoria*, *Some Like It Hot*, *Sylvia Scarlett*, *I Was a Male War Bride*, Kate Clinton, Reno, Pee-Wee Herman, Kids in the Hall, Funny Gay Men). But the queerness of comedy consists of far more than humorous representations of queerness. Let's face it, as a genre, comedy is fundamentally queer, since it encourages rule-breaking, risk-taking, inversions and perversions in the face of straight patriarchal norms. Although you could argue that most comic gender and sexuality rule-breaking is ultimately contained or recuperated by traditional narrative closure (as it attempts to restore the straight *status quo*), or through the genre's "it's just a joke" emotional escape hatch, the fact remains that queerness is the source of many comic pleasures for audiences of all sexual identities.

While comedy can be queer in numerous ways, not all of these are specific to producing or reading comedy *as* comic. Queer reading strategies involving the sociopolitical, star cult, gossip/extratextality, *auteurism*, identification and erotics are employed across mass culture texts and personalities. On the other hand, camp, a distinctively queer strategy for reading comedy as comic, is also used to humorously read not-intended-to-be-comic texts and performers, like Bette Davis or *Valley of the Dolls*. What follows in this essay is an attempt to cover a number of queer approaches to comedy by using *The Women* as an illustrative text. Why *The Women*? Because it is a traditional comic narrative film, albeit an unusual one in certain respects (its all-woman cast, its gay director, its lengthy Technicolor fashion show insert). In addition, *The Women* has been the subject of a wide range of print and conversational readings in queer cultures as a cult film.[2] As with any cult film, queer readings of *The Women* are often set within the context of (sub)cultural gossip, publicity, and other extratextual information. For example, part of the way many queer audiences understand the "bitchy" comedy of *The Women* has to do with knowing something about the long-standing professional animosity between Joan Crawford and Norma Shearer; or the fact that director George Cukor was gay; or that the director and many of the stars were *Gone With the Wind* rejects;[3] or about how the press at the time attempted to exploit much of this information in order to promote an on-the-set feud between Crawford and Shearer, while at the same time characterizing Cukor as the alternately dispirited and harrassed mediator for a jealously temperamental cast of 135 women.[4]

Camp Readings

Gossip, publicity and other extratextual information are also important to queer comic readings of films, because considering extratextual material often helps create the conditions for camp readings. Extratextuality can foster a certain camp distance and irony towards narrative and characters by encouraging a passionate involvement in "behind-the-scenes" news about the production and the actors. Camp: almost everyone has heard of it, many have tried to define it, but few have succeeded in capturing on the printed page what camp is.[5] At most, I think, you can descriptively approach and encircle camp. Camp is sometimes a reading strategy ("in the eye of the beholder") and sometimes an approach used in constructing texts or performances (and sometimes it is both). Camp's central interests are taste/style/aesthetics, sexuality and gender—or, rather, sexuality as related to gender role-playing (via style codes). Camp's mode is excess and exaggeration. Camp's tone is a mixture of irony, affection, seriousness, playfulness and angry laughter. Camp's politics can be reactionary, liberal or radical, depending on the example you are considering and your ideological agenda as a reader. But one thing about camp is certain—at least for me. Camp is queer. There is nothing straight about camp.

While camp is queer, not all queers are camp or do camp. On the other hand, straight-identifying people can use camp strategies in producing or reading cultural texts. But try as they might to neuter or to heterosexualize it, camp remains a queer thing, even when it is employed to homophobic ends. After all, it is not as if queers have not done self-oppressive, homophobic (and misogynistic) camping themselves. So to go camping in culture is to place yourself within queer discourses which comically consider a wide range issues through their connections to ideologies of taste/style/aesthetics, gender and sexuality. While camp's ironic humor always foregrounds straight cultural assumptions and its (per)version of reality, and therefore seeks to denaturalize the work of dominant (patriarchal, heterocentrist) ideologies, its political agenda is not always progressive. Camp's position and that of the camp reader, however, are in some way non-, anti-, or contra-straight: camp is queer.

The camp in *The Women* begins with its notorious credit sequence, which, as one critic points out, compares the world of women to a "vast bestiary" with dissolves linking animals to each actor-character.[6] Women are not just like animals here, they arise from various animals. This overly literal representation of patriarchy's metaphoric connection of women and nature is audaciously funny and ridiculous to many queer viewers—it is campy. But the political ends of this camp depend upon the reader. It is misogynist if you decide the intent of the sequence is to ridicule straight women rather than the cultural paradigms that compare them to animals. Even apart from any camp reading, however, genre considerations make it difficult to determine the intent of an excessive sequence like *The Women*'s credit sequence. After all, is not the point of much comedy to exploit excess and exaggeration? So most critical statements about comic "intentions" actually express particular ideological interpretations of a text's comic message(s). Certainly, one general camp reading of *The Women* has been built around laughing at the idiotic extremes of straight women's attempts to catch and keep straight men. This reading would not be particularly concerned with how the (offscreen) patriarchy surrounding these women might force them to go to such extremes.

Another general camp reading of the film does consider this sociopolitical context, however. Taking its cue from the film's juxtaposition of the credit sequence with the beauty salon sequence that follows, this approach encourages a less misogynistic reading of the film's excesses. Considered together, the opening sequences expose a central cultural paradox about gender that queers any straight reading of the film. For while the credit sequence tells us that women are (like) animals, that they are natural forces, the salon scenes insist women are artificial, that they are carefully constructed for certain gender and class roles. The film's opening campily establishes the idea that culture demands a "naturalized artificiality" or an "artificial naturalness" of women. This ideological catch-22 would inform certain camp responses to the film's subsequent comic revelations about women.

These misogynistic and feminist interpretations of *The Women* do not exhaust the range of camp readings queers perform on the film. Besides those readings which understand characters either as representing something essential about straight women or as representing the cultural construction of straight women, there are also a variety of cross-gender approaches which have been the source of great pleasure and great ideological tension for gay men. These cross-gender interpretations are carried out in two forms which are opposite sides of the same cultural coin: (1) seeing the women characters (and/or the actors) on the screen as "really" being gay men, and (2) seeing gay men as being *like* the female characters or performers. But feminist questions about appropriating women's images and queer questions about capitulating to straight paradigms that pejoratively define homosexuality as always being about gender "inversion" can arise when gay men read women stars and characters as if they were somehow also representing gay men.

As you might expect by this point, there are no simple analyses of the pleasures and politics of cross-gender identification for gays, lesbians and other queers. For example, gays who identify with (or who identify other gays as) Sylvia—Rosalind Russell, Crystal—Joan Crawford, or Mary—Norma Shearer might be identifying with certain shared, positive qualities in these characters and stars (wit, determination, stylishness, and so on), or they might see themselves and other gays as being in, or being culturally forced into, the places of these bitchy or masochistic characters and stars. The complicated humor involved when gays conduct camp readings of *The Women* within this latter cultural position finds its perfect expression when showgirl Miriam Aarons (Paulette Goddard) reminds Shearer's Mary Haines, "Heck, a woman's compromised the day she's born!" Since patriarchal, heterocentrist culture see gay men as women wannabes and women-substitutes, this line, spoken as a half-bitter, half-resigned wisecrack, needs little translation to make it register with gay spectators culturally trained as cross-gender readers.

So within any of the general camp reading strategies of *The Women* outlined above, the politics of the camp connected to the text or the reader can become contested ground, often negotiated scene by scene and character by character, as readers move between different camp positions, sometimes cued by textual codes, sometimes by their cultural background. In terms of characters and camp politics, the most complicated and problematic figure in *The Women* is Sylvia Fowler, particularly as performed by Rosalind Russell. Russell recalls in her memoirs how, while testing for the part, she played Sylvia in three distinct styles: "drawing-room comedy," "realistically" and "flat out, in a very exaggerated style."[7] To her amazement, Cukor insisted Russell play the "very, very exaggerated version" throughout the film, in contrast with the rest of the cast.[8] The director also told Russell he wanted Sylvia to be outrageous, even within the context of a farce, because he wanted audiences to like her, despite any malicious things the narrative had her do.[9] For Pauline Kael, the resulting performance is an "all-out burlesque of women as jealous bitches," that is, a caricature of a stereotype.[10] Critic Carlos Clarens finds Russell's Sylvia is "somewhat like a female impersonator trying to crash the powder-room."[11]

The readings of Sylvia suggested by Kael, Clarens, Cukor's directions and Russell's initial response also hint at the varied ideological positions camp allows. Russell is astonished by (and indicates elsewhere in her autobiography that she was initially resistant to) Cukor's insistence that Sylvia be played as a grotesque, while Kael hails the performance as a brilliant use of camp in the service of deconstructive masquerade. Cukor wanted Sylvia to be a larger-than-life, bitchy woman that audiences (particularly queer audiences?) could laugh at, but he was also concerned that Sylvia be someone audiences liked *because* of her unrelenting outrageousness. Finally, Clarens indicates that, for gay audiences at least, the campy laughter in this case is less directed at (straight) women than at gays, as Sylvia is being read as a woman-as-gay-man, or, perhaps more precisely, a drag queen among straight women. Even considering just the two gay responses to Sylvia as a camp figure (Clarens's and Cukor's), the ideological bottom line remains uncertain. For while in Sylvia's case, the camp caricature and laughter might work to satirize cultural clichés (the aggressively envious woman, the dishing drag queen), it also has the potential to disempower through misogyny and gay self-hate.

Cukor and Auteurism

Director George Cukor's cross-gendered *auteurist* reputation as a "woman's director" forms the background for understanding his complicated response to the camp elements in Sylvia and throughout the rest of the film.[12] Designer Edith Head once invoked a "third sex" paradigm to describe Cukor, when she observed in an interview, "If you were going to star in a film, who would you want to direct you—a man or a woman? I think I'd choose George Cukor myself."[13] Most writing about Cukor has not so much aligned him with both or neither gender(s), as identified him with women, particularly strong women actors. I find it difficult to believe that it is sheer coincidence that Cukor is both gay and the director of many films (*Dinner at Eight, Sylvia Scarlett, Camille, The Women, The Philadelphia Story, Born Yesterday* and *A Star is Born*) and stars (Joan Crawford, Judy Garland, Rosalind Russell, Katharine Hepburn, Jean Harlow and Greta Garbo) central to queer cults.

The cross-gendered critical labels which have been used by critics, even sympathetic ones, in order to dismiss Cukor as a serious *auteur* have strong and disturbing parallels to the process by which women and queers are labeled, categorized and dismissed within mainstream culture. Thus Cukor is discussed as "just" a woman's director; theatrical; concerned with costuming, decor and aesthetic detail; committed to style, glamour and chic; and a dialogue director. One strategy by which Cukor has been recently (re)claimed as a gay *auteur* takes these traditionally cross-gendered characteristics, as well as his uses of camp, as signs of a positive difference in the director's work.[14] But this is not to say that all queer *auteurist* readings of Cukor and his films will consider these qualities as positive ones. Indeed, there is much in Cukor interviews and biographies (particularly Patrick McGilligan's *George Cukor: A Double Life*) to suggest the director was often ambivalent about both camping and his identification with women actors or characters.[15]

While acknowledging the possibility for *auteurist* readings of Cukor and his films which examine their expression of misogynistic and/or gay (self-) oppressive themes, I will briefly indicate certain points within a more affirmative construction of Cukor-as-gay-*auteur*, focusing in particular on camp and cross-gender identification with reference to *The Women*. For one thing, Cukor's affinity with the women actors in the film appears to have created such rapport between cast and director that the group improvised on the set, something rare in Hollywood at the time, and came up with such inspirations as the multipaneled mirror image of Sylvia in Mary's dressing room, and the Countess DeLave's cry "la publicité" as she bemoans her public embarrassment at a nightclub.[16]

Cukor's cross-gender identification appears to have expressed itself "theatrically" in the decision to preface the narrative proper with an extended version of the original play's Scene Two exposé of a beauty and health salon as Frankenstein laboratory. This scene foregrounds, from the start, the idea that social identities are culturally constructed, and that the characters, consciously or not, are role-playing gender, sexuality and class parts throughout the narrative. This woman-as-man-made motif is later picked up in the lengthy fashion show sequence, which initially depicts *haute couture* incongruously within stylized reconstructions of "everyday situations," but which finally associates both high fashion and the daily world of bourgeois women with/as the products of a mad scientist's expressionistic laboratory (models with electrodes on their gloves parade before giant retorts and circular glass tubing).

Encouraging the audience's awareness of women actors with strong star images playing characters for whom role-playing is important is perhaps the central (and often campily *mise-en-abyme*) thematic in Cukor's work, visible in such films as *Girls About Town, What Price Hollywood? Our Betters, Dinner at Eight, Sylvia Scarlett, Camille, Zaza, The Women, Susan and God, The Philadelphia Story, A Woman's Face, Two-Faced Woman, Her Cardboard Lover, Keeper of the Flame, Adam's Rib, A Life of Her Own, Born Yesterday, The Actress, It Should Happen to You, A Star is Born, Les Girls, Heller in Pink Tights, Let's Make Love, The Chapman Report*, and *My Fair Lady*.[17] Cukor often signals an implied antiessentialist position on identity, in particular women's gender identity, by an antinaturalist visual aesthetic that is often trivialized by critics who call the director a "stylist."

For *The Women*, Cukor seems to have developed many of the film's antinaturalistic touches from the long and garish Technicolor fashion show he claims he was forced to incorporate into the otherwise black-and-white film. In interviews, the director says he found it impossible to introduce any "nuance" into the segment, faced as he was with the prospect of garish color processing and Adrian's "tacky" creations.[18] From the evidence on screen, however, it appears Cukor became perversely inspired by Adrian and Technicolor, pushing the kitschy color and couture into the realm of camp satire by emphasizing surreal details or adding bizarre touches to

Butch Women and Camp Costumes: Joan Fontaine, Rosalind Russell, Florence Nash and Phyllis Povah in *The Women* (1939).

the staging (monkeys in a cage wearing the same creations as the women feeding them peanuts; tracking into a close-up of a decapitated hand which serves as the clasp for a beach jacket; the "mad scientist's lab" finale.)

Cukor's campy use of Hollywood's kitschy style extends into the rest of the film's *mise-en-scène*. Objects like Sylvia's bejeweled "Seeing Eye" dress and a series of feminized phalluses (ornamental decorative hands, perfume bottles) suggest a campy commentary on studio "realism." Things which typically function as unobtrusive background elements are here unexpectedly and disconcertingly foregrounded. The visual outrageousness of these objects, we come to realize, is really only a slight exaggeration of the glamourized realism MGM set designer Cedric Gibbons and costume designer Adrian display throughout the film. Camp production and readings always have this potential for conducting critiques from within, as camp takes up the styles, the technologies and the narratives of mainstream culture, and denaturalizes them through irony and excess. By doing this, camp establishes queer discursive spaces which reveal how (mass) culture's partiarchal, heterocentrist agendas are hidden in plain sight on the surfaces of its "realistic" representation.

Lesbian Readings, Queer Pleasures

Something else is "hidden in plain sight" on the surfaces of *The Women*'s comic narrative: a lesbian agenda which finds in the tensions and the camaraderie between the all-women cast a rich source for cultural criticism, identification and erotics. Until recently the social history of lesbian film and mass culture spectatorship largely took the form of anecdotes, letters, diaries, gossip and daily conversations. Most of this oral history remained within lesbian communities. The "Lesbians and Film" special section in *Jump Cut*'s March 1981 issue marked an important step in making this lesbian cultural work visible in a journal with both straight and queer readers. The introductory essay by Edith Becker, Michelle Citron, Julia Lesage and B. Ruby Rich, and "Hollywood Transformed," a series of interviews conducted by Judy (later Claire) Whitaker are particularly valuable sources for material about lesbian readers and mainstream films like *The Women*.[19] Both pieces consider how identification (both cross-gender and same-gender), erotic desire and "subtexting" allow lesbian readers to derive varied pleasures from stars, characters and narratives. Although not mentioned in these works, camp has also been a means by which some lesbian readers have understood the products of dominant culture. In discussing the development of her queer identity, Sue-Ellen Case remarks that, besides cross-gender identification, "a multitude of other experiences and discourses continued to enhance my queer thinking. Most prominent among them was the subcultural discourse of camp which I learned primarily from old dykes and gay male friends I knew in San Francisco."[20]

As I have already discussed camp readings and *The Women*, and cross-gender identification is discussed later, I will confine my remarks here to same-gender identification, desire and (sub)texting in lesbian readings of *The Women*. Certainly, any film in which, for once, straight men are the ones literally out of the picture is a promising text for lesbian appropriation. More than two hours of frames filled with the sights and sounds of women energetically sparring with and supporting each other generate enough emotional intensity to make the idea of "compulsory heterosexuality" with invisible men seem pallid and uninteresting by comparison.[21] Besides, as Kayucila Brooke and Jane Cottis suggest, in their video *Dry Kisses Only*, even the confrontations and arguments between women in mainstream films like *The Women* might be understood by lesbian viewers as being more indicative of the ways in which women have been forced by patriarchy into the role of rivals, rather than of any fundamental hatred and jealously between women.[22]

Within these lesbian cultural reading practices, Syliva once again becomes a key figure. While at times her excesses might appear to serve patriarchal heterosexuality in her divisive role as gossiping "bitch," she also provides a model of fast-talking assertiveness and independence which the other characters follow at one time or another. Sylvia also connects the upper-class characters with Crystal Allen, a working woman, in a sisterhood of aggressive "bitchery." The Sylvia-Crystal-Mary triangle is especially important within lesbian and other queer readings, as it reveals that much of Sylvia's bitchery is actually motivated by sexual jealousy over her cousin Mary. Heterocentrism encourages us to read Sylvia's machinations as part of a plot to destroy Mary's marriage to Stephen Haines, because Sylvia cannot stand to see someone in a happy relationship when her own marriage is not fulfilling. But Sylvia's actions in the film can be read as easily—and as justifiably—as attempts to break up Mary's marriage (and later her bonds with other women) in order to have Mary all to herself.

Indeed, in a scene at a Reno "divorce ranch," Mary reminds Sylvia that Sylvia does not love her husband just before Sylvia has a "catfight" with her supposed rival, Miriam. Heterosexual competitiveness does not quite explain the intensity of Sylvia's attack on Miriam (which includes a moment when Sylvia licks her lips as a prelude to biting Miriam's thigh). The film suggests there is something, and someone, else motivating Sylvia as she yells at Mary after the fight, "You're on her [Miriam's] side. . . . You'll be sorry when you need a girlfriend!" Soon after, in an attempt to make Mary jealous, Sylvia becomes Crystal's new best girl-friend. To make matters more erotically complicated and provocative here, we might recall that Sylvia's first encounter with Crystal occurs when she decides to take a look at Stephen's mistress. With this excuse, Sylvia (along with her friend Edith Potter) places herself in Stephen's position as she prowls a store, avidly gazing at likely candidates in the perfume department to determine who is the most attractive. Within the confines of a traditional narrative, this cross-gendered positioning "allows" Sylvia to direct an erotic gaze at other women.[23]

Women Looking at Women

This narrative strategy is one of many in the film which attempts to frame and contain moments of women looking at other women through references to the straight male gaze—or, rather, by counting on audiences to function within straight cultural paradigms which tell them women only look at other women as heterosexually "feminine" role models or as heterosexual rivals. But while these strategies allow for and encourage such straight readings, how does anyone know for certain that all the characters who are looking at other women are straight, or are looking

Women Looking at Women: Phyllis Povah, Rosalind Russell, and Joan Crawford in
The Women.

at women only for straight reasons? Maybe these moments represent
lesbian or bisexual cross-gender gazing: that is, they are moments when
women are covering themselves by using the excuse of looking at women
from a male position in order to fulfill their own pleasures and desires.
Besides, not all narrative moments of women gazing at other women's
bodies in *The Women* can be fully explained as being filtered through
straight female, or even cross-gendered, positions. The fashion show
begins with a woman exhorting other women to "study the flow of the
line as it responds to the ever-changing flow of the female form divine."
And Sylvia is not in any sort of straight or cross-gendered queer position
when she first arrives at the Reno divorce ranch and looks Miriam up
and down (this before she knows anything about Miriam's involvement
with Howard or her friendship with Mary). Could not characters like
Sylvia be closeted lesbians or bisexuals?[24] The signs are there for queer
readers.[25] Besides, if having sex with men, being married and having
children are not indisputable signs of heterosexuality in life, why must
they be so in films?

Then there is the figure of Nancy Blake, author, feminist ("another lecture on the modern woman") and big-game hunter who favors tailored suits, and who enjoys goading Sylvia about her clothes, her marriage and her jealousy over Mary. "Her happiness gets you down, doesn't it Sylvia? . . . Because she's content. Content to be what she is . . . a woman." Branding Sylvia a "female," that is someone playing at being a "real" (read: heterosexual) woman, Nancy dubs herself "that which nature abhors, an old maid, a frozen asset"—"old maid" being a common euphemism at the time for a lesbian. As with the "mannish lesbian" professional women in many 1930s and 1940s Dorothy Arzner films, Nancy represents a masculine-coded yet woman-identified position, implicitly suggesting you do not have to take Stephen's (or any man's) place to cast an erotic gaze at Mary (or any woman).[26] At one point, for example, Nancy responds to Sylvia's closeted, backhanded compliment regarding a picture of Mary in the paper ("Trust Mary to be photographed from her best angle") by remarking, "Best angle, my eye, it doesn't half do her justice."

"*My* eye," Nancy's dyke look, is also present among spectators who are not looking at the women in the film as heterosexual models for how to be appropriately "feminine." In addition to erotic gazing, lesbians and other queerly-positioned women in the audience might look at the women in a film like *The Women* as models of strength, wit or femme-ininity. As with gay and queerly-positioned male spectators, this identification often centers on stars as well as characters. Andrea Weiss discusses the importance of star cults to lesbian cultural readings of films.[27] Performers like Greta Garbo, Marlene Dietrich, Katharine Hepburn, Bette Davis, and more recently Julie Andrews, Sigorney Weaver, Kathleen Turner and Jodie Foster often structure lesbian readings of narratives as star texts through processes of identification and desire.

As in gay star cults, strength, a sense of ironic humor or the ability to be caustically witty are among the qualities most prized in lesbian star cults. As one of Whitaker's interviewees declares,

> I loved *All About Eve*, particularly because I had a crush on Bette Davis, a wonderful model. She's a strong bitchy woman who knows what she wants and gets it and yet stayed human and sensitive. I was particularly interested to see her pitted against another woman and to see a whole bunch of other great tough women, like Thelma Ritter, in the film.[28]

This tribute also fits *The Women*, in which Joan Crawford, Rosalind Russell, Paulette Goddard and Norma Shearer play strong, witty women. Determination and a sharp wit (if not always a bitchy wit) were central to Crawford's and Russell's existing star images. Their lesbian followings have been built on these qualities, as well as a certain butchness which

"You know, that's the one good thing about divorce—You get to sleep with your mother:" Virginia Weidler and Norma Shearer in *The Women*.

emerges more dramatically in Russell's "boss lady" films of the 1940s and in Crawford's *Mildred Pierce* and *Johnny Guitar*. Shearer and *The Women* costar Joan Fontaine also have dyke followings, but for being model femmes, generally soft-spoken, yet gradually revealing a core of strength in the face of adversity (see especially *Marie Antoinette* and *The Barretts of Wimpole Street* for Shearer, and *Rebecca* and *Frenchman's Creek* for Fontaine).

Mothers and Bitches

In *The Women*, Shearer's character's intense relationship with her daughter, "little Mary," and with her own mother provides another opportunity for lesbian identification and erotics which are culturally rooted in the maternal.[29] Introduced in matching tailored riding outfits, Mary and her daughter engage in some horseplay themselves, with "little" Mary filming her mother "on the bias" with a home movie camera before trying to mount her for a "horseback ride." Soon afterward, dressed in a robe and with her husband's pipe in her mouth, Mary has a window-seat cuddle with her daughter, during which the latter asks jealously, "Do you love him [her father] more than me?" "Well, that's a different kind of love," Mary replies. These mother-daughter erotics culminate later in the film when "little Mary" gets into her mother's bed one night: "You know, that's the one good thing about divorce—you get to sleep with your mother." In this context, it makes sense that Mary decides to confront Crystal only after she has been told that Crystal has been trying to gain her daughter's affection. Mary also seeks love and comfort from her mother when faced with Stephen's infidelity. "It's rather nice to have you need mother again," Mary's mother exclaims at the end of a scene in which Mary has spend a good deal of the time with her head in her mother's lap.

This two-generation matriarchy is rather short-lived, however, as a bedroom scene with Mary, "little Mary," and Mary's mother segues into the Casino Roof powder-room sequence, during which Mary devises a plan to win her husband back. This sequence not only concludes the film, it marks the final showdown between straight and queer—producers, readers and (sub)text(s)—over the meaning of the comedy in *The Women*. Taken straight, the bitchy wit, repartee and arch role-playing (of actors and characters) is being used to restore Mary's marriage by putting Crystal back in her working-class place. But Sylvia's supposedly unacceptable "drag queen" bitchery is also being redeemed as a source of empowerment for "nice" straight women like Mary. While the irony of all this bitchy camping seems lost on the characters, it isn't lost on many queer readers. Even though she is locked in a closet (!) by the other women at one point, Sylvia's dyke/drag queen is ultimately vindicated as their imitation of her becomes the sincerest form of flattery.

But the film does not end here. As Mary begins to rush out for a conventional heterosexual happy-ending clinch, a newly "out of the closet" Sylvia (sporting a rag-mop wig) tries one more time to keep Mary from Stephen by reminding her of her "pride." This is something Mary herself had made a compelling case for earlier, in the face of her mother's advice to ignore Stephen's affair. At one point the narrative suggests Sylvia "is right" when she advises women, particularly married women, to "hang on to" their own money as their "only protection." Now, Sylvia tries to say the same thing about a woman's spiritual independence from men and marriage that she has said about their economic independence. But Mary, caught up in the machinations of a capitalist, patriarchial narrative, cannot recognize Sylvia's echoing of her own sentiments.

However, while bitchy, dykey, drag queen Sylvia is unable to stop Mary from returning to a conventional heterosexual marriage, Cukor and his collaborators are able to comment on this "happy ending." As with the opening of the film, a dialectic is set up which uses campy irony to queer the finale. While following the structure of the original play, Cukor and company use strikingly different styles of performance, sound and *mise-en-scène* in order to contrast the vivid, high-key and fast-paced look and sound of the action in the powder room with the ultrasentimental, glamourous final shot, in which Mary, supported by an angelic choir, leaves Sylvia in the doorway. Gliding toward the camera with an ecstatic look on her face, Mary finally flings open her arms and rushes offscreen (as church bells ring) to abandon herself to a man who really is not there.

In an excellent feminist reading of *The Women*, Deborah Fried says of this scene: "The fadeout just before the man shows up to meet his wife's triumphant welcome . . . is playfully censored. It's an odd coyness, as if the embrace of husband and wife were not a proper subject for the movies."[30] From a queer perspective, a heterosexual (re)union is not the "proper subject" for this particular movie, as it would threaten the "all-women" pleasures of the preceeding two hours or so. Depicting heterosexuality, particularly using heterosexual clinches to close narratives, is, however, the proper subject for most traditional films—indeed it is *the* subject. So the exclusion of an embrace and kiss from even the final shot of *The Women* seems much more than an "odd coyness" on the part of Cukor, and scriptwriters Anita Loos and Jane Murfin. They make heterosexuality, for once, the invisible, connotated (if not fully unspeakable) subject of a Hollywood movie, and humorously underline this point through camp style. Heterosexuality as *amour fou* has rarely been depicted so wittily—or so queerly—in a Hollywood comedy as it is in the final moments of *The Women*.

Notes

Introduction

1. Rick Altman, *The American Film Musical* (Bloomington: Indiana University Press, 1987), pp. 93–94.

2. James Agee, *A Death in the Family* (New York: Bantam, 1969), p. 19.

3. Agee, p. 19.

4. Walter Kerr, *The Silent Clowns* (New York: Alfred A. Knopf, 1975), pp. 9–10.

5. Kerr, p.10.

6. Kerr, *ibid.*

7. Graham Petrie, "So Much and Yet So Little: A Survey of Books on Chaplin," *Quarterly Review of Film Studies*, vol. 22, No. 4, 1977, pp. 468–483. William Paul has similarly suggested the role which repression plays in altering our memories and descriptions of comic moments in Chaplin's films in order to avoid contemplating the more scatological or, in Paul's words, "anal" dimensions of his humor. See William Paul, "Charles Chaplin and the Annals of Anality," in Andrew S. Horton, ed., *Comedy/Cinema/Theory* (Berkeley: University of California Press, 1991), pp. 109–130.

8. On the concept of popular memory, see Lynn Spigel, "Communicating with the Dead: Elvis as Medium," *Camera Obscura*, 23, May 1990, pp. 177–205.

9. Steve Seidman, *Comedian Comedy: A Tradition in Hollywood Film* (Ann Arbor: UMI Research, 1981).

10. Frank Krutnik, "The Clown-Prints of Comedy," *Screen*, July–October 1984, pp. 50–59; Peter Kramer, "Derailing the Honeymoon Express: Comicality and Narrative Closure in Buster Keaton's *The Blacksmith*," *Velvet Light Trap*, Spring 1989, pp. 101–116; Henry Jenkins, *What Made Pistachio Nuts?: Early Sound Comedy and The Vaudeville Aesthetic* (New York: Columbia University Press, 1992).

11. Gerald Mast, *The Comic Mind: Comedy and the Movies* (New York: Random House, 1976); Donald McCaffrey, *Four Great Comedians* (New York: Barnes, 1968).

12. McCaffrey, p. 152.

13. McCaffrey, p. 165.

14. Robert C. Allen and Douglas Gomery, *Film History: Theory and Practice* (New York: McGraw-Hill, 1985), pp. 73–74. Allen and Gomery cite Gerald Mast as their primary example of a critic working within this "masterpiece" tradition.

15. Mast, p. 20.

16. McCaffrey, p. 142.

17. Charles Malland, *Chaplin and American Culture: The Evolution of a Star Image* (Princeton: Princeton University Press, 1991); Charles Musser, "Work, Ideology and Chaplin's Tramp," in Robert Sklar and Charles Musser, eds., *Resisting Images: Essays on Cinema and History* (Philadelphia: Temple University Press, 1990), pp. 36–67.

18. Robert Darnton, *The Great Cat Massacre and Other Episodes in French Cultural History* (New York: Random House, 1984), pp. 77–78.

19. For similar criticism of auteurism, see Graham Petrie, "Alternatives to Auteurs," *Film Quarterly*, Spring 1973, pp. 27–35.

20. Peter Wollen, *Signs and Meaning in the Cinema* (London: Secker and Warburg, 1972).

21. Andrew Sarris, "Toward a Theory of Film History," in John Caughie, ed., *Theories of Authorship* (London: Routledge and Kegan Paul, 1981), p. 65.

22. David Bordwell, Janet Staiger and Kristin Thompson, *The Classical Hollywood Cinema: Film Style and Mode of Production to 1960* (New York: Columbia University Press, 1985), p. xiv.

23. Mary Beth Haralovich, "Sherlock Holmes: Genre and Industrial Practice," *Journal of University Film Association*, Spring 1979, pp. 53–57.

24. Haralovich, p. 53.

25. See, for example, Richard Alan Nelson, "Before Laurel: Oliver Hardy and the Vim Comedy Company, a Studio Biography," in Bruce A. Austin, Ed., *Current Research in Film: Audiences, Economics and Law*, vol. 2 (Norwood: Ablex, 1986), pp. 136–155; and Jon Gartenberg, "Vitagraph Comedy Production," in Eileen Bowser, Ed., *The Slapstick Symposium* (Brussels: Federation Internationale Des Archives du Film, 1988), pp. 45–48.

26. Paul Seales, " 'A Host of Others': Toward a Nonlinear History of Poverty Row and The Coming of Sound," *Wide Angle*, vol. 13, No. 1, January 1991, pp. 72–103.

27. Bordwell's approach runs counter to the push towards identifying so-called progressive genres, an approach examined in Barbara Klinger, "Cinema/Ideology/Criticism Revisited: The Progressive Genre," in Barry Keith Grant, ed., *Film Genre Reader* (Austin: University of Texas Press, 1968), pp. 74–90.

28. On *film noir*, see Bordwell, Staiger and Thompson, pp. 74–77. On animation, see Donald Crafton, *Emile Cohl, Caricature, and Film* (Princeton: Princeton University Press, 1992), and *Before Mickey: The Animated Film, 1898–1928* (Cambridge: MIT, 1982). On vaudeville and early sound comedy, see Jenkins, *Nuts*.

29. John Cawelti, *The Six-Gun Mystique* (Bowling Green: Bowling Green University Press, 1971) p. 54.

30. John G. Cawelti, *Adventure, Mystery and Romance: Formula Stories as Art and Popular Culture* (Chicago: University of Chicago Press, 1976), p. 10.

31. *Adventure*, pp. 35–36. See also Thomas Schatz, *Hollywood Genres: Formulas, Filmmaking and the Studio System* (New York: Random House, 1981). *Film Musical*, see especially chapter one.

32. Raymond Durgnat, *The Crazy Mirror: Hollywood Comedy and the American Image* (New York: Delta, 1969), p. 19.

1. Genre, Narrative and the Hollywood Comedian

1. This chapter is a reformulation of an earlier article—"The Clown-Prints of Comedy," *Screen*, vol. 25 Nos. 4–5, July-October 1984; pp. 50–59—which was a response to Steve Seidman's book, *Comedian Comedy: a Tradition in Hollywood Film* (Ann Arbor: UMI Research Press, 1981). This chapter owes a substantial debt to the semantic and semiotic acumen of Patricia Marshall. I would also like to thank Steve Neale, the editors of this volume, Henry Jenkins and Kristine Karnick, and my honors classes at Aberdeen University for valuable suggestions on comedy, comedians and Hollywood.

2. For an influential consideration of the formal features of the classical narrative film, see David Bordwell, Janet Staiger and Kristin Thompson, *The Classical Hollywood Cinema: Film Style and Mode of Production to 1960* (Columbia University Press, New York (1985), pp. 1–84.

3. To describe the form of entertainment spectacle presented by vaudeville and burlesque, Henry Jenkins has used the term the "vaudeville aesthetic" (" 'Fifi Was My Mother's Name': Anarchistic Comedy, the Vaudeville Aesthetic, and *Diplomaniacs*," *The Velvet Light Trap*, No. 26, Fall, 1990, p. 3). As Jenkins suggests, "Vaudeville's push towards the intensification of affective experience" was at the expense of realist principles of narrative and characterization (p. 8).

4. Peter Kramer: "Vitagraph, Slapstick and Early Cinema," *Screen*, vol. 23, No. 2, Spring 1988, p. 101. Further consideration of silent slapstick can be found in the essays collected in *The Slapstick Symposium*, ed. Eileen Bowser, New York: The Museum of Modern Art/Federation Internationale des Archives du Film, 1988).

5. Kramer, p. 101.

6. Steve Neale, in *Popular Film and Television Comedy*, Steve Neale and Frank Krutnik, (London: Routledge, 1990), p. 5.

7. In the US, the theatrical tradition of "genteel" comedy—the plausible comedy of manners, morals and sentiment—clearly suited the burgeoning cinema's desire to secure a more respectable, middle-class audience. The earliest genteel comedy films—featuring such performers as John Bunny and Flora Finch—represented an emphatic shift from the slapstick tradition. The renewed investment in slapstick attractions by Mack Sennett from 1912 did not serve simply to displace the genteel mode, for during the 1910s, slapstick and genteel comedy both continued to develop within the context of the short film (cf. Steve Neale and Frank Krutnik, pp. 115–120). Subsequent stars associated with the genteel mode included Mary Pickford, Douglas Maclean, Johnny Hines, Sidney Drew and Lucille McVey (Mr and Mrs Drew) and Douglas Fairbanks (who combined genteel comedy with stunts and adventures).

8. Although displaced by the prominence of the feature film, the slapstick short persisted until long after the introduction of sound. There continued to be a place for short subjects within cinematic exhibition contexts: The Three Stooges, for example, made their last short for Columbia in 1958 (and thereafter many cinema shorts and performers were "recycled" on television).

9. Hollywood's investment in Broadway and vaudeville performers was also encouraged by their exposure on the increasingly popular medium of broadcast radio. In the late 1920s and early 1930s, radio drew extensively upon vaudeville talent. For a discussion of radio comedy and its use of vaudeville talent, Arthur Frank Wertheim's *Radio Comedy* (New York: Oxford University Press, 1979) is highly recommended (especially pp. 12–15 and pp. 87–94). For the shifting relations between the radio and film industries, see Richard B. Jewell's article "Hollywood and Radio: competition and partnership in the 1930's," *The Historical Journal of Film, Radio and Television*, vol. 4, no. 2, 1984, pp. 125–139.

10. Henry Jenkins, *What Made Pistachio Nuts?: Early Sound Comedy and the Vaudeville Aesthetic* (New York: Columbia University Press, 1982), pp. 137–141.

11. Jenkins: "Fifi," p. 4.

12. Jenkins: "Fifi," p. 23.

13. Jenkins, "Fifi," p. 9. A similar degree of standardization was evident in broadcast radio comedy at this time (cf. Wertheim p. 263 ff).

14. Jenkins: "Fifi," p. 23.

15. Jenkins: "Fifi," p. 24.

16. Currently in preparation is a book-length study of Jerry Lewis's film career, entitled *A Burlesque of an Idiot: Jerry Lewis and the Comedian-Comedy*. I argue there that Lewis's self-directed films manifest a studied deformation of conventional procedures of gag comedy and narrative structure, to the extent that they represent a significant shift away from the structuring principles of the formalized comedies. In particular, the identity thematic is taken to a particularly obsessive, self-reflexive extreme. For further consideration of this phase of Lewis's career, see Michael Stern: "Jerry Lewis b. Joseph Levitch, Newark, New Jersey, 1926 res. Hollywood," *Bright Lights*, vol. 1, No. 3, Summer 1975; Scott Bukatman: "Paralysis in Motion: Jerry Lewis's Life as a Man," *Camera Obscura*, No. 17, Fall 1988; Michael Selig: "*The Nutty Professor*: A 'Problem' in Film Scholarship," *The Velvet Light Trap*, No. 26, Fall 1990.

17. Competition from broadcast television has contributed to the widespread redefinitions of the role and character of comedy in mainstream cinema. From its inception, television invested substantially in comedy, incorporating and adapting many preexisting comic forms. But the presentation of performer-centered comedy in the broadcast media tends to be much more atomistic, characterized not by the feature-length narrative but by the sketch, the stand-up routine, the short sitcom or variety show. Television has also provided more widespread exposure for comic performers long marginalised in the cinema—for women like Lucille Ball, Goldie Hawn and Rosanne Barr, for black comedians like Eddie Murphy, Bill Cosby and Britain's Lenny Henry. Many comedians who have become familiar in the home-based broadcast media have subsequently transferred, with varying degrees of success, to the cinema.

18. Christian Metz: "Story/Discourse," trans. Michael Taylor *Psychoanalysis and Cinema* (London: Macmillan, 1982), p. 92.

19. Leo A. Handel, *Hollywood Looks at its Audience* (Urbana: University of Illinois Press, 1950), p. 45.

20. cf. John Ellis, *Visible Fictions* (London: Routledge and Kegan Paul, 1982), chap. Six.

21. In the musical film, the fit between star and role is often legitimized by casting the star within a diegetic context of performance (the world of theatre, for example). In the formalized comedies, comedians are occasionally cast as professional entertain-

ers—for instance, the Bob Hope-Bing Crosby *Road* series (1940–1962); the Dean Martin-Jerry Lewis films *Jumping Jacks* and *The Stooge* (1952); Danny Kaye's *Knock on Wood* (1954); and Lewis's *The Patsy* (1964)—but this is by no means essential as a motivation for "impromptu" performance scenes.

22. Seidman, p. 30.

23. Seidman, pp. 27–40. There are, of course, more evident examples of auteur-comedians—for example, Buster Keaton, Charlie Chaplin, Harry Langdon, Jerry Lewis and Woody Allen have all operated as both performer and filmmaker (writing, producing, directing). At issue here is at what points within the comedian film the comic performer can be said to shift from star to "enunciative subject"—that is, when the "enunciative feint" of profilmic direct address gives rise to (and is exceeded by) the "enunciative faint" of "authorial" recognition.

24. This fantasy of the comedian's deviation from convention is charged with a high degree of narcissism. Both Chaplin and Jerry Lewis repeatedly sentimentalize the misfit figures they impersonate, parading their inner worth, and demanding its recognition and acceptance by the spectator. It is often the case that this sentimental demand to be loved substitutes for the necessity of social integration. Where this is so, the comedian figure's very difference from cultural codification can be displayed as a sign of his creative talent (ideally to be recognized as such by the spectator, if not by the characters with whom he comes into conflict). Narcissism, of course, also pervades Groucho Marx's assault upon the procedures and protocols of the "normal" social world. Although his style is more acerbic, Groucho still mobilizes a basically individualistic fantasy of living in defiance of the cultural rules. Instead of submitting to the adult responsibilities of social living, the comedian harkens back to the liberty and irresponsibility of childhood. He asserts a childlike capacity to play, seeking—often in a blatantly fantastical manner—to reshape the world in accordance with his own desires. Whether the comedian-figure ultimately succumbs to or resists integration, this fantasy of living in defiance of the rules and demands of everyday life remains one of the major sources of the pleasure offered by the comedian-centered film.

25. Seidman, p. 5.

26. This is made clear by the Hope and Crosby *Road* films. The simple plot of the series—from *The Road to Singapore* (1940) to *The Road to Hong Kong* (1962)—was "always this: the boys are in a jam, as many jams as possible, and they have to clown their way out" (William Robert Faith: *Bob Hope: a Life in Comedy* (London: Granada, 1983), p. 142). Crosby commented: "The jams are plotted in the script and although they're bogus situations and on the incredible side, they are important because they hold the story together and provide a framework for our monkeyshines. Gags can't be played against gags; they have to be played against something serious even though the serious stuff is melodramatic. Hope and I invent many of these gags from predicaments as we go along" (quoted by Faith, p. 142).

27. Seidman, pp. 79–118.

28. cf. Seidman, pp. 70–76.

29. For further discussion of this film see Seidman, p. 134.

30. Bosley Crowther: review of *The Delicate Delinquent*, *The New York Times*, July 4, 1957.

31. Andrew Sarris: *The American Cinema: Directors and Directions, 1929–1968* (New York: E.P. Dutton, (1978), p. 243).

32. A polarization between "ideal" and "inverted" masculinity was fundamental to the Martin-Lewis team from the beginning. In his autobiography, Lewis wrote:

> Since time immemorial, there has never been a two-act in the business that weren't two milkmen, two food operators, two electricians, two plumbers, and for the first time here we have a handsome man and a monkey. . . . That was the premise. And that is precisely how we played it. Not only onstage, but whenever the mood struck. (Jerry Lewis and Herb Gluck: *Jerry Lewis in Person* [New York: Atheneum, 1982], pp. 142–3)

In their live act, Martin's relaxed, self-confident crooning was persistently interrupted by Lewis's strangulated voice and excessive, directionless energy. Lewis created a grotesque, "subhuman," comic persona, often wearing a simian hairpiece and an oversized set of false teeth (Hal B. Wallis and Charles Higham: *Starmaker* (New York: Macmillan, 1980), p. 139). Not that Martin was always simply a straight-man to this disruptive "monkey"—for he would occasionally join Lewis's madcap disruptions, invading the audience and running amok, stealing food and drink, throwing comic insults, and smashing plates. Whereas in their nightclub act Martin would oscillate between the roles of straight-man and funny man, in the team's films there is a much more straightforward division of labor between crooner and comedian, between handsome man and monkey. Martin does not serve as agent of comic disruption but as foil to and yardstick for Lewis's deviations.

33. Prior to their teaming, Martin and Lewis had negligible solo careers. Dean Martin had a straight singing act. Lewis already possessed a show-biz history—his parents were vaudevillian song-and-dance team Rae and Danny Lewis. As a child, Lewis occasionally joined his parents onstage, and in his teens he developed a comic "record act" which involved exaggerated lip-synching to popular and operating songs. He took this act round nightclubs and entertainment houses through the early 1940s.

34. The two female partners in *Sailor Beware* mirror the terms of difference inscribed in the Martin-Lewis partnership. Melvin's girlfriend, Hilda Jones (Marion Marshall), not only possesses the same surname as the Lewis character, but she is also equally as childlike. The woman Al/Martin is paired up with—French star Corrinne Calvert, playing herself—is, like her man, a singer. Like is paired with like, and this serves to minimize the importance of heterosexual differences when measured against the familiar differences between the two men.

35. Molly Haskell: *From Reverence to Rape: The Treatment of Women in the Movies*, (London: New English Library, 1974), p. 66.

2. Comedy, Melodrama and Gender

1. This essay is taken from *The Unruly Woman: Gender and the Genres of Laughter*, forthcoming from the University of Texas Press. Another section of *The Unruly Woman* was published as "Roseanne: Unruly Woman as Domestic Goddess" in *Screen* 31.4 (1990): 408–19.

2. Melodrama is perhaps as slippery a term as comedy. For my purposes I will be using it to refer to a set of narrative conventions loosely associated with "the woman's weepie" or "woman's film" and with the television soap opera.

3. *Moonstruck* begins when Loretta (played by Cher) accepts a marriage proposal from Johnny, a safe man ("a big baby") whom she doesn't really love. Almost immediately, she meets Ronny (Nicolas Cage), his estranged and tempestuous brother. Both Loretta and Ronny were wounded—he, literally—by their first experiences with love. Sparks

fly between them. Loretta tries to resist but gives in to her love for him, seeing his favorite opera, *La Bohème*, with him. Meanwhile, Loretta's mother Rose (Olympia Dukakis) has been suffering because her husband Cosmo has withdrawn from her and taken a mistress. In the final scene, Johnny breaks up with Loretta, Cosmo makes up with Rose, Ronny proposes to Loretta and she accepts. While occupying the position of high culture within the film, *La Bohème* actually represents the efforts of Italian composer Giacomo Puccini (1858–1924) to popularize opera by drawing its characters from ordinary life rather than heroic myths—in other words, to shift opera's generic mode from tragedy to melodrama. *La Bohème* tells the story of Mimi, a sickly seamstress, and Rudolpho, an impoverished artist. After a brief period of love, the couple quarrel and separate, Rudolpho returns to his bohemian friends, and Mimi dies.

4. This topic was the focus of a double issue of *Camera Obscura* ("The Spectatrix"), which includes contributions from more than fifty feminist film and television scholars. In *The Desire to Desire*, Doane also writes of "apparent blockages" in contemporary feminist theory (5, 7).

5. Closely related to such laughter is women's use of spectacle to disrupt the male gaze and exert their own. As Mary Russo suggests in "Female Grotesques: Carnival and Theory," the taboo against "making a spectacle" of themselves is also available to women as a potential source of power.

6. I borrow the term "genres of laughter" from Laura Mulvey, although as Norman Holland suggests, laughter does not define comedy and comic forms so much as it "hovers in their vicinity" (16).

7. These exceptions include Mary Russo, who has argued provocatively for the importance of the carnivalesque to feminist theory and practice; Patricia Mellencamp, who has kept the study of comedy on the feminist agenda since her early work on Lucille Ball and Gracie Allen and, most recently, in *High Anxiety: Catastrophe, Scandal, Age and Comedy*; and Lucy Fischer, who wrote the first extended feminist analysis of theories of narrative comedy and their relation to film. See, also, Ramona Curry's work on Mae West, Pamela Robertson's on camp, Shari Roberts's on Carmen Miranda, and Candace Mirza's on classical Hollywood romantic comedy.

8. This *topos*, I believe, provides the occasion for a project Mary Ann Doane has called for, one that "works on" the "tropes of femininity" stylized and valorized by melodrama. (See especially pp. 176–183 in *The Desire to Desire*.) Such work, or play, is evident in the sexual ambiguity of certain stars commonly associated with classical Hollywood romantic comedy (Katharine Hepburn and Cary Grant, for example). On Grant, see Britton and Cohan. Social historian Natalie Zemon Davis's influential "Women on Top" first introduced me to the concept of female unruliness and gender inversion. I use "gender inversion" in place of Davis' "sexual inversion" to avoid the ambiguity of the latter term, which is also associated with homosexuality.

9. Tragedy's persistence as an aesthetic and conceptual category enhances its value as a touchstone for discussions of other genres, such as melodrama and romantic comedy. For a compelling example of recent feminist scholarship on tragedy, see Kintz.

10. I am grateful to Robin Blaetz for introducing me to the concept of explanation by emplotment. According to Hayden White, the meaning of an event or series of events is determined by the narrative form into which it is cast or "emplotted." Blaetz demonstrates how fictional accounts of the life of Joan of Arc construct her as a romantic heroine by emplotting her story in melodrama rather than tragedy. On melodrama, see Gledhill.

11. Even Aristotle acknowledged the difficulty in making an evenhanded comparison between comedy and tragedy: The history of tragedy is well known, but "comedy has had no history because it was not at first treated seriously" (*Poetics*; in Lauter, 14).

12. See Woodward (71–72) for similar argument about the lack of critical attention to film comedy. For examples of early genre criticism, see Solomon and Kaminsky. For film criticism on the left, see Ryan and Kellner.

13. Horton describes this kind of comedy as "pre-Oedipal," which he distinguishes from "Oedipal" comedy, a kind of comedy that, like romantic comedy, moves toward accommodation (10–12). Dana Polan notes a similar tension in screwball comedy, which, he writes, "would seem an eminently dialectical genre" because it combines a notion of comedy as "aspiration" with another of comedy as "materialization" ("The Light Side of Genius," 136).

14. This kind of comedy is variously called structural comedy (Gerald Mast), situation comedy (Steve Seidman), man-versus-woman comedy, couples comedy and romantic comedy. Variations of it have also been called crazy comedy (Peter Wollen) and screwball comedy. I prefer romantic comedy because, especially in its cinematic forms, the genre is deeply dependent on the thematics of romantic love.

15. This canon includes Mack Sennett and the Keystone Kops, Fatty Arbuckle, Harold Lloyd, Harry Langdon, Charlie Chaplin, Buster Keaton, Laurel and Hardy, the Three Stooges, the Marx Brothers, W. C. Fields, Jerry Lewis and Dean Martin, Bob Hope, Bing Crosby, Peter Sellers, Dudley Moore, Mel Brooks, Albert Brooks, Monty Python, Cheech and Chong, Woody Allen, Robin Williams, Dan Akroyd, the Belushi brothers, Chevy Chase, Steve Martin, Eddie Murphy, Danny DeVito and others.

16. Most studies of comedian comedy, such as Seidman's, note the hero's "sexual confusion" but give scant attention to larger issues of gender. Frank Krutnik acknowledges the misogyny and latent homosexuality in the male comedy team, but does not develop his suggestive remark that the "sexual specificity" of comedian comedy is "most blatantly indicated by the veritable absence of *female* comedians" ("The Clown-Prints of Comedy," 57). For recent examples of scholarship recovering the work of women in comedian comedy, see Jenkins's "Don't Become Too Intimate With that Terrible Woman" and *What Made Pistachio Nuts? Early Sound Comedy and the Vaudeville Aesthetic.*

17. Those romantic subplots, of course, exist in nearly all mainstream Hollywood films. Bordwell, Staiger and Thompson found that in ninety-five out of the one hundred classical Hollywood films they surveyed, romance figured in at least one story line (16).

18. U.S. culture's glorification of youth usually affirms the freedom of the *male* youth (Huck Finn and Tom Sawyer) from the domestic confines imposed by home and mother, who becomes a repressive guardian of morality whether in comedy (W. C. Fields) or melodrama (the "Uplifters" in Griffith's *Intolerance*).

19. While the essential structure of the New Comedy plot that underlies most romantic comedies has endured since the days of early Greek and Roman drama, various ideologies, including Christianity and Courtly Love, have been layered onto it in succeeding centuries and altered the meaning of the couple's union. In the twentieth century, with the increased idealization and fusion of marriage and romantic love, the union of the couple has come to signify the satisfaction of all personal desire. I do not argue here for a reconsideration of the institution of romantic love but for a look at other tensions and possibilities that coexist with it in its narrative representations.

20. Such was the case in the 1930s and early forties, I believe, when a series of films, most notably *It Happened One Night* (Capra, 1934), *Bringing Up Baby* (Hawks, 1938), *Ball of Fire* (Hawks, 1941), and *The Lady Eve* (Sturges, 1941), exploited the feminist potential latent, but not necessarily developed, in romantic comedy.

21. Frye published his most ambitious book, *The Anatomy of Criticism*, a little more than a decade before the social and political upheavals of the late 1960s. Charged with idealism and formalism, his work soon fell out of critical favor until thirty years later, when Fredric Jameson reclaimed for materialist cultural criticism Frye's ideas about the relation between works of the imagination and the social world. According to Frye, that relation is most fully realized in the forms of comedy and romance, which express wish-fulfillment rather than anxiety-fulfillment, and so "educate" the imagination in the direction of social transformation.

22. Liminality is tied to the notion of thresholds and borders, where what is fixed becomes unstable. Turner writes: "For every major social formation there is a dominant mode of public liminality, the subjunctive space/time that is the counterstroke to its pragmatic indicative texture" (34–35).

23. Cavell short-circuits his efforts to deal with female desire by failing to incorporate feminist theory and criticism into his work. See Tania Modleski's critique of Cavell in *Feminism Without Women*, pp. 8–10.

24. See Neale and Krutnik (133–36) for a discussion of the relation between romantic comedy and romantic melodrama.

25. Much of my thinking about mothers in melodrama and romantic comedy is derived from Naomi Scheman's "Missing Mothers/Desiring Daughters: Framing the Sight of Women," a response to Stanley Cavell's analysis of melodrama and what he calls the "comedies of remarriage." I am grateful to Leland Poague for directing me to her article.

26. The 1990 remake of the film makes even more of Stella's unruliness by casting Bette Midler in the part, an actor more unambiguously and consistently coded as "outrageous" than Stanwyck.

27. Much postclassical Hollywood romantic comedy has been marked by an interest in melodrama similar to *Moonstruck*'s, but from a point of view that sentimentalizes the male hero [for example, *Green Card* (1990), *Pretty Woman* (1990), *Frankie and Johnny* (1992) and *Sleepless in Seattle* (1993)]. These films, in fact, tend to appropriate the feminized genre of melodrama in the service of a suffering, beleaguered masculinity. See Frank Krutnik's " 'The Faint Aroma of Performing Seals': The 'Nervous' Romance and the Comedy of the Sexes." See also Henderson, Neale and Shumway.

28. Sally Potter's revision of *La Bohème* from Mimi's point of view in her film *Thriller* (1979) anticipates Loretta's disbelief at why the heroine has to die.

3. Funny Stories

1. Craig Hutchinson, as quoted in Epes Winthrop Sargent, "The Photoplaywright," *Moving Picture World*, May 16, 1914, p. 962.

2. Buster Keaton and Charles Samuels, *My Wonderful World of Slapstick* (New York: Da Capo Press, 1982), p. 176, as quoted in Kevin W. Sweeney, "The Dream of Disruption: Melodrama and Gag Structure in Keaton's *Sherlock Junior*," *Wide Angle*, vol. 13, No. 1, January 1991, p. 104.

3. Sumner Smith, "Harold Lloyd, a Real Showman, Discusses Comical Comedy," *Moving Picture World*, November 11, 1912, p. 36.

4. Tom Gunning, "The Cinema of Attractions: Early Film, Its Spectator and the Avant-Garde," in Thomas Elsaesser with Adam Barker, eds., *Early Cinema: Space, Frame, Narrative* (London: BFI, 1990), p. 59.

5. Gunning, pp. 56–62.

6. David Bordwell, Janet Staiger and Kristin Thompson, *The Classical Hollywood Cinema: Film Style and Mode of Production to 1960* (New York: Columbia University Press, 1985), pp. 159–161.

7. Henry Jenkins, *What Made Pistachio Nuts: Early Sound Comedy and the Vaudeville Aesthetic* (New York: Columbia University Press, 1992), p. 96. For a fuller discussion of the vaudeville aesthetic, see also the section on performance in this volume.

8. Bordwell, Staiger, Thompson, pp. 161–163.

9. *Ibid.*

10. Quoted in Bordwell, Staiger, Thompson, p. 178.

11. In 1908 the comic short averaged two to three hundred feet. By the spring of 1910, none of the comic shorts listed in *Moving Picture World* fell under five hundred feet, and a significant number exceeded one thousand feet. A similar rise in the number of productions resulted in an average of twenty-four comedies per week in 1911 and forty-three per week in 1912. Henry Jenkins, "Film Comedy Before Mack Sennett: Some Observations," unpublished manuscript.

12. Jenkins, "Film Comedy Before Mack Sennett."

13. For example, in *Madam's Fancies* (Pathe Freres, December 1907), an "indulgent" husband takes his rather extravagant wife on a shopping spree, and much of the humor springs from the overburdened husband's efforts to transport her purchases home. The trip goes well until, on reaching the house, the husband trips and the whole load breaks apart.

14. Jenkins, "Film Comedy Before Mack Sennett."

15. The Sennett myth has been summarized by Kent Eastlin: "The comedies that had reached the screen, other than some of those in which Sennett had a hand at Biograph, were almost completely influenced by the stage. There was no true motion picture comedy form, precedent or technique. It was a clear field and what Sennett did with it . . . is what gave the Keystones their impact on the movies of the day and on motion picture comedy for all time to come." Kent Eastlin, "Introduction," Kalton C. Lahue and Terry Brewer, *Kops and Custards: The Legend of Keystone Films* (Norman: University of Oklahoma Press).

16. Peter Kramer, "Vitagraph, Slapstick and Early Cinema," *Screen*, Spring 1988, pp. 99–104.

17. David Bordwell and Kristin Thompson, *Film Art: An Introduction* (New York: McGraw Hill, 1993), pp. 173–179.

18. Bordwell and Thompson, p. 178.

19. Bordwell and Thompson, pp. 178–179.

20. Bordwell and Thompson, pp. 81–82.

21. See, for example, James Harvey, *Romantic Comedy in Hollywood from Lubitsch to Sturges* (New York: Knopf, 1987); Ted Sennett, *Lunatics and Lovers* (New York:

Limelight Editions, 1985); Elizabeth Kendall, *The Runaway Bride: Hollywood Romantic Comedy of the 1930s* (New York: Anchor Books, 1991).

22. Brian Henderson, "Romantic Comedy Today: Semi-Tough or Impossible?" in Barry Keith Grant, ed., *Film Genre Reader* (Austin: University of Texas Press, 1986), pp. 309–328.

23. Henderson, p. 309.

24. Tzvetan Todorov, *Genres in Discourse* (Cambridge: Cambridge University Press, 1990), pp. 13–26.

25. Todorov, pp. 17–18.

26. Todorov, p. 18.

27. Alistair Fowler, *Kinds of Literature: An Introduction to the Theory of Genres and Modes* (Cambridge: Harvard University Press, 1982), pp. 106–111.

28. Todorov, pp. 19–20.

29. Gerald Mast, *The Comic Mind: Comedy and the Movies* (Chicago: University of Chicago Press, 1979). Mast's eight categories include (1) young lovers succeed in marrying despite various obstacles; (2) parody of other genres; (3) plot in which a single mistake produces utter chaos; (4) an investigation of the workings of a particular society; (5) the picaresque; (6) a sequence of gags; (7) the heroic endeavor; (8) the discovery of a lifelong error.

30. Jerry Palmer, *Logic of the Absurd* (London: BFI, 1987), p. 28.

31. Gerald Else, *Aristotle's Poetics* (Ann Arbor: University of Michigan Press, 1970), pp. 27–28.

32. Northrop Frye, *Anatomy of Criticism: Four Essays* (Princeton: Princeton University Press, 1957), pp. 43–52.

33. Kathleen Rowe, "Comedy, Melodrama and Gender: Theorizing the Genres of Laughter," in this volume.

34. Frye, p. 173.

35. See, for example, the introduction to Part III in this volume.

36. Madhev Apte, *Humor and Laughter: An Anthropological Perspective* (Ithaca: Cornell University Press, 1985), pp. 31–32.

37. Steve Seidman, *Comedian Comedy: A Tradition in Hollywood Film* (Ann Arbor: UMI Research Press, 1981), pp. 64–71.

38. *Ibid.*

39. Apte, p. 32.

40. Richard Bjornson, *The Picaresque Hero in European Fiction* (Madison: University of Wisconsin Press, 1977), p. 3. See also Robert Alter, *Rogue's Progress: Studies in the Picaresque Novel* (Cambridge, MA: Harvard University Press, 1964); Alexander Blackburn, *The Myth of the Picaro: Continuity and Transformation of the Picaresque Novel, 1554–1954* (Chapel Hill: University of North Carolina Press, 1979).

41. Bjornson, pp. 6–7.

42. Bjornson, p. 11.

44. Terry Palmer, *The Logic of the Absurd* (London: BFI, 1987) p. 144.

45. Palmer, pp. 141–142.

46. Kevin W. Sweeney, "The Dream of Disrruption: Melodrama and Gag Structure in Keaton's *Sherlock Junior*," *Wide Angle*, vol. 13, no. 1, January 1991, p. 105.

47. Sweeney, p. 108.

48. Crafton, pp. ---.

49. Crafton, pp. ---.

50. Tom Gunning, "Responses to 'Pie and Chase'," in this volume.

51. Sylvain du Pasquier, "Buster Keaton's Gags," *Journal of Modern Literature*, April, 1974, p. 275.

52. Pasquier, p. 276.

53. Pasquier, p. 276.

54. Noel Carroll, "Notes on the Sight Gag," in Andrew S. Horton, ed., *Comedy/Cinema/ Theory* (Berkeley: University of California Press, 1991), p. 26.

55. Steve Neale and Frank Krutnik, *Popular Film and Television Comedy* (London: Routledge, 1990), pp. 44, 57.

56. Peter Kramer, "Derailing the Honeymoon Express: Comicality and Narrative Closure in Buster Keaton's *The Blacksmith*," *The Velvet Light Trap*, No. 23, Spring 1989, pp. 101–116.

57. Bordwell and Thompson, pp. 173–179.

58. Jenkins, *Nuts*, pp. 104–106.

4. The Origins of American Film Comedy

1. Neil Harris, *Humbug, The Art of P.T. Barnum* (Chicago: University of Chicago Press, 1973), pp. 57, 72–89. Charles Musser discusses the relevance of the operational aesthetic to early film exhibition in *High Class Moving Pictures: Lyman H. Howe and the Forgotten Era of Traveling Exhibition, 1880–1920* (Princeton: Princeton University Press, 1991).

2. *Film Catalogue*, International Film Company 1897–98, p. 13, in Charles Musser et al., *Motion Picture Catalogues by American Producers and Distributors 1894–1908, A Microfilm Edition* (Frederick MD: University Publications of America, 1985).

3. Georges Sadoul, *Histoire generale du cinema* Tome I *L'invention du cinema 1832– 1897* (Paris: Editions Denoel, 1945), pp. 250–252. See also Georges Sadoul, *Lumière et melies* (Paris: L'Herminer, 1985), p. 49. Sadoul indicates Vogel's strip had two versions, one with nine images and one with six. Since Vogel does not draw frames around his sequential images, this is perhaps open to debate. By my count the version Sadoul reprints in *Histoire generale* on p. 251 shows at least seven different stages in the story. Interestingly, in terms of theories which relate cinematic techniques to comic strip layout, Vogel's strip is closer to cinematic styles of nearly two decades after Lumière, since it clearly shows the equivalent of an elegant shot reverse between the second and third image, switching from the rascal in the foreground, as he steps on the hose, to a view with the gardener in the foreground, as he examines the nozzle.

4. The classical Hollywood film is described in David Bordwell, et al., *The Classical Hollywood Cinema: Film Style and Mode of Production to 1960* (New York: Columbia University Press, 1985). Henry Jenkins has discussed the somewhat deviant relation certain forms of film comedy have to this model in *What Made Pistachio Nuts?:*

Early Sound Comedy and the Vaudeville Aesthetic (New York: Columbia University Press, 1992).

5. Noel Carroll's intricate and insightful essay, "Notes on the Sight Gag," in *Comedy/ Cinema/Theory*, ed. Andrew Horton (Berkeley: University of California Press, 1991) has proposed a logical schema underlying the sight gag and also makes a tentative historical judgment that early film comedy was dominated by slapstick rather than sight gags (pp. 25–26). I think that my analysis of the mischief gag undermines Carroll's dichotomy. Are mischief gags therefore sight gags? If we mean by this visual rather than verbal gags, undoubtedly. The logical schema that Carroll uses to define the sight gag conflict between two different interpretations which are present in the film image, seems more appropriate to the later gags of Keaton, Lloyd and Chaplin that he analyzes in the essay. However, when Carroll describes the gag of watching someone slip on a banana peel as "involving a conflict between the protagonist's unaware interpretation (there is no danger on this sidewalk) and our own awareness of the banana peel," he is clearly using the schema in a way that is applicable to mischief gags. In this essay I am less involved in specifying a single underlying logic for gags than in describing surface structures and their historical metamorphoses. But it would seem my essay shows that Carroll's sight gag is as old as the cinema, and probably more important from the start than simple slapstick. Sadoul says of *L'Arroseur arrosé:* "The gag, cinema's comic effect, which has such a glorious future before it, was born with this film." Sadoul, *Histoire generale,* p. 252 (my translation—the French have adopted the English word "gag").

6. Henri Bergson, "Laughter" in *Comedy,* ed. Wylie Sypher (Garden City: Doubleday, 1956), pp. 98–99.

7. Dates for the early American films in this essay come primarily from two sources. Copyright dates come from Kemp Niver, *Motion Pictures from the Library of Congress Paper Print Collection 1894–1912* (Berkeley: University of California Press, 1967). Production dates for Biograph film come from Kemp Niver, *Biograph Bulletins 1896–1908* (Los Angeles: Locare Research Group, 1971), pp. 423–454, which gives production dates from the Biograph Cameraman's Record.

8. Tom Gunning, "The Cinema of Attractions: Early Film, Its Spectator and the Avant-Garde" in *Early Film: Space Frame Narrative,* ed. Thomas Elsaesser (London: BFI, 1990).

9. Donald Crafton, "Pie and Chase: Gag, Spectacle and Narrative in Slapstick Comedy" in this volume.

10. Crafton, p. 111.

11. Crafton, p. 108.

12. See Tom Gunning, *D. W. Griffith and the Origins of American Narrative Film: The Years at Biograph* (Champaign: University of Illinois Press, 1991).

13. Eileen Bowser first isolated the subgenre of the explosion film in her essay "Preparation for Brighton—The American Contribution" in *Cinema 1900–1906 An Analytical Study* vol. I, ed. Roger Holman (Brussels: FIAF, 1982).

14. Musser, *High Class,* p. 196.

15. See Crafton's analysis of Charley Chase's *His Wooden Wedding* on pp. 112–116.

16. For a detailed discussion of the way gags can be subordinated to plot and character, see Peter Kramer, "Derailing the Honeymoon Express: Comicality and Narrative Closure in Buster Keaton's *The Blacksmith,*" *The Velvet Light Trap,* No. 23, Spring 1989, pp. 101–116.

17. On *lazzi*, see Mel Gordon, *Lazzi: The Comic Routines of the Commedia dell'Arte* (New York: Performing Arts Journal Publications, 1983), esp. pp. 4–5.

18. Brooks MacNamara notes the lifting of this well-worn routine from circus and minstrel shows in his catalogue essay, " 'Scavengers of the Amusement World: Popular Entertainment and the Birth of the Movies" in *American Pastimes* catalogue (Brockton: Brockton Art Center—Fuller Memorial, 1976) p. 18. McNamara has also located a sausage machine sketch presented as a shadow play in Frank Dumont, *The Whitman Amateur Minstrel Guide and Burnt Cork Encyclopedia* (New York: M. Whitmark and Sons, 1899), pp. 146–49. I thank Brooks McNamara for his erudition, which is matched by his generosity.

19. The desire to produce longer films in the period 1907 to 1909 produced some exceptions to this rule, and a number of films linked together a series of one-shot gags all created by the same device. Vitagraph produced a number of these, such as *The Thieving Hand*, (1908) or *Liquid Electricity* (1907).

20. "The comic is that side of a person which reveals his likeness to a thing, that aspect of human events which, through its peculiar inelasticity, conveys the impression of pure mechanism, of automatism, of movement without life." Bergson, "Laughter," p. 117. If, in this section, I tend to agree with Bergson's connection of the comic with the mechanical, I would stress two differences between our approaches. First, I see this as a historical phenomenon of an age saturated with the mechanical, and secondly, as my citation of Kleist and Twain indicate, I do not agree with the sentence that follows the above: "Consequently it [the mechanical nature] expresses an individual or collective imperfection which calls for an immediate corrective. This corrective is laughter, a social gesture that singles out and represses a special kind of absentmindedness in men and events."

21. Walter Kerr, *The Silent Clowns* (New York: Alfred A. Knopf, 1975), p. 147.

22. Kerr, *Silent Clowns,* pp. 144, 149.

23. David Kunzle, *The History of the Comic,* vol. II *The Nineteenth Century* (Berkeley: University of California Press, 1990), p. 290. John L. Fell, *Film and the Narrative Tradition* (Berkeley: University of California Press, 1986) also details the relation between the comic strip and the cinema, although he deals more with the protocinematic nature of the graphic medium.

24. Crafton, "Pie and Chase."

25. Reproduced in *The Smithsonian Collection of Newspaper Comics,* ed. Bill Blackbeard and Martin Williams (Washington and New York: Smithsonian Institution Press and Harry N. Abrams, 1977), p. 113.

26. Reproduced in *Rube Goldberg: A Retrospective* (New York: Putnam Publishing Group, 1983), p. 62.

27. Philip Garner, "Introduction" in *Rube Goldberg,* pp.17–18.

28. In ways that are different from each other (and different from my own viewpoint) both Bergson and Carroll also discuss the role that absentmindedness or inattention plays in comic gags. See Bergson, "Laughter," pp. 155–56, 187, Carroll, "Sight Gags," p. 30.

29. Rudi Blesh, *Keaton* (New York: Collier Books, 1966), p. 350.

30. Daniel Moews, *Keaton: The Silent Features Close* (Berkeley: University of California Press, 1977), p. 71.

31. Heinrich von Kleist, "On the Marionette Theater," in *German Romantic Criticism,* ed. A. Leslie Willson (New York: Continuum, 1982), pp. 240, 244.

32. Mark Twain, "Life on the Mississippi," in *Mississippi Writings* (New York: The Library of America, 1982), p. 297.

33. Twain, "Life on the Mississippi," p. 298. I thank Louis Schwartz for directing my attention to this Twain story.

5. Gag, Spectacle and Narrative

1. This somewhat grizzled text requires a bit of explanation. In early 1985, Eileen Bowser proposed a "Slapstick Symposium," which would be held in conjunction with a congress of FIAF (The International Federation of Film Archives). Those of us in the New York vicinity were able to preview a selection of films at the Museum of Modern Art. Ms. Bowser's concept, original and elegantly simple, was that each presentation would be not just a paper, but rather a running commentary integrated with projections of complete films. This was spectacularly successful as live performance at the symposium, which took place May 2–3, 1985, but proved nettlesome when the time came to produce written papers. Besides the shift from an informal verbal mode to written discourse, the presenters/authors had to cope with the inaccessibility of the films for many of the readers.

   Meanwhile I was asked to re-present the talk at the Columbia University Seminars at the Museum of Modern Art. I was fortunate to have Tom Gunning, who had participated in the Slapstick Symposium, as my respondent on November 14, 1985. His reactions, suggestions and criticisms, as well as those of others at the symposium and the seminars, were incorporated into the 1988 publication of the proceedings.

   Since 1985, of course, the slippery banana peel has been the subject of much serious study, and likewise the study of narrative and narration in cinema has developed. Although I considered writing a completely updated revision for the present anthology, I ultimately rejected the idea. Nevertheless, I have made some changes of emphasis which I believe will clarify some murkiness in the original.

   I would like to dedicate this essay to Eileen Bowser, on the occasion of her retirement from the Museum of Modern Art in 1993.

2. See for example, Dan Kamin's chapter "The Magician," in *Charlie Chaplin's One-Man Show* (Metuchen: Scarecrow Press, 1984), pp. 37–55; David Madden, *Harlequin's Stick, Charlie's Cane: A Comparative Study of Commedia dell'Arte and Silent Slapstick Comedy* (Bowling Green, OH: Popular Press, 1975); François Mars, *Le Gag* (Paris: Editions du Cerf, 1964); Jean-Paul Simon and Daniel Percheron, "Gag," in Jean Collet, et al., eds., *Lectures du film* (Paris: Editions Albatros, 1980), pp. 104–107.

   Other useful works include Andrew Horton's anthology, *Comedy/Cinema/Theory* (Berkeley: University of California Press, 1991); Steve Seidman, *Comedian Comedy: A Tradition in Hollywood Film* (Ann Arbor, MI.: UMI Research Press, 1981); Gerald Weales, *Canned Goods as Caviar: American Film Comedy of the 1930's* (Chicago: University of Chicago Press, 1985); Steve Neale and Frank Krutnik, *Popular Film and Television Comedy* (London; New York: Routledge, 1990); and Henry Jenkins, *What Made Pistachio Nuts?* (New York: Columbia University Press, 1992).

3. "Charlie's Gold Coast Triumph," *New York Times*, quoted in *Film Daily Yearbook* 1926, p. 15.

4. Gerald Mast, *The Comic Mind: Comedy and the Movies* (Indianapolis: Bobbs-Merrill, 1973), pp. 39, 53.

5. David Bordwell, *Narration in the Fiction Film* (Madison: University of Wisconsin Press, 1985), p. 53. Bordwell's answer is also yes, but qualified. Such elements are "excess" (citing Kristin Thompson's analysis of *Ivan the Terrible*) and "whatever its suggestiveness as a critical concept, excess lies outside my concern here."

6. Brett Page, *Writing for Vaudeville* (Springfield, MA: The Home Correspondence School, 1915), p. 98 fn. Thanks to Henry Jenkins for bringing this book to my attention.

7. Noël Carroll's six categories of sight gags are a useful catalogue ("Notes on the Sightgag," in Horton, ed., *Comedy/Cinema/Theory*, 25–42). His defining principle is based on the construction of conflicting interpretations in the visual organization of a scene.

8. Carroll's distinction between verbal and visual jokes ("Notes on the Sightgag") is generally, but not always, valid. He argues: "Sight gags differ from verbal jokes. Verbal jokes generally culminate in a punchline that at first glace is incongruous by virtue of its appearing to be nonsense. . . . One is initially stymied by the incongruity of the punchline, which leads to a *re*interpretation of the joke material that makes it comprehensible. Sight gags also involve a play of interpretations. But with sight gags, the play of interpretation is often visually available to the audience simultaneously throughout the gag: the audience *need not* await something akin to the punchline in a verbal joke to put the interpretive play in motion" (p. 27). There are many examples of gags that deliver just such a "punch" due to a surprise cut or change in *mise-en-scène*, prompting a reinterpretation analogous to the one Carroll describes in verbal humor.

9. Sergei Eisenstein, "Montage of Attractions," in Jay Leyda, ed., *The Film Sense* (New York: Harcourt, 1947), pp. 230–231.

10. Eisenstein, "The Unexpected," in Leyda, ed., *Film Form* (New York: Harcourt, 1949), p. 23.

11. Tom Gunning, "The Cinema of Attraction: Early Film, Its Spectator and the Avant-Garde," *Wide Angle* 8, 3/4, 1986, p. 64.

12. Andrew Horton states succinctly, "No plot is inherently funny. Put another way . . . any plot is potentially comic, melodramatic, or tragic, perhaps all three at once" ("Introduction," *Cinema/Comedy/Theory*, p. 1).

13. Steve Neale, "Melodrama and Tears," *Screen* 27, 6, November–December 1986, p. 7.

14. *His Wooden Wedding* is available from Blackhawk Films. Other players are Gale Henry, Fred deSilva, John Cossar. Photographed by Glen R. Carrier. Edited by Richard Currier. Running time: 24 minutes at 24fps. Released December 20, 1925.

15. The throwaway function of marriage in this film is another good way to distinguish the short from the feature. In *His Wooden Wedding* it is a perfunctory motive, almost a gag in itself; in Keaton's *Seven Chances* it is a "narrativized" orchestration of delays that build in intensity. Horton notes that "Most screen comedy concerns romance . . . of one form or another, and romance requires personal compromise and social integration, as traditionally represented in the final marriage" ("Introduction," *Comedy/Cinema/Theory*, p. 11). The lack of character development, a hallmark of the slapstick short, precludes all but the most brusque references to social integration, whereas the feature foregrounds character development.

16. The passenger is a stereotypically sexist "old maid" character.

17. Neale, "Melodrama and Tears," p. 12.

18. In a melodrama—or in an "integrated" comedy feature like *City Lights*—the "lost time" of the story is not wasted, because there has been some intangible gain. For example, a character may have gained maturity, or self-knowledge, or may have survived a rite of passage, or two people's affection may have grown into love. In slapstick the characters are cartoonlike and the plots too shallow to encourage the kind of empathy that leads to melodramatic recuperation. In slapstick shorts, lost time is seldom recovered.

19. Thanks to Peter Demetz for translating the Czech titles on the print back into English for me.

20. Richard Koszarski, *An Evening's Entertainment: The Age of the Silent Feature Picture 1915–1928* (New York: Charles Scribner's Sons, 1990).

21. "Narration refers not to what is told, but rather to the conditions of telling—to the overall regulation and distribution of knowledge in a text. . . ." (Edward Branigan, "Diegesis and Authorship in Film," *IRIS* 7, 2nd semester 1986, p. 38).

7. Hollywood Romantic Comedy

1. Rick Altman, *The American Film Musical*, (Bloomington: Indiana University Press, 1987), pp. 12–15.

2. James Harvey, *Romantic Comedy in Hollywood, from Lubitsch to Sturges*, (New York: Alfred Knopf, 1987), p. xi.

3. Harvey, *op. cit.,* pp. xi–xii.

4. Ted Sennett, *Lunatics and Lovers*, (New York: Limelight Editions, 1971), pp. 14–15.

5. Thomas Schatz, *Hollywood Genres*, (New York: Random House, 1981), p. 150.

6. Harvey, *op. cit.,* pp. xi–xii.

7. Peter Rabinowitz, "The Turn of the Glass Key: Popular Fiction as Reading Strategy," *Critical Inquiry*, March 1985, pp. 420–421.

8. Susan Fiske and Linda Dyer, "Structure and Development of Social Schemata: Evidence from Positive and Negative Transfer Effects," *Journal of Personality and Social Psychology*, 48, No. 4, (1985), pp. 839–840.

9. David Bordwell has posited film viewing as a dynamic psychological process, manipulating a variety of factors, among them "prior knowledge and experience: Everything, from recognizing objects and understanding dialogue to comprehending the film's overall story utilizes previous knowledge." David Bordwell, *Narration in the Fiction Film* (Madison, WI: University of Wisconsin Press, 1985), p. 33.

10. Gordon Bower, "Experiments in Story Comprehension and Recall," *Discourse Processes*, 1 (1978), pp. 229–230.

11. Bower, pp. 213–231.

12. Bordwell, p. 48.

13. Jean Mandler, "A Code in the Node: The Use of a Story Schema in Retrieval," *Discourse Processes*, 1 (1978), pp. 14–35; Gordon Bower, John Black and Terence Turner, "Scripts in Memory for Text," *Cognitive Psychology*, 11 (1979), pp. 177–220.

14. Arthur Asa Berger, "Humor: An Introduction," *American Behavioral Scientist*, 30, No. 1 (1987), p. 6.

15. For Bergson's approach, the opposition is between the living and the mechanical, with incongruity located in the imposition of the mechanical on the living; see Elder Olson, *The Theory of Comedy* (Bloomington: Indiana University Press) 1968, p. 6; Schopenhauer viewed the cause of laughter to be "simply the sudden perception of the incongruity between a concept and the real objects which have been thought through in some relation, and the laugh itself [to be] just the expression of this incongruity." See especially Patricia Keith-Spiegel, "Early Conceptions of Humor: Varieties and Issues," in *The Psychology of Humor: Theoretical Perspectives and Empirical Issues*, ed. J. H. Goldstein (New York: Academic Press, 1982), pp. 4–39. This position can also be seen in Kant, writing that "laughter is an affectation arising from the sudden transformation of a strained expectation into nothing." See especially Immanuel Kant, *Critique of Judgement*, trans. J. H. Bernard (London: MacMillan, 1892), part I, Div. 1, 54; see also Paul McGhee, "On the Cognitive Origins of Incongruity Humor: Fantasy Assimilation versus Reality Assimilation," in *The Psychology of Humor*, pp. 64–79.

16. Jerry Suls, "Cognitive Processes in Humor Appreciation," in *Handbook of Humor Research*, vol. 1, Basic Issues, eds. Paul McGhee and Jeffrey Goldstein (New York: Springer-Verlag, 1983), pp. 39–57.

17. Keith-Spiegel, pp. 15–32.

18. In Berlyne's study subjects were asked to categorize humor according to degrees of comprehension (i.e., easy, moderately difficult, difficult, difficult, impossible). Subject preferences indicated that moderately difficult humor was the most appreciated. In contrast, humor that was easily comprehensible made no demands on the subjects' intellectual capacities, and created no rise of arousal. Similarly, difficult jokes produced bewilderment "without any hope of prompt clarification." See Daniel Berlyne, "Humor and its Kin," in *The Psychology of Humor*, pp. 47–50.

19. S. Schacher has suggested that "cognitions arising from the immediate situation as interpreted by past experience provide the framework within which one understands and labels his feelings." Schacher further concludes that the way in which the subject processes information available at the time of arousal determines the specific nature of the affective experience. See S. Schacher, "The Interaction of Cognitive and Physiological Determinants of Emotion State," cited in Paul McGhee, "On the Cognitive Origins of Incongruity Humor," pp. 63–64; A compatible model advanced by George Mandler argues that emotional experience occurs in consciousness. Verbal expressions of emotion, for example, depend on prior mental states and on direct environmental categorization. He argues that emotional behavior is composed of two segments: a nonspecific arousal of the nervous system, and a cognitive appraisal of the general situation; see George Mandler, *Mind and Emotion* (New York: John Wiley and Sons, 1975), pp. 66–67; see also Craig Smith and Phoebe Ellsworth, "Patterns of Cognitive Appraisal in Emotion," *Journal of Personality and Social Psychology*, 48, no. 4 (1985), pp. 813–836.

20. Bordwell, pp. 30–33.

21. Vladimir Propp, *Morphology of the Folktale*, 2nd ed., trans. Laurence Scott. (Austin: University of Texas Press, 1968).

22. Propp, p. 19.

23. Propp, pp. 19–24.

24. Propp, pp. 79–83.

25. David Bordwell, "ApProppriations and ImPropprieties: Problems in the Morphology of Film Narrative," *Cinema Journal*, 27, No. 3 (Spring 1988), p. 11.

26. Bordwell, "ApProppriations," pp. 6–7.

27. Bordwell, "ApProppriations," p. 17.

28. Bordwell, *Narration in the Fiction Film*, pp. 48–53.

29. Stanley Cavell, *Pursuits of Happiness: The Hollywood Comedy of Remarriage*, (Cambridge: Harvard University Press, 1981), pp. 113–114.

8. Acting Funny

1. James Agee, "Comedy's Greatest Era," in Gerald Mast and Marshall Cohen, eds., *Film Theory and Criticism* (New York: Oxford University Press, 1974), p. 439.

2. Robert Warshow, *The Immediate Experience* (New York: Atheneum, 1975); Gilbert Seldes, *The Seven Lively Arts* (New York: Barnes, 1924).

3. Richard deCordova, "Genre and Performance: An Overview," in Barry Keith Grant, ed., *Film Genre Reader* (Austin: University of Texas Press, 1986), p. 129. Since he wrote his essay, there has been an explosion of studies of film performance, acting and stardom. A key work in this new scholarship has been deCordova's own book, *Picture Personalities: The Emergence of the Star System in America* (Urbana: University of Illinois Press, 1990). Other recent works dealing centrally with performance, acting and the star system are Christine Gledhill, *Stardom* (London: Routledge, Chapman and Hall, 1992); James Naremore, *Acting in the Cinema* (Berkeley: University of California Press, 1988); Richard Dyer, *Stars* (London: BFI, 1981); Robert E. Pearson, *Eloquent Gestures: The Transformation of Performance Style in the Griffith Biograph Films* (Berkeley: University of California Press, 1992).

4. James Naremore, *Acting in the Cinema*, pp. 68–82.

5. Richard Dyer, *Stars*.

6. Roland Barthes, "The Grain of the Voice," in Simon Frith and Andrew Goodwin, eds., *On Record: Rock, Pop and the Written Word* (New York: Pantheon, 1990), p. 295.

7. Bordwell, Staiger and Thompson, p. 71.

8. Naremore, p. 77. See also his study of Chaplin's performance in *The Gold Rush*, pp. 114–130.

9. For a fuller discussion of these different comic subgenres, see Jenkins, *Nuts*, pp. 127–152.

10. Steve Seidman, *Comedian Comedy: A Tradition in Hollywood Film* (Ann Arbor: UMI Research Press, 1979), p.54.

11. Seidman, p. 55.

12. Vadim Uraneff, "Commedia dell'Arte and American Vaudeville," *Theatre Arts*, October 1923, p. 326. For a fuller discussion of the vaudeville aesthetic, see Jenkins, *Nuts*, chaps. two and three.

13. On the comic theory of Drew and Sargent, see Jenkins, *Nuts*, chap. two.

14. Seidman, pp. 5–6.

15. See, for example, Peter Kramer, "Vitagraph, Slapstick and Early Cinema," *Screen*, Spring 1988, pp. 99–104; Peter Kramer, "Derailing the Honeymoon Express: Comicality and Narrative Closure in Buster Keaton's *The Blacksmith*," *Velvet Light Trap*, Spring 1989, pp. 101–116. See, also, Frank Krutnik's essay in this anthology.

16. Parker Tyler, "High, Low, Comedy Jack, and the Game," in *Magic and Myth of the Movies* (London: Secker and Warburg, 1971), pp. 56–74.

17. Tom Gunning, "The Cinema of Attractions: Early Film, Its Spectator and the Avant-Garde" in Thomas Elsaesser with Adam Barker, eds., *Early Cinema: Space, Frame, Narrative* (London: BFI, 1990). See also Gunning's essay in this collection.

18. David Robinson, "The Italian Comedy," *Sight and Sound*, Fall 1986, pp. 105–122; David Robinson, "The Rise and Fall of the Clowns: The Golden Age of French Comedy, 1907–1914," *Sight and Sound*, Fall 1988, pp. 99–102.

19. Peter Kramer, "Vitagraph, Slapstick and Early Cinema," pp. 99–104.

20. Gerald Mast, *The Comic Mind: Comedy and the Movies* (New York: Random House, 1976).

21. "Sectional Sure-Fire Yarns are Out; Favor Stories National Scope," *Variety*, October 20, 1931, p. 2.

22. See Jenkins, *Nuts*, chap. nine; Kathleen K. Rowe, "Roseanne: Unruly Woman as Domestic Goddess," *Screen*, Winter 1990, 31, 4 408–419; Shari Roberts, " 'The Lady in the Tutti-Frutti Hat', Carmen Miranda, a Spectacle of Ethnicity," *Cinema Journal*, 32, 3, 1993, pp. 13–23; Pamela Robertson, " 'The Kinda Comedy that Imitates Me': Mae West's Identification with Feminist Camp," *Cinema Journal*, 32, 2, 57–72.

23. On Lewis, see Jean Pierre Coursodon, "Jerry Lewis," in Jean Pierre Coursodon and Pierre Sauvage, eds., *American Directors* (New York: McGraw-Hill, 1983), 2:189–190; Dana Polan, "Being and Nuttiness: Jerry Lewis and The French," *Journal of Popular Film and Television*, 1984, pp. 42–46; Claire Johnson and Paul Willemen, eds., *Frank Tashlin* (Edinburgh: Edinburgh Film Festival, 1973).

24. Jacques Aumont, Jean-Luc Comolli, A. S. Labarthe, Jean Narboni and Sylvie Pierre, "A Concise Lexicon of Lewisian Terms" in Claire Johnson and Paul Willemen, *Frank Tashlin*, pp. 89–129.

25. Michael Selig, *"The Nutty Professor:* A 'Problem' in Film Scholarship," *Velvet Light Trap*, Fall 1990, pp. 42–56.

26. Tyler, pp. 66–67.

27. On the conception of generic evolution, see John G. Cawelti, *"Chinatown* and Generic Transformation in Recent American Films," in Barry Keith Grant, ed., *Film Genre Reader* (Austin: University of Texas Press, 1986), pp. 183. Many of the other essays within the Grant anthology deal with issues of generic evolution, including those by Rick Altman, Barbara Klinger and Tag Gallagher.

28. On Hepburn, see Janet Thumim, " 'Miss Hepburn is Humanized': The Star Persona of Katharine Hepburn," *Feminist Review*, Autumn 1986, pp. 71–104; Andrew Britton, *Katharine Hepburn: The Thirties and After* (Newcastle upon Tyne: Tyneside Cinema, 1984). On Grant, see Andrew Britton, *Cary Grant: Comedy and Male Desire* (Newcastle Upon Tyne: Tyneside Cinema, 1984). On Monroe, see Richard Dyer, *Heavenly Bodies: Film Stars and Society* (New York, St. Martins, 1986).

29. Britton, *Hepburn*, p. 1.

30. For a study of Capra which is particularly attentive to the role of diagetic performance, see Raymond Carney, *American Vision: The Films of Frank Capra* (Cambridge: Cambridge University Press, 1986).

9. The Keystone Film Company

1. Delimiting the scope of this study to Keystone during its Mutual period (1912–1915) was a historiographical decision based on several factors. Keystone and NYMPCo.'s departure to form Triangle reflects a larger trend in the American industry at this time: the displacement of the distribution alliances organized around single reels and daily releases (e.g., Mutual, Universal, General Film) by the rise of the feature film. As Gerald Mast rightly points out in his periodization of Sennett's career, the Keystone-Triangle films took on a more polished, less anarchic look, due in large part to higher budgets and an overall attempt to produce a classier, higher quality product. Gerald Mast, *The Comic Mind* (New York: Bobbs-Merrill, 1973), pp. 44–45.

   Moreover, though the studio remained essentially intact under Sennett's leadership into the early 1930s (despite Sennett having lost the legal rights to the name "Keystone" in 1917), the original Mutual Keystone was by far its most innovative and influential incarnation. By 1915, the slapstick boom had branched off in different directions at a variety of studios, and after this point the Sennett studio no longer retained the dominant position in the genre that it held during the early period. Triangle's misguided management decisions—its exclusive distribution to a handful of affiliated, upscale theaters, and its expensive recruitment of theatrical stars who proved less popular than established film stars—almost certainly contributed to the decline of Keystone's dominance of the slapstick field. Regarding Triangle, see also, Kalton Lahue, *Dreams for Sale: The Rise and Fall of the Triangle Film Corporation* (Cranbury, NJ: A. S. Barnes & Co., 1971); and Richard Koszarski, *An Evening's Entertainment: The Age of the Silent Feature Picture, 1915–1928* (New York: Charles Scribners' Sons, 1990), pp. 66–68.

2. Jay Leyda, "California Slapstick: A Definition," in *The Slapstick Symposium*, Eileen Bowser, ed. (Brussels: Federation Internationale des Archives du Film, 1988), pp. 1–3.

3. While some historians have pointed to contemporaries of Keystone and Sennett as comparably important, trade press coverage of the time clearly held Keystone to be the preeminent company in developing and popularizing the new slapstick comedy. Many celebrate Hal Roach as a superior producer to Sennett, but Roach did not really start regular production until 1915. Jean Mitry cites Al Christie and the Nestor Company as predecessors to and possible influences on Keystone; however, published film synopses and the few surviving films which I have viewed indicate that Nestor's 1911–12 output was not devoted solely to comedy, and that their comedies were not built around action and violence in the Keystone fashion. See Mitry, "Mack Sennett," in *Anthologie du Cinema*, Tome III (Paris: L'Avant-Scene), pp. 182–83. For an example of trade press predictions of slapstick's imminent decline, see Louis Reeves Harrison's review of Keystone's *The Little Teacher* in *Moving Picture World*, July 3, 1915, p. 79. Harrison ends his review by noting that "the day of farce comedy is getting rather dim."

4. The Pordenone Festival of Silent Cinema presented a Sennett retrospective as part of its 1983 program, and the Italian journal *Griffithiana* devoted an accompanying special issue to Sennett. This issue consisted mainly of Italian translations of American trade journal and fan magazine articles, with original articles by Davide Turconi, Steven Higgins, Maryann Chach, Anthony Slide and others. *Griffithiana* No. 12/13/14/15, October 1983. The 1985 FIAF-sponsored Slapstick Symposium at the Museum of Modern Art devoted much attention to 1910s (and earlier) slapstick, though none to Keystone specifically. The papers delivered at the Symposium are collected in *The Slapstick Symposium, op. cit.*

5. Walter Kerr, *The Silent Clowns* (New York: Alfred A. Knopf, 1975).

6. James Agee, "Comedy's Greatest Era," *Life*, September 3, 1949; reprinted in *Agee on Film* (New York: McDowell, Obolensky Inc., 1958), pp. 2–19. Other major works I would consider part of this tradition include David Robinson, *The Great Funnies* (London: Studio Vista, 1969); Kalton Lahue, *World of Laughter: The Motion Picture Comedy Short, 1910–1930* (Norman: University of Oklahoma Press, 1966); Donald McCaffrey, *4 Great Comedians* (New York: A. S. Barnes and Company, 1968); Gerald Mast, *The Comic Mind*; William K. Everson, *American Silent Film* (New York: Oxford University Press, 1978), chap. 15: "Comedy." Kalton Lahue has published two books on Sennett and Keystone which clearly fall into this tradition: Kalton Lahue and Terry Brewer, *Kops and Custards: The Legend of Keystone Films* (Norman: University of Oklahoma Press, 1968); Lahue, *Mack Sennett's Keystone* (New York: A. S. Barnes and Company, 1971). This critical tradition also included countless monographs on individual comedians, and non-English language studies not cited here. Grouping these authors together and debating certain of their assumptions is not meant to disparage their work. Despite its historiographical shortcomings, Kerr's *The Silent Clowns* remains one of the most elegant and provocative works of genre criticism, and Robinson's *Chaplin* is an excellent professional biography. David Robinson, *Chaplin* (New York: McGraw-Hill, 1985).

7. Kerr, p. 62.

8. Kerr, p. 62. William K. Everson similarly states that "the comedic values of the early Mack Sennett Keystones have always been grossly overrated. Sennett's sight gags are easily presented out of context, and often erroneously suggest that the movies are equally good all the way through." William K. Everson, "Videotape Review: *The Original Keystone Comedies,* vol. 4," *Video Review* (May 1985), p. 83.

9. Kramer, "Vitagraph, Slapstick and Early Cinema," *Screen*, vol. 29, No. 2 (Spring 1988), pp. 101–103. Steve Neale and Frank Krutnik, *Popular Film and Television Comedy* (New York: Routledge, 1990), pp. 120–131. Each argues essentially that the 1920s slapstick features represent not the apotheosis of the genre's steady maturation and progress, but rather an integration or "hybridization" of the slapstick short's action- and performance-centered comedy with classical Hollywood feature film conventions of narrative, characterization and romance. Kramer's article, ostensibly a review of the 1987 Pordenone Festival of Silent Cinema, presents a useful outline for a nonteleological, industrially contextualized history of silent film comedy.

10. Eileen Bowser, *The Transformation of Cinema, 1907–1915* (New York: Charles Scribner's Sons, 1990), pp. 179–181; Bowser, "Subverting the Conventions: Slapstick as Genre," pp. 13–14. Tom Gunning describes a similar shift in Biograph comedy in 1908–1909 and attributes it to similar causes. Gunning, *D. W. Griffith and the Origins of American Narrative Film* (Champaign: University of Illinois Press, 1991), p. 141.

11. For example, Richard Abel and Thierry Lefebvre have both informed me that Gaumont's 1912–13 "Onesime" comedies, to which the Keystones have often been compared, were never released in the United States market (though these films were exported to England, where the character was renamed "Simple Simon"). Kristin Thompson discusses American companies' efforts to diminish the distribution of European films in the U.S. market in *Exporting Entertainment: America in the World Film Market, 1907–1934* (London: British Film Institute, 1985), pp. 1–27.

12. Bowser, *The Transformation of Cinema*, pp. 179–181.

13. *Variety*, November 21, 1913, pp. 8, 15.

14. On *Moving Picture World*'s consistent preference for "polite" situation comedy over "vulgar" slapstick, see Henry Jenkins, *What Made Pistachio Nuts?: Early Sound Comedy and the Vaudeville Aesthetic* (New York: Columbia University Press, 1992), pp. 48–58.

15. *Moving Picture World*, May 3, 1913, p. 489.

16. See, for example, the *World* review of *Love and Rubbish*, July 19, 1913, p. 321.

17. *Moving Picture World*, June 7, 1913, p. 1033.

18. Tino Balio lists the Strand's opening-night program in *The American Film Industry*, Tino Balio ed. (Madison: University of Wisconsin Press, 1985), p. 112. See also: *Variety*, June 12, 1914, p. 20; *The New York Times*, July 14, 1914, p. 9. Rothapfel defended his use of slapstick on the Strand's programs in an interview with *Moving Picture World*, December 12, 1914, p. 1511.

19. *Motography*, October 24, 1914, p. 566.

20. Some early 1913 films, such as *Hide and Seek* and *The Bangville Police*, might be considered transitional films between the narrational comedy of the earliest Keystones and the knockabout comedy of the later Keystones. The comedy in these films revolves around narrative misunderstandings, with violent comic action entering only toward the end of the film, when the Keystone Cops appear. More commonly, however, this comic violence pervaded a Keystone film from start to finish.

21. Kerr, p. 74.

22. Quoted by Walter Kerr, p. 63.

23. Umberto Eco, "The frames of comic 'freedom'," in *Carnival*, Thomas A. Sebeok, ed. (New York: Mouton Publishers, 1984), pp. 1–9.

24. Eco, p. 1.

25. Eco, p. 2.

26. T. G. A. Nelson, *Comedy: An Introduction to Comedy in Literature, Drama, and Cinema* (New York: Oxford University Press, 1990), pp. 89–102.

27. Nelson, pp. 89, 91.

28. Nelson, p. 89.

29. Nelson, p. 91.

30. Mast, pp. 53–54; Kerr, p. 113; Douglas Gilbert, *American Vaudeville: Its Life and Times* (New York: Dover, 1940), p. 61. Lahue and Brewer note that these "films' subjects would be heartily condemned today." *Kops and Custards*, p. 34. For the sake of fairness, I wish to make clear that I am *not* accusing any of these critics of condoning or downplaying the racism in the films or vaudeville acts. Nor do I wish to imply that film historians should devote more energy to condemnation of offensive material in past films or that such humor might not have more complex cultural meaning and appeal. Rather, my point is that, far from being unconscious and noticeable only to modern, progressive sensibilities, the use of ethnic and racial stereotypes was integral to Keystone's style of comedy and was widely discussed and criticized *at the time*.

31. *Motography*, February 7, 1914, p. 86; February 21, 1914, pp. 127–28; March 7, 1914, p. 168; *Moving Picture World*, April 18, 1914, p. 337.

32. *Moving Picture World*, October 25, 1913, p. 355.

33. Ben Singer, "Female Power in the Serial-Queen Melodrama: The Etiology of an Anomaly," *Camera Obscura*, No. 22 (1990), pp. 91–129.

34. Sennett's Biograph film *Hot Stuff* (1912) relied on essentially the same sort of comedy, with Sennett playing a rejected suitor who disrupts a party by pouring Tabasco sauce into a tray of taffy as it cools on a window sill. An earlier Griffith Biograph comedy, *Her First Biscuits* (1909), also relied on facial expressions of disgust and nausea for humorous effect. Griffith's 1908–09 comedies often contained elements of earlier film comedy as well as elements which reappeared in 1910s slapstick. As Tom Gunning has pointed out, however, Griffith increasingly incorporated these comic elements into more narrative-oriented, middle-class situation comedies, such that the comedy in *Her First Biscuits* depends equally on an overall joke about the middle-class housewife's poor cooking. Gunning, *D. W. Griffith and the Narrator System: Narrative Structure and Industry Organization in Biograph Films, 1908–1909* (Ann Arbor: UMI, 1988), pp. 404–409.

35. *The American Motion Picture Directory: A Cyclopedic Directory of the Motion Picture Industry, 1914–15* (Chicago: American Motion Picture Directory Co., 1915), p. 8.

36. *Moving Picture World*, February 14, 1914, p. 784; *Motography*, July 25, 1914, p. 126.

37. Robert Sklar, *Movie-Made America* (New York: Random House, 1975), p. 109. Records of the activities of the Chicago censorship board, as published regularly in *The Chicago Tribune* in 1914, show Keystone and other comedy production companies receiving a less-than-average number of censorship citations from that particular board.

38. "Tempo—The Value of It," *Wid's Films and Film Folk: An Independent Guide for Film Patrons*, October 7, 1915, p. 1. This was the fifth issue of Wid Gunning's then-weekly magazine, which went through several incarnations before becoming *Wid's Film Daily*. Gunning did not sign individual articles, presumably because he wrote everything which appeared in the magazine at this point.

39. "Tempo—The Value of It," p. 1.

40. In figuring Average Shot Lengths, I have excluded all intertitles (but not inserts) from my calculations. This method differs from that used by some other researchers, which may result in slightly different figures. My calculations are based on a projection speed of sixteen frames per second, which strikes me as correct for these films—though, of course, actual projection speed varied widely in actual theatrical screenings at the time.

41. This latter problem poses especial dangers for analyzing Keystone films, since these films remained popular and marketable as revivals for years after their initial release. Fortunately, some late 1914 and almost all 1915 Keystones released through Mutual survive in reliable versions in the Library of Congress's Paper Print Collection. Though paper print deposits were legally no longer necessary in 1914–15, Keystone apparently chose to begin using this copyright method in the wake of massive illegal duping of its films. The 1912–14 Keystones survive in much smaller percentages, and the extant films often survive in several versions with different footage, editing and intertitles. Some of the techniques used in reediting Keystones for rerelease make any attempt to figure ASL problematic. For example, W. H. Productions, which rereleased dozens of Keystones in the late 1910s, edited single reels down to 700–800 foot lengths, not simply by eliminating whole shots and scenes, but also by actually trimming a few frames off the beginning and end of each shot! Bo Berglund

has called my attention to this practice and the difficulties that it poses for accurate analysis of Keystone editing styles (letter to the author, March 22–23, 1992). Paolo Cherchi Usai has also discussed this practice more generally in a paper entitled "The Film It Might Have Been, or The Analysis of Lacunae As an Exact Science," delivered at the Society for Cinema Studies conference, Los Angeles, May 23–26, 1991. In the early 1920s, Tri-Stone Pictures rereleased several Charlie Chaplin Keystones with original footage sacrificed to make room for obnoxious gag titles written by Syd Chaplin—up to 75 per reel—often interpolating as many as five new intertitles into the middle of what had been a single shot.

42. *Moving Picture World*, July 5, 1913, p. 12 (advertisement).

43. *Moving Picture World*, April 26, 1913, p. 366.

44. *Motion Picture News*, January 16, 1915, p. 31; January 23, 1915, p. 31. *Moving Picture World*, February 20, 1915, p. 1126. *Motography*, May 1, 1915, p. 709. Bo Berglund has pointed out to me that this second Keystone feature project was eventually released in 1922 under the title *Oh, Mabel Behave*. Letter to the author, October 8, 1992. Berglund's gracious correspondence has been extremely helpful to my ongoing research.

45. Richard deCordova, "The Emergence of the Star System in America," *Wide Angle*, vol. 6, no. 4 (1985), pp. 4–13.

46. Kramer, p. 100.

47. Kramer, 101. Steve Seidman, *Comedian Comedy: A Tradition in Hollywood Film* (Ann Arbor: UMI Research Press, 1981).

48. Both of these terms would be distinct from details of *character* unique to a specific film's diegesis, such as the comedian's job or marital status. Developing a consistent comic persona does not require having a consistent character from film to film. For example, Harold Lloyd's *comic persona* remains consistent across his 1920s features. However, we do not assume he is the same *character* from film to film, and thus we are not confused by his having different relatives, different hometown, different job, etc. in each film. Serials and series films (e.g., the *Thin Man* films), as well as televison situation comedies, on the other hand, involve consistent characters across multiple films or episodes.

49. With the possible exception of comic strip adaptations such as the Happy Hooligan, Buster Brown and Foxy Grandpa series, which might be said to have comic personas without stars.

50. English translation: "Rosalie and her loyal furniture," "Onesime debuts in the theater." It remains unclear to what degree audiences knew, or at what point they began to know, the names of the performers as distinct from the names of the comic personas. More research needs to be done on this body of films.

51. At the same time, Keystone's films did not identify cast members in screen credits, a practice which continued (with a few exceptions) until the studio became part of Triangle.

52. A secondary line of Sterling Co. films continued the popular child comedies featuring Jacobs which Keystone had begun producing in late 1913. As with the adult line, the Sterling Co. child comedies apparently focused far more on Jacobs' performance alone, whereas the Keystone films featured more ensemble performances by a group of children. The dearth of extant prints of Keystone and Sterling child comedies makes such generalizations problematic. As far as I know, only the Sterling Company's 1914

It's a Boy survives (at the Library of Congress) from this body of films. This hypothesis is based mainly on published plot descriptions and articles about these films.

53. *Moving Picture World*, March 7, 1914, pp. 1196–1197.

54. *Moving Picture World*, April 11, 1914, p. 153.

55. *Moving Picture World*, March 7, 1914, p. 1283. As I have noted above, Sennett had by this time dropped regular directing duties to become an Ince-like supervising producer, but he did indeed increase his number of screen appearances after Sterling's departure, after not having appeared on-screen in several months.

56. *Moving Picture World*, March 21, 1914, p. 1557. For the sake of space, I have avoided trying to reproduce the variable spacing and different typefaces and sizes used in the ad.

57. See, for example: David Robinson, *Chaplin* (New York: McGraw-Hill, 1985), pp. 114–115. Chaplin scholars have debated over the years the question: in which film did Chaplin first wear his "Tramp" costume? Most agree that he did not wear it in *Making a Living* but did in *Kid Auto Races at Venice* and *Mabel's Strange Predicament*. Though *Kid Auto Races* was released earlier, Robinson has argued that *Predicament* may have been shot first. *Chaplin*, pp. 113–14. Bo Berglund has presented a case for *Kid Auto Races* in a more recent article. Berglund, "The Day the Tramp Was Born," *Sight and Sound*, vol. 58, No. 2 (Spring 1989), pp. 106–112. A surviving Keystone release book in the Aitken Brothers Papers clarifies this question. This document gives production dates of January 6–12, 1914 for *Mabel's Strange Predicament* and January 10 for *Kid Auto Races*. Chaplin's role in the former film was too large to have been shot all in one day (presumably the studio did not shoot on Sunday, January 11). Thus Chaplin began filming *Mabel's Strange Predicament* earlier. New York Motion Picture Company Film Release Book: 1912–1917, Aitken Brothers Papers, Vol. 76, p. 66, Wisconsin State Historical Society, Madison.

58. *Variety*, April 30, 1915, p. 16.

59. *Motion Picture News*, January 16, 1915, p. 31.

60. *Motion Picture News*, March 6, 1915, p. 21.

61. Obviously, the definition of a "long take" cannot be determined by the duration of the shot alone. My definition of this technique in Keystone films takes into account both the duration of the specific shots *and* their function of highlighting a comedian's extended performance. The Sennett Biograph films and early Keystones often include shots longer than 30 seconds, but these usually function to show a lengthy series of narrative events within a single space in tableaux fashion, and thus would not fit my definition of this technique in the 1914–15 Keystones.

62. Most early examples of this technique occur in Charlie Chaplin's films under other directors in his first few months at Keystone—*Making a Living*, *Kid Auto Races at Venice*, *Mabel's Strange Predicament*, *His Favorite Pastime*, *Twenty Minutes of Love* and *Caught in a Cabaret*. This raises the question of how much we may attribute the development of this technique in Keystone's films to Chaplin's influence. The status of extant prints from this period makes a comparison of Chaplin films and other Keystone films difficult. Whereas all but one of Chaplin's Keystone films survive, very few prints of Keystone films *without* Chaplin from January to June 1914 have survived. Even if this technique was used primarily for Chaplin's performances at first, we might ask whether Chaplin conceived and insisted on this technique, or whether other Keystone personnel fashioned this technique as a way of adapting to and showcasing particular qualities of Chaplin's stage-honed performance style. In

his 1964 autobiography, Chaplin claims that he pressured and convinced Sennett and Lehrman to leave the long take of his hotel lobby performance in *Mabel's Strange Predicament* intact when the latter were reluctant to allow such a lengthy shot to run uninterrupted. *My Autobiography* (London: Penguin, 1964), pp. 146–47. However, these memoirs have a deserved reputation for being factually unreliable and more than a little self-serving. Though available evidence does not allow for more than speculation, I doubt that Chaplin could have successfully insisted on such a striking innovation in the studio's style during his first few weeks on the job, in films for which he had no control over scripting, shooting and editing. The fact that all Keystone records indicate that Mabel Normand directed *Mabel's Strange Predicament,* rather than Sennett, as Chaplin claims, casts further doubt on Chaplin's account. "Keystone Releases [March 1913 to March 1917]," p. 3, Mack Sennett Papers, General files, The Margaret Herrick Library, Academy of Motion Picture Arts and Sciences, Los Angeles. (Kalton Lahue reprints this document, with unfortunate and unacknowledged omissions and additions, in the appendix to *Mack Sennett's Keystone,* pp. 291–300.) Also, New York Motion Picture Company Film Release Book: 1912–1917, Aitken Brothers Papers, vol. 76, p. 66, Wisconsin State Historical Society, Madison. Almost all Chaplin scholars continue to list Lehrman and/or Sennett as the director of this film, in essence discounting the original studio documents in favor of Chaplin's anecdote told fifty years later. Interestingly, Chaplin's first few films as director do not employ this technique nearly as much as these early films under other directors. Later in 1914, however, Chaplin pursued this long take style even further in films such as *Dough and Dynamite* and *His Musical Career,* as well as in his later Essanay and Mutual films.

63. Again, the survival of some films in reedited, reintertitled prints often makes it difficult to examine this aspect of Keystone's style. For example, the National Film Archive in London holds an incomplete but original Keystone release print of *The Masquerader* which opens with a 97-foot shot of Chaplin and Arbuckle drinking and applying makeup in a dressing room. Bo Berglund informs me that this opening shot runs 107 feet in a different print he has seen (letter to the author, October 8, 1992). However, the print of this film circulated by the Museum of Modern Art includes only two short snippets of this original long take. Surviving prints of *His Trysting Places* which derive from the version reedited and retitled by Syd Chaplin in the 1920s open with what appears to have originally been an uninterrupted three-minute shot of Charlie Chaplin and Normand in a kitchen. In this version, five intertitles have been interpolated into the shot. The Blackhawk print of this film is missing this opening entirely.

64. Some might challenge the historical relevance or appropriateness of using the term "long take" to refer to films of 1914–15. Shots of a duration that would later be considered quite long—longer than, say, a minute—were not uncommon in much preclassical cinema, especially before 1912–13. The use of the term "long take" would not be especially germane in discussing most films of this period, since this duration was more the norm than the exception. The term "long take" has traditionally been employed in a relative rather than absolute sense, denoting a reaction against a dominant style rather than simply the use of shots beyond a designated length. It is this historically contextualized sense, however, which I find most useful to an analysis of shifting film styles at Keystone. The use of this technique represented a significant departure from the rapid editing and rapid action which was so integral to Keystone's distinctive studio style, and which other slapstick producers emulated. As I have argued, this stylistic shift must be seen in relation to broader institutional shifts at the studio and in the American industry.

65. Robinson, *Chaplin*, pp. 127, 697–98. Robinson's shot breakdown is incomplete, missing (1) an opening scene in which Chaplin flexes his muscles and Swain accidentally drinks varnish, and (2) the final chase ending up in the harbor. This final sequence is missing from many prints of the film. However, the print available for rental from EmGee Films, which has been compiled from various source material, contains this sequence. This is probably the most complete print available of this film.

66. Comparison of these trends manifests the necessity of complementing the use of ASLs with analysis of the functions which different cutting rates may serve. *Hogan's Aristocratic Dream*, an example of this long take/comedian performance style with an ASL of 18.6 seconds, employs a wholly different style of comedy and filmmaking than *The Deacon Outwitted* (January 1913), a typical early Keystone prank narrative, with an almost identical ASL.

67. Kerr, pp. 70–72. It should be noted that Keystone's owners did not eschew paying huge salaries to star comedians on principle, especially once plans to form Triangle began. In June 1915, Keystone hired Weber and Fields to a contract potentially more lucrative than that which Essanay had given Chaplin, and Bauman ordered Sennett to attempt to lure Chaplin back to Keystone "regardless of cost." *Moving Picture World*, July 3, 1915, p. 68. Letter, Charles O. Bauman to Mack Sennett, June 14, 1915, in the Mack Sennett Papers, General files, Correspondence folder, Academy of Motion Picture Arts and Sciences, Margaret Herrick Library, Los Angeles. It is also important to keep in mind that Sennett was a minority (33%) owner of Keystone between 1912–15, and did not make all studio policy decisions on his own. Adam Kessel, Charles Bauman and Charles Kessel each owned 19% (giving NYMPCo. officials a 57% majority), and Thomas Ince owned 10%.

10. The Making of a Comic Star

1. I want to thank Henry Jenkins for his judicious editing and general support and Hugh Marles and Martin Stollery for their help during the writing of this article.

2. Title of an important 1958 essay by Christopher Bishop (*Film Quarterly*, vol. 12, No. 1, pp. 10–15), and a 1970 documentary on Keaton.

3. *The Saphead* warrants critical attention both because Keaton's performance in it stands out from his other work in the 1920s, and because its narrative has striking similarities with the ten classic feature films Keaton directed between 1923 and 1928. For example, paternal interference with the Keaton character's romance links *The Saphead* to *The Three Ages* (1923), *Our Hospitality* (1923), *Sherlock Jr.* (1924), *Battling Butler* (1926), *The General* (1927) and *Steamboat Bill Jr.* (1928). Furthermore, like several of Keaton's later features, *The Saphead* revolves around a case of mistaken identity. Bertie must overcome his self-inflicted reputation as a gambler and carouser, and confront false allegations that he fathered an illegitimate child, in order to win his father's approval for his marriage. Similarly, due to a failure of communication and/or a rival's machinations, the protagonist appears to be a thief in *Sherlock Jr.*, a coward in *The General*, an insincere suitor in *Seven Chances* (1925), and a famous boxer in *Battling Butler*, his romance being threatened by these misunderstandings in each case. Most importantly, in *The Saphead*, as in Keaton's other classics, the happy end is preceded, and facilitated, by a series of spectacular feats of physical action, in which the protagonist overcomes tremendous obstacles (mostly to save the girl and/or her father), thereby proving his worth in their eyes, and casting all misunderstandings aside. These feats include a battle with cannibals

in *The Navigator* (1924), a cattle drive across Los Angeles in *Go West* (1925) and a series of athletic performances in *College* (1927). In *The Saphead*, Bertie engages in a frantic and acrobatic buying spree at the New York Stock Exchange.

4. Gilberto Perez, "The Bewildered Equilibrist: An Essay on Buster Keaton's Comedy," *The Hudson Review*, vol. 34, No. 3 (Autumn 1981), p. 350.

5. For accounts of the history and strategies of auteurist film criticism, see David Bordwell, *Making Meaning: Inference and Rhetoric in the Interpretation of Cinema* (Cambridge, MA: Harvard University Press, 1989), pp. 43–70, 157–61; and John Caughie, ed., *Theories of Authorship* (London: Routledge and Kegan Paul, 1981). These accounts, however, are mainly concerned with theoretical debates about the concept of authorship, rather than with its application in practical criticism, especially in popular writing such as some of the Keaton criticism discussed here. Notable exceptions to this focus on directorial control include Patrick McGilligan, *Cagney: The Actor as Auteur* (San Diego: Barnes, 1982) (rev. ed.), Joyce Rheuban, *Harry Langdon: The Comedian as Metteur-en-scène* (Rutherford: Fairleigh Dickinson University Press, 1983).

6. Donald McCaffrey, *Four Great Comedians: Chaplin, Lloyd, Keaton, Langdon* (London: Zwemmer, 1968), p. 88.

7. Walter Kerr, *The Silent Clowns* (New York: Alfred A. Knopf, 1975), p. 126 (emphasis in the original).

8. David Robinson, *Buster Keaton* (London: Thames & Hudson, 1970) (2nd revised ed.), p. 42; and David Robinson, *Buster Keaton: A Hard Act To Follow* (London: Thames/Channel 4, 1987), p. 10 (booklet accompanying Kevin Brownlow and David Gill's television series of the same title).

9. Kevin Brownlow, *The Parade's Gone By* (New York: Ballantine Books, 1970), p. 551.

10. This relation between a core corpus and marginal films is also characteristic of most genre studies. See for example the discussion of "exclusive" and "inclusive" definitions of a generic corpus in Rick Altman, "A Semantic/Syntactic Approach to Film Genre," *Film Genre Reader*, ed. Barry Keith Grant (Austin: University of Texas Press, 1986), pp. 26–40.

11. George Wead and George Lellis, *The Film Career of Buster Keaton* (Boston: G. K. Hall, 1977), p. 7.

12. Book-length studies of Keaton's work always concentrate on a selection of his classic feature films. Daniel Moews, *Keaton: The Silent Features Close Up* (Berkeley: University of California Press, 1977); cp. William Orr Huie, *Buster Keaton's Comic Vision: A Critical Analysis of Five Films*, unpublished PhD thesis, University of Texas at Austin, 1975; Noel Carroll, *An In-Depth Analysis of Buster Keaton's "The General,"* unpublished PhD thesis, New York University, 1976; Charles Wolfe, *Spatial Disorientation and Dream in the Feature Films of Buster Keaton*, unpublished PhD thesis, Columbia University, 1978. *The Saphead* is not discussed by Huie, Wolfe and Carroll. Moews refers to it only briefly in the Preface (p. vii). John Montgomery makes a few misleading statements on the film in his *Comedy Films* (London: George Allen and Unwin, 1954), p. 154. Mast does not mention it at all in *The Comic Mind: Comedy and the Movies* (New York: Bobbs-Merrill, 1973). Wead's and Lellis's bibliography does not list a single critical essay dedicated to *The Saphead*, only a few newspaper reviews. Even Kevin Sweeney's recent analysis of *Sherlock Jr.* and the problems Keaton encountered when extending his comedy

from shorts to features mentions *The Saphead* only in passing in a footnote, rather than discussing it as a possible prototype. Kevin Sweeney, "The Dream Of Disruption: Melodrama and Gag Structure in Keaton's Sherlock Junior," *Wide Angle*, vol. 13, No. 1 (January 1991), pp. 104–120.

13. For discussions of *The Saphead* in the wider context of Keaton's career in the late 1910s and early 1920s, see Rudi Blesh, *Keaton* (New York: Macmillan, 1966), pp. 83–152; Kevin Brownlow and David Gill, *Buster Keaton: A Hard Act To Follow*, three-part television documentary, Thames/Channel 4, 1987, Pt. 1; Brownlow, *op. cit.*, pp. 549–57; Robinson, 1970, *op. cit.*, pp. 23–44; Tom Dardis, *Keaton: The Man Who Wouldn't Lie Down* (London: Andre Deutsch, 1979), pp. 36–70.

14. Robinson, 1970, *op. cit.*, p. 42.

15. Dardis, *op. cit.*, pp. 66–7; Blesh, *op. cit.*, pp. 142–3. These writers fail to mention that the protagonist's transformation in later films goes well beyond the brief spurt of activity which the still-ignorant and manipulated Bertie engages in at the end of *The Saphead*; the classic features tend to show the Keaton character ultimately gaining an understanding of the situation, and then taking control of it in the climactic action sequence.

16. Robinson, 1970, *op. cit.*, p. 42; Blesh, *op. cit.*, p. 144

17. For information on Hart, see obituaries in *New York Times*, *Variety* and *New York Herald Tribune*, May 24th, 1950. That Keaton was a client of Hart's during this period is confirmed by a memo sent by Hart to the Shubert brothers on March 27, 1917. This is contained in the Max Hart file (No. 4147), General Correspondence 1910–1926 box, Shubert Archive, New York. For information on *The Passing Show of 1917*, see Sally Barnes, "Preliminary List of Shubert Revues," *The Passing Show. Newsletter of the Shubert Archive*, vol. 3, No. 1 (Winter 1979), unpaginated.

18. The Comique Film Corporation had been registered with the New York State Bureau of Incorporation on August 26, 1916, with a capital stock of $100,000, which was owned by Arbuckle and Joseph Schenck, who acted as company president and whose brother Nicholas was the company secretary. Incorporation record, No. 1306–83, Bureau of Incorporation, Albany, New York.

19. Buster Keaton with Charles Samuels, *My Wonderful World of Slapstick* (New York: Da Capo, 1982), pp. 91–4; Blesh, *op. cit.*, pp. 84–89. For release dates and other filmographic information, I rely on Maryann Chachs filmography in Dardis, *op. cit.*, which is partly based on Sam Gill's Arbuckle filmography in David Yallop, *The Day the Laughter Stopped: The True Story of Fatty Arbuckle* (New York: St. Martins Press, 1976).

20. On the marginal status of physical comedy in Broadway revues, see George Jean Nathan, *The Popular Theatre* (New York: Alfred Knopf, 1918), pp. 114–21, 198–202; and Marsden Hartley, *Adventures in the Arts. Informal Chapters on Painters, Vaudeville and Poets* (New York: Boni and Liveright, 1921), pp. 155–61. Arbuckle's and Chaplin's contracts are discussed in Andy Edmonds, *Fatty. The Untold Story of Roscoe Fatty Arbuckle* (London: Macdonald, 1991), pp. 99, 114; Yallop, *op. cit.*, pp. 61–3; David Robinson, *Chaplin: His Life and Art* (London: Paladin, 1986), pp. 156–60.

21. *Chicago News*, September 27, 1916; *Chicago Post*, September 26, 1916; *Detroit Tribune*, undated clipping; unidentified clipping dated September 27, 1916; all in Arbuckle file (MFL+n.c.2754, 10–79), Billy Rose Theater Collection (BRTC), New York Public Library, New York.

22. Mabel Normand was the first to make this move in 1916 and 1917. She was given a separate production unit within the Keystone outfit, which produced her first feature, *Mickey*, and she then moved on to the Goldwyn studio, which specialized in quality features, for a series of full-length comic dramas. On Normand's features, see Betty Harper Fussell, *Mabel: Hollywood's First I-Don't-Care-Girl* (New York: Limelight, 1992), pp. 93–120. Keystone's earlier production of a feature-length comedy, *Tillie's Punctured Romance* (1914) was a vehicle for vaudeville and Broadway star Marie Dressler; here, Chaplin and Normand served merely as supporting players. Cp. Kalton C. Lahue and Terry Brewer, *Kops and Custards: The Legend of Keystone Films* (Norman: University of Oklahoma Press, 1968), pp. 81–88. Arbuckle made the transition to features in 1919. Higher production costs and Arbuckle's unproven appeal in longer and more serious films motivated him and Schenck to hand over Arbuckle's feature debut to Famous-Players/Paramount, which was experienced in handling such properties, and also able to spread the risk more widely. Cp. Peter Kramer, "Vitagraph, Slapstick and Early Cinema," *Screen*, vol. 29, No. 2 (Spring 1988), pp. 98–104. For debates on, and trends in, slapstick comedy in American cinema of the 1910s and 1920s, see, for example, Henry Jenkins, *What Made Pistachio Nuts?: Early Sound Comedy and the Vaudeville Aesthetic* (New York: Columbia University Press, 1992), pp. 48–58.

23. According to an agreement of March 9, 1920, Arbuckle received $1,500 per week from Comique and 35% of the company's profits. Under a second employment contract with Famous-Players, signed on March 10, he received a salary of $3,000 a week commencing on April 12, 1920. All information about these contracts is taken from a report on Arbuckle's agreements submitted on September 26, 1933, probably to Joseph M. Schenck. The document is contained in Tom Dardis's collection, which he kindly gave me access to.

24. For information on Schenck, see, for example, Alan Hynd, "The Rise and Fall of Joseph Schenck," series of three articles in *Liberty Magazine*, June 28, 1941, July 5, 1941, and July 12, 1941; Jack Spears, "Norma Talmadge," *Hollywood: The Golden Era* (New York: Barnes, 1971), pp. 105–39, 397–400; DeWitt Bodeen, "Constance Talmadge," *From Hollywood: The Careers of 15 Great American Stars* (New York: Barnes, 1976), pp. 137–53.

25. For documentation of shares in Comique held by the Loew family see, for example, incorporation record, No. 2405–59, Bureau of Incorporation, Albany.

26. On the Shuberts see, for example, Jerry Stagg, *The Brothers Shubert* (New York: Random, 1968); and Brooks McNamara, *The Shuberts of Broadway* (New York: Oxford University Press, 1990). Schenck's correspondence with them is preserved in file No. 1372, General Correspondence 1910–1926 box, Shubert Archive.

27. Cp. Yallop, *op. cit.*, p. 61, and Edmonds, *op. cit.*, p. 95.

28. For appearances by the Keaton family act in Loew theaters, see, for example, review of show at Loews American Roof Theater, *New York Morning Telegraph*, May 17, 1916.

29. The above-mentioned entertainment entrepreneurs were all active in more than one medium: Schenck in amusement parks, small-time vaudeville and film production; the Shuberts in legitimate theatre, vaudeville and film production. The Shuberts were amongst the original backers of Loews' small-time vaudeville circuit. See Kevin Lewis, "A World Across From Broadway: The Shuberts and the Movies," *Film History*, vol. 1, No. 1 (1987), pp. 39–51; Robert C. Allen, *Vaudeville and Film 1895–1915: A Study in Media Interaction* (New York: Arno, 1980), pp. 238–43.

30. There are doubts about *A Reckless Romeo,* which is usually listed in Keaton filmographies but actually seems to have been made by Arbuckle at Keystone in 1916, although it was the second Comique short released due to a special arrangement with his former studio. Cp. Gill's filmography in Yallop, *op. cit.,* pp. 314–5.

31. The contract is referred to in an authorization signed by Keaton on October 30, 1922, concerning the direct payment of a part of his salary to his wife. This authorization is contained in Tom Dardis's collection.

32. Agreement between Keaton and Buster Keaton Productions, Inc., of September 1924, pp. 1, 3; contained in Kevin Brownlow's collection, which he kindly gave me access to.

33. This observation is based on an examination of numerous press clippings contained in a variety of clippings files on Buster Keaton and Roscoe Arbuckle, mainly from the Billy Rose Theater Collection, New York Public Library, and the Daniel Blum Collection, Wisconsin Center for Film and Theater Research, University of Wisconsin-Madison; I have also checked reviews of Arbuckle's films in *Variety* and the *New York Times.*

34. The film was finally released on April 11, 1921, when, after a successful run of releases, there was a shortage of new Comique product due to an injury of Keaton's.

35. See John C. Tibbets and James M. Welsh, *His Majesty the American. The Cinema of Douglas Fairbanks, Sr.* (New York: Barnes, 1977).

36. On Metro, see, for example, Jackson Schmidt, "On the Road to MGM: A History of Metro Pictures Corporation, 1915–1920," *The Velvet Light Trap,* No. 19 (1982), pp. 46–52.

37. For further information on June Mathis, see Richard Koszarski, *An Evening's Entertainment: The Age of the Silent Feature Picture, 1915–1928* (New York: Scribner's, 1990), pp. 239–41.

38. The scripts and a summary of the play on which they were based are contained in the MGM script collection at the University of Southern California (USC).

39. The date of the contract is taken from an internal MGM/Loews's report written by Katherine Barnes for Mark Avramo. It is contained in the MGM collection at the University of Southern California. The press release is contained in Buster Keaton file, William Seymour Theater Collection (WSTC), Princeton University Library, Princeton. Although this clipping is not clearly identified, it can be assumed that it was issued by Metro, possibly with the help of a Comique publicist. According to standard contracts, the distributor was responsible for the advertising and publicity concerning the films it distributed. See, for example, agreement between Comique and Associated First National Pictures, Inc., about the second series of Keaton two-reelers, dated August 1, 1921, pp. 18–19 (Warner Brothers Archives, WSTC).

40. James Agee, "Comedy's Greatest Era," *Agee on Film* (London: Peter Owen, 1963), pp. 2–19.

41. For an account of the vaudeville aesthetic by which slapstick performance was informed, see Jenkins, *op. cit.,* chap. 3.

42. For a contemporary account of what was initially expected of Keaton's screen performance, see "Papa Joe's Worthy Succesor" (*sic*), *New York Morning Telegraph,* April 8, 1917. The article promised that Arbuckle would hit Keaton even harder than his father had done. I have explored in more detail the effect of Keaton's transition from vaudeville to cinema on his performance in "Mediated Violence: Buster Keaton's Performance on Stage and Screen," paper presented at the 1990 SCS conference.

43. Cp, Janet Staiger, "The Eyes Are Really the Focus: Photoplay Acting and Film Form and Style," *Wide Angle*, vol. 6, No. 4 (1985), pp. 14–23; Roberta E. Pearson, *Eloquent Gestures: The Transformation of Performance Style in the Griffith Biograph Films* (Berkeley: University of California Press, 1992); Eileen Bowser, *The Transformation of Cinema, 1907–1915* (New York: Scribners), chap. 6.

44. See, for example, John Emerson and Anita Loos, *Breaking Into Movies* (New York: James A. McCann, 1921), chap. III; Tamar Lane, *Whats Wrong with the Movies* (Los Angeles: Waverly, 1923), pp. 137–41.

45. Cp. entry on Crane in *Who was Who in the Theater* (Detroit: Gale Research, 1978).

46. Unidentified newspaper clipping, December 26, 1915, William H. Crane biographical clippings file, Harvard Theater Collection (HTC), Cambridge, MA.

47. *New York Sun*, February 28, 1916, unpaginated clipping, Crane file, HTC.

48. unidentified clipping, dated March 5, 1916, Crane file, HTC.

49. Unidentified clipping, dated November 27, 1917, William H. Crane/Roles clippings file, HTC.

50. *David Harum* (Famous Players, 1915, 5 reels). After *The Saphead*, Crane appeared in *Souls for Sale* (1923), *Three Wise Fools* (1923) and *True as Steel* (1924).

51. *Boston Sunday Globe*, July 26, 1925, unpaginated clipping, Crane file, HTC.

52. MGM script collection, University of Southern California (USC). A revised script, probably written in April, contains certain changes (for example, the deletion of a prologue with Nick, at the age of 40, taking on Agnes as his ward in the desert of Arizona), yet the dual focus of the narrative remains in place. If anything, Mrs. Opdyke's role, and with it Nick Van Alstyne's romance, have become more important.

53. On New Comedy and its importance for the history of comedy on stage and screen see, for example, Northrop Frye, *Anatomy of Criticism. Four Essays* (Princeton: Princeton University Press, 1957), pp. 163–86; David Grote, *The End of Comedy: The Sit-Com and the Comedic Tradition* (Hamden: Archon, 1983), pp. 17–55.

54. On Fairbanks's performance in the 1910s, see Tibbets and Welsh, *op. cit.*, especially chaps. 1–3.

55. The Henrietta is a mine Nick co-owns with Jim Hardy, an old friend from Arizona who appears at the film's beginning to tell Nick that he has finally struck gold. Nick decides to put shares in the mining corporation on the market. At the same time, his son-in-law Mark, an unsuccessful stockbroker, receives a letter from his old, now-destitute love Henrietta, asking for help. When he ignores her request, she takes drastic measures: On her deathbed she sends a messenger with Mark's letters to Nick's house, asking him to take care of their child. Meanwhile, Bertie, who joins the nightlife wherever he can, displaying trophies of his (supposed) exploits in his room, has collected pictures of Henrietta, a well-known dancer. Although he has never actually met her, this apparent connection helps Mark to set him up as the addressee of the dying Henrietta's letters, and thus as the father of her child. Because Mark, who would like to have Nick's commissions, has asked Rose to put in a word for him, Nick puts him in charge of the sale of Henrietta shares when he leaves on his trip after the disrupted wedding. Knowing that he has not much time left before his ploy will be uncovered, Mark manipulates the price of the Henrietta shares so that he will be able to make a fortune, ruining Nick in the process. When Bertie, spending his time at the stock exchange because he was told to go into business, hears men shouting "Henrietta," the name that brought him disaster, he naturally wants to shut them up. Nick's regular broker Watson Flint, who has realized what

Mark is trying to do, tells Bertie that he can silence people by saying "I take it" to everyone who utters the offensive name, which is precisely what he does. The share price recovers and Nick's business is saved.

56. It is possible to see *The Saphead* as a comedian comedy, which foregrounds the comedian's performance as a spectacular attraction in its own right, while at the same time narrativizing it as the expression of the comic character's unresolved personality which the film's story works to normalize. Keaton's deadpan signals the comedian's distance from the dramatic task of convincingly characterizing Bertie, and Bertie's passivity in turn appears as a refusal to fulfill the role of protagonist. In the end, these tensions are partially resolved through Bertie's decisive action at the stock exchange and his social integration through paternal acceptance, marriage and fatherhood. While I partially go along with this generic analysis, I do not believe that Keaton brought any well-known preestablished comic persona to the film, and instead used the film precisely to define such a persona and to develop an appropriate performance style. On comedian comedy, see Steve Seidman, *Comedian Comedy: A Tradition in Hollywood Film* (Ann Arbor: UMI Research Press, 1981); Frank Krutnik, "The Clown-Prints of Comedy," *Screen*, vol. 25, No. 4–5 (July–October 1984), pp. 50–59; Peter Krämer, "Derailing the Honeymoon Express: Comicality and Narrative Closure in Buster Keaton's *The Blacksmith*," *The Velvet Light Trap*, No. 23 (Spring 1989), pp. 101–16.

57. *New York American*, February 17, 1921, unpaginated clipping in scrapbook MWEZ x n.c.18,201, Billy Rose Theater Collection (BRTC), New York Public Library at Lincoln Center, New York. This piece was probably written by the theater critic, whereas an earlier, positive review focusing on Keaton and mentioning Crane only once is likely to have been penned by a regular film critic or derived from a press release (*New York American*, February 14, 1921).

58. *New York Evening Telegram*, February 14, 1921, unpaginated clipping, MWEZ x n.c.18,201, BRTC; cp. for example *New York Morning Telegraph*, February 14, 1921, and *New York Herald*, February 14, 1921. Similarly, the involvement of Winchell Smith, the writer and stage director, was frequently mentioned, emphasizing the film's links to a tradition of quality in the theater.

59. *Variety*, February 18, 1921, p. 40. The *New York Times* noted that "(a)s a cinematographic work the picture may claim distinction in some of its scenes, but limps along through many others with the feeble aid of words." (February 14, 1921, p. 12:2).

60. *New York Times*, February 14, 1921, p. 12:2.

61. *New York Morning Post*, February 15, 1921, MWEZ n.c.18,201, BRTC; cp. *New York Tribune*, February 14, 1921, *ibid.*: ". . . the silliest picture we ever saw."

62. *New York American*, February 17, 1921, *ibid.*

63. Unidentified clipping, *ibid.*

64. *Photoplay*, May 1921, unpaginated clipping, Kevin Brownlow collection.

65. *New York Globe and Commercial Advertiser*, February 14, 1921, MWEZ n.c.18,201, BRTC. Cp. *New York Herald*, February 14, 1921: "Keaton saves the essentially inane character from becoming aggravating." *Photoplay* attributes the strategy of ironic exaggeration to Winchell Smith.

66. *New York Journal*, February 14, 1921, *ibid.*

67. *New York Herald*, February 14, 1921, MWEZ n.c.18,201, BRTC. Others simply, and approvingly, called Keaton's performance "slapstick" or "nonsense" making people laugh. See *New York Globe and Commercial Advertiser*, February 14, 1921,

ibid.; "Buster Keaton's Nonsense Keeps You Chuckling," *New York Daily News*, February 14, 1921, *ibid*. Here these terms were used neutrally, if not positively; for the *New York Herald*, however, "slapstick" had a negative connotation.

68. *New York World*, February 14, 1921, *ibid*.

69. A hint at what was at stake in this differentiation was given by the *New York Evening Mail*, when it pointed out that Keaton's role and actions were basically childlike and, in their childish innocence, "guaranteed inoffensive." The possibility of offense, as well as slapstick's particular appeal, were related to those members of the audience who had not yet reached, and those who had gone beyond, the seriousness of maturity: "grandma and all the children can be taken in perfect safety." The realistic drama, which framed this infantile entertainment, however, was addressed to adults, dealing with their more mature concerns, which dominated in the end: "as he (Bertie) winds up with a wedding and two children, it must be presumed that he is no longer a child." (*New York Evening Mail*, February 15, 1921, *ibid*.)

70. *New York Times*, February 14, 1921, p. 12:2.

71. *New York Daily News*, February 15, 1921, MWEZ n.c.18,201, BRTC. The same ambiguous feelings about Keaton's characteristic work as an acrobatic comedian were articulated in many other reviews. One stated that, in *The Saphead*, Keaton was "rescued for a time from a life of slapstick." (*New York Herald*, February 14, 1921, *ibid*.)

72. *New York Journal*, February 14, 1921, *ibid*.

73. Elizabeth Peltret, "Poor Child," *Motion Picture Classic*, vol. 13, No. 1 (March 1921), pp. 64, 96–7.

74. Unidentified clipping in Buster Keaton file, Daniel Blum Collection; cp. for example his "sober views on marriage" in "Before and After Taking," unidentified clipping in Keaton file; and Willis Goldbeck, "Only Three Weeks," *Motion Picture Magazine*, vol. 22, No. 9 (October 1921), pp. 28–9, 87.

75. Dardis, *op. cit.*, pp. 109–56.

11. Mae West and Film Censorship

1. Records of the Production Code Administration (PCA), a section of the Motion Picture Producers and Distributors Association (MPPDA) colloquially called "the Hays Office," are housed, organized in case files by film title, in the Margaret Herrick Library of the Academy of Motion Picture Arts and Sciences, Beverly Hills, California. My thanks go to the staff there for their assistance, as well as to Barbara Scharres, director of the Film Center of the School of the Art Institute, who invited me to give the public lecture in which I first presented some of the material developed here. Thanks are also due Chuck Kleinhans, Kate Kane and Gene Bild for discussing concepts of comedy and star image with me and commenting on drafts of the essay, and the participants of my film and TV comedy course at the University of Illinois, for insightful criticism of the essay in progress.

2. I make the detailed argument that leads to these conclusions in my essay, "Mae West as Censored Commodity: The Case of *Klondike Annie*," *Cinema Journal* 31.1 (1991), pp. 57–84, especially 57–58 and 66–74.

3. For a well-theorized discussion of this point, see John R. Grooch, "What is a Marx Brother?: Critical Practice, Industrial Practice, and the Notion of the Comic Auteur," *Velvet Light Trap* 26 (1990), pp. 28–41. For an analysis of how social and aesthetic

transgression functions as a comedic convention, see Steve Neale and Frank Krutnik, *Popular Film and Television Comedy* (London: Routledge, 1990), pp. 4, 86–94, 151–52.

4. The text of the Code is reprinted in several film encyclopedia; (see, for example, Cobbett Steinberg, *Film Facts* (New York: Facts on File, 1980), pp. 389–98. For an analysis of how the Code embodied middle-class values, see Ramona Curry, "Power and Allure: The Mediation of Sexual Difference in the Star Image of Mae West" (diss., Northwestern University, 1990), pp. 166–75. See, also, Lea Jacobs, *The Wages of Sin: Censorship and the Fallen Woman Film, 1928–1942* (Madison: University of Wisconsin Press, 1991).

5. Mae West, *Goodness Had Nothing to Do with It* (New York: Macfadden–Bartell, [1959] 1970), pp. 45–46, 107, 164.

6. Philip K. Scheuer, "Town Called Hollywood: Mae West to Dance in Next," *Los Angeles Times*, June 27, 1943: 2+. Another *Los Angeles Times* columnist had previously presented this explanation of West's comedic style, during early production for *Goin' to Town*: Edwin Schallert, " 'Films Should Be Fit for Children to See'," *Los Angeles Times* September 23, 1934. That West exhibits a wisecracking style in her debut film role in *Night After Night* (1932), *prior* to the filming of the *Diamond Lil* adaptation, contradicts Scheuer's and Schallert's (and West's own) accounts or at least the dating of this development of her comedic style.

7. Wingate to Harold Hurley (Paramount's liaison to the Studio Relations Committee), November 29, 1932, *She Done Him Wrong* PCA case file.

8. Breen, February 20, 1936, *Klondike Annie* PCA case file.

9. *Goin' to Town* was produced by William LeBaron and directed by Alexander Hall; the story is by Marion Morgan and George B. Dowell, screenplay by Mae West. West made ten films from 1932 through 1943, of which eight are distinctly her star vehicles; after the age of seventy-five, West appeared in two further films, *Myra Breckinridge* (1970) and *Sextette* (1978). *Goin' to Town* is available for rent in 16mm copy from Swank Motion Pictures and, as of the one hundredth anniversary of West's birth in August 1993, is a recent videotape release.

10. For the detailed argument that leads to these conclusions, see Curry, "Mae West as Censored Commodity."

11. *Goin' to Town* PCA case file. The project bore the working title *Now I'm a Lady* for about two months after its initial submission for PCA script approval; its replacement, *How Am I Doin'?* continued as the working title through April 1935, shortly before the film's release.

12. See *Variety* May 22, 1935, pp. 9–10; and May 29, 1935, pp. 9–10. Headlines above almost all of the city-by-city movie business reports acclaim *Goin' to Town* as the highest-grossing film of the week.

13. McCarthy, "Goin' to Town," *Motion Picture Herald*, May 11, 1935: 54. It is noteworthy that Martin Quigley, coauthor of the Motion Picture Production Code of 1930, was editor-in-chief and publisher of this journal. For a discussion of Quigley's engagement in the discourse surrounding censorship of West subsequent to this production, see Curry, "Mae West as Censored Commodity," pp. 69–74.

14. Letter from E. Robb Zaring of the Methodist and Episcopal Church to the Production Code Administration, n.d., *Goin' to Town* case file.

15. For an extended analysis of PCA policies and operations at the time *Goin' to Town* was made, see Jacobs, especially pp. 106–131.

16. Breen to Paramount, January 16, 1935, *Goin' to Town* case file.

17. Breen to Paramount, January 16, 1935; Paramount to PCA, Jan. 24, 1935; Breen interoffice memos January 25 and 26, 1935, *Goin' to Town* case file.

18. West, p. 137.

19. On this point, see also Donald Bogle, *Toms, Coons, Mulattoes, Mammies, and Bucks,* (New York: Viking Press, 1989 [1973]) p. 62. For discussion of the issue of a contemporary fetishized blonde's use of actors of color as a mark of sexual transgression, see Curry, "Madonna from Marilyn to Marlene: Pastiche and/or Parody," *Journal of Film and Video* 42.2 (1990), pp. 15–30, especially 19–20 and 26–29.

20. *Belle of the Nineties* PCA case file. There may also have been resistance in the U.S. South to West's extended on-screen interactions with her black maids. While the reduced African-American presence in West's films after 1934 can also be explained in terms of the geographic shifts in the stories' settings, the settings may have been influenced by extracinematic considerations. On this, see Jacobs, pp. 89 and 177–78.

21. This line was altered in performance from the version Paramount initially submitted for PCA review: "Hi, de, o, love is *dealin' me aces.*" *Goin' to Town* case file, January 16, 1935. The new phrasing effaces implications of promiscuity (if the word "aces" is taken to mean "good *men*," as in "flying aces") and of card gambling.

22. Schallert, " 'Films Should Be Fit'."

23. For discussion of such reactions to West's subsequent production, *Klondike Annie,* see Curry, "Mae West as Censored Commodity," pp. 61–64 and 75–77.

24. The *Goin' to Town* file contains reports from censor boards in Ohio, Maryland, Massachusetts, Virginia, Pennsylvania, New York and Kansas, Canadian provinces Alberta and Quebec, and England, Australia and Italy; the latter country outright rejected the film. The decisions these censor boards took affected prints shown not only within these states, but also in adjoining states which for film distributors constituted the same sales region. For example, the prints cut to meet specifications for Massachusetts were also distributed to Rhode Island, Vermont and New Hampshire. See Ira Carmen, *Movies, Censorship, and the Law* (Ann Arbor: University of Michigan Press, 1967) p. 129, as well as Jacobs, pp. 30–39.

25. The dialogue about West/Cleo's divorcing her husband, as well as the romantic scene between Cleo while married and Carrington, were eliminated by Quebec censors. The strong influence of Catholicism in that province may have had a bearing on the decision, as may also have been the case in Italy. (Italy was, of course, under Fascist rule at the time as well.)

26. George Eells and Stanley Musgrove, *Mae West: A Biography* (New York: William Morrow and Co., 1982), pp. 160–61.

27. Sigmund Freud, *Jokes and Their Relation to the Unconscious,* trans. James Strachey (London: Hogarth Press and Institute of Psycho-analysis [*sic*], 1960 [first published 1905]). Subsequent page number references to this work are in parentheses in my text.

28. In addressing West's dialogue as jokes, I do not disagree with Steve Neale's position that film comedy is not reducible to jokes, but rather must be seen as "a sequence, a *narration* of jokes and joke-like structures." See Steve Neale, "Psychoanalysis and Comedy," *Screen,* 22.2 (1981), p. 34. Neale and coauthor Frank Krutnik develop

this point in their book, *Popular Film and Television Comedy*, pp. 43–61, especially 47–49.

29. "Mae West: 1971 Interview and Christmas Songs" (San Franciso: The Mind's Eye, 1985), audiotape. This and others of West's radio performances and interviews, which extensively reprise witticisms from her films, are available on audiotape for sale and at public libraries. Of the many published collections of Mae West quips and jokes drawn from her films, see, for example, *The Wit and Wisdom of Mae West* ed. Joseph Weintraub (New York: G. P. Putnam, 1967). See, also, *Quotable Women: A Collection of Shared Thoughts* (Philadelphia: Running Press, 1989).

30. Besides the African-American maids who appeared as West's "straight-men" and occasional butt of jokes in her early films, another female character type also functions as the target of West's hostile jokes: morally rigid or snobbish upper-class women. The character, Mrs. Crane Brittany, and the upper-class friends she brings to call on and condemn West's character as a nouveau riche interloper are examples in *Goin' to Town*. An example in *My Little Chickadee* is the character, Mrs. Gideon (Margaret Hamilton), a small-town meddler and defender of female virtue who gets West's character run out of town. The aggressive jokes aimed at the upper-class women contribute to the recurrent narrative trajectory of West's films, which celebrate the American ideal of ever-increasing wealth and status, but simultaneously take a populist view in criticizing the exclusivity, intolerance and pretentious mannerisms associated with the upper classes.

31. See, for example, Claire Johnston, "Women's Cinema as Counter-Cinema," *Notes on Women's Cinema*, ed. Johnston (London: SEFT, 1973), reprinted in *Movies and Methods*, vol. 1, ed. Bill Nichols (Berkeley: University of California Press, 1976), pp. 208–17, especially 211–12. See, also, Joan Mellen, *Women and Their Sexuality in the New Film* (New York: Horizon, 1973), pp. 229–43, and Marjorie Rosen, *Popcorn Venus: Women, Movies and the American Dream* (New York: Coward, McCann and Geoghegan, 1973), pp. 150–55. For an oblique rebuttal of Johnston's position, see Molly Haskell, *From Reverence to Rape: The Treatment of Women in the Movies* (New York: Holt, Rinehart and Winston, 1974), pp. 115–18.

32. See, for example, Elizabeth Yeaman, "Mae West's Purified Picture Scores Hit," *Citizen-News* Aug. 18, 1934.

33. Johnston, pp. 211–12.

34. These performative gestures are of course not unique to West, but derive from conventions of "comedian comedy." On this comedic subgenre, see Neale and Krutnik, pp. 103–107. These and many other authors mention West as the sole female practitioner of comedian film comedy. Certainly, in the 1930s and subsequently, other female performers appeared in star-centered film (and later TV) comedy (e.g., Fanny Brice, Gracie Allen, Lucille Ball); however, West stood out in the 1930s— and retrospectively stands out for contemporary audiences of "classical Hollywood cinema"— as a rare female star of her stature who acted in a self-referential comedic style, repeatedly drawing attention to herself as a known performer.

35. For a widely discussed argument about relations between voyeurism in the cinema and sadism, see Laura Mulvey, "Visual Pleasure and Narrative Cinema," *Screen* 16.3 (1975), pp. 6–18. For an argument about relations between cinematic pleasure and masochism, see Gaylyn Studlar, *In the Realm of Pleasure: Von Sternberg, Dietrich and the Masochistic Aesthetic* (Urbana: University of Illinois Press, 1988), especially pp. 9–49.

36. See, for example, Haskell, pp. 115–16; Rosen, pp. 152–53, Mellen, pp. 230–39, and, for a more recent discussion, Rosetta Reitz, "Mae West, Queen of Sex." *Hot Wire* 4:2 (1988), pp. 40–41.

37. For the earliest available description of Mae West as a female impersonator in print, see George Davis, "The Decline of the West," *Vanity Fair* May 1934, pp. 46, 82. See also Parker Tyler, *Sex Psyche Etcetera in the Film* (New York: Horizon Press, 1969), p. 20; and Tyler, *Screening the Sexes: Homosexuality in the Movies* (Garden City, New York: Doubleday, 1972), pp. 2, 14–15; as well as Eric Braun, "Doing What Comes Naturally," *Films and Filming* October 1970, pp. 27–32 and Braun, "One for the Boys," *Films and Filming* November 1970, pp. 38–42. I discuss West's function as a female impersonator at length in "Power and Allure," chap. 5.

38. See, for example, "Dancer's Story of 'Marriage' Irks Film Star," *Los Angeles Examiner*, April 25, 1935; Louella O. Parsons, "Eva Tanguay Backs Mae in Dispute Over Husband, " *Los Angeles Examiner*, April 26, 1935. Before this time, West's age had been a matter of some media and public speculation. The 1935 British film *Thirty-Nine Steps* (directed by Alfred Hitchcock) makes a joke of such speculation, as a raucous audience member calls to a memory expert performing on stage: "How old is Mae West?"

39. "At Last 'Mr. Mae' Gets Recognition," *Los Angeles Examiner*, July 8, 1937, p. A1. West subsequently sued for and was granted a divorce; the court found that she was exempt from paying any settlement to Wallace, who, following the nationwide publicity following the discovery of their 1911 marriage license by a public employee in Milwaukee, had sought a share of West's wealth as community property. On Wallace's claims, see, for example, "Actor Who Claims He Is Stars Ex-Husband Bares Story of Romance," *New York Herald*, April 23, 1935; and "Mae West Sniffs at 'Husband's' Suit, *New York Times*, February 28, 1936, p. L19.

40. On this point, see Jacobs, pp. 23–24 and 106–31, especially 130–31.

41. Breen, February 20, 1936, *Klondike Annie* PCA file.

42. That Mae West was "censorable" is an element of her persona that has persisted for decades after her performances last faced censorship in the 1940s. West was adept at exploiting this element of her image: for example, West recorded a comedic song (probably in the 1950s) entitled "That's All, Brother" that begins with the rhymed observation, "Now those censors say I'm naughty and no dice, But I've heard it said what's naughty *can* be nice." The lyrics recount in a succession of double entendres the ways that her performance, even as "Snow White" or "Little Red Riding Hood," might elicit censorship. The song appears on at least two currently available audiocassettes: "Mae West: Sixteen Sultry Songs" (New York: Rosetta Records, 1987) and "Mae West" (San Franciso: The Mind's Eye, 1985).

43. A recent example of the discursive formation of comedy's meaning was the controversy surrounding the CBS sitcom, *Murphy Brown*. Conservative Republican Vice President Dan Quayle's denunciation of the program in 1992 enhanced its public reception as "socially progressive" and "feminist," even though a close textual analysis of the program reveals that it only superficially or weakly promotes such positions.

44. The card was printed by West Graphics in San Francisco in 1987; Ed West is credited with the concept; Charles Pierce impersonates Mae West.

12. Performance Anxiety and Male Dread

1. The plot of *Unfaithfully Yours* centers around Sir Alfred, a noted conductor, who has recently returned from an extended stay abroad. Sir Alfred has suggested to his

brother-in-law, August Finchler, that he should "keep an eye on my wife" while he is away, a suggestion Finchler took to justify the hiring of private detectives to trail her. A detective report, which Sir Alfred initially refuses to read but later must confront, suggests that his wife, Daphne, may have had an affair with Tony, his private secretary. Sir Alfred becomes hysterical with jealousy, and while conducting a performance of three musical selections, he fantasizes about possible responses. In the first fantasy, he imagines killing Daphne and framing Tony for the crime. In the second, he gives her the freedom to pursue her love. In the third, he challenges Tony to Russian roulette. When Sir Alfred tries to enact these fantasies, he succeeds only in demolishing his apartment and destroying his dignity. Daphne tells him that she went to Tony's apartment late at night because she suspected that her sister, Barbara, might have been there. Sir Alfred accepts her explanation and the two embrace in the film's final scene.

2. Janey Place, "Women in Film Noir," in E. Ann Kaplan, ed., *Women in Film Noir* (London: BFI, 1978), pp. 35–67.

3. Sigmund Freud, *Jokes and Their Relation to the Unconscious* (London: Penguin, 1976). My discussion of Freud draws heavily on Steve Neale, "Psychoanalysis and Comedy," *Screen*, 22, n2, 1981 pp. 29–43.

4. Richard Corliss, *Talking Pictures: Screenwriter in the American Cinema* (New York: Penguin, 1974), pp. 59–60.

5. Sandy Sturges, ed., *Preston Sturges on Preston Sturges* (New York: Simon and Schuster, 1990), p. 307.

6. My discussion of the context of the film's production and its links to Sturges' personal life draw primarily on Diane Jacobs, *Christmas in July: The Life and Art of Preston Sturges* (Berkeley: University of California Press, 1992). See, also, James Curtis, *Between Flops* (New York: Harcourt Brace Jovanovich, 1982), and Donald Spoto, *Madcap: The Life of Preston Sturges* (Boston: Little, Brown and Company, 1990). For sustained discussions of the film, see James Harvey, *Romantic Comedy* (New York: Alfred A. Knopf, 1987); and Mark J. Williams, "Preston Sturges and Noir Comedy: Re-Historicizing an 'Auteur'," Masters Thesis, University of Southern California, 1987.

7. For a particularly lurid and gossipy treatment of this scandal, see Kenneth Anger, *Hollywood Babylon* (New York: Dell, 1981).

8. Karen Horney, "The Dread of Woman," *International Journal of Psychoanalysis*, vol. 13, 1932, p. 353.

9. Horney, p. 356.

10. For a useful discussion of the possibility of male masquerade, see Chris Holmlund, "Masculinity as Multiple Masquerade: The 'Mature' Stallone and the Stallone Clone," in Steve Cohan and Ina Rae Hark, eds., *Screening the Male: Exploring Masculinities in Hollywood Cinema* (London: Routledge, Chapman and Hall, 1993), pp. 213–229.

11. On the discussion of the difference between the phallus and the penis, see Richard Dyer, "Don't Look Now: The Instabilities of the Male Pin-Up," *Screen*, pp. 61–72.

12. Karen Horney, "The Dread of Woman," *International Journal of Psychoanalysis*, vol. 13, 1932, p. 349.

13. Parker Tyler, *Magic and Myth in the Movies* (London: Seckes and Warburg, 1971) also provokes a more acute and overt "dread of women" within his description of female comic performers, such as Cass Daley, Joan Davis and Betty Hutton: "These comedienne's styles are systematizations of mere sexual frustration, song and dance

being weapons to transfix and magnetize the desired male object. The grossness and violence become laughgetters through the logical incongruity lying in the transfer of aggressiveness from male to female. Innately the female feels the dislocation involved in any excessive energy required to attract the male, and her spiritual horror of her unnatural role creeps into her style. . . . To arrive at a parallel phenomenon of female aggressiveness and violence we should have to go to the insect world of the bee and the preying mantis." p. 68. For Tyler, as for many men, the figure of the laughing and joking woman is a truly dreadful one.

14. Tyler, p. 58.

15. Significantly, as masculinity has become an important focus for feminist and queer scholarship, the hypermasculinity of the heroic myths of the warrior (Schwarzenegger, Stallone) remains the dominant focus. Steven Cohan and Ina Rae Hark's anthology, *Screening the Male*, for example, includes essays on the construction of male identities and the performance of masculinity within the action film, the historical epic, the horror film, the swashbuckler and the musical, but makes only passing references to comic texts. Here, the anthology simply follows the example of Steve Neale's early essay, "Masculinity As Spectacle: Reflections on Men and Mainstream Cinema," reprinted in Cohan and Hark, *Screening the Male,* which provides the foundation for that collection. For an useful overview of recent work, across a number of disciplines, on masculine identity, see Peter Middleton, *The Inward Gaze: Masculinity and Subjectivity in Modern Culture* (London: Routledge, Chapman and Hall, 1992). Notable exceptions to this neglect of the comic male spectacle would be the portfolio of essays on Pee-Wee Herman found in Constance Penley and Sharon Willis, eds., *Male Trouble* (Minneapolis: University of Minnesota Press, 1993) and Peter Lehman's "Penis-Size Jokes and Their Relation to Hollywood's Unconscious," in Andrew Horton, ed., *Comedy/Cinema/Theory* (Berkeley: University of California Press, 1991), pp. 43–59.

16. Paul Smith, *Clint Eastwood: A Cultural Production* (Minneapolis: University of Minnesota Press, 1993), p. 173.

17. Smith, p. 173, derives the term from Nina Baym, "Dramas of Beset Manhood" in Elaine Showalter, ed., *The New Feminist Criticism* (New York: Pantheon, 1985).

18. Andrew Britton, *Cary Grant: Comedy and Male Desire* (Tyneside-by-the-sea; Tyneside Cinema, 1984). The pages in Britton's short monograph are not numbered.

19. Harrison, like Grant, was both a dramatic and comic actor. At the film's release, Harrison was known to American audiences primarily through two films, one a romantic drama (*The Foxes of Harrow*) and the other a romantic comedy (*The Ghost and Mrs. Muir*).

20. *Collieshangie* derives from a Scottish term which literally refers to a brawling tangle of Collie pups. Here, I use it to evoke an image not as a contradiction (a fairly static image) or a palimpsest (which evokes historic change) but as something noisy dynamic, mobile, in constant struggle, ever changing. I see the term as consistent with my conception of masculinity as a process rather than a structure of identification.

21. Sturges, p. 307.

22. A fuller analysis of these three musical pieces would suggest that each of these themes can be traced back to heroic male myths, though the specific analysis of these selections is beyond the scope of this paper. I am indebted to Martin Marks for helpful comments and conversations about the role of music within this film, a topic which he hopes to explore in a future essay.

23. Scott Bukatman, "Paralysis in Motion: Jerry Lewis's Life as a Man," in Horton, (ed.), *Comedy/Cinema/Theory* pp. 188–205. Sir Alfred's humiliation is amplified in the scene by the witness, first of the female operator who comes on the phone every time he trips over the line, and later by Daphne, who sees the destruction his rampage has caused.

24. Jacques Attali, *Noise: The Political Economy of Music* (Minneapolis: University of Minnesota Press, 1985), p. 6.

25. For useful discussions of the impact of these sociological shifts on postwar Hollywood cinema, see Frank Krutnik, *In a Lonely Street: Film Noir, Genre, Masculinity* (London: Routledge, Chapman and Hall, 1991); Dana Polan, *Power and Paranoia: History, Narrative and the American Cinema, 1940–1950* (New York: Columbia University Press, 1986); Brandon French, *On the Verge of Revolt: Women in American Films of the Fifties* (New York: Frederick Ungar, 1978).

26. Richard Dyer, "Resistance Through Charisma: Rita Hayworth and *Gilda*," in E. Ann Kaplan, ed., *Women in Film Noir*, p. 91.

27. The definitive study of the films in that tradition is Mary Ann Doane, *The Desire to Desire: The Woman's Film of the 1940s* (Bloomington: Indiana University Press, 1987).

28. Jacobs, pp. 369–370.

29. Tony, the presumed other man, Sir Alfred's faithful assistant, also remains a cipher, ever present yet invisible. Sturges gives him few lines and those are largely functional and reactive; he tells us little about his background or his personality. We are to see him as, much like Daphne, a projection of Sir Alfred's tumultuous emotional states.

30. Many people claim that they trust Daphne from the outset, blaming the later events on proliferating misunderstandings and miscommunications. Such a reading would be consistent with the romantic comedy tradition to which the film belongs, yet would find minimal concrete support in the film itself. Consider how the same lines and actions might be read in a *film noir*, where genre expectations work the opposite way, intensifying our distrust of the seductive wife. Sturges's film combines multiple genres and multiple expectations, playing them against each other in such a way as to intensify Sir Alfred's confusion and to preserve Daphne's enigmatic qualities. As a result, our experience of the film will be different depending upon how much stress we place upon these differing genre expectations. My reading does not deny the possibility that Daphne may be innocent, but I want to stress the *noir*-like ambiguity which surrounds her language and behavoir.

31. Kristine Brunovska Karnick, "Commitment and Reaffirmation in Hollywood Romantic Comedy," in this volume.

32. Edward Branigan, "The Point-of-View Shot," in Bill Nichols, ed., *Movies and Methods*, vol. II (Berkeley: University of California Press, 1985).

13. Comedy and the Social World

1. Dana Polan, "The Light Side of Genius: Hitchcock's *Mr. and Mrs. Smith* in the Screwball Tradition," in Andrew S. Horton, ed., *Comedy/Cinema/Theory* (Berkeley: University of California Press, 1991), pp. 140–141.

2. Charles Musser, "Work, Ideology and Chaplin's Tramp," *Radical History Review*, 41, April 1988, pp. 37–66.

3. Charles Musser, "Ethnicity, Roleplaying and the American Film Comedy: From *Chinese Laundry* to *Whoopee* (1894–1930)," in Lester Friedman (ed.), *Unspeakable Images: Ethnicity and the American Cinema* (Chicago: University of Illinois Press, 1991).

4. For a useful overview of this new tradition, see Lynn Hunt (ed.), *The New Cultural History* (Berkeley: University of California Press, 1989).

5. Carroll Smith-Rosenberg, "Davy Crockett as Trickster: Pornography, Liminality and Symbolic Inversion in Victorian America," *Disorderly Conduct: Visions of Gender in Victorian America* (New York: Oxford University Press, 1985), pp. 90–108.

6. Mary Douglas, "Do Dogs Laugh?," *Implicity Meanings: Essays in Anthropology* (London: Routledge & Kegan Paul, 1975), pp. 83–88.

7. James Agee, "Comedy's Greatest Era," *Agee on Film*, Vol. 1 (London: Peter Owen).

8. For a fuller account of this discourse, see Henry Jenkins, *What Made Pistachio Nuts?: Early Sound Comedy and the Vaudville Aesthetic* (New York: Columbia University Press, 1992).

9. Richard Barton, "The Mistimed Laugh," *Bellman*, May 19, 1917, p. 544.

10. Mary Douglas, "Jokes," *Implicit Meanings* (London: Routledge and Kegan, 1975).

11. Mikhail Bakhtin, *Rabelais and His World*, trans. Helene Iswolsky (Bloomington: Indiana University Press, 1984).

12. Bahktin, p. 7.

13. Bahktin, pp. 7–8.

14. Umberto Eco, "The Frames of Comic 'Freedom'," in A. Sebeok ed. *Carnival!* (Berlini Mouton, 1984), pp. 1–9.

15. Eco, p. 4.

16. Eco, p. 5.

17. Eco, p. 6.

18. Eco, p. 8.

19. Mary Russo, "Female Grotesques: Carnival and Theory," in Teresa de Laurentis, ed., *Feminist Studies/Critical Studies* (Bloomington: Indiana University Press, 1988).

20. Natalie Davis, quoted in Russo, p. 215.

21. See William Paul, *Laughing, Screaming: Modern Hollywood Horror and Comedy* (New York: Columbia University Press, 1994); Andrew Horton, ed., *Comedy/Cinema/Theory* (Berkeley: University of California Press, 1991).

22. Victor Turner, "Liminal to Liminoid, in Play, Flow and Ritual," *Rice University Studies*, 3, 1974, pp. 53–92.

23. David Kunzle, "World Turned Upside Down: Iconography of a European Broadsheet Typo" ??? in Barbara A. Babcock, ed., *The Reversible World: Symbolic Inversion in Art and Society* (Ithaca: Cornell Univesity Press, 1978) pp. 88–90.

24. Lewis Jacobs, quoted in Arthur Knight, *The Liveliest Art* (New York: New American Library, 1959), pp. 241–242.

25. Knight, p. 241.

26. Andrew Bergman, *We're in the Money*, (New York: Random House, 1981), pp. 133–134.

27. James Harvey, *Romantic Comedy in Hollywood, from Lubitsch to Sturges*, (New York: Alfred Knopf, 1987), pp. xi–xii.

28. Musser, p. -.

29. Musser, p. -.

30. Lent, p. -.

31. Wes Gehring, *Screwball Comedy: Defining a Film Genre*, Ball State Monograph #31, (Muncie, IN: Ball State University, 1983).

32. Ernest R. Groves, quoted in Lent, in this volume, p. -.

33. Ralph A. Brauer, "When the Lights Went Out—Hollywood, the Depression, and the Thirties," *Journal of Popular Film and Television*, vol. VIII, No. 4, Winter 1981, pp. 18–27.

34. Brauer, p. 20.

35. Brauer, pp. 24–25.

36. Alexander Doty, "Queerness, Comedy, and *The Women*," in this volume, p. -.

37. D.A. Miller, "Anal Rope," in Diana Fuss, ed., *Inside/Out: Lesbian Theories, Gay Theories* (New York: Routledge, 1991).

38. Christopher Craft, "Alias Bunbury: Desire and Termination in *The Importence of Being Earnest*," *Representations*, Summer 1990, N. 31, pp. 19–46.

14. The Comedy of Remarriage

Thanks to Sumiko Higashi, Miriam Hansen, Paolo Cherchi-Usai and Lynne Zeavin for their generous assistance in the preparation of this article. An earlier version, "DeMille, Divorce and the Comedy of Remarriage," appeared in Paolo Cherchi-Usai and Lorenzo Codelli, eds., *The DeMille Legacy* (Pordenone: Edizioni Biblioteca dell'Immagine, 1991) for Le Giornate Del Cinema Muto in Pordenone, October 1991. Initially written while I was on a National Endowment for the Humanities fellowship, this study has been expanded and revised for the present anthology with assistance from Laura Wexler and Franny Nudelman of the American Studies Working Group at Yale University. It is part of a series of articles I have been writing on film comedy and its relation to the social transformation of twentieth-century America. This includes "Ethnicity, Roleplaying and Film Comedy," in Lester Friedman, ed., *Unspeakable Images: Ethnicity and the American Cinema* (University of Illinois: 1991), pp. 41–81; and "Work, Ideology and Chaplin's Tramp," in Robert Sklar and Charles Musser, eds., *Resisting Images: Essays in Cinema and History* (Philadelphia: Temple University Press, 1990), pp. 36–67.

1. William Paul, *Ernst Lubitsch's American Comedy* (New York: Columbia University Press, 1983); Gerald Weales, *Canned Goods as Caviar: American Film Comedy of the 1930s* (Chicago: University of Chicago Press, 1985); James Harvey, *Romantic Comedy in Hollywood, from Lubitsch to Sturges* (New York: Knopf, 1987); Ed Sikov, *Screwball: Hollywood's Madcap Romantic Comedies* (New York: Crown Publishers, 1989); Elizabeth Kendall, *The Runaway Bride: Hollywood Romantic Comedy of the 1930s* (New York: Knopf, 1990).

2. Walter Kerr, *The Silent Clowns* (New York: Alfred A. Knopf, 1975). Breaks with this approach are beginning to appear, notably a recent study by Henry Jenkins, which has sought to show how vaudeville-based comedy of the 1930s is rooted in this earlier period: *What Made Pistachio Nuts?: Early Sound Comedy and the Vaudeville Aesthetic* (New York: Columbia University Press, 1992).

3. A similar observation has recently been made by Steve Neale and Frank Krutnick, *Popular Film and Television Comedy* (London: Routledge, 1990). Parallel problems exist with the study of other genres, such as the Western (see Tag Gallagher, "Shootout at the Genre Corral: Problems in the 'Evolution' of the Western," in Barry Grant, ed., *Film Genre Reader* (Austin: University of Texas, 1986), pp. 202–215.

4. Stanley Cavell, *Pursuits of Happiness: The Hollywood Comedy of Remarriage* (Cambridge, MA: Harvard University Press, 1981), pp. 18–19.

5. Bill Rothman, a close associate of Cavell, informs me that Cavell purposefully excluded this film from his survey.

6. Michael Fischer, *Stanley Cavell and Literary Skepticism* (Chicago: University of Chicago Press, 1989), particularly pp. 80–94.

7. Jean-Louis Comolli, "Technique et idéologie," *Cahiers du cinema*, 229 (May 1971), pp. 4–21; 230 (July 1971); pp. 231 (August–September 1971), pp. 42–49; 233 (November 1971), pp. 39–45; 234/235 (December 1971, January–February 1972), pp. 94–100; 241 (September–October 1972), pp. 20–24. For a challenge to Comolli's approach, see Kristin Thompson and David Bordwell, "Linearity, Materialism and the Study of Early American Cinema," *Wide Angle* 5:3 (1983), pp. 4–15.

8. Cavell acknowledges the role that adaptations of plays performed in the comedies of remarriage that he celebrates. To justify the priority he gives to these films over their theatrical predecessors, Cavell makes an argument about adaptation which, while not without interest, questions the genre's ability to move across forms (Cavell, *Pursuits of Happiness*, pp. 24–25). By somewhat different routes, I come to a similar conclusion that the comedy of remarriage is first and foremost a Hollywood genre.

9. In this respect, a distinction between formations and origins is helpful. Tracing cinema's origins can often takes us back to Plato's cave, but an examination of its formation will force the historian to look at the immediate conditions and pressures that made it possible and brought it into being.

10. George Blaisdell, "Edwin S. Porter," *Moving Picture World*, December 7, 1912, p. 961.

11. Diane Koszarski, *The Complete Films of William S. Hart: A Pictorial Record* (New York: Dover, 1980), pp. ix–xxiv, 27, 31.

12. Richard Slotkin is only the latest historian to cite *The Great Train Robbery* as the first Western. Acknowledging Owen Wister's *The Virginian* as "the paradigm text of the Western film genre" (p. 169), he fails to offer any kind of detailed, meaningful, historical progression from the 1903 train robbery film to Hart's Westerns. This is no coincidence: the connection is slight. As a result, Slotkin, like numerous predecessors, jumps over the Westerns made between 1903 and 1914; in contrast, his knowledge and interest in relevant literature of this period is extensive (Slotkin, *Gunfighter Nation* [New York: Macmillan, 1992], pp. 231–252.)

13. A brief comparison between the comedy of remarriage and the western in relation to Porter and DeMille raises the question of authorship within a framework formulated by Michel Foucault. As with Edwin S. Porter vis à vis the film western, Cecil B. DeMille can be credited as the progenitor or author of a notable genre, the comedy of remarriage (Michel Foucault, "What is an Author?" in Paul Rabinow, ed., *The Foucault Reader* [New York: Pantheon Books, 1984], pp. 101–120]. That is, DeMille's claims to authorship are properly associated with 1) a distinctive and often rigorous style evident in films of the late 1910s and early 1920s that bear his name, 2) justified by his central role in the creative process as director *and* production chief,

and 3) determined by industry discourse and his relative position of power within the Hollywood industry that enabled that discourse to benefit his person and persona. But he also can be said to author this genre in the way that Sigmund Freud might be said to have authored the discourse of psychoanalysis. If Porter did indeed make "the first western," his creation of this new film genre was relatively modest since it merely involved the adaptation of narrative elements found on stage and elsewhere. This process of adaptation was so routine in the early 1900s that other studios could have easily duplicated Porter's achievement independently of his influence (or vice versa). In contrast, the process of authoring this comic genre of remarriage proved a much more difficult and original achievement for DeMille. It is not that I have any illusion that this essay on the comedy of remarriage will provide the last word on its formative moments. Additional texts of a similar kind can easily be found from the 1919–1929 period. It is quite possible that there are somewhat earlier examples of this narrative trope and that I have overemphasized DeMille's contribution to the genre's formation. However, I would be very surprised if some future cultural historian found that the genre was flourishing before World War I.

14. Roderick Phillips, *Putting Asunder: A History of Divorce in Western Society* (Cambridge, England: Cambridge University Press, 1988), p. 516.

15. Paul H. Jacobson and Pauline F. Jacobson, *American Marriage and Divorce* (New York: 1959), p. 90.

16. Phillips, *Putting Asunder*, p. 517.

17. William L. O'Neill, *Divorce in the Progressive Era* (New Haven, CT: Yale University Press, 1967), p. 40.

18. Nelson Manfred Blake, *The Road to Reno* (Westport, CT: Greenwood Press, 1962), pp. 229–230.

19. Herbert Spencer, *The Principles of Sociology*, 3rd ed., 2 vols (New York: 1892), 1:753, cited in O'Neill, *Divorce in the Progressive Era*, p. 97.

20. O'Neill, *Divorce in the Progressive Era*, p. 164.

21. Robert Sklar, ed., *The Plastic Age, 1917–1930* (New York: Braziller, 1970), pp. 1–24. The ways in which World War I was a pivotal moment in the history of divorce is evident from Cecil B. DeMille's *For Better, For Worse* (1919). Pediatric surgeon Edward Meade (Elliot Dexter) longs to marry Sylvia Norcross (Gloria Swanson)— as does Dick Burton (Tom Forman). Both men are patriotically joining the army to fight in Europe, but Dr. Meade is pressured into remaining a civilian in New York because the shortage of doctors threatens the lives and well-being of many young children. Feeling Edward is a coward, Sylvia switches her affection to Dick, who induces her to marry him so he will have someone to fight for while he is "over there." Sylvia eventually recognizes that Edward did a truly courageous thing by staying in New York. After learning that Dick was apparently killed in action, she becomes emotionally reattached to Edward. Dick is not dead but badly wounded and scarred. When he returns just before Sylvia and Edward are to announce their engagement, it is too late for her to change her affections yet again. Try as she might, Dick's scars disgust her. In fact, Betty Hoyt (Wanda Hawley) has loved Dick all along and finds his scars touching. The choice is clear: everyone must either live out their lives in misery because of some empty principle of marriage, or they must rearrange their marital relationships. The latter choice is quickly taken. Here war acts as a catalyst that induces hasty marriages and separates newly formed couples. During its course, husband and wife change in profound ways both emotionally and physically. Old beliefs in the sanctity of marriage cease to be viable as a result.

Divorce becomes a necessity, a godsend. This was not DeMille's first film to articulate a new attitude toward divorce. This honor must go to *Old Wives for New*, released in May 1918, before the war had even ended.

22. Patricia King Hanson et al., eds., *The American Film Institute Catalog of Motion Pictures in the United States: Feature Films, 1911–1920* (Berkeley: University of California Press, 1988), 2: 297.

23. DeMille had made this film earlier under the title *The Golden Chance* (1915).

24. Sumiko Higashi, *Cecil B. DeMille: A Guide to References and Resources* (Boston: G. K. Hall & Co., 1985), p. 32.

25. Sumiko Higashi, "Melodrama as a Middle Class Sermon: *What's His Name*," in Paolo Cherchi-Usai and Lorenzo Codelli, eds., *The DeMille Legacy*, pp. 224–248.

26. "Old Wives for New," *Variety*, May 24, 1918.

27. "Old Wives for New," *Variety*, May 24, 1918.

28. Media Mistley, "Why Husbands Leave Home, An Interview with Cecil B. DeMille," *Motion Picture Classic*, July 1918, p. 55.

29. Lary May, *Screening Out the Past: The Birth of Mass Culture and the Motion Picture Industry* (New York: Oxford University Press, 1980), p. 204. See, also, Robert Sklar, *Movie-made America* (New York: Random House, 1975), pp. 91–95; and Higashi, *Cecil B. DeMille*, pp. 28–33.

30. Elaine Tyler May, "The Pressure to Provide: Class Consumerism, and Divorce in Urban America, 1880–1920," *Journal of Social History*, 12 (1978), pp. 180–193. Such themes are foregrounded in DeMille's films, such as *The Golden Chance* (1915), *The Whispering Chorus* (1918) and *Forbidden Fruit* (1920, a remake of *The Golden Chance*).

31. Charles Higham, *Cecil B. DeMille* (New York: Scribners, 1973), pp. 67–68.

32. "Old Wives for New," *New York Telegraph*, May 26, 1918, p. 5E (Part II).

33. Joseph McBride, *Hawks on Hawks* (Berkeley: University of California Press, 1982), p. 14.

34. "Don't Change Your Husband," *Moving Picture World*, February 8, 1919, p. 310. Comedies of remarriage existed outside the cinema, but discourse around the films never referred to them. The status of the remarriage comedy as a genre is an interesting one. In some respects its domain is relatively narrow, like the tramp comedies of silent cinema rather than slapstick comedy, or film comedy in general. Genres obviously function on different levels. Comedies of remarriage have generally been a subset of the sophisticated romantic comedy. Moreover, many films are part of more than one genre. Thus Chaplin's *The Kid* is not only a tramp comedy but it also revived, however briefly, the bad boy comedy.

35. *Motion Picture News*, February 1, 1919, p. 726.

36. Miriam Hansen, "Pleasure, Ambivalence, Identification: Valentino and Female Spectatorship," *Cinema Journal* 25 (Summer 1986), pp. 6–32; Gaylyn Studlar, "The Perils of Pleasure? Fan Magazine Discourse as Women's Commodified Culture in the 1920s," *Wide Angle* 13:1 (1991), pp. 6–33; Sumiko Higashi, "Ethnicity, Class and Gender in Film: DeMille's *The Cheat* (1915)," in Lester Friedman, ed., *Unspeakable Images: Ethnicity and American Cinema* (Urbana: University of Illinois Press, 1991), pp. 112–139. See, also, Mary Ann Doane, *The Desire to Desire: The Woman's Film of the 1940s* (Bloomington: Indiana University Press, 1987), particularly chap. 1, for a discussion of female spectatorship.

37. Sigmund Freud, *Medusa's Head* (1940 [1922]) in *The Standard Edition of the Complete Psychological Works of Sigmund Freud* (London: Hogarth Press, 1955), pp. 273–274. This Medusa figure is most concentrated in the figure of Sophy in *Old Wives for New*, but the spectre of a controlling or dominating woman crops up throughout DeMille's work.

38. Henri Bergson, "Laughter" in Wylie Sypher, ed., *Comedy* (John Hopkins University Press, 1956), p. 105.

30. Wylie Sypher, "The Meaning of Comedy," in *Comedy*, p. 193.

40. *Ibid.*, p. 143.

41. Adela Rogers St. Johns, "The Confessions of a Male Vampire," *Photoplay*, March 1919, pp. 28–30.

42. Mistley, "Why Husbands Leave Home," p. 55.

43. Adela Rogers St. Johns, "What Does Marriage Mean?" *Photoplay*, December 1920, pp. 28–31.

45. "The Confessions of a Male Vampire," p. 30.

46. Kenneth McCaffey "Introducing the 'Vampette'," *Photoplay*, March 1919, p. 47.

46. "Why Change Your Wife," *Variety*, 30 April 1920.

47. Bergson, "Laughter," p. 119.

48. Needless to say, the hypothetical spectators in these DeMille films are always heterosexual. Shoe fetishism for DeMille is the kinkiness that covers over anxiety about other "orientalist" forms of sexual orientations, notably homosexuality. For a pertinent consideration of this subject, see chapters 11 and 12 of Miriam Hansen, *Babel and Babylon: Spectatorship in American Silent Film* (Cambridge: Harvard University Press, 1991).

49. Bergson, "Laughter," p. 137.

50. "The Shadow Stage," *Photoplay*, May 1920, vol 17, No. 6, p. 64.

51. Edward W. Said, *Orientalism* (New York: Pantheon, 1978), pp. 1–6, 186–190.

52. *Ibid.*, 188.

53. This orientalism is already present in DeMille's *The Cheat* (1915), where the Japanese's ivory merchant's acquisition of objects is associated with Edith Hardy's unfulfilled sexual longings and unrestrained consumerism—her acquisition of dresses and other luxuries at a moment when her husband is potentially overextended in his investments. In this prewar film, orientalism has a strong negative association that would change in DeMille's postwar films. See Higashi, "Ethnicity, Class and Gender in Film," p. 112–139.

54. For an investigation of orientalism and the cinema, see Ella Shohat, "Imagining Terra Incognita: The Disciplinary Gaze of Empire," *Public Culture* 3:2 (Spring 1991), pp. 41–70; Shohat, "Gender and the Culture of Empire: Toward a Feminist Ethnography of the Cinema," *Quarterly Review of Film and Video*, 13: 1–2 (Spring 1991), pp. 45–83, and Antonia Lant, "The Curse of the Pharaoh; or How Cinema Contracted Egyptomania," *October* 59 (Winter 1992), pp. 87–112.

55. See Said, *Orientalism* p. 114.

56. These words are actually spoken by Robert Gordon to his wife in a moralizing lecture that parallels the narrator's stance *vis-à-vis* the female spectator. Clearly Robert

Gordon is the favored character, the sympathetic protagonist, in this film. His point of view is very close to that of the narrator.

57. "Why Change Your Wife," *Variety*, April 30, 1920.

58. "The Screen," *New York Times*, April 26, 1920, p. 18.

59. Bergson, "Laughter," p. 190.

60. "Why Change Your Wife," *Moving Picture Word*, March 6, 1920, p. 2389.

61. "French Give Donnay Drama," *New York Times*, November 5, 1918, p. 11. See also: "Hopwood Writes a High Moral Farce," *New York Times*, August 28, 1918, p. 5; " 'The Saving Grace,' with Cyril Maude," *New York Times*, October 1, 1918, p. 11;"French and American Morals in Farce," *New York Times*, August 18, 1918, p. 6C and "From the New Plays," *New York Times*, October 8, 1918, p. 2D.

62. "Front Page Melodrama Revives," *New York Times*, January 15, 1919, p. 9.

63. (Robert) Burns Mantle, ed., *Best Plays of 1919–1920* (Boston: Small, Maynard & Co, 1920); (Robert) Burns Mantle, ed., *Best Plays of 1920–1921* (Boston: Small, Maynard & Co, 1921). This series of annual "Best Play of . . ." publications began with the 1919–1920 theatrical season. Since *New York Times* theater reviews are not always as thorough in outlining the plots of a given play, this shift may not have been quite as extreme as my consulted information suggests. *Enter Madame*, which premiered in August 1920 and ran for 350 performances, was another play from this period that verges on being a comedy of remarriage: the husband of a world-famous prima donna is weary of their life apart, and seeks a divorce with plans to marry a more domestically inclined widow. His wife returns and declares her own desire for a new husband. In the end, however, they are reconciled. *Enter Madame*, was also chosen as one of the best plays of that year by Mantle, who had a fine appreciation for this particular narrative trope.

64. Others would include *The Silver Fox* (September 5, 1921), *The Circle* by Somerset Maugham (September 12, 1921), *Lilies of the Field* (October 4, 1921), *Danger* (December 22, 1921), *The Married Woman* (December 24, 1921).

65. Burns Mantle, ed., *The Best Plays of 1921–1922* (Boston: Small, Maynard & Co., 1922), 421.

66. "Love and Alimony," *New York Times*, August 7, 1923, p. 20.

67. Alexander Woolcott, "The New Richman Comedy," *New York Times*, September 19, 1922, p. 14.

68. Arthur Richman, *The Awful Truth: A Comedy in Three Acts* (New York: Co-National Plays, Inc., 1930). The film is a relatively free but also typical Hollywood play-film adaptation, in that it uses information provided by dialogue in the play as a basis for creating earlier scenes in the film (as with *Twentieth Century*, for example).

69. "The Screen," *New York Times*, July 2, 1925, p. 12.

70. "Changing Husbands," *Variety*, June 25, 1924; Iribe had designed many of the sets for DeMille's earlier films. He had a falling out with DeMille in 1926.

71. Cavell, *Pursuits of Happiness*, p. 157.

72. "A Dual Role," *New York Times*, June 23, 1924, p. 22.

73. "Changing Husbands," *Variety*, June 25, 1924.

74. "The Idle Class," *Variety*, September 30, 1921, p. 36; "Bringing Up Baby," *New York Times*, March 4, 1938, p. 17.

75. Bill Rothman, a close associate of Cavell, informs me that Cavell purposefully excluded this film from his survey.

76. Stephen Neale, *Genre* (London: British Film Institute, 1980), p. 19.

77. Gerald Mast, *Howard Hawks, Storyteller* (New York: Oxford University Press, 1982), pp. 203–204. For an examination of the way John Barrymore's persona is transposed from film to film, see Marian E. Keane, "John Barrymore's Acting on Stage and Film" (Ph.D dissertation, New York University, 1991).

78. Mast, *Howard Hawks, Storyteller*, p. 208.

79. "Critical Reviews and Comments," *Moving Picture World*, February 8, 1919, p. 803.

80. "Special Service Section on *Don't Change Your Husband*," *Motion Picture News*, February 1, 1919, p. 728.

81. At what point in the 1920s did the industry, critics and moviegoers more generally become aware of the "remarriage picture" as a implicit genre and not simply a particular kind of film by a particular author? Here DeMille's retreat from the genre in the mid-1920s, the film versions of hit plays and Lubitsch's corresponding contribution could be investigated still further.

82. Stephen Neale and Frank Krutnik, *Popular Film and Television Comedy* (London: Routledge, 1990), pp. 136–141.

83. Warren Susman, *Culture as History* (New York: Pantheon, 1984), pp. 271–285.

84. John Higham, "The Reorientation of American Culture in the 1890s," in *Writing American History: Essays on Modern Scholarship* (Bloomington: Indiana University Press, 1970), pp. 73–102.

85. T. J. Jackson Lears, "From Salvation to Self-Realization: Advertising and the Therapeutic Roots of the Consumer Culture, 1880–1930," in Richard Wightman Fox and T. J. Jackson Lears, eds., *The Culture of Consumption: Critical Essays in American History, 1880–1980* (New York: Pantheon, 1983), p. 4.

86. Lears, "From Salvation to Self-Realization," p. 24.

87. Lears, "From Salvation to Self-Realization," p. 22.

88. Lears, "From Salvation to Self-Realization," p. 29.

15. Gender Relations in Screwball Comedy

1. Other examples of films that addressed the new relationship between men and women were the Fred Astaire-Ginger Rogers series of musicals (beginning in 1933) and *The Thin Man* series of detective stories (beginning in 1934). Both featured costarring couples, whose verbal repartee and active physical relationships (involving dancing and detecting) showed that love included fun and friendship, as well as romance. The recurrent pairing of the same stars in both the Astaire-Rogers musicals and *The Thin Man* series, however, the more elite realms in which they lived, and the more specialized expertise they exhibited, restricted the impact of their message regarding the possibilities of redefined gender relations for those middle-class, nondancing, nonsleuthing Americans.

2. The term "love-companionship" was used by Ernest R. Groves, *Marriage* (New York: Holt, 1933), p. 6.

3. According to the Lynds' 1925 study of Muncie, Indiana, periodicals (including *The Saturday Evening Post, American Magazine, Ladies' Home Journal, McCalls*, and

Women's Home Companion) operated more powerfully than books to shape the practices, manners and outlook of a city; they also mentioned that the "most potent single agency of diffusion from without shaping the habits of thought in Middletown in regard to marriage" was the advice columnist Dorothy Dix. Robert S. Lynd and Helen Merrell Lynd, *Middletown: A Study in American Culture* (New York: Harcourt, Brace and World, 1929), pp. 239 and 116 (note 10).

4. Lynd and Lynd, *Middletown* 239; Margaret Ferrand Thorp, *America at the Movies* (New Haven: Yale University Press, 1939), p. 5; the female spectator and consumer is also discussed by Miriam Hansen, *Babel and Babylon: Spectatorship in American Silent Film* (Cambridge: Harvard University Press, 1991), pp. 114–25, 245–68.

5. Steven Seidman, *Romantic Longings: Love in America, 1830–1980* (New York: Routledge, 1991), p. 71.

6. Seidman, pp. 71–72; he adds that, according to contemporary sources, for marriages entered into from 1922–1926, the chance of divorce climbed to one in five or one in six; Lynd and Lynd, *Middletown*, p. 149; Peter Gabriel Filene, *Him/Her Self: Sex Roles in Modern America* (New York: NAL, 1974), p. 164.

7. Seidman, p. 73.

8. For a discussion of the larger cultural context in which these changes occurred, see Seidman, pp. 66–74.

9. Filene, p. 164; Nancy Woloch, *Women and the American Experience* (New York: Knopf, 1984), p. 443.

10. Frank Capra, *The Name Above the Title: An Autobiography* (New York: Macmillan, 1971), p. 164, acknowledged *The Taming of the Shrew* (the prototypic battle of the sexes) as the model for *It Happened One Night*.

11. Thomas Schatz, *Hollywood Genres: Formulas, Filmmaking, and the Studio System* (New York: Random House, 1981), p. 150.

12. Stanley Cavell, *Pursuits of Happiness: The Hollywood Comedy of Remarriage* (Cambridge: Harvard University Press, 1981), p. 85. He discusses the concerns of comedy in his introductory chapter.

13. Lewis Jacobs, *The Rise of the American Film: A Critical History* (New York: Harcourt, 1939) p. 535; Ted Sennett, *Lunatics and Lovers: A Tribute to the Giddy and Glittering Era of the Screen's 'Screwball' and Romantic Comedies* (New Rochelle, NY: Arlington House, 1973), p. 14.

14. Andrew Bergman, *We're in the Money: Depression America and Its Films* (New York: Harper, 1971), pp. 132–148; Schatz, pp. 150–185. Robert Sklar, *Movie-Made America: A Cultural History of American Movies* (New York: Vintage, 1975), pp. 187–188; Karyn Kay, " 'Part-Time Work of a Domestic Slave,' or Putting the Screws to Screwball Comedy," *Women and the Cinema: A Critical Anthology*, eds. Karyn Kay and Gerald Peary (New York: Dutton, 1977), p. 319; Jim Leach, "The Screwball Comedy," *Film Genre: Theory and Criticism*, ed. Barry K. Grant (Metuchen, NJ: Scarecrow Press, 1977), p. 77; and Andrew Sarris, "The Sex Comedy without Sex," *American Film* 3:5 (1978), p. 11. For typical contemporary film reviews of *It Happened One Night*, see: *The Literary Digest* 117 (March 10, 1934), p. 38; *Nation* 138 (March 14, 1934), p. 314; *New Republic* 78 (May 9, 1934), p. 364.

15. Sklar discusses this methodological pitfall in a more generalized analysis in Robert Sklar, "The Imagination of Stability: The Depression Films of Frank Capra," *Frank Capra: The Man and His Films*, eds. John Raeburn and Richard Glatzer (Ann Arbor: University of Michigan Press, 1975), p. 125.

16. Sklar "Imagination," p. 125.

17. Obvious and direct links between screwball comedy and popular periodical fiction exist. The magazine story "Night Bus," was the basis for *It Happened One Night*, and the Hagar Wilde story, "Bringing Up Baby," originally appeared in *Collier's* (April 10, 1937). Also see Note 67.

18. Cavell (p. 16) posits that the screwball comedy required the creation of a new woman and that this phase of cinema history is bound up with a phase in the history of the consciousness of women.

19. Linda Gordon, *Women's Body, Women's Right: A Social History of Birth Control in America* (New York: Grossman, 1976), p. 190.

20. Paula S. Fass, *The Damned and the Beautiful: American Youth in the 1920's* (Oxford: Oxford University Press, 1977), pp. 21–22; G. Stanley Hall, "Flapper Americana Novissima," *Atlantic Monthly* 129 (1922), pp. 774–775.

21. Fass, p. 23.

22. Lary May, *Screening Out the Past: The Birth of Mass Culture and the Motion Picture Industry* (Chicago: University of Chicago Press, 1980), p. 203.

23. Hall, p. 775; Fass (pp. 119–123) develops the rise of the youth culture of the 1920s as originating as a college phenomenon that "trickled down" to the high schools later in the decade.

24. Lynd and Lynd, *Middletown*, pp. 160–161 and 267–268 .

25. In spite of Charlotte Perkins Gilman's radical statements that economic independence was the crucial ingredient in women's freedom, women were still unable to attain this freedom in the 1920s because of the structural biases and inequalities of the labor market. See Charlotte Perkins Gilman, *Women in Economics: A Study of the Economic Relation between Women and Men as a Force in Social Evolution* (Boston: Small, Maynard, 1899); and Alice Kessler-Harris, *Out to Work: A History of Wage-Earning Women in the United States* (New York: Oxford University Press, 1982), pp. 217–49.

26. Mary P. Ryan, "The Projection of a New Womanhood: The Movie Moderns in the 1920s," *Our American Sisters: Women in American Life and Thought*, eds. Jean E. Friedman and William G. Slade (Boston: Allyn and Bacon, 1976), p. 381; Woloch, p. 458. Molly Haskell, *From Reverence to Rape: The Treatment of Women in the Movies* (New York: Penguin, 1974), p. 45, notes the time lag in movies, and that it was not until the early 1930s that the revolutionary spirit of the 1920s, at least in the questioning of marriage and conventional morality, took hold. Elsie Clews Parsons "Changes in Sex Relations," *Our Changing Morality: A Symposium*, ed. Freda Kirchwey (New York: Boni, 1924), p. 41, also notes that the movies are a "great . . . vehicle of traditional manners and morals."

27. Ryan, pp. 368–370. The correspondence of the Production Code and the origins of screwball comedy has been treated by Sarris and Haskell, and results in a more oblique treatment of the sexual dimension of love in these comedies, which will be discussed later in this essay.

28. Thorp, pp. 5, 70–71.

29. Angelus Rouge Incarnat, Max Factor Makeup, Vitality Health Shoes, Canned Pineapple: *McCalls* (March 1934), pp. 140, 135, 141, 38.

30. Max Factor advertisements: *McCalls* (March 1934), p. 135 and (April 1934), p.142; Lux soap advertisements: *McCalls* (March 1934), back cover and (May 1934), p. 37.

31. General Mills, *Vitality Demands Energy*, 1934, cited in Jane and Michael Stern, *Square Meals* (New York: Knopf, 1984), p. 11.

32. Fass, pp. 262–70; Seidman, p. 71. Fass pp. (264, 268) points out that petting was an elaborate code of "eroticism with very clear limits of permissible expression" which was "distinctly marriage-oriented."

33. Kessler-Harris, pp. 217–49; see quote from Fass in Note 32.

34. William Chafe, *The American Woman: Her Changing Social, Economic, and Political Roles, 1920–1970* (New York: Oxford University Press, 1972), p. 100; Marjorie Rosen, *Popcorn Venus: Women, Movies, and the American Dream* (New York: Coward, McCann & Geoghegan, 1973), pp. 104, 144; Susan Ware, *Holding their Own: American Women in the 1930s* (Boston: Twayne, 1982), p. 187; Haskell, p. 82.

35. June Sochen, "Mildred Pierce and Women in Film," *American Quarterly* 30 (Spring 1978), p. 12; (Susan) Elizabeth Dalton, "Women at Work: Warners in the 1930s," in *Women and the Cinema: A Critical Anthology*, eds. Karyn Kay and Gerald Peary (New York: Dutton, 1977), p. 267. Neither the 1920s films featuring the flapper, nor the 1930s films featuring the screwball heroine, were intended as feminist statements. What is surprising is not, as many contemporary feminist film critics state, that Hollywood films supported the traditional, male-biased *status quo*, but that, in spite of this bias and the basic conservatism of the film industry, women were depicted as freer and subject to less societal restrictions. For writers who critique these films for their incorporation of male biases, as opposed to being truly liberated statements, see Dalton and Kay. Ware (p. 187) implies that the marriage is tacked on at the end, and speculates whether the audience could see the independent woman beyond the conventional ending. She infers that the endings are not integral parts of the narratives.

36. Ryan, p. 375; Woloch, p. 458. Wealthy, leisured heroines appear in *It Happened One Night, Bringing Up Baby, My Man Godfrey, The Awful Truth, The Philadelphia Story* and *Holiday*.

37. For the economic role of women during the Depression, see Kessler-Harris, pp. 250–272; Ruth Milkman, "Women's Work and the Economic Crises," *A Heritage of Her Own: Toward a New Social History of American Women*, eds. Nancy F. Cott and Elizabeth H. Pleck (New York: Simon & Schuster, 1979), pp. 507–541; Lois Scarf, *To Work and To Wed: Female Employment, Feminism, and the Great Depression* (Westport CT: Greenwood Press, 1980), pp. 43–65, 86–109.

38. A study of popular women's magazine fiction in the 1920s and 1930s upholds this view: successful marriage was a "constantly reiterated theme" that was magnified in contrast to women's publicly changing role, while women with successful careers suffered for that success in the realms of love and affectional relationships. Patricke Johns-Heine and Hans H. Gerth "Values in Mass Periodical Fiction, 1921–1940," *Mass Culture: The Popular Arts in America*, eds. Bernard Rosenberg and David Manning White (New York: The Free Press, 1957), p. 229.

39. Babe Bennett, the newspaper reporter in *Mr. Deeds Goes to Town*, quit her job before she (in her "real" persona) and Deeds reconciled at the end of the film; in most of the films the incompatibility of work and home is made through inference. Only in the two films where the woman's **career** is equated in importance with the

man's (*His Girl Friday* and *Woman of the Year*), and where the conflict between the realms of work and home are incorporated into the larger ideological conflict between the leading couple, is the return of the woman to the female sphere left in question.

40. Maureen Honey, "Images of Women in 'The Saturday Evening Post' 1931–1936," *Journal of Popular Culture* 10 (1976), pp. 353.

41. Honey, pp. 353–355.

42. Honey, pp. 355–356.

43. Woloch, pp. 402–403.

44. Hall, p. 776.

45. *Woman's Home Companion* (January 1934), p. 73.

46. *McCalls* (February 1934), p. 95.

47. Ryan, p. 378.

48. The idea of zany physical (screwball) activities as substitutes for, or sublimations of, female sexuality due to Code restrictions is dealt with by Sarris (pp. 11–13) and Haskell (p. 125).

49. Cavell coined the term "comedy of equality" to refer specifically to the screwball comedies concerned with the issue of remarriage; this is to differentiate them from Old Comedy where the woman is dominant, and from New Comedy where the man is dominant. Haskell (p. 130) also refers to these films as battles of equals, as does Sarris (p. 11).

50. Woloch, pp. 407–408. Examples of marriage manuals and college texts include: *Our Changing Morality: A Symposium*, ed. Freda Kirchwey (New York: Boni, 1924), particularly Ludwig Lewisohn's "Love and Marriage," p. 200; Margaret Sanger, *Happiness in Marriage* (New York: Brentano's, 1926); Judge Ben B. Lindsay and Wainwright Evans, *The Companionate Marriage* (New York: Boni & Liveright, 1927); advice columns dealing with marriage were written for the daily papers by Dorothy Dix, as cited by Lynd, *Middletown*, p. 116 (note 10) and James McGovern, "The American Woman's Pre-World War I Freedom in Manners and Morals," *Our American Sisters*, pp. 345–365.

51. Sanger, p. 20; Parsons, p. 40; Lewisohn, p. 200; Floyd Dell, "Can Men and Women Be Friends?" in *Our Changing Morality: A Symposium*, p. 184; Lindsey, p. 263.

52. Groves, p. 6. This accompanied a redefinition of women's sexuality. Also see Gordon, pp.186–245; Seidman, pp. 73–77.

53. Seidman, pp. 73, 79.

54. Groves, p. 36.

55. Sanger, pp. 47–48.

56. Martha Wolfenstein, "The Emergence of Fun Morality," *Mass Leisure*, eds. Eric Larrabee and Rolf Meyerson (Glencoe, Illinois: The Free Press, 1958), pp. 93–94.

57. Babington (p. 13) wrote, "Impersonation . . . becomes in these films almost a necessary sign of the heroine's refusal to play overdefined roles." This is also true of the male characters; in *Bringing Up Baby* David Huxley's fiancée Miss Swallow had even warned him not to forget who he was as he departed for the ill-fated golf game with Mr. Peabody. Bruce Babington & Peter William Evans, *Affairs to Remember: The Hollywood Comedy of the Sexes* (Manchester: Manchester University Press, 1989).

58. Francis Sill Wickware, "The American Thing," *Woman's Home Companion* (January 1934), pp. 24–25, 65–66.

59. Brooke Hanlon, "Marriage is Like That," *McCalls* (January 1934), pp. 10–11, 25–26, 28.

60. Mary C. McCall, Jr., "I'll Give You a Ring Someday," *McCalls* (February 1934), pp. 10–11, 94–96, 101.

61. Cover, *McCalls* (February 1934).

62. Groves, p. 13.

63. This idea of complementariness appears in much Howard Hawks criticism, both in relationship to characters within the comedies, and to the dual nature of his work as a whole. See particularly Peter Wollen, *Signs and Meaning in the Cinema* (Bloomington: Indiana University Press, 1972), pp. 74–115. The idea is not related to the screwball genre in general, nor to contemporary ideas about marriage.

64. I will discuss the use of language and argument in screwball comedy later in this essay.

65. Dorothy Parker, "The Sexes," in *Here Lies: The Collected Stories of Dorothy Parker* (New York: Viking, 1939), pp. 11–18.

66. Parker, "Here We Are," *Here Lies,* pp. 51–66.

67. Hagar Wilde, "Bringing Up Baby," *Collier's* (April 10, 1937) reprinted in *Bringing Up Baby*, ed. Gerald Mast (New Brunswick: Rutgers University Press, 1988), pp. 235–248.

68. The absence of children in the screwball comedy is partially accountable by the fact that these are courtship stories, but even in the remarriage variations treated by Cavell, children are missing. This supports the contemporary ideology of love-companionship by downplaying the former procreative rationale for marriage to focus on sexualized love as the meaning and justification for marriage. Seidman, p. 82.

69. Parker "Too Bad," *Here Lies*, p. 92.

70. Sarris, p. 9.

71. Leach, p. 76.

72. Leach, p. 77.

73. Leach, p. 84.

74. Jacobs, pp. 535–536.

75. Thorp, p. 76.

76. See Cavell's chapters on *It Happened One Night* (pp. 73–109) and *Bringing Up Baby* (pp. 113–132); Sarris, pp. 13–14; Haskell, p. 130; Leach, pp. 77–78. The dancing in the Astaire/Rogers films can also be read as a substitute for overt sexuality.

77. For example: *It Happened One Night, My Man Godfrey, Bringing Up Baby, His Girl Friday, Mr. Smith Goes to Washington, Meet John Doe.*

78. All direct quotes are from the films.

79. Babington, p. 28.

80. Haskell, p. 125. It is notable that both partners participate in screwball antics; they are not just the domain of the female character.

81. Babington (p. 9) writes of the mutual swaying around the brontosaurus in final scene in *Bringing Up Baby*, "The scene once more emphasizes their antic harmony and,

at the same time, suggests the obvious connotations of rhythmic excitement followed by surrender and climactic fall in the all too familiar patterns and cycles of the act of love itself."

82. Cavell, p. 86.

83. Cavell, p. 88.

84. Cavell, p. 88.

85. Lynd and Lynd, *Middletown in Transition*, p. 176.

86. Lynd and Lynd, *Middletown in Transition*, pp. 178–179.

87. Lynd and Lynd, *Middletown in Transition*, p. 262. There was widespread concern in the early 1930s that the movies were having a profound (and negative) influence on the beliefs and attitudes of young viewers, but contemporary studies provided contradictory evidence of this. While the Lynds believed in the strong influence exerted by the movies, and Forman believed they were a "school of conduct," and influenced behavior and attitudes (particularly regarding sex), others indicated that while actions were imitated, other factors were more important in influencing the conduct and attitudes of children. Foreman, p. 155; Frank K. Shuttleworth and Mark A. May, *The Social Conduct and Attitudes of Movie Fans* (New York: Macmillan, 1933), p. 83.

88. Seidman, p. 73.

16. Queerness, Comedy, and *The Women*

1. I am using "queer" in this essay in two ways: (1) as an inclusive "group" term that refers to gays, lesbians, bisexuals and those with other nonheterosexual, nonstraight sexual desires, identities and politics, and (2) in relation to cultural production and reception to suggest a range of nonheterosexual, nonstraight expressions and responses that can be articulated by anyone, regardless of their stated sexual identity. My use of "queer" in this second sense becomes complicated as I believe it is still important to distinguish specifically lesbian, gay, and bisexual production and response from other types of queer production and spectatorship. When it is not being used as a unifying term, then, queer is used in this essay to describe either the nonstraight production and spectatorship of straight-identifying people, or those aspects of lesbian, gay, bisexual (and other nonstraight people's) production and responses that are not aligned with their sexual identity. For example, while lesbians might take "lesbian" pleasure in the (sub)text of *The Women*, gays, bisexuals and straights would find "queer" pleasures in this lesbian (sub)text. See my book *Making Things Perfectly Queer: Interpreting Mass Culture* (Minneapolis: University of Minnesota Press, 1993) for a more detailed account of these ideas.

2. *The Women*'s screenplay was written by Anita Loos and Jane Murfin, based on the play by Clare Boothe Luce. This film has been remade twice—once by gay director R. W. Fassbinder as *Frauen in New York* (1972, Gdr Television). I label *The Women* a "cult film" because its status within segments of the queer community fits the definition of cult films as films which have developed an enthusiastic band of repeat viewers who know most scenes and dialogue by heart, and for whom the text has special meaning(s). As Danny Peary notes in *Cult Movies* (New York: Dell, 1981). "Cultists believe they are among the blessed few who have discovered something in particular films that the average moviegoer and critic have missed—that something that makes the pictures extraordinary" (xiii). The following, very selective, list will give you some sense of the range of queer (gay, lesbian, bisexual and so on) cult

films: *Desert Hearts, The Wizard of Oz, Jeanne Dielman, 23 Quai de Commerce, 1080 Bruxelles, Aliens, All About Eve, Gentlemen Prefer Blondes, Some Like it Hot, Whatever Happened to Baby Jane? Calamity Jane, Thelma and Louise, Scorpio Rising, Female Trouble, Madchen in Uniform, Sylvia Scarlett* and *Christopher Strong*.

3. Joan Crawford, Norma Shearer and Paulette Goddard had been considered for the role of Scarlett O'Hara in *Gone With the Wind*. Goddard had actually been signed for the part before producer David O. Selznick met Vivien Leigh, who would ultimately play Scarlett. In addition, *The Women* cast member Joan Fontaine had been asked to test for the part of Melanie Hamilton. Rumor has it that she wanted the lead role and would not consider playing Melanie, telling Selznick to try sister Olivia de Havilland instead (who eventually played Melanie). Cukor was the original director of *Gone With the Wind*, and a number of scenes he directed remain in the final version. His dismissal from the film has been the subject of much gossip and speculation. Some sources claim costar Clark Gable did not like being directed by a "faggot" who paid more attention to the women in the cast than to him. For accounts of Cukor's involvement with *Gone With the Wind*, see Patrick McGilligan, *George Cukor: A Double Life* (New York: St. Martin's Press, 1991); Richard Harwell, "Introduction," *GWTW: The Screenplay* (New York: Collier, 1980), pp. 7–44; Roland Flamini, *Scarlett, Rhett, and a Cast of Thousands: The Filming of Gone With the Wind* (New York: MacMillan, 1975); Ronald Haver, *David O. Selznick's Hollywood* (New York: Alfred A. Knopf, 1980); Gavin Lambert, *GWTW: The Making of Gone With the Wind* (Boston: Little, Brown & Co., 1973); and Rudy Behlmer, ed., *Memo from David O. Selznick* (New York: Viking, 1972).

4. Typical of the publicity surrounding *The Women* at the time of its release is a *New York Times* piece, "Mr. Cukor: A Man Among 'The Women'," which reports the rumors of a Crawford-Shearer feud, and calls Cukor the only man in Hollywood who "dared tackle the job of bossing 135 women at one time"—a task which included keeping "all guerrilla warfare outside the studio gates." *New York Times*, October 1, 1939, rpt. in *New York Times Encyclopedia of Film*, vol. 3 (1937–1940), eds. Gene Brown and Harry M. Geduld (New York: Times Books, 1984), n.p.

5. The following works include many approaches to defining and discussing camp: Esther Newton, *Mother Camp: Female Impersonators in America* (Chicago and London: University of Chicago Press, 1972/1979); Andrew Ross, "The Uses of Camp," *No Respect: Intellectuals and Popular Culture* (New York and London: Routledge, 1989), pp. 135–170; Philip Core, *Camp: The Lie That Tells the Truth* (New York: Delilah Books, 1984); Oscar Montero, "Lipstick Vogue: The Politics of Drag," *Radical America* 22, No. 1 (January–February 1988), pp. 35–42; Carole-Anne Tyler, "Boys Will Be Girls: The Politics of Gay Drag," *Inside/Out: Lesbian Theories, Gay Theories*, ed. Diana Fuss (New York and London: Routledge, 1991), pp. 32–70; Jack Babuscio, "Camp and the Gay Sensibility," *Gays and Film*, ed. Richard Dyer (New York: New York Zoetrope: 1984), pp. 40–57; Andrew Britton, "For Interpretation: Notes Against Camp," *Gay Left* 7 (1978–1979); Sue-Ellen Case, "Toward A Butch-Femme Aesthetic," *Discourse* 11, No. 1 (Fall–Winter 1988–1989), pp. 55–71, rpt. in *Making a Spectacle: Feminist Essays on Contemporary Women's Theatre*, ed. Lynda Hart (Ann Arbor: University of Michigan Press, 1989); Sue-Ellen Case, "Tracking the Vampire," *differences* 3, No. 2 (1991), pp. 1–20; Al LaValley, "The Great Escape," *American Film* 10, No. 6 (April 1985), pp. 29–34, 70–71; Seymour Kleinberg, *Alienated Affections: Being Gay in America* (New York: St. Martin's Press, 1980), pp. 38–69, 118–156; Christine Riddiough, "Culture and Politics," *Pink Triangles: Radical Perspectives on Gay Liberation*, ed. Pam Mitchell

(Boston: Alyson, 1980), pp. 14–33; Derek Cohen and Richard Dyer, "The Politics of Gay Culture," *Homosexuality: Power and Politics*, ed. Gay Left Collective (London and New York: Allison and Busby, 1980), pp. 172–186; Susan Sontag, "Notes on Camp," *Against Interpretation* (New York: Farrar, Straus, Giroux), pp. 275–292; Mark Booth, *Camp* (New York, Quartet, 1983); Judith Butler, *Gender Trouble: Feminism and the Subversion of Identity* (New York and London: Routledge, 1990), pp. 128–149; Vito Russo, "Camp," *Gay Men: The Sociology of Male Homosexuality*, ed. Martin P. Levine (New York: Harper and Row, 1979), pp. 205–210; Robin Wood, "The Dyer's Hand: Stars and Gays," *Film Comment* 16, No. 1 (January–February 1980), pp. 70–72; Jeffrey Hilbert, "The Politics of Drag," *The Advocate* 575 (April 23, 1991), pp. 42–47; Lisa Duggan, "The Anguished Cry of an 80s Fem: 'I Want to be a Drag Queen,' "*OUT/LOOK* 1, No. 1 (Spring 1988), pp. 62–65; Pamela Robertson, " 'The Kinda Comedy That Imitates Me': Mae West's Identification with the Feminist Camp," *Cinema Journal* 32, No. 2 (Winter 1993), pp. 57–72; Michael Musto, "Old Camp, New Camp," *Out* No. 5 (April/May 1993), pp. 32–39.

6. Carlos Clarens, *George Cukor* (London: Secker and Warburg/BFI, 1976), p. 64.

7. Rosalind Russell and Chris Chase, *Life is a Banquet* (New York: Random House, 1977), p. 80.

8. *Ibid.*, p. 80.

9. *Ibid.*

10. Pauline Kael, *5001 Nights at the Movies: A Guide from A to Z* (New York: Holt, Rinehart and Wilson, 1984), p. 660.

11. Clarens, *George Cukor*, p. 63.

12. Robert Lindsey, reporting on a December 1976–January 1977 retropective of Cukor's films at the Regency Theater in New York, felt that it was "appropriate" the retrospective open with *The Women*, but reminded readers that while Cukor was "best known in Hollywood as a 'woman's director' " the term "has nothing to do with being a ladies' man." "A Festival to Honor George Cukor," *The New York Times*, December 24, 1976, rpt. in *The New York Times Encyclopedia of Film*, vol. 11 (1975–1976), eds. Gene Brown and Harry M. Geduld (New York: Times Books, 1984), n.p.

13. Virginia Wright Wexman and Patricia Erens, "Clothes-Wise: Edith Head," *Take One* 5, No. 4 (October 1976), p. 13.

14. Current reevaluations of Cukor's films in the context of gay culture include Richard Lippe, "Authorship and Cukor: A Reappraisal," *CineAction!* No. 21–22 (Summer–Fall 1990), pp. 21–34; and the chapter "Whose Text Is It Anyway?: Queer Cultures, Queer *Auteurs*, Queer Authorship" in my book *Making Things Perfectly Queer* (cited earlier). Patrick McGilligan's *George Cukor: A Double Life* (cited earlier) also contains critical material connecting gay culture, Cukor's "homosexuality" (he disliked the term "gay"), and his films.

15. Lindsey's *New York Times* article quotes Cukor's response to being called a "woman's director":

> "Woman's director!" Mr. Cukor said the other day in Los Angeles, a trace of annoyance in his voice. "Well, I'm very pleased to be considered a master of anything, but remember, for every Jill there was a Jack. People like to pigeonhole you—it's a short-cut, I guess, but once they do, you're stuck with it." (n.p.)

16. George Cukor, interviewed by Charles Higham and Joel Greenberg for *The Celluloid Muse: Hollywood Directors Speak* (New York: Signet, 1969), pp. 60–78, mentions

improvisations on the set of *The Women*; while Russell and Chase's *Life is a Banquet* recalls spontaneous changes in staging and the last-minute addition of bits of business for characters, in a chapter on the film (pp. 80–85).

17. Debra Fried's excellent feminist analysis, "The Men in *The Women*" takes up the theme of women role-playing (self-consiously or not) in the film. But recognizing Cukor's gayness and its possible relation to women's role-playing in this film becomes particularly crucial at moments during Fried's analysis, when she appears to conflate him with the straight male characters who are offscreen. Discussing scenes where characters record themselves with a home movie camera, for example, Fried notes:

> A movie character handling a movie camera is readily interpreted as in some sense a surrogate for the movie director. . . . But when this character is a woman taking a picture to certify an event for a man who never shows up in the film . . . the identification between the onscreen filmmaker and the offscreen one becomes vexed. . . . The woman with the camera reminds us of the man with the camera recording this specious image of woman as image maker. . . . [I]n the woman's hands the movie camera becomes a device by which she may stage her own image for the unseen male viewer. *Women and Literature*, vol. 4, *Women and Film*, ed. Janet Todd (New York: Holmes and Meier, 1988), p. 51.

While agreeing that the women in the film are to some extent constructing their home movie images for straight male viewers, both home movie sequences also reveal that the women (and the cross-gender-identifying gay director behind the other camera) resist fully catering to straight male pleasures. Little Mary films her mother's horse race victory "on the bias," even though Mary implies her father will not like it done that way. During the screening of the Bermuda home movies filmed by Mary and her mother, the offscreen commentary of Mary, her mother, and Little Mary reveals that they are enjoying the home movies in their own ways ("You look pretty pretty, mother," little Mary remarks over a shot of her mother lying on the beach). Little Mary asks about showing the film to her father only after the "women-only" showing is over.

18. While most accounts, including Cukor's own in a number of interviews, suggest the director collaborated on the fashion show even though he did not want it in the film, McGilligan's biography claims that the sequence was "filmed by someone else." McGilligan doesn't cite a specific source for this information, although he does say in his notes that he reviewed "individual production files of Cukor's films" for MGM "during the span of his contract years," which would include *The Women* (p. 363). If Cukor did not film the fashion show, the camp effects I discuss in this section are less in the eye of the gay *auteur* than in that of the queer spectator (or perhaps other queers working on sets and costuming for *The Women*). Whether attributable to directorial intent, the work of other queers on the production team, general studio style, or the queer spectator, however, the camp and its potentially satiric effects remain.

19. Edith Becker, Michelle Citron, Julia Lesage and B. Ruby Rich, "Lesbians and Film: Introduction," *Jump Cut* 24/25 (1981), pp. 17–21; rpt. in *Jump Cut: Hollywood, Politics and Counter-Cinema*, ed. Peter Steven (New York: Prager, 1985), pp. 296–314; Judy (Claire) Whitaker, "Hollywood Transformed," *Jump Cut* 24/25 (1981), pp. 33–35; rpt. in *Jump Cut: Hollywood, Politics and Counter-Cinema*, pp. 106–118.

20. Sue-Ellen Case, "Tracking The Vampire," *differences* 3, No. 2 (Summer 1991), p. 1.

21. The term "compulsory heterosexuality" comes from Adrienne Rich's essay "Compulsory Heterosexuality and Lesbian Existence," *Signs* 5 (1980), pp. 631–660; rpt. in *Powers of Desire: The Politics of Sexuality*, ed. Christine Stansell and Sharon Thompson (New York, Monthly Review Press, 1983), pp. 177–203.

22. This video combines mock-academic discussions, "lesbian-on-the-street" interviews and cleverly edited clips from films like *The Great Lie*, *Johnny Guitar*, *All About Eve*, *Madchen in Uniform* and *The Hunger*, to reveal the variety and complexity of lesbian culture's work with/in mass culture.

23. Fried also discusses the film's attempts to mark the female gaze within the film as really that of a straight male. Discussing the department store sequence, Fried concludes:

> Since they [Sylvia/Russell and Edith/Phyllis Povah] have never seen Crystal, in order to find her they must inspect every likely candidate through the eyes of a temptable man. . . . Our first shot of Crawford [Crystal], then, is from Russell and Povah's point-of-view, but they have consigned their point-of-view to the man, or temporarily borrowed it from him. This is not to say, of course, that the shot of Crawford from their point-of-view implies that they find her desirous or alluring as a man would—they make it plain that they find her a contemptible mansnatcher—but they must mark her out as the proper object of their contempt by first seeing her as she must look in the eyes of a desiring man. (pp. 60–61)

While Edith's point-of-view in this scene might be explained within Fried's terms, I think Syliva's is not so easily contained. For one thing, by this point the narrative has established that Sylvia is jealous of Mary's happy marriage, so would she fully "find [Crystal] a contemptible mansnatcher"? Certainly her *public* pose would convey shock and dismay, so it might *appear* that her gazing at Crystal and the other women was motivated by contempt. Even if Sylvia and Edith's gazing was motivated by dislike, however, this gaze would have to be different from one the one Fried feels they are "temporarily borrowing" here—that "of a desiring man." As my reading in this essay indicates, I think Sylvia is using this rather incoherent spectatorial position (contemptuously surveying the women in the store from the position of a desiring straight male) as a pretense to mask her own queer (lesbian or bisexual) desires— and perhaps Edith is doing the same thing (Edith has the first line in the scene: "Gorgeous torso, dear! Maybe that's little Crystal!"). Besides this, assuming cross-gender positions is one queer gazing strategy that has a long history in lesbian and gay cultures. It may be an ideologically problematic practice (as is made clear in Fried's article), but it happens. So characters in *The Women*, as well as women in the audience, just may be looking at Crystal and other women in the film from a position understood as being *like* that "of a desiring man," but not exactly *as* a desiring man.

24. Queer readings of the entire narrative could also recognize the film as a "(closet) lesbian" or a "bisexual" narrative. In the first case, since the affectional charge of the narrative is rooted in the interactions between women, and since these same-sex intensities are the audience's central source of pleasure in the narrative, a film like *The Women* might be said to have a "lesbian" narrative, whether the characters are coded or read as lesbian or not. Of course, this use of "lesbian" to describe a narrative's emotional and erotic temper is based upon a particular understanding of the qualities and characteristics that go into defining what is "lesbian." By other definitions, film narratives like *The Women* would remain "straight," or perhaps be only "hypothetically" lesbian (to borrow Chris Straayer's term from "*Voyage en*

Douce, Entre Nous: The Hypothetical Lesbian Heroine," *Jump Cut* No. 35 [1990]: 50–57).

A narrative might be understood as "bisexual" when both opposite gender and same gender emotional and erotic intensities are consistently made important to the working out of a narrative. Rather than see "heterosexual" narrative elements as necessarily placed in opposition to (or in tension with) "homosexual" narrative elements, this bisexual approach to narrative would consider these elements together as simultaneously viable narrative possibilities for characters, as well as simultaneously viable sources for an audience's pleasure. To a great extent, *The Women*'s narrative contains the elements of bisexual construction described above.

25. Sylvia has a telling queer wisecrack when she announces to Nancy Blake and Peggy Day, "I'm on to my Howard. I wouldn't trust him on Alcatraz—the mouse!" This quip simultaneously suggests that her husband is gay or bisexual (she wouldn't trust him sexually in an all-male prison/he's a "mouse," which a slang term for a young woman); that Sylvia is lesbian or bisexual (if her statement is read as a displacement of her own closeted desire); and that their marriage may be a so-called "lavender cover-up" for both of them.

26. For discussions of Dorothy Arzner and the "mannish lesbian" figures in her films, see Judith Mayne, "Female Authorship Reconsidered," in *The Woman at the Keyhole: Feminism and Women's Cinema* (Bloomington and Indianapolis: Indiana University Press, 1990), 89–123; Judith Mayne, "Lesbian Looks: Dorothy Arzner and Female Authorship," *How Do I Look?: Queer Film and Video*, eds. Bad Object-Choices (Seattle: Bay Press, 1991), 103–143; and Sarah Halprin, "Writing in the Margins," *Jump Cut* No. 29 (1984).

27. Andrea Weiss, "A Queer Feeling When I Look at You: Hollywood Stars and Lesbian Spectatorship in the 1930s," *Stardom: Industry of Desire*, ed. Christine Gledhill (London and New York: Routledge, 1991), 283–299.

28. Whitaker, "Hollywood Transformed," 33.

29. Mother-daughter bonding has been celebrated in lesbian culture long before socio-cultural and psychoanalytic analyses of it, of course. In the face of anthropological and psychoanalytic accounts in the past two decades, however, at least two understandings of the lesbian erotics of the maternal have developed: (1) These erotics suggest that lesbian sexuality is "regressive" and a case of arrested development, and (2) These erotics suggest the need to radically rethink current socio-cultural and psychoanalytic paradigms which (re)inscribe a phallic and patriarchal order. Feminist and lesbian work in many areas has begun to consider this second line of thought and its implications for everyone, not only lesbians. For example, in film studies Gaylyn Studlar's *In the Realm of Pleasure: Von Sternberg, Dietrich, and the Masochistic Aesthetic* (Urbana and Chicago: University of Illinois Press, 1988) uses Gilles Deleuze's work in order to reconsider audience pleasure and desire from within maternal paradigms. For an interesting application of the mother-daughter mythos to lesbian work, see Rosemary Curb, "Core of the Apple: Mother-Daughter Fusion and Separation in Three Recent Lesbian Plays," *Lesbian Texts and Contexts: Radical Revisions*, ed. Karla Jay and Joanne Glasgow (New York and London: New York University Press, 1990), 355–376. Noted in Curb's bibilography are some important references for this topic, including Adrienne Rich, "Compulsory Heterosexuality and Lesbian Existence," *Signs* 5 (1980), pp. 631–660; Adrienne Rich, *Of Woman Born: Motherhood as Experience and Institution* (New York: Bantam, 1976); Nancy Chodorow *The Reproduction of Mothering: Psychoanalysis and the Sociology of Gender* (Berkeley: University of California Press, 1978); Carol Gilligan *In a Different Voice: Psychologi-*

cal Theory and Women's Development (Cambridge: Harvard University Press, 1982); Coppelia Kahn, "The Hand That Rocks the Cradle: Recent Gender Theories and Their Implications," *The (M)other Tongue: Essays in Feminist Psychoanalytic Theory*, ed. Shirley Nelson Garner et al. (Ithaca, N.Y.: Cornell University Press, 1985), 72–88; and Azizah al Hibri, "Reproduction, Mothering, and the Origins of Patriarchy," *Mothering: Essays in Feminist Theory*, ed. Joyce Trebilcot (Totowa, N.J.: Rowman and Allenhand, 1983), 81–93.

30. Fried, "Men in *The Women*," 47.

Index

List of Contributors

HENRY JENKINS is Head of Film and Media Studies at MIT. He is the author of *What Made Pistachio Nuts?: Early Sound Comedy and the Vaudeville Aesthetic* and *Textual Poachers: Television Fans and Participatory Culture*.

KRISTINE BRUNOVSKA KARNICK is Assistant Professor of Communications and Director of Telecommunications at Indiana University, Indianapolis.

FRANK KRUTNIK is a lecturer in Film and English at the University of Aberdeen, Scotland. He is the author of *Popular Film and Television Comedy* (with Steve Neale) and *In a Lonely Street: Film Noir, Genre, Masculinity*.

KATHLEEN ROWE teaches media studies at the University of Oregon. She is the author of *The Unruly Woman: Gender and the Genres of Laughter* (forthcoming).

TOM GUNNING teaches film at Northwestern University, and is the author of *D. W. Griffith and the Origins of the American Narrative Films: The Early Years at Biograph*.

DONALD CRAFTON is a Professor of Communications Arts at the University of Wisconsin-Madison and Director of the Wisconsin Center of Film and Theatre Research. He is the author of two books on animation history.

DOUGLAS RIBLET is a Ph.D candidate at the University of Wisconsin-Madison.

PETER KRAMER teaches film and cultural studies at Staffordshire University.

RAMONA CURRY teaches film history and theory and popular culture in the Department of English at the University of Illinois Urbana-Champaign.

CHARLES MUSSER teaches cinema studies at New York University and Columbia University. His trilogy on early cinema in the United States includes *Before the Nickelodeon: Edwin S. Porter and the Edison Manufacturing Company*, *High Class Moving Pictures: Lyman H. Howe and the Forgotten Era of Traveling Exhibition*, and *The Emergence of Cinema: The American Screen To 1907*.

TINA OLSIN LENT teaches film and women's studies at the Rochester Institute of Technology.

ALEXANDER DOTY is an associate professor of film and mass culture at Lehigh University. His book, *Making Things Perfectly Queer: Interpreting Mass Culture*, was published in 1993.